OSCAR'S GHOST

OSCAR'S GHOST

OSCAR'S GHOST

The Battle over Oscar Wilde's Legacy

LAURA LEE

AMBERLEY

First published 2019

Amberley Publishing
The Hill, Stroud
Gloucestershire, GL5 4EP

www.amberley-books.com

British Library Cataloguing in Publication Data.
A catalogue record for this book is available from the British Library.

ISBN 978 1 4456 9078 0 (paperback)
ISBN 978 1 4456 6259 6 (ebook)

Typesetting and Origination by Amberley Publishing.
Printed in the UK.

Contents

About the Author

Oscar's Ghost is Laura Lee's twentieth book. In addition to her non-fiction works, she has written two novels and the children's book, *A Child's Introduction to Ballet*. She lives in the Detroit metropolitan area. She has researched the Oscar Wilde circle and the feud between Ross and Douglas over several years.

Introduction

Of course you will never dream of fighting a duel for me: that would be awful
and create the worst and most odious impression.
Oscar Wilde in a letter to Lord Alfred Douglas, 3 June 1897[1]

This is a story about stories. On its most basic level, *Oscar's Ghost* is about Oscar Wilde's life and how its telling affected the lives of two people whom fate had cast as characters in it. But it is also about other stories: the stories told in courtrooms masquerading as the 'whole truth'; the stories we tell ourselves to create an identity; stories we tell others to carve out a place in the community; stories that marginalised groups tell themselves to make sense of their difference; and the stories society relies upon to explain a moment in history. *Oscar's Ghost* explores how all these stories interact and what happens when contradictory narratives collide.

Wilde famously said, 'There is no such thing as a moral or immoral book.' That may be, but he was wrong when he argued that his stories could have no effect on people. His own life proved him wrong. There is nothing more powerful or potentially dangerous than a story. By telling stories we connect with others, build a reputation and beyond that, create a legacy. After death, all that remains is a story. It is by imagining one's legacy that one tries to answer the great question: what is the meaning of my life?

In prison, Wilde was consumed with the notion that not only his reputation, but his legacy, was tarnished. It was an unbearable thought. Unwilling 'to sit in the grotesque pillory' for all time, he took up his pen to try to re-write the ending that gave his entire life story its meaning. The result was a long essay in the form of a letter to his lover, Lord Alfred Douglas.

At that moment, Wilde was too immersed in his own suffering to consider the effect publishing such a document might have on the person with whom his life was so fatefully intertwined. He did not stop to think that he was writing Douglas's legacy as well as his own, and thus unwittingly shaping the course of the young man's life. Written in a period of great torment, the document came to be known as *De Profundis*. At 50,000 words, it is longer than *The Picture of Dorian Gray*. It can be viewed as the first biography of Lord Alfred Douglas, and the least objective. Prison authorities could see that this was no ordinary letter and they did not let him send it.

Never an entirely personal document, *De Profundis* was a combination of passages that were private and passages Wilde wanted to disseminate to the wider world. So he handed the manuscript to his friend Robbie Ross, who went on to become his literary executor. We can only speculate on what verbal instructions Wilde gave Ross at that meeting. The only accounts of the hand-over come from Ross himself in the context of legal actions. The adversarial system is not famous for producing subtle, nuanced stories. What we do know is that Wilde told his friend, while he was still in prison, that his manuscript was the most important thing he had ever written, and as such Ross was determined to protect it – and equally tempted to leak its contents. We also know the letter was never read by its intended recipient while Wilde was alive.

The first time Douglas learned of these piercing and exaggerated grievances was a decade after Wilde's death when they were produced as evidence in a libel trial that Douglas had instigated. Douglas had the misfortune of catching a glimpse of his unflattering legacy before he'd lived the greater part of his life. Through the veils of imposed secrecy surrounding a criminalised love – and the intricacies of copyright – Ross, a man who now disliked Douglas, had complete control of all of Wilde's writing, including *De Profundis*. He donated the manuscript to the British Museum with instructions that it not be released until 1960. It was a time bomb. Douglas's story had been wrenched from his control. It seemed to be set, no matter what he did, no matter how he proved himself. He did not wish to be placed forever in the grotesque pillory any more than Wilde did. The course he took to remedy the intolerable situation was dictated by an inheritance of volatile personality. It was not pretty.

This is also a story about story tellers. Wilde and his friends were not impartial observers. They were 'creative types' all. None could resist a touch of embellishment. Mihaly Csikszentmihalyi, author of the book *Creativity*, did an extensive study of the personalities of creative people and he concluded that the one trait that made them different from average people is their 'complexity'.

> ... they show tendencies of thought and action that in most people are segregated. They contain contradictory extremes – instead of being an 'individual', each of them is a 'multitude'. Like the colour white that includes all of the hues of the spectrum, they tend to bring together the entire range of human possibilities within themselves ... creative persons definitely know both extremes and experience both with equal intensity and without inner conflict.[2]

Csikszentmihalyi found that creative people seek one another out. They seem to need to be in the company of others who share the same struggles and who value the same 'divergent' things. Wilde, Ross and Douglas were all 'divergents'. They contained multitudes.[3]

This is, of course, why so many contemporary writers take Wilde on as a subject. It is a wonderful challenge to try to find the topic sentence of him. Each depiction of Wilde is the product of someone's fascination with some aspect of the man and its tension with other aspects. While many biographers have understood this when it comes to Wilde, few have extended it to his friends. For decades, partisans of Douglas or Ross have defended mutually contradictory stories about who was to blame for their feud. They have tended to paint the two men as Wilde's good angel and his bad angel. The either/or narratives meant that the point of view of one or the other needed to be minimised or challenged, and that of the other cleansed and contextualised.

Douglas was especially complex because he suffered from mental illness. One's impression of him was profoundly shaped by the mood he was in when he was encountered. There was an even-keeled, well-mannered, charming Douglas who was excellent company. Then there was the manic Douglas, nervous, mischievous and full of creative energy. He was apt to get his companions into trouble. There was a depressed Douglas who was sullen, negative and petulant. Finally, there was the hyper-manic Douglas who was irrational, furious and abusive. This Douglas would be most evident in stressful periods in his later years. He was destructive.

Ross was much less famous than his larger-than-life friends. Ironically, Douglas's vilification of Ross did more to cement his image as selfless, responsible, and wise than anything else could have. Douglas's vindictiveness made people rush to Ross's defence, with a few buckets of whitewash when necessary. Douglas's means of trying to expose Ross's sexuality were morally suspect, and a fair-minded person is thus inclined to discount anything he alleged. As a result, Ross's rough edges have been smoothed. There was too much evidence to deny his sexuality entirely. In keeping with the biases of the day, however, Ross was presented as the 'good' kind of homosexual – discreet – while Douglas was the bad kind, 'flaunting it'. ('I defy you to name even one youth of the lower class with whom I "flouted acquaintance",' Douglas once complained.)[4]

Thus we have a rather curious popular biography of Ross, who, at 17, was bold enough to seduce Oscar Wilde, a famous, married man. He was then almost ruined by a homosexual scandal involving a teenager but after Wilde's time in prison he had no sex life to speak of and was shocked by and disapproving of Wilde and Douglas's vices, while at the same time being the primary recipient of their letters about them. He was the centre of the community of homosexual men without engaging in any of the practices that scandalised society. That story makes little sense. Yet the depiction tends to persist even among people who would praise Ross for defending Wilde and condemn Douglas for becoming a religious moralist. Many of the crimes that Douglas alleged against Ross are hardly worth refuting today. Ross attended a Christmas party where men danced with each other? It would be more shocking if he had not.

As with Douglas, there were widespread, contradictory reports about Ross's personality. While researching her dissertation on Ross, it seemed to Edra Bogle that 'there were two Robert Rosses.'[5] One Ross was the 'good angel' who was always wise and advised Wilde to do the right thing, while Douglas, the 'bad angel', prodded him to do the wrong. He was entirely selfless, honest, and compassionate. If he had one fault is was that he was far too giving. The other Ross was a jealous sycophant who would lie, cheat and blackmail to weasel his way into a prominent role in society and destroy his romantic rival. Frank Harris allegedly called him 'a rascal of the first water', and Harris's friend, a publisher of banned books called Samuel Roth, described Ross as 'skinny, dark and aggressive, and probably the most conscienceless liar in England in his day. He had the sort of luck which rarely attends liars. He was believed throughout the greatest part of his lifetime.'[6]

Ross was indeed a teller of tall tales, who surrounded himself with complex, difficult people. He liked gossip and meddling in his friend's affairs. He was a tireless caregiver and sometimes a dirty fighter. He was generous except when he was not. He was quiet and unassuming, and also a formidable presence. When he entered a room people assumed he was the one in charge, but some of his closest friends never mentioned him in their memoirs. He launched numerous artists' careers by encouraging them, making introductions and finding them backers. He was like a second father to Wilde's younger son. He also used the contents of Douglas's private letters, written in the period of their greatest intimacy, to expose his past.

Stories are not only about individuals, but also communities. What does it mean to be 'a man'? Does he have to prove himself in battle or in bed with women? What does it mean to be English? Do all members of a nation have to live the same way, to have the same religion, the same lifestyle? What should we do with those who do not or cannot conform? What communities discuss more than anything else is what it means to be 'us'. In our story we will encounter men who loved men and the stories they told to explain their difference. Some will sound familiar to modern ears, some were quite different. It is important to bear in mind, when judging the actions of our ancestors, the over-familiar but useful quotation from L. P. Hartley, 'The past is a foreign country. They do things differently there.'

While they were in widespread agreement that the official narrative of sin and criminality did not accurately reflect their lives, homosexuals had a number of ways of conceptualising their place in society. In the 20th century a more fluid notion of sexual desire was being replaced by an increasingly medicalised narrative of biological determinism. Some are born heterosexual and some homosexual. But there were older, still powerful, notions of homosexuality as vice and sin, a forbidden appetite that must be suppressed as an alcoholic would avoid drink.

It is important to bear these differences in mind when considering the behaviour of our characters, especially the mid-life religious conversion of Douglas. Ross and his circle were not living and promoting what modern LGBT activists do, nor was Douglas reacting against 'gay culture' or biologically determined 'homosexuality', a word that was not yet current at the beginning of our story. Ross, like Wilde, was an adherent of the Greek paederastic model of sexual mentorship. There are aspects of this culture that align with modern gay culture and aspects that are troubling to us today. I have opted to use the term 'homosexual', which is more culturally neutral than 'gay'. In doing so, I do not mean to imply that these historical figures viewed themselves through the binary, medical lens.

While on the subject of language, torn between ways of referring to our protagonists, by their first name/nickname or last, I have opted to allow a mix to stand. There are times when, speaking of friendship, only the intimacy of the nickname will do, and in those cases I used Bosie, Robbie and Oscar. In other contexts, the legal arena or the office, it seems out of place.

Finally, I had to rein in my enthusiasm and make a few cuts. My original concept was not to assume knowledge of Wilde's dramatic life story. This required a lot of exposition, and with so many Wilde biographies available, it is unnecessary. For the purposes of this book, it is enough to know that Wilde was a homosexual in an era when sexual activity between men was illegal. When his lover Lord Alfred Douglas's father objected to their relationship in a dramatic fashion, Wilde tried to stop him by suing for criminal libel. This backfired when the trial revealed his extensive relations with male prostitutes and other boys. His incarceration for the crime of gross indecency and subsequent early death is one of the great tragedies of the literary world, and one that had far-reaching implications for the people who loved him.

1

'He Lieth for His Name Is Shame'

> In all his life [Oscar] has never written me a letter that was unkind or at
> least unloving and to see anything terrible in his handwriting written directly
> to me would almost kill me.
> Lord Alfred Douglas in a letter to More Adey, 1897[1]

In April 1913, the High Court was packed and full of reporters for the sensational case, 'Douglas v. Ransome and Others'. In the front row, right next to the defendant, author Arthur Ransome, sat Wilde's friend and literary executor, Robert Ross. Lord Alfred Douglas, who at 43 still had a surprisingly youthful appearance, was suing Ransome for libel over his *Oscar Wilde: A Critical Study*. The book was, for the most part, a literary analysis of Wilde's work but it contained a reference to an unnamed youth who had lived off Wilde, ruined him, and then abandoned him when the playwright had no money. Anyone who knew the rudiments of the Wilde story knew that the youth was Douglas. Ransome's source was an unpublished portion of Oscar Wilde's prison manuscript, *De Profundis*.

Sir Henry Alfred McCardie for the defence handed Douglas a manuscript on loan from the British Museum. It consisted of twenty foolscap folios, four sides each. The first page had the header 'H. M. Prison, Reading' followed by the handwritten words 'Dear Bosie'.[2]

'How does it come to be produced from the British Museum?' asked the judge.

'It was given to the museum by Mr Ross, the literary executor of Wilde and they accepted it,' a member of the defence team said. 'Mr Ross published parts of it, and the unpublished parts are here.'

McCardie handed the document to Douglas and asked if he recognised the handwriting.

How could he not? It was the same hand that had written 'This is to assure you of my immortal, my eternal love for you ... Our love was always beautiful and noble, and if I have been the butt of a terrible tragedy, it is because the nature of that love has not been understood.'[3]

It was the hand that had written, 'I shall be eternally grateful to you for having always inspired me with adoration and love ... My passion is at a loss for words, but you can understand me, you alone.'[4] And 'It is perhaps in prison that I am going to test the power of love. I am going to see if I cannot make the bitter waters sweet by the intensity of love I bear you.'[5] And after that test, 'Do remake my ruined life for me, and then our friendship and love will have a different meaning to the world.'[6]

Douglas acknowledged that he recognised the handwriting of Oscar Wilde and handed the document back to McCardie. McCardie then began reading from a typescript copy prepared for the trial by Robert Ross. It was 130 pages long with annotations in Ross's hand. McCardie had underlined passages to emphasise when reading.

'Dear Bosie, after long and fruitless waiting I have determined to write you myself, as much for your sake as for mine.'[7]

Douglas stood in the witness box and listened to a letter he had never read when Wilde was alive. The first he knew of the full document was when his solicitor received a copy of the typescript in preparation for the trial. Until he learned otherwise in Ransome's biography, he had assumed a published version of De Profundis was an extract from a letter not to him, but to Ross. Douglas had even written a review of that version, never knowing its true history.

McCardie continued: 'If there be in it one single passage that brings tears to your eyes, weep as we weep in prison where the day no less than the night is set apart for tears ... Ah! You had no motives in life. You had appetites merely. A motive is an intellectual aim.'

Douglas remained standing. 'My life, as long as you were by my side, was entirely sterile and uncreative. And with but a few intervals you were, I regret to say, always by my side.' McCardie started to become hoarse and he passed the manuscript to Justice Charles Darling to continue. Darling recounted to the riveted courtroom how Douglas ruined Wilde's ability to make art, that he was vain and reckless and brought him to financial ruin, that when he thought of their friendship he felt 'ashamed ... It was intellectually degrading to me.' Fifteen minutes had gone by and Douglas was visibly shaken. He asked the judge if he could sit down. The judge said he did not wonder why he wanted to do so and gave him permission. Darling's voice, too, began to give out and he passed the document on to J. H. Campbell.

'But most of all I blame myself for the ethical degradation I allowed you to bring on me ... my will power became absolutely subject to yours. It sounds a grotesque thing to say but it is none the less true. It was the triumph of the smaller over the bigger nature. It was a case of the tyranny of the weak over the strong.'

Douglas asked the judge if he might be excused from the court. The judge asked if he was unwell. He said he was not ill, but that he did not want to hear any more. The judge ordered him to stay put. The London newspapers would all publish gleeful accounts of Douglas's discomfort on the stand the next morning.

'Do you really think that at any period in our friendship you were worthy of the love I showed you, or that for a moment I thought you were? I knew you were not ... You were my enemy: such an enemy as no man ever had.'

The letter was so long that the court concluded its business for the day and scheduled a continuation of the reading for the next. As the reading continued the court was so wrapped up in the drama it was a while before the judge noticed Douglas was not in his place. He sent two wardens out to find him. Ten minutes later they reappeared with Douglas in tow. He was clutching a Bible. The judge asked him why he had not been in court.

'I asked my council to ask you if I might go out, and he said it was not necessary to ask you and I might go,' Douglas replied.

'I suppose you did not wish to hear what was read,' said the judge.

'Yesterday you volunteered the remark after hearing the first part read, when I wanted to go out, you were not surprised that I wished to do so.'

'No I did not,' the judge snapped. 'I said I did not wonder why you wanted to sit down. Now, I may tell you this. You are the plaintiff in this case, and if you leave the court again while you are a witness I will give leave for a judgement to be entered against you.'

'I apologise.'

Douglas took his seat and McCardie continued where he had left off. Douglas listened as the ghost of Wilde mocked his 'undergraduate verse'. The poem he claimed was amateurish had been written as a love token for Oscar, and he had praised it in the most lavish terms at the time.[8]

> But thou, my love, my flower: my jewel, set
> In a fair setting, help me, or I die,
> To bear Love's burden; for that load to share
> Is sweet and pleasant, but if lonely I
> Must love unloved, 'tis pain; shine we, my fair,
> Two neighbour jewels in Love's coronet.

As the reading went on Douglas looked down and flipped through the pages of the New Testament.

The narration dragged on and on. Eventually the jury had had enough and they asked that the reading be stopped. Speaking on behalf of Douglas, Cecil Hayes asked that the reading continue because, he said, the tone of the letter becomes less bitter as it goes on and it would become clear that Wilde was subject to dark prison moods that clouded his perception. But the judge, too, had had enough of *De Profundis* and so the reading came to an end.

It was not true that Douglas had abandoned Wilde. He had been forced to separate from him by pressure from, among others, Robert Ross himself. Yet the only way he could prove this was by revealing love letters that would incriminate him as a homosexual, a crime punishable by hard labour in prison. Anything too warm could make him guilty of gross indecency. Anything not warm enough proved the libel. He was paradoxically accused both of loving Wilde too much and of loving him too little. It was a tight-rope no one could walk without falling. Wilde's accusations from beyond the grave had to remain unanswered. The court would officially endorse the view that Douglas was an untalented, unintelligent, self-centred scoundrel who never loved anyone but himself and who lived off Wilde, ruined him in a vendetta against his father and then abandoned him when the money ran out.

Robert Ross had set it all in motion. Douglas would have his revenge.

2

Café Royal Days

[Robbie Ross is] one of my greatest friends and one of the best fellows that ever lived.
Lord Alfred Douglas, letter to his brother Percy, 1893[1]

In the 1890s, London was the centre of the world. From 1800 to 1890 the population soared from less than a million to more than four million. Its streets were literally becoming electric, with gaslight being replaced by the brasher glimmer of electricity. The well-lit streets and the dark corners were shared by immigrants, new arrivals from the country, criminals and hustlers, wealthy merchants and the viscounts and earls who ran a vast empire with territory from Australia to India and Canada, and all across the African continent. University students full of bold new ideas mingled with established artists, journalists and poets within the mirrored walls of the Café Royal. It was in the 'luxurious, convenient, unconventional' Café that one could find 'rest from the pompous and distressing unrealities of a great city'.[2]

The prime spot in the Café was a chipped marble table at the end of the grill in the Domino Room. This was the favoured spot of Oscar Wilde. Here the combined effects of copious quantities of red and yellow wine (as Oscar insisted on describing it) and the haze of Egyptian cigarette smoke created a dream-like atmosphere appropriate for a clientele of artists. Wilde's drink of choice was whiskey and soda, the famous absinthe only an occasional affectation. Known as the greatest conversationalist of his day, his musical voice had an almost hypnotic effect as he narrated tales that would eventually be reworked into his society plays. Young poets sat on the fringes, hoping for an introduction and a few words of advice from one of the greatest celebrities of the day.

Wilde enjoyed the company of students and surrounded himself with admirers that outsiders called his 'disciples'. They, in turn, referred to him only half-jokingly as 'the Divinity'.[3] Much like a modern fan community, the Wilde disciples were influenced as much by him in his absence as in his presence. They imitated his style of dress, mannerisms and sense of humour. They would lift their eyes in mock horror, gesture in surprise and speak with a flippant tone of amused self-adoration, full of pleasing paradoxes, verbal nonsense and aesthetic philosophy. They included some of that generation's most brilliant scholars and poets, as well as some notorious rogues.

Together, this circle created a Victorian version of a Greek symposium. The original symposium featured lots of food and drink and great minds leisurely discussing philosophical questions in the company of *hetairai*, high-class female prostitutes, slaves and boys who would service them sexually should the desire arise. It was a place to celebrate erotic beauty and to use it as inspiration for new heights of intellectual achievement.

Wilde's community had its own set of moral values, which elevated art above all. Being a colourful personality was much more valued than what the outside world called respectability. This was an intoxicating and appealing image of what life could be for a young man who loved men and quite a departure from the options open to him in the outside world: shame, suicide, prison. Their playful secret language, full of inside references and innuendo appealed not only to 'inverts' but to those whose sexual preferences were more traditional or perhaps vaguely defined. Ada Leverson, Aubrey Beardsley and Max Beerbohm all enjoyed their working knowledge of the Wilde circle's code. It made them feel like members of a secret society open only to the most imaginative. Max used the playfully affectionate language of the circle in his letters to his best friend Reggie Turner, a lawyer and writer Wilde would one day dub 'the boy snatcher of Clements inn'. Yet Max was, himself, a confirmed 'mulierast'. That word had been coined by Robert Ross, known to intimates as Robbie or Bobbie, an impish, witty and charming young man, wise beyond his years. Robbie created the word by combining the Latin *mulier*, or woman, with the suffix from paederast. It filled a linguistic gap because the word 'heterosexual' was not yet current.[4]

Robbie had a way of steering a conversation without appearing to do so at all. He surrounded himself with the imaginative and eccentric, and when there was a lull, he could toss in a simple word or observation that would set the grand personalities off on flights of fancy. He made the funny funnier, the bold bolder and he encouraged playful, taboo talk. Ross liked to tell others who were 'so' (as it was described at the time) that he had been the first man to sleep with Wilde. He winked at the stories that he had picked the writer up in a public lavatory. This may or may not have been true, but these kinds of tales served as a sort of insiders' gossip, stories that created bonds of intimacy between men who shared a common secret.

Wilde's constant companion, Lord Alfred Douglas, stood out among the 'disciples'. Although Bosie, as he was known to his close friends, was an Oxford undergraduate, he looked (and often acted) more like a teenager. He was fortunate to embody a particular Greek ideal of golden, youthful beauty that was especially celebrated by his peers. (That said, his fabled beauty was exaggerated by Wilde. The dazzling effect of his blue eyes was dimmed by an oddly shaped nose.) Always perfectly dressed, he had a confidence and sense of mischievous play that some found magnetic and others appalling. Max found him to be 'pretty' and 'charming' but 'obviously mad'.[5] He loved action. He was athletic, roguish and glamorous. He was a de facto member as Oscar had chosen him and he was always at the master's side. He was *in* the circle, but he was never entirely *of* the circle.

Well-born and proud of it, Bosie was not a natural Bohemian. He enjoyed his station in life and the privileges he was heir to. He had no desire to see society transformed except when it came to outmoded views of sexual behaviour. As the son of a Marquess (even a scandalous one like John Sholto Douglas) his name had been a fixture in the society pages since he was 14. He was 'abnormally, damnably, touchingly conceited' about his literary talent.[6] As this observation by Max suggests, it was a brand of narcissism that could be oddly appealing. Bosie had the capacity to be as generous one moment as he was selfish the next, as playful and childlike today as he was stubborn and domineering tomorrow.

Years later, George Bernard Shaw would walk with an older and wiser Robbie as he described the attraction Wilde had for some young men. Shaw (who had a bitter relationship with his own father) was inspired by the conversation to write about mentors like Wilde, 'The influence they can exercise on young people ... in whom a natural bent towards art has always been baffled and snubbed, is incredible to those who have not witnessed and understood it. He (or she) who reveals the world of art to them opens heaven to them. They become satellites, disciples, worshippers of the apostle.'[7] Their common secrets, and a mutual love of the world of art as revealed by Wilde, created a fast intimacy between Robbie and Bosie. Robbie had never known his father and Bosie had been disappointed and hurt by his. Both had chosen a new father figure in the person of Oscar. They were brothers.

Late in his life, Robbie would write somewhat ruefully to his friend Christopher Millard that besides his long-time partner Freddie Smith, Oscar Wilde and Alfred Douglas were the two people for whom he had made sacrifices, implying his friendship with Bosie was one of his most important relationships.[8]

3

Robbie

There was something of Don Quixote in him, and a little of Malvolio.

Edmund Gosse[1]

Robert Baldwin Ross was an illustrious name in Canada, evoking a family history that included two of the nation's most prominent politicians, Robert Baldwin and the Honourable John Ross. Our Robbie was the second child of that name born to John Ross and his wife Augusta Elizabeth Baldwin, known to friends as Eliza. The first child was born in 1854 and died three days after his second birthday. An older sister, named Maria-Louisa, had been born in 1852 and had also died in infancy. After that there were four more surviving children, Mary-Jane, Jack, Alexander and Lizzie before the surviving Robbie was born in Tours, France, on 25 May 1869. The esteemed name was perhaps a too much for him, throughout his life he was known to friends by the diminutive 'Robbie'.[2] He explained the nickname with a highly embellished (probably fictional) tale that appeared in a 1910 issue of *The Bystander*:

> I used to see that bleak old sage [Thomas Carlyle] when I lived as a child in Chelsea. I regarded him with extraordinary aversion and fear ... He patted my head on several occasions and addressed me in language generally incomprehensible to my little Cockney ears. One day he inquired my name. I replied that it was 'Bobby'. He animadverted thereon, in words I do not profess to remember, and urged that it should be 'Robbie' – a reminiscence, no doubt, of Burns. This was faithfully reported by my nurse on returning home, and from that day I was called 'Robbie'.
>
> One day I was sent to post a letter. I suppose I was older; thoroughly unconscious, as always, of anything ahead, I cannoned into Carlyle. The impact lay me flat on the pavement, where I yelled for some minutes, though soothed eventually by England's great thinker. And then – this is the point of the story – Carlyle dived into his pockets, produced a halfpenny, and said kindly, 'Here is a bawbee for Bobbie.' He had quite forgotten (and this hurt me) that my name had been changed out of deference to his opinion. I have the halfpenny to this day. When Mr Carlyle died I was put into deep mourning. He was the first, and perhaps the most interesting, of all my street acquaintances.[3]

Robbie's mother, Eliza, had not had a happy childhood. She was ignored by her father and treated as a servant by her grandmother. One of her family duties was to carry a large Bible to her grandmother's room and to read to her from it. After a while the Bible would be laid aside and the girl would be sent to fetch a snuff box, which the old woman used 'for her health's sake'. At twelve she was sent away to live in the Ursuline Convent in Quebec. This upbringing produced for Robbie a strict mother with an 'extraordinary knowledge of the Bible', who believed in raising her children with a fair but firm hand.

Robbie would also inherit from her a nervous disposition and weakness for stress-induced illness. Eliza's wedding was to be a grand affair, three special chairs had been ordered for the most prominent guests, the Governor-General and his family. Eliza was so nervous that the day before she broke out with what the doctors diagnosed as erysipelas, but which family members said was 'really a form of gout in her head'. Consequently, the grand wedding was called off and the couple were married in private on 4 February 1851.

The Ross home near Toronto was modelled on an English country estate. John Ross corresponded with most of the leading political figures of his day and came back from travels abroad with oil paintings, the latest literature and tales of new operas, but Robbie would have no memory of this.

In 1865, Ross suffered a series of financial losses. In the same year his son Aleck lost an eye playing with a bow and arrow. Ross moved his family to England where he believed doctors might have more advanced techniques to help preserve his son's sight. After a few months in London, the Ross family settled into a country home in Tours, France. It was here that Robbie and his younger sister Maria Elizabeth were born. Soon thereafter the political situation began to destabilise in the build-up to the Franco-Prussian War and the family returned to their country house in Toronto. John Ross died there on 31 January 1871. Robbie was not yet two years old. The death took its toll on Eliza, who had another attack of her bizarrely named skin ailment. Eldest daughter Mary, now 26, was left to run the household. After Eliza recovered, she devoted all of her love and energy to the two toddlers. (The older boys were now away at boarding school.)

In April 1872, the Rosses moved to England. As the baby of the family, Robbie was doubly spoiled, both by his mother and older siblings. Although 'a delicate child', Robbie learned to swim, row, bicycle and play cricket. He was educated in a series of boarding schools including Landroyd House in Surrey and another school in Edinburgh. He studied the classics with an emphasis on Greek and Latin.[4] In 1884, Aleck finished his studies at Cambridge, and Robbie was taken out of school and spent much of the year travelling Europe with his family. Robbie and his mother were primarily based at the Grand Hotel in Vavey, Switzerland. Robbie was also able to get up to a bit of mischief on a ten-day trip with his brother Jack in Mainz. They were arrested for trespassing and fined sixty marks. As Robbie would later tell it, in his own imaginative fashion, they narrowly escaped being jailed as spies.[5]

The trip helped to fuel Robbie's life-long interest in art. He wrote long letters to his siblings about the works he saw and how they inspired him. He also saw a theatrical production that had a profound effect on him. Performed in a wooden theatre behind the post office, with the Alpbach river running by to cool the Alpine air, the Innsbruck Passion Play was a seven-hour drama, but to young Robbie it 'seemed like two'. It was a lavish production with 200 actors in 'marvellously correct and artistic' costumes. Cannon blasts announced each act. (There was an hour for refreshments before the crucifixion.) The play was divided into sixteen 'representations' beginning with a tableau-vivant depicting a scene from the Old Testament foreshadowing the narrative of Christ. The tableaux were, as one reviewer put it, 'as near perfection as can be imagined'.

After the orchestra, a band of angels all clad in white had played an overture, there was a prologue, choral music and wordless representations of sin, its chastisement and the promise of redemption. Then there was Jesus, played by an actor with 'a noble face, fine figure, long black hair, a demeanour full of repose and dignity and a distinct musical voice'. There were people of all ages shouting Hosannnas and waving branches. The moralising Pharisees looked on 'with a sort of envious satisfaction' as Jesus sealed his own fate by turning the tables of the money changers. There was Peter's denial, the death of a despairing Judas, the crucifixion and the descent from the cross copied from Reubens, closing at last with a giant tableau representing the risen Christ with the whole ensemble on stage. Robbie called it 'the most beautiful and remarkable thing I have ever seen'.[6]

Around this time Robbie decided to become a Catholic. Although his mother spent part of her youth in a Catholic convent, she emerged a devout Anglican. She had a puritan streak, believed in 'providence' and that virtue was rewarded and vice punished. Robbie later gave a comic description of the type of instruction found in his boyhood textbooks:

> In a semi-geographical work called *Near Home; or, Europe Described*, published by Hatchards in the fifties (though my friend, Mr Arthur Humphreys, denies all knowledge of it), I can recall many stereos of dialectic cast in a Socratic mould:–
> Q. What is the religion of the Italians?
> A. They are Roman Catholics.
> Q. What do the Roman Catholics worship?
> A. Idols and a piece of bread.
> Q. Would not God be very angry if He knew the Italians worshipped idols and a piece of bread?
> A. God IS very angry.[7]

From an early age Robbie recognised that he was different, and understood what that difference was. By the time he was 13, he already knew he was not destined to marry or have children. When his oldest brother Jack became engaged he wrote a letter to his mother,

> I shall be very careful in my will that I leave my property to Jacks and Mary children [sic] ... Very soon we shall here [sic] of Alick's engagement.[8] Then I sincerely hope Lizzie's – and then I sincerely hope Not mine but will live with you dear Oiseau in a large house when I gain my reputation by being an oculist and saving one of the family Royal. Take cataracts off the eyes of the queen and restore her sight and when my guineas roll in. That is my life which I have pictured before myself and to live with you the rest of my days. I am very glad that Jack has married for the great house of Ross will not become extinct.[9]

In fact, neither Jack nor Aleck had children, but the Ross name was saved when Mary's son changed his name from Jones to Ross by deed poll in 1918.

Robbie understood that it was in his nature to commit what the church called sin. In his mother's conception of the universe, there were good people and bad people. If this notion was true, Robbie was born pre-condemned. He wrestled with this idea in his teenage years, producing youthful poems on the theme. Unlike Bosie, who would struggle his whole life with the conflict between faith and desire, Robbie managed to reconcile his Catholicism and his sexuality at a young age without any great difficulty. By his late teens, Robbie had fully accepted his love of males and was enthusiastic in the exploration of his desires.

In 1886, Robbie was staying with his brother Aleck and studying to follow in his (and brother Jack's) footsteps as a Cambridge scholar. On 16 November the brothers attended a performance of Shelley's verse drama, *Hellas*. *The Times* described it as a 'monotonous recital of the entire poem'. Robbie found the experience thrilling, if not for the poetry, then at least for the celebrities in the audience: Robert Browning, Frederic Harrison, Walter Pater, Rider Haggard and most enchanting of all, Oscar Wilde.

How and precisely when Robbie went from observing Wilde from afar to enjoying his company in a much more close and personal manner is not known, but not long after the *Hellas* performance, seventeen-year-old Robbie seduced the thirty-two year-old writer. Wilde was a married man with two young sons. He was already a celebrity – but little more than just that – famous more for his fame than for any great literary success. If Robbie was not Oscar's first male lover, Oscar certainly led Robbie and a number of his friends to believe he was. (Wilde was always less concerned with the truth of a story than of the effect it had on his audience.)

There was certainly hero worship in Robbie's initial attraction to Wilde. Oscar was not beautiful. Max Beerbohm kept a private character book with notes on his impressions of people. Max saw Oscar as being 'like an enormous dowager', 'schoolboy' or 'wax statue'. He made an impression with his curled hair and his 'fat white hands' with pointed fingers decorated by huge rings. In spite of his 'heavy shoulders' he had a 'cat-like tread'. He was 'effeminate but [with the] vitality of twenty men ... magnetism ... authority ... deeper than repute or wit ... hypnotic'. Oscar's views on art and experience, his charm and wit and the musical quality of his voice weaved a spell. It was 'a mezzo voice, uttering itself in a leisurely fashion with every variety of tone.'[10]

Oscar's conversational brilliance is the stuff of legend. It produced a reaction that people from all walks of life described as magical. He was a master story teller, a great wit, and excellent at repartee, but what made him even more remarkable was how he drew other people out and made them feel more brilliant themselves. He was complimentary and encouraging of Robbie's artistic pursuits. He listened to him as if he were a peer, not a teenager. The puckish young man was exactly the breath of fresh air Wilde needed at that moment. Although he had genuinely fallen in love with his bride Constance, the novelty of marriage had worn off and he was looking for a new adventure. Around the time of his first son Cyril's birth, he had written to a male friend that he felt there was no longer such a thing as a romantic experience, only the memory of romance and a desire for it. His marriage had become 'a curious mixture of ardour and indifference. I myself would sacrifice everything for a new experience, and I know there is no such thing as new experience at all.'[11]

How wrong he was. There is no documentation of the development of Robbie and Oscar's friendship. If there were love letters between them, they have long since been burned. Although there is no way to know for sure, most biographers agree that the sexual aspect of their relationship did not last long and was probably not a major part of their relationship (if it continued at all) when Ross became a lodger at the Wilde's red brick Queen Anne-style home at 16 Tite Street in Chelsea. He stayed for three months in 1887.

Ross had been living with his mother as he crammed for Cambridge. Eliza wanted to continue her travels and did not want to leave her son in the city by himself. Presumably it was Robbie who suggested Wilde might be a suitable chaperone, and his mother agreed. So he went to live as a paying tenant occupying one of the three bedrooms on the third level just below the room that had once been Wilde's study but was now a nursery for the toddler Cyril and the nursing baby Vyvyan. Constance was as enchanted by Robbie's wit, charm and intelligence as Oscar had been.

When Ross came into his life, Wilde's showmanship had won him headlines, but as is the case with most who court fame, he was seen as a bit of a hack. He had yet to find any real literary success. His first volume of poetry had been widely panned and parodied. The Oxford Union had even rejected a presentation copy after accusations of plagiarism. His plays *Vera* and *The Duchess of Padua* were flops. To make ends meet, Wilde took a job as editor of *Lady's World*. (He renamed it *Women's World*) but he was still having a hard time paying the bills, Robbie's rent notwithstanding.

If Wilde could have found a way to make a living from his universally acknowledged talent for talk, he would probably never have written a thing. He sat down to write with difficulty, and always fleshed out his literary works in conversation first. Robbie came up with the idea of writing down the best of Wilde's table talk in a notebook. Much of what he captured found its way into the comic plays that would one day bring their author his greatest commercial success.

In the evenings the men would retire to the front section of the first floor drawing room. The chamber was divided by folding doors with the back section taken up by a painted grand piano that Constance sometimes played. They called the front section 'the smoke room'. It was decorated in the latest fashion with a deep red and gold textured wallpaper known as Lincrusta-Walton, designed to simulate pressed plaster. There, as they smoked endless cigarettes, the friends would discuss Shakespeare, Pater, poetry and ancient Greece. (Cigarettes were a conspicuous luxury the poor could not afford.) They both liked to play with ideas 'as children play at ball – not football – but the old game of catch'.[12] They would try out a position, then its opposite, sometimes simultaneously.

Ross was an entirely new and different type of sounding board. He was not only witty and worldly, their conversation crackled with sexual innuendo and fantasy. These passionate, provocative talks would usher in a new stage in Wilde's development as a writer. 'Although not himself a creative person, [Ross] had, in those days especially, a genius for friendship,' wrote William Rothenstien. 'He had a delightful nature, was an admirable story-teller, and a wit; above all he was able to get the best out of those he admired.'[13] Osbert Sitwell, who knew Ross later in life, remembered his 'rather purring voice' with a 'slight transatlantic roll of the r'. His charm had a powerful effect on friends. His sense of humour was remarked upon by all who knew him, but unlike Wilde, whose epigrams have stood the test of time, Ross's humour was too much of the moment to be remembered. He enjoyed a good pun, and was current on all of the latest trends and artists, most of whom, as is the nature of art, are unknown to us a century later. Sitwell was impressed by the 'intoxicatingly subversive element' in Ross's conversation. It was 'provocative in the extreme in its refusal to accept other people's rags and tags of ideas. An implicit attack on authority.'[14] He was also, according to Edmund Gosse, a 'dangerous listener ... With attentive affability he would allow the fabric of assumption to reach its height, and then destroy it with a single stroke.'[15]

Robbie and Oscar were both fascinated by literary and artistic forgeries. They were both, in some sense, artistic forgers themselves, creating respectable public personas that were at odds with the secret desires that polite society despised (and, perhaps, feared). Dissembling held a natural fascination. Together they found a way to view their enforced secrecy and fractured selves not as oppressive but as artistically enriched. Knowing better than most that the public 'self' was a mask, they were able to see identity as a form of play.

As a young man Wilde had kept a notebook with clippings on the poet Thomas Chatterton, who had composed poems he claimed were the works of a 15th-century Bristol monk, his own fictional creation. Wilde believed his forgery 'came from the desire of artistic self-effacement'.[16] Thus, it was a perfect example of art for art's sake. By impersonating someone else, he was not bound by his own identity and could express artistic truths more fully. Ross would take up the theme of forgery in a story called 'How We Lost the Book of Jasher,' which would one day be published in an Oxford publication, *The Spirit Lamp*, edited by Lord Alfred Douglas. In this story the protagonist burns down a museum in order to preserve the mystery of a forged archaeological find. Oscar's forgery-themed essay 'Pen, Pencil and Poison' was also written in this period. It dealt with Thomas Wainwright, 'a forger of no mean or ordinary capabilities, and ... a subtle and secret poisoner almost without rival in this or any age'. Wilde concludes, 'there is no essential incongruity between crime and culture.' Ross's creative approach to history (as illustrated by his school book 'memory') inspired one of Wilde's most acclaimed essays, 'The Decay of Lying'. Both writers believed 'There is such a thing as robbing a story of its reality by trying to make it too true.'

Robbie's sexual openness inspired Wilde to tap into his forbidden fantasy life. The result was a story of Shakespeare's attraction to a boy actor. 'The Portrait of Mr. W. H.' had many of the themes that would animate both Wilde and Ross's work: artistic forgery, faith in fiction and the added element of the male muse. It was, Wilde told Ross, 'half yours, and but for you it would not have been written.'[17] A passage from that story captures the flavour of the conversation that inspired it:

> I had been dining with Erskine in his pretty little house in Birdcage Walk, and we were sitting in the library over our coffee and cigarettes, when the question of literary forgeries happened to turn up in conversation. I cannot at present remember how it was that we struck upon this somewhat curious topic, as it was at that time, but I know that we had a long discussion about Macpherson, Ireland, and Chatterton, and that with regard to the last I insisted that his so-called forgeries were merely the result of an artistic desire for perfect representation; that we had no right to quarrel with an artist for the conditions under which he chooses to present his work; and that all Art being to a certain degree a mode of acting, an attempt to realise one's own personality on some imaginative plane out of reach of the trammelling accidents and limitations of real life, to censure an artist for a forgery was to confuse an ethical with an aesthetical problem.[18]

In autumn 1888, Robbie moved out of Tite Street to begin his university career. Although it began with great optimism, and congratulations from Oscar, it came to an abrupt and violent end in March 1889. A group of students accosted him and threw him into a fountain. It was not friendly hazing. The 'ducking incident' would have long-lasting repercussions.

Robbie's brothers had both enjoyed their time at Cambridge. Aleck had studied at Caius College and older brother Jack at Trinity. Robbie chose King's College because he wanted to study history. Until 1861, scholarships at King's were restricted to Etonians, and in 1885 its high-born graduates still made up a large portion of the student body. As a privately educated outsider, Robbie would have found it hard to fit in in the best of circumstances. On his admission Robbie made two claims that can most generously be described as 'aspirational'. (The university used the term 'false statements'.) He said he belonged to the Church of Rome, which may have been true in his heart but would not be actually true for another five years. He also said he was a member of the Savile Club, which he attended frequently *as a guest* with his brother Aleck, a member. Although he had not been officially admitted to the club, he had been proposed for membership by the playwright and critic W. E. Henley. These white lies would feed into the notion, among his detractors, that Robbie Ross was a social-climbing poseur.[19]

When Robbie started at Cambridge he had known Wilde for two years and had been introduced by him and by his brother Aleck to many of the most celebrated writers of the day. Wilde had sung Robbie's praises to Oscar Browning, a history fellow at King's. Browning, known as 'the O. B.' to students, was a singular character. He was a snobbish name-dropper, gregarious, loud and eccentric. He took a strong personal interest in his students, helping them find jobs or lending them money. He received thousands of letters from students he had helped, but his tendency to favour certain boys, those who had the most beautiful faces, was a cause of concern at times to those in academic authority. His career as a master at the prestigious Eton school ended after allegations of improprieties with a male student. A major scandal was averted and he had been allowed to move on to Cambridge. The real reason for his departure from Eton was never made public.[20]

Ross struck up an intimate friendship with Browning. The following year they would vacation together on the Isle of Wight with a poor, young apprentice sailor. Ross described the lad as 'very beautiful and very charming'. According to Browning's biographer 'both men spoilt and petted him' and at some time sex 'had crept into' the relationship between Browning and the sailor.[21]

Ross arrived at Cambridge with a worldly confidence that struck not a few of his fellow students as cocky condescension. His Bohemian, aesthetic style did not sit well either. His Eton-educated peers, Robbie would (ill-advisedly) write, 'whose conservative prejudices are something more than mere sentiment, may regret the admission of non-Etonians into the place, [but] we believe it was the salvation of the college ... among those who battered down the doors for admission under the new regulations, there came some of the most undesirable ... Not only the long-haired, but the short-haired and the no-haired came – the purely social and the socially pure.'[22]

Robbie found a place among fellow writers and befriended Walter Murray Guthrie of Trinity College. Eton-educated Guthrie was the son of the Governor of the Bank of England. Though outwardly conservative, he was also friendly with Browning, and knew something of his 'artistic' side. The two friends decided to produce an anonymous paper called *The Gadfly*. It was, in the words of their later publication *The Granta*, 'written on Tuesday, printed on Wednesday, published on Thursday, sold on Friday, suppressed on Saturday, and wept for on Sunday'.[23] The publication was shut down after a single issue in large part because of a fake interview with Oscar Browning that lampooned his aesthetic pretensions. Robbie had not been the author of the Browning piece, it was actually written by Guthrie, who Browning never suspected was the *Gadfly's* editor.[24] The brash article was probably intended as an affectionate parody by two young men who had not quite mastered the boundaries of what was appropriate among friends and what could be shared with a wider public. Browning was not amused, and he believed he knew who was to blame. The article bore the fingerprints of Robbie Ross. Guthrie, meanwhile, was 'helping' Browning ferret out the literary scoundrel. He took a pledge with a group of Browning's supporters that 'they would never wash nor shave until they had brought condign and personal vengeance on the head of the editor of *The Gadfly*.'[25] The college authorities were not amused either. One of the fellows, a student named E. H. Douty, took it on himself to identify the editor. He also suspected Ross and put pressure on him to confess, but he never managed to prove anything.

After the demise of *The Gadfly*, Guthrie decided to take his teasing to a new level. He had heard that Browning was planning to bring out a serious educational journal called *The Granta*. Guthrie registered the title himself, and put up posters advertising the new student publication. When Browning saw the posters he was, in his own words, 'horrified' at the 'act of literary piracy'. His own journal never appeared.[26] *The Granta*, subtitled 'A College Joke to Cure the Dumps', appeared during an election for dean of the college. Ross wrote an article making fun of the college's conservative culture, telling his fellow students who they should support and, in a particularly undiplomatic move, he used the opportunity to lash out at Douty, who was hoping to be appointed to the office of dean:

> Mr Douty, last term, endeavoured, without success, to play the part of an undignified Lecoq. Owing to his detective energies, the Undergraduates failed to discover the King's correspondent of the Gadfly, and his semi-official interference disgusted even the Senior Proctor. So that even those who had been loudest in their threats of vengeance against the (then-unknown) long-haired Freshman, were as eager to protect him against the pomposity and officiousness of an amateur policeman.[27]

This was the final straw for Douty, and a group of his incensed friends decided it was time to teach the arrogant, aesthetic freshman a lesson. But this was no spur-of-the-moment impulse. The students sought the advice of a junior tutor, Arthur Tilley, the older brother of one of the members of the posse, for advice on how to punish Ross without harming their own futures. Rumour had it Browning was in on the discussions as well, but he vehemently denied it.

On 8 March, as Ross was walking back from the dining hall he was set upon by Douty's friends. They grabbed him and threw him into the fountain. When the deed was done, they went off laughing to the dining hall where they enjoyed a celebratory dinner with Tilley. When the college authorities reviewed the incident they concluded that both the assailants and Ross had broken college rules and they decided to take no action. Their inaction incensed Ross more than the original ducking had.

Ross was deeply traumatised by the event. He suffered, in the words of Browning, '... a violent brain attack, the result of the outrage preying on his mind'.[28] He became so distraught that he contemplated suicide and was sent back to his mother's home to recover. Over the Easter break, his family did their best to console Robbie, but he continued to suffer 'attacks' and to stew in an unremitting depression. He returned to college in April, determined to get justice. He told Browning that he had consulted with solicitors and he would sue if Tilley and the ringleaders were not disciplined. His determination not to let the matter rest forced students and members of the administration alike to take sides.

John Nixon, professor of Classics and a member of the disciplinary council, was one of those who felt the matter should not be swept under the rug. Although he feared he was putting his own position in jeopardy by criticising a tutor, he submitted a detailed report on 14 May, arguing that 'lynch law cannot be tolerated in civilised society and any encouragement of it by a responsible officer seems to be inexcusable.' Nixon was not a personal fan of Ross's, but, he wrote 'A natural disgust at the personalities of modern forms of society journalism ought not to blind him or us to the offensiveness and harm of retaliation by personal violence.'[29] In the end, the College Council decided that it would be in the best interest of the college if the matter was put to rest without any official sanctions. It was settled by having Tilley issue a public apology to Ross in the dining hall, a humiliation from which Tilley was said to have never recovered.

One intuitively suspects there was more behind the ducking than college politics. It was after this event that Ross decided to tell his family about his sexual orientation. Although they loved and supported him as much as ever, his sexuality was a cause for concern and discussion. Like most families of the time, Robbie's relatives were not inclined to believe that such deviant desire was part of his natural makeup. They instinctively looked for a cause, an interloper with a sinister influence, and a moment when he had been corrupted. Brother Aleck believed Ross was turned by one of the headmasters at boarding school. Ross's niece Ethel, six years his junior, would write to Margery Ross in 1949, 'I have a very strong feeling that he must have been one of those who are tragically turned or rather set in that direction by early influences and not born with the strong tendency thereto, i.e, a lack of the balance of the masculine and feminine within them.'

Ross was shuttled off to Edinburgh, supposedly far from the wicked influences of London. Aleck helped him with his start by introducing him to W. E. Henley, editor of the *Scots Observer*. Henley hired Robbie to write book reviews and to do various other low-level literary chores. His work there would eventually qualify him to join the Society of Authors. From his lodgings in Rutland Square, Robbie wrote to Oscar Browning. Tilley's dining hall apology had not satisfied him, and he was still dreaming of revenge. His plan is revealing in light of later events. If Tilley were to be appointed lecturer in Classics, Ross said he would publish full details of the ducking incident, 'at all events,' he wrote, 'I shall act in such a way as to make it incumbent on Tilley to bring an action against me. You can tell the Council that you know (privately) that if any attempt to bring Tilley back is successful that I shall make the whole thing public.'[30]

In early February 1890, Ross developed peritonitis and was sent back to London to recover under his mother's care. By the time he recovered, Henley had transferred the *Scots Observer* to London, and Robbie was able to stay and to visit Oscar Wilde from time to time. (Wilde's time was now increasingly occupied by a handsome young poet named John Gray.) Oscar was starting to enjoy the fruits of his new artistic labours. The Ross-inspired *Portrait of Mr. W. H.* had been released the previous July and June saw the publication of both *The Decay of Lying* and the first published version of *The Picture of Dorian Gray*.

Dorian Gray caused a strain between Ross and his editor, as Henley disapproved of the tone of Wilde's latest works and never missed an opportunity to pan them. Robbie felt quite differently. He wrote to Oscar: 'Even in the precincts of the Savile, nothing but praise for *Dorian Gray*, though of course it is said to be very dangerous. I heard a clergyman extolling it, he only regretted some of the sentiments of Lord Henry as apt to lead people astray.'[31]

4

Bosie

And, indeed, the whole book seemed to him to contain the story of his own
life, written before he had lived it.
The Picture of Dorian Gray, Oscar Wilde[1]

Sitting in a small bedroom overlooking the deer park in Oxford's 'New Buildings'
(built in the 18th century), a baby-faced undergraduate 'still as much at heart a
schoolboy' opened the cover of his favourite novel for the fifth time.[2]

Lord Alfred Douglas was never a serious student, but he could stay up half
the night discussing topics that interested him – the two most interesting being
poetry and boys. One of his favourite conversation partners was Lionel Johnson,
an old friend (and bedfellow) from his days at boarding school, now a talented
poet at New College, Oxford. He had, Bosie said, 'a mania for not going to bed'
and he could speak 'in the most brilliant way up till five o'clock in the morning'.
Johnson had read a book that had stunned him so much he had written a poem,
in Latin, to its author. 'In Honorem Doriani Creatorisque Eius' ('In Honour of
Dorian and His Creator') contains the lines:

> Here are apples of Sodom, here are the very hearts of vices, and tender sins.
> In heaven and hell be glory of glories to you who perceive so much.[3]

The Picture of Dorian Gray was Gothic horror, crackling with rebellious wit and
sensuality, laced throughout with philosophy in a way that Johnson had never
before found in a popular novel. It bore the stamp of its long genesis in that very
college in Oxford; with its veiled allusions to the controversial don, Walter Pater,
and allusions to Greek myth evoking the secret associations they held for a certain
subculture of students. Johnson was certain that Dorian would weave the same
spell over Bosie and he lent him his copy. The book had a 'terrific effect' on Bosie,
who would read it fourteen times in a row. 'For years it produced the same effect
every time I read it.'[4]

> I believe that if one man were to live out his life fully and completely, were to
> give form to every feeling, expression to every thought, reality to every dream –
> I believe the world would gain such a fresh impulse of joy that we would forget
> all the maladies of mediaevalism, and return to the Hellenic ideal.

It was a clarion call to action, to imagine what it would mean to live life to the full and 'give form to every feeling'. What could be more intriguing to a man of twenty just beginning to explore his sexuality, a delicious and forbidden kind of love, which the author of this book clearly understood? Dorian, like Douglas, had a beautiful, perfect exterior that disguised a sinister, secret inside. To his friends at Oxford, Bosie appeared to have no shame or fear. He came across as 'an erratic and most attractive person, defiant of public opinion, generous, irresponsible and extravagant'.[5] He was the rake who had cards printed which read: 'Lord Alfred Douglas presents his compliments to ... and regrets that he will be unable to ... in consequence of ...' When he had spent a late night drinking and discussing poetry instead of doing his work, he would fill out the card thus and leave it for one of the dons: 'Lord Alfred Douglas presents his compliments to *Professor Smith* and regrets that he will be unable to *show up an essay on the Evolution of the Moral Idea* in consequence of *not having prepared one.*'[6]

He had a special brand of arrogance that many people found charming. 'Damnably, touchingly conceited', as one half-enamoured friend described him.[7] Wilde would later compare Douglas, approvingly, to Narcissus, the character in Greek mythology who became so infatuated with his own reflection in a pool of water that he sat gazing at it until he turned into a flower.[8] Like Dorian, Douglas felt his beautiful facade hid something dangerous and ugly, thus he was always at pains to defend it. (He would one day famously use the word 'shame' in two of his poems to describe love between males. In a later sonnet, he would compare his desires to a tree rotting from the inside.)

> Eternal youth, infinite passion, pleasures subtle and secret, wild joys and wilder sins – he was to have all these things. The portrait was to bear the burden of his shame. That was all.

More than anything else, he was intrigued by the notion of remaining forever young. For he longed to remain a carefree, innocent boy for the rest of his life. He would, on his 21st birthday, be 'so overcome with melancholy' at the thought of his 'vanished youth' that he retired after dinner to his bedroom and wept. 'When you go to heaven,' he would one day write, 'you can be what you like and I intend to be a child.'[9]

The life-long nickname 'Bosie' hearkens back to childhood. Alfred Bruce Douglas was born on 22 October 1870, the third of five children of the ninth Marquess of Queensberry, John Sholto Douglas and his wife Sibyl née Montgomery. He was named for his maternal grandfather, Alfred Montgomery, whose fabled good looks he had inherited, and Lord Robert Bruce, one of his father's friends from the Royal Navy, who was also his godfather. His name reflects two warring aspects of his own identity, a strong, athletic absolutist and a delicate-looking, poetic and musical aesthete. Alfred was the apple of his mother's eye. She spoke to him using an affectionate Scottish term for 'boy' – 'boysie', which his infant tongue transformed into 'Bosie'. (His sister Edith had a similar nickname, 'Wommy' meaning 'little woman'.) The only family member who objected to the appellation was his namesake grandfather. He never called his grandson anything but Alfred, and made fun of the 'ridiculous name Bossy' pretending he did not know to whom the name referred. To all of his other friends and family members, he was Bosie and he would remain, in name, a boy until his death in his seventies.[10]

The initial attraction between Sibyl Montgomery and John Sholto Douglas could only have been physical, because there were few people in the world who had less in common. Queensberry was an energetic, athletic, risk-taker. Sybil was more focused on books and art than the practical matters of the world around her. Bosie inherited from his mother a passion for fine arts, music, literature and ballet and from his father a talent for sport, an interest in horses and hunting and a stubborn, confrontational streak. As a child he was, in his own words, 'frightfully spoilt' by his mother. ('Frightfully' was one of his favourite words.)[11]

Douglas loved the hierarchical world into which he was born. What was not to like? It put him at the centre of the universe. Although his biographers have made his relationship with Oscar Wilde the central conflict of his life, Douglas himself thought the biggest cross he had to bear was being born an aristocrat just as the aristocracy was losing its power.

Of his social class David Cannadine, author of *The Decline and Fall of the British Aristocracy* has written: 'As late as the 1870s [the year of Douglas's birth] these patricians were still the most wealthy, the most powerful, and the most glamorous people in the country, corporately, and understandably, conscious of themselves as God's elect ...'[12] They had been born into a position that liberated them from the compromising pursuit of money. They had the leisure to think great thoughts, hold essential political posts, engage in art, and assist the less fortunate; noblesse oblige. Their marriages were business arrangements, consolidating fortunes and titles. Their households were small villages of butlers, valets, cooks and maids.

The Prince of Wales, later King Edward, was a good friend of his maternal grandfather and namesake Alfred Montgomery and was a regular guest in the Douglas household. When HRH stopped by, he would joke with young Lord Alfred and tease him in a good-humoured way. There was no question that the young man would grow up to have a significant voice in world affairs and that the events of his life would be recorded for posterity. Raised with the help of French nurses and waited on by a bevy of servants (I believe that is the correct collective noun), it must have seemed the world had been made just to have him in it. It was not a question of whether he had been singled out as special by society, objectively he had been. The only question was why.

Douglas learned all of the proper skills for a man of means. He was schooled with impeccable manners, he knew how to dress properly for each event and time of day, he learned to ride horses, write poetry, compose music, play the piano and sing. By the traditional definition, a 'gentleman' was a man with no occupation. Money was a fact of life. It was like the air one breathed. The idea that money could actually dry up, or that one had to trouble oneself much about where it came from, was entirely foreign to Bosie. *That* would be a slow and painful education. In later years Bosie would often make the mistake of writing things for the (middle class) public as though they shared his aristocratic values and assumptions, alienating them when he wanted to gain their sympathy. He truly did not understand that people born without silver spoons might find it hard to sympathise with his brand of 'hardship'.

'The lot of a younger son with the courtesy title of "Lord" and no money is indeed a miserable one,' Douglas wrote in his autobiography. 'I believe the most constant cross I have had to bear is precisely that of having been born, and having had to go all my life being, a lord without money.' (Being *not* a lord without money was beyond his ken.)[13]

He was, as was the habit among those of his class, sent to a series of boarding schools arriving, aged fourteen, at Winchester College, where he first met Lionel Johnson. (By this time, the name Lord Alfred Douglas was already a fixture of the society pages, listed among the guests at various balls and fetes.) Older than

Eton, Winchester, officially known as Collegium Beatae Mariae Wintoniensis prope Winton ('The College of the Blessed Mary of Winchester, near Winchester', for those without a satnav), was a forcing ground of social privilege. It had a tradition of scholarship dating back to its founding in 1382. A Winchester scholar was considered to be the cream of the academic crop and a future member of the ruling class. And then there was Bosie. Never more than a passable scholar, he was nevertheless clever enough to get through without taxing himself overmuch, popular enough to make important social contacts, and athletic enough to earn himself a few minor accolades.

He described his time at the college as 'one long joyous "rag" ... Life was simply one long dream of joy and fun.' Always ready for mischief, Bosie was called more than his fair share of times to the headmaster's office to report for a 'licking' with a birch 'but as Dr. Fearon ("the Bear"), misled by my appearance, cherished the delusion that I was a youth of almost angelic virtue, he never, except on one occasion, carried out the sentence.' When his youthful looks failed to spare him that last time, Lionel Johnson happened to be 'Prefect of Hall' that week and 'officiated in the usual attendant capacity.' Bosie bragged of his hiding to his 'circle of admirers' in the dormitory. 'I ... felt that I was nobly carrying on the old Wykhamical traditions.'[14]

As a boy in boarding school, Bosie had formed a number of strong emotional attachments with other boys. One student, an American who 'fascinated' him, used to call him 'Puppy Dog'.[15] This was perhaps a reference to his most outstanding feature, his puppy dog eyes. It may also have been an early recognition of a trait that would define Douglas throughout his life. In friendship he was, indeed, much like a puppy dog. Anyone who showed affection or flattery earned his complete loyalty, devotion and child-like trust. That is, until he felt he had been betrayed, in which case he would growl and snap like an angry terrier and then, usually, he would come back wagging his tail, expecting to be forgiven. He was not at all discerning about his friend's motivations. If he liked a person, he was highly malleable, frequently gullible and prone to being swindled or led astray.

Bosie gloried in the nickname 'puppy dog' from his 'friend of the heart'. A teacher caught wind of this and thereafter would tease Douglas by calling him an Italian greyhound. 'This used to fill me with rage and grief, and often reduce me to tears.' It was the first time words of endearment between Douglas and an intimate friend would be appropriated by an authority figure and used against him. It would not be the last.

The first fleeting glimpse of love came in the summer term of 1887. Bosie came down with German measles and was quarantined for three weeks in the sick house. Among his fellow patients was a boy named Maurice Turner, the son of one of the house dons, two years his junior. The boys were in adjacent beds and experienced what Bosie would later describe as a 'violent mutual attraction' and love at first sight.

> During the whole of that blissful three weeks when we remained in the Sick-House we were inseparable. In the golden summer weather we walked about with arms entwined or lay in the long grass with stone bottles of ginger beer, and talked, and talked, and told each other stories, real or imaginary. Maurice ... freed from the cramping inhibitions of public-school taboos and conventions, became a natural child and sang songs he had learnt in the nursery. Some of them stick in my memory to this day, after more than fifty years ... Our friendship ... was entirely innocent and idyllic, but it was sentimental to the last degree, which was very far from being the case with most friendships between

older and younger boys in my day at Winchester ... To this very hour it gives me a sharp pang in the heart to remember [Maurice leaving the Sick-House] ... I threw my arms around his neck, and while Miss D'Arcy [the school matron] looked on sympathetically we embraced and mingled our tears, knowing full well that owing to the idiotic and rotten conventions of public-school life ... we would hardly ever be able to see each other except in the distance. We both cried bitterly as we embraced, and I shall never forget the kindness and sympathy of Miss D'Arcy, who, being a good woman, saw nothing to reprehend in two boys kissing each other and shedding tears at parting.[16]

Bosie recounted this scene late in his life, remembering it as the only time he fully experienced his ideal of pure, innocent love with another boy. He called that year 'the star-year of my eternity'.

At Winchester, Douglas was also introduced to the common practice of sexual play with fellow classmates. Initially he found this shocking and upsetting, but he adjusted quickly and came to be an enthusiastic participant. Most of the boys who engaged in such activities were fundamentally heterosexual. They involved their friends in order to explore their own bodies, not because they had any emotional interest in one another. Bosie would later write in his autobiography that some of these youthful sexual relationships were 'innocent' and some were not. He did not spell out the difference, but reading between the lines it is clear. What marked a relationship as 'not innocent' was falling in love. Playing with another boy's body was tolerated as long as it was kept secret. Being another boy's *lover* was shameful. 'Immorality there might be, but sentiment no!'[17]

Thus Bosie, who was inclined to fall in love with other boys, learned to operate in a world of unwritten but understood relationship categories. There was strictly physical play; naughty but also excusable for a temporary period when women were not available, such as at boarding school. Then there was the loving platonic friendship, in which two boys or men could be entirely devoted to each other and even attracted to one another, as long as there was no sexual activity. When the physical and romantic lines merged, you had trouble. (This division continued into adult life where respectable people knew about, and were willing to turn a blind eye to, the uses to which some of their members put male rent boys, as long as no one talked about it or allowed themselves to be caught. They could also find no reasonable objection to strong bonds of affection between men which had no sexual impropriety. Two men gazing at one another in public with an unconcealed combination of affection and lust, on the other hand, could not be tolerated.)

As he entered university, Bosie grew into a highly eligible young man. He was a complete renaissance man, a sportsman who enjoyed shooting, rowing, football and fly-fishing, as well as a talented pianist, singer and poet. He attended the balls and dinner parties that were standard fare for one of his class. He was presented to many young ladies. The corseted and coy creatures did little to stir his heart, but they were pleasant enough company and he even managed to develop small crushes on one or two.

As a matter of propriety, young society ladies, all chaperoned and protected, did not express their appreciation of a man's physical beauty. They did not pursue. They did not praise too highly. They could never hint at lust. To desire and express desire was the prerogative of men. Bosie, who loved to be pursued and adored, found girls vastly inferior to boys when it came to love. To be fully worshipped, mind, body and soul, was to be the object of male, not female desire. No woman could compete with the male gaze. He would marry one day, of course; preferably a woman with a small fortune to complement his unfunded title. A good marriage would provide him a lifetime income and support him as a poet. If it was not too much to ask, he hoped that when the time came he would love his bride. In any case, he was still young, and he had lots of time to play before he would have to face such questions. He would make the most of it.

In his last year of Winchester, he had also discovered what he now believed was his life's calling: poetry. In this art form Bosie found another benefit. Through the structure of poetry, especially the sonnet, he was able to give voice to his deepest emotions. When writing letters or prose his passions would run away with him. He had trouble staying on topic and knowing what was better left unsaid. By forcing himself to slow down and focus on form, he could harness his overwhelming emotions and create something of beauty. The octet of Douglas's *Sonnet on the Sonnet* is, in many ways, an expression of how Bosie related to the world throughout his life:

> To see the moment holds a madrigal,
> To find some cloistered place, some hermitage
> For free devices, some deliberate cage
> Wherein to keep wild thoughts like birds in thrall;
> To eat sweet honey and to taste black gall,
> To fight with form, to wrestle and to rage,
> Till at the last upon the conquered page
> The shadows of created Beauty fall.[18]

He was a man of unruly passions, an inheritance they say, of the 'mad bad' Douglas line. He would spend his life in search of a structure, a 'deliberate cage' to constrain his wild thoughts and feelings.

When he was in a good mood he could not sit still. He would fidget and pace, jump up and sit down. When angered, he could not contain the emotion, he would explode and then the storm would pass, but not without leaving hard feelings in its wake. It was an aspect of his personality he would have to wrestle with his entire life.

Given his family history of mental illness, it is likely that Douglas suffered from what a modern psychologist would diagnose as bipolar affective disorder. Wilde's description (in *De Profundis*) of Douglas's personality reads like a textbook description of the illness: 'long resentful moods of sullen silence' followed by 'sudden fits of almost epileptic rage'.[19] Bipolar disorder consists of dramatic mood swings from deep depression at one end of the scale to mania on the other. Between these two poles there is hypomania, a less severe form of mania. In this state a person feels pleasant, productive, attractive, interested in the world and interesting to the world. When this crosses into mania thoughts start to race, self-esteem is inflated to a grand extreme, small slights morph into persecution complexes, judgement becomes poor and behaviour becomes reckless. The episodes can last for weeks, months or even years at a time and do not necessarily run in predictable cycles.

Douglas was aware of his own turbulent emotions at an early age. The closest he came to explaining how these tempers felt from inside was the 1891 poem 'A Summer Storm,' '... but lo! one note/Of harsh discord, one word of bitterness, And a fierce overwhelming wilderness/Of angry waters chokes my gasping throat.'[20] These tempests were dramatic and sometimes frightening to observers, but thankfully they were fairly rare, most often brought on when Douglas was rejected or felt he had been betrayed. Lady Queensberry wrote to Wilde early in his relationship with Bosie to warn him about this side of her son's personality. Initially, Wilde found her account hard to believe. Many of his friends never encountered his temper. If they eventually did, they were stunned.

To keep the wild thoughts in thrall, Douglas sought external structures, absolute moral codes, and protective mentors, whom he allowed to guide and shape him. He lived his life always in search of a cause or religion, something to which he could dedicate himself, mind, body and soul. 'It has been the passion of my life to sacrifice myself for others, to find and fight for "lost causes" (which I never believe to be really lost), to affront unimaginable odds, and never to admit that I was beaten ... Whatever I have done in life has been done in obedience to an overpowering instinct.'[21]

When he read *Dorian Gray*, Bosie discovered his first great cause: Wilde's philosophy of seeking out sensation and experience. He would believe it more than Wilde ever did himself.

5

Oscar and Bosie

> Oscar and myself are merely ordinary people who are very fond of one
> another and very anxious to live peacefully, joyously and happily and without
> scenes and tragedies and reproaches and all that sort of thing.
>
> Lord Alfred Douglas to his mother, 1894[1]

Robbie was used to relating to older people and was intellectually self-assured
beyond his years. Bosie, by contrast, was still immature. An essay he wrote
when he was editor of the Oxford publication *The Spirit Lamp* underscores this.
Published one year after Bosie and Oscar met, it is called 'An Undergraduate on
Oxford Dons.' It is an extended complaint about the tediousness of dons. It has
the tone of a Holden Caulfield or even a modern teenager complaining about
systems which he has no hand in creating and no way to escape, someone who
does not yet feel he has the power to make choices about his own life.[2]

If the dons were something for Bosie to endure with impatience, they were
something else entirely to Oscar. The intellectual stimulation of Oxford had a
profound and lasting impact on the young writer. Walter Pater's *The Renaissance*
struck young Oscar like a bolt from on high. The book had been controversial
when it was published in 1873. The Bishop of Oxford attacked it for its
neo-paganism and hedonism. It shaped Oscar's imagination more than any other
single work. Years later, he would refer to it as 'that book which has had such
a strange influence over my life.' The Conclusion (which Pater would leave out
of the second edition in case it be 'misunderstood') was so important to him
that he committed it to memory.[3] Pater wrote that our selves are fluid over
time but that 'Every moment ... some mood of passion or insight or intellectual
excitement is irresistibly real and attractive to us – for that moment only. Not the
fruit of experience, but experience itself is the end.' The sentence that particularly
piqued Oscar's imagination was 'To burn always with this hard, gemlike flame,
to maintain this ecstasy, is success in life.' 'Flamelike' became one of Oscar's
favourite adjectives. He would also quote the line 'In a sense it might even be said
that our failure is to form habits' in *De Profundis*. Pater ends by noting that death
is inevitable, but we have the interval to fill with experience:

> Of such wisdom the poetic passion, the desire of beauty, the love of art for its
> own sake, has most. For art comes to you proposing frankly to give nothing
> but the highest quality to your moments as they pass, and simply for those
> moments' sake.[4]

By the time he came to Oxford, Wilde had already won a Berkeley Gold Medal, the highest academic award given by Trinity College, Dublin. He went on to win a Newdigate Prize for his poem *Ravenna* at Oxford. Bosie's academic achievements were less Olympian, consisting of his working just enough to avoid being thrown out. He was threatened with expulsion for poor performance on exams in Divinity and Holy Scripture. Though he did succeed in hiring a pony and going jumping with his brother whenever he could.[5]

Wilde and Douglas both studied 'Greats', the classical grounding specific to Oxford, which focused on Ancient Greek and Roman culture and history, classical languages and philosophy. They read Plato's *Symposium*, the first extended philosophical discussion of love in the Western world. In Plato's conception, love was aroused by beauty – specifically male beauty. Its celebration of male-male love was an eye-opener for many undergraduates. Bosie was especially fond of the part of the *Symposium* that wrote of 'men of debased temperament whose love is directed towards women rather than boys.'[6]

In February 1892, Campbell Dodgson would write to Lionel Johnson of the difficulties he faced tutoring Bosie. 'We argue for hours in favour of different interpretations of Platonism ... Bosie is beautiful and fascinating but quite wicked. He is enchanted with Plato's sketch of democratic man, and no arguments of mine will induce him to believe in any absolute standards of ethics or anything else. We do no logic, no history but play with pigeons and children that drive by the sea.'[7] Bosie would thus have to receive the benefits of an Oxford classical education second-hand, filtered through the mind of Oscar Wilde.

This is not to say that it was Oscar who introduced Bosie to what was then called Uranian culture. There was, at this time, a discernible counter-culture that coursed through the all-male environs of the universities. It celebrated youthful male beauty over the female in its art, poetry, song and discourse. Bosie wrote to his mother that he discovered these ideas 'two years' before he met Wilde.[7] He considered them to be the natural product of his Oxford education. Many years later, after he had rejected his early Uranian views, he would come to believe that Plato should be dropped from the university curriculum. 'I have always maintained that to teach boys, at Oxford, to read Plato is a very risky proceeding.' Impressionable young minds might, he feared, make the same mistake in interpretation he had.[8]

Although Bosie was just an undergraduate, Oscar already knew something of him through their mutual friend Lionel Johnson. Johnson believed his two friends would get on well, and he arranged a meeting in June 1891. Oscar, who was taking a break from writing *Lady Windemere's Fan*, did not make a great first impression. Stuffed into an elaborate frock coat, he seemed to Bosie rather 'comic-looking' and 'too fat for beauty'. But it was the second impression that counted. That was when Oscar started to speak, weaving spells with his melodious voice: Without any apparent effort 'he exerted a sort of enchantment which transmuted the ordinary things of life and invested them with strangeness and glamour ... He had a way of looking at life, and a point of view, which were magical in their effect.'[9]

Bosie finished the evening enchanted and Oscar did too, but it was not love at first sight, at least not for Bosie. It would be another six months before they would become inseparable. In the meantime, Bosie said Oscar pursued him with ardour. (Bosie called it a 'long, patient and strenuous siege'.)[10] That is certainly how it appeared to him, but Oscar remembered things differently. His wooing was not all that specific. He was, at this time, sending his compliments to many young men and making each of them feel he was the only person in the world.

Once Oscar handed Bosie a sonnet called *The New Remorse* which began with the line 'The sin was mine; I did not understand.' Bosie never realised that it had not only been written well before, it had already been published in a slightly different form under the titled *Un Amant de Nos Jours*. Bosie was so certain that it had been written for him, he asked the readers of his autobiography to look at it for insight into the nature of their relationship. He believed, until the end of his life, that the sonnet was the best Wilde had written. This would not, incidentally, be the last time Wilde recycled the poem. In 1899, shortly before his death, Wilde dedicated it to a young Bohemian named Christian Gauss. The version Wilde presented to Gauss was renamed 'Ideal Love.'[11]

The sentimental friendship did not prevent Oscar from working his magic on another young writer, André Gide. Wilde met Gide in November 1891 on a trip to Paris where he would write most of his play, *Salome*. Wilde had a profound effect on the twenty-two year old who found him 'radiant'. His accounts of the experience and his own emotions mirror, in many ways, the effect that Wilde had on both Robbie and Bosie. He told Gide, 'You listen with your eyes.' Gide suspected Wilde 'prepared his conversation in advance' but that did nothing to lessen its charm. Each of them, he said, was a 'sincere actor ... for each was acting out his own character.'

Gide publicly denied that this was a physical seduction. He claimed at the time of this meeting he was unaware of Wilde's sexuality. Of course, the pages for the months of November and December were torn out of his 1891 journal, so it is hard to know for sure. Their conversations were, however, a siege on his soul. Wilde was, Gide said, 'always trying to instil in you a sanction for evil'. He preached the virtues of hedonism, how it was the artist's duty to make his life a masterpiece and to do so he must be open to all experience and every form of vice. Gide was most impressed, as Robbie had been, with Oscar's thoughts on the virtues of lying. 'I don't like your lips,' he told Gide, 'they are straight like those of someone who has never lied. I want to teach you to lie, so that your lips may become beautiful and twisted like those of an ancient mask.'[12]

In the first months of their relationship Bosie had the impression that Oscar was completely infatuated with him even though he was still involved with the poet John Gray and was also romancing a staff member at his publisher's, a neurotic young man named Edward Shelley, whom he described as having 'an intellectual face'.[13] Bosie knew nothing about this at the time, although he would meet Shelley later.

That all changed in May 1892. Oscar rushed to Bosie's aid like a knight in shining armour. Bosie was facing his first brush with blackmailers and he was terrified. (In *De Profundis* Wilde would refer to the episode as the 'Oxford mishap.') Bosie confided in his brother, Percy, who wrote to Wilde for help. Wilde consulted his solicitor George Lewis. Lewis was well-known as the guardian of the secrets of the well-placed and well-to-do, up to and including the Prince of Wales. He neutralised the threat for £100. The details of the blackmail were thus successfully hushed up. (We'll examine what it might have been later.) Word reached Bosie's father, who called it 'infamous conduct' and a 'horrible story'.[14]

Our protagonists saw it differently. To them it was the beginning of a classic romance, the damoiseau in distress, in need of the guidance and protection of an older lover. Their physical relationship began one evening after dinner at the Savoy, a play, and then supper at the Lyric Club. Bosie confessed to Frank Harris in a 1925 letter,

> I was filled up with drinks by the time I got back to his house at almost two o'clock in the morning. There were more drinks and more conversation. After

about two hours discussion he induced me to stay the night in a spare bedroom. In the end he succeeded in doing what he had wanted to do ever since the first moment he saw me. Wilde treated me as an older boy treats a younger one at school, and he added what was new to me and was not (as far as I know) known or practised among my contemporaries: he `sucked' me. Much as I was fascinated by Wilde and much as I really in the long run adored and was 'crazy' about him. I never liked that part of the business. It was dead against my sexual instincts which were all for youth and beauty and softness. After a time he tumbled to the fact that I didn't like it at all and only consented to it to oblige him, and he very soon cut it out all together.[15]

To modern ears, a sex-less relationship is assumed to be incomplete. In the Greek erotic tradition, however, the lack of sexual expression confirmed rather than negated their love. The Symposium shaped the fantasies and love-scripts of many young men who were attracted to other men, including that of Oscar Wilde. In this script an older man takes a beautiful young man under his wing. The older man acts as the younger man's mentor and protector and the young man acts as the older man's muse. In the Greek model, the older man is expected to have more erotic feeling towards the younger than the other way around. As Simon May explains in *Love: A History*, in the ideal form of Greek love,

The young man was supposed to respond only with philia – an attachment of admiring friendship – not physically. According to Greek erotic convention, the junior party was to submit to the older man's advances only after a decent period of resistance. And he was not to enjoy the ensuing sex. Instead he was expected to lack – or failing that, to control – all erotic feelings of his own to the point where he was able to sustain a flaccid penis even in circumstances where this might be thought impossible. He would smile charmingly and look demurely elsewhere while his lover was permitted to rub his penis between the young man's legs, but to avoid penetrating any bodily orifice. (Full-blown intercourse between men is seldom mentioned in Greek literature.)

If a relationship truly blossomed, it transcended its erotic beginnings and evolved into a perfect intellectual friendship that leads to a 'pregnancy of the soul' producing great works of art and creative achievement.[16]

Physical expressions of their love were rare, Bosie wrote in his autobiography, 'but they did occur spasmodically ... They were completely discontinued about six months before the final catastrophe, and were never resumed after he came out of prison. Wilde always claimed his love for me was ideal and spiritual ... I Ionestly, I believe he thought this to be true and meant what he said. In any case I am perfectly certain that his love for me, such as it really was before he went to prison, was the nearest he ever got to a pure and spiritual love.'[17]

Bosie may not have been quite as ambivalent about sex with Wilde as he would have people believe. Copies of the witness statements in preparation for the Oscar Wilde trial were recently uncovered. One of the statements, not used in court, reveals that the governess of Wilde's children discovered a carelessly discarded letter from Bosie to Oscar signed 'your own loving darling boy to do what you like with.' (As much as Douglas is criticised for his carelessness with private letters, it is worth noting that it must have been Wilde who left this one where it could be seen.)[18]

In any case, Bosie's *description* of their sex life corresponds to an ideal of love that he, at this time, shared with Oscar. 'It was a perfect love, more spiritual than sensual, a truly Platonic love, an artist's love for a beautiful soul and a beautiful body.'[19] When Wilde was asked, in his criminal trial for gross indecency, to explain Douglas's poem 'Two Loves' he gave what would become a famous speech. It was, ironically, a very bad summation of the theme of the poem, which was about young love. It was, however, a perfect summation of how he saw his relationship to the poet who had written it.

'The love that dare not speak its name,' Wilde said, 'is that deep, spiritual affection that is as pure as it is perfect ... It is beautiful, it is fine, it is the noblest form of affection. There is nothing unnatural about it. It is intellectual, and it repeatedly exists between an elder and a younger man, when the elder man has intellect, and the younger man has all the joy, hope and glamour of life before him.'[20]

Bosie 'adored' Oscar, who would one day speak of Bosie before an unsympathetic court and say that he had 'only loved one friend in my life'.[21] In Oscar, Bosie found someone to nurture and protect him, who could write him poetic words of love and compliment his beauty. This appealed to the child-like side of his nature. He wished to be cared for and complimented much as a woman is traditionally loved by a man. He would later write to Robbie that his ideal would be for all of his money to go directly to Oscar so that he would be entirely dependent on him.

Yet he had an equally strong, 'masculine' side, which desired to be dominant and powerful. The child Bosie and the absolute, uncompromising man Douglas were difficult for any single partner to reconcile or satisfy. In this relationship, Bosie was able to be dominant with other young men with Oscar's encouragement. He could then return to Oscar and be the darling boy, protected, admired and nurtured.

Oscar was not looking for a relationship with an equal when he chose Bosie. He was drawn, in large part, to a quality that Shaw called Bosie's 'blazing boyishness', a sense of carefree adventure unencumbered by the stress of family life and career, two pressing realities which occupied so much of Oscar's daily attention. 'I like those who may be called idle and careless,' Wilde would later say in one of his criminal trials, and this was no doubt true. Bosie was happy to play the part. He 'adopted the attitude of *enfant gâté* (spoiled child) with considerable delight and some amusement.'[22]

Bosie had something to teach Oscar too. While the taciturn Pater and the tedious dons wrote glorious phrases about seizing the moment and debated nuances of particular Greek verbs, he was out riding horses, drinking brandy, playing music, making love. His impulsiveness, his sense of fun and his disregard of convention unconsciously embodied the spirit of Pater's *Renaissance*: 'With this sense of the splendour of our experience and of its awful brevity, gathering all we are into one desperate effort to see and touch, we shall hardly have time to make theories about the things we see and touch.'[23]

Bosie lived almost entirely in the moment. He had a sense of humour that was quite different from Oscar's but they made each other laugh and they inspired each other's work. They had in common a sense of unashamed arrogance. Bosie, who was used to being praised for his physical beauty, was moved that Oscar 'recognised that besides a beautiful body I possessed a beautiful soul.'[24]

The summer after the blackmail incident, Oscar headed off on a family vacation at Grove Farm near Cromer. The idea was that a relaxing stay on the Norfolk coast would help him focus on finishing *A Woman of No Importance*. After a pleasant couple of weeks building sand-castles with his sons (now seven and five) he became bored. In late September, Oscar invited Bosie who sped to his friend's side. He spent an enjoyable week with the Wilde family before Constance departed with the children to visit a friend. Bosie's arrival put Oscar in good spirits. He wrote a letter to a friend saying 'I find Cromer excellent for writing and golf still better.'25

'Playing golf' is the only echo of this holiday that makes its way into *De Profundis*, and it probably suggested more to Bosie than to any of the letter's other readers, for they were not alone on the links. They were joined by a boy called Jack who was probably around thirteen. Information about Jack comes from a letter read out in the Ransome trial, but which the British press were too polite to print. The Australians believed their readers were less easily shocked. The Sydney *Truth* included the full text and described Jack as being connected to the Wilde case, although he does not seem to have been. (The full title of the sensational *Truth* article was 'De Profundis! Oscar Wilde and Lord Douglas. "Times" Book Club Sued. Wilde's Weird, Woeful Tale. Lord Alfred Douglas's Letters. "The Song of Two Loves." An Abnormal Aristocratic Atavist.')

Bosie's letter makes for disturbing reading, if indeed the sexual connotations placed on it in court are true. Jack was a caddy or in some way connected to the golf course. After writing that he feared Jack might have forgotten him, Bosie said he 'meant to come and play golf' but that he had not had the opportunity. 'Perhaps I shall be able to come down soon. Is there any golf going on now or is it all over?' Jack was not, however, based in Cromer, so he must have come along with Bosie. 'Have you ever been over to Cromer since the time you were with me?' he asks. Jack and Bosie seem to have corresponded for a while, as Bosie was reminded of Jack by looking at some old letters. His age can be guessed by the fact that Bosie says, 'I suppose you have grown quite big now, but I hope you have not changed much.' He enclosed 'the present of a sovereign' with his note and asked 'Will you write to me like a good boy?' The letter was signed 'Yours affectionately, Alfred Douglas.'26

There is one uncomfortable aspect of Uranian culture that is sometimes glossed over. To a Uranian poet, a perfect muse was a teenager, maybe fourteen to sixteen years old. The boys were to some extent viewed as objects of longing because they were unobtainable, but it is clear that these ideals shaped the fantasies and views of the men who wrote raptures about their beauty. There was, of course, no age of consent for sex between males. It was strictly illegal. To get an idea of what age the larger society deemed a consenting adult we can look to the same law that had only recently criminalised 'gross indecency between male persons'. It also raised the age of consent for girls from 12 to 16. (In France the age of consent was still 13.) Frank Harris, the American journalist and a good friend of Wilde's, objected to the new law. He felt that it was ridiculous because it outlawed sexual activities with a girl under the age of 13 'even with her own consent' and – still more absurd – girls under sixteen even if they 'tempted'.27

One of the many ironies in the Oscar Wilde story is that if he had been tried under the Sexual Offences Act of 1967, which finally decriminalised sex between men, he would have received a five-year sentence rather than the two-year sentence he did. The law that decriminalised gay sex set the age of consent at 21 and almost all of Oscar's partners mentioned in court were younger than that, the youngest being 16 and 17. (In 1994, the age of homosexual consent was lowered to 18 and then, in 2000, to 16 bringing it in line with the age of heterosexual consent.)

The Victorians had Janus-like notions of childhood. It was they who created the mythos of the beatific, innocent child. (An image that is easier to maintain when the daily childcare is left in the hands of servants). On the other hand, they were notoriously tolerant of child labour – eight- and nine-year-olds worked in factories and mines. As Oscar Wilde would later detail in a letter on prison conditions, children of this age were routinely sent to prison and faced sentences as harsh as those endured by adults. Thus the rich child was protected, coddled and idealised, the working class child was seen as a small adult to be exploited for labour and feared as a potential criminal.

During Wilde's criminal trials, even though most of his partners were in their teens, their ages were never much of an issue for the court. It was only their gender and social class that provoked outrage. A medical professional who examined Wilde in prison wrote in his report that the prisoner 'practised the most disgusting and odious of criminal offences with others of his own sex and that too not with one or two individuals of a better station in life, but apparently with the most casual acquaintances of comparatively low social position.'[28]

There is evidence that Bosie, Robbie and Oscar all had sexual encounters with teenagers. (As, no doubt, did Reggie Turner, if his nickname 'the boy snatcher of Clements Inn' is anything to go by.)

Young Jack seems to have been behind either Bosie's eventual expulsion from Oxford or the 'Oxford mishap'. Bosie's nephew, the 11th Marquess of Queensberry, attributed both the Oxford blackmail incident and his expulsion to his 'passion for little boys'.[29] He was in a position to know, or at least to have heard informed family gossip. His father, Bosie's brother Percy, was Bosie's closest confidant.

In the Ransome trial, the 'Jack' letter was tied to an incident at Magdalene College. Shortly after the letter was read in court, Bosie accused the solicitors Lewis & Lewis, who were then acting for Ross and who had briefly acted for Queensberry, of sharing confidential material that Queensberry had gathered for his prosecution of Wilde. Bosie would certainly have known the context of the letter. If he thought it had come from his father, the letter, or one like it, must have been provided to Queensberry in the course of one of the two Oxford scandals.

Queensberry referred to the expulsion in a telegram to Percy a few years later. He called it the 'hideous story of A at Oxford' which he had up to then 'suppressed'.[30] Percy was aware of the first blackmail attempt at Oxford and had been instrumental in getting Wilde to come to his brother's aid, but he did not know the specifics.

In *De Profundis*, Oscar would blame his loss in court on the fact that his friend and solicitor Sir George Lewis did not represent him. He claimed that the relationship was ruined because of the 'Oxford mishap'. If the *De Profundis* account is true, and Lewis was appalled by the Oxford blackmail incident, it is important to remember that Oscar was not. Quite the contrary. He fell in love.

6

Devotion and Admiration

No one at the time thought it of sufficient historical importance to record the auspicious moment when Robert Ross first shook hands with Lord Alfred Douglas. Years later, in a deposition, Robbie would remember that he met Bosie in 1893. Ross's first major biographer Maureen Borland gave the following characterisation to that event: 'Wilde did not introduce Ross to Douglas until early 1893; he knew Robbie would never play a subordinate role to Douglas and he delayed the meeting as long as he could.'[1] But the 1893 date may be a case of faulty memory. Early in his relationship with Bosie (in May or June of 1892), Oscar wrote to Robbie:

> My dearest Bobbie,
> Bosie insisted on stopping here for sandwiches. He is quite like a narcissus – so white and gold. I will come either Wednesday or Thursday night to your rooms. Send me a line. Bosie is so tired: he lies like a hyacinth on the sofa, and I worship him.[2]

Oscar's letter makes it clear that if Robbie didn't already know Bosie, he certainly knew *of* him. The fact that he chose to write to Robbie about his new relationship so early on does not easily lend itself to the conclusion that he wanted to keep one a secret from the other. Douglas and Ross had been part of the same young social circle for some time.

Bosie wrote that he met Robbie about eighteen months after the Cambridge 'dunking incident'. Robbie met Max Beerbohm and Reggie Turner in 1892 and it is likely that he also met Bosie around the same time. Although he would later testify in court that he met Ross through Wilde, Bosie's description in his *Autobiography* makes it sound as though he met Robbie through Max and Reggie. They probably met at a gathering that included all of these friends.

In any case, Oscar did not need to keep Robbie away. He was pursuing other interests. After he left Cambridge, Robbie worked steadily towards his goal of becoming a writer and his ultimately more successful role as a friend and facilitator of a growing circle of artists. In 1891 the editor of the *Saturday Review*, Walter Pollock, suggested that Robbie work with the translator More Adey to write an introduction to a new edition of Charles Robert Maturin's *Melmoth the Wanderer*. (Maturin was, coincidentally, Oscar Wilde's great-uncle.)

Adey, ten years Robbie's senior, was then working under the pseudonym William Wilson. He had done a verse translation of Ibsen's *Brand* which was produced at the Court Theatre. He also contributed to the translation of *The Intruder* by Maurice Maeterlinck. Osbert Sitwell found him to be an 'intensely fantastic character'. At this time Adey was a small man with a full beard and a receding hairline that made him look older than he was. Many people found something exotic and slightly eastern European in his aspect. At the time Sitwell knew him, he evoked a 'colour drawing of Lenin as he would have been rendered through the etherealised vision and by the etiolative hand of Burne-Jones.'[3]

The character of Lord Henry Wotton in Wilde's *The Picture of Dorian Gray* may have been named from Adey's family estate, a Queen Anne manor known as Under-the-Hill in Wotton-under-Edge, Gloucestershire. He studied at Keble College, Oxford. Keble was for members of the Anglican Church, a large number of whom were expected to go on to ecclesiastical careers. Adey was ejected from the college in 1879 when he converted to Catholicism. He earned his BA and MA as an unsupported student.[4] He was a kind and gentle man, intensely private and non-confrontational and yet he had far-left political views. He was, Sitwell said, 'so ineffective as to be incapable of hunting a midge (but) it pleased him to dramatise himself to himself as a dangerous anarchist.'[5]

Robbie and More developed the kind of close friendship where their names were often spoken together. That year they moved into a shared home on Church Street in Kensington and would live together for the next 15 years. Although they were almost always in each other's company, More used to irritate Robbie sometimes. He was absent-minded, 'vague'. He often lost track of the time of day. Robbie liked to stay up late and talk, but More was such a night owl that he would come home from work in the early hours of the morning and expect Robbie to take him out to dinner. He often woke the housekeeper in the middle of the night to send her out to buy him cigarettes.[6]

Early Ross biographers were at pains to downplay his sexuality and did not elaborate on the nature of the relationship between these two. Bosie described their living situation in an 1897 letter as 'a sort of ménage'. It was the same expression he used on another occasion to describe his own living situation with Oscar Wilde in Naples and his home with his wife Olive.[7] The reasonable, though unproveable, conclusion is that Adey was the first of Robbie's two long-term committed romantic relationships.

Adey was but one of many new friends Robbie was making at this time. He was attracted to colourful characters with personalities and habits that shone as bright as (and sometimes brighter than) their artistic abilities. He was a devoted friend and champion to many. He also enjoyed gossip and involved himself in his friend's emotional dramas. He was always ready to jump in and offer support and assistance, but his interventions often straddled the fine line between helping and meddling. A common phrase in his friends' letters is 'Don't tell Bobbie,' which highlights his propensity to overstep his bounds. Siegfried Sassoon said Robbie often acted at 'the risk of being thought a busybody ...'[8]

Robbie's sexual encounter (or encounters) with Oscar had not been the beginning of a love affair. By his own account, Robbie would not really get to know Oscar well until 1891. ' ... there were long intervals when I never saw him,' Robbie wrote of Oscar, 'and he never corresponded with me regularly until after the downfall ...'[9] It was not until the trials themselves that Robbie's loyalty, compassion and practical assistance would truly bond them.

Whenever it began, a friendship developed between Robbie and Bosie in the long period that Wilde and Douglas were inseparable. Bosie was delighted by the 'slender, attractive, impulsive boy.' Although he lacked any great physical beauty, he had an appealing, vulnerable quality. He struck Bosie as being 'like a kitten.' He was also impressed by his wit, intelligence and social graces. 'When you had ten minutes' conversation with him you went away with a pleasing feeling that you were really an important person, and that Ross appreciated it, and would never be likely to forget it.'[10]

The attraction was mutual. Bosie was very much Robbie's type: an aspiring poet with a complex personality and a certain carelessness as to the exigencies of everyday life. Robbie's caregiver nature, and his attraction to drama explains his relationship with Bosie as well as Oscar. 'Bosie liked Ross then,' wrote Rupert Croft-Cooke. 'He took him about more than Wilde had ever done.'[11] They were frank and bold in their letters to one another, recounting experiences they could share with few others.

'Ross was by way of being devoted to me in those days,' Bosie recalled in his *Autobiography*. 'If I had followed his example and kept the letters he wrote to me, I could have showed that he professed devotion and admiration for me in as extravagant terms as those used by Oscar.'[12]

Like Bosie, Robbie was a man of moods. The main difference between them was that Bosie directed his rages outward. Robbie turned inward. They were both prone to over-reaction when they felt rejected by a friend. Bosie typically reacted with a mixture of hurt and haughty outrage, retreating to the comfort of his title to protect him from such indignities. His bitterness and anger were usually short-lived (as most of his moods) except when he categorised someone as a real enemy, in which case he could be unrelenting. Robbie, by contrast, held onto his hurts. He would stew and complain bitterly to other friends, trying to bring them around to his point of view. 'If Douglas was a Jekyll and Hyde character then it must be said so was Ross,' wrote Borland. 'And there perhaps is the cause of their quarrels. They were both so alike, spoilt, arrogant, charming, generous, witty and utterly unforgiving of each other's faults.'[13]

To the Victorians, homosexuality was a crime not principally because it was contrary to scripture, but because it was a corruption that undermined civilization and threatened the cohesion of society. Edward Gibbon's *Decline and Fall of the Roman Empire* had argued that Rome had collapsed because men became effeminate and unwilling to fight in the military. This made homosexuality not only distasteful but also a threat to the empire. (An article on the Wilde trials in *The Sun*, which ran with the headline 'Wilde's Career Ended' referred to this idea. 'The growth of evil among certain classes of this country is appalling ... it becomes evident that no other means will suffice to check and destroy the vice which undermined the civilization of the ancient Romans.')

Oxbridge-educated homosexuals found a counter-narrative in the story of Greece's brave Theban soldiers who fought beside their younger male lovers (the new recruits were known as ephebes). They remained undefeated until the Battle of Chaerona in 338 B. C. E. Where Plato's *Republic* advanced the idea that the love of an older man for a younger could lead to wisdom that would improve the world, the Theban bands showed that such men could be bold, brave, and beneficial to society. This was the idea behind the secret group known as the Order of Chaeronea founded in 1897 by the sexologist and prison reform advocate George Ives.

The use of evasive language, secret codes and initials rather than names in Ives' diaries make it difficult to know how the order operated and who belonged to it.

Both Robbie and Bosie were central figures in the counterculture of homosexual men. Oscar and Bosie were both allegedly members of the Order. Robbie was not, although he was in sympathy with 'the Cause'. He called Ives 'St. George,' but the two men did not really click. When Robbie died in 1918, Ives wrote in his diary 'I've known him for 20+ years but we seldom met, both parties having tastes far asunder, and each having nerves though in a different way. Poor Robbie got dreadfully irritable, in fact he rasped me unbearably, and I kept right away for the sake of peace.'[14]

Bosie was thrilled by the modern ideas he was encountering. When he took over the Oxford publication the *Spirit Lamp*, he transformed it into a showcase of the works of Uranian poets and advertised it to 'all who are interested in modern life and the new culture', an insider's term for a philosophy of life that elevated, rather than denigrated, male-male love. Robbie contributed his tale of forgery, 'How We Lost the Book of Jasher.' Max Beerbohm made his debut in its pages. Other contributors included John Addington Symonds, Lionel Johnson and Charles Kains-Jackson, who had been responsible for a similar transformation as editor of *The Artist and Journal of Home Culture*. Almost every issue of that magazine during his tenure included poems with Greek imagery and odes to beautiful male youths. (Kains-Jackson, reportedly a member of the Order, was a solicitor and also an expert on agriculture and in that capacity he published articles with titles like 'History of the International Corn and Wool Trade.')[15] The world of Oxford academics was drifting farther and farther away in the eyes of the forward-looking Bosie.

If Oscar admired Bosie for his courage, the feeling was mutual. Bosie wrote to Kains-Jackson in September 1893:

> Perhaps nobody knows as I do what [Oscar] has done for the 'new culture', the people he has pulled out of the fire and 'seen through' things not only with money, but by sticking to them when other people wouldn't speak to them. He is the most chivalrous friend in the world, he is the only man I know who would have the courage to put his arm on the shoulder of an ex-convict and walk down Piccadilly with him, and combine with that the wit and personality to carry it off so well that nobody would mind.[16]

Bosie also did what he could to help the fallen. He wrote to Ives a number of times begging him to publicise the deaths of men who had committed suicide after being accused of indecent acts with young men. He wrote to Kains-Jackson for legal advice to help a man waiting trial for a similar offence.[17] Robbie corresponded with Kains-Jackson as well on issues related to 'the cause'. Robbie was acting as a liaison, sending financial support from his eccentric friend Count Eric Stenbock to the exiled homosexual artist Simeon Solomon.

In April 1894, *The Artist* included Bosie's 'Prince Charming', a love poem for a 16-year-old boy. Immediately following, under the initials PC, was Kains-Jackson's 'The New Chivalry', a full-throated advocacy of the New Culture. The revolution would not be restricted to decriminalising sexual relations between males, it would be a complete cultural shift – part religion, part art, part social and political change.

Kains-Jackson argued that the 'youthful feminine ideal' was being replaced with the 'exaltation of the youthful masculine ideal'. The old paradigm of married love for the purposes of procreation made sense in a world that was under-populated, but that now that England was militarily strong, it was no longer necessary to encourage reproduction. The nation was free to embrace a more spiritually evolved culture. It would be a distinctly bisexual world, where men would have free choice to love either sex, but would most often choose boys because of their superior intelligence.

Relationships in this new civilization would be modelled on Plato with an older partner and a younger, 'the tenderness of ... one who has endured for him that has yet to endure ...' When this form of love was celebrated, the entire nation would rise to a new level of spiritual and intellectual development.[18]

Douglas was a true believer. He wrote to Kains-Jackson from Wilde's chambers in St James and praised the article as 'brilliant and daring'; perhaps too daring. The April 1894 edition was to be Kains-Jackson's last as editor.

7

The First Battle of Salome

As Bosie and Oscar's relationship developed, Robbie was encouraging. He received from both (and presumably sent) breathless letters about boys. Robbie was also sometimes called upon to smooth out disputes between them. Exactly why Oscar proposed, in 1893 that Bosie should translate his play *Salome*, originally written in French, is a bit of a mystery. Wilde was, after all, a native English speaker himself and he would know better than anyone else what he meant to say. Maybe he believed Bosie understood his play, and its author, better than most and he wanted to see what kind of poetry he would bring to it. Bosie did, after all, praise the language of *Salome* in his review of the text in *The Spirit Lamp*, comparing it to 'the tones of different instruments, suggestion, suggesting, always indirectly, till one feels that by shutting one's eyes one can best catch the suggestion.'[1]

The most satisfying explanation is also the most romantic. The notion of Platonic pregnancy of the soul inspired Wilde to make *Salome* a joint creation with his muse. As Wilde wrote of Shakespeare's relationship to his own muse, the actor Willie Hughes, '... we cannot marvel that he so worshipped one who was the interpreter of his vision, as he was the incarnation of his dreams ... This was indeed a subtle element of pleasure, if not of passion, and a noble basis for an artistic comradeship.'[2] Whatever he was thinking, it proved to be a mistake, as did Robbie's suggestion of Aubrey Beardsley as illustrator.

Beardsley was Robbie's first major artist cause; he made introductions, tried to enlist critics to review Beardsley's work, supported him and offered him practical assistance. Aubrey's fragile health brought out Robbie's caregiving instincts and over the next few years he would offer invaluable support to the artist and his family. Although Robbie would publicly call Beardsley's desire to shock a 'boyish failing for which he may be forgiven', Robbie's life-long attraction to eccentric artists and their work suggests he did not disapprove of art that pushed the boundaries at all.[3]

C. Lewis Hind, editor of *The Studio*, had asked Beardsley to draw a sketch to illustrate a review of Wilde's *Salome*. Beardsley chose to depict the climax of the play, Salome kissing the severed head of John the Baptist. He produced a drawing as dazzling in its simple, elegant composition as it was horrible in theme. Salome seems to float in a cloud among an abstract background of overlapping circles, her black hair is unruly and wild and her expression is viciously satisifed as she brings the disembodied head towards her lips. From the severed neck drops a flow of blood into a lily pond and the foot of the picture. It is both dreamlike and visceral, and it was far too much for his editor. When Hind saw it he 'nearly had a fit' and refused to publish it.[4]

The drawing did have its admirers, among them Robbie, who arranged a meeting between Beardsley and Wilde, Wilde was convinced that Beardsley should do illustrations for the English-language edition of his play. The honeymoon between Beardsley and Wilde did not last. Privately, Beardsley and Beerbohm enjoyed mocking and parodying Oscar. There is good reason to believe Robbie also enjoyed talking behind Oscar's back. He was, after all, one of the young men behind the taunting of his mentor Oscar Browning at Cambridge, so he was not averse to a bit of affectionate roasting of men he admired. In November 1893 Beardsley felt emboldened to write to Robbie about Oscar and Bosie that 'both of them are really very dreadful people.'[5] The unkind parodies and the obscene details in some of Beardsley's *Salome* drawings bothered Wilde and led to some tense negotiations.

Meanwhile Bosie, who had translated *Salome* with great enthusiasm, had sent his results to John Lane. When Oscar saw the proofs, he was upset by what he called (in *De Profundis*) the 'schoolboy faults'. Robbie would later tell Oscar that Bosie felt 'humiliated' at having his work returned 'like a schoolboy's exercise'. It would be an absurd understatement to say Bosie did not take criticism well. The disagreement ended in a major row during which Bosie said he was 'under no intellectual obligation of any kind' to Oscar.[6] This angry outburst clearly struck a nerve with Oscar, who would replay the incident in his mind years later in prison.

Oscar and Bosie each turned to friends to act as intermediaries. Bosie turned to Robbie, who pleaded his case. Oscar would later claim Robbie said Oscar was 'expecting far too much intellectually' from his friend.[7] This may be true, although it sounds more like the criticism Oscar usually lobbed at Bosie himself when he was angry with him.

While much has been made of Bosie's temper, much less has been said about Oscar's own style of argument. Bosie's outbursts were dramatic and unpredictable, but they were straightforward. He would shout whatever he thought at the moment, no matter how unfair or extreme. The mood would pass, and he would come back and apologise for losing his head. When Oscar was angered his attacks were much more understated, and much more devastating. The same skill that made him a brilliant conversationalist could be used as a weapon. 'There was nothing at that time, nor I believe since, the least like Oscar Wilde dominating a dinner table,' the actress Elizabeth Robins wrote. 'He did what he liked with people. He could make them shine, he could make them shrink.' He was, she said, 'brilliant beyond the power of report, overbearing yet urbane, unless crossed and then most alarming.'[8]

Oscar had, according to Bosie, a 'ferocious will about many things'.[9] When Oscar wanted to put Bosie in his place, he would compare his young lover negatively to his past loves (especially John Gray) or compare his conversation to that of his more intellectual friends (especially Robert Ross). For example, Douglas told biographer A. J. A. Symons that he didn't know much about Wilde's friend Carlos Blacker 'except that he was a great friend of Oscar's ... He used to disapprove of me, according to Oscar's account, & Oscar used to quote him when he wanted to be disagreeable. "Carlos Blacker says etcet." I once said to Oscar "I don't believe there's no sich [sic] person."'[10] Whether the topic of Bosie's intellectual ability had entered the subject because of Oscar or Robbie, Robbie had other lines of defence. He told Oscar that 'no matter what [Bosie] wrote or did' he was 'absolutely and entirely devoted' to him.

Kains-Jackson also received telegrams from both parties asking for his help, and did his part to smooth things over, also arguing for the inclusion of some of Beardsley's more controversial drawings.[11]

Bosie wrote to John Lane and said, 'I have decided to relinquish the affair altogether. You and Oscar can arrange between you as to who the translator is to be. My private opinion is that unless Oscar translates it himself, he will not be satisfied.'[12] After he rejected Bosie's translation, Oscar handed *Salome* over to Beardsley to fix. He liked his version even less. In the end, Oscar decided to use Bosie's base text and make the corrections he wanted himself. Bosie did not accept this version was his work and he asked to have his name removed as translator. A compromise was reached. Instead of listing Douglas as the translator, the 1894 text would appear with a dedication 'To my friend Lord Alfred Bruce Douglas the translator of my play.'[13] Ross or Kains-Jackson had managed to persuade Bosie, as he would write to John Lane,

> The dedication which is to be made to me is of infinitely greater artistic and literary value than the appearance of my name on the title-page. It was only a few days ago that I fully realized that the difference between the dedication of *Salomé* to me by the author and the appearance of my name on the title-page is the difference between a tribute of admiration from an artist and a receipt from a tradesman.[14]

After Oscar's death, in 1906, Robbie published an updated version of the play. It was released with the title *Salome: A Tragedy in One Act Translated from the French of Oscar Wilde.* Yet there is no mention anywhere of who did the translation. This is because Douglas had written to Lane on 6 July 1906 asking to have the dedication removed from the title page. 'Oscar Wilde ... revised the translation to the extent of taking out from it most of the elements of original work on my part.' In a note in the second edition of his *Autobiography*, Bosie also said although the translation of *Salome* was usually attributed to him, he viewed it as Wilde's work, not his.[15]

Bosie was unaware that Robbie had, at any rate, quietly substituted the earlier text with an entirely new translation. Most people who knew the history of *Salome* assumed the anonymous translator of the 1906 edition was Douglas. In 1910, a version that bibliographer Christopher Millard called 'the Ross edition' appeared in the United States with the title 'Salome translated from the French of Oscar Wilde by Lord Alfred Douglas.' From that point on, publishers printed the 1906 Ross translation believing it was Douglas's 1894 text, when, in fact it was not.[16] Years later, Robbie wrote to Frank Harris commenting on his biography of Wilde, and said it was 'at my insistence' that Douglas's name was removed from the title page. He conveyed this information to Harris as if it were a secret. (Robbie often shared 'secrets' with people as a way to get them to be the first to publicise something he did not want to appear to have originated.)[17]

Thus we have two competing narratives about the translation of *Salome*. Bosie's is that he and Oscar had creative differences and that Oscar rejected his work and used what was essentially his own translation. The second is that Bosie's work was incompetent, but used anyway because Oscar didn't want to hurt his feelings and that Robbie quietly solved the problem by commissioning a new translation. Of the two accounts, Bosie's is better documented, but Robbie's has been more widely believed. In any case, the battle over *Salome* created waves throughout their circle of friends. 'I had a warm time of it between Lane and Oscar & Co,' Beardsley wrote to Ross. 'For one week the number of telegraph and messenger boys who came to the door was simply scandalous.'[18]

The message contained a double entendre. Of course there had been a flurry of furious messages, but the allusion to 'telegraph boys' also called to mind the 1889 Cleveland Street scandal, in which it was revealed that a number of post-office messengers were moonlighting at a male brothel. Beardsley was not only saying that emotions ran high ...

8

Feasting with Panthers

It was like feasting with panthers. The danger was half the excitement.
Oscar Wilde, *De Profundis*.[1]

Much ink has been spilled over the question of whether Robbie or Bosie lured Oscar to the types of companions that would lead to his downfall. No one involved was considerate enough to historians to create documentation of any such illegal activities. The story that Bosie introduced Oscar to what they called 'rough trade' has won out. Bosie, of course, denied it. In all of this debate one important and seemingly obvious point was lost. Oscar had more than two friends. What is more, he did not need to be *lured* to the red light district by anyone. He had been attracted to the dark eroticism of the slums long before he met either Robbie or Bosie. He was encouraged in this interest (and surpassed in enthusiasm for it) by his long-time friend Robert Harborough Sherard.

Wilde and Sherard met in Paris in the spring of 1883 when Sherard was 22 and Wilde 28. They were then both ambitious, aspiring writers. For the first two months of their friendship they were together constantly. They dined together every day; long, lingering meals that lasted from noon to 3 A. M. Sherard was always broke. It is easy to see why Oscar was drawn to him. The handsome, athletic blond was, both in appearance and temperament, a lot like Lord Alfred Douglas. His emotions were often extreme. He fell alternately into melancholy, rages and periods of intense activity. Like Douglas, Sherard valued his friend's ability to lift him out of suicidal depressions. Oscar taught him 'the gladness of things ... the possibility of great and buoyant happiness in the world.'[2]

He had a habit of getting into duels, and not literary ones. By the time Oscar met him, he'd been wounded in the leg after a fight in Naples with a man who had ogled his girlfriend. Also like Douglas, Sherard was a man of unrestrained sexual appetites, although his were focused on women.

Sherard was probably the man who took Oscar to the Eden Music Hall where he engaged the services of one Marie Aguetant, a well-known prostitute who was later murdered.[3] On Wilde's 1884 honeymoon, Sherard took his friend out on the town to see some of the most notorious bars in Paris including the Château Rouge, a famous criminal haunt located beneath the 'Salle des Mort', a flop house for drunks, beggars and orphans, 'a room full of ragged men who looked, in slumber, more like corpses than human beings, and upon whom Oscar gazed in horror and wonder.'[4]

Pierre Louys described a memorable Paris outing with Sherard in a letter to André Gide of 2 October 1891. Their adventures in Les Halles continued until

50

dawn and ended with them sharing bacon and oysters with a pair of syphilitic, 16-year-old prostitutes. Francis Gribble, one of Sherard's fellow writers at the *Daily Graphic*, was treated, along with Rowland Strong of the *Morning Post*, to a tour of some of his favourite Parisian dives. He suggested they wrap up the evening in an area with a reputation as a den of thieves. Strong warned Gribble not to go, 'He'll get mixed up in a fight,' Strong said, 'You won't have the least idea what the row is about, but you'll feel obliged to join in, and you're pretty sure to get hurt.'[5]

Homosexual activity was, however, inexorably linked with this enticing, dangerous world. Criminalising desire had the unintended effect of eroticising criminality. Whether or not Oscar acted on these impulses at this early date, they were certainly a long-running part of his fantasy life. Oscar had been developing a hedonistic philosophy since his student days at Oxford when he read Walter Pater's advice to burn with a 'hard, gemlike flame.' Harris, who believed Bosie introduced Oscar to 'the streets' pointed out in his *Oscar Wilde* that every incident mentioned in Oscar Wilde's trial occurred in 1892 or later, after Oscar had met Bosie. Of course, this does not prove that Oscar had no experience with prostitution before then, only that he had never before been caught.

There is an oft-repeated tale of a turning point in Oscar's life. The story comes from Ada Leverson. Back when Oscar was still an attentive, newly-wed husband, he took Constance shopping at Swan and Edgar's, a famous department store facing Piccadilly Circus. As husbands have done from time immemorial, he waited outside as she lingered over skirts and feminine garments. As he stood, enjoying the sunny May morning a 'curious, very young, but hard-eyed creature appeared, looked at him, gave a sort of laugh, and passed on. He felt he said 'as if an icy hand had clutched his heart'. He had a sudden presentiment. He saw a vision of 'folly, misery and ruin'.[6]

Even if this anecdote is apocryphal, it illustrates an important point. If he had wanted to engage a male prostitute, Oscar would certainly have known where to find one. As Leverson's tale reveals, Swan and Edgar's was not only one of the most elegant shops in London, it also overlooked one of the city's most notorious pick-up spots. Piccadilly's reputation was such that it was almost enough to convict Wilde's co-defendant Alfred Taylor of gross indecency when he was forced to admit before the jury that he 'frequently walked through Piccadilly'. The theatre district was likewise a well-known centre for prostitution of all types. The bar at the St. James Theatre, where *Lady Windemere's Fan* and *The Importance of Being Earnest* were staged, was especially notorious.[7]

If Bosie did introduce Oscar to the streets, it must have been a big part of Oscar's attraction, just as Robbie's openness had once attracted him. There is, however, some reason for scepticism and it comes from Wilde's own hand. Of the blackmail attempt at Oxford, Wilde would write (in *De Profundis*) 'The gutter and things that live in it *had begun* to fascinate you. That was the origin of the trouble in which you sought my aid.' This suggests that Bosie's foray into 'the gutter' was new at that time and that it developed in the course of his friendship with Oscar, not before.[8]

When A. I. Tobin and Elmer Gertz were writing *Frank Harris: a Study in Black and White*, Harris and Douglas had been sparring over shared history for some time and the authors patiently corresponded with the two writers in an ultimately vain attempt to get to the final truth behind the two touchy characters' aggressive pronouncements. Gertz was a celebrated attorney who approached the case with a lawyer's eye, trying to weigh the evidence as he might in court. One of the main bones of contention was whether Bosie introduced Oscar to prostitution. The authors recorded, rather mysteriously, that Bosie had furnished them with 'absolute proof that he had nothing to do with Oscar's introduction to catastrophic vices'. They did not, however, elaborate on what that proof might have been.[9]

Bosie was certainly sexually experienced when Oscar met him, but a reputation for wickedness need not have come from back alleys. Having any sexual experience with another male made one wicked and criminal in the Victorian world. Bosie was to become highly promiscuous. Before he met Oscar, however, most if not all of his encounters – however many there may have been – were probably with other students, not 'rough trade'.

The most likely reason that Bosie would have suddenly developed a fascination for the gutter after he met Oscar was that it was inspired by Oscar himself. As Bosie wrote in his *Autobiography*:

> Even before I met Wilde I had persuaded myself that 'sins of the flesh' were not wrong, and my opinion was of course vastly strengthened and confirmed by his brilliantly reasoned defence of them, which may be said almost to have been the gospel of his life. He went through life preaching the gospel which he puts into the mouth of Lord Henry Wotton in Dorian Gray. Wilde was, in fact, a most powerful and convincing heresiarch.
>
> He preached that it was the duty of every man to 'live his own life to the utmost,' to 'be always seeking for new sensations,' and to have what he called 'the courage' to commit 'what are called sins'.
>
> I am trying to be fair to Wilde and not to make him responsible for 'corrupting' me more than he did. All the same, I must say that it strikes me now that the difference between us was this: that I was at that time a frank and natural pagan, and that he was a man who believed in sin and yet deliberately committed it, thereby obtaining a doubly perverse pleasure. I was a boy and he was a blasé and very intellectual and brilliant man who had immense experience of life. Inevitably I assimilated his views to a great extent.[10]

Robbie believed the Hellenic/Hedonistic philosophy as much as Bosie did. Some time after Wilde's trials, the poet R. C. Jackson wrote to Oscar Browning:

> Today I lunched with Mr Ross ... & he made terrible things known to me, respecting the person we spoke about [Wilde] ... The while he gave myself information which saved linking my name with such a foul and detestable person – he appeared to think nothing of such foul enormities saying, 'Michael Angelo, Shakespeare, J. A. Symonds, Pater & many others were equally admirers of the same sort of thing' – that was his excuse to me.[11]

Although there is no evidence that Robbie was involved with the particular circle that featured in Wilde's trials, what evidence there is suggests that Robbie was not a stranger to any of the behaviours of his friends: cross-class sexual entanglements, sharing sex partners with friends, prostitution and sexual activity with teenagers. In the course of their later battles, Bosie would seek out the testimony of a Scotland Yard inspector who swore that he had patrolled the Vine Street area of Piccadilly for fifteen years and 'had known Ross during all those years as an habitual associate of sodomites and male prostitutes'.[12]

Oscar had another friend whose role in his downfall has rarely been examined. His name was Maurice Salis-Schwabe and his arrival ushered in both Oscar and Bosie's most ardent period of sexual experimentation and the first major conflicts in their relationship. Handsome, with dark hair and a square jaw, he was a charismatic character who made friends quickly and easily. Schwabe was born on 14 October 1871, the oldest of six children to General George Salis-Schwabe and his wife Mary. His paternal grandfather Salis Schwabe was a German Jewish cotton merchant who immigrated to Middletown, converted to the Unitarian religion, bought a local mill and made a fortune. His wife Julia became a noted philanthropist and founder of schools. One of their other children, Julia Rosetta (Maurice's aunt), married Sir Frank Lockwood, who would become Solicitor General, a fact that will become highly relevant as we go on. Maurice grew up in a home full of servants including a governess, nurse, nurse maid, cook, kitchen maid, parlour maid and a page. At some point in his life, Schwabe considered joining the priesthood (at least according to his mother) but he was destined for a very different career.[13]

The Labouchere amendment, section 11 of the Criminal Law Amendment Act of 1885, which made 'gross indecency' between male persons a crime, criminalised for the first time sexual acts between consenting adults in the privacy of their own homes. This aspect of the law was not popular, and a number of editorials appeared in both legal and lay journals, but few respectable people were inclined to make it their cause célèbre for fear of being thought guilty of 'unnatural practices' themselves.[14] It came to be known as 'the Blackmailer's Charter'. Those in the legal profession predicted that fear of prosecution for private acts would lead to a whole new market for blackmail but that juries would be reluctant to convict people for activities that took place in private regardless of the letter of the law. Both of these predictions proved true.

Even though it figured in two highly prominent cases, the Cleveland Street prostitution case and the trials of Oscar Wilde, the Labouchere amendment did not lead to an increase in prosecutions of same-sex activity. Long before Labouchere, under common law, any *attempt* to commit a crime was viewed as an offence. Therefore, an 'unnatural' touch could be defined as an attempt to commit sodomy and prosecuted.[15]

In fact, author Graham Robb calls the amendment 'the biggest non-event' in the history of laws affecting homosexual men. Conviction rates in the decade before and after the amendment were practically identical.[16] But criminal prosecution was not the main fear of homosexual men. They were equally terrified of the loss of reputation, being expelled from their clubs, and being estranged from their families. This allowed blackmailers to ply their trade even though arrest rates for such crimes remained stable.

The problem with an inconsistently enforced law is that it creates opportunities for people to use the threat of arrest for their own purposes. While the police monitored known homosexual haunts and sometimes made lists of known homosexuals, they were not inclined to make arrests. Arrests were almost always the result of a specific complaint and they were often used by homosexual men as revenge against other homosexual men. As Robb noted 'many lovers' quarrels ended with an anonymous letter to the vice squad.'[17] In a similar vein, the law would one day prove to be a highly effective club with which Douglas and Ross could bludgeon one another.

One of the reasons blackmail surged in the years 1885 to 1900 had to do with another law. The Elementary Education Act of 1870 mandated compulsory education in England and Wales for children between the ages of five and thirteen. By 1900, 97 per cent of the population of England and Wales was considered literate. This meant that for the first time there was a large population of people both desperate enough to turn to crime and able to read a misplaced letter and make use of it.[18]

Illicit sexuality required deception and some people, like Schwabe, discovering a talent for dissembling, decided to make it a career. In the eyes of the law, a man who slept with another man in his own bedroom was as much of a criminal as someone who stole your diamonds, or swindled you out of a fortune with fraudulent business ventures. If one was going to be a criminal, one might as well engage in crime's more lucrative forms.

Schwabe made a life-long career out of leading others down the primrose path. He would become an internationally wanted member of a band of cardsharps and blackmailers and may have been a police informer and spy. He made introductions that ended in theft, hosted sex parties that ended in blackmail and founded dubious businesses that ended in charges of fraud, always against other members of the criminal organisation, not himself. Most of the time, his marks never realised that he had been involved in their mishaps. In fact, some backed him in multiple businesses.[19] Croft-Cooke's description of Schwabe as a 'fat talkative queen with glasses and a pronounced giggle' hardly did him justice.[20]

It is unclear how Schwabe met Wilde. It seems as though he actively sought out the friendship, as Croft-Cooke describes him as 'a busy ambitious young man … intrepid in making contacts and indefatigable in that pursuit.'[21] However they met, it was some time before February 1892. Schwabe was part of the green-carnation-wearing crowd at the premiere of *Lady Windemere's Fan.* Schwabe shared something with Oscar that Robbie and Bosie (at least at this time) did not, an attraction to crime. In spite of Oscar's later claim, Bosie was never attracted to 'the gutter' in particular, he was attracted to sex in general, and his tastes happened to be illegal. The attraction to the thrill of criminality was initially all Oscar's.

Schwabe brought the blackmailers that we know of into Oscar's life. He introduced him to Alfred Taylor who would stand trial alongside Wilde for procuring, and thanks to the discovery of some long-lost love letters, we now know that Bosie fell passionately (though perhaps only briefly) in love with Schwabe. Although the exact timing is unknown, their sexual relationship began while Bosie was still a student at Oxford. Bosie called Schwabe 'my darling pretty boy'. With only Bosie's side of their correspondence still in existence, it is impossible to know whether Schwabe returned his feelings, but the letters reveal that they were close enough for Schwabe to have visited Bosie's mother's home in Salisbury at least once. The warm and tender side of their relationship is, unfortunately, not nearly as well documented as their more reckless recreational activities.

In the summer of 1892, Schwabe took Oscar to afternoon tea in an incense-scented room above a disused bakery on Little College Street, Westiminster. There Oscar met Taylor who was known to open the door to his flat himself instead of leaving that task to a servant. This was something court officials would later find suspicious, but not nearly as incriminating as his habit of greeting men by calling them 'dear'. Schwabe and Taylor had a great deal in common, both were gossipy with feminine mannerisms, a taste for rough lads and a willingness to make cross-class introductions. In the words of Croft-Cooke, 'From that time onwards Taylor and Schwabe, who had hitherto shared their discoveries, competed in introducing young men to Oscar. Many of them were dangerous; Schwabe seems to have been grossly careless about this and Taylor quite idiotic, but Oscar liked danger and encouraged them both.'[22] They often worked together, with Taylor scoping out willing young men and Schwabe arranging seemingly safe places for the introductions. (Little College Street had only a single spring mattress raised slightly from the floor.)

Shortly after the Wilde-Taylor introduction, Schwabe had picked up a charming 17-year-old at the Knightsbridge roller skating rink. Freddie Atkins was an occasional Music Hall actor with a winning grin, a 'vulgar but sprightly personality' and extensive experience in entrapment and blackmail. He had pale eyes, loose fair hair and a winning sense of humour. (In court, he would give his occupation as 'comedian.') Atkins called himself Dennis, St. Dennis or Denny. Working with an accomplice named James Dennis Burton, also known as Watson, Atkins would go to the public urinals and other notorious pick-up spots and get someone to take him home, at which point Burton, claiming to be his uncle, would barge in and demand money for his silence. Their con was famous enough in certain circles that Burton was known as 'Uncle Burton'.[23]

Denny and Uncle Burton had a falling out and it was during their separation that Atkins met Schwabe. Schwabe was quite taken with Atkins, who entertained him with tales of his experiences as a billiard-maker and bookie's clerk. Given Schwabe's later career, the cons and the crime were undoubtedly part of the charm. Schwabe was attached to Atkins for several months and the young man visited his rooms off Margaret Street almost every day. 'Freddy does not seem to have regarded Schwabe as a prospect,' wrote Croft-Cooke, 'but rather as a friend, even a collaborator.'[24]

Schwabe's relationship with Bosie was also heating up at this time. In one of the recently discovered love letters Bosie wrote, 'I love you as much as I did at Bournemouth & Oxford, more.'[25] Bournemouth is probably a reference to a trip Bosie took in early November 1892. Having suffered an attack of jaundice, Bosie went to recuperate at the Royal Hotel and invited Oscar along. If Schwabe also turned up, and he and Bosie had a passionate encounter, it is worthwhile to note that this was also the occasion of Oscar and Bosie's first serious fight. It can only be speculation, but it seems a fair guess that the trigger for their first serious argument was Bosie's unconcealed love for Schwabe, or his annoyance that the older man had intruded upon it. Whatever had been the cause of the fight, the rancour did not last long.

Atkins became a regular at Alfred Taylor's rooms and brought a new friend into the mix, an attractive, fair-haired young man named Alfred Wood. Wood was an unemployed clerk, new to prostitution and blackmail. Bosie entertained Wood several times at chambers in Jermyn Street, probably Schwabe's place.[26] Wood pilfered a number of compromising letters from Oscar to Bosie and others as well. He passed them on to partners to extract sums from the famous playwright. Thankfully for them both, only one of the letters found its way into the courtroom, but that one letter was damaging enough. Oscar found it all frightening but thrilling. He thought the blackmailers were 'wonderful in their infamous war against life'.[27]

9

The Perils of Respectable Society

> It is not the perfect but the imperfect who have need of love.
>
> Oscar Wilde, *An Ideal Husband*[1]

Bosie and Oscar fell into a pattern in their relationship where they would fight and Bosie would storm off, pour all of his emotion into a bitter, cathartic letter, and then, having cooled off, he would weep and beg for forgiveness. In these moments, he appeared to Oscar as a vulnerable, hurt child. Oscar always loved Bosie most in the moments that he could play the ephebe. Bosie learned that Oscar responded when he was at his most childlike, dependent, irresponsible, needy. He cultivated those traits. Oscar learned that being with Bosie meant surfing an unending sea of moods, and he adapted to that. In agreeing to take back Bosie after his blow-ups and their fights, Oscar had made a decision (although there were times when he questioned it) to accept all of the pain that came with the pleasure of having him in his life. Although he did not use such modern terms, Oscar understood that Bosie suffered from a form of mental illness. 'I was always terribly sorry for the hideous temper to which you were really a prey.'[2]

Eventually, except in particularly dramatic cases, they would skip the apologies all together. After an outburst, Bosie would simply calm down, come back and they would both behave as though it had never happened. On at least one occasion, a perfectly attired Bosie arrived for a dinner party in high spirits only moments after Oscar had received a foul letter from him written in a rage. Oscar put the letter in his pocket, and tried to enjoy the meal. It would be years before Bosie realised that some of these letters 'hurt him much more keenly than I had intended'.[3]

Oscar was one of the few people who could draw Bosie out of his depressions. Bosie called him 'a supreme consoler' and thought if he had become close to Queensberry, Oscar might have cured his father of his foul moods.[4] If Oscar had serious reservations about the relationship, Bosie seems to have been mostly unaware of it, or at least not to have taken it too seriously. Oscar found Bosie's extremes and changeability fascinating. For someone always seeking novel sensation, Bosie was a stimulating, infuriating, exhausting and inspiring partner.

If Bosie was difficult to live with, so was Oscar. With few exceptions all of the people Oscar became close to became disillusioned with him, including Robbie. Even Bosie would eventually be disillusioned, but it would not be until years after Oscar's death. 'To be a friend of Oscar Wilde's was a mixed blessing and a risky investment,' wrote Ashley H. Robins, who speculates that the writer suffered from histrionic personality disorder. 'If one humoured him and praised him, and listened attentively and appreciatively to him, then he could be charming and effusive. But if one criticised him or opposed his wishes, he could be abrasive and obnoxious.'[5]

After one dramatic falling out, Bosie begged Oscar to take him to the Savoy, where they had dined a year before on the night they first made love. Oscar responded to that romantic request and rented a suite consisting of two bedrooms and a sitting room. Wilde's was Room 362, which had a connecting door to Douglas's room, 361. There Bosie entertained a young man in his bed, something that did not go unnoticed by the hotel staff. This could have been Schwabe. We now know, thanks to the long-lost love letters (which we will come to shortly), that Schwabe slept with Bosie at the Savoy. He may not, however, have been the mysterious bed partner, and might have checked in separately and had his own room. At the time he wrote his letter to Schwabe, Bosie had checked out and then returned to the Savoy. Nostalgia drew him down to room 123 where, he told Maurice 'we used to sleep together.' Oscar had not checked out of the hotel in the intervening period, and assuming he had not changed rooms, he would not have to 'go down' to the room where he slept with Schwabe if it was the suite he shared with Oscar.

By now Bosie had fallen deeply in love with Maurice. He also adored Oscar, and wanted to hold onto them both. Although there was no expectation between Oscar and Bosie (or for that matter between Bosie and Maurice) that they would be monogamous, Bosie's depth of feeling for Maurice had to have created some tension and must have been a factor in their arguments in this period. Bosie liked to tease Oscar. He could make Oscar seethe by bringing up a hotel concierge who referred to Oscar as 'votre papa'.[6] This takes on new hues in light of the revelation in his letter to Maurice that a valet at the Savoy called him 'votre cousin'.

After a week or so at the Savoy, Bosie and Oscar argued again, and Bosie stormed off back to Salisbury to be comforted by his mother. It is not clear whether these events are connected, but they happened in this sequence: a member of the hotel staff saw a young man in Bosie's bed, Bosie quarrelled with Oscar, and Schwabe found it prudent to take a sudden trip to Australia. Schwabe cabled or wrote Bosie to tell him he was sailing from Plymouth on 1 March 1893. Bosie wrote a long letter on mourning paper from his mother's house starting on the evening of Sunday, 5 March addressed to 'My Darling Pretty':

> My darling pretty boy, I do love you so much & miss you every minute; as long as you were here in England I didn't mind so much not being with you, but now that you have gone right away, I miss you all day & all night. I really love you far more than any other boy in the world, and shall always be your loving boy-wife, or your 'little bitch' if you prefer it. Do write to me as soon as you can ... and tell me if you still love me at all. Please darling never take off the bangle I sent you, & write to me as often as you can. If I possibly can I'll come out & join you in Egypt when you are on your way back. Everybody is so sorry you have gone in London, but no one is so sorry as me.
>
> Have you found someone nice on board. I am longing to hear. I hope it is not rough ... I feel that I want to cry, goodbye now my dear darling beautiful Maurice; I send you all my love and millions of kisses all over your beautiful body.
>
> I am your loving boy-wife,
> Bosie

The letter concluded on 9 March. He told Maurice about Wood's blackmail and called him

> ... the worst blackguard of all the renters in London ... I have seen nobody new lately. My boy here seems to have quite disappeared. I wish I was with you on the ship, we would have a splendid time, & have the same cabin. What is your cabin fellow like?
>
> I always think of you every night when I go to bed, please do the same for me. That is if you still love me any more as I do you. I love you just as much as I did at Bournemouth & Oxford, more.
>
> One more goodbye darling Pretty. With heaps of kisses, & love from your Ever loving boy-wife
> Bosie[7]

Bosie also wrote to Oscar from Salisbury, begging for forgiveness. The exact date of his letter is unknown, but it seems to be just before he started composing his letter to Schwabe. Oscar's reply called the letter 'delightful, red and yellow wine to me' but it asked Bosie not to make scenes because he could not stand to see him 'so Greek and gracious, distorted with passion' or 'listen to your curved lips saying hideous things to me'. In spite of the rancour, he called him 'the divine thing I want, the thing of grace and beauty' and concluded 'Why are you not here, my dear, my wonderful boy?'[8]

Oscar did not go to Salisbury because Bosie and his mother were by then en route to Thuringia, Germany, for three weeks before the next semester at Oxford. Bosie meanwhile had had a response from Maurice and wrote his reply on 17 March. He spoke of a boy he'd 'got into communication with ... his father has consented to our writing to one another. I have not...' (The thought is left unfinished.) He signed off: 'Goodbye now my darling boy, I will write again next week. With heaps of love & kisses. Ever your most loving Boy-wife, Bosie.'[9]

Throughout 1893, Ross and his two friends shared more than letters about beautiful boys. They shared the boys themselves and compared notes. This behaviour was not peculiar to the Wilde circle. It was common in the larger community of homosexual men to share partners to increase the intimacy of friendships.[10] Any one of the friends could have brought ruin to Wilde. In fact, it was very nearly Robbie, not Bosie, who set that chain of events in motion. Oscar was fooling himself when he romanticised the danger of the criminal element. Respectable society, it turns out, was the more dangerous place. Rent boys might blackmail you, but they were unlikely to turn over their evidence to authorities. What is more, a mark who was sent to jail was a mark who could no longer be induced to pay. The real danger was if a father of means discovered that a man had been involved with his son. This may have been what Alfred Taylor meant when he told Oscar that Bosie would prove 'far more fatal' than any of the 'common lads' he met on Little Church Street.[11]

In April, 1893 Robbie went to Bruges over Easter to visit Oscar Browning's brother-in-law Biscoe Wortham. There he met 'a nice-looking, well-mannered, rather attractive boy a little over sixteen, of no particular strength of character'. His name was Claude Dansey and he was the son of a retired Lieutenant-Colonel in the Life Guards.[12] Robbie corresponded with the young man for some time before finally inviting him to stay with him at his mother's house in Onslow Square in July1893.

Robbie wrote to Bosie about his new friend. Browning would later tell Harris 'The letter contained the word "Boy".' This was enough to send Bosie running.

'On Saturday the boy slept with Douglas, on Sunday he slept with Oscar. On Monday he slept with a woman at Douglas's expense. On Tuesday he returned to Bruges three days late (for the new term).'[13] Max Beerbohm recounted the events with a little more drama in a letter to Reggie Turner:

> ... the garcon entretenu, the schoolboy Helen 'for whom those horned ships were launched, those beautiful mailed men laid low,' was the same as him of whom I told you that he had been stolen from Bobbie by Bosie and kept at the Albemarle Hotel: how well I remember passing this place one night with Bobbie and his looking up sadly at the lighted windows and wondering to me behind which of the red curtains lay the desire of his soul.[14]

The student's late arrival for the new term aroused suspicion. Wortham intercepted the boy's letters, which included one from Dansey to Douglas, and a letter and presents from Douglas to Dansey. These, he told Browning, 'left absolutely no doubt of the relations which existed between them'. With the letter in front of him, the student had no choice but to confess to everything.[15]

Wortham was horrified by his discovery and wrote to Browning, not realising that he was reporting everything to his friend Robbie. Wortham said the youth 'formed the acquaintance of a young man, a friend of Mr Ross's, with whom he afterwards stayed at the Albemarle, and with whom he admits (the boy I mean) that he behaved in an indecent manner.'[16] This revelation horrified the Worthams, who up to then had trusted Robbie with their two sons. Mina Wortham had, just in the past summer written to Robbie to tell him how much she valued his friendship with the boys. Now she was revisiting everything.

Browning was well aware that his nephew had a friendship with Ross. Phillip had sent him a letter in November saying that he'd written to Ross asking if he could go see him, and again in December mentioning that Ross had invited him to go to the theatre.[17] After repeated questioning by Biscoe, Philip confessed that one morning before breakfast,

> I was in my night shirt. He was in his pyjamas: he put me on the bed. He had me between the legs. He placed his **** between my legs. He did it on three occasions. When I was staying in London with him on a second occasion. The 3rd time was in his rooms at Church St. It was when I was reading with Mr Edwards. I went to London and spent the night there from Windsor.

Wortham shared this report 'in its naked hideousness' with Browning: 'You will be as much horrified as we are, I doubt not.' His main concern was that Philip's name might come out.

> The details of the case of this boy here are too horrible. Ross is simply one of a gang of the most brutal ruffians who spend their time in seducing and prostituting boys & all the time presenting a decent appearance to the world. Two other persons besides himself are implicated in this business.[18]

One of the 'two other persons' in this scandal was Douglas. The third is generally believed to have been Wilde. One biography of Browning speculates the third party was More Adey, but this is unlikely given his role as a neutral intermediary. Browning continued to share the Worthams' confidences with Robbie, warning him of Philip's confession and about the Worthams' fears that he had improper relations with the younger son, Toddy, as well. Ross denied ever having sex with the Wortham boys in a letter to Browning:

> I was also confronted by Philip who repeated his story. It is an absolute fabrication. If it were true I would certainly not attempt to conceal it from *you*, as you must know perfectly well. From what you have often told me about Mr Wortham & what *you know yourself* about him it is in your power to free the whole affair of its more serious aspects without compromising yourself in any way.

Given his close relationship with Browning, this seems persuasive, but McKenna believes Ross did, indeed, have sex with both boys. A few days later Mina wrote again to her brother in a state of great relief. Nothing improper had occurred between Toddy and Mr Ross. He had answered all his father's questions entirely to their satisfaction. But Toddy had not been telling the whole truth. He had certainly written to Robbie, and may have had a physical encounter with him, but as More Adey told Browning, all Toddy's letters to Robbie had been safely burnt and there was now no evidence to connect them.[19]

On Browning's advice, Bosie and Robbie chose the bold strategy of travelling to Bruges to meet with Wortham in person. Wortham told Robbie and Bosie that he had 'documentary evidence' of their misdeeds. The family's main concern was that they might have letters from Dansey and their sons in their possession. Robbie later told Browning he had no letters from Dansey which could not be read in public. Perhaps the same could not be said of Bosie. According to Wortham, when he first asked Bosie to return any letters he had received from Dansey he replied, 'Why should I?'[20]

When it was clear they would not be able to talk their way out of the mess, and with not one but two fathers threatening legal action (Dansey's father was threatening to go to the authorities as well) they consulted George Lewis. Lewis told the outraged parents that if Ross and Douglas were brought to trial, Dansey and perhaps the Wortham boys would also be implicated in the crime of gross indecency. The publicity would destroy their reputations. Wortham, worried about his own sons' futures, persuaded Dansey's father not to press charges. Adey and Browning both acted as intermediaries. There was an exchange of incriminating letters. Wortham also returned Douglas's presents through Adey and the matter was put to rest.[21]

Dansey, however, had been expelled over the scandal. He grew up to be the vice-chief of the Secret Intelligence Service, and Jay Robert Nash, the author of an encyclopedia of spies, suggests that it was the youthful experience of having his mail intercepted that made him distrustful and secretive, refusing to put anything in writing if he could avoid it; skills he would put to good use in the secret service.[22]

Robbie had been unable to keep the scandal a secret from his own family. Dansey's father contacted the Rosses asking for compensation for his lost tuition, room and board. They decided it would be best for all if Robbie went abroad. He was shipped off to Davos, Switzerland, where his older brother Jack lived with his wife. In January 1894, Robbie wrote to Bosie for sympathy, referring to Rev. Biscoe Wortham by the name of the bullying headmaster from Dickens' *Nicholas Nickleby*, Wackford Squeers.

> I am not allowed to live in London for two years. As the purse strings are in their hands, and a stoppage is threatened, I have to submit … the worthy

Rev Mr Squeers wrote a full and particular account of how things were to my brother. It was news to him as [More Adey] had hitherto concealed everything, but the trouble with the noisy military gentleman. My elder brother here gets letters about the disgrace of the family, the social outcast, the son and brother unfit for society of any kind, from the people at home.[23]

Bosie and Robbie remembered this close call and when the threat of another scandal from an outraged father loomed, they assumed that the Marquess of Queensberry, while a bit mad, would not be foolish enough to tarnish his own family name and to risk destroying his own son by exposing Wilde.

10

Family Values

I have in my blood the love of a scene and a tragedy, but I am convinced it is
a mistake, and certainly in our family of all families somebody ought to make
a determined stand against it.

Lord Alfred Douglas to his mother, 1894[1]

In the eyes of the British public, The Marquess of Queensberry, John Sholto
Douglas, was, indeed, 'a funny little man'. Like Oscar Wilde, he courted
publicity for his unconventional views of life. Middle class readers loved to
follow newspaper stories about his latest outbursts and rampages. He was,
to them, a comic anti-hero. His bursts of irrational violence, public threats to
horsewhip his adversaries, well-known womanising and scandalous views on
religion and free love made him no ordinary peer. He 'assaulted the police,
and swore and cursed at every one and everything in a way that would make a
costermonger blush.'[2]

Bosie's relationship with his father was never simple hate. As a boy he
had worshipped his mostly absent father, then well-known for his sporting
prowess. Queensberry was the very model of Victorian manliness. A horseman
of some accomplishment he was best known for his association with one sport
in particular: boxing. The 'Queensberry Rules' introduced the mandatory use
of gloves and the code of conduct helped change the image of boxing from a
savage free-for-all to an athletic competition. To friends he was known as Q, in
contrast with his ancestor 'Old Q'. While his sullen moods, eccentric behaviour
and outbursts of temper were legendary, his close friends recognised another
side of Q. 'In his buoyant, boyish, irresponsible way he enjoyed life like a youth,
and was always ready to take part in a frolic, play a practical joke, or share an
escapade with men thirty years his junior.'[3]

By the time Bosie was born, the honeymoon between Sibyl and Queensberry
had ended. They had an acrimonious divorce in 1886. From then on Queensberry
would 'hover over the family like some rumbling unpredictable cloud that might
either storm or reveal sunshine.'[4] When Q occasionally did find himself in the
company of one of his children he didn't know how to communicate. 'He was
an embarrassing person to be with, because he had a disconcerting way of not
listening to and completely ignoring what one said,' Bosie wrote. 'He sat there in
silence and smoked a cigar, conversation not being encouraged and one's remarks
being received with stony silence.'[5]

Perhaps as a result, Bosie would be attracted throughout his life to people who were described as excellent conversationalists, Oscar Wilde being the best. Robbie also appealed to Bosie as 'a man of brains and ability, and a good talker'.[6] Later Bosie would marry Olive Custance, a poet also known as a brilliant conversationalist, and he would become attached to a rough-hewn business partner, T. W. H. Crosland, a famous raconteur.

Bosie was one of the few people who failed to recognise how alike he and his father were. In his 1938 book *Without Apology*, he described his father's personality as 'childlike ... He was kind and generous enough, in his own selfish way, but he was incapable of discussing anything without losing his temper, or of understanding any point of view which did not coincide with his own.'[7]

In particular, he remembered the way his father used to fight with his Uncle Beau (Sir Beaumont Dixie). The way they would 'quarrel and argue and then have almost tearful reconciliations, struck me even then (I was about thirteen at the time) as very babyish as well as screamingly funny.'

Once on such a visit Q had been playing the piano, plunking out notes with one finger. Uncle Beau pushed him aside and began to pound on the piano making fun of Q's musical efforts. A quarrel ensued and in a few minutes they were 'hurling abuse' at one another. Finally, Bosie's father, 'pale with rage', stormed out of the house 'slamming the front door behind him with such force that all the china ornaments in the drawing-room rattled.'

> Uncle Beau took this quite calmly, 'He'll soon come back,' was all he said, while he went on 'playing the piano,' and sure enough, about half an hour later, my father came back into the room, and gloomily sitting down, began to read a paper. After a few minutes Uncle Beau said 'Come along, "Q" dear old boy, let's go out and have a game of tennis.' My father replied stiffly, 'No thank you. I don't feel inclined to play.' But Uncle Beau, ignoring this, went out into the garden and wound up the net ... a few minutes later my father came out and joined us, and a game was soon in full swing.[8]

Around the time of his public and shameful divorce, Queensberry had become an outspoken advocate for his own agnostic form of religion that emphasised living on through the souls of one's children rather than in a heavenly afterlife. He was sharing this revelation wherever he could out of a 'feeling of sacred duty to the welfare and advancement of mankind'. It was adjudged in a different light by the public and the press.[9]

He became president of the British Secularist Union and he spread the gospel of no Heaven with impressive evangelical zeal. He gave talks, published pamphlets and wrote to newspapers on several continents. In our more secular culture, it is hard to appreciate how shocking this was. Secularism made him, in the language of an earlier time, a pervert. The word 'pervert' literally means 'to turn away from' and was once almost exclusively applied to people who turned away from religion. (The word didn't start to take on a sexual connotation until it was popularised by Havelock Ellis's *Sexual Inversion* published in 1897.)[10]

Although his agnosticism made him unpopular with 'the establishment' it made him a hero in the community of freethinkers. T. H. Bell, a fellow freethinker, met him in the Edinburgh office of the *Agnostic Journal*. He found Queensberry to be 'pleasant and well-read'. Queensberry contributed to the paper, both financially and with content. Bell described him as 'a man of intellect and ability'.[11]

The Agnostic Journal printed the part of a speech he had been prevented from delivering to the Scottish peers. It does indeed show that Queensberry had a keen mind. Particularly interesting in the speech, given his own son's later dramatic conversion from 'paganism' to Catholicism, is a part where Queensberry talks about the time he was a Christian in his youth and how devoted he was.

> My Lords, I have no desire to be posing as a hero; but at my time of life ... I can afford to tell a true story of my youth in defence of myself, and showing that then, as now, I never had any fear of giving expression to the highest thought that was in me of that which I considered to be true ...[12]

He continued his mission to spread the gospel, interrupting a performance of Tennyson's 'Promise of May' to object to the dialogue given the character Edgar, a fictional freethinker. This caused a flurry of mocking coverage in the newspapers, and until the Wilde trials it was his most enduring public image.

In 1893, Queensberry unveiled the latest philosophy he wished to share with the world in a lecture at Price's Hall in Piccadilly. The title was 'Marriage and the Relation of the Sexes, and address to women.' He had printed up a companion pamphlet which the ladies in the hall could buy for sixpence. According to the *Pall Mall Gazette*, Queensberry's speech was 'intermittent, full of hills and valleys, short cuts and unexpected corners'. He kept his eyes glued to his script, and had a serious manner. It was 'impossible to imagine a joke thriving in his vicinity'.[13]

His position was that current marriage laws were against basic human nature. Compulsory monogamy led to prostitution and all of its dire consequences. What he advocated was not, he said 'polygamy' but 'a kind of plurality of marriage'. Instead of having sexual relations with one woman for life, society should acknowledge mistresses and their children in a form of legal concubinage.

Ironically, with the exception of the genders of the people involved, Oscar and Bosie were at this time living something approaching Queensberry's ideal. They were devoted to one another, and each at times described their relationship in marriage-like terms.[14] They also accepted and encouraged sexual relationships outside their union. Queensberry certainly did not recognise these similarities.

Ultimately, what condemned Wilde was not risky behaviour with prostitutes and blackmailers, nor the rumours about his sexuality, nor jealousy over his fame, nor shocked reactions to *Dorian Gray*; although they all played their parts. What sealed his fate was far more simple: a loving glance.

Bosie had never been one to conceal his emotions. When he was angry he lashed out, when he was joyful he laughed with abandon and when he was in love, everyone could see it. Wilfred Blunt, after dining with Oscar and Bosie, wrote 'I did not quite understand the full character of his relations with Oscar though they were plain enough. It was difficult to realise that there could be passion felt for one so physically repulsive as Wilde was, yet the fat sensual man had already thoroughly debauched the boy, as a girl is debauched, mind and body.'[15] These rumours inevitably reached Queensberry, who now tried to end the friendship with renewed zeal.

This only made his equally stubborn son dig in his heels. The more Queensberry threatened to thrash Bosie if he found him with Oscar, the more determined Bosie was to be seen in the very restaurants where his father had made a scene. He wrote his father taunting letters, telling him where he and Oscar would be and daring him to come and try something.

On 1 April Queensberry found the two men together at the Café Royal. Wilde invited Queensberry to join them, but knowing why Bosie had been expelled from Oxford, Queensberry was not inclined to overlook the admiring glances and inside jokes that passed between them. 'With my own eyes I saw you both in the most loathsome and disgusting relationship as expressed by your manner and expression,' he wrote. 'Never in my experience have I ever seen such a sight as that in your horrible features. No wonder people are talking as they are ... If I thought the actual thing was true, and it became public property, I should be quite justified in shooting him on sight.' The letter was signed 'Your disgusted so-called father'.[16]

Bosie answered with a taunting telegram: 'What a funny little man you are!' A telegram was a public rebuke, for the servants who handled it could see exactly what had been written. He was pleased with himself for this impertinence. The poet John Betjeman, who knew Bosie late in life, remembered him as an excellent raconteur who was especially entertaining when he told stories about his father.[17] There is every reason to believe that Bosie entertained Robbie with such tales and that the 'screaming scarlet marquess' as Wilde called him, was a regular comic figure in their banter along with such figures as Rev. Squeers and the noisy military gentleman. Animated tales about standing up to his crazy father found a welcome audience among young men who also had to deal with parental disapproval. The telegram 'What a funny little man you are' was famous enough in his circle to find its way into Robert Hichens 1894 satirical novel *The Green Carnation*.[18]

The novel depicts a barely disguised Douglas as 'Lord Reggie'. Hichens noticed the religious fervour with which Douglas embraced the ideas he received from Wilde, and one observation about 'Lord Reggie' is especially prescient:

> There was something so young about him, and so sensitive, despite the apparent indifference to the opinion of the world, of which he spoke so often, and with such unguarded emphasis. Sometimes she tried to think that he was masquerading, and that a travesty of evil really concealed sound principles, possibly even evangelical tendencies, or a bias towards religious mania.[19]

Queensberry, like his son, preferred to do battle on a public stage. He answered the telegram on 3 April calling Bosie 'You impertinent young jacknapes' and threatened to give him the 'thrashing' he deserved. 'Your only excuse is that you must be crazy. I hear from a man at Oxford that you were thought crazy there, and that accounts for a good deal that has happened. If I catch you again with that man I will make a public scandal in a way you little dream of; it is already a suppressed one. I prefer an open one, and at any rate I shall not be blamed for allowing such a state of things to go on.'[20] He threatened again to cut off Bosie's allowance, something which only made his son more determined.

The family quarrelling expanded. Everyone was forced to take sides, and Queensberry, who had alienated each of his sons for different reasons, was usually the odd man out. Percy and Bosie were always united, but Francis managed to earn some of Bosie's ire by refusing to show support of his relationship with Oscar by dining publicly with them.

Francis was advancing in his political career at a rapid pace. The Liberals were anxious to increase their numbers in the Upper House, and they looked to the twenty-six-year-old who was then the prospective Liberal candidate for the Northern Burghs. Elevating him to the Upper House would require giving him a British peerage. While Queensberry was a Scottish peer, he had never been given a British peerage. It was an unusual step to elevate someone so young, who had no record of achievement to speak of. It could be seen, moreover, as a deliberate snub of Queensberry who had not been so honoured. Thanks to the patronage of Lord Rosebery, then Foreign Secretary, on 22 June 1893, Francis Douglas, Viscount Drumlanrig, was created Baron Kelhead and given his own seat in the House of Lords.

The promotion seemed to come out of nowhere, and the newspapers expressed bewilderment. *The New York Times*, however, thought it a good move calling Drumlanrig 'the only sane adult ... which that family has contained for a long time.'[21]

The press speculation was nothing compared to the gossip in society, and Queensberry became increasingly convinced that there had been a conspiracy to embarrass him. He concluded that it must have been set in motion by Alfred Montgomery, a figure who loomed large in every Q conspiracy, as Ross would one day for his son. Queensberry was not the only one with conspiracy theories. There had long been rumours about Rosebery's sexual preference and a persistent rumour began to circulate that Rosebery and Drumlanrig were lovers. It doesn't matter whether the rumours were true or not (there are proponents of both sides), what matters is that Queensberry believed them. He went on a rampage, stalking Rosebery.

On 6 August 1893, he wrote a letter to Rosebery that opened 'Cher fat Boy ... this shall be my concluding letter to you.' (Rosebery no doubt thought this was a shame as his letters had been such a delight.) He said the 'savoury odour of your Jew money bags has too delicious a fragrance to allow me to expect any justice in high quarters.' He taunted him to skip rope because it would be 'good for your fat carcass' and that he had a 'pounding ball', which he had inscribed in black letters 'The Jew pimp,' which he was punching daily. He said it would be a 'hell of a race' and that Rosebery might win 'by a foreskin', the anti-Semitism of the remark being undimmed by its confusion over which faith undergoes the covenant of circumcision.

Queensberry followed Rosebery to a resort in Bad Homburg to give him a whipping. The police found him walking up and down outside Rosbery's lodgings announcing what he planned to do to 'that b-y pimp' and that 'b-y b-r Rosebery.' (Stratmann suggests that the missing letters be filled in as 'bloody pimp' and 'bloody bugger.') Given the rumours that were already circulating about him, and his father's attacks on Rosebery, Francis's reluctance to take on Bosie's battle is understandable.[22]

It all came to a head on 30 June 1894. The Marquess arrived at Wilde's Tite Street house with a pugilist friend. Being confronted at his home was a serious escalation and it jarred Wilde. The following Wednesday, Oscar met Bosie's cousin, the MP George Wyndham. His advice was that Oscar should drop Bosie. Indeed, this is probably the only thing that would have stopped Queensberry, but Oscar was not willing to do this. Legal action seemed the only option.

Wilde would later claim, in *De Profundis*, that George Lewis did not represent him in his libel case because Bosie's 'Oxford mishap' had shocked him and it ruined their friendship. This is unlikely. Lewis did not shock easily. He was known as the keeper of society secrets. When Lewis retired in 1909 he had all of his papers burned. He was highly sought after, and was able to turn down cases. Yet he had been perfectly willing to assist Douglas and Ross in the unpleasant Dansey matter, which happened after the Oxford mishap.

Relations between Wilde and George Lewis had become strained by 1895, but it had little to do with Bosie. Back in 1890, Wilde's good friend Carlos Blacker speculated on some sort of business in America. The enterprise went bust and he lost a great deal of money. To make matters worse, he had encouraged his friend

Henry Pelham-Clinton, Duke of Newcastle, to invest as well. Newcastle believed the entire thing was a con and publicly blamed Blacker for it. The matter was so damaging to Blacker's reputation that he fled to Paris with his new bride. Lewis was Newcastle's solicitor. The legal negotiations dragged on for two years and in 1894 Wilde offered to help. He met personally with Norfolk but both the duke and Lewis found his 'intervention in the delicate matter' inappropriate, and it 'served to put further distance between Wilde and his once close friend and adviser George Lewis.'[23]

The real reason Lewis could not take Wilde's case against Q was a conflict of interest. Queensberry had already engaged him. The keeper of society secrets was the first person Queensberry had thought to call to represent him in a delicate divorce proceeding that called his manhood into question.[24] His young second wife had filed for divorce on the grounds of non-consummation and impotence. After an embarrassing medical exam, the marriage was dissolved in July 1895 for reasons of 'the frigidity, impotency and malformation of the parts of generation of the said Respondent'.[25]

Robbie suggested his own solicitor, Charles Humprheys of the firm of Humphreys and May. On 11 July, Humphreys sent a letter to Queensberry saying his client had been 'most foully and infamously libelled' in letters to his son. He asked him to retract his libels and apologise for them, if not, Humphreys said, his client would sue.[26] Queensberry called his bluff. He refused to apologise and told them to take whatever action they wanted. Wilde did nothing. This only emboldened Queensberry. A few weeks later, Oscar wrote to Bosie that the Marquess had made a scene at the Café Royal.[27]

From August 1894 to February 1895 there was a break in the action as Oscar took a family vacation to Worthing. Bosie made three long visits there and Oscar came to visit him once in Dieppe. Events that autumn, however, conspired to re-energise Queensberry. In October 1894, Francis Douglas died from a gunshot wound while on a hunting trip. Although it was reported as an accident, it was widely believed to have been a suicide.[28]

There need not have been any scandal or intrigue behind it. Bipolar illness ran in the Douglas family, and a person who is suffering from depression can become suicidal without a definable reason. That does not stop the people who are left behind from looking for one. Queensberry blamed homosexual intrigue between Rosebery and Drumlanrig. A short time after his son's death he wrote to Alfred Montgomery saying the fault lay with 'the snob Queers like Rosebery'. He wrote 'I smell a Tragedy behind all this and I have already got Wind of a more startling one.'[29]

As always, it was Robbie who stepped in to pick up the pieces. Increasingly, that meant dealing with Constance Wilde. In 1893, Constance referred to Robbie as Mr Ross in her letters. By the time *The Importance of Being Earnest* was in rehearsal she called him 'my dear Robbie'.

During the rehearsals of Earnest, with constant financial worries, a family to care for, an emotional lover to console and a mad marquess stalking him, its author had been under a great deal of stress. He was, in the words of the actor/producer George Alexander's biographer, 'fractious. His interruptions were so continuous that no scene could be taken through from the beginning to the end.'[30]

Alexander finally had to throw Wilde out of the rehearsals for his own play. With the burden of rehearsals lifted, Oscar decided to get away with Bosie to Algiers. Constance was staying in Babbacombe with her friend Lady Mount-Temple. She was running out of money and Oscar had left her no way to contact him. She got in touch with Robbie asking him if he could get a message to her husband. He replied by offering to help her with money from his own pocket.

She wrote back calling Robbie 'a real friend' but told him she could hold out financially until Oscar returned.[31]

Oscar returned for the Earnest premiere leaving Bosie in Algiers a few days longer. By now, anyone who knew Queensberry also knew about his vendetta against Wilde. They also remembered how Queensberry menaced Rosebery, how he had humiliated his family with his tracts on free love, and most famously, how he had disturbed a theatrical performance to pontificate on religion.

No one wanted a repeat performance of the *Promise of May* incident, so when George Alexander learned that Queensberry had purchased a seat for the premiere of *The Importance of Being Earnest*, he cancelled the ticket and returned his money. That was not enough to deter him. He arrived at the stage door with a large bouquet of turnips and carrots.

With Bosie safely out of the country, Oscar felt confident that he could bring charges against his nemesis and end the torment. 'I feel now that, without your name being mentioned, all will go well,' he wrote to Bosie in Algiers. Ross's solicitor, Humphreys, tried to collect statements from the staff of the St. James Theatre, but with Earnest doing brisk business, Alexander did not want his theatre involved in the dispute.

On 28 February 1895, Humphreys wrote to Wilde to tell him the bad news that Alexander would not help, but he added, 'the only consolation we can offer you now is that such a persistent persecutor as Lord Queensberry will probably give you another opportunity sooner or later of seeking the protection of the Law.'[32]

11

Posing Somdomite

'Litigation' derives from two Latin words, litis and ago. The first, litis, means contention, strife, a quarrel. Ago means 'to go.' ... And litigiosus, whence our word 'litigious,' referred to a person full of strife. Litigation, then, is strife.
                                                                Jerome Frank, *Courts on Trial*.[1]

That very day Oscar walked into the Albemarle Hotel, asked for his messages, and was handed an envelope containing one of Queensberry's calling cards on which a message was scrawled. It clearly began 'For Oscar Wilde' and ended with the misspelled 'somdomite.' The words between were barely decipherable and scholars continue to squint at them and debate them. Sidney Wright, the hall porter at the Albemarle testified in magistrate's court that he had read it as 'For Oscar Wilde ponce and sodomite.'[2] It was only at this hearing that Queensberry chimed in to state that he had actually written 'posing as sodomite'.

Oscar and his friends probably also read the more inflammatory text in the message. (What does 'posing as sodomite' mean anyway?) In Police Court Wilde would testify that he had read the card 'as well as he could'.[3] If he was being accused of being a ponce and sodomite it was, strictly speaking, true to say he had been libelled. If the reports of his sexual tastes are true (biographers Neil McKenna and Richard Ellmann both claim that Wilde did not practise anal sex) he was not a 'sodomite', nor was he a 'ponce', which literally means a procurer or pimp. Of course, parsing that particular distinction in court would not have helped him much. Even so, the burden of proof of an actual claim of sodomy was much higher than one of ... whatever posing as sodomite means.

Wilde's first act after receiving the card was to send a note to Robbie. It was delivered by hand at 6:40 the same evening. He told Robbie about the card with 'hideous words on it,' and said he felt he had no choice but to file a criminal prosecution. He apologised for 'trespassing ever on your love and kindness' and made a plan to meet with Robbie that night and Bosie the next day, but Bosie arrived first. Together, the three friends decided that they would go to see Humphreys the next day and file charges. According to Bosie, Robbie recommended Humphreys because he had helped avert the Dansey matter.[4]

Perhaps it was his misreading of Queensberry's card that made him swear to Humphreys that there was no truth whatsoever in the charge. More likely he told him it was a lie because he knew Humphreys would not file criminal charges against a man he knew to be innocent, and he wanted his stalker to be stopped by the only means he saw at his disposal. Whatever his reasons, it was a tactical error because Humphrey's team went into court entirely unprepared for what would await them.

Years later, Robbie would insist that he had encouraged Oscar not to file charges against Queensberry, but this does not appear to be the case. The context of the later statement is important, Robbie made it as part of his deposition for the Ransome trial where the defence was trying to prove that Douglas ruined Wilde. He did not testify in the case, but his statement was preserved in the Clark Library. Robbie rarely spoke publicly about the Wilde case, and his only biographies were written decades after both he and Bosie had died. The biographers relied heavily on his statement for biographical details. There appear to be no contemporary accounts of Robbie urging Oscar not to take the action. This narrative would become more and more fixed as the battle between Ross and Douglas wore on, but in 1895, having no psychic ability, none of the friends could imagine the unlikely events that were soon to unfold.

Bosie was thrilled that his father was going to get his just deserts. While the ink was still drying on the warrant, he sent a press release to James Nicol Dunn, editor of the *Morning Post*.[5] On 2 March 1895, the Marquess of Queensberry was arrested at Carter's Hotel. He was taken to Vine Street police station and then to the Great Marlborough Street magistrates' court to be charged. George Lewis did his job on behalf of his client putting it on the record that 'there is nothing against the honour of Lord Queensberry.'

'You mean to say that you have a perfect answer to the charge?' the magistrate asked.

Lewis did not answer directly and pivoted to the subject of bail. 'I ask you sir, to allow his lordship to be at large on entering his own recognizances in the sum of £1000.'[6]

In that moment (if not before) it must have become clear to Lewis that he had a terrible conflict of interest. Representing Bosie in the Oxford mishap and the Dansey matter had given him far too much privileged information. It would be unethical to use that information against his old friend even if he wanted to. Nor could he zealously defend Queensberry while pretending not to know it. As soon as the court rose, Lewis told Queensberry he could not go on representing him. Queensberry had to scramble to find a new attorney.

He engaged the solicitor Charles Russell who recommended Edward Carson to argue the case in court. Like Wilde, Edward 'Ned' Carson attended Trinity College, Dublin. When Wilde heard he would be going up against Carson, he famously said, 'I am sure he will do so with all the added bitterness of an old friend.' One of his memorable paradoxes, it has survived much longer than it would have if he had uttered the more historically accurate, 'I am sure he will do so with all the added bitterness of a passing acquaintance.'

Carson was certainly aware of Oscar Wilde in his days at Trinity. The year he sat the entrance examination, 1871, Wilde carried all of the academic prizes, he earned a scholarship and was generally feted for his scholarly excellence. Carson had to work much harder to get moderate grades. He never much liked the celebrated aesthete.[7] Wilde remembered their school days enough to know that Old Ned, who had retained the Dublin accent that Oscar had worked hard to shed, was not his intellectual match. He had every reason to believe that he could out-speak him and that his wit would rule the day. Wilde was, after all, the man of whom the poet Theodore Wratislaw said, 'if he had ordered me to commit a murder, his talk almost would have persuaded me.'[8]

Initially, Carson didn't think Queensberry had enough evidence to sustain a plea of justification. Although Queensberry would later speak of his card to Wilde as a brilliant trap, it was more of a lucky shot in the dark. For months he had been attacking in all directions hoping something would finally stick. When Wilde finally did file charges against him, Queensberry had nothing to justify his statement but rumours, innuendo and some flowery letters from Oscar to Bosie that proved nothing illegal.

Russell tried to shore up the case by hiring private detectives to search for hard evidence. They discovered that Wilde had stayed in the same hotels as Douglas on many occasions, and that the staff in some of these places had stories to tell. The information could sink Wilde, but it would destroy Bosie along with him. Queensberry did not, contrary to Bosie's belief, want to destroy his son.

Private investigators eventually led Queensberry to Alfred Taylor's rooms. He no longer lived there, but he had not paid the rent and his landlady had a box with some of his belongings, among them a cache of revealing letters that led to some of the men Taylor had introduced to Wilde. With this information, Queensberry had the ammunition to attack Wilde while leaving his son's behaviour out of it. Charles Russell approached Carson again. It was still not going to be an easy case. All of the proposed witnesses were accomplices, but Carson was persuaded that Wilde was trying to have an innocent man sent to jail and he agreed to take the case.

The big mystery at the centre of nearly any biography of Oscar Wilde is why he took legal action against Queensberry when he knew it would likely land him in prison. The answer is actually quite simple. He didn't. He was fully convinced that he was going to win his libel suit. It is only in retrospect that the action was an obvious disaster. Wilde's sentence was the most severe he could get and was, therefore, one of the *least likely* outcomes of the case.

When they filed the charges, Oscar and Bosie assumed the trial would be about their relationship with *each other*. They were well prepared to defend that. In fact, in his first criminal trial Wilde's speech about the 'love that dares not speak its name' prompted applause in the courtroom. If this had been the basis for Queensberry's case, they most likely would have won and it would have been a footnote in Wilde's biography. (And if Wilde had died peacefully in his sleep after a long career, there would be far fewer biographies of Wilde.)

After the magistrate's hearing was out of the way, Oscar and Bosie went off on a week-long vacation in Monte Carlo, comfortable that they could defend their relationship and pleased that they would free themselves of Queensberry's interference once and for all. 'I saw Humphreys today,' Bosie wrote to Percy on 11 March. 'He says everything is splendid and we are going to walk over.'[9]

Although he was of age, no one involved in the case treated Bosie as a man. Queensberry's team would argue that he was led astray by Wilde. Wilde, meanwhile, acted at all times to shield and protect his 'own boy' from his abusive father. Only Bosie seems to have thought of himself as an adult and as Wilde's partner in the legal action. He always called it 'our case'. Win or lose, he believed, they were in it together.

The common view that everyone but Wilde and Douglas could see the lawsuit was a suicide mission is bolstered by an often repeated account of Frank Harris's pre-trial meeting with Oscar Wilde, at which George Bernard Shaw was present. Harris, who had gotten inside information through journalistic contacts, knew that Queensberry had been employing private investigators and he had an idea of the type of information he was planning to unleash. He indeed urged Wilde to drop the case. (He had also urged him to drop Bosie, and couldn't figure out why that was difficult for him.) But one man is far from 'everyone'. In fact, many of Wilde's friends and supporters were behind him. A common view in many early accounts was that Wilde was being egged on by his circle of admirers.

Willie Wilde told Sir Edward Sullivan that his brother had 'surrounded himself ... with a gang of parasites who praised him all day long.' Frank Harris felt that Oscar would not drop the case because 'it would have involved breaking away from his associates and from his friends.'[10] Harris told a number of people that Oscar was surrounded by parasites, and there is good reason to believe he counted Robbie among them.[11]

Bosie may have been leading the charge, but he was far from alone. 'Why is Robert Ross not equally blamed,' Bosie whined to Elmer Gertz years later. 'Since he gave the same advice & actually took Wilde to his own solicitor who also gave the same advice? Why is it always I that am blamed & no one else?'[12]

When Oscar finally saw the list of names in Queensberry's claim of justification a couple of days before the trial, it certainly gave him pause. But the simple fact is, at this point he had no choice. If he dropped the libel case, it was as good as admitting he was guilty. Queensberry would turn over his information to the police for a criminal prosecution. Even if he did not give his evidence to the police, Queensberry could sue Wilde for malicious prosecution or simply go on slandering him until his reputation was ruined. Oscar was afraid that Queensberry would not stop until he had been ruined or Bosie had been driven to suicide. Unless he was willing to drop Bosie, the only hope was to win the case entirely.

If precedent was anything to go by, they had a good chance. It was unlikely that any of the people listed in Queensberry's plea of justification could be compelled to appear in court. On the off chance that they did, there was very little chance they would admit to committing crimes. Finally, even if they did testify, most of them were prostitutes and blackmailers, and the testimony of such characters was routinely dismissed.

An interesting contrast is the arrest of the actor and producer George Alexander six months after *The Importance of Being Earnest* closed, with Oscar Wilde's name famously removed from the playbills. (It was replaced on 11 May with a play called—I am not making this up – 'The Triumph of the Philistines.')[13] Alexander (who had refused to put up bail for Wilde) was arrested by a policeman who said he had seen the actor 'having connexion' with 'a disorderly person', 24-year-old Elizabeth Davis. The witness, according to reports, 'having indiarubber on his boots' (and being therefore quiet) was able to get within five yards of the distracted pair before they noticed him. Even though a policeman saw the act with his own eyes, and the woman admitted that Alexander gave her money for sex, the court found her testimony unreliable and preferred Alexander's explanation that he had been sitting with his wife in his house writing a letter, when the urge struck him, at almost one in the morning, to go visit the friend in person. He stepped out of his house (did he mention his wife was in the house?), the 'unfortunate woman' appeared and begged for money and he gave it to her. The policeman decided to write up the event with a less damaging charge of 'disturbing the peace'. After a number of witnesses vouched for Alexander's good character, the magistrate decided to 'give him the benefit of the doubt' and discharge him. The woman was bound over for future good behaviour. When Alexander returned to the theatre after what was viewed as a horrible mistake and gross miscarriage of justice, he was greeted with cheers.[14]

Before the Wilde trials Agnus McLaren wrote in *Sexual Blackmail: A Modern History* (of course there is a book on the history of sexual blackmail):

> The official blackmail story was unabashedly constructed to defend the propertied ... Judges distrusted poor children who claimed to have been abused and took an obvious delight in sentencing young men who attempted to extort a few pounds to up to ten years in prison ... The courts for the most part did not want to know if the blackmailers made up their stories or if the victims actually had engaged in homosexual practices ... The courts were certainly heterosexist and homophobic, but the evidence suggests that their concern for maintaining propriety and protecting property could override their desire to root out indecency.[15]

In her biography of Oscar's wife Constance, Franny Moyle reports that in the days leading up to the hearing, Constance was entertaining guests at her home and seemed to be in great spirits. Moyle has trouble explaining this, as she assumes Constance had to have known she was on the eve of destruction. She suggests that the accounts must have the wrong dates, or if they do not '... it may suggest that there was a last-minute display of bravado by the Wildes.'[16] There is a much simpler explanation. Constance was in good spirits and acting like everything was normal because she did not know a disaster was looming.

12

'Upon His Evidence the Only Hope Now Rested'

> It is most difficult for a wit to be agreeable; so, if you allure a witness into indulging his taste for comicality, you may be sure that he will offend at least one of a tribunal of thirteen.
>
> Justice Charles Darling, *Scintillae juris*[1]

On the morning of 3 April 1895, Oscar Wilde stepped into a carriage and pair and headed off for a courtroom that was packed to capacity. The trial between the eccentric peer and the famous playwright was the hottest show in London. The tiny courtroom was not suited for its new role as a theatre. That is not to say that it did not possess a certain theatricality on an average day, with its robed and bewigged officials on elevated seats. The judicial wig was an anachronism even in Wilde's day. Thus an advocate of the New Civilization was walking into a world whose customs were a call to tradition and the preservation of ancient ways. There were more wigs than usual in the court that day. Barristers who had no attachment to the case wore their professional garb to be sure they would be allowed in. Between the off-duty barristers and the reporters, there were few seats available for the curious layman.

Finally the star of the show, Oscar Wilde came on the scene, with the glamorous Lord Alfred Douglas at his side. He looked confident, healthy and in good spirits and 'seemed to have been browned by other suns than those of England'. Both Wilde and Queensberry were dressed in overcoats with velvet cuffs. Wilde also carried a 'strange, very tall, but conical shaped silk hat.'[2]

Mr Justice Henn Collins was running late. As the crowd waited, someone made a joke about 'The Importance of Being Early', causing some scattered laughter.[3]

Finally there were three knocks on the door, everyone rose and the judge entered dressed in the traditional scarlet robe and wig. He was followed by the High Sheriff of London carrying a sword. The barristers bowed to the judge and he to them and then the judge sat down. He took up a bouquet of flowers, which had once been supplied as a protection against the plague but which was now only an ornament to the ceremony.

When the judge had taken his seat, he noticed Lord Alfred Douglas in the court. As a potential witness, he was not allowed to hear the testimony and was asked to leave. Bosie touched Oscar's arm and gave him a pleading look as though he expected him to intervene, but he did not. Bosie was escorted out by an usher.

Wilde was represented by Sir Edward Clarke, Mr Charles Mathews and Mr Travers Humphreys. The Marquess of Queensberry by Edward Carson,

Charles Gill and Arthur Gill; also present in court were two attorneys who were observing on behalf of Percy and Alfred Douglas. And unbeknownst to Wilde or Clarke, in another part of the building were the rent boys Charlie Parker and Alfred Wood, ready to testify at a moment's notice.

According to a deposition given for a later legal case, Robbie was also in court. He attended under a subpoena from Queensberry, and travelled to the Old Bailey in the same car as Oscar and Bosie. Robbie was not a public figure, and did not turn up in any of the newspaper accounts of the trial. He was not called upon to testify, and I was not able to find independent confirmation that there was such a subpoena.

It is curious that Robbie being subpoenaed to give evidence against Wilde was never mentioned in any contemporary context, not by Robbie or Bosie or other friends like Max, Reggie and More Adey. As a close friend of Bosie, Robbie would have been a risky witness for a father who was determined to keep his son's bad behaviour hidden. There is no evidence that the Queensberry legal team ever took a statement from Robbie or offered him any incentives to testify. It would be unusual for a legal team to call someone if they did not have a strong idea in advance of what he had to say. What is more, it seems unlikely, had Ross been called to testify for Queensberry, even under subpoena, that it would not have formed one of Bosie's later grudges against him and been mentioned.

That said, being called to testify in the Wilde case as a witness for Queensberry is a strange lie to tell. It does not seem as though it would advance Robbie's interests. The only reason he might have had to obfuscate was that at the time he made this statement he was arguing he had always discouraged Wilde from taking legal action against Queensberry and that Bosie was solely to blame. If he admitted that he had not only recommended an attorney, gone with Wilde to file charges, and also attended the libel trial, it might have undermined his argument. Another possibility is that saying he was in the witness room, rather than the courtroom, allowed him to say he was there but had not heard the testimony and therefore couldn't comment on it. One way or another, it is likely that Robbie was also at the court house as the trial was taking place.

If Queensberry had actually accused Wilde of *being* a sodomite, his trial and the events that followed would have unfolded differently. As it stood, to win his case in court, Queensberry would have to prove that Wilde *posed* as a sodomite, but this was only half of the matter. In a justification defence for libel the defendant had to prove not only that the statement was true, but that it was *in the public interest* to make it. That it was vital for the public to know that Wilde seemed kind of gay (a modern translation of 'posing sodomite') was not actually an easy case to make.

The crux of the Queensberry team's public interest argument was that Wilde's 'pose' was a corrupting influence on young men like Lord Alfred. The 'pose' mattered because it could charm readers into doing the real thing. This argument drew on two popular anxieties. One had to do with growing literacy among the great unwashed. The elites no longer had a monopoly on reading, and they feared that people of less breeding would be able to read, but not contextualise, questionable matters. Perhaps a gentleman could read *Dorian Gray* without being corrupted, but what about a mill worker or railway porter?

This was combined with a Victorian obsession with the new practice of hypnotism, which they described using words like mesmerism and magnetism.

The idea that one person could control the mind of another was a staple of Gothic fiction of the era. Wilde gave warm reviews to a number of sensational pot-boilers on the subject of mesmerism when he was editor of *The Woman's World* in the 1880s. He reviewed Violet Fane's *Helen Davenant*, a novel about a murder committed by someone who was being controlled through hypnotism, saying, 'This is the supreme advantage that fiction possesses over fact ... It can make things artistically probable ... by force of mere style, [and] compel us to believe.' The notion was also popular in pornography. The year Wilde and Douglas met saw the publication of *The Power of Mesmerism: A Highly Erotic Narrative*, a book available by request in certain Holywell Street shops.

One year before Wilde's trials George du Maurier published his second novel, *Trilby*. The first modern best-seller, it had been published first as a serial in *Harper's Monthly*. The book version was released first in the United States and became the number one best seller of 1894, its most enduring contribution to the culture being Svengali. The marketing team behind the novel promoted the character of Svengali and the public fascination with mind control. Svengali was portrayed as physically repulsive and dirty, and in the casual anti-Semitism of the times as 'of Jewish aspect,' but he is so musically gifted that, through art, he could capture another person's soul.[4]

Wilde, too, was consistently described as physically unattractive, comic or even repulsive until he started to speak and then he would 'weave spells'. Was he a real-life Svengali? Was he like Lord Henry Wooton of his own *Dorian Gray*, teasing out dark impulses that should remain forever buried? No one was a better symbol of those anxieties than the impeccably dressed, blue-eyed, baby-faced blueblood at Wilde's side.

In order to support this theory of influence, the defence's plea of justification focused on Wilde's works, in particular *The Picture of Dorian Gray*, which was alleged 'to describe the relations, intimacies and passions of certain persons of sodomitical and unnatural habits, tastes and practices'. Wilde's contribution to *The Chameleon*, 'Phrases and Philosophies for Use of the Young' was accused of 'subverting morality, corrupting youth, and encouraging vice'.[5]

Before he took on those topics, Clarke, still taking his client's word that there was no truth to Queensberry's claims, reminded the jury of Queensberry's 'Promise of May' outburst over Carson's objection. The judge ruled that it might be relevant in explaining Wilde's subsequent actions towards Queensberry. 'Whether Lord Queensberry is at all times responsible for his actions is a matter upon which you, I think, may possibly have your doubts at some time before this case ends.'[6]

Queensberry glared at Wilde from the dock. Throughout the proceedings he would occasionally combine his look of utter contempt with subdued, angry muttering. The first witness was not Oscar Wilde but Sidney Wright, the porter from the Albemarle Club. He testified that Queensberry had left a card for Wilde, but when he was asked what the card said he replied, 'I looked at the card but I could not understand what was written upon it.' Highlighting, once again, what a bizarre case this was – a man standing accused of a libel that no one could clearly read or understand.[7]

Next Wilde was called to the witness box, he swore his oath and kissed the Bible. While he was being quizzed by his own counsel he was at his most engaging, and at first it seemed that his plan of charming the jury and verbally outwitting his opponents might be working.

Then it was time for Wilde's old schoolmate Edward Carson to ask the questions. He established with his questions what Clarke had already admitted in his opening statement, that Wilde and Douglas had been inseparable and had stayed in numerous hotels together both in England and abroad.

With that done, most of the opening day was taken up with a discussion of art and whether or not an artist was responsible for how his work was received by the audience. Bosie's poems from *The Spirit Lamp* and *The Chameleon* were read as evidence that he had been corrupted. He would forever feel it was an injustice that he had not had the opportunity to explain his own state of mind.

While the subject of the case was still art, Wilde held his own. 'Everybody laughed,' wrote Edward Majoribanks, 'the jury were as delighted with their places as if they had been given free seats for *The Importance of Being Earnest*.'[8] Even as the subject progressed from poetry and plays to back rooms and blackmailers, Wilde kept the sympathy of the court.

The journalists on hand that day focused on the entertainment value of it all and were prepared to give Wilde the benefit of the doubt. 'Epigrams in the box,' read one headline, 'The witness speaks like one of his own characters.'[9] They praised the 'wonderful intellectual force and flow of perfect language with which he had defended his positions.'[10] Things would change dramatically the following day.

Wilde arrived 10:10 and talked and laughed with his second counsel Charles Mathews about the newspaper coverage of the case. Questioning resumed at 10:30. Now Wilde would have to discuss the company he kept. Carson questioned Wilde on his relations with Alfred Taylor, the young men he met through him, and two other boys with whom he'd been associated.

Asked to explain what he was doing in the company of grooms and valets, Wilde maintained that he knew nothing of class distinctions and had a 'passion to civilize the community'. There were at this time a number of well-known social reformers who wrote about exploited dock workers and 'rough lads'. Sherard was not the only journalist who professionalised his fascination with the underworld. Although Wilde's reasons for seeking the company of such lads were less than altruistic, he could conceivably convince a jury that he was only trying to save London's poor youths with his benevolent influence. The tactic had been tried successfully in prostitution cases before.

Carson now dropped his bombshell. He told the court that one of Taylor's men, Charles Parker, was present in the building and ready to testify. This elicited an audible reaction from the gallery, and must have thrown Wilde off, for shortly thereafter, the exhausted playwright, in a feeble attempt at wit, made the biggest mistake of the entire trial; (and arguably one of the biggest mistakes of his life.) Carson asked him about Walter Grainger, a sixteen-year-old servant of Lord Alfred Douglas. Wilde, in spite of his pose as a socialist man of the people implied that he took no notice of the young man because he was a waiter. 'I never dined with him. If it is one's duty to serve, it is one's duty to serve; and if it is one's pleasure to dine, it is one's pleasure to dine.'

'Did you ever kiss him?'

'Oh, dear no. He was a peculiarly plain boy. He was, unfortunately extremely ugly. I pitied him for it.'

'Was that the reason why you did not kiss him?'

Wilde recognised immediately what he had done, but there was no way to recover. His wit and repartee eluded him as Carson pressed him doggedly.

'Was that the reason why you did not kiss him? ... Did you ever put that forward as a reason why you never kissed the boy? ... Why, sir, did you mention that this boy was extremely ugly?'

'If I were asked why I did not kiss a door-mat, I should say because I do not like to kiss door-mats. I do not know why I mentioned that he was ugly, except that I was stung by the insolent question you put to me ...'

Carson would not be put off.

'Why did you mention his ugliness? ... Was that the reason why you should say the boy was ugly?'

Wilde gave a number of half-formed answers. 'You sting me and insult me and try to unnerve me; and at times one says things flippantly when one ought to speak more seriously. I admit it.'

'Then you answered flippantly?'

'Oh yes, it was a flippant answer.' And a fatal one.[11]

By the time Carson ended his cross-examination Clarke had been completely blind-sided. He did his best to recover with the only tools at his disposal. From the beginning, he had not wanted to make Queensberry's fractured relationship with his family an issue. When he believed his client was innocent, he did not think it would be necessary because the lack of evidence against Wilde would speak for itself. Now realising that his client had not told him the whole truth, he felt the only option was to try to demonstrate that Queensberry was not motivated by public interest at all, and that his attacks on Wilde were part of an on-going family feud.

Instead of calling Douglas to the stand, which would have opened him up to cross-examination, he read Queensberry's abusive letters into the record. If he had done this at the opening of the trial, perhaps it would have been effective, as it would have made Queensberry's erratic nature much more prominent, and it might have led the jury to suspect anything Queensberry alleged before they even got to Wilde's testimony. Now, with Wilde's implied confession that he kissed boys (so long as they weren't ugly) still reverberating through the court, it was too little, too late.

Bosie went to his grave believing that if he had been put in the witness box he could have turned the libel case around and Wilde would not have gone to jail. Bosie was not the only one who thought it was a mistake that he had not testified; according to his biographer, Edward Carson thought so as well.

'Everybody then expected Clarke to call Lord Alfred Douglas,' Majoribanks wrote, 'whose friendship with Wilde was the prime cause of the whole case ... There was a great surprise when Clarke closed his case ... All who had followed the case were amazed at Clarke's decision. The last letters had been Alfred Douglas' correspondence, not Wilde's. The strikingly handsome youth had sat beside Wilde all through the trial, coming to the Court and leaving with him in his brougham. Why was Clarke not calling him? ... on ordinary rules of advocacy, an obvious refusal to call a relevant witness, who was visible to all in Court, was calculated to do as much harm as any deadly cross-examination of that witness.'[12] Majoribanks was mistaken that Douglas sat beside Wilde in the courtroom. He had been excluded precisely because he was likely to be called on to testify. His arrival and departure with Wilde each day, however, had made a strong impression.

That the prosecution rested without presenting anyone to corroborate Wilde's account created the impression that there was no one who could. Carson took advantage of this. He asked why Taylor had not been called as a witness for the prosecution if he could provide an innocent explanation for Wilde's meetings with his companions.[13] He also brought up (without naming him) Maurice Schwabe, who had been alluded to a number of times in the trials, but whose name had been concealed, written on a piece of paper. Carson suggested that the only reason Wilde mentioned this mysterious person was because he could not be questioned as he was out of the country.[14]

Bosie would take this to heart. After the libel trial he tried to persuade Schwabe to come back and testify in Wilde's criminal trial. His unwillingness to do so left Bosie feeling abandoned and betrayed. During Wilde's imprisonment, Douglas wrote an article in Wilde's defence which he intended to publish in the *Mercure de France*. In it, he named Schwabe, 'This youth was, in many respects, unwittingly responsible for Mr Wilde's troubles ... If Schwabe would have appeared in court, his testimony would have greatly strengthened Mr Wilde's case. He did not come forward, and all efforts to trace him have been unsuccessful. Mr Wilde ... refused to avail himself of this piece of information ... In light of what has happened, I have no scruples in divulging it now.'[15]

Carson effectively contrasted Wilde's self-aggrandizing statements about the elite position of artists in society with his contention that he was so blind to social distinctions that 'even a street Arab' was excellent company. He compared *The Picture of Dorian Gray* to Douglas's poems in the *Chameleon* and drove home the point that one must have inspired the other, and that it was terrible to think that a young man 'upon the threshold of his life' could be turned 'under the domination of' Oscar Wilde to the 'frightful subject of the passion of man for man'.[16]

Carson would do more. He would prove that Wilde not only looked the part, he lived it. After revisiting Wood's blackmail attempt he announced that Wood was also in the building and ready to testify. This brought a gasp from the crowd.

'Everybody in Court seemed conscious that they were assisting at a great tragedy, the fame of which was indeed already ringing through the world,' wrote Majoribanks. 'The climax of the drama had not been reached, but it now seemed to all certain and foredoomed. Even the cultured Judge, who had been obviously impressed, amused and delighted with Oscar Wilde on the previous day, sat with his head buried in his hands.'[17]

Because Bosie had not testified, Carson was able to make the uncontested claim that 'Lord Queensberry's son is so dominated by Wilde that he threatened to shoot his own father.'[18]

Bosie insisted he be given a chance to respond to this, and Marjoribanks wrote 'indeed, upon his evidence the only hope now rested.'[19] Clarke refused. This may have been because Wilde wanted to protect Bosie and keep him out of it. It may also have been because Clarke understood it was too late. Art and its influence had been on trial as much as Wilde had. In the narrative the defence had created, Douglas was Trilby to Wilde's Svengali; Dorian to Wilde's Lord Wooton. Under such circumstances, a spirited defence of Wilde was as good as condemnation.

The depth of Bosie's 'unnatural' devotion to Oscar was clear to anyone who looked. A couple of weeks after the libel case, as officials weighed the decision of whether or not to charge Douglas alongside Wilde, prosecuting counsel Charles Gill wrote, 'Having regard to the fact that Douglas was an undergraduate at Oxford when Wilde made his acquaintance, the difference in their ages and the strong influence that Wilde has obviously exercises over Douglas since that time, I think that Douglas, if guilty, may fairly be regarded as one of Wilde's victims.'[20]

The director of public prosecutions, Hamilton Cuffe, was of the same mind. He believed Douglas was 'a person of weak character' and that Wilde 'induced' the undergraduate 'to enter on these evil practices ... by admiration for Wilde's intellect and literary abilities' and that from then on Wilde 'exercised almost absolute sway and control over this young man.' Under these conditions he 'fell' and never had 'the force of will or character to emancipate himself from his degrading submission to Wilde whom, no doubt, he still regards with the utmost devotion and affection.' The hope was that once Wilde was safely behind bars, Douglas would see the 'iniquity' of his lifestyle.[21]

The powers of the world would eventually succeed in forcibly separating the couple and causing Douglas to see the iniquity of his ways, but it would not happen until years after Wilde's death. Unlike Hamilton Cuffe, history would not judge this a positive development in Douglas's life.

As the second day drew to a close, Wilde was in a very different position than he had been a day before. His legal team was split on what to do next. Clarke, still reeling at being caught so off-guard, didn't know how he could proceed in a defence he did not believe. His junior, Charlie Mathews thought it was not their job to determine whether Wilde was guilty, only to give him the best defence possible. They still had a chance to win by attacking the credibility of the witnesses one by one. The courts usually did not take much stock in the testimony of blackmailers and prostitutes. Clarke would prove highly effective in Wilde's criminal trials challenging their testimony and it is possible he could have carried the day in the libel suit if he had not been so demoralised. There were no clear right or wrong answers, but one thing was certain, the stakes were now very high for their client.

Wilde was in a state of shock and could not decide whether he should keep going or withdraw the case. We can only imagine the conversations between Oscar and Bosie that night. If Bosie urged him to fight on, he disregarded the advice. In the end, as most legal battles do, it all came down to money. If they followed Mathews' course the case would drag on. At best, to examine and cross-examine all of the witnesses on Queensberry's list would take three or four days. Queensberry's expenses were also mounting. So the lead counsels made a gentlemen's agreement that if Wilde dropped the case, Queensberry would not take the matter any further.

The crowds were gathered outside the Old Bailey again on the third day of the case Regina v. Douglas, but their mood was decidedly changed. Inside, Carson was beginning his opening speech for the defence. Edward Clarke sat looking miserable but Wilde was not in the courtroom.

At the beginning of Carson's speech, Clarke had gone out to consult with his client, who was in another room. He returned and interrupted the proceedings by touching Carson's sleeve. They began to talk in whispers. Carson then sat down and gave Clarke the floor. Clarke's statement boiled down to this: while not admitting that Wilde *was* a sodomite, based on the literary evidence alone it was reasonable to say that he *seemed* that way. Under those circumstances, a father might use the word 'posing' in his attempts to protect his son. Even giving Wilde the benefit of the doubt about his sexual behaviour, a jury could return a verdict of 'not guilty' based on how things *seemed* rather than on what they were. Clarke was concerned that if this happened, the 'not guilty' would be interpreted to mean Wilde was guilty of the more serious offence and so with his client's approval he was prepared to submit a verdict of 'not guilty'. And so it was legally established that Wilde 'had posed as a sodomite' and that Queensberry had published his statement 'for the public benefit'.

There is a great deal of evidence that the witnesses in the libel trial were paid, in some cases handsomely, for their testimony. Based on their letters and editorials, Wilde's friends believed the fix was in and that Wilde would otherwise have been victorious in court – a stark contrast to the later view that Wilde's downfall was inevitable. Could Wilde have prevailed if he had seen the libel trial through to the end? Could Douglas's testimony have changed the outcome? We can never know. What we do know is that those questions would haunt Bosie for the rest of his life.

Another important side effect of the aborted libel trial, and one that is extremely relevant to the battle to come between Ross and Douglas, was that it created the uncontested notion that Wilde was a malevolent force who 'wilted the golden youth of London ...'[22] In his quest to rehabilitate Wilde, Ross would have to counter that narrative.

13

Criminal Trials

Rule 5 – A man hanging on the ropes in a helpless state, with his toes off the
ground, shall be considered down.

Queensberry rules of boxing

If there was a gentlemen's agreement between Clarke and Carson, it did not last long. Queensberry seems to have assumed that a 'not guilty' verdict would force Wilde to leave the country and end the relationship with his son. He sent a message to Wilde, 'If the country allows you to leave, all the better for the country, but if you take my son with you I will follow you wherever you go and shoot you.'[1]

It became immediately apparent, however, that Bosie had no intention of leaving Oscar's side. So as soon as Queensberry was discharged, Charles Russell sent a letter to the Director of Public Prosecutions, Hamilton Cuffe, including the shorthand notes of the trial and copies of all of their witness's statements.[2]

When word got out that Wilde would be arrested, both of his friends flew into action; Robbie conveyed the news to Constance, broke into Tite Street to gather incriminating letters, and got Oscar a change of clothes, which he was not allowed to deliver. Bosie tried to get his influential contacts to help, tried to raise bail – which was in the end not granted – and pleaded his case to the press.

Public reaction was instantaneous and dramatic. They were not inclined to wait for a verdict to make up their minds on the case. Bosie called it 'a veritable Walpurgis night ... The thing was in the air, the atmosphere was impregnated with cruelty'. In a breathtaking display of self-absorption, he added. 'I don't know how I was able to stand it ...'[3]

Bosie was still frustrated (as he would remain for the rest of his life) that he had not been able to speak for himself in the libel case. He continued to see himself as Wilde's partner, and in a letter to *The Star* he argued on behalf of them both and portrayed them both as suffering from Philistinism and prejudice. The public, needless to say, did not accept Douglas as Wilde's partner.

Clarke had his own misgivings about the decision to withdraw the libel case, and agreed to represent Wilde pro bono. Alfred Taylor, who had also been arrested to be tried as Wilde's conspirator, was represented by the solicitor Arthur Newton. It was widely rumoured than an arrest warrant for Lord Alfred Douglas was soon to follow. George Wyndham made some discreet inquiries on the status of his nephew and wrote to the Hon Percy Scawen Wyndham (George's father) on 7 April. He learned that while 'W is certain to be condemned' due to hostile public feeling 'among all the classes', there was not going to be a case against

Bosie. But because he had 'associated himself with W up to the last moment' and was 'spoken of as having known the witnesses who will be called' it was felt that it would be best for him to go abroad.

> Bosie took it very well. He thought I was going to ask him to go at once, and began by saying that nothing on earth would make him leave London until the trial was over. You may be sure that nothing will: he is quite insane on the subject ... If W was released, Bosie would do anything he asked, and no entreaty from you or his mother would weigh with him. But W is humanly speaking, sure to be imprisoned. I told Bosie so; and he agreed that it was almost certain ...[4]

Three days after his arrest, Oscar wrote to More and Robbie from Holloway Prison asking them to express his gratitude to the Leversons and Mrs. Bernard Beere and to inform his clubs that he resigned his membership. 'Bosie is so wonderful,' he wrote. 'I think of nothing else. I saw him yesterday.'[5]

Robbie wanted to stay in England and help Oscar. Eliza Ross, however, having already weathered two near scandals that had threatened to derail her son's life was not willing to let him take such a risk. She offered to pay £500 towards Oscar's defence costs, and to support Lady Wilde, if Robbie would leave the country. Robbie was a practical man who also possessed a more strongly developed sense of self-preservation than did Bosie. He reluctantly crossed the English Channel with Reggie, settling just across the border at the Hotel Terminus at the Gare Maritime in Calais.

Bosie stayed. He visited Oscar in prison every day, brought him books, and seems to have talked him down from contemplating suicide. 'You write that it is my duty to you and to myself to live in spite of everything. I think that is true. I shall try and I shall do it,' Oscar wrote.[6] In the Ransome trial, Bosie testified that Oscar told him he would only live through the ordeal if Bosie stuck with him.[7] He told journalists he intended to take a house near the prison and live there until Wilde was released.[8]

Bosie made himself a nuisance with every solicitor and society figure he thought could help Oscar in any way. Wilde wrote to Sherard in Paris that nothing but Bosie's daily visits 'quickened [him] into life'. To another friend he wrote '... sometimes there is sunlight in my cell, and every day someone whose name is Love comes to see me, and weeps so much through prison-bars that it is I who have to comfort him.'[9]

Oscar's lawyers, on the other hand, were less enamoured of the hovering, vibrating youth, who was constantly haunting their offices. They insisted he should go abroad. Clarke was savvy enough to recognise the visual effect the slim, gold-haired angel at Wilde's side produced on a jury and he feared what the impetuous young man might say if he were ever to take the stand.

In the end, no one but Oscar could persuade Bosie to leave. They met for the last time in Newgate prison next to the Old Bailey, where Oscar was being held while awaiting a decision of the Grand Jury. 'The last time I saw him,' Bosie would later tell More Adey, 'he kissed the end of my finger through an iron grating at Newgate, and begged me to let nothing in the world alter my attitude and my conduct towards him.'[10]

There was a flurry of activity before Bosie finally set sail on 24 April. Max Beerbohm was at the Leversons with him on the night before his departure and described it to Reggie Turner:

> The scene that evening at the Leversons was quite absurd. An awful New Woman in a divided skirt (introduced by Bosie) writing a pamphlet at Mrs. Leverson's

writing-table with the aid of several whiskey-and-sodas; her brother – a gaunt man with prominent cheek-bones from Toynbee Hall who kept reiterating that 'these things must be approached through first principles and through first principles alone!' two other New Women who subsequently explained to Mrs. Leverson that they were there to keep a strict watch upon New Woman number one, who is not responsible for her actions: Mrs. Leverson making flippant remarks about messenger-boys in a faint undertone to Bosie who was ashen-pale and thought the pamphlet (which was the most awful drivel) admirable – and Mr Leverson explaining to me that he allowed his house to be used for these purposes not because he approved of 'anything unnatural' but by reason of his admiration for Oscar's plays and personality. I myself exquisitely dressed and sympathising with none.[11]

Before he left London, Bosie sent Arthur Newton a check for £50 to help with Taylor's defence. He admired Taylor's courage and loyalty. Like those who would testify against Wilde, Taylor had been offered immunity from prosecution, but he refused and risked a maximum prison sentence of two years hard labour rather than compromise his sense of honour. 'I felt sorry,' Douglas wrote, 'that Taylor should be left as he was: in prison, quite penniless, unfriended and undefended. So I sent Mr Newton a cheque and asked him to do the best he could for Taylor with such a small sum.'

Ashley Robins, author of *Oscar Wilde: The Great Drama of His Life* notes that there is no evidence that Wilde himself ever expressed remorse or regret for the role he played in Taylor's arrest and imprisonment. Nor does his correspondence include any acknowledgement of the sacrifice Taylor made on Wilde's behalf.[12]

Bosie was not the only agitated, outraged friend to fight with the press over its treatment of Wilde. As soon as he heard of Wilde's arrest, Sherard sent a telegram from Paris offering to help. When he heard some English ex-pats expressing delight over Wilde's fate, he became incensed and he went around proclaiming the writer's innocence (often while falling down drunk) to all who would listen.

Early in their relationship Sherard had felt nervous and uncomfortable when Wilde kissed him and insisted he call him 'Oscar,' but he quickly put his doubts out of his mind. More than fifty years later, he insisted to a childhood friend that he 'never had the faintest idea that my looks attracted him.'[13]

He would later also reconsider the time that Oscar planned to have his aesthetic 'first period Oscar' locks cut in a new 'Neronian' fashion. He persuaded Sherard to go with him and have his hair curled the same way. Oscar had fond memories of the outing. He would later write to his friend that '... society must be amazed and my Neronian coiffure has amazed it.'[14] Looking back years later, Sherard shuddered to think that the hairdressers must have imagined them to be 'two English dolly boys getting ready to go on the boulevards in quest of lucrative "pick ups".'[15]

In 1895, however, he believed Oscar innocent. Oscar had, on his honeymoon, talked so much and with such detail about the joys of sex with his wife that even the far-from-sensitive Sherard had asked him to stop. It never occurred to Sherard that this might have been overcompensation, nor did he find it odd that Oscar seems to have spent more time with him on his honeymoon than he did with his new bride.[16]

He was ultimately persuaded of his friend's heterosexuality, ironically, by what must have been Oscar's attempts to flirt with him. Some of his letters to Sherard are as effusive as those he wrote to Bosie. 'Your letter was a loveable as yourself' he wrote before waxing about 'memories of moonlight meanderings, and sunset strolls' and concluding that he would accept the dedication of his friend's book of poems because he could not refuse 'a gift so musical in its beauty, and fashioned by one whom I love so much as I love you.' A month later he described his friend's letters as 'iridescent ... I think of you often, wandering in violet valleys with your honey-coloured hair.'[17]

In spite of these profusions, Oscar had never made a pass at him (at least not one that he could allow himself to acknowledge) and so he believed the letters to Bosie that turned up in the libel trial must have been innocent as well. *In The Real Oscar Wilde* he would argue that his friend was 'in the habit of writing extravagant letters, which those who received them took for exactly what they were, effusions partly humorous, partly pathetic, but obviously insincere and written as literary essays in epistolary style.'[18]

Sherard subscribed to an 'inversion' model of homosexuality. Inverts were assumed to have the drives, desires and personalities of the other gender. The confused Sherard, in his many writings defending Wilde against the charge, would point to occasions on which he acted in manly ways as proof that he could not possibly have loved boys. Example: 'For my own part I never saw anything in Oscar Wilde to justify the charge of effeminacy against him. He always impressed me as a man, a man of masculine bent of mind. To begin with, I always considered him a genius, and genius is never associated with what is feminine.'[19]

These arguments were designed as much to convince their author as the public, for there are a number of episodes that suggest he had some doubts. On 12 April 1895, the French writer Edmond de Goncourt encountered Sherard in a bar weaving, spilling his drink and threatening to break the neck of a *Le Figaro* journalist who had written negatively about Wilde. Goncourt asked Sherard if he believed was was guilty, and the drunken Sherard shouted that he 'did not worry what his friends did in water closets'.[20] One of those who was treated to an earful was James Richards MacCarthy, a twenty-seven year-old clerk of the British Consul, who accused Sherard of being a 'faux journaliste et pederaste'. Sherard sued for libel and won, receiving damages of 1,000 fr.

Robbie and Bosie clearly wanted to spend their exile together, but familial interference – from Robbie's mother – would make this a constant challenge. Bosie settled in Calais and sought out Robbie and Reggie. He learned that they had moved on to Rouen, and he telegraphed asking them to come back and join him, which they did.

Oscar's friends followed the news of Wilde's trials, a day after the fact, in the newspapers. Bosie read with disgust that his poem 'Two Loves' with its line about the 'love that dares not speak its name' was used as evidence of deviance in the proceedings. The associations were so painful to him that he refused to allow the poem to be reprinted in his lifetime. He must have been bolstered, however, to read Wilde's answer, which caused an outburst of spontaneous applause in the gallery. Max Beerbohm, who was in the court that day, wrote to Reggie Turner that Oscar 'never had so great a triumph, I am sure.'[21]

About the third day of the trial, Bosie read about the testimony of a staff member at the Savoy. He immediately telegraphed Sir Edward Clarke offering to give him 'certain information' though it was compromising to himself. Clarke did not find this at all helpful.

Wilde's legal team was optimistic about their chances. Traverse Humphreys believed a jury would be unwilling to prosecute a man for acts that took place in private. 'As it was put by a legal friend of mine,' he wrote, 'We shall see which the jury dislike most – section 11 (the Labouchere Amendment) or Oscar Wilde.'[22] They were, it seems, divided on the issue. The case ended with a hung jury.

Oscar was finally released on bail on 7 May, but Queensberry, having heard a rumour that his son was back in England and planning to reunite with Wilde, was not prepared to let him have a night's peace. His friends followed Wilde from hotel to hotel, threatening the managers if they gave him a room. He finally retreated to his mother's house on Oakley Street in Chelsea where he collapsed on a camp bed at midnight.

Sherard had rushed to Wilde's side and was buzzing around the house proud to be able to do 'menial work for my friend'. This consisted mostly of fetching him glasses of claret. Bosie was no longer encouraging Oscar to stay and fight. He was begging him to come join him on the continent. Sherard recalled some of the letters that Bosie sent him (which Willie had seen and kept teasing his brother about) '... a curious medley of attractions was set out. There was moonlight on the orange-groves and there were other inducements which need not be particularised.'[23]

Bosie wrote from Paris on 15 May, 'Do keep up your spirits, my dearest darling. I continue to think of you day and night, and send you all my love. I am always your own loving and devoted boy Bosie.'[24]

Now Oscar was being prodded on by another highly influential force, his mother, who believed he would win. She told him, 'If you stay, even if you go to prison, you will always be my son, it will make no difference to my affection, but if you go, I will never speak to you again.'[25] The Wildes were not the only ones who thought Oscar would be vindicated. Gossip around the courtroom was that 'there is evidently but slight chance of his conviction.'[26]

Oscar responded to Bosie with an emotional letter explaining why he could not join him in Paris. Douglas wrote in 1929:

> It made me weep at the time, and even now I don't like to think of it, but I have thought since, a hundred times, that it was an insane thing not to go ... Oscar said in his letter that he could not 'run away' and 'hide' and 'let down' his bails ... He wrote: 'A dishonoured name, a hunted life are not for me to whom you have been revealed on that high hill where beautiful things are transfigured.' He also, pathetically, thought that he had 'a good chance of being acquitted' at the second trial.[27]

The press coverage of the third trial was lighter than that of the first. The public had already heard the shocking revelations about blackmailers and rent boys. They'd already had the fun of seeing the arrogant poser brought down to size, and there was nothing novel in a repeat performance.

Lockwood did not expect to win. The Friday before the verdict he was asked about the case at the House of Commons and he said, 'He will be acquitted, I am sorry to say.' As the jury deliberated, he told Clarke, 'You'll dine with your man in Paris tomorrow.'[28] *The Chicago Tribune* also expected a not guilty verdict, 'public feeling having somewhat reacted in [Wilde's] favour during the trial.'[29]

It was Robbie's 26th birthday, and Bosie and Robbie were together at the Hotel de la Poste when Oscar was given the maximum sentence for the crime of gross indecency, two years hard labour. The verdict ran in the *Chicago Tribune* under the headline, 'Result is a Surprise'. The friends were shocked by the outcome, and were certain it could only have been the result of political pressure and coercing of witnesses. Although Bosie would be the most vocal champion of this point of view, letters from More Adey show that he was not alone.[30]

Sherard, who had not had the stomach to attend the trial, came to the Old Bailey on the final day with his friend Ernest Dowson. When the verdict was read he jumped up to castigate the judge, but Dowson pulled him down.[31] The scene outside the court would become the stuff of legend. Sherard, in his 1905 biography of Wilde, would describe men and women dancing 'an ungainly farandole, where ragged petticoats and yawning boots flung up the London mud in *feu de joie*, and the hideous faces were distorted with savage triumph.'[32] If this is what happened, the reporter for the *Illustrated Police News* did not see it. 'Outside a large crowd had assembled,' he wrote, 'but there was no demonstration.'[33]

In the end it was not Bosie, but Sherard who moved permanently to England and took up residence close to Wandsworth Gaol in order to be near Oscar. Meanwhile, Bosie, almost in the role of the appreciative spouse, wrote a letter to Wilde's counsel Sir Edward Clarke thanking him for his 'noble and generous and superb efforts on behalf of my friend'.[34]

Queensberry rather naively thought his court victory meant the end of his son's relationship with Wilde and that he would now return to his natural heterosexual state. He wrote to Bosie and offered to restore his allowance if he renounced Wilde and he suggested that Bosie go to the South Sea Islands because there were 'plenty of beautiful girls there'. Bosie did not take him up on the offer.

14

While Wilde Was Away

The New Chivalry ... will not fear to bare its errors to loving eyes. And will
not grudge even shame if so be it may save the beloved from the like.
Charles Kains-Jackson, *The New Chivalry*

One of the formative experiences of Robbie's life happened on his vacation
to Switzerland with his mother in 1884. Eliza was a strict Protestant who
expected proper behaviour from her children (and who had, Robbie would
report to his brother, packed eight toothbrushes for the two of them). One of
their fellow guests at the Grand Hotel in Vevey was a young woman who had
scandalised the crowd with ostentatious flirting. She was now being treated,
throughout the hotel, as persona non grata. The conservative, Bible-quoting
Mrs Ross may not have approved of the young woman's indiscretion, but she
was even more offended by the scapegoating that followed. She made a point
of bowing to the young woman whenever she passed. For the rest of their
stay, mother and son took great pleasure in being visibly kind to her. The
instinct to come to the aid of the vilified or rejected would remain with Ross
throughout his life.[1]

After Wilde was sent away, many of Robbie's friends gave him the sensible
advice to drop Wilde and move on. Typical was Edmund Gosse who wrote: 'Now
the great thing is to forget. Your action throughout, so far as I understand it has
been Quixotic and silly but honourable. In this dark world no one can do more
than walk by the light of his conscience. If it is any pleasure for you to know it,
you preserve all our regard (my wife's and mine), and in future, calmer times we
shall both rejoice to see you and give you any support we can, if you ever want
support.'[2]

This was not something Robbie was willing to do. The innkeeper and author
John Rowland Fothergill, who had met Robbie through his brother Aleck,
described the Wilde circle at this time. At first he tried to mimic the affectations
of the group at Robbie's house 'in the company of homosexuals' but he
found them silly. 'Oscar Wilde was in prison and they were without a leader.'
He reported that Robbie's clique often spoke of 'the cause' but without Wilde's
direction 'they simply didn't know what they were doing.'[3]

The lack of direct communication with the prisoner would lead to numerous
comedies (or more accurately tragedies) of errors during the two years of Wilde's
imprisonment. Oscar's friends all wanted to help him, but could not directly
ask him how to do it. Each well-intentioned friend came up with his own plan,

many of them were at odds with one another. Some did more harm than good. Ross and Adey believed the best thing they could do for Oscar was to deal with his bankruptcy and ensure he had a stable income when he got out of jail. Accordingly around this time, they made a plan to buy Oscar and Constance's marriage settlement. This did not work as well as they intended. (More on this later.) Sherard, still believing that Wilde was innocent (and heterosexual), thought the most important thing was to save his friend's marriage. Bosie, on the other hand, believed the most important thing was to tell the world how much Oscar loved him and how noble and pure that love was.

In one of his last letters to Bosie, Oscar had written that it was his duty to set the record straight. 'Those who know not what love is will write, I know, if fate is against us, that I have had a bad influence upon your life. If they do that, you shall write, you shall say in your turn, that it is not so. Our love was always beautiful and noble, and if I have been the butt of a terrible tragedy, it is because the nature of that love has not been understood.'[4] Bosie took up the challenge with great bravado.

He wrote letters to every high level dignitary he could think of, up to and including Queen Victoria. He also wrote to his brother Percy asking him to use the family's political connections to try to get Oscar's sentence reduced and suggested they could bribe the wardens at Pentonville to get extra food sent in. Oscar's friends Adele Schuster and More Adey were using various contacts to try to influence prison personnel and were also considering bribes. All that these efforts managed to achieve was the transfer of the prisoner from Pentonville to Wandsworth.

Shortly after the verdict, Robbie's mother got wind of the fact that he was back with Bosie and ordered him to leave Rouen. He travelled to Dieppe and was joined by 'a gourmet of great personal beauty' named Maurice Gilbert, a blonde charmer Bosie had sent his way. He enjoyed his company until he was called back to England for the funeral of his brother Jack's wife, Minnie, on 28 May. As it seemed he was in no immediate danger of arrest, he decided to stay, although he would, over the next two years, make frequent visits to Bosie and Reggie on the continent.

Neither Bosie nor Robbie renounced their sex lives during the trial or its aftermath. Bosie and Oscar had never been sexually exclusive and so being faithful, as Bosie understood it, was not maintaining celibacy until Oscar's return. Rather it was remaining devoted to both Wilde and 'the cause'. Being loyal to the cause meant partaking in the sacrament of sex. Robbie's public profile was such that he was able to enjoy Gilbert's company without drawing the attention or disapprobation of the neighbours or the media.

The same could not be said of Bosie. In Le Havre, Bosie rented a boat and hired two young sailors as crew. This did not escape the notice of the neighbours or the press. A journal accused him of corrupting the local youth after which he received a series of anonymous letters saying he was being watched by detectives and would be expelled from France.[5] Bosie responded with a proud and petulant letter to the editor. In the immediate aftermath of the trials, Bosie had a great deal of company. He filled his staff with at least some servants who were 'so' and he had a series of sympathetic visitors.[6]

One was Charles Hickey, a 22 year-old Bosie described as a friend of Reggie's and Robbie described as a 'great friend' of Bosie's. (McKenna believes he had sex with all of them.) Lady Queensberry sent him the money to join the gang at Rouen. (When Hickey was brought up against him later in court, Robbie claimed that Hickey took the money and did not join them.)[7]

Another visitor was a young poet named James H. Wilson. Not much is known about him, but his poetry suggests he was in sympathy to 'the Cause,' if not an actual member of the Order of Chaeronea. He was fired up by the great injustice and determined to publish a defence of Wilde, 'Some Gentle Criticisms of English Justice', under the pseudonym 'I. Playfair'. The contents were so obviously inspired by Bosie that many people assumed he wrote it. Wilson wanted it to be a series of articles in *Reynold's Newspaper*.

Adey's response to Wilson reveals some of the difficulties he and Robbie faced, as homosexuals sympathetic to Bosie, but aware of the need to stay hidden to protect Wilde's interests (as well as Bosie's and their own). Adey explained that, as one of Wilde's friends, he had to take up a public attitude of 'cold reserve and indifference'.

> I am equally the friend of Mr Wilde and Lord Alfred Douglas, but this is not the case with many people who are most anxious to help Mr Oscar Wilde. I think that allusions *at this time*, to the exceptional friendship existing between them are calculated to prejudice Mr Wilde's cause in the eyes of those who are friends of his and *not* of Lord Alfred. At present it is necessary to emphasize rather Mr Wilde's excellent understanding with his wife, and not his romantic friendship with Lord Alfred Douglas, with which I sympathise so cordially and which Mr Playfair so eloquently describes.[8]

The 'at this time' emphasised by Adey highlights his, and presumably Robbie's, strategy for helping both Bosie and Oscar. They would work *in the short term* to re-establish Oscar's relationship with his wife and to gain the support of as many members of polite society as they could. Eventually, when the furore had died down, if they still felt the same, Oscar and Bosie could discreetly resume their relationship.

Bosie had his own strategy. He was not prepared to listen to anyone who told him to be patient. 'That is my idea of the way of saving Oscar and to get him out,' he wrote to Ada Leverson. 'Don't wait till "the time is ripe" &c&c&c: but go on trying and never stop worrying everyone possible.'[9]

Bosie cherished the letters Oscar had sent him during the trials. He prayed over them and kept them under his pillow. He felt guilt and remorse over the events that sent Wilde to prison[10] but Wilde's letters reassured him that 'the unjust gods alone' were to blame. Wilde, who always liked to see himself as the central character in a grand drama, had crafted a narrative about the trials which Bosie believed entirely. (Wilde no doubt believed it at the time as well.) Theirs was the grand love story. Wilde was willing to suffer anything to protect his beautiful young love, and not even prison could end their devotion to each other. 'My sweet rose, my delicate flower, my lily of lilies, it is perhaps in prison that I am going to test the power of love. I am going to see if I cannot make the bitter waters sweet by the intensity of love that I bear you,' Wilde had written just before the verdict was rendered.[11]

Before Wilde went to prison they had talked about Bosie's plans to publish his first collection of poetry. Bosie said he would dedicate it to Oscar, and Oscar had encouraged him to do so. So Bosie worked with more dedication and focus than he had on anything in his life to finalise the manuscript, which he hoped would 'pay a hopeless debt'. This was the poem Bosie wrote for the dedication:

TO OSCAR WILDE
What shall I say, what word, what cry recall,
What god invoke, what charm, what amulet,

To make a sonnet pay a hopeless debt,
Or heal a bruised soul with a madrigal?
O vanity of words! my cup of gall
O'erflows with this, I have no phrase to set,
And all my agony and bloody sweat
Comes to this issue of no words at all.
This is my book, and in my book my soul
With its two woven threads of joy and pain,
And both were yours before they were begun.
Oh! that this dream would like a mist unroll,
That I might look upon your face again,
And hear your kind voice say: 'This was well done.'[12]

As Bosie worked on his poetry, Robbie's literary ambitions were put on temporary hold. Wilde's fate had been sealed as much by his writings and his literary success as by his sexual peccadilloes and this had a profound effect on the friend whose conversations had shaped *The Portrait of Mr. W. H.* He had become wary of revealing the erotic energy that feuled his youthful creativity, but he found that he had trouble writing anything 'in which the heroine is not a beautiful boy.'[13]

When he finally did return to writing, he focused almost entirely on satire and criticism, forms that reveal less about their authors. Although he would gain some prominence in this field, most of his real creative energy would be devoted to advancing the careers of other artists.

In August Bosie left France for Naples to visit his grandmother, Fanny Montgomery (nee Wyndham), who had been separated from her husband and children when she became a Catholic. He took a small villa at Sorrento, and had the company of Charles Gatty, but the extrovert poet found it isolating. Gatty had not read Oscar's books and 'understands nothing of our dear familiar cliches', he wrote to More Adey in a letter begging him and Robbie to come visit him. He told them they would pay nothing for lodging, and the place was 'supremely lovely'. He concluded 'Do come and save me from despair.'[14]

Because all of Oscar's homosexual friends had fled to France, the first to visit him in prison, on 26 August, was Sherard. What his friends learned from Sherard upset them all. Bosie wrote to Andre Gide on 22 September, 'I do nothing and I think nothing. I only wait … I am very unhappy. Yesterday I had terrible news about Oscar. I am told he is suffering terribly, that he can't sleep and doesn't have enough to eat.'[15]

Robbie characteristically channelled his worry into practical action. When he learned Oscar was dreading being examined in bankruptcy court more than anything else, he started a drive among Oscar's friends to help pay his debts. In the end, Robbie was not able to collect enough to forestall the bankruptcy and he returned the contributions to the benefactors. Bosie's style was different. He was passionate, self-centred, chivalrous and frustrated by Robbie's advice to be patient. Robbie was frustrated by Bosie's complete lack of interest in practical matters like finance.

Oscar had believed he would be able to communicate with Bosie on a regular basis through his solicitor. This was not possible. After one month of good behaviour the prisoner was allowed only one letter. After that he was allowed only one letter every three months. Bosie wrote and asked for permission to correspond with the prisoner, and waited impatiently for his reply. He was hurt when Oscar was forced to deny the request. He had decided to send this only letter not to Bosie but to his wife, Constance.

Bosie's jealousy of Oscar's (other) spouse was clear. In his frustration, he wrote a letter to Ada Leverson, the gist of which was that he was Oscar's real 'family' – not Constance. His request for permission to write to Oscar had come back with a letter from the Governor of Wandsworth Prison. 'It appears from this letter that Oscar had the power to correspond with me but that he deliberately preferred not to.' He could not understand why he had not heard from Sherard since his prison visit and why Oscar had not sent a message. 'I am so afraid that some secret influence has been brought to bear on Oscar, or that he has been told some lies about me. It seems quite inconceivable that he should prefer to correspond with his "family" than with me without some very strong reason of which I know nothing. Altogether I am in utter misery and despair. Gatty is going away and I shall be left alone again as neither More nor Bobbie will come out to me. I really wish Oscar and I were both dead.'[16]

Robbie seems to have talked him down from this, but when Bosie finally did receive a letter from Sherard, it did little to allay his fears. Sherard had told Oscar about a forthcoming article Bosie had written for the *Mercure de France* which was to include excerpts of some of Wilde's letters. This was probably not done as a warning, as has often been assumed, but rather as a positive example of action on Oscar's behalf. Sherard, at this time, was a firm believer in the benefits of publicity. On this occasion, for example, he had arranged for a reporter from the *Westminster Gazette* to meet him so he could give an interview outside the prison gates. And he was about to initiate a libel action against the *Evening News* for its commentary on his previous libel action. He thought the suit would expose the 'cowardice' and 'hypocrisy' of the public when it came to Wilde.[17]

When Oscar heard about Bosie's planned article, he was horrified. He told Sherard to put a stop to it. He, too, had been longing for news from Bosie, but this was upsetting. What letters was he planning to quote? What would they reveal? Sherard couldn't tell him. It filled him with frustration and anxiety and he told Sherard to make sure the publication was stopped.

Sherard was happy to have something constructive to do for Oscar. He managed to get the article withdrawn and he sent a strongly-worded letter to Bosie which, predictably elicited a belligerent reply. Bosie told Sherard that his interference was 'exceedingly impertinent and in the worst possible taste' and in a follow up letter he threatened to shoot him 'like a dog'.[18]

The *Mercure de France* offered to publish Bosie's article without the letters, but he felt there was no point. Up to that point, Bosie had been welcomed with open arms into the circle of French poets and Bohemians who wrote for the *Mercure*. When word of Wilde's disapproval leaked to the *Mercure* circle, however, many of its members, who had enjoyed association with Bosie primarily for the connection to Wilde, dropped him like a hot potato.[19]

Bosie justified his article to Robbie, 'My object was to try and raise the case out of the gutter to its true level of the greatest romantic tragedy of the age. The case was tried by a jury of shopkeepers. I wanted to appeal to a jury of artists or men of letters.'[20] (This was one of the letters which would routinely show up in court cases in the years to come.)

Bosie fell into a depression, which he described in a 13 November letter to Andre Gide. He apologised for taking so long to respond to Gide's 'generous and kind' letter. 'The fact is I have been so afflicted with misery and disgust with life that I live like an animal and I have almost no energy to write a word ... I have found that almost everyone is ignoble and a blackguard.' He added in a postscript that he had had almost no news from his dear Oscar. 'They tell me he is sick and in the prison hospital. This is the best thing that could have happened because at least in the hospital he will be cared for and nourished.'[21]

Robbie, after hearing reports of Bosie's depression from both Adey and Leverson, went to Capri to stay with Bosie, in defiance of his mother's wishes. Bosie had rented the upper floor of the Villa Federico, and Robbie remained there as his guest for about two months. The visit did much to lift Bosie's spirits. He wrote to Gide 'I have a great friend with me who is also a great friend of my poor Oscar. Although I am still very unhappy I can tell you that I feel better and less desperate.' Robbie had told Bosie about the petition to free Oscar, and this gave him a bit of hope. He told Gide that the news reassured him 'these days of misery and torture for my friend will not last long.'[22]

Robbie must have tried to get him to stop obsessing over Oscar and accept the situation, but this he could not do. When Bosie learned that Adey was going to visit Oscar he sent him a long letter, begging him to pass on a message to Oscar.

The arrival of Bobbie has cheered me up a great deal, we are doing well and the weather is very nice.

Of course I know everything and I know from what I have heard from Bobbie that my instinct is right and Oscar has changed about me. I am writing to you now, dear More, unknown to Bobbie, to beg you to do what you can for me with Oscar. If only you could make him understand that though he is in prison he is still the court, the jury, the judge of my life and that I am waiting hoping for some sign that I have to go on living. There is nobody to play my cards in England, nobody to say anything for me, and Oscar depends entirely on what is said to him, and they all seem to be my enemies ...

I am not in prison but I think I suffer as much as Oscar, in fact more, just as I am sure he would have suffered more if he had been free and I in prison. Please tell him that. Can't you tell him this and tell him to send me some message? If you could only show him a photograph for a minute I think it might give him back his soul again. Do try and do this; there is a little photograph of me in a cap and gown at Oxford that Bobbie had. How can he expect anything from his wife, what did she do for him when he was in trouble and how can he have changed so?

The only thing that could make his life bearable is to think that he is suffering for me because he loved me, and if he doesn't love me I can't live and it is so utterly easy to die. Do work for me, More, and even if you cut him to the heart and make him unhappy you will only be doing him good if you can only make him love me again and know that he is being martyred for my sake. It is such a joy for me to suffer anything for him. Tell him that I know I have ruined his life, that everything is my fault, if that pleases him. I don't care. Doesn't he think that my life is just as much ruined as his and so much sooner? I am drivelling now, so good-bye and do something for me.[23]

By the time More received the letter, he had already visited Oscar, so he was not able to pass along Bosie's plea. He did try to comfort his friend, however, writing 'You must try to show the love which I know you have for him by the most difficult of all things – waiting.'[24]

Bosie would be mocked (and deservedly so) for saying that he suffered more waiting for Oscar than Oscar did in prison, but later, in a a more balanced mood (and in a less quoted letter), he expressed a similar sentiment with less self-pity: 'Perhaps if I were in prison myself I should be infinitely happier,' he wrote to

W. T. Stead in November 1895. 'What makes me more unhappy than anything else is the feeling that my friend is bearing nearly all the burden and I so comparatively little. People look upon me as the victim of his superior age and wisdom and therefore an object of pity, while they reserve their execration for him. All this is so utterly wide of the real truth. So far from his leading me astray it was I that (unwittingly) pushed him over the precipice. He lived 36 years without seeing me and then I came and dragged into his life all the influences of our morbid half insane heritage which reaches its highest point in that terrible father of mine.'[25]

Unable to send letters to Oscar, Bosie continued to look for other ways to get messages through. He learned that his friend would be taken out of prison for a bankruptcy hearing (to pay the debts he had incurred suing Bosie's father). Bosie could not yet risk returning to England, but he asked a solicitor who would be present to pass along a secret message using the playful nicknames he and Oscar had used in their love letters.[26] He no doubt imagined that Oscar would smile to remember and to know that Bosie was still thinking of him and still loved him.

15

Pit of Shame

This too I know – and wise it were
If each could know the same –
That every prison that men build
Is built with bricks of shame.

The Ballad of Reading Gaol

The events recounted in the previous chapter appeared quite different from Oscar's side of the prison bars. Oscar's admission to Pentonville Prison would give him nightmares for years. He was strip-searched to ensure nothing was hidden on his body and then ordered to bathe in a dirty tub, which other prisoners had used before him. After drying himself with 'a damp brown rag' he was sent for a medical examination where he was certified as fit for light labour, which meant he would be assigned to pick oakum and sew mail bags. He was then issued his prison uniform with black arrows indicating that it was government property and the 'Scottish cap' that would cover his face when he walked the prison grounds so he could not communicate with other prisoners. He would be referred to only by his cell number, not his name.

The first three months of a prisoner's incarceration were designed to be as punitive as possible. The 13 x 17-ft cell, where Oscar spent his days alone, was furnished with a hard plank which sat directly on the floor, a small table for his eating utensils and a metal bucket to use as a toilet. At one time prison cells had been equipped with latrines, but they had been taken out because the prisoners used the pipes as a means of communication. Oscar received an allotted ration of six gallons of water per day to be used for both washing and drinking. Little natural light came into his chamber. The cell window consisted of fourteen small opaque panes of glass situated so far up the wall that the prisoner could not gaze out of it.

There he suffered the effects of undernourishment, insomnia and isolation. The prison diet, consisting mostly of porridge, unbuttered bread, a bit of greasy bacon and weekly cold meat, was not enough to sustain him and it produced an unpleasant side effect, diarrhoea. This not only weakened him but also made the air in the cell putrid.

Also painful was the lack of intellectual stimulation. In the first three months, the only reading material available to a prisoner was the Bible, a prayer-book and a hymn-book. In these dismal surroundings Oscar's life rotated on a wheel of mind-numbing repetition, picking oakum in silence in his cell day after day.

Modern psychologists who have studied the effects of solitary confinement have reported negative effects in more than eighty per cent of prisoners including intrusive thoughts, irrational anger, confused thought processes, and difficulty with concentration and memory. Sometimes when isolated prisoners are given an opportunity to interact with other people, they can't do it.[1]

Between the 1830s and 1850s idealistic prison chaplains brought in a new emphasis on rehabilitating, rather than punishing prisoners. If prisoners could use their time productively, by learning to read if they could not, and studying the Bible, they would come out with a firm moral foundation and be less likely to re-offend. The key to this, argued Reverend John Field, was to keep prisoners free from the negative influence of other prisoners. In solitude, a prisoner would be forced to reflect on his crimes and thus his hard heart would be softened and prepared to receive God. This made sense in theory, but when put into practice, prison officials noticed that isolated prisoners tended to go insane. So they reduced the maximum time prisoners were allowed to be in solitude from the first eighteen months of their sentence to the first nine.

As part of this noble experiment, hard labour was stopped and replaced with schooling. By the time Wilde arrived in prison, however, the pendulum had swung back the other way. His generation of reformers wanted the focus to be put squarely on punishment with an emphasis of hard labour, hard board and hard fare. So when Wilde entered Pentonville he encountered a system that was the worst of both worlds. Prisoners were still kept in isolation, but they were also required to perform hard labour in the solitude of their cells and, unlike in the previous era, there would be no schooling.[2]

On 12 June 1895, R. B. Haldane, one of the prison commissioners, decided to pay a visit to Wilde. Haldane had known Wilde at the peak of his success, and he had become concerned about newspaper rumours that Wilde was losing his mind in prison. When he first entered the cell Wilde refused to speak. 'I put my hand on his prison-dress-clad shoulder and said that I used to know him and that I had come to say something about himself ... I would try to get for him books and pen and ink.' At this Wilde burst into tears.' This was, of course, completely against prison rules, and the prison's governor objected, but the reading restrictions were nonetheless lifted.[3] He received fifteen books in all.

On 26 August 1895 a representative of the Official Receiver had his first meeting with Wilde's creditors. This was weighing heavily on Wilde's mind when he had his first prison visit from Sherard. Already, the idea of being seen in public in his diminished state horrified him. The following week, Wilde's solicitors received a special visiting order to take a statement from Wilde in connection with his bankruptcy. Wilde, in good times, had paid little attention to his finances. Now he had to go through, line by line, and account for everything he had spent in those more carefree days. He remembered the gifts he had showered on Bosie, the expensive meals and the lavish hotel suites. The reminder of who he had been contrasted bitterly with who he was now.

A few months before, an auction of Wilde's household goods had taken place. The Marquess of Queensberry was insisting upon recovering his court costs. Wilde was most worried about his personal papers and manuscripts, and Robbie had broken into the house in an attempt to recover some of his works in progress, but to no avail. When he got there he found that someone had been there before him. Wilde's manuscripts were scattered about. (One theory is that it was one of Queensberry's men who had rummaged through the papers trying to make sure no incriminating letters from Bosie would ever be found.) At the auction, gawkers rummaged through desks and stole personal letters and unpublished plays. The autographed books and presentation copies Wilde had collected over a lifetime sold in lots of £2 each. Along with the regular dealers at the sale were a number of artists who knew exactly what they wanted – Wilde's famous blue china and his collection of original paintings and artwork.

The Leversons managed to buy a few paintings of Bosie that Oscar had commissioned, but manuscripts of *Salome* and *Dorian Gray* were scattered to the winds. Beautifully bound editions of his father's and mother's works were now gone forever. All of Wilde's worldly goods sold for under £300, less than half of what he owed to Queensberry.[4]

As the meeting wrapped up, the clerk pulled a piece of paper out of his pocket, looked at it and then leaned across the table speaking in a low voice. 'Prince Fleur de Lys wishes to be remembered to you.'

Wilde stared at him.

'Prince Fleur de Lys wishes to be remembered to you,' he repeated, adding 'The gentleman is abroad at present.'[5]

When Oscar finally remembered the terms of endearment, and understood the message, he laughed bitterly. Bosie, still living abroad, had no idea how tone-deaf his playful secret message would seem – coming, as it did, at the very moment Oscar was confronted with just how much he had lost: his family, his good name, his history, his writing and all of his worldly goods.

On 24 September the day that Oscar had been dreading finally arrived. He was forced to appear in public as a prisoner at his hearing in Bankruptcy Court. Wilde's trustee, Arthur Clifton, was shocked at how thin he was. Oscar was 'very much upset and cried a good deal'.[6]

The hearing was short. Wilde's solicitors mentioned Robbie's effort to obtain donations from friends and said they believed their client would be able to pay all the creditors 20s in the pound. None of the creditors objected, so the examination was adjourned for seven weeks.

A crowd had gathered at the court to goggle at the famous prisoner. Oscar's humiliation was profound. Robbie stood among them for a chance to glimpse his friend. As Wilde would later write, 'before the whole crowd, whom an action so sweet and simple hushed into silence, he might gravely raise his hat to me, as, handcuffed and with a bowed head, I passed him by. Men have gone to heaven for smaller things than that.'[7] Oscar fell in love with Robbie on that day.

The stress of the bankruptcy hearing, on top of the sleeplessness, seclusion, and hunger had taken its toll on Oscar's health. Ten days after the hearing he collapsed and was taken to the infirmary. He was still there when he received an official request from Bosie through the Governor of the prison to publish extracts of his love letters in his *Mercure de France* article. The idea that Bosie would think to publish such intimate and personal letters was yet another horrible exposure. He immediately refused the request. He was nearing a total breakdown.

On 14 October Sherard was allowed to visit prisoner #13090 as an emergency to try to prevent divorce proceedings. He suggested that he might be able to help Oscar by writing an article for the *Daily Chronicle* to call attention to his condition in prison. In the stark text of officialdom, the warder whose job it was to monitor the conversation reported 'The prisoner expressed himself as not being in favour of this course, and the prisoner seemed very averse to any publicity of this kind.'[8]

The governor was nevertheless alarmed by this report, and he wrote to the head of the Prison Commission, Sir Evelyn Ruggles-Brise, suggesting that Wilde be moved to a country prison 'in view of the apparent intention to make the prisoner the subject of newspaper agitation.'

Edouard Conte, a French journalist who visited with Sherard, shortly thereafter wrote to More Adey, 'I saw him in the infirmary at Wandsworth on Monday. He is a perfect wreck and he says he will be dead before long.'[9]

A few days later, Oscar's sister-in-law Lily Wilde was permitted to visit to impart some very bad news. Oscar's mother was making out her will and was not expected to live long. On 12 November 1895 Oscar was taken from Wandsworth prison in handcuffs to court to be declared bankrupt. If he wished to shun publicity, it showed little desire to shun him. A reporter from the *Labour Leader* was on hand for the spectacle and noted in its pages that the prison authorities had 'cut his hair in a shocking way and parted it down the side and he wears a short, scrubby, unkempt beard.'[10]

At the bankruptcy hearing, Robbie, in the role of a business manager, managed to get a half-hour meeting with Oscar. Although he had worked tirelessly in the previous months to line up enough subscribers to fend off the bankruptcy, the drive had fallen short. When Oscar sat down across from Robbie, he was horrified by what he saw. He had lost a shocking amount of weight and the only subject on which Oscar spoke calmly, without breaking into tears, was death.[11]

Prison authorities were just as worried about publicity, but for different reasons. Thanks to Sherard, they were becoming increasingly concerned about leaks to the press about their famous ward's condition. The last thing they wanted was to have Wilde die or waste away on their watch. They decided that the best course of action was to transfer him to Reading Gaol. In a country prison it was less likely that 'irregular communications may pass (through prisoners on discharge) with outside agitators.'[12]

One of the worst days of Oscar Wilde's life was 20 November 1895, the day he was sent from Wandsworth Prison to Reading Gaol.[13]

> From two o'clock till half-past two on that day I had to stand on the centre platform at Clapham Junction in convict dress, and handcuffed, for the world to look at. I had been taken out of the hospital ward without a moment's notice being given to me. Of all possible objects I was the most grotesque. When people saw me they laughed. Each train as it came in swelled the audience. Nothing could exceed their amusement. That was, of course, before they knew who I was. As soon as they had been informed they laughed still more. For half-an-hour I stood there in the grey November rain surrounded by a jeering mob ... For a year after that was done to me I wept every day at the same hour and for the same space of time.[14]

Sherard had, of course, come to catch a glimpse of his friend. He was treated to a terrible spectacle. The first man who recognised the prisoner shouted 'By God, that's Oscar Wilde,' and then spat in his face.

On his arrival at the prison, a warden observed the fallen poet had 'a hopeless look in his eyes.' The warden had the unpleasant task of clipping the prisoner's hair, which had grown longer with natural curls. This was 'the last drop in the cup of sorrow and degradation which he had to drain to the bitter dregs.'[15]

The new book Oscar found waiting in cell C.3.3., *Friendly Advice to a Prisoner* written by Rev. John Field (the man behind the 'separate system' of prison organisation) did little to lift his spirits. From then on, the warden recalled, Wilde was a man who 'seldom lifted his bowed head of shame to smile'.[16]

Psychologist and author Ashley H. Robins believes that after this dramatic experience Oscar 'developed a minor form of post traumatic stress disorder in which there was the recurrent experiencing of the traumatic event and the avoidance of situations likely to arouse recollections of it'.[17]

Although Oscar now had a lighter and more pleasant work-load – bookbinding and gardening – his life was made miserable by the prison governor, Henry B. Isaacson, a retired Royal Marines lieutenant-colonel, who ran the penitentiary with strict military precision and no tolerance for bending the rules. Wilde called him a 'mulberry-faced dictator ... a great red-faced, bloated Jew who always looked as if he drank, and did so.'[18]

Isaacson was, as it happens, not a Jew. He was, however, a stern disciplinarian and an absolutist. Wilde would later tell Gide that Isaacson was 'very harsh because he was entirely lacking in imagination.' A lack of imagination is, interestingly, the same charge he would soon level at Alfred Douglas in *De Profundis*. When Robbie visited the prison, he had a long talk with the governor about Oscar's health. Robbie found him to be 'polite and amiable' and 'he impressed me favourably.'[19]

After Oscar was sent to prison, all joy left Lady Wilde. Her despair was deep, and from then on she never left her room and allowed few visitors. She fell ill and as she lay dying in her bed, sent a request that her son be allowed to visit her. When she heard it had been refused she said, 'May the prison be of help to him!' She died on 3 February 1896 and left instructions that no one attend her funeral.[20]

Constance, knowing how devastated Oscar would be, requested the right to visit so that she could tell him the news herself. The tragic circumstances drew them back together. He appreciated her compassion and comfort and he confessed his weakness for Bosie to her. He explained it in paternal terms. He said he felt protective of Bosie and wanted to save him from his abusive father and his smothering mother. He compared Bosie to his own sons contrasting Sibyl's mothering of Bosie with his hopes and fears for Constance, who was now, like Sibyl, raising her sons without a father in the house. Constance was shaken by Oscar's condition, and she left feeling sympathetic and willing to consider reconciliation.[21]

With the exception of the visit from Constance, which had been allowed on compassionate grounds, Wilde had the right to one visit each quarter from two friends. Sherard (of course) had made the first visit shortly after Wilde's arrival. The visiting area at Reading was, in his words, 'in a degrading kind of rabbit hutch over which a wire netting was nailed, as though for the caging of an animal ... The hutch was almost in complete darkness ... I am sure that Wilde was glad of it, for further to hide his face from my eyes, he put a blue handkerchief over his mouth and cheeks. No doubt disfiguring growths of hair were thus masked.'[22]

Indeed, a warder reported that Wilde had grown to dread visits from his friends. News that he was to receive a visitor would make him a nervous wreck. Oscar had nothing but time to sit in silence and think about the enormity of his loss, how foolish he had been with his money, and the contrast between Bosie's life now and his own. It was around this time that a new governor came to Reading and allowed Wilde to have a pen and writing paper.

16

Continual Longing

While he was in prison, my whole life can be described as a continual longing
to see him again.

Lord Alfred Douglas[1]

In 1896, as he looked back on the ugliness of the previous year, Bosie was having a
spiritual crisis. He was disillusioned with the men who had spoken with such force
about 'the cause' using militaristic terms, who seemed to have lost their nerve as
soon as a real opportunity for 'battle' presented itself. He had written to Kanis-
Jackson after Wilde's arrest, 'Can you do anything or suggest anything at this
terrible moment? ... Do you know no strong fearless man who will stand up?'[2]

Like Oscar, he spent lots of time imagining what would have happened if
things had been different, if only ... If only he had been allowed to testify in the
libel case. Maybe he could have saved his friend. Above all he was ashamed of his
own cowardice. His greatest regret was standing down in the Wilde case.

Later in *Oscar Wilde: A Summing-Up*, he imagined what might have happened
if he and Oscar had stood side by side in the dock and said 'Yes, we are lovers.
We are not ashamed of it.'

> He got a maximum sentence and of course lied all the way through the case by
> denying things which he not only had done, but would, in argument, anywhere
> outside a court of law, have defended to the last as perfectly justifiable. So what
> did he gain? Nothing at all. He rather lost heavily, because he missed the chance
> of striking a blow for justice by telling the truth and saying what he passionately
> believed ... If I myself had had the sense and the nerve to put him up to it in
> those far-off days, when he would have done anything in the world I asked
> him to do, he might have tried it; and I would have gone into the witness-box
> for him ... and between the two of us, neither of us being without brains and
> courage, we might have made a certain amount of history. I don't believe he
> would have got off even so, but we would have at least 'put up a terrific show,'
> and the result could not possibly have been worse than it was.[3]

Victorian Hellenism offered little consolation when you were torn from someone
you loved and felt rejected by the world. It did not do much to address feelings of
sorrow, guilt and powerlessness. Christianity, on the other hand, had a lot to say
to those who were in pain and grieving. But all of this was wrapped in a package

Bosie could not yet accept. He was not yet ready to submit to a sterile, celibate life for the consolations of Christianity. What is more, neither philosophy had a vision of a 'beautiful, fine, noble' love between men that was spiritual and also sexual. The young man was spiritually adrift. As he wrote in his poem 'Rejected':

And now I am lost in the mist
Of the things that can never be,
For I will have none of Christ
And Apollo will none of me.[4]

In May, Robbie travelled to Reading with Sherard. He brought with him messages from Bosie, still in exile on the continent, and others. Robbie, who had been helping Bosie prepare his first book of poetry, thought news of it would cheer Oscar. He was taken aback that Oscar seemed to have no interest the messages. What Robbie saw upset him so much that he wrote a choppy, breathless letter to More Adey, intended also for Bosie, on the train journey back to London:

The remarkable part of the interview was that Oscar hardly talked at all except to ask if there were any chance of his being let out, what the attitude of the press and public would be, as to whether any of the present Government would be favourably disposed towards him. He cried the whole time and when we asked him to talk more he said that he had nothing to say and just wanted to hear *us* talk. That as you know is very unlike Oscar ... Asked did we think his brain seemed all right? Feared that confinement [might] deprive him of his mind. It was a constant dread. Found Greek and Latin writers gave him headache and that his thoughts wandered. Could only read a little ... When I told him that Bosie's poems were coming out and that I had messages in letter which I showed through bars. He said 'I would rather not hear about that just now.' He listened to the names I read out with some attention. (Those who sent messages through Bosie, self, you or Sherard.) ... He sent no individual message to anyone ... He seemed to take no interest in literary or artistic news that we told him, but seemed to talk to himself while we did so ... our proud cheerfulness did not seem to amuse poor Oscar at all and our attempts to talk of cheerful things were a total failure ... I have omitted one or two wandering remarks, which it is difficult to convey to you the impression they produced on me. They were odd disconnected remarks that had no bearing on any subject we spoke of nor were any of them of any importance. For instance he asked me suddenly, 'Where are you going for the summer.' I thought it had reference to Bosie or to his possible release and followed up on both trails but without any result ... I firmly believe ... he is sinking under a broken heart ... I should say that 'Confinement apart from all labour or treatment had made him temporarily silly,' that is the mildest word that will describe my meaning. If asked whether he was going to do. It seems quite possible within the next few months ... I have endeavoured to be judicious and have no reason to exaggerate to you and Bosie.[5]

Bosie was becoming more and more determined to return to England and visit Oscar. Sibyl had consulted her solicitor as to whether or not it would be safe for him to return. His reply was a 'most emphatic' no.[6] Bosie did not care. Robbie's report upset him, and he wrote to Robbie to say that no matter what anyone said he was going to return to England and see Oscar. Robbie replied that he did not think a visit was a good idea. Not only was it risky for Bosie, a visit could do nothing but harm Oscar's chances for an early release, which they still believed was in the works.

A few days later Oscar wrote a note to Robbie apologising that he had been a poor conversationalist. It was clear that the visit had thrown him. He said he had not been expecting him until the following day and now '[a]nything sudden' upset him. He asked Robbie to tell 'Douglas' that he 'could not accept or allow' a dedication and that the idea was 'revolting and grotesque'. He also asked Robbie to collect a number of his love letters, and the gifts he had given Bosie – books and jewellery. His instructions were curious. He wanted Robbie to get them from Bosie and keep them so that he could destroy them himself unless he died in prison, in which case Robbie was to destroy them. He asked Robbie to copy out the letter for Douglas so that he could have 'no loophole of escape ... He has ruined my life – that should content him.'[7]

Robbie did as he was told, but the mission could not have given him any pleasure. Bosie was absolutely devastated, 'deprived of all power of thought and expression'. But having heard Robbie's report of Oscar's mental state, he refused to return any of the gifts. In his grief, Bosie turned to the one person who always provided unconditional love – his mother.

The next time Robbie saw Oscar (with the ever-present Sherard) on 29 May, he tried to plead his friend's case. Not wanting to write in a letter that would be seen by the prison censors, or to speak about the matter out loud, Robbie wrote on a piece of paper for Oscar to scan. The message was not preserved, but it said something to the effect that Oscar's harsh treatment of Bosie had disturbed some of his friends and estranged their sympathies from him. This elicited a stern rebuke from Oscar in a letter the next day, and even more harsh condemnations of Bosie. He wrote that he was more ashamed of his friendship with Alfred Douglas than for his connection to prostitutes. (Much of the text of this letter is virtually identical to passages in *De Profundis*.)[8] Robbie would not make the mistake of pleading Bosie's case to Oscar again.

Bosie refused to give up his faith in Oscar's love. As he wrote to More Adey:

> ... [Oscar] warned me that all sorts of influences would be brought to bear upon me to make me change; but I have not changed. From the first to last I have been absolutely consistent and absolutely the same. I shall not change now. I decline to listen to anything he says while he is in prison. If he really means what he says and if he is really not mad, he is not the same person that I knew and he is not Oscar, the Oscar to whom I shall always be faithful and who belongs to me quite absolutely. When lovers quarrel, they return to each other their letters and presents. I and Oscar were lovers, but we have not quarrelled, and as I have not asked for a return of my letters and presents he cannot ask for his. If Oscar really meant what he says now, I should despise him utterly, for no meanness could be lower, and I should be obliged to think that what many people over and over again told me about him is true.
>
> But I do not believe that he means what he says, and I regard what he says as non-existent. I ignore the cruel insults and unmerited reproaches which I am told his lips have uttered against me. I attribute them simply to an evil and lying spirit which at present inhabits Oscar's body, a spirit born in an English prison, out of English 'prison discipline,' and which I hope in spite of everybody and everything to ultimately cast out of him. But even if I shall never cast it out, even if Oscar's body is always to be inhabited by this thing, even if the last time I saw Oscar I really said goodbye to him for ever and ever (at least in this world), I should still

love and be faithful to my own Oscar, the real one, and I should always refuse to take notice of English prison spirits. I daresay you think I am talking nonsense, but I mean every word I say, and that is enough on this subject.[9]

This put Robbie in an impossible position as he tried to maintain his friendship with Oscar, who had made it absolutely clear he wanted nothing to do with Bosie, and with Bosie, who wanted nothing else but to be with Oscar. Robbie must have tried again to carry out Oscar's instructions, because he received the following letter from Bosie dated 4 June 1896:

... with regards to the letters. I cannot give them up to anyone. The possession of those letters and the recollection they may give me even if they can give me no hope, will perhaps prevent me from putting an end to a life which now has no raison-d'etre. If Oscar asks me to kill myself I will do so, and he shall have back my letters when I am dead. Till he asks me that I could not give up the letters which are part of my life, and now the only part that is not quite poisoned and ulcerated. What I will do is this: I will put them in a packet and seal them, and I will write on the outside: 'In case of my death this packet is to be destroyed unopened.' The whole shall be locked in my despatch box. More than this I cannot do. The letters he wrote me while he was out [on] bail I have carried in a case every day. I have slept with them under my pillow. Morning and evening I have kissed them and prayed over them. To give up this ritual will cost me more than I can say, childish though it may appear. ...

Your affectionate friend, Bosie [10]

Robbie's response no longer exists, but it is clear that he tried to persuade his friend that Oscar did, indeed, want to end things with him and that it would be better for him to accept this. The stresses of the previous year had done nothing to improve Robbie's health, and in late June he underwent surgery to remove a kidney that had been damaged in childhood. It was a hazardous operation, but his fears were allayed by the fact that his doctor, Sir Frederick Treves, was a pioneer in the field. It required a month of hospitalisation and Robbie was not sure he would survive it. One of the letters he wrote before undergoing the knife was to Constance Wilde. He wrote to assure her that he wanted to be her friend.

Robbie remained gaunt and fragile-looking for some time after the operation. His hair, which had been cut short for the procedure, never grew back properly. At the age of twenty-seven, he described himself to friends as 'middle age and balding'.[11]

Ada Leverson visited Robbie on 15 July and was startled by how thin he was. When she mentioned that Adey was going to visit Oscar in prison, for some reason this upset him a great deal, and she ended up writing to Adey apologising for being so tactless as to mention it.

Robbie wrote to Bosie around this time to advise him, once again, to let Oscar go and move on. On 15 July 1896, Bosie responded, 'It certainly was a surprise to me that you do not think Oscar Wilde and I should ever be together again. If Oscar Wilde only loves me half as much as I love him – if he comes out of prison nothing in the world will keep us apart. All friends and relations, all their plots and all their plans will go to the winds once I am alone with him again and am holding his hand.'[12]

On one of his prison visits, Adey had also urged Oscar not to be too hard on Bosie, but it had no effect. So he tried to to shield Bosie from the worst of the onslaught he knew Oscar was preparing for him. Bosie lashed out at the messenger. He accused More and Robbie of siding with the enemy and 'playing Queensberry's cards for him'. The religious content of his letter is striking:

> What you are working for I don't know and I don't understand, but the inconsistencies of both you and Bobbie I may tell you quite frankly I put down to the baleful influence of the Catholic Church. The fact of belonging to and really believing in that institution puts such a gulf between you and Bobbie on the one hand and real pagans with a real sense of the supremacy of Greek love over everything else such as Oscar and I, that it is impossible for you to understand what I think about it, and what Oscar would think if he were in his normal condition ... I tell you both that when I get the chance I will fight with any weapons I can find ... It requires all my previous knowledge of you to refrain from saying that all this about 'being better for Oscar and I not to meet' et cet is canting humbug. But as it is, I am content to call it Popish weakness coupled with social cowardice.[13]

Jealousies, petty arguments and griping continued to plague Oscar's circle of friends. Sherard was now telling everyone that the Leversons were to blame for Oscar's misfortune because they had put him up in their home instead of urging him to flee the country. Robbie, following Oscar's prison tone, was blaming Bosie and he had managed to bring the Leversons around to his point of view.

The French actor and theatrical producer Aurelien Lugne-Poe visited the Leversons in September, and when he returned to France, he met up with Bosie and gave him a report of the visit. Bosie wrote to More Adey on 27 September saying that Lugne-Poe had told him the Leversons 'abused' him very much and 'told him that I prevented Oscar from going away when he was out on bail.' Bosie said he wrote a 'very nice' letter to Leverson asking for 'some explanation'. He concluded that he was 'very fond of both' the Leversons and was 'much distressed at their quite inexplicable conduct'.[14]

Robbie meanwhile encouraged Bosie to focus on promoting his poetry. Bosie's first book had finally been published on 30 October 1896 with no dedication. It had sold well in France without any special publicity and this seems to have had a positive effect on its author.

Robbie knew Bosie well. He tried to lift him out of his malaise, and get his mind off Oscar, by appealing to his fighting spirit. In contrast to the cautious long-term route he was to take with Oscar Wilde's work, he advised Bosie to take a public stand, advertise his work in the London papers and send copies to reviewers there 'even if they are to be slated.' (Hyde speculated that Robbie did this in order to sabotage Bosie, but this is highly unlikely. When the British edition was published, Robbie was its champion, sending copies to friends, praising the anonymous author and asking for their opinions.)[15]

In spite of their differences of opinion over Oscar and his wishes, Robbie and Bosie remained close. Robbie continued to be one of Bosie's main confidants regarding his adventures with boys and the risks that came with it. On 18 November 1896 Bosie wrote:

> My dear Bobbie ... A beautiful sailor boy with whom I had had adventures appeared a few days ago at my house accompanied [by] an enormous strapping woman about six feet high who spoke French and who was supposed to represent his mother and a small timid man, who looked thoroughly frightened, to represent the father. I was at lunch when the cook announced them. I at once divined (and subsequently found I was right) that the woman had been specially

retained from a neighbouring lupanar. [Described as a brothel in court.] The woman commenced by weeping bitterly and groaning and saying she had to speak to me on a most serious matter. I said at once 'Voyons madam ... je ne peux pas vous permettre de rester ici' – that means 'Clear out' – She replied that she intended to remain or return with the Police. I took her gently but firmly by the shoulder saying 'Allons Madam Foutez le camps tous les trois' – that is 'Clear out, all three of you' – and pushed her out of the door, the other two following meekly. I have not seen anything of them since. The whole proceeding was so naïf and pastoral that I was more in love with the boy than ever and am making desperate efforts to find him again. This system of blackmailing will not and cannot, I think, survive but the world will never grow tired.

Your affectionate friend, Bosie [16]

In February 1897, Ross and Sherard made another visit to Wilde in Reading. Sherard became jealous, and believed he had fallen out of favour when Oscar asked him to move away so he could have a private conversation with Robbie. There were a number of issues Oscar might have wished to discuss privately. He and Adey were in the middle of negotiations over his wife's life interest and were, Oscar believed, collecting funds from benefactors for him to live on after his release. He might also have wanted to talk to him about Bosie or about the letter he had started writing to him that month. He told More Adey, in a letter dated 18 February, that it was 'the most important letter' of his life and that he hoped 'to have it finished by Tuesday'.[17]

17

De Profundis

If Bosie's *Mercure de France* article had gone to press, the French audience would have read his affirmation: 'One thing that saves us from the deepest misery, and renders all of our sufferings bearable: the knowledge, nay the certainty that neither my friend nor myself regret in the slightest what brought it about – that is to say, our friendship ... in spite of everything, he is happy to have known me; and if he had those last four years to live again, he would not wish to change anything which he has done, no more than I.'[1]

Unbeknownst to Bosie, in the confines of a prison cell, Oscar had re-written his story with a new moral. Bosie was still at the centre of his grand narrative, but he was no longer Juliet. He was Judas.

The only official account of the writing of *De Profundis* comes from the new Governor of Reading, Major J. O. Nelson. According to this version of events, Wilde was given one sheet of paper to write on at a time, and it had to be handed back when he was through with it. Ian Small, editor of the Oxford University Press *Complete Works* edition, for various textual reasons – including the fact that only two of the twenty sheets of paper finish at the end of a sentence – believes the story is unlikely. Nelson would later admit to relaxing prison regulations for Wilde in other ways, to a degree that could have cost him his job or worse. Nelson, contrary to the rules, brought Wilde a daily newspaper, conveyed notes between him and other prisoners, and smuggled hot soup into his cell. The most important thing he did, however, was to propose to the Commissioners that Wilde should receive a strong, coarsely bound manuscript book for his use. Simply having a pen and a notebook began to soothe his mind.

De Profundis was written over an extended period resulting in what Wilde himself called '... this letter in its changing, uncertain moods, its scorn and bitterness, its aspirations and its failure to realise those aspirations.'[2]

One section, later known as 'the published part', is a philosophical essay on individualism, humility and Christ as Artist. We will deal with this part later. Now our focus is on what came to be called 'the unpublished part', a semi-public letter to Bosie. The letter is at times personal and raw and at other times self-conscious and aware of an audience. Prison had not destroyed Wilde's ability to write. He paints a vivid portrait of his perspective at that moment, coloured by all of the trauma he had experienced in the previous year. *De Profundis* is an exceedingly literate cry of pain.

Author Regenia Gagnier has noted that Wilde's letter has some elements common to most prison literature in which a narrator often speaks with grandeur and authority, and often addresses dialogue to someone he loves. Those who have endured solitary confinement suffer from intrusive, repeating memories and are prone to 'endless dialogues from former scenes from the life world'. One prisoner, who Gagnier quotes, calls such thinking 'deprived memory': 'I think about each remembered thing, study it in detail, over and over … Finally it changes and begins to tear itself free from facts and joins my imagination … Every memory has an element of pain or disappointment.'[3]

Three main issues were preying on Oscar's mind as he wrote *De Profundis*. The first was the fact that Bosie had not written him a letter. The second was his bankruptcy and the humiliations surrounding it. Third, that he was now viewed by the public as a vile corrupter of young men. He comes back to each of these subjects time and time again. Nearly all of the episodes and anecdotes he chooses to relate about his relationship with Bosie come back in one way or another to Oscar's financial generosity, Bosie's lack of appreciation of it, the resulting damage to his good name, and not having a single letter from him.

Oscar's feelings towards Bosie at this time were complicated. Contrary to what it might at first seem, *De Profundis* is not a break-up letter. Oscar still, very much, wanted to be with him. Yet his statements to Adey and Ross about Bosie at this time were uniformly negative, even exhibiting a paranoia that Bosie, as if by sorcery, is somehow still directing every negative event in his life.

In the process of writing, the letter had grown from a private communication into a public declaration. From the beginning, Wilde imagined the first audience for this work as Ross and Adey. Eventually he was writing for the public at large. For this audience, he wanted to overturn the Svengali narrative: 'your father will always live among the kind pure-minded parents of Sunday-school literature, your place is with the Infant Samuel, and in the lowest mire of Malebolge I sit between Gilles de Retz and the Marquis de Sade.'[4] Bosie became a fictional character, their life together like a drama 'inspired by real events'.

Wilde brings up the 'Oxford Mishap' again and again in *De Profundis*. He emphasises this to show that Bosie was already 'corrupted' before they became intimate. Wilde also highlights the times he thought about ending the relationship and depicts a dynamic in which Bosie is constantly in pursuit, and he is constantly trying to escape. The explanations and justifications of his actions, and the anger and recriminations, make up such a large part of the letter that the 'record of bitter moments' overwhelms the more loving parts. Had he written the story of his friendship with Bosie at another time, he might have focused on the moments of joy rather than pain. (Indeed, there was such a record once, before Bosie burned his love letters.) In prison, he could produce only a story of suffering.

The *De Profundis* claim that Bosie had forgotten all about him and was off somewhere enjoying the sun was a record of Oscar's fears, not the facts. People who were not personally acquainted with either man (such as the jury in the Ransome libel trial) would, of course, have no way of knowing that. The idea that Bosie had abandoned him loomed large in Wilde's mind, even though it should have been clear that he had not.

Wilde admits he knew Bosie had tried to write to him, but that he had been forced to reject the initial request himself.[5] He must also have suspected the prison authorities would frown on communication with Bosie. Prison regulations of the time stated that 'the permission to write and receive letters is given to prisoners for the purpose of enabling them to keep a connection to their respectable friends, and not that they may be kept informed of public events.'[6] From the point of view of prison authorities, Bosie was not a *respectable* correspondent. It was only in the relaxed environment of Reading under Nelson that Oscar could write to him 'with perfect freedom'. In the conclusion to his letter he gives Bosie instructions on how to write to him and tells him that he can feel free to say whatever he wants precisely because he knew such a thing would not have been possible before.

In the course of the writing, he had communication from Bosie through other people. *De Profundis* reports that Bosie was sending messages to Oscar through More Adey, asking if he could give Oscar some money to repay his debts. He knew as well that Bosie had refused to surrender the gifts and letters Oscar had sent him. He had learned from Robbie how devastated Bosie was by his message. Robbie had shared some of Bosie's exact words on the subject with him. If he wanted a letter from Bosie, all Oscar had to do was to put him on a list of people from whom he would like to receive communication, and send a message through Ross or Adey saying 'tell him to write.' If he had done so, Bosie would have written in a heartbeat. Why didn't he?

It seems he didn't want to have to ask. He had put his entire life on the line in order to be with Bosie, and he wanted Bosie to do the same. He wanted him to overcome all obstacles, even those he created himself. 'Even if I had not been waiting but had shut all the doors against you, you should have remembered that no one can possibly shut the doors against Love for ever.'[7]

Elsewhere in the text (it appears early, but was perhaps written later, as scholars think the letter went through various stages of composition) Wilde expanded on this thought, asking what would have happened if their situations were reversed. If Bosie had been sent to prison, he said, 'I would have written none the less, so that you should have known that at any rate there were always letters waiting for you.'[8]

In the context of the prison document, nothing Bosie does is good enough. Oscar criticises him both for writing an article that was too personal and for another that was too rigid and formal. He is chided for not communicating and then despised for the quality of the messages he does manage to get through. Wilde admits in *De Profundis* that he knew why Bosie had written his *Mercure de France* article (he had told Bosie to plead his case) and planned to dedicate his poems to him (he had already agreed that he should do so). Even so, he is furious at the way these things were done. Whatever valid objections he might have had to Bosie's actions on his behalf, they were magnified in light of his distress at losing control of his own public image.[9]

When Oscar wrote to Robbie and told him to get his love tokens back from Bosie, it was not because he wanted to end the relationship. It was to provoke a reaction. Bosie had not responded directly to Oscar's shocking letter to Robbie because he still believed he was not allowed to, and he now also believed Oscar did not want to hear from him. Instead, he wrote to his mother about his hurt feelings. When Oscar received news of this he was hurt again and this leads into a section of *De Profundis* in which he criticises Bosie's relationship with his mother.

It was only after all of this 'long and fruitless waiting' that Wilde decided to write a letter so powerful that Bosie would have no choice but to respond. By writing it, Oscar exorcised his demons and reclaimed his sense of self.

Wilde once famously said he only put his talent into his writing, but his genius into his life. For his entire adult life, from his days in Oxford, to the moment of his arrest, his greatest artistic creation had been the persona of Oscar Wilde. *De Profundis* follows its author through the grieving process as he mourns 'Oscar Wilde's' death. He is angry, he rails against the injustice, he weeps and finally he accepts his fate. He comes to see that the carefree Bosie he loved is dead as well. What remains is the love these two ghosts have for one another, and the desire to face their uncertain future together.

After all of the recriminations, Oscar still imagined his future with his own darling boy. He envisioned a meeting with Bosie, in 'some quiet foreign town like Bruges'. It is notable that he thought the reunion would be arranged through Robbie. Where once they were separated by a 'chasm of achieved Art and acquired culture', they were now separated by 'the chasm of sorrow', but 'to Love all things are easy.' He asked Bosie to tell him about the dedication he'd planned for his poems. 'If it is in prose, quote the prose; if in verse, quote the verse. I have no doubt that there will be beauty in it ... Remember also that I have yet to know you. Perhaps we have yet to know each other.'[10]

18

The Life Interest

All bad art is the result of good intentions.

Oscar Wilde[1]

Bosie was not the only one whose attempts to help Oscar backfired in a spectacular fashion. Having been unsuccessful in getting enough subscribers to prevent Oscar's bankruptcy, Ross and Adey now set their sights on guaranteeing an income for their friend and protecting his relationship with his two sons. Had they done nothing, there is a good chance Oscar would have been reunited with them. Instead, Ross and Adey's efforts, conducted out of love and devotion with the best of intentions, drove a wedge between Oscar and his wife. They reduced the amount of the annuity she had been willing to give Oscar from £200 a year to £150 and they very nearly lost that as well.

The legal issues require explanation. Until the Married Women's Property Act was passed in January 1883, about a year before the Wildes' marriage, women had no legal right to property, nor to the custody of their children. Upon marriage, everything a woman owned became her husband's to dispose with as he saw fit. The man of the house had the sole right to make decisions about his children's care unless he was proven unfit by a court order. Women from privileged backgrounds had a means of protecting their property rights by drawing up a marriage settlement prior to the wedding day. This contract would give the wife the right to control the property she brought to the marriage.

Although the new act meant that women had the right to control their property in any case, many women, including Constance, continued to draw up marriage settlements spelling out their separate property rights. Constance's settlement was fairly standard for its day. She accrued interest from the investment of her personal property, called a life interest. If she died before Oscar did, the life interest would be paid to her husband for the duration of his life and then, upon his death, it would go to the children. There was often a clause that guaranteed that in the event of a husband's bankruptcy the life interest would bypass the receiver and be put in trust for the children. Unfortunately, there was no such clause in their settlement and the life interest became an emotionally charged personal asset of Wilde's bankrupt estate.

At the time of the bankruptcy, the marriage settlement was yielding an income of about £800 a year. There was another interesting wrinkle. When Oscar and

Constance married, Constance gave Oscar a loan of £1,000 from her marriage settlement with an interest of five per cent a year. When they were happily married, it made little difference that he had never made a payment on that loan. But by August 1895, Oscar now owed £1,558, making Constance her husband's largest creditor.[2]

The Official Receiver demanded that the life interest be sold to satisfy Wilde's creditors. Now that Wilde's income had stopped, the life interest was the only thing that would secure the futures of the Wilde boys. Thus Constance intended to buy it back. Adey and Ross had the same idea. They wanted to give it to Oscar so *he* could bestow it on his children.

Ernest Leverson advised Ross and Adey not to bid against Constance because it would cause a rift between Oscar and his family. The trust was actually safer in Constance's hands, as anything Wilde owned was at the mercy of the Official Receiver. Yet Oscar's friends bid against her anyway, inflating the price. This led to a falling out between Leverson and Ross.[3]

Oscar's friends contacted Constance's legal team in an effort to come to an amicable agreement. They worried that if Constance had full control, she might not allow Oscar to see his sons. Also, if they did not secure a guaranteed income in the form of the life interest, Oscar would be dependent on his wife's good-will. Constance, understandably, wished to protect her parental rights and was not ready to give unlimited trust to the convict husband who had betrayed her. She insisted that there would be no agreement unless she retained sole custody of the children.

When Constance visited Reading to bring Oscar word of his mother's death she also consulted her solicitors and appointed her cousin, Adrian Hope, as her executor and named him the beneficiary of her will to put her personal estate in trust for the benefit of the children. In the event of her death, she appointed him guardian until the children reached their majority.

The deal, as outlined by Constance's solicitor Mr Hargrove, was that Oscar's friends would withdraw their opposition to her purchase of the life interest, and give her full control of the children. In consideration, she would give Oscar one-third of the income from the settlement in the event of her death and during her lifetime provide him with £200 a year. Oscar agreed to this reasonable arrangement, and wrote at once to Robbie telling him to stop contesting the life interest.

Robbie and More, for whatever reason, decided to ignore Oscar's direct instructions and continued to bid. Perhaps they were driven by the fact that their petition to raise money for Oscar on his release had failed. Oscar was, as yet, unaware of this and they may have hoped that they could break this bad news to him in tandem with the good news that they had secured the life interest.

Constance had also heard rumours about the petition. She and her legal team continued to act under the mistaken assumption that two or three thousand pounds would be waiting for Oscar when he got out. With proper investment of that sum, her annual allowance would be largely unnecessary and was more than generous. Constance did not believe Robbie's explanation, in a June letter, that there was a rumour Queensberry was planning to make a bid on the life interest.

She did not know whether this interference came from Oscar or if the friends were acting on their own. It would not have been out of character, certainly, for Oscar to present one pose to her while behaving entirely differently to others. She told Robbie that if they continued to act against her regarding the life interest, she would take back her offer to support Oscar with an allowance.

More and Robbie did not realise that the balance of power had shifted. Constance did not have to provide for Oscar at all. If she chose to divorce him, the life interest would be void. Then she could go to court and be granted sole custody of her children without any concessions. So far, she was hoping to avoid this, but Oscar's friends continued to push her in that direction.

From here Adey took up the negotiations through the intermediary of Adela Schuster, a friend of both of the Wildes, who had generously donated £1,000 to Oscar during the trials. Schuster had been happy to help Wilde, provided she could be sure she was not doing an injustice to Constance. When she read the instructions that Robbie had ignored, she decided not to support them and tried, without success, to convince Adey to listen to Oscar.

Shuster wrote to Adey in March, 1896. She said she was certain Constance would keep her promise and reminded him that she was the victim. She begged him to back down 'First because it is just and right and secondly for Oscar's sake ...'[4]

Adey, it seems, did not much care for Constance. Schuster responded to one of his letters saying that she did not suspect him of 'allowing any personal dislike you may have of Mrs. Wilde to influence you in this matter.' She reminded him, once again, that Constance was the 'injured person' and that they should defer to her for that reason, even if Oscar's interests suffered for it.[5] Adey could not suspect Schuster of being against Oscar. She was, in the midst of all of this negotiation, scheming with him to gain influence with prison chaplains and doctors to look after their friend. Their plans included various means of influence up to and including outright bribery.[6] Even so, Adey did not take Schuster's advice.

Adey was, at this time, circulating a petition to secure Oscar's early release, and he knew that the most important signature was Constance's. He sent a message to her through Schuster asking for her cooperation, to which she responded that she would 'tear herself into little bits' to assist in Oscar's release provided his friends drop their bid on the life interest.[7] Adey believed if he explained to Constance directly why he was acting as he was, she would see the wisdom of his ways. Constance's reply no longer exists, but it is clear that she stood her ground. It shocked Adey so much that he asked Schuster if it could be a forgery. Schuster assured him it was not. She warned him in an August 1896 letter that if he and his friends kept interfering, they would drive a wedge between Oscar and Constance. She reminded him that Oscar would be dependent on her good will when he got out, and this was not helping Oscar's cause.

Ross and Adey could not be swayed by Shuster, Constance, or even Oscar. They were determined that the only course of action was to buy the life interest, the price of which had now doubled. Adey wrote to Oscar and tried to persuade him not to agree to Constance's terms. He suggested that Constance was being advised by enemies and that he should not sign any legal documents that would diminish his parental rights. Oscar continued to be open to the idea of appointing a guardian to ensure the well-being of the boys in the event of Constance's death. In a September letter he suggested Arthur Clifton. Clifton declined. If Constance heard about this manoeuvre, it would have been yet another sign that Oscar had lied to her and was acting against her.

In October, Adey and Ross offered the Official Receiver £50 for a half-share in the life interest, with the assumption that Constance would buy the other half. The Official Receiver agreed in December, which prompted Hargrove to write directly to Oscar. He said if this bid was not withdrawn, Constance's offer of an allowance, which had now been reduced to £150, would be rescinded entirely. Oscar did not react well to taking orders from his wife. It persuaded him that Adey had been right and she was receiving advice from people who were against him. Still believing that Ross's subscription of £2,000 or more was forthcoming, he decided to take a hard line. Adey wrote to his solicitor outlining Oscar's demands. He expected to be paid an annuity of £200 a year from Constance, plus he wanted one-third of the life interest with no conditions concerning his domestic arrangements whatsoever.

If they did not receive this, they would offer the official receiver £50 for half of the life interest with an option of buying the second half, or £75 for the entire interest. Adey said he was was willing to go up to £100 for the whole thing. The offer of £75 was accepted and The Ross/Adey team secured the life interest. It was not worth the paper it was printed on.

The moment of good will that Oscar and Constance had shared had been squandered. There was nothing left for her to do but to go to court to have Oscar removed as legal guardian of his children and to file for divorce, thus invalidating the life interest. When Oscar learned about this turn of events he was furious at how Ross and Adey had bungled his affairs. He proclaimed Adey 'incapable of managing the domestic affairs of a tom-tit in a hedge for a single afternoon.'[8]

His outbursts towards Ross and Adey – especially Adey – have usually been characterised as grossly unfair given their hard work and good intentions. Yet they had made a serious mess of things. They defied Oscar's wishes when he was powerless to act on his own behalf and unravelled a very favourable agreement between him and his wife. As things stood after his friends' help, he was the proud owner of a worthless life interest, he had no chance to see his children, and no income at all. Even worse, if Constance carried through with her threat of divorce, she would have to go into court and prove that Oscar had committed sodomy. This would result in another humiliating legal ordeal and in the worst case scenario, more prison time.

Fortunately, no one believed this was in the children's best interest and so the lawyers for all sides came to an agreement. They hammered out a deal for judicial separation. Ross and Adey signed over the life interest to Constance. In return Oscar would receive an allowance of £150 a year, a sum that would continue after her death. Because trust between the couple had been so badly battered, her solicitor saw fit to include a clause that said she could discontinue the allowance at her discretion if Wilde was 'guilty of any moral misconduct or notoriously consort with evil or disreputable companions ...'[9]

Bosie was not the only one to receive an angry prison letter from Oscar. Towards the end of his prison term, when he was able to receive more communication from the outside world, Oscar was finally able to learn more about the actions his friends had been taking on his behalf and he did not approve of all of them. He attacked most of the people who had tried to help him, including Ernest Leverson, More and Robbie. Reggie Turner rebuked Oscar for some of what he wrote to, and about, his friends. 'The most beautiful thing I have ever known is Bobbie's devotion to you. He has never had any other thought than of you; he has only looked forward to one thing, the time when he will be able to talk to you freely and affectionately again. It is very rare to find such complete devotion, and I fear, dear Oscar that you have gone very near to breaking his heart.'[10]

In spite of Oscar's angry outburst, Adey continued to negotiate on his behalf. In a letter to Holman dated 14 May 1897, he expressed his concerns about the implications of the phrase 'moral misconduct', which was overly broad and might be used to interfere in his private conduct rather than public activities that might legitimately affect Constance. He also advised Oscar not to sign anything until he had received a letter of condonation forgiving his past homosexual activities. This would provide him a safeguard against any new divorce claims in the future.

Oscar's lawyer, Hansell, warned him that under the terms of this agreement, his allowance would stop if he ever resumed his relationship with Douglas. At that moment Oscar was unconcerned about this. It would not be long, however, before this clause would come back to haunt him.

19

A Curious Way of Expressing his Disinclination

When Oscar was once again a free man, Robbie wanted to meet him at the prison gates. Oscar asked him not to come. He didn't want his friend to see him in that context. More Adey came alone, bringing a number of items his friends had collected for Oscar: a dressing case provided by Reggie Turner with the initials S. M. for his new *nom de guerre*, Sebastian Melmoth; from Robbie and Frank Harris a wardrobe of clothes; and from More Adey, hats, gloves, socks, handkerchiefs, mother-of-pearl studs and toiletries such as tooth powder, toilet water, lotion, French soap and a hair tonic called Koko Marikopas, which would disguise the fact that his hair was turning white.

Oscar emerged in high spirits, intoxicated with his new freedom. All of his fears about being seen vanished, and his friends' fears that he would be changed did too. He was as witty and proud as ever. He talked so much that he and Adey missed their train, much to the disappointment of Robbie and Reggie waiting at the Hotel Sandwich in Dieppe.

They prepared the room, arranging books they had collected, brightening the space with flowers and ordering wine and sandwiches. The honoured guest finally arrived at half past four in the morning. Robbie and Reggie found him to be in 'childish spirits'. According to Robbie, one of the first things Oscar did when he saw him was to hand him the manuscript of *De Profundis*. We will talk about this element of the story in much greater length later.

They spoke until nine in the morning, at which point the exhausted Robbie had to lie down for a nap. Everyone was exhausted except Oscar. They met at noon for lunch and then went sightseeing. Oscar had an appreciation for nature that Robbie had never seen before, describing everything with vivid adjectives. Over the next few days the friends travelled through the country, looking for the cosy country inn that Wilde had imagined as his post-prison home. Reggie and Robbie made this trek on bicycles. They had tried to get Oscar to ride one, but he could not manage it, and so he and Adey travelled in a comfortable carriage.

Robbie told Hesketh Pearson that Oscar could never be persuaded to speak about his childhood. 'In fact, he rarely, if ever, spoke of his own life at all. But, very strangely, just after he came out of prison, for several days he continually reverted to his boyhood. Reggie Turner and I were, of course, burning to hear all about his life in prison, and we were perpetually bringing his thoughts back from the one topic to the other.'[1]

After about two weeks in Dieppe, Oscar travelled to Berneval, France, and Robbie went with him to help him get settled. They stayed in a spacious hotel suite made up of eight rooms and enjoyed excellent dinners. Robbie tried to rein in Oscar's pre-prison spending habits, preventing him from dissipating all the resources he had on luxurious perfumes. During this sojourn, Oscar and Robbie made love. After Robbie returned to England, Oscar wrote him a long, affectionate letter. It was now Robbie who he called 'Dear boy' and who had the 'heart of Christ'. He said Robbie could heal and help him. 'No other friend have I now in this beautiful world. I want no other.'[2]

Around this time, *The New York Times* ran an optimistic article on Wilde written by its Paris correspondent Rowland Strong, a friend of Bosie and Robbie. (Strong will continue to pop up in the strangest episodes of this story.) The article quotes an unnamed friend. Based on the tall tales and the emphasis on Oscar's spiritual growth in prison, which echoes *De Profundis,* the friend must have been Robbie. (Sherard, who was also in Paris, would not have said anything so romantic about Douglas, and Adey and Turner would not have told such a fiction.)

The article makes prison sound like a writer's retreat. It claims Wilde learned two new languages and drew up the plans of two comedies in prison and that the first book he would write post-prison would be a novel. Wilde left prison determined to be 'truer to his artistic self in the future'. The article mentioned that Douglas was residing temporarily in Paris 'where he is very popular in the best literary and artistic circles for his poetic talent is undoubted and he has a great fascination of manner.' Their 'common friend' explained that there would be no meeting between the two men. 'Their souls may speak to each other,' the friend said, 'but nothing more.'[3]

After his release from prison, Oscar could have taken over his own business and legal affairs, but he preferred to have More and Robbie act as liaisons with the various lawyers. On 10 May More Adey had received a warning from solicitors Parker, Garrett & Holman:

> Lord Queensberry has made arrangements for being informed if his son joins Mr Wilde and has expressed his intention of shooting one or both. A threat of this kind from most people could be more or less disregarded, but there is no doubt that Lord Queensberry, as he has shown before, will carry out any threat that he makes to the best of his ability.[4]

Queensberry had also threatened to have Bosie institutionalised if he ever returned to England. Adey certainly conveyed this information to Oscar, but for the moment, he was not concerned about it. He was not yet thinking about reuniting with Bosie. He was excited to get back to work.

He met and drank with Leonard Smithers, the publisher of the avant-garde, decadent and erotic. He specialised in 'anything that the others are afraid of.' This included everything from finely bound translations from French and Latin to illegal pornography. In the Victorian era, antique book dealers, Smithers among them, were often fronts for a trade in erotica. Police were as much aware of their existence as they were of the habits of some of the clients they served.[5]

Smithers had taken up many of the decadent writers who had been dropped by John Lane and the Bodley Head in the backlash following the Wilde trials and he continued the tradition of taking great care in all of the aspects of the presentation of his texts, producing beautifully bound and illustrated volumes. Wilde called him 'the most learned erotomaniac in Europe'.[6] Wilde made plans, over drinks and warm conversation, to have Smithers publish his next book, which turned out to be *The Ballad of Reading Gaol*. In addition to the Ballad, Smithers would obtain the rights to put out print versions of *An Ideal Husband* and *The Importance of Being Earnest* in 1899.[7]

Bosie was also optimistic. Once Oscar was free to receive his letters, Bosie quickly disabused his friend of the notion that he had not wanted to write. His letter does not survive, but according to Bosie it said, 'I am told that you now hate me and do not wish to see me or have anything to do with me, but all the same I write to tell you that I have not changed to you, in spite of all the efforts that have been made to put me against you, that I have remembered and kept my solemn promise to stick to you through thick and thin, and that I long to see you again.'[8]

Whether it represented his true feelings on this communication or not, Oscar wrote to Robbie about 'Bosie's revolting letter'. Oscar claimed the letter prevented him from sleeping. It was so revolting, in fact, that he read it multiple times. He said he had 'a real terror' of Bosie's 'evil influence' and that 'To be with him would be to return to the hell from which I do think I have been released. I hope never to see him again.'[9]

Over the next couple of days, Oscar wrote Robbie two more letters full of business, flirtation and expressions of his horror of Bosie. 'Bosie can almost ruin me ... His letters to me are infamous.'

Probably on the same day, Oscar wrote to Bosie. The letter has not survived but it seems Bosie did not like what Oscar had to say. He responded with a 'bitter' letter.[10]

On 2 June, Oscar wrote a long letter to Bosie. Based on this reply, Bosie had written to him about the French production of *Salome*, mounted by his friend Lugne-Poe while Wilde was in prison. Bosie was apparently trying to find work for Oscar, and had suggested that Lugne-Poe produce his next play. This was probably the fabled 'Pharoah' which Oscar came out of prison determined to write, and yet never put on paper. Oscar liked the idea of a triumphant return to the French stage with a play on a Biblical theme, but knew that Lugne-Poe could not pay him, and he needed some quick cash. Bosie had also suggested Oscar might write for *Le Journal,* and appears to have been acting as an intermediary with some contacts there. Oscar wanted to do this work, but was concerned about giving his address to anyone.[11] He noted that he had read Bosie's poems with 'pleasure and interest'. He wrote again the next day, and the next. He said, 'Don't think I don't love you. Of course I love you more than anyone else. But our lives are irreparably severed, as far as meeting goes. What is left to us is the knowledge that we love each other, and every day I think of you, and I know you are a poet, and that makes you doubly dear and wonderful.'

He closed saying that he would write again later that night.[12]

Most of Bosie's letters to Oscar at this time have been lost, but Wilde described them later in a letter to Robbie. The letters contained 'assurances of eternal devotion ... entreaties that I should always live with him ... offers of all his life and belongings' and described, Wilde said, 'his desire to atone in some way for the ruin he and his family brought upon me.' Wilde's bitterness seemed to have vanished.[13] Yet he would, over the next few weeks, consistently write about Bosie to Robbie in the harshest terms.

When Andre Gide met Wilde in Berneval, Wilde told him one story about his plans to reunite with Bosie, while writing something else entirely to his friend. Wilde told Gide that Bosie wrote him 'horrible letters'. He said Bosie wanted to pick up where they left off and was ready to take on the whole world. He didn't understand Oscar's reluctance. This was undoubtedly true. It was not mentioned but also true that Oscar was not putting up much resistance.[14]

Shortly thereafter, Gide met Douglas in Paris and told him what Wilde had said. Bosie told him that he knew Oscar very well and that he was 'incapable of suffering boredom' and 'never did anything great in solitude.' (This was quite true.) He showed Gide a stack of letters that confirmed Wilde was writing to him every day. He read the most recent letter to Gide. It said Wilde was working on a play called *Pharaoh*, and that he wanted to finish it so he could make a triumphant entrance to Paris instead of slinking in as a criminal. As Gide described it, Oscar urged Bosie to 'let him finish his *Pharaoh* in peace; that then he would return, return to him.' Gide remembered the last 'glorious sentence' – 'And then I shall be King of Life once more!'[15]

Wilde may have told Gide that Bosie's letters were 'horrible', but he did not go so far as to describe Bosie himself that way. In Wilde's existing letters to others, Bosie is usually described in glowing terms. It is only in letters to Robbie that you find Oscar saying that Bosie is revolting and fills him with horror. It is unclear why he chose to present his feelings in this way to Robbie. If the act was entirely for the benefit of lawyers, he could have told Robbie the truth.

Oscar had handed *De Profundis* to Robbie, and perhaps he felt some embarrassment at doing something that so contradicted the views he had expressed while in prison. Certainly he sensed that Robbie would not approve of the reunion, given all he had read. The most compelling reason was that he loved Robbie, and he seems to have believed if he kept his devotion to Bosie from Robbie he could please them both. From whatever combination of these motivations, the result is that he painted a very different picture of his feelings to each of his friends.

On 5 June, Oscar wrote Robbie that 'Bosie telegraphs daily.' He quickly corrected saying 'This is an exaggeration.' What he failed to mention to Robbie was that he answered the messages and that he was writing just as often.[16]

Robbie may have suspected something was up when Oscar wrote that he wanted his own house, or perhaps he heard something from More Adey, who was with Bosie. The tone of Robbie's letters became more business-like. Oscar tried to charm him: 'As regards people living on me in the extra bedrooms; dear boy, there is no one who would stay with me but you.'[17]

But the next day Oscar was writing to Bosie saying 'My dearest Boy, I must give up this absurd habit of writing to you every day. It comes of course from the strange new joy of talking to you daily ... Dear boy, I hope you are still sweetly asleep: you are so absurdly sweet when you are asleep.' He signed off 'En attendant, yours with all love.'[18]

A few days later, Wilde wrote to his 'dear honey-sweet boy' to come see him in Berneval on 18 June. He said he had a bathing costume for him, and that he should pack a straw hat and flannels. He also asked him to bring him lots of cigarettes and books. He said he had been thinking of a suitable pseudonym for him and was divided between 'Le Chevalier de la Feleur-de-lys' and 'Jonquil du Vallon', eventually settling on Jonquil. He referred to himself as 'that strange purple shadow who is known as Sebastian Melmoth.' In his *Autobiography*, Bosie described this as being 'just like the old Oscar'.[19]

When Wilde's solicitor Mr Hansell heard of the proposed reunion, he threatened to resign. He must have conveyed his concerns about Queensberry's threats to his client. Whatever he said shook Oscar enough that he wrote to Bosie to tell him it was not yet safe to meet.

Bosie, frustrated and disappointed, suspected there was a conspiracy afoot, and he blamed Adey. Adey had made the legal arrangements with Constance, which had put Oscar in a 'ridiculous and ignominious position'. Bosie's letter claims More promised that under the terms of the agreement he could meet with Oscar and resume his relationship with him, and this would not be considered 'bad conduct' on Oscar's part. As we saw earlier, More was always working as something of a go-between, even a double agent, trying to restore Oscar's relationship with his family while also supporting the relationship between the two men. So it is likely that he had said something like this to reassure Bosie.

Now the young man felt betrayed and sent an angry letter. When More received it he was coming down with pneumonia and he left it to Robbie to answer on his behalf. After working for years on the practical financial and legal matters while his lordship went off to fight quixotic, counter-productive battles, the responsible one had had enough of the prodigal. He certainly was not going to let him unload on his ailing friend who had worked so tirelessly and selflessly on behalf of both Oscar and Bosie. Robbie took credit for the deal with Oscar's wife and stood by his choices. He said he was writing an account that 'gives the dilemma in which we were placed'. If Bosie was not satisfied, their lawyer could send him a complete account of the proceedings about the marriage settlement in which Bosie heretofore had taken so little interest. Robbie said even though More had not particularly liked Oscar before the trial, he had put in a great deal of time and money to help him. Robbie added that he could have no feeling or regard for Bosie at all until he withdrew his offensive remarks about More.[20]

'At all events I should have thought you had good taste enough under these circumstances not to write the sort of things you do, though I can easily understand and sympathise with your irritation and annoyance at any arrangement which deprives you of seeing Oscar,' he wrote. He suggested that if Bosie wanted to be with Oscar, then he should support him financially and then the allowance from Oscar's wife would not be an issue. Then 'he will have the added pleasure of your perpetual society and your inspiring temper for the future.'[21]

Bosie knew about Robbie's sexual reunion with Oscar. He now suspected Robbie had a personal motive for keeping them apart. He sent Robbie's letter to More Adey, along with one from himself. He ruefully thanked Robbie for letting him know that he was responsible for what had happened, 'and in the letter I read between the words his own satisfaction that after all I have been baffled of my long hope and long expectation.'

He wrote to More again on 30 June saying that he had been overwhelmed by insulting letters from Robbie and that one of them was fourteen pages long. He said he had no choice but to end the friendship. 'It seems to me that he is possessed by an extraordinary spirit of animosity and vindictive hatred towards me.'[22]

Then something occurred to Bosie. Hadn't Robbie said he was sending a long explanation of the legal process? He went and retrieved the thick envelope he had cast aside and saw immediately that there was a reason the letter was fourteen pages long. It was the explanation Robbie had promised. Oops. Whatever was in that document, it persuaded Bosie that More had not been trying to break up his relationship with Oscar. His letter changes tone in mid-stream as a presumably shame-faced Bosie writes: 'I have read it through & I can only say that I think you are absolutely blameless and quite justified (& Bobbie too in that matter) ... I can only repeat that I am very sorry that I wrote to you as I did.'[23]

The fourteen-page explanation does not survive, but Ross and Adey had done nothing to try to keep their friends apart. They were the messengers, that is all, and the blow-by-blow account of the negotiations satisfied Bosie. Around this time Bosie also learned that Queensberry's detectives had been monitoring Oscar since he left prison, which explained his reluctance to meet.[24]

More replied, trying to make peace. Bosie answered with more apologies. He asked More to remember what he had been through, that he had been separated from the person he loved most and that he had been longing to see him again for two long years; then within sixteen hours of the planned reunion a telegram came calling it off. He said he was further baffled and hurt by the cool letter from Robbie making a point of saying he was responsible for keeping them apart when he thought he was on his side. 'I say remember all this, and I do not think you will find it very hard to forgive my sudden irritation, my rudeness, my bad taste (call it what you like), and remember that as soon as I knew that I had wronged any one I was ready to make ample amends.'[25]

He also wrote to Robbie:

13th July 1897
My dear Bobbie, Your letter only reached me this morning though it is dated Saturday. It will be all right about Oscar. Though of course it is evident that he must have thought something had suddenly occurred which made it necessary to postpone my visit you say he knows always that I was to be allowed to see him but I knew that too, Hence all this row .... You may not know that there were paragraphs in several French papers and the *New York Herald* saying that Oscar and I had been 'the object of much interested attention at the races on Sunday last'. There followed imaginary description of how we looked and what we did, etcet. Oscar at first thought that Hansell had seen these and that was his reason for writing as he did. You will seem to cling to the idea that Oscar doesn't want to see me. The wish is father to the thought. But you must admit that if he doesn't want to see me, he has a curious way of expressing his disinclination. When a man writes to one and invites one to come and see him, and says that he trembles with ecstasy at the joy of seeing one again it requires a subtle mind like yours to detect symptoms of his unwillingness to see one.[26]

It would take a subtle mind, indeed, if Robbie were reading Oscar's letters to Bosie, to imagine he was anything but overjoyed at the prospect of reunion. In reading Oscar's letters to Robbie, on the other hand, it required no exegesis at all to imagine Oscar was reluctant. Bosie, knowing nothing of what Oscar wrote to Robbie, believed that Robbie must be in a state of wilful and obstinate denial for personal reasons he could only begin to imagine.

In early August Robbie visited Oscar for 10 days and was joined by Robert Sherard. He left with the impression that Oscar was not planning to see Bosie. He and Aleck travelled to County Donegal, Ireland, to visit friends.

On 24 August Oscar wrote to tell Robbie that Bosie had said he did not have forty francs to come to see him and since then he had not written. This cannot be true. Four days later Bosie boarded a train and headed to Rouen. He carried with him gifts for Oscar including a silver cigarette case, engraved with a stanza from Donne's 'Canonization'. With its reference to the Phoenix, it celebrated both Oscar's emergence from prison and the rekindling of their love.

> The Phoenix riddle hath more wit
> By us, we two being one are it.
> So to one neutral thing both sexes fit,
> We die and rise the same and prove
> Mysterious by this love.[27]

Even Bosie knew where the triumphant love story should have ended: on a train platform in France. Oscar is waiting there. Bosie gets off the train. Oscar sees his beautiful young love and bursts into tears. They walk all day arm-in-arm in perfect joy. Bosie wrote in his autobiography that he had always felt that if they had both died after that, it would have been the perfect love story. (The 1997 film, *Wilde*, indeed, chose to end the story at this point.) After that honeymoon, they secretly made plans for the marriage. They would live together in Naples.

On 31 August, Oscar wrote to his own darling boy saying that his 'only hope' of 'doing beautiful work' was being with him. 'Everyone is furious with me for going back to you, but they don't understand us. I feel that it is only with you that I can do anything at all. Do remake my ruined life for me, and then our friendship and love will have a different meaning to the world.'[28]

When he got back from Ireland, Robbie learned that Oscar had seen Bosie. Although Robbie had not planned to see Oscar again that year, he made a special trip to Rouen to speak to him face to face. Oscar looked Robbie in the eye and said he had no intention of going to Italy with Bosie. But the plans were already underway.[29]

Naples was an ideal destination for a number of reasons. It was possible to live well on much less money than in London or Paris. It was one of the most densely populated cities on the Mediterranean and home to a number of world-class theatres and opera houses. It was also a favourite vacation spot for English gentlemen who enjoyed the companionship of Italian boys. The idea that Italy was a decadent place dated back at least a century, when John Dennis called the nation a land in which 'idolatry has set up its headquarters ... the home of the sodomite and the pope.'[30]

It was so well known in this regard that sodomy was sometimes referred to as 'the Italian vice'. Ironically, because this reputation attracted so many sex tourists, in Italy they called it 'the English vice'. Four years after the La Bouchere Amendment was passed in England, Italy had decriminalised same-sex acts. The Zanardelli code made official what was only custom in England, that same-sex relations were acceptable as long as they did not create 'querela di parte' – a public scandal. Years later, during the Ransome trial, Justice Charles Darling would ask the defending counsel 'Are you aware, Mr Campbell of the reputation of Naples?'[31]

On 15 September Wilde left for Paris and a few days later joined Bosie in Naples. They must have known that they were risking Wilde's allowance by making this move, but Bosie was convinced that his brother, who always believed he was on the verge of coming into a fortune, would support them if all else failed.

Robbie felt betrayed on many levels. Foremost was the fact that the man who had written him words of love a few months before had not trusted him enough to tell him the truth. He had lied over and over about his feelings for Bosie. Not only that, Oscar did not appreciate the years of work that Robbie and More had put into facilitating Oscar's return to respectable society nor how cruel he was being to his wife. Just that week Carlos Blacker had written to Oscar to say that Constance had agreed to see him in October. Now all of that work was for nothing. Oscar was delusional in his belief that he could live with Bosie while being supported by his long-suffering wife. As all of this was happening, Robbie had read *De Profundis*. He was dismayed that Oscar would want to return to the drama of Bosie. Robbie not only believed the relationship was unhealthy, he thought Oscar had a long life ahead of him, and assumed that the only way he could resume his career was to return to his wife and *appear* to have repented of his sins.

To Robbie, Wilde explained this reunion in an apologetic fashion.

My going back to Bosie was psychologically inevitable ... I could have lived all my life with you, but you have other claims on you – claims you are too sweet a fellow to disregard ... Of course, I shall often be unhappy, but still I love him: the mere fact that he wrecked my life makes me love him.[32]

Oscar liked this last line and would frequently reuse it. This 'what can I do?' helplessness was clearly for Robbie's benefit, because *De Profundis* shows Oscar always intended to be reunited with Bosie. To Reggie he painted a rosier picture: 'I love him, and have always loved him,' he said. After repeating his line about loving him for ruining his life, he said that with 'the first of all the young poets of England' at his side he could now 'do lovely work'.

So when people say how dreadful of me to return to Bosie, do say no – say that I love him, that he is a poet, and that, after all, whatever my life may have been ethically, it has always been romantic, and Bosie is my romance. My romance is a tragedy of course, but it is none the less a romance, and he loves me very dearly, more than he loves, or can love anyone else, and without him my life was dreary.[33]

If Oscar thought an apologetic letter would be enough to soothe Robbie's feelings he was mistaken. Robbie could not believe anything Oscar said. Of the letters Robbie wrote to Oscar during this period, only one phrase survives: 'Remember always that you committed the unpardonable and vulgar error of being found out.' Oscar said the letters distressed and angered him and didn't keep them.[34] Two months after begging Bosie to 'remake my ruined life for me,' he wrote to Robbie, 'As you remade my life for me you have a perfect right to say what you choose to me ...'[35]

Based on Oscar's response, Robbie had proposed that he continue to handle Oscar's business but that they keep things on a purely professional basis. Oscar replied that of course he wanted Robbie to handle his business and that he wanted his friendship too. Oscar tried to ignore Robbie's anger and to write to him in friendly terms. For the next two months, Robbie only wrote to him on business matters.

If Robbie's romantic love for Oscar had been briefly rekindled, it was now over. When Oscar suggested using the lines 'When I came out of prison ... You met me with love,' as a dedication to *The Ballad of Reading Gaol*, Robbie wrote to Smithers he was sure 'dear Oscar meant to tell me and Douglas and two or three other people that each was intended. That only amuses me.'[36]

Shortly after 25 September, Oscar and Bosie rented the Villa del Guidice at Posillipo, a fashionable part of town. None of Wilde's works had been translated into Italian, so his reputation in Italy was entirely based on his scandalous trial. Resistance to the Wilde/Douglas reunion was widespread. They even received a visit from a representative of the British Embassy. He had come to let Douglas know that England did not approve of the living arrangement. Apparently Lord Rosebery had rented a villa nearby and the Embassy worried about how his new neighbours might reflect on him. When they refused to leave, the British Consul in Naples, Eustace Neville-Rolfe, investigated the matter, and sent Rosebery a letter marked 'Very secret'. He had heard that Wilde was going by the name 'Sebastian Mothwell' [sic] and that 'he looks thoroughly abashed, much like a whipped hound.' He did not think he posed any threat.[37]

Initially, the couple were quite content. They pooled their financial resources, what was brought in by one was available to both. (Wilde's description of Douglas's letters in *De Profundis* as 'a strange mix of romance and finance' isn't a bad description of marriage.) Their Naples villa was beautiful with a terrace overlooking the sea and marble steps leading down. They employed a cook, a maid and two additional servants. Bosie was impressed that in Naples he could feed himself, Oscar and the staff for only twelve francs a day. The downside was that the villa was full of rats, and Bosie refused to stay there until they were taken care of. He temporarily rented a room in a villa across the street. Not only did they engage the services of a ratter, they took the additional step of having a local sorceress burn incense and mutter rat-chasing incantations. They were initially both prolific; Oscar was finishing work on *The Ballad of Reading Gaol*, hoping to have *Salome* translated into Italian and performed in Italy, and promoting Bosie's sonnets.

Bosie and Robbie both gave Oscar advice on the ballad. Bosie's view was that he encouraged Oscar towards greater artistic sincerity, whereas Robbie always encouraged artificiality. Robbie did believe it 'was natural to Wilde to be artificial ... when he wrote of serious things.'[38] But it seems both friends advised him to tone this down, each in his own fashion. Robbie, in particular, thought Oscar used too many overwrought adjectives and he thought the ballad should have ended at 'And outcasts always mourn.' He shared his dislike of the ballad with a number of people, whereas Bosie considered it to be one of Oscar's best works. Their different perspectives were coloured by their relations with the poet. For Bosie, the ballad was the product of their brief, happy honeymoon. For Robbie, it was the product of laborious and contentious negotiation at a time when he was most disillusioned.

Oscar wrote to Reggie expressing great happiness with Bosie. 'Somehow, he is my life: of course, he is unchanged: he is just what he was: kinder, and more considerate in a thousand ways: but still the same wilful, fascinating, irritating, destructive, delightful personality. If we had money we would be all right ...'[39]

Oscar told Smithers, 'He understands me and my art, and loves both. I hope never to be separated from him. He is a most delicate and exquisite poet, besides – far the finest of all the young poets in England ... He is witty, graceful, lovely to look at, loveable to be with.'[40] For a short period Oscar seemed to delight in writing to friends using the word 'we.'

It was not long, however, before word of the reunion spread. As Robbie had expected, it sent shockwaves through Oscar's remaining circle of 'respectable' friends who were appalled at his stubborn refusal to become heterosexual. The backlash was strong and immediate.

Oscar was not one to be controlled by anyone, and when his wife wrote saying she 'forbade' him to live with Bosie, it made him so mad that simply describing the letter later made him turn white and tremble with rage. His response to her was, given the circumstances, impolitic. The lawyers were called, and they found that Wilde was in breach of their agreement and cut off his allowance. Bosie's mother also threatened to cut off his allowance, which was almost three times that provided by Constance.

In rehabilitating the literary Oscar Wilde, Robbie faced what we today might call a serious branding problem. Even before he went to jail, Oscar had a hard time persuading publishers to invest in him. Until the society plays, he never had a real commercial hit. As a jobbing writer, his work was so eclectic that editors didn't know where to place him or how to market him. His literary reputation was mixed and incoherent; his fame based on the now poisonous persona of Oscar Wilde. Robbie was determined to change that. He took a smart, patient, long-term approach. Unfortunately, his biggest nemesis was Wilde himself. He kept sabotaging any effort to present him as reformed, respectable and not dangerous to read.

Wilde was no longer in a position to think long-term. His main priority was to get income as quickly as possible. He was negotiating with an American agent called 'Pinker' on the publication of *The Ballad of Reading Gaol*, and had also persuaded Smithers to let the poem be published serially in a British newspaper to give him a larger, and more immediate, income.

Robbie was against the idea of publishing the Ballad serially. He thought newspaper sales would jeopardise its chances as a book. He was chiefly concerned with how the British public would receive the new Oscar Wilde. He hoped that someone would pick it up and serialise it in America so that Oscar could make some quick income without undercutting its potential in England. His frustrations with Oscar were showing in an October 1897 letter to Smithers. Unable to persuade Oscar to think long-term, he tried to enlist Smithers in preventing serial publication. 'I hope you will refuse to publish [the ballad] at all if the market is going to be spoiled by having it published in an English newspaper. I am really sick of it and I should think you must be by this time, as you have had all the trouble.'[41]

Meanwhile, Robbie was stuck in the middle of the battle between Oscar and Constance's lawyers. Oscar's argument was that Bosie could not be referred to as a 'disreputable person' in a legal sense as he had never been charged or convicted of anything and he was well bred and well born. He argued, likewise, that he and Bosie had no control over whether they were reputable or not, as it is other people's talk that gives someone a reputation. His criticism was valid, as he would go on to prove by openly consorting with the lower elements of society. It was Douglas's notoriety that offended, not his actual morality or social status. All of this was beside the point. Oscar was wilfully blind to the fact that his wife could not be expected to support him while he lived with the male equivalent of a mistress – the man who had torn her family apart.

As the money ran out, Oscar's letters became more irritable and full of self-pity as he grumbled about his poverty, the difficulty in selling his poem and the unfairness that art and love could be circumscribed by a want of money. Meanwhile, Robbie wrote him letters that were alternately cold and business-like or acrimonious. On at least one occasion, Bosie defended Robbie when one of his letters had angered Oscar, saying that some of the words that offended him were probably meant as a joke.[42]

In early November, Oscar was told his allowance would be stopped. What angered him more than anything was hearing that More and Robbie had agreed that Bosie was, for the terms of the agreement, a 'disreputable person'. If loving men was a crime, More and Robbie were as guilty as he and Bosie were. He wrote a long, angry letter to More.[43]

Two days later, Oscar had calmed down and he wrote to Robbie to ask if he thought the lawyers might restore his allowance if he would agree not to live with Bosie in the same house. He could agree to that, but he would not agree never to see him again. Robbie responded, but his answer seems to have focused mostly on the ballad, not the personal drama. Oscar also wrote to More asking him to pass along the compromise that he would stop living with Bosie, but could not agree to 'cut him' or not see him.

In the midst of all of this, Robbie continued to work with Smithers on literary business. Somehow Bosie had gotten wind of Robbie's letter to Smithers, urging him not to allow publication of the ballad in serialised form. Bosie interpreted this as more evidence that Robbie was behind the plan to starve them out. He wrote a letter to that effect to a mutual friend and word got back to Robbie.

Robbie was tired of being blamed for being unable to do the impossible. Oscar's lack of trust in his business judgement was the final straw. On 25 November he wrote a letter to Smithers saying he had 'ceased to be on intimate terms' with Wilde.[44] Oscar responded diplomatically to Smithers with words crafted to be conveyed to his pouting and bitter friend.

Shortly thereafter Lady Queensberry joined the long list of those trying to force the couple to separate. She had determined to cut off Bosie's allowance if he did not leave Oscar. With no money coming in on either side, they had little choice. 'It is proposed to leave me to die of starvation, or blow my brains out in a Naples urinal,' a bitter Oscar told Smithers.[45]

How could people think it was more moral to make him a lonely, impoverished outcast than to let him be happy and productive with Bosie? But Oscar's plaint was no use, the resistance against them was too great – though they each made it clear that they planned to remain fixtures in each other's lives. Bosie had his allowance restored, and got his mother to agree to let Oscar stay on in Naples and to provide him with £200.

When he was leaving Oscar at Naples, Bosie wrote to his mother laying out the moral question as he saw it; what if he were to tell his friend,

> 'I cannot come and live with you now. I lived with you before and stayed with you and lived on you, but that was when you were rich, famous, honoured and at the summit of your position as an artist, now I am very sorry of course, but you are ruined, you have no money, you have hardly any friends, you have been in prison (chiefly, I admit, on my account and through my fault), you are an ex-convict, it will do me a great deal of harm to be seen about with you, and besides that my mother naturally objects to it very strongly, and so I'm afraid I must leave you to get on as best you can by yourself ...'

Sincerely and frankly, is this what you would have me write? Apparently it is. But darling Mama, all my love for you and all my gratitude for your immense love of me could not make me a cad and a snob and a low filthy hypocrite, and a vile crawling time-server and a dirty coward, such as I would have been if I had written in that way. Please observe that I take no credit to myself for coming back to my friend when he asked me, though some people might say that it was courageous, and certainly I have had to pay dearly for it, if only that it has cost me the first really deliberately cruel and unkind letter that you have ever written to me. But I take no credit at all, it seemed and it seems to me the plain natural thing to do if I wished to have any kind of respect for myself or differentiate myself in any way from the lowest and vilest people in the World …[46]

Oscar wrote a letter as well. His was to Robbie:

Bosie, for months, by endless letters, offered me a 'home.' he offered me love, affection and care, and promised me that I should never want for anything. After four months I accepted his offer, but when we met at Aix on our way to Naples I found that he had no money, no plans, and had forgotten all his promises. His one idea was that I should raise money for us both. I did so, to the extent of £120. On this Bosie lived, quite happily. When it came to his having, of course, to repay his own share he became terrible, unkind, mean and penurious, except where his own pleasures were concerned, and when my allowance ceased, he left …

It is, of course, the most bitter experience of a bitter life; it is a blow quite awful and paralysing, but it had to come, and I know that it is better that I should never see him again. I don't want to. He fills me with horror.[47]

Beyond the fact that Oscar and Bosie had lived together in Naples, there is little in this letter that is true. Oscar was as big a spendthrift as his partner, if not worse, and Bosie had left him at Naples with the greatest reluctance while ensuring he had a home and money on which to live. There was no suggestion prior to this that Bosie was not paying his share, in fact, his allowance was much larger than Oscar's. Given his larger income, he was surely paying a larger share of the expenses at the villa. The feelings he expresses about Bosie are not echoed in any of his other correspondence or conversations with friends. It was this letter, quoted in Ransome's biography of Wilde, that would incite Bosie fourteen years later to sue for libel. But Bosie did not yet know of it in 1910, when he claimed that Oscar told him at Naples, 'If you leave me, I shall go to hell headlong.'[48]

The only explanation is that it was written to persuade his wife's lawyers that he had truly broken with Bosie. He had already written letters to a number of Constance's friends saying that they were no longer living together, but he received no responses. A bitter note in a private letter to Robbie, on the other hand, might be believed. The letter had its intended effect. Shortly thereafter, Constance did agree to restore his allowance.

Robbie was probably in on this plan. Bosie was also sending him letters about the arrangement. 'My mother wrote yesterday that she agreed to the terms of my proposals,' he wrote. 'So I accordingly left Oscar and I am under a pledge never again to reside in the same home or hotel with him.'[49]

A few days after he arrived in Rome, Bosie wrote another letter to his mother that contradicted the feelings he had expressed only a few days before. It is impossible to say whether Bosie was sincere when he told his mother that he was miserable in Naples and that he hid it even from himself. 'I am glad, O so glad! to have got away, to have escaped,' he wrote. ' … Even when I got here I persuaded myself that I was miserable and that I wanted to go back and I wrote to you in that sense.' His insistence that he was suddenly and completely over Wilde came with detailed instructions about the money she was to send to him. Even then he combined it with this vow:

> Don't think that I have changed my mind about him or that I think him bad or that I have changed my views about morals. I still love and admire him, and I think that he has been infamously treated by ignorant and cruel brutes. I look on him as a martyr to progress. I associate with him in everything. I long to hear of his success and artistic rehabilitation in the post which is by his right at the very summit of English literature, nor do I intend to cease corresponding with him or not to see him from time to time in Paris or elsewhere. I give up nothing and admit no point against him or myself separately or jointly.

Perhaps he did want to be free. There was a weariness in his letter, 'I am tired of the struggle and tired of being ill-treated by the World,' he wrote, 'and I had lost that supreme desire for his society which I had before, and which made a sort of aching void when he was not with me.' He also started to sense that 'he didn't really wish me to stay and that it would really be a relief to him if I went away.'[50]

The desire to fight the world to be together was gone. On the other hand, it is not clear that this was a 'break-up' either. Their relationship had never been monogamous and was not based on sex. So these usual measures can't be used to determine if they were still a couple. Although they never lived together again, after a short hiatus they fell back into their comfortable old pattern. They dined together, went to the theatre together, shared boys with each other, and there were periods in which they saw each other so regularly they might as well have been living together. Oscar's letters continued to be full of references to Bosie.

'At that time,' wrote T. H. Bell, 'I was not aware of any break between Wilde and Douglas. My recollection, very dim now after all these years during which I attached no meaning to the matter, is that the name of Douglas did come into the conversation I had with Wilde.'[51]

In 1900, shortly after Oscar Wilde's death, Bosie wrote to his brother, Percy, 'I was afraid you might think I had changed my mind about him in later life. I never did and he was the same to me, always my dearest and best friend, although I found it absolutely impossible to see him as much as formerly in the face of the avalanche of slander and grief of relations etc. both on his side and mine.'[52]

Bosie said he remained in love with Oscar until he read the unpublished parts of *De Profundis* in 1912. He did not start looking for a bride until after Wilde's death, which suggests he could not move on while Wilde was alive. The grand drama of their romance had ended but it was replaced by a warm, everyday emotion.

Vincent O'Sullivan, who visited Oscar in Naples just after Bosie left, said Oscar spoke of 'certain grievances which he thought he had against Douglas. They were of a personal, not of a material, order, and seemed to me rather dramatised. He never blamed Douglas before me for leaving Naples; indeed, he seemed to think there was nothing else for him to do. That he had formed no implacable grudge against Douglas is certain, for I dined with them both a long time after in Paris.'[53]

This description stands in stark contrast to a conversation with Wilde that Ross described to Smithers. Robbie visited Oscar in Paris not long after the separation. He said Wilde spoke bitterly of Bosie and that his complaints were mostly about money.[54]

By the time Bosie left Oscar at Naples the two friends had entirely different understandings of what had transpired there. Bosie believed he and Oscar had lived a great love story and that it was only the interference of moralists that forced them to part. He believed Oscar admired his poetry and intellect and that he needed him as his muse to create beautiful work. This is what Oscar told Bosie, and wrote to many others. Bosie continued to believe that the ordeal of the trials and the period that followed had been theirs together. His proudest accomplishment, central to his entire sense of self, was how he had stood by Oscar through thick and thin. Robbie, on the other hand, believed Bosie had always been the pursuer in the relationship; that Oscar did not want to reunite with him, but he had not been strong enough to resist because he was damaged and weak from his time in prison. This is what Oscar told him.

In later years, when biographers began to call, they would naturally trust the word of the apparently objective, dispassionate literary executor over that of the self-interested, and ill-tempered ex-lover.

20

Luxuriating in Tragedy

I was appalled at what people were saying about him. I did not say I was
appalled at the vice.
Robert Ross, on Oscar Wilde, testimony in Ross v. Crosland

After Bosie moved out, Oscar fell into a deep depression. He told O'Sullivan
that a short time after Bosie went away he thought of suicide.[1] His letters to his
agent were also full of veiled threats of suicide. Bosie also fell into a depression.
Ross wrote to Wilde's agent at this time that Douglas seemed to have lost
interest in people.[2]

In early January, Bosie wrote to Oscar complaining about how much better
life had been in Naples, both in terms of expenses and recreational opportunities.
'The annoyance of living in this town and not having any money to live the way
one would like is perpetual. The facilities of Naples are so enormously superior.
Here I have simply not the energy of going to the trouble of doing that sort of
thing. Since I left Rome, there have only been three occasions, and unbridled
chastity is telling on my health and spirits.'[3]

Robbie was spreading gossip about Oscar's break from Bosie. He told
Smithers that Oscar told him *The Ballad of Reading Gaol* described his life
with Bosie in Naples, not prison. If Oscar did say this behind Bosie's back, it
is equally possible that he grumbled about Robbie to Bosie. Robbie, some time
after Oscar's death, told Frank Harris that he had never felt Oscar really liked
him. Oscar's gossip about each friend to the other set the stage for what was to
happen in years to come.[4]

Oscar stayed in the Villa through February 1898 and then moved to France
and settled into the Hotel de Nice in the rue des Beaux Arts in Paris. It was a
short walk from the more elegant Hotel du Quai-Voltaire where he had stayed
when he first met Sherard – but miles away in terms of prestige and comfort. By
spring, Oscar had returned to a scaled-down version of his previous life. Oscar
and Bosie went to Nogent, in part because Oscar had unpaid bills to escape
in Paris. Oscar wrote to Robbie, telling him the town was lovely and that he
was enjoying Bosie's company, but he made a point to mention that Bosie was
returning to Paris each night.

In March 1898, Oscar wore out his welcome at another hotel. He moved
to the Hotel D'Alsace run by Jules Dupoirier. For a debtor in disreputable
exile, he was an arrogant man. Dupoirier, who came to like his tenant and

to be a true blessing to him in his last days, described Sebastian Melmoth as 'not at all pleasant'. Mr Melmoth never spoke to the servant, Jules Patuel, only directly to the owner. He arrived with two valises, one stamped with the initials S. M. They were heavy, loaded with books, and Dupoirier carried them up to the third floor himself. The playwright occupied two adjoining rooms, one was his study and the second the bedroom. The price for these rooms, which he rarely paid, was 65 francs a month. Dupoirier was not fond of Douglas either. He described him as too much of a nobleman to speak to a common fellow like himself. Ross, he said, had a different character. 'He was a pleasant, obliging fellow.'[5]

Wilde was a late sleeper, and had a consistent breakfast order of a lamb chop and two hard-boiled eggs. This he took around the time most people have lunch. He usually went out with friends in the evening and would come home around 2 or 3 in the morning. He sent Dupoirier to the Avenue de l'Opéra four or five times a week to fetch him 'an astounding cognac', which cost 28 francs a bottle.

Oscar gave his innkeeper the impression that he was working regularly. 'He used to work all night long,' Dupoirier told Sherard. He believed Wilde was producing articles, but that the person who employed him was not sending him the money he was owed.[6] Most of his money and meals, however, came from the many friends, mostly French and English writers, who invited him to dine with them. He frequented some of the most upscale restaurants in the area, including the Café de Paris.

In order to pay for his appetites Oscar continued to insist his wife owed him money. He believed she should pay him arrears for the period when he had lived with Bosie. He wrote a letter to Robbie on 17 March 1898 making the false claim that Lady Queensberry had not given him any money when Bosie left, adding that furthermore Bosie owed him £500, 'a debt of honour'.

Knowing how money slipped through Oscar's fingers, Robbie did his best to control his finances, doling out funds little by little so that they might last. Robbie, in his fatherly role, would tell people to give Oscar clothing, or to buy him a meal, but not to give him money. If they were determined to give Oscar money, they should route it through him. Oscar was always trying to work around Robbie's financial control.[7]

Although Robbie gave advice to Oscar – Oscar called it lecturing – he did not advise him to stay away from Bosie, only to try to be more discreet. His nagging was on three topics: Oscar's drinking, his spending and his lack of interest in work. The nagging was affectionately exaggerated by Oscar, who seemed rather to miss it when it did not come. Throughout the latter part of 1897 and into 1898 Ross tried his best to set boundaries with Wilde. He corresponded with him and visited him infrequently and tried to limit conversation to business. 'Robbie learned to detach himself to some extent from Oscar,' wrote Bogle, 'not to mind his criticism too much, and to go ahead and do what he considered best, whether or not Oscar objected.'[8]

In May Oscar had an operation on his throat, and Bosie was the only one of the old gang who was there during his recuperation.[9] Any hard feelings between Robbie and Bosie had passed, and Oscar felt free once again to regale Robbie with tales of their mutual friend and his sexual adventures. Bosie and Robbie, meanwhile, wrote each other intimate, chatty letters about boys and other topics of interest.[10]

Oscar had emerged from his depression as strong and defiant as ever. He no longer felt any need to please society. Bosie said Oscar's lifestyle was 'notorious and he was quite open about it. He was hand in glove with all the little boys on the boulevard. He never attempted to conceal it. Oscar believed, as may other eminent people do, that he had a perfect right to indulge in his own tastes. He would not thank you for trying to make people believe it was otherwise.'[11] Bosie, who lived nearby in a flat that Oscar had helped to furnish, was no stranger to the boulevards either.

The company of renters suited Oscar for a number of reasons. Being fellow outcasts, they would not reject or shame him. Making these habits known to his respectable friends served a purpose in itself. He wanted to make it clear that even if they had succeeded in keeping him from living with Bosie, they had not saved him. Anyone who was to be his friend would have to accept that fact.

Oscar would sometimes lament and sometimes revel in his exclusion from society. As a general rule, those who were least sympathetic to Oscar's relationship with Bosie saw an unhappy, debauched man. Oscar made it a point in this period to reject anyone who was not willing to accept Bosie as part of his life.

Those who were most sympathetic to that friendship were also the most likely to report that they found Oscar, in his last years, to be drinking and spending too much, but overall – content. Bosie wrote in 1905:

> I give it as my firm opinion that Oscar Wilde was, on the whole, fairly happy during the last years of his life. He had an extraordinarily buoyant and happy temperament, a splendid sense of humour, and an unrivalled faculty for enjoyment of the present. Of course, he had his bad moments, moments of depression and sense of loss and defeat, but they were not of long duration. It was part of his pose to luxuriate a little in the details of his tragic circumstances … he painted an image of himself, destitute, abandoned, starving even. (I have heard him use the word after a very good dinner at Pillard's); as he proceeded he was caught by the pathos of his own words, his beautiful voice trembled with emotion, his eyes swam with tears; and then, suddenly, by a swift, indescribably brilliant, whimsical touch, a swallow-wing flash on the waters of eloquence, the tone changed and rippled with laughter, bringing with it his audience, relieved, delighted, and bubbling into uncontrollable merriment.[12]

Reading only Oscar's letters to Robbie throughout this period, one is struck by the contradictions in his attitudes about Bosie. He sometimes speaks of him in the most derogatory terms, and yet he mentions him constantly, seems to always be in his company and asks for reports of him whenever he is not there. There are only two reasonable explanations for this. The first is that he was a liar. The second is more intriguing and it is that for Oscar, the fact that Bosie was 'terrifying,' 'evil,' and 'revolting' did not preclude his being in love with him.

To illustrate this notion, we turn to one of the less savoury events of Oscar Wilde's last years: his acquaintance with a man who was described as 'the most marvellous, audacious & wonderful canaille that it was possible to imagine, either in fiction or history & capable of any & every villainy, including murder.'[13] When Oscar arrived in Paris, the country was divided by the Dreyfus Affair. Alfred Dreyfus, a Jewish artillery captain had been falsely accused of giving secrets to the Germans. He was tried for treason, was found guilty on the evidence of a handwriting expert and, before a howling mob shouting anti-Semitic epithets, exiled to the Devil's Island penal colony off the coast of French Guiana. He was kept in solitary confinement, manacled to his bed at night. Dreyfus's wealthy family could not accept the verdict, and they continued to fight to prove his innocence. A critical breakthrough came when a fellow officer recognised the handwriting on the crucial note as belonging to Ferdinand Esterhazy. Esterhazy looked in every way the villain. The Hungarian had black hair, a huge moustache and shifty eyes. He was also an arrogant, malicious, gambler and womaniser who augmented his military salary by running a brothel.

Wilde found him to be excellent company. He told Esterhazy that he should not feel guilty about condemning an innocent man to the horrors of a prison colony because 'the innocent always suffer ... Besides, we are all innocent until we are found out. It is a poor, common part to play and within the compass of the meanest. The interesting thing surely is to be guilty and wear as a halo the seduction of sin.'

Esterhazy was impressed by this argument and he stood up in the restaurant and said, 'Why should I not make my confession to you? I will. It is is, Esterhazy, who alone am guilty. I put Dreyfus in prison and all France cannot get him out.'[14]

Wilde continued to socialise with Esterhazy after his confession, along with Bosie and Maurice Gilbert, who had spent time with Robbie and Reggie before settling in for a time as Wilde's new narcissus. What Wilde actually thought of the Dreyfus affair is hard to discern. Bosie was an anti-Dreyfusard (as were Frank Harris, Rowland Strong and Robert Sherard), although he admitted in an 1898 letter to Wilde that things looked rather bad for his side. It is not clear from the letter whether he believed Wilde agreed with him or not.[15] At the very least, he did not think Wilde would be shocked by his opinion. Sherard was not much better at defending his friend against the charge of anti-Semitism than he was against homosexuality. He explained that Wilde's sympathies were, of course, with Dreyfus. He liked Jews. 'The Jews,' he used to say, 'are the only people who lend money.'[16]

By dining with Esterhazy, Wilde was once again feasting with a panther. Esterhazy was thrillingly immoral – like Dorian Gray, who killed to experience the sensation, or Salome, who asked for the head of John the Baptist on a plate. He had fired Wilde's literary imagination. Fascinated with criminality, he spent his days attending the trial of a couple who had murdered a debt collector and his nights at The Kalasaya, 'a bar with sodomist outcasts who were sometimes even dangerous in other ways.'[17] He was writing again, although his tales would never end up on paper.

Meeting with the young novelist Wilfred Hugh Chesson around this time, Wilde said his work was 'all in his head'. He told Chesson 'I do not doubt that there are as wonderful things in my future as there are in my past.' He spoke about a drama about a murder staged in a theatre frequented by criminals, described an execution by guillotine he claimed to have witnessed, and contemplated the morgue. He asked, 'Have you ever noticed a thief's hands? How beautiful they are? How fine and delicate the tips? They must be fine and delicate to take the watch from your pocket without your knowing.'

But this was only half of the picture. In their pleasant afternoon together, they discussed art and artists in depth. They talked about religion and Wilde's attraction to Christianity. Chesson witnessed the writer's warm relationship with local children and Oscar mesmerised him with stories and parables.[18]

In conversation, O'Sullivan said, Oscar studied his partner's mood and 'adapted himself to it'. Once he and Wilde were having a conversation about

Rossetti, an artist both men admired. For some reason it struck O'Sullivan to see how his friend would respond if he suddenly started to disparage the artist. At first Wilde stopped and seemed displeased, but in only a moment he had shifted to this new position and 'was developing brilliant variations on the theme that Rossetti was a foreigner and did not know the English language.'[19]

Thus Wilde's conversation reveals as much about who he thought his audience was as it does about who *he* was, or how he felt. The gossip-loving Robbie, his friend Harold Nicholson recalled, 'so delighted at the eccentricities of his friends that he actually encouraged them to be more eccentric than they really were.'[20]

That it was fun to shock Robbie, and Robbie enjoyed being shocked, is evident in some of the letters that Bosie wrote to him as well. The most outrageous of them no longer exist, but they were quoted in the Ransome libel case. (Presented together in one case, they create a disturbing image of their author.) In a particularly offensive example, Bosie tells Robbie that he has written a poem about the devil that Robbie would probably find blasphemous. He added that there were reflections on the Deity and the Saviour in it and that the Deity's affection for the Jews was enough to justify all that was said. In a courtroom in 1913, Bosie would say this was 'a horrible thing to have written' but that he could not understand why Ross had kept the letters all these years.[21]

It was in the great tradition of the decadent school to seek the beauty in danger and sin. As Wilde was attracted to Catholicism, so too was he attracted to the criminal and horrible, cruelty for its own sake. 'If Esterhazy had been innocent,' he told translator Henry Davray, 'I should have had nothing to do with him.'[22]

Chesson remembered an evening he spent with Wilde in this period. At the end of the night, he told Wilde he thought his life was 'a harmony of two extremes, very rare and very valuable. 'Yes,' Wilde replied, 'artistically it is perfect; socially most inconvenient.'[23]

Whether or not Oscar, really did delight in decadence, he relished presenting himself to Robbie as the perfect artist. For the young disciple with whom he had invented tales of forgery and crime, who was close enough to Count Stenbock, the eccentric writer of erotic, macabre vampire stories to be mentioned in his will, and who suggested the bizarre and transgressive work of Aubrey Beardsley would be perfect for *Salome*, Oscar struck a decadent pose. Oscar was a Romantic, wrote O'Sullivan. 'The romantic point of view was that the poet is vowed to disaster; or if the wine of success comes to him in a brimming goblet, it turns to ashes as he drinks.'[24]

In this context, Bosie was sin – beautiful in his horrendous tempers, his red-faced outbursts of swearing and invective, his prowling after rent boys. Oscar was drawn to Bosie not in spite of his flaws but because of them. Bosie was exhausting, frustrating perfection for someone who wanted to experience the heights and the depths of life; to burn with a gemlike flame. Wilde's excessive expressions of disgust and loathing about Bosie in *De Profundis* and in his letters to Robbie sometimes seem to have been ripped from the pages of Gothic fiction. Wilde was rapturously horrified. Romanticising the drama of the pain was as much a pleasure as were the gilded expressions of love and affection. Just as Robbie was intimate enough to hear tales of the boulevard boys, he was intimate enough for Oscar to reveal his attraction to the ugly side of his beloved.

21

Oscar's Last Years

Bosie was becoming homesick for England. In late September 1898 he had gotten word from Herbert Asquith that no charges had been filed against him and that none were likely to be filed. In March 1899, he went home to stay with his mother in Cadogan Place. He was busy working with a pair of publishers who were going to put out his poems. The first was Grant Richards, who was planning an English edition to be called *City of the Soul* and published anonymously. The main difference between the English and the French edition was that two of the poems that had been used in court against Oscar Wilde, 'In Praise of Shame' and 'Two Loves,' with the line about the 'love that dares not speak its name', were omitted. Their use in the trials had given Bosie a distaste for them.[1]

If Bosie had harboured any resentment against Robbie for his handling of Wilde's affairs it was long gone, and if Robbie was resentful of Bosie for his lack of help with financial matters, it didn't show. When Bosie finally returned to England, the two friends spent most of their time together. Bosie wrote to More Adey that he 'practically lived' at Robbie's house.[2] Oscar missed Bosie. He wrote to Robbie asking after Bosie and complaining that he had only written to him once.[3]

In September and October, Reggie and Robbie decided to take a tour of Florence, Rome and Naples. Not wanting to be badgered for money, they purposely avoided stopping in Paris to see Oscar.[4]

Oscar, although he spoke a great deal about plays he had in his head, was focused on the publication of his old works, which he hoped would bring in fast cash. Although much has been made of Wilde's lack of literary output after his time in prison, this was not, in fact, a change from his early days. Oscar had always found it hard to sit down and write. He worked out his fictions over dinners, honing his stories over periods of years. T. W. H. Crosland described Wilde's writing habits, as told to him by Douglas:

> The truth is that he would begin a work with great zeal and fury and apply himself to it and to the contemporaneous consumption of cigarettes and whiskies till he became utterly exhausted. As a rule, he completed what he had begun in a series of spurts and with periods of easy donothingness between whiles. On the other hand, there were occasions when he got stuck, and he got stuck over more than one of his plays. This is merely to say that he was like any other artist.[5]

He was of the old folk tradition, where stories were acted out, embellished and improved upon by the reactions of the audience. Those who spent time with Oscar in his last years all report that his powers as a narrator were intact. As in the old days, he could hold listeners spell-bound and if he could have passed the hat and made his living that way, there is a good chance he would never have written a word. There were similar long, dry spells in his early career such as the three-and-a-half year period from May 1883 when he had returned from his U. S. lecture tour until the end of 1886. This was almost exactly the length of time of his release from prison until his death.[6]

Oscar wrote to a number of friends in melancholy moods saying he would never write again, but his time in prison had not directly created this state of mind. His lack of motivation post-prison was similar to that of his pre-prison life. Now he had a new explanation for it. If he had lived longer, many of his table stories would undoubtedly have become essays, short stories or plays and more of his negotiations would have yielded results.

In March 1899, Oscar went to Switzerland to visit Harold Mellor, the twenty-six-year-old son of a wealthy industrialist. Mellor was a 'discreet' Uranian. He 'has Greek loves, and is rather ashamed of them,' is how Wilde put it.[7] Oscar was soon bored with Mellor and his standard of living – serving beer with meals instead of more expensive wine. So he left, settling in a village called Santa Margherita near Genoa. There were not enough boys and not enough wine here either, and he wrote to Robbie begging him to visit. This, he finally did in May. He found Oscar, to no great surprise, drunk and in debt. Robbie paid his debts, bought him a rail ticket, and took him back to Paris, where they spent several days together. Robbie lectured Oscar about his drinking and 'he quite reformed for six months.'[8]

One thing he did not lecture Oscar about was his sex life, which continued on much as in the old days. After Robbie's rescue, he went right back to Italy to stay with Mellor. (On further reflection, he decided he was not so boring.) Robbie visited him in Rome in March and April. There they cavorted with a boy named Omero.

In Rome, they had also discussed Catholicism. Oscar asked Robbie to find him a priest who could instruct him on how to become a Catholic. Robbie was not sure Oscar was serious. He also despaired of finding a priest in Rome who would be intelligent enough to answer all of Oscar's questions.

In the years following the Wilde trials, Queensberry's reputation had taken a beating. He had become an outcast, banished in part for the sin of creating a public scandal. The newspapers went back to treating him as an eccentric crank, printing critical accounts of his family feuds with Percy and Sholto, who had earned his father's wrath for marrying an American music hall performer. He sent long, rambling letters to the US papers with his views on the Civil War and was mocked for his new obsession with bicycles.[9]

In December, Bosie learned that his father was seriously ill, and he went to see him. Queensberry cried, embraced his son, called him his 'darling boy' and promised to restore his allowance. The reconciliation was short, a week later, an abusive letter arrived. Queensberry had changed his mind and said he would not give Bosie a penny until he knew what his son's relations were now with 'that beast Wilde'. Bosie replied with a bitter letter of his own, and that was the last communication between father and son. Queensberry died on 31 January 1900.[10]

Queensberry died richer than was supposed. Although he sold all of the family land, his fortune upon his death was sworn at £307,000, about as much as he succeeded to on the death of his father in 1858.[11] Bosie inherited £15,000 from the estate, of which he received £8,000 immediately. He and Percy returned to Paris to visit Oscar.

Queensberry's death did not mark the end of his son's conflicted feelings. Bosie opened his autobiography not with a tale about Wilde or poetry, but with reminiscences about his father. 'The thought which has only recently occurred to me is a terrible one,' he wrote in *Without Apology*. 'Did my father really love me all the time, as I certainly loved him before he turned against me, and was he only doing what Oscar says in his great Ballad all men always do, killing the thing he loved? Didn't we all three, Wilde, my father, and I, do it, more or less?'[12]

Ross always insisted his feud with Douglas was related to business not personal matters. In a 1918 letter to Oscar's son Vyvyan, he placed the feud's genesis in June 1900, shortly after the death of Queensberry. Ross claimed he had offered Douglas a half share in all of Wilde's future royalties if he would pay off Wilde's remaining debt. 'His chief hatred of me was due to the fact that he had ignored my belief in the commercial possibilities of the estate and refused my sporting offer.'[13]

This claim deserves some scrutiny, as the only evidence that the offer was made comes from Ross. Ross was determined to pay off Wilde's bankruptcy, and when Douglas inherited his share of the family fortune, he certainly wanted him to use part of it to pay the debt and support Wilde.

No one at the time could know how successful Ross would be at rehabilitating Wilde and creating a market for his work, not even Ross. In 1897 Ross wrote to the publisher Leonard Smithers about Wilde, 'I do not think his work has any market value, but I may be quite wrong.'[14]

During his life Wilde had a hard time getting commercial recognition. As a playwright he was eclipsed by Sydney Grundy and R. C. Carton. (Who?) Grundy had nine plays with runs of 100 nights or more, making him the most successful theatrical writer of his day. Carton wrote six plays that ran for more than 100 nights. As a novelist Wilde was far outsold by writers like Marie Corelli, rarely discussed today. Even when Wilde did have some success, it rarely came with a big pay cheque. He never published a book that could be considered anything like a 'best seller' until *The Ballad of Reading Gaol*. At the height of his fame Wilde was largely considered to be a popular writer but not a great artist. His society comedies were light and unserious, exactly the type of things you would not expect to be immortal. What happened was just about the *least likely* thing that could happen.

Ross could not have offered Douglas the copyrights to Wilde's past works at that point even if he had wanted to. They belonged to the Official Receiver. As for future works, one would assume that Wilde would have to agree. If they did discuss this, there is no record of it in his existing letters to Ross. In any case, at that time Wilde was hardly prolific, and no one knew that better than his close friends. To buy a share in Wilde's future earnings in June 1900 did not seem like a wise investment. (Had they still been living together in Naples, however, Oscar and Bosie would have been pooling their resources and the 'sporting offer' would have been unnecessary.)

If Robbie was critical of Bosie's financial contributions at this time, he remained diplomatic about it. As late as 1902, Robbie told Wilde's supporter Adela Schuster that Douglas (presumably Bosie, although he could be referring to Percy) had promised to pay Wilde's Paris debts but that he'd failed to do so 'through no fault of his own'.

What Ross did suggest, according to the documentary evidence, was that Douglas set up an annuity for Wilde. Royalties and copyrights do not appear to have been part of the discussion.

Many years later, Frank Harris would publish a biography of Wilde, with Ross's help. It has been widely criticised for its literary style, which invents direct quotes as a narrative device, and for its content, which bolsters his own importance. Douglas *hated* Harris's biography. He fought to keep it from being published in England, and he worked with Harris and later George Bernard Shaw as the writers tried to come up with a version Douglas would find satisfactory.

There was one incident in the Harris book that offended Bosie the most. After Queensberry's death, Oscar invited Bosie to the Café de la Paix. Robbie had suggested to Oscar that now Bosie had his inheritance, he should ask him to set up an annuity of £2,000 from his estate. (About £22,000 today) This would give Oscar a regular income and would make him no longer dependent on his wife's estate if he did anything to upset the administrators of the fund.

Something went wrong, however, in the way Oscar presented the idea to Bosie. It sparked one of Bosie's rages. What struck a nerve seems to have been a suggestion that Bosie owed him for the ruin his family had brought on him. This was probably not the first time he had heard this complaint. As Oscar recounted the argument to Robbie, Bosie 'went into paroxysms of rage, followed by satirical laughter' and said Oscar had no claim of any kind on him.[15]

Harris happened to be staying in Paris along with Bosie and Oscar and he saw each of them shortly after the blow up. Harris quotes Bosie, two days later: 'I do not see that there is any claim at all,' and spitting the word 'claim' as if the very word maddened him.' The word 'claim' must have come from Oscar and was at the heart of Bosie's anger.[16]

Two pages later Harris tells Bosie that Oscar seems to blame him for egging him on in the libel trial. (Given how the Harris book was written, Wilde may have said something like this to Harris or Harris may have gotten the idea that Oscar felt that way from a conversation with Robbie or one of Oscar's letters to Robbie. In which case, this dialogue was fictional.)

'How did I know how the case would go?' Bosie snaps in the book. 'Why did he take my advice, if he didn't want to? He was surely old enough to know his own interest ... he is simply disgusting now ...'[17]

In his letter to Robbie, Oscar describes Bosie as 'revolting' and 'mean, and narrow, and greedy'. He says he is 'disgusted' and considers Bosie's refusal to be an 'ugly thing' that 'taints life'. He also threw in a few negative comments Bosie had made about Robbie's attitude towards money for good measure, contrasting Robbie's goodness with Bosie's badness.[18] Bosie's memory of the argument differed from Wilde's. He said he had just given Oscar £40 (in another source it was £80) and that he 'whined and wheedled and wept' to get more.[19]

In the letter to Robbie, Oscar quotes Harris as saying 'One should never ask for anything: it is always a mistake.' He suggested that Oscar should have had Robbie make the suggestion. This is quite different in tone to the conversation as it appears in Harris's biography. There is no way Harris could have appreciated all of the subtext in that quarrel between lovers. (Harris admits as much himself.)

'He could earn all the money he wants if he would only write; but he won't do anything,' Harris quotes Bosie as saying. 'He is lazy, and getting lazier and lazier every day; and he drinks far too much. He is intolerable.'[20] Bosie admitted in his 'setting the record straight' preface to the 1930 edition of the Harris biography that he might well have called Oscar 'an old prostitute'.[21]

As usual, however, the mood soon passed and had no lasting effect on his relations with Oscar. If Harris had not been around to witness it, the whole thing would probably have been forgotten. The sad fact is that at this time, Oscar was sinking deeper and deeper into addiction. He drank to excess and spent every penny that fell into his hands on liquor and rent boys. His friends were at a loss.

Oscar had always been a heavy drinker. Back in 1893, Max Beerbohm had written to Reggie Turner, 'I am sorry to say that Oscar drinks far more than he ought: indeed the first time I saw him, after all that long period of distant adoration and reverence, he was in a hopeless state of intoxication.'[22] Robbie's brother Aleck attributed Wilde's downfall to 'hock and seltzer,' noting that in the years leading up to his arrest he was seldom sober.[23]

He also enjoyed other drugs, including hashish, which he tried on an infamous trip to Algiers in January 1895. According to Wilde's Paris friend, the symbolist writer Marcel Schwob, during an 1891 visit Wilde 'never stopped smoking opium-tainted cigarettes.' He was also, 'A terrible absinthe-drinker, through which he got his visions and desires.'[24] Ross, incidentally, was also addicted to Egyptian cigarettes. His were probably tobacco rather than the opium-laced variety favoured by Wilde. In his Paris years, Wilde preferred the Dutch liqueur Advocaat, along with brandy and absinthe. He had a high tolerance, as Ellmann reports, 'They did not make him drunk, but they offered him consolation.'[25]

Alcoholism ran in his family. His father Sir William Wilde had been a heavy drinker at the end of his life. His brother Willie died at age forty-six from the effects of chronic alcoholism. After Willie's death in 1899, Robbie got Oscar to sober up for a few months. 'Had circumstances permitted me to be with him more than I was,' Robbie said, 'I might have done something with him as he liked being ordered about by people whom he knew were fond of him.'[26]

This goes a long way to explaining Bosie's furious pronouncements that Oscar could support himself if he were not so lazy. He and Robbie had different styles, but it seems that Robbie in his gentle, thoughtful way, and Bosie in his direct and brutal way, were both ordering Oscar around out of love. Robbie, Bosie and Harris each tried to support Wilde without giving him the means to drink himself into a stupor. Wilde griped to each of his friends about the stinginess of the others.

Yet Bosie believed Robbie did the right thing in doling out funds to Oscar. Years later, when he had little love left for Robbie, he wrote, 'I do not blame Ross at all for his cautiousness about the money and for his, unfortunately fruitless, efforts to make it last a little longer than it did. In this respect he certainly acted entirely in Oscar's interests and with the best motives.'[27]

T. H. Bell, who knew Wilde in his last year, found he had 'nothing left in him of responsibility, truthfulness or common honesty.' Robbie complained to him of Wilde's ingratitude. Bell was impressed by Robbie's loyalty, given how he had been treated. 'It is evident that there must have been something at one time, if there was not much of it left in his last period, that drew to the man those good friends who stood by him.'[28]

Bell felt that Wilde was too much for his friends to handle. He needed someone who was

> ... qualified to get hold of Wilde, sober him up and get him out of his usual haunts and off to some quiet establishment far from his companions and the cafés ... He should, in short, have had a combination nurse, guardian and amanuensis. It would have required a great deal of tact, patience and sympathy. It is possible enough that with all of these it might not have succeeded. But in no other way, as all of us knew, was there a chance of getting him to write anything.[29]

The tragic consequence is that when Oscar was struck by his fatal illness, and sensed that he did not have long to live, few of his friends believed him.

22

Either the Wallpaper ...

As the racing season ended in August 1900, Bosie and his brother Percy planned to go to the Scottish Highlands for the beginning of the grouse shooting season. Before he left France, Bosie had dinner with Oscar at the Grand Café in the Boulevard des Capucines. Oscar was in a good mood and they laughed as in the old days. Then Oscar suddenly became grave and told Bosie he did not think he would live to see the new century. Bosie did not take this seriously. He said goodbye and promised to mail a cheque from Scotland, which he did a few days later. He had no idea that would be the last time he would ever see Oscar.[1]

A month later, Wilde was feuding with Harris over a play called *Mrs Daventry*. Harris had written the script from an idea of Wilde's. Both writers felt they had been cheated by the other, and in his last days Oscar was insisting that Harris owed him a share of the proceeds on the play.

On 10 October 1900, Oscar underwent surgery to prevent a chronic ear infection from spreading into his brain. The operation, performed under chloroform, was not only extensive but also expensive. If Robbie's account is correct, Oscar downplayed its seriousness, not even mentioning it to him until it had already happened. The doctors initially believed the procedure had been a success, and that the patient was on his way to a full recovery, but the invisible bacteria was still advancing towards his brain.

Oscar was, as Robbie put it, 'as he always was at least twice a year, financially embarrassed' and spent his last days writing long, angry letters to Harris about his play and the money be believed he was owed.[2]

'The Morgue yawns for me,' he wrote to Harris. 'I go and look at my zinc bed there.' He telegraphed Robbie, 'Terribly weak. Please come.' Both friends thought these were the typical overly dramatic expressions of a man who wanted money and attention.

Robbie came over from London and met Oscar on his birthday, 16 October. Oscar had lots of company, Reggie was there, as were Aleck Ross and Willie's widow Lily, with her new husband. The audience did much to lift Oscar's spirits. On 29 October, Oscar was finally well enough to leave his bed. He insisted on going to a café with Robbie. Robbie lectured him for ordering absinthe, but took it as a good sign that things were returning to normal.

The next day, when he and Robbie went for a drive, Oscar felt dizzy and they went back to the hotel. The doctor reassured Robbie, on 6 November, that the patient was improving, but Oscar did not agree. He was certain he was dying. In spite of the morphine prescribed and injected by his nurse, he was in constant pain. Only opium relieved it. He combined this with champagne.

Oscar's physician, Dr Tucker, 'a silly, kind, excellent man', after getting permission from Oscar to discuss his health with Robbie, said his patient was doing much better. His professional advice was that Oscar should write more and drink less. If he did not, he could not expect to live more than five years. A second doctor was a bit less optimistic, but also advised Robbie that he should encourage Oscar to stop drinking. The doctors were left with the impression that Robbie was the man who handled Oscar's affairs, and that he was the one to consult on any important matters.[3]

On 6 November, Robbie wrote to Bosie. According to Bosie, Robbie told him that Oscar was sick, but that it was nothing serious, and that he was worried about money. Robbie's account is essentially the same, although he claimed to have written that Oscar was 'very ill' but mostly emphasised that he was worried about his debts. Six days later, Robbie said goodbye to Oscar, because he had to go meet his mother in the south of France, a journey of about 17 hours by train. His friend's emotional pleas were not enough to persuade him to cancel the trip. After Robbie left, Oscar's health took a turn for the worse.

From this point on, Reggie, with the help of the hotel owner, Dupoirier, kept a vigil at Oscar's bedside. When Reggie left for the night, Dupoirier would sleep in an armchair facing Wilde's bed. On 25 November, it became clear to the doctors that his ear infection had crossed into the brain and that there was nothing more they could do. They stopped injecting him with morphine and in the absence of family had Reggie sign a certificate saying he had been informed of their diagnosis. Over the next few days, Oscar had periods of lucidity and periods of delirium in which he would speak nonsense.[4]

On 26 November, Reggie wrote to Robbie, telling him to come back. He was still holding out hope that Oscar would recover although the doctors were giving him little reason for optimism. Oscar was rude to and difficult with the doctors, but kind to Reggie. 'I myself cannot help thinking he may yet live to furnish Frank Harris with another plot, but I may be quite wrong.' Reggie wrote. He also asked Robbie to write to Bosie because he did not have his address.[5]

Later that day Oscar took another turn for the worse. He was running a high fever and babbling incoherently. Reggie wired Robbie, 'Almost hopeless.'

The next day he wrote again, asking Robbie to send directions as to whom he should contact if Oscar died. Oscar was not an easy patient. He refused to let the doctors put mustard plasters on his legs and he made difficult scenes with them. The doctor told Reggie he could not continue treatment if he was not paid, and Reggie (although he had no money to speak of) said he would be responsible for the expense. He wanted to know how to contact the guardian of Wilde's children and asked Robbie again how to get in touch with Bosie. He said he had written the day before to an old address on the off chance the letter would reach him.

The following day Maurice Gilbert arrived. He found it hard to stay in the room with the dying Oscar. Oscar tried to get out of bed, he asked Reggie to get a Munster to cook for him and added that one steamboat was very like another. The SS *Munster* was a ship that serviced routes between England and Ireland. Oscar wanted to go home.[10] As Reggie was applying an ice pack to his head, Oscar said, 'You dear little Jew, don't you think that is enough?' He suddenly added, 'Jews have no beautiful philosophy of life, but they are sympathetic.' He told Reggie that he should be a doctor because he always wanted people to do what they didn't want to do. The master conversationalist continued to speak, but his words lacked meaning. Reggie found it 'very terrible'.[6]

Reggie received Robbie's reply to the 'almost hopeless' wire and wired back telling him that he had no time to lose. The doctors were reluctant to deal with anyone but Robbie. Reggie also wrote to another friend asking him if he could reach Bosie. By now Oscar had lost his sight, and Dupoirier sat at his bedside and read poetry out loud to him.[7] When Robbie arrived on 29 November, Oscar had gone quiet. Reggie was a wreck. Robbie immediately went out to find a priest.

Father Cuthbert Dunne, a thirty-one year-old native of Dublin, who happened to be living in Paris and attached to St. Joseph's Church, responded to the call. Robbie did not mention the name of the dying man, but explained that he had always wished to join the Catholic Church and that he was certain it was his dying wish to be baptised. Whether Oscar was conscious enough to make this choice is highly debatable. Dunne described him as being in 'a semi-comatose condition'. He had leeches on either side of his forehead in a ridiculous attempt to relieve the pressure of blood on the brain. Dunne said even in this condition he could be roused and when he was, he gave signs of being 'inwardly conscious. He made brave efforts to speak, and would even continue for a time trying to talk, though he could not utter articulate words ... From the signs he gave, as well as from his attempted words, I was satisfied as to his full consent.'[8] Reggie, on the other hand, believed that while Oscar's death was a horrible experience for the people who had to watch him suffer, he was not aware of what was going on himself.[9]

After these ministrations, according to Robbie's account, he sent wires to Harris, to the children's guardian and to Bosie. At about 5:30 the next morning the 'death rattle' began. It was a sound like the turning of a crank. Oscar's eyes were non-responsive and foam and blood came from his mouth. Reggie and Robbie passed the time destroying (presumably incriminating) letters.[10]

When Harris received Robbie's wire, he gave money to T. H. Bell to take to Paris. Before he left, Harris told him that Oscar was only ever 'ill' until he had some money in his pocket. He instructed Bell to give the money to no one but Oscar, because he was surrounded by parasites and blackmailers. If he found that he was not really sick, he should continue the negotiations. If he found he was drunk, he was to hold the money until he was sober and get his signature as proof that he had received the money.[11]

At about noon, the ragged breathing ceased. Robbie and Reggie went to Oscar's bedside. He exhaled a long deep breath and then it was finished. Reggie said, 'He's dead.' Robbie nodded.[12] Oscar Wilde died at 10 minutes before 2 pm on 30 November 1900.

The main account of Oscar Wilde's last days is a long letter written by Robbie to More Adey on 14 December 1900. The letter appeared in several editions of Frank Harris's *Oscar Wilde* and in slightly different versions in other publications. In the mid-1960s, the Clark Library purchased a version in Ross's own handwriting. The original in the form of a letter has not surfaced, but the earlier version owned by the Clark Library reveals that some fascinating revisions were made before the publication of the now familiar account. Ross seems to have made the changes in the printed version himself, for a typescript with most of the changes exists at the University of Texas corrected in Ross's handwriting. As the text was given to Harris to publish, the reason for one of the changes is obvious. The earlier version was more critical of Harris and his financial dealings with Wilde.

More significant, for our purposes, is a change in a part of the story where Robbie tells the ailing Oscar he has to leave the next day, just before he left him in Reggie's care. 'While we talked the post arrived with a very nice letter from Alfred Douglas enclosing a cheque. It was in response to my letter. Oscar cried a little & then recovered himself.'

This is how the Harris version continues:

> About 10:30 I got up to go. Suddenly Oscar asked Reggie and the nurse to leave the room for a minute, as he wanted to say good-bye. He rambled at first about his debts in Paris: and then he implored me not to go away, because he felt that a great change had come over him during the last few days. I adopted a rather stern attitude, as I really thought that Oscar was simply hysterical, though I knew he was genuinely upset at my departure. Suddenly he broke into a violent sobbing, and said he would never see me again because he felt that everything was at an end – this very painful incident lasted about three-quarters of an hour. He talked about various things which I can scarcely repeat here. Though it was very harrowing, I really did not attach any importance to my farewell, and I did not respond to poor Oscar's emotion as I ought to have done ...[13]

In the earlier version this reads, with my italics added for emphasis:

> He rambled at first again about the £200, the amount of his debts in Paris, then he asked me not to go away. That he felt a great change had come over him. I adopted a rather stern attitude as I really believed Oscar was simply hysterical & nothing more. Suddenly he broke into violent sobbing and & said he would never see *him* again. That he felt everything was at an end. This lasted about ¾ hour. He talked about various [things] not necessary here to repeat. Though it was very harrowing I really did not attach any importance & did not respond to poor Oscars [sic] emotion as I perhaps should have done ...[14]

The him/me substitution could have been, as Bogle interpreted it, a slip of the pen. But there is another possibility: Oscar's emotional break-down and his three-quarters of an hour of sobbing were triggered not by Robbie's departure, but by Bosie's letter. Oscar was devastated because he knew he was dying and he would never see *Bosie* again.[15] Robbie would always reproach himself for his response. He became 'rather stern' with Oscar, chalking his behaviour up to hysteria from the morphine.[16]

Publicly, once their feud had begun, Bosie would blame Robbie for delaying contact and preventing him from seeing Oscar one last time. The charge was only made in retrospect, after he had decided that Ross was evil. At the time he was grateful for Robbie's steadiness and ability to take charge.

Bosie's official story was that he left Paris for Scotland in August and did not return to France until he received news of Wilde's death. He had received one letter from Robbie saying that Oscar had been sick but was doing better, and then a day later he received a cable that he had died. This criticism is unfounded. Ross's reassuring letter was written on 6 November when Oscar was going out with Robbie and drinking too much absinthe. Robbie genuinely believed he was on the mend. By the time he realised he was wrong, it was too late to summon Bosie.

Bosie had been unaware of Oscar's operation. He wrote to More Adey shortly after Oscar's death, 'It seems so beastly that I couldn't have seen him before he died, and nobody told me a word about his illness till the day before his death when it was too late.'[17]

What Bosie failed to mention is that he could have seen Oscar again between August and his November death. It was not Robbie, but his own lusts that got in the way. Bosie had returned to Paris sometime in mid-October. After his father's death, Bosie had used some of his inheritance to buy a stable in Chantilly. He probably came to France to check in on his horses, and may have planned to visit Oscar, but fate intervened.

Bosie, at this time, still had some inheritance money to blow through, and was in the mood for an amorous adventure. As a Parisian journal gleefully reported a few days later, 'he paid handsomely for his Socratic fantasies.' *Le Journal*, while identifying him only as Lord X, nevertheless did little to disguise his identity. It mentioned that the gentleman in question had brought a certain well-known English poet to two years hard labour.

At a cabaret in Montmartre, Bosie met two twenty-four year olds, Alfred Marquet and Auguste Audeux. The pair was 'well known to the police'. Douglas was also well known to them. The young men engaged Bosie in some financial negotiations, which the British press (which did identify him) euphemistically referred to as inducing him 'to interest himself in the career of a youth they had with them.' He arranged for a rendezvous at 2 pm the next day at a hotel in the Quartier de l'Europe. (In *Le Journal's* account, the boy was not with the procurers and Bosie met him only the next day to discover he was rough and emaciated from vice.) As soon as he got into the room with the boy, Marquet and Audeux charged in, pushed him to the ground and beat him up. As the boy looked on laughing, one of the men held a revolver to his head (in the British version) while the other took his watch, chain, rings and wallet, which contained about 20,000 francs. All together, the value of the loot was about a thousand pounds. They left him lying on the floor and went off to celebrate. *Le Journal* crowed that the attackers had demonstrated the superiority of French boxing, a sly reference to the Queensberry rules.

Bosie did not report the incident right away, fearing scandal. The attackers no doubt assumed he never would go to the police. Eventually, however, he decided that the system would work for him. The assailants were found in a nearby cabaret where they were spending lavishly and toasting with champagne. After he had retrieved his property and what was left of his money, he fled the country. According to the journal, he had departed the day before the article went to print.[18]

None of the newspaper accounts of Bosie's attack mention the exact date on which it occurred. The *Journal* story describes it as happening 'a few days ago'. It describes a delay of only one day before reporting the incident and says that he left the country a day before the article went to print. The tone of the article is too gossipy to accept the details entirely at face value. Bosie may have delayed much longer than the newspaper reported. He may have come back to France for Oscar's birthday gathering, but suffered the attack before he could attend. Fear and shame would have prevented him from making a public appearance with bruises still on his face. Robbie would have known the reasons for Bosie's departure and would likely have been sympathetic. For that reason, his 6 November letter probably downplayed the seriousness of Oscar's illness, and told Bosie that he was in good hands.

Whether the attack happened earlier or later, Bosie's 'very nice letter' and cheque, which arrived on 12 November, would have contained an explanation of his early departure. This would explain Oscar's deep emotion at losing the chance to see 'him' one more time. It would also explain Robbie's references to things 'not necessary here to repeat' and his desire to change the account for a wider audience than himself and More.

Bosie must have received the telegram from Robbie on 29 or 30 November. It told him to come quickly because Oscar was dying. As he made his travel arrangements, he sent a message to Robbie. 'Give him my undying love and affection' it said. The fastest route from Edinburgh to Paris consisted of two eight-hour legs.[19] There was no way he could have made it back to Paris in time. Before he could board his train, he received a second telegram telling him the great love of his life was dead.

During the Ransome trial, the defence, in its closing argument, twice mentioned that Bosie had sent Wilde 'the deathbed message'. The fact that Bosie had 'sent a message of undying love' to Wilde on his deathbed was reckoned evidence of deviancy in the trial.[20]

Robbie never told Bosie about the 'harrowing' conversation with Oscar because under the circumstances, it could only have caused him more pain. Robbie regretted that he had not taken Oscar's appeals seriously at the time. If he had responded to the emotion, as he later believed he 'should have done', he would have contacted Bosie right away, but he had believed Oscar was just being melodramatic. Everyone had.

Robbie wrote to his sister Mary on 12 December 1900 that he felt Oscar's death 'most horribly. One becomes fond of people for whom one has sacrificed a good deal. As I wrote to Alex I fear I sacrificed other people's feelings as much as anything else.'[21] Robbie would have to convince himself, as much as anyone, that he had made the right choices for Oscar Wilde.

23

The Aftermath

And alien tears will fill for him
Pity's long broken urn
For his mourners will be outcast men
And outcasts always mourn
The Ballad of Reading Gaol

T. H. Bell arrived in Paris with a cheque from Harris in the early afternoon of 30 November 1900. He had been instructed to go straight to Oscar's room and not to speak to any of the blackmailers and parasites who surrounded him. He was to report back to Harris whether Oscar was drunk or sober and whether he was only feigning sickness.

He walked down a dingy street near the Beaux-Arts to what he described as a fourth-class hotel. He went in the side entrance and encountered a cleaning woman. He asked her for directions to Sebastian Melmoth's room. He was surprised by her startled reaction. She pointed up the stairs. When Bell came to the room he was surprised again to find the door ajar. Inside was a Catholic nun in a white habit sitting with candles burning before her and next to her in the bed was the lifeless body of Oscar Wilde. He had died about two hours before.

The cleaning woman must have gone to fetch the landlord, for he arrived a few moments later. He assumed that Bell was a member of Wilde's family come to pay the hotel bill. 'Wilde owed him quite a sum,' Bell wrote, but the landlord 'spoke of his guest with a feeling which I could see was quite genuine.'[1]

No one else was there. Robbie was out making funeral arrangements, which were greatly complicated by the fact that it was illegal in France for a non-citizen to register at a hotel under an assumed name. The authorities wanted an inquest to determine if the man's death was murder or suicide.

When Robbie and Reggie returned to the hotel, Bell was suspicious of them. 'Some of the warnings I had received from Harris may have showed in my face, for I remember that after I had told them who I was we remained rather cool and reserved to each other, till I gradually saw that I had not to do with blacklegs or hangers-on but with men who had been with Wilde because they were really his friends. One of them was Robert Ross.'[2]

Shortly thereafter the French journalist Henri Davray arrived. After he reassured Bell that the money would not have prevented Oscar's death if it had arrived earlier, Bell returned shell-shocked to England. He did not stay for the funeral.

Robbie was accompanied by the district doctor who examined the body and 'everybody in the hotel & after a series of drinks & unseasonable jests the district doctor consented to sign the permission for burial,' Ross wrote. Next, Ross said 'the revolting Juge de Paris' came to seal up the effects. According to Ross, he asked how many collars Oscar had and the value of his umbrella. Knowing his reputation as a fabulist, Ross added 'This is quite true & not a mere tale of mine.'[3]

Robbie had already seen to Oscar's personal papers, burning letters that might be problematic for their writers, stashing others that might have historic, legal or literary importance.[4] Some of Oscar's effects remained in the hotel. The umbrella stayed behind, along with a shirt embroidered with the initials S. M. for Sebastian Melmoth – it had been in the laundry. There were also two trunks of books and magazines and a set of false teeth. Dupoirier kept them as souvenirs and in the years that followed would show them to the many curiosity seekers who wanted to visit the hotel where Wilde had died.[5]

Dupoirier, with the help of one of the Catholic sisters, washed Wilde's body and dressed him in his nicest suit. He looked 'calm & dignified,' Ross said, adding that there was 'nothing horrible about the body until about 6:30 in the evening when decomposition set in rapidly.' The doctors advised Ross to have the remains placed in a coffin immediately. At 8:30 more visitors arrived and a rosary that had been a gift from More to Robbie on his own conversion was placed around Oscar's neck. The nuns placed a Franciscan medal and some flowers in the coffin, which was then sealed and covered with a white sheet and flowers. A crucifix, candles and holy water were placed by Oscar's side. This was what the scene looked like when Bosie arrived.

Shortly after Wilde's death, Robbie wrote to More Adey and paid tribute to Reggie's selfless care of their dying friend. His praise of Reggie also acknowledges that it was understood Bosie was the most necessary person to contact, 'Reggie Turner had a far worse time of it than I or anyone else had as he experienced all the horrible incertainty [sic] the appalling responsibility of which he did not know the extent. He only knew my address & could not communicate with Douglas direct.'[6] Robbie also had a difficult time dealing with matters related to Wilde's sons. Adrian Hope, their guardian, still distrusted Robbie after the conflict over the life interest and would only discuss legal matters with him through solicitors.[7]

Robbie had the presence of mind to order a wreath of laurels to represent the people who had admired Wilde but who could not be reached in time for the ceremony. In light of Dupoirier's kindness, Robbie and Reggie were both anxious that the outstanding hotel bill be paid. Harris agreed to take care of it, but he did not come through in the end.[8]

Bosie had arrived in Paris emotionally drained and exhausted from his journey and he was pleased that Robbie, with whom he was 'on terms of great friendship', was there to take charge of all of the arrangements. Bosie took care of much of the expense of the funeral, splitting the costs with 'another friend' of Oscar's.[9] Robbie told Bosie that he had come across some letters and papers of Wilde's, but that there was nothing there that was of any importance. He asked Bosie what he wanted to be done with them. There was no question that Bosie was Oscar's significant other – the one who needed to be consulted about such matters. But Bosie did not, at that moment, have any idea what to do with them and he was happy to turn the problem over to Robbie. As Bosie had no objection, Robbie felt empowered to act as Wilde's literary executor, a role that Wilde had once asked him to take on in a letter, but which he would not officially hold until 1906. Bosie would not realise for many years that among the papers Ross took that day were his personal letters to Oscar.[10]

Bosie acted as chief mourner at Oscar's funeral, marching first behind the hearse in the procession to the Church of Saint Germain-des-Prés. He was followed by Reggie and then Robbie in line, then Dupoirier and the servant to whom Wilde had once refused to speak, Jules Patuel. There was a low mass and then the coaches departed for the cemetery at Bagneux. The first coach was for the priest, the next carried Bosie, Reggie, Robbie and the hotel proprietor. Following the official procession was a cab full of journalists who had not been invited.[11] Father Cuthbert Dunne officiated at the burial service.

Bosie had a bad feeling about the religious tone of the ceremony, but he was too overcome by grief to say anything about it at the time. 'It certainly seemed to me then, and for many a long day afterwards, that the sun had gone down,' he wrote.[12] To his brother, Percy, he wrote 'The world seems to be greyer now that he is dead. He was always kind and generous and gentle and forgiving.'[13]

In the wake of Oscar's death, Bosie's spiritual crisis became more pronounced. He wrote to More Adey trying to come to terms with the idea that he would never see Oscar again. His language suggests that he wanted to believe in an afterlife and held out some hope. But even if what he called the Roman Catholic 'tomfoolery' was correct, it offered him no consolation because the same religion that offered a glimpse of heaven promised that people like him and Oscar were damned to hell.[14]

In these letters, Bosie blamed Christian morality for Wilde's death and scorned the notion that the playwright had undergone a death-bed conversion to Catholicism, which he felt negated everything Wilde had stood for in life. A few years later, however, after he had become a Catholic himself, the death-bed conversion would become extremely important to him. It meant that Oscar was in heaven and they would be re-united after all.

> I am miserable and wretched about darling Oscar ... It seems to get worse every day ... I suppose Bobbie is consoled by the R. Catholic tomfoolery, though why he should be I don't know, for he knows perfectly well that Oscar was never really received at all ... and even if he was according to your Church he is certainly damned. I suppose Bobbie is sustained by the thought of meeting him in 'Hell.' Please don't mind my talk. I know it won't offend you as it would Bobbie and it is a vent to my feelings which I have had to bottle up. I did so loathe the idea of his 'being received' on his deathbed ... My dear More what is to be done with one's life? I simply don't know. I am utterly sick of the whole business.

Shortly thereafter he elaborated his viewpoint about the deathbed conversion. It was a violation of the pagan religion in which Bosie was still working hard to maintain faith. And inevitably, Bosie felt that he should have been asked before anyone made such a decision for the ailing Wilde.

> Still I suppose it doesn't make much difference. It is only a matter of sentiment. I shall feel exactly the same if somebody (with the best intentions) published an exhaustive work whereby he proved that Oscar was entirely guiltless of the charges brought against him, and that he was really a confirmed and secret mulierast. I love Oscar's faults and vices just as much as his virtues and splendours, because they are all part of him and part of his intellectual attitude

towards life. He was as a matter of fact the most complete sceptic imaginable, and would never have bowed his intellect to any dogma or any form of religious belief, however fine. He was never in his life self-convicted of sin, which is the touchstone of religious belief. He was proud of the so-called sin or crime for which he was persecuted, and he was in fact a martyr to a new Humanism of which Christianity in any form is the deadliest and most powerful enemy ... The moment he becomes a Christian and professes Christianity, he admits that he was wrong, and that the morality whose Vicar on earth is, say, Mr Justice Wills, is justified.[15]

The disagreement did not cause a rift between Bosie and Robbie. In it, however, can be seen the main ingredients that would form the basis of most of their later misunderstandings.

First, it indicates that Robbie often viewed his artist friends – Oscar and Bosie especially – as children for whom he played the role of responsible adult. As he wrote to William Rothenstein on 11 December: 'I feel poor Oscar's death a great deal more than I should, & far more than I expected. I had grown to feel, rather foolishly, a sort of responsibility for Oscar, for everything connected with him except his genius, & he had become for me a sort of adopted prodigal baby.'[16]

Seeing himself as an adult surrounded by children, he made decisions and carried them out based on his own conscience without consulting others. We have already seen that he sometimes went against Wilde's wishes when he disagreed with them.

Second, Bosie, who saw himself as the true spouse in Oscar's life, felt that he should be treated as such by others, even though society did not permit him to make such a claim. In this case, he felt that he was the one who knew Oscar best and he should have been consulted on the question of his deathbed wishes.

Finally, Bosie and Robbie had some fundamentally different ideas about what Oscar would have wanted based on the different sides that he revealed to each of them. To accept one friend's understanding of Oscar was to belie the other's. Robbie was a Catholic and Oscar often spoke to him about Catholicism and expressed interest in converting. Robbie had never taken these requests too seriously, but when it came time for the last rites, he believed he had been wrong to dissuade his friend and that the best thing to do was to call a priest. Bosie, on the other hand, always needed a noble cause and he had found it in Wilde's Greek philosophy. He believed Oscar was as devoted to The Cause as he was and that this was his true religion. Whether this was true or not, Oscar did not discourage Bosie from believing it.

In the immediate aftermath of Oscar's death, Robbie considered writing a memoir 'done with discretion'. He imagined the audience would consist mainly of Oscar's family and friends. But when he was actually approached by the publisher Arthur Humphreys with a proposal to do a book, he changed his mind.[17]

Humphreys responded with the suggestion that Robbie write a joint memoir of Wilde along with Douglas and Harris, an idea that can only have been proposed by someone who did not know these men well. Robbie must have laughed as he replied that although he was good friends with Douglas and knew Harris a little, the three of them could never collaborate as their views were so diametrically opposed. He suggested, however, that if Humphreys wanted to produce such a book himself, he would offer him whatever assistance he needed.[18]

24

Olive and Freddie

... of all the motives of dramatic curiosity used by our great playwrights, there is none more subtle or more fascinating than the ambiguity of the sexes.

Oscar Wilde, *The Portrait of W. H.*[1]

After Oscar's death, Robbie went to recuperate with his mother at Menton, France. He stayed with her through the winter. He, like Bosie, felt that an era in his life had ended and he was not sure what he would do next. The visit was not as relaxing as he had hoped. His mother's physical and mental health were both poor, and Robbie, whose own health had been taxed by the stress of recent events had trouble maintaining his patience. His sister Mary's daughters took on some of the burden, reading to Mrs Ross so Robbie could spend time at museums, renewing his interest in art.[2]

He was still in France in early May when William Rothenstein wrote to him with an opportunity to start the next chapter. John Fothergill wanted to sell his share of the Carfax Art Gallery. Rothenstein thought Ross, with his rare combination of business acumen and understanding of artists, would be the ideal candidate.

In the summer of 1901, Robbie paid Fothergill about £400 to buy the gallery and its already established business relationships with artists. He took over the job of selecting the art works from Rothenstein. More Adey came on board as manager with Arthur Clifton continuing to manage the business.[3] The Carfax was one of the first small galleries that focused on the works of contemporary, living artists rather than the old established masters. Under Ross's stewardship the Carfax became 'influential out of all proportion to its size'.[4]

One of his first exhibits was a showing of Max Beerbohm's caricatures. Max was sceptical that his work would generate any sales, and so he was not terribly concerned with the gallery's percentage. When Max sold some of the works intended for the gallery prior to the show, he offered the Carfax a cut, but Robbie responded that the notion was 'quite absurd'.[5] As he became more established, Robbie would amend his casual approach. He had conflicts with a number of friends over the years due to hard-line stances on business matters.

In the previous year, Bosie had lost two childhood friends, his father and Oscar Wilde. It was time to grow up. His inheritance was nearly gone – spent on horses, boys, brandy, Oscar and a terrible investment scheme put forward by Frank Harris.

Harris was the type of man Bosie found to be attractive company, a great raconteur who dominated any room. Bosie admired him because he was '"a hell of a man", one who was capable of knocking out a prize-fighter in a street "scrap"; who had been a cowboy, a mining prospector and a lot of other romantic things and, as he had often told me, a dead shot with a gun or a rifle ... I admired him for very much the same reasons as, long before, when I was a child, I admired my father.'[6] The two extreme, changeable personalities had an on-again-off again friendship.

A short time after Wilde's death, Harris persuaded Bosie to invest his inheritance in a casino scheme. He misled Bosie into believing that he had been given permission to run two casino games banned under French law. Bosie advanced him £2,000 for stock, believing he was acting as a co-investor but he had actually purchased Harris's own stock, which meant the funds were legally transferred directly to Harris not as working capital but to pay off his own investment in a failing business. Harris also managed to extract a similar amount from Percy. When Bosie finally realised how the money had been squandered he was understandably angry. Harris promised he would return the investment, but he never did. Although Bosie was initially willing to forgive Harris and overlook the incident, it remained a point of resentment that would come out whenever they disagreed.[7]

Realising that his inheritance was not going to last his lifetime, the next stage in his development, according to his social script, was marriage to an eligible woman of breeding. Bosie's public role in the Oscar Wilde scandal had lessened his prospects, but he was not entirely un-marriageable. The record shows that there were a few (no doubt fairly desperate) fathers who sent their daughters in his direction. Yet they somehow failed to catch Bosie's eye. Wilfrid Blunt tried to make a match between the wayward aristocrat and his daughter Judith. Blunt had become estranged from his daughter after she caught him planning an affair with one of her friends, her contemporary. Blunt thought a marriage would be beneficial to both problem children, it would get the upset Judith out of the house, and it would pave the way to social respectability for Bosie. Also, they both liked horses. This common interest did not lead to wedded bliss.[8]

Even so, marriage was inevitable, and Bosie's family made plans for him to travel to America to find a suitable bride with money to compliment his title. Bosie was not looking forward to his American journey, nor to the future it promised for him, but he saw little choice in the matter. His future began to look brighter, however, when he started corresponding with Olive Custance. It began with a fan letter. Custance wrote complimenting Bosie's poetry in the most flowery terms and he responded.

Bosie was impressed by the work of the 'girl poet' and he enjoyed her attention and praise of his work and his physical beauty. She showered him with gifts, flowers, jewellery and praise. 'I read Shakespeare's sonnets and wondered why people should have worried so much who they were written to,' she wrote in one letter. '... because, you see, I know it was you ... Shakespeare must have met you in another world!'[9] (The ellipses are in the original, as Custance used them as an all-purpose form of punctuation.) The ardent praise of the letters reminded him of those he had once regularly received from Oscar Wilde. She even called him, as Oscar had, 'My Own Boy'.

To get an idea of how bold and rare feminine praise of a man's beauty was, years later when he wrote his autobiography and included some of Olive's letters, Bosie felt the need to defend these expressions by saying 'this admiration of the girl for the boy is in itself beautiful and brave and right and classic, even if it does not commend itself to modern stupidity.'[10] Up to then, Bosie had not known it was possible to be the object of a woman's desire as he had often been the object of a man's. When she sent him poems that he had inspired, he had the satisfaction once again of being a male muse. He fell 'desperately in love'.[11]

Olive Eleanor Custance was born 7 February 1874, the older daughter of Colonel Frederic Hambleton Custance and his wife Eleanor.[12] Hers was a wealthy and respected family, descended on her mother's side from Francis Bacon. In spite of this upbringing, she found her spiritual home in the world of 'decadent' poets. Like her male counterparts, she read Pater, Swinburne and Wilde. She had read Wilde's *Intentions* so many times she practically had it memorised. She also idolised Lord Byron and identified with him. When she was depressed, she would stay in her room and pretend to *be* him. She said she was '*possessed* by these people of [her] imagination'.[13]

Although Olive experimented with lesbian eroticism, her real attraction was not to women but to men with feminine qualities. She identified with Oscar Wilde, a brilliant writer who enjoyed both the social privileges of maleness and the pleasure of loving men. She was steeped in the decadent poetic culture and responded to the homoerotic imagery of the beautiful boy, and also to the idea of being accorded the right of a man to gaze on a beautiful figure and express desire and longing for him or her.

In 1890, when she was sixteen Olive met the poet John Gray (then Oscar Wilde's twenty-five year-old lover) at a party. For Olive it was love at first sight. She called him her 'Prince of Poets' and sent him her work, seeking advice. They corresponded a little, but he remained a distant and beautiful fantasy figure. She followed Wilde's trials with interest, and told her mother at that time that Bosie was the only many she would ever marry. This did not sit at all well with her parents.

Olive began writing poems as a teenager. She was published in the *Yellow Book* next to Baron Corvo's homoerotic work.[14] Her first book, *Opals*, was published in 1897, but most of its contents had been written before she was seventeen years old. She had her book plate designed by Aubrey Beardsley. When she did not sign her letters Opal, she sometimes styled herself 'Wild Olive'. Beardsley called her 'Silly little O' for her habit of sending him long letters full of frivolity, sweeping decorative lettering and eccentric punctuation.[15] Bosie, who liked to think of himself as a child, responded much more favourably to her playfulness.

One admirer of her work was an American writer living in Paris, Natalie Clifford Barney. She discovered Olive through her poetry probably in 1901. Up to then, Olive's rebellious side had been satisfied entirely in the realm of fantasy. While she liked to imagine living a Wildean existence, she also enjoyed the comforts of her respectable life.

Barney, though slightly younger than Olive, was much more bold. By the time she contacted Olive, she had already published a controversial poetry collection, *Quelques Portraits – Sonnets des Femmes* consisting entirely of love poems she had written to other women. They were a bit much for her father, a rich businessman from Cincinnati. When he read *Quelques Portraits* he was so outraged that he bought several copies to destroy them.

Barney was in the market for a new translation of Sappho, and John Lane suggested she might like *Opals*, the first book from a promising young poetess. Natalie responded to the artistry and a certain fluidity of gender she sensed in the collection. She sent the author a copy of her own work. If the gift was a question, Olive was unambiguous with her answer. She replied with a poem she had written:

> For I would dance to make you smile, and sing
> Of those who with some sweet mad sin have played,
> And how Love walks with delicate feet afraid
> Twixt maid and maid.[16]

Barney was at the centre of a circle of literary and artistic women who admired the dandies and decadents of the fin-de-siecle. They identified with Wilde and his love for Douglas. An off-chance meeting with the author when she was a child was one of Barney's formative experiences. She recalled it in slightly different versions in her 1929 memoir *Aventures de l'esprit* and in an interview she gave in 1969. She described it as her 'premiere aventure'. Wilde saw the five-year-old being teased by a group of boys at a seaside resort. He sat her on his knee and told her a story. Barney dressed as Wilde's fairy-tale *Happy Prince* for the portrait she used as the frontispiece of her first book of explicitly lesbian-themed poetry, published in 1900. She had written to Wilde in jail 'hoping to comfort him as he had comforted me'.[17] She would go on to have an affair with Wilde's niece Dolly.

At the time she received the suggestive poem from Olive, Natalie was involved in a passionate affair with the poet Pauline Tarn, better known by her more exotic pen name Renée Vivien. The relationship had begun in 1899. There was no conflict for Natalie, who did not believe in monogamy (Pauline had somewhat different views on the subject). Natalie immediately wrote to Olive that she should come to Paris and the three of them would form a commune and live like Sappho on Lesbos. This piqued Olive's imagination. She travelled to Paris with her aunt Lady Anglesey and their neighbour Freddie Manners-Sutton, the 21-year-old son and heir of the Viscount of Canterbury. A strange love triangle developed on that trip. Natalie was infatuated with Olive, who mostly teased her, as she was infatuated with Bosie, whom she did not yet know. Meanwhile, Freddie was trying, with little success, to court Natalie. He ordered an elaborate engagement ring for her with diamonds and an enamel peacock eye in the centre representing his coat of arms. She told him she could not marry him because she loved Olive. Freddy didn't care about that. Pauline was miserable and jealous over all of the attentions her lover was lavishing on the guests, especially Olive. She went off on her own to write bitter poems about Natalie.

> The moon slanted over you, grazed you
> It showed you hideous beneath your beauty.
> I saw on your mouth the withered smile of an old whore.[18]

Pauline got called away to care for a dying friend. Natalie took the opportunity to escape to Venice with Olive. Natalie's lack of compassion would compel Pauline to break up a few months later.

Barney complained once that her lovers were more interested in 'mot a mot' than in 'corps a corps'. This certainly applied to Olive. They had a brief fling, but Olive was not enamoured. She hung a picture of a statue of Antinous, the favourite of the Roman Emperor Hadrian, over her bed. She said it reminded her of Bosie, to whom she had just started writing. When Olive complained that her father would never allow her to marry someone like Bosie, Natalie suggested, perhaps only half joking, that she would marry him herself and they could live together in a ménage à trois.[19] Shortly thereafter, Olive returned to England and Natalie went to America.

Bosie was not instantly attracted to Olive, but then he had not been physically attracted to Wilde either. When she sent him a photograph of herself dressed as a boy, he was intrigued by the androgynous figure in the photo and the playful fantasy Custance deftly created about him/her. She called her character 'The Page'. Much of their courtship took place through the post, which fuelled the fantasy. She became, as W. H. had for Shakespeare, the master-mistress of Bosie's passion and they carried out a series of secret meetings. Some of these meetings were facilitated by Robbie, who gave them the use of an upper room in the Carfax.[20] Olive was chaperoned by her maid to keep it all above board. In person their talk was 'delicate and shy'.[21]

Olive was well versed in the language of Greek love. The fact that she presented herself to Bosie in the guise of a boy told him she understood him. Whereas Oscar had hidden his sexuality from his wife, Bosie made it clear in his letters to Olive that he had only loved boys and that she was the only girl he had ever been attracted to.[22]

Their relationship, too, conformed to a Platonic ideal. As Simon May wrote in *Love: A History*, 'Love between a man and a woman, (symposium) speakers hold, is no starting point for spiritual growth … for sexual intimacy leading to spiritual friendship and pregnancy of the soul – they might both need to pretend that she is a boy, or at least ignore the fact that she isn't.'[23]

As time went on, Bosie became intrigued by Custance's femininity. His letters to her stop mentioning 'the Page' and asking her to dress up like a boy. He shifts into ultra-feminine terms of endearment for his bride ('darling tiny little girl'). While his letters to Custance lack some of the fire of the letters he wrote to Schwabe in his youth, the playful affection in them is genuine and there is no reason to disbelieve Bosie's assertion that the marriage began as a passionate romance. They had what we would today call a 'queer' love affair, something that was much misunderstood in their time, as it is still today. Bosie was delighted to discover that there was a woman of his own class that he could love, and that there was a whole new aspect of his sexuality he had yet to explore. (He had engaged in some isolated experiments with professional women prior to this.)[24] The cherry on top was that, being heterosexual, the intriguing affair would appear quite respectable and allow Bosie to return to society without compromising his happiness.

Unfortunately, the match seemed impossible. Olive's father, Colonel Custance was a war hero, a retired member of the Grenadier Guards when he joined the Norfolk Militia which he commanded in the Boer War, earning a C. B. for his services.[25] Known by his tenants as 'The Old Man', he was a skilled fisherman who bred trout on his estate. He contributed a chapter on breeding to the book *The Trout* by the Marquess of Granby.[26] Beyond that he was little involved in literature either as a writer or a reader. There was also a comic aspect to his demeanour. He was quite deaf and carried a large ear-trumpet wherever he went. When it was not in use, it bulged in his greatcoat pocket. He was fond of motoring and he drove at high speeds sounding his horn loudly so that everyone knew to get out of his way.[27] Custance was strict, opinionated and expected his word to be law. He saw much better things for his daughter than to marry someone with Douglas's reputation. Yet the very hopelessness of the situation sparked an adventurous sense of 'you and me against the world' in the young lovers. Just before he left for America to seek his dollar princess, Bosie sent a locket to Olive containing a lock of his hair. Olive encouraged Bosie to meet Natalie Barney in Washington DC.

Bosie's family did what they could to minimise his chances of encounters with journalists, having him sail into Portland, Maine, rather than one of the major east coast cities. His first stop was Boston, which he found pleasant thanks to the fact that he met some nice boys from Harvard University. From there he travelled to Toronto and back to the United States via Buffalo, New York, so he could see Niagara Falls. He wrote to Frank Harris from the luxurious Queen's Royal Hotel at Niagara asking him if he could make any introductions to the litterati of that city. The new friendships did not materialise.[28] Barney's prediction proved accurate. Bosie had a miserable time in Buffalo. Retreating to the Iroquois Hotel he wrote to Olive '… why did I ever come to this country of third rate snobs and prigs?'[29] The first rate snobs and prigs were yet to come.

Bosie moved on to New York City, where he finally drew the attention of reporters. 'Lord Alfred Douglas, who has registered in New York as Mr A. B. Douglas, says he has put aside his title for there is no order of nobility in the United States. He desires when in Rome to do as Rome does.'[30]

Next on his itinerary was Washington DC, where he planned to meet Barney for the first time. As their correspondence became increasingly affectionate, Olive had a certain ambivalence about her early plan to have Barney marry Bosie. She wanted her friends to meet, but but the idea of the seductive Barney encountering the object of her affection also made her jealous, and she responded by sleeping with Pauline Tarn and sending a copy of one of her love letters to Bosie. Given that Bosie was just about to meet Pauline's ex, the letter could also have been a fiction – a ploy to make both parties jealous.

On 1 November 1901 Bosie replied that he had torn up the love letter.

> I wish you wouldn't send me her love letters to you. I don't like them and I think it is rather unkind of you. I shan't forgive you unless you write by return of post and say you love me more than her and more than anyone else! I have not seen Natalie, but I am sure I shall like her very much, but please don't think for an instant that I shall fall in love with her. You don't seem to realise that you are the only girl I have ever loved or even looked at seriously. Do you imagine that because I have found out how sweet and lovely one girl is I shall immediately go and fall in love with others? It is far otherwise I assure you. I have never known anyone like you and I am homesick for you sometimes you darling sweet little girl.[31]

Barney's parents were not keen on her spending time with the scandalous lord, but she would not be deterred. She found ways to meet with him in secret; a favourite method was to go for a ride with him in a carriage and talk for hours. Their relationship was fun and flirtatious, and there were rumours that they were engaged, but there was no truth to them. For a social outcast, Bosie seemed to have no trouble making friends in Washington. On 14 January 1902, for example he wrote to Barney saying 'I will bring Frank completely clothed to lunch, and if necessary he can be completely unclothed afterwards.'[32]

Whether there was any of the physical play that this message suggests can only be a matter of speculation, but whatever it was, it was not love. 'I like her very much, but as to falling in love with her that is absolutely out of the question,' Bosie reported to Olive. He went on to reassure her that there was no chance of that because Olive was an exception to his usual affections. ' … you are a darling

Baby and you are exactly like a boy and you know perfectly well that I love you better than anyone else, boy or girl.'[33]

As in New York, Bosie signed the register at the Raleigh Hotel (one of the grandest in Washington) 'A. B. Douglas, London, England.' He did not escape detection by reporters, however, because he was, according to the hotel staff 'a conspicuous figure' – much better dressed than the average guest. Some of the less discreet members of the staff told the *Washington Post* that Douglas was entertained by 'members of the smart set' and that he stayed out every evening very late. *The Post* concluded its article by mentioning Douglas's relationship with Wilde. 'It is not known how long Lord Douglas will remain in this city. At the British Embassy last evening no information could be obtained regarding his visit.'[34] This publicity led to the most unpleasant episode of Bosie's American journey.

In the late 19th Century, police had been generally indulgent of same-sex behaviour between consenting adults as long as it did not draw undue attention. Then Oscar Wilde happened. As W. T. Stead commented in June 1895, Wilde's trial ' ... has forced upon the attention of the public the existence of a vice of which most of us happily know nothing.'[35] Now that it knew something, the British public was gripped with what Sir Thomas Macaulay famously called 'one of its periodic fits of morality.'

Prosecutions for buggery and gross indecency shot up in the early 20th Century both in England and the United States. It was then, in the words of Graham Robb, 'the Dark Ages began.'[36] This was the period in which Douglas had to build a career and start his adult life. Wilde had a public reputation prior to the trials, but Douglas's public reputation was formed *by* the scandal. His name evoked no other associations. In the years after the trials, the names Oscar Wilde and to a lesser extent Lord Alfred Douglas served as a shorthand for homosexual vice.

For example, in 1901 the Earl of Yarmouth, who went by the stage name Eric Hope, sued the *New York Sun* for libel over an article that suggested he had no money, had given up looking for a bride and that he had been shunned from English society after it was discovered that he had dressed up in feminine clothes and posed as a ballerina in Australia. The defence in the case, trying to demonstrate that Yarmouth was a degenerate said, 'We will show you that this man associated with Lord Alfred Douglas ...'[37] The Earl denied categorically that he knew Douglas.[38]

Of course, nothing had ever been proved about Bosie's relationship with Oscar. He had not been arrested and had no criminal record. He was free and he was still a gentleman with a fluctuating but enviable access to money and influential associates. His was not a life of constant abuse or discrimination, but what he did experience was difficult none the less. Slights and scorn came on a regular basis. They came when he least expected them, and often from the people he least expected.

Whenever he felt he had put the worst of the scandal behind him, something would happen out of the blue and knock him off his axis. For the rest of his life he would endure laughter, innuendo, social slights, and jokes at this expense and anyone who so wished could dismiss him or his arguments with a wave of the Wilde wand. Wilde had experienced one great, poetic tragedy. Bosie's tragedy was slow and continuous, an un-ending series of small diminishments.

On 17 December, Bosie entered the Metropolitan Club, a fashionable establishment where he had been welcomed with an honorary membership because his cousin, Percy Wyndham, the Second Secretary of the British Embassy, was a member. He had been happily socialising there for about two weeks, and fashionable people had clamoured to meet a visiting lord. When it became known that Douglas was *the* Lord Alfred Douglas of the Wilde affair 'an earthquake struck fashionable society, and as a result there was a general closing of doors and a vehement denial that he had ever been entertained within certain portals.'[39]

When Bosie walked into the club that day he had no idea that the membership committee had been chattering about whether his honorary membership should be revoked in light of his 'connection with a disgraceful scandal.' One of the members who opposed his continued membership saw Bosie sit down for a drink. He made an offensive comment about Wilde in a voice loud enough for Bosie to hear. Bosie finished his drink and left the club. Later he went to his cousin's rooms and told him what had happened. That very day Wyndham had received a letter from the committee asking him to explain his introduction of Douglas. Wyndham was an honourable man and he replied that Douglas was his cousin and a guest and that no explanation was needed. The British ambassador tried to make up for the slight by having Douglas escort Lady Pauncefote to a public concert and a dinner party at the embassy.[40] Bosie appreciated the kindness of the people at the embassy, but he thought it best to move on.

'The cause of his going, it is understood, is what he considered an unseemly interest in his movements while in Washington,' reported the *Washington Post* without any apparent self-reflection. Wyndham told the reporters that Douglas had left for New York to escape them. 'I am sure he intended to remain longer, but he is such an unassuming person, naturally, that it was very distasteful to him to be sought continually by interviewers.'[41]

He found no peace in New York, as the newspapers there had picked up the Metropolitan Club story. Never one to retreat from an argument, Bosie wrote a letter to the *New York Herald* responding to its story and defending his friendship with Wilde. He said he did not think his friendship before and after the trial 'constitute a serious indictment against my character, either as a gentleman or a Christian.'[42]

He had not entirely vented his spleen, so he channelled his bitterness into sonnet form. 'The New World' decried the 'Malice and Envy and vain boasting pride' of the continent, and advised the Americans to take the old virtues of 'Kindness and Courtesy' and use them as guiding lamps. 'Then would thy country be a New World indeed.' He sent this work off to the *New York Herald* to be published just before he left the country for good. He would later admit in his autobiography that he did not consider this particular sonnet to be one of his best works.[43]

In spite of a number of introductions to rich heiresses, he had not become friendly with any of them, certainly not friendly enough to want to marry one. He told Olive 'It might have been different if I had met a nice heir.'[44]

Olive's fling with Pauline was not the only relationship she had pursued while Bosie was busy searching for a rich wife. By the time he got back to England, Olive was being courted by the highly suitable George Montagu, later Earl of Sandwich and earlier a 'fair-haired, blue-eyed, pretty boy with engaging manners' who Bosie used to bully when they were both students at Winchester. (Bosie considered this teasing a form of affection. Montagu saw it differently.)[45] In any case, they were friends and had spent a fair amount of time together after Bosie returned to London after his exile. They remained, in Bosie's words, 'almost inseparable' until Montagu's family arranged to have him stand for Parliament, at which point Bosie's status 'a disreputable person' reared its head again. Montagu was forced to disassociate himself from Bosie or ruin his chances of election.

Bosie considered this to be 'the blackest treachery' and responded in a predictable fashion to the act of moral cowardice. He wrote two nasty letters to Montagu spelling out what he thought of him in no uncertain terms. He received no reply. Finding this not enough of a catharsis, he wrote a sonnet called 'The Traitor' which compared Montagu to Judas Iscariot.[46] (He was one of many who would receive such an honour.)

Olive did not discourage Montagu. She enjoyed his company, in part, because he could do a spot-on impression of Bosie. She 'liked him very much' but did not love him. Still, if Bosie was not available, he seemed like a reasonable choice.[47]

Bosie returned from America in January 1902 as George Alexander was attempting a revival of *The Importance of Being Earnest*. Olive suggested the play would be the ideal vehicle for a bit of Bunburying. She had taken two stalls for a matinee performance in February, and told her parents she was going with Montagu. She wrote to Bosie asking him meet her there instead.[48] If he did meet her, it was probably an eventful encounter. Olive's son Raymond was born nine months later.

Olive did not end her relationship with Montagu. He gave her many persuasive (and true) reasons why he would be a much better husband than Bosie, and thinking there was no hope with her first choice, she finally agreed to marry him a few weeks later.

When Bosie heard the news he was shocked, and asked to meet Olive immediately to plead his case. They met secretly at Kettner's Restaurant (where Wilde had once passed a preserved cherry to the lips of one of Alfred Taylor's boys.) Olive told Bosie she had only agreed to marry her rival because she thought Bosie was determined to marry an American. He told her he had given up on that idea because he was in love with her. They still faced the overwhelming hurtle of her parents disapproval. They were not going to be any more open to the idea of Bosie as a son-in-law now that she was engaged to someone else. They decided they had only one chance, they had to elope immediately or they would be separated forever.

On 4 March 1902, the very morning that the Custances received a letter from King Edward congratulating them on the engagement of their daughter to George Monatgu, Olive packed a small bag and handed it to her maid to smuggle out of the hotel where she was staying. She told her mother that she was going to spend the day visiting her former governess. She met the maid at the train station, picked up her bag and went to the church where Bosie was waiting. His family was far more pleased at the union than the Custances would be. (Percy Wyndham famously observed, 'Anything short of murder in the Douglas family is a source of congratulation.')[49] Bosie's mother gave him a diamond ring for the bride, £200 for the honeymoon, and the promise of an allowance. His sister Lady Edith Fox-Pitt came with a carriage and his friend Cecil Hayes, who would go on to act as his barrister in the Ransome case, was the witness. After the ceremony was finished, Bosie noticed that Robbie had come in quietly and watched the event from the back pews. Bosie was surprised to see him. He always felt that Robbie disapproved of the marriage.[50]

Bosie's was not the only marriage plan Robbie opposed, incidentally. Around the time that he was arranging Max Beerbohm's showing at the Carfax Gallery, Robbie took an interest in the artist's romantic life. Six years before, Max had become engaged to the actress Grace 'Kilseen' Conover. Max described her in a letter to Reggie Turner as 'a dark Irish girl of twenty, very blunt and rude who hates affectation and rather likes me.' After describing his love for her, and his intentions to woo her in rather lukewarm terms he implored Reggie 'Do be sympathetic.'[51]

Max's family had mixed feelings about the union. While they disliked her abrasive personality and considered her common, they were pleased that she put to rest rumours about Max's sexuality and 'diverted' him from 'an unfortunate set – dangerous friends.'[52] About the only thing they did like about Conover's bluntness is that she'd told Max directly that his relationship with members of the Wilde circle was harming him.

Max's infatuation with Kilseen was short-lived. They were great friends, and would be so for the rest of their lives, but there was no real passion on Max's part. He was in no hurry to close the deal but was also unwilling to break it off. In 1899, Ross had already written to William Rothenstein saying 'Max looks more unmarried than ever and poor Kilseen does not look particularly engaged. I feel so deeply for her.' In 1901 he invited Kilseen to lunch to address the 'difficult subject.' Kilseen wrote later saying that she appreciated the 'kindness' in his concern. 'I won't say any more about it. I feel mean discussing it even. Mean to Max, for either I should not discuss it, or I should break it off. But all the arguments on the earth cannot undo the last six years. All I ask Max' friends is not to judge him too unkindly ... I don't want the added unhappiness of thinking that Max has lost any of his friends through me.'[53]

In spite of Ross's intervention, the engagement dragged on until 1903 when Max fell in love with another woman, Constance Collier, and finally freed Kilseen. His letter to Reggie alludes to Robbie's tendency to gossip and stir his friends up: 'Please don't breathe to Bobbie or anyone about my engagement to Constance ... The position of fiancée to Max Beerbohm is a rather ridiculous position, after poor Miss Conover's experience, and I don't want Constance to be placed in it publicly.'[54]

If Robbie disapproved of Bosie and Olive, it was nothing compared to the 'fearful rumpus' (in Bosie's words) the marriage elicited from the Custance family when they discovered Olive had rejected a wealthy heir to an earldom for a penniless, scandalous third son of an equally scandalous father. While the happy couple honeymooned in Paris, Custance ran off to Scotland Yard asking to see his lordship's police file. He was surprised to find that no such file existed.[55]

The couple lived on the continent at first, but after a reconciliation with Custance, they came back to England where their son Raymond Sholto Douglas was born on 17 November. Natalie Barney and Freddie Manners-Sutton were named godparents.[56]

Sutton had no ill-will about losing Natalie's affections to Olive. He was a frequent dinner guest, and between the years of 1904 and 1906 his name appears so frequently in Bosie's letters and in Olive's diary it seems as though he practically lived at their house. Bosie counted Sutton as one of his greatest friends.[57]

Robbie was also falling in love again. By 1903 he was nearly the age Oscar had been when they had met. No longer the ephebe, his attraction to older men gave way to pleasure in the company of the younger. In his middle years, Robbie's lifestyle mirrored in many ways, that of Oscar in his prime. Like his mentor, Robbie enjoyed the society of men of a younger generation who he encouraged in their artistic pursuits. His role as Wilde's champion and friend made him the focal point of the community of well-educated homosexuals. They would meet and discuss poetry, art and sex as the Wilde circle had in the old days at the Café Royal. Robbie's relationship with More Adey graduated into a warm, platonic friendship and Robbie was drawn to an attractive young man who he could love and mentor in the Greek tradition. That man was Frederick Stanley Smith, 'Freddie' to his intimates.

Smith was born on 27 May 1885, the seventh child of a skilled tradesman, the printer George Thomas Smith and his wife Selina Eleanor. Like most boys of his background, he went off to work at the age of fifteen, getting a job as a merchant's clerk. He was, like Robbie, interested in literature and attracted to the ritual and theatricality of the Catholic mass. He served as an acolyte at St. James Church where he was also a member of the choir and part of the church dramatic society, which mainly performed the works of Shakespeare.

Robbie would later testify in court that he met Smith in 1905 when he was acting under the name Stanley Smith in an amateur production of Oscar Wilde's *Salome*. Smith played a small part, the role of the 'First Jew.' Robbie had come to see the performance in his role as Wilde's executor.

In his courtroom account, Robbie testified 'I remember Stanley Smith – I remember meeting him very vividly because I was surprised to find that the old man was only a boy of 20 or 21; he was just 20 at the time I believe.'[58]

This was likely a cover story designed to provide an unsympathetic court with a legitimate reason that a man of Robbie's position would socialise with a much younger, working-class clerk. (Social class would be, as it had been in the Wilde trials, a major issue in court.) Robbie actually met Freddie through the network of men who loved men, probably in late 1903.[59]

The initial draw was sexual attraction. It would later be alleged that Robbie, in September 1903, 'corrupted' both Freddie and his cousin Reggie Smith and that he 'habitually committed sodomy and acts of gross indecency with said boys.' This is plausible given what we know about the Dansey case in which a much younger Robbie allegedly seduced two brothers. Freddie was, at the time, living in the basement of a house belonging to his female cousin, a charwoman. Reggie was her son.[60]

Robbie had taken rooms in Sheffield Gardens early in 1903. On 23 March, Charles Ricketts wrote Robbie and teased him about 'setting up a new establishment in Sheffield Gardens with your "nearest and dearest friend" and keeping his old address on Hornton Street 'merely to go there and complain.'[61]

Smith did not, however, move to the Sheffield Gardens address. He stayed with his cousins until 1904, when he became part of an unconventional family with another lover, George Ives. (Sexual exclusivity was not the norm in their social circle.) Ives had fallen in love with the young man, although the feeling may not have been mutual.

Ives was then living in a comfortable home in Adelaide Road, which he had inherited from his grandmother. It was a villa in suburban area of semi-detached homes yet sufficiently Bohemian due to its close proximity to artist's studios and galleries. It had become a favourite location for poets and musicians, 'a city refuge for those who fled Phillistinism [and the] intolerable respectability of more conventional London.'[62]

Ives shared his large residence with a number of working class friends and servants who he referred to by affectionate nicknames and who he considered to be his family with himself in the role of 'mother hen.' The relationships with the men usually began as sexual affairs, but usually quickly became platonic. There was 'Kit,' James Goddard, who had been a servant for the Ives family for years, and apparently at one point George Ives' bedfellow. Goddard married and his wife, Sylvie, and two children were welcomed into the brood. They acted in the role of traditional live-in servants, but Ives considered them to be family.

There was also Harold Bloodworth, called 'Pug,' a former footballer who would remain in the home until Ives death and eventually inherit it. A warm but troublesome alcoholic, Stanley Saunders or 'Elephant' made life more interesting, as did Freddie, dubbed 'The Baabe' by Ives. Along with this core there were other working class men who came and went, living with Ives for anything from a few weeks to a few years, often moving on when they married. Their roles were fluid, shifting, in Matt Cook's words, 'from (possible) lovers to sons and, in bed, to comrades ... He did not think about his acknowledged love for them in terms of sex and coupledom.'[63] Ives was accepting, if not entirely thrilled about, his 'sons' outside relationships. He watched the budding relationship between the Baabe and Robbie with wistful acceptance.

Like most of the people to whom Robbie was drawn, Freddie was charming, creative and temperamental. During his relationship with Smith, Ives's diary is full of references to Freddie's youth, his cutting remarks, his habit of staying out late and his difficult personality.

In the intelligent but disadvantaged Freddie, Robbie discovered an ideal partner, someone who he could introduce to the world of art and literature. Freddie responded to this as powerfully as Robbie had with Oscar.

In Robbie's company, Freddie was beginning to speak in a more educated manner about literature and art and to carry himself differently. Robbie showered his love with gifts and attention. As their relationship progressed, members of the church dramatic society began to notice that Freddie was flush with cash and started wearing a large ring of which he was exceedingly proud. By June 1905, Freddie was spending more and more time with Ross and less with Ives.

The opportunity for Robbie to act as caregiver bonded the two men, and made Freddie's split from Ives inevitable. In July, Freddie had come down with a fever and Robbie nursed him at his house. Shortly thereafter the pair went on vacation together in Switzerland and from then on were inseparable.[64]

25

The Return of Maurice Schwabe

Whatever bitterness Bosie had felt about Maurice Schwabe's refusal to return and speak on Wilde's behalf in his trials, it was quickly forgiven. In 1902, a newly married Bosie wrote to his wife from Brighton (which he described as devoid '... of any but the lower middle classes of whom there are swarms, but all the same it is nice as the weather has been so lovely'). He said he 'had promised Schwabe to go to Italy with him till Friday ...' – a three-day stay. '... I am going to ask Maurice Schwabe to bring his yacht to Weybourne, it would be great fun to have it there. It is a sailing yacht but a good size and comfortable.'[1]

There is no record of what Olive thought about her husband's relationship with Schwabe or what she knew about their history. Many of the men of Bosie's social circle did not see marriage, fatherhood and homosexual desire as incompatible. Even among heterosexual couples, men and women of Bosie's social class largely inhabited separate spheres. A man did not expect his wife to be his primary source of companionship. His social life centred around sport and the gentleman's club. A father's role was to be a good provider and to pass along an honourable name, and there was nothing inherently contradictory between those goals and same-sex desire as long as one remained discreet.

George Ives seriously contemplated having children with a woman named Matilda 'Tilly' Hayes with whom he had a sexual friendship that lasted decades. Ives wrote in his diary that he was physically attracted to Hayes but 'not the romantic love; no girl can win that from me.' She, however, insisted upon marriage as a condition of having his children, and he did not want to get married. He decided against fatherhood, not because of his sexual orientation, but because he was not sure he could support a child financially while maintaining two households.

The poet and advocate of same-sex love, John Addington Symonds, did maintain two households, one for his wife, who was aware of his relationships with men, and a second home in Venice for his lover Angelo Fusato – along with Fusato's wife and children. Designer Charles Ashbee's wife knew about her husband's male lovers before their engagement and did not see any reason it should prevent them from having a family.[2] We don't know if the Douglases had such an understanding.

After Schwabe's adventures in Australia, he had returned to England in 1896, and spent some time studying mining and the Dutch language before leaving again for South Africa in 1898, one of many ambitious young men seeking his fortune in the gold boom.[3]

'South Africa in those days was still regarded as a wild land where men went to seek fortune and adventure,' wrote Montagu Pyke, who would one day become Schwabe's business partner. 'But it was also the land to which most of the "remittance" men went, to while away their lives in drinking, fighting and thieving. They were the n'er-do-wells of wealthy families who were paid by their relations to keep out of England, and the Colony, and the Transvaal at that time had become rather notorious ...'[4]

The mining team would relax in Nice and that was how Schwabe wound up in Monte Carlo where he met a man who went by the name Baron von Koenig.[5] Koenig was really Rudolf Stallmann (sometimes spelled Stallman) a man of many aliases. He came from a family of wealthy Berlin jewellers and had interests in mines in the Portugese Macequence colony near Transvaal. The South of France was an excellent hunting ground for card sharps and blackmailers during the season. There you could find all manner of well-born youths looking to kick over the traces.

'If the nineties were "naughty" the Edwardian era was a worthy successor to the nineties,' wrote Pyke of these holidays. 'The young moderns think they know how to live today, but I don't think they could have taught the young men and women of those days anything; rather the contrary. I know of wild midnight parties and scandalous orgies among the best people of several lands, and I hardly think these have their counterpart today.'[6]

Stallmann was in the early stages of a long and notorious career which would involve theft, confidence tricks and espionage.[7] He was tall, slim and ruggedly handsome with thick, jet-black hair that skimmed his perfect collar. His dress sense 'showed a fussy correctness which came perilously close to being prissy. He saw himself, however, as "spruce and elegant."'[8]

He was flirtatious and magnetic. He had a way of making anyone in his company feel as though he was a close friend. He belonged to a number of good clubs where he played cards under various names. He was 'Always extremely well groomed, apparently well bred, with agreeable manners, a delightful fund of anecdote, plentifully supplied with ready money, frequenting the best hotels, occupying the best cabins on steamers &c, [he and his international team of swindlers] found no difficulty in picking up acquaintances and sooner or later this led to card games, with the ultimate result that the strangers were victimised, in some instances to a very large amount. In most cases the victims said nothing, preferring the loss of their money to the ridicule which they felt they would be subjected to at having allowed themselves to be duped by men who are professional crooks.'[9]

Stallmann's syndicate was said to be organised 'like a limited liability company', divided into sections of a few members each, to which particular spheres of activity were allotted by the central management ... At intervals general meetings were held in London or Paris and the spoils distributed in regular proportions. Members who gathered information on potential marks passed it on to others to carry out the cons, a process they called 'wiring.' An example of a 'wiring' advisory was recorded in the German publication *Illustrierte*. 'Parents wealthy, loves to play, homosexual.' This last bit of information was important so the team would know what type of bait to dangle in front of the victim. Sometimes they employed beautiful women (usually wives or mistresses of the swindlers) to lure their marks. For those immune to such charms, the team could offer other varieties of sexual temptation.[10] This was one of Schwabe's specialities.

Schwabe travelled the world with Stallmann and other associates, and would be monitored by police on a number of continents for years. Not only would he be suspected of shady business dealings and card sharping but also blackmail and facilitating the crime of gross indecency. 'The eldest of the Schwabs [sic] is said to have a fine house in the West End of London,' the *Evening Standard* would later report, 'where orgies are enacted in the entertainment of select visitors.'[11]

Some time before 1905, Bosie and Sutton started to spend much of their free time with Schwabe. In a trial a few years later, Bosie would describe Schwabe as 'an old friend' and said he and Sutton 'went constantly' to Schwabe's flat. 'It was a free and easy bachelor's flat where one could go and have a drink and a smoke. We went there often, sometimes together and sometimes separately.'[12] If Olive had been a boy, Bosie would have brought her along on his visits. But such a thing was not appropriate for a respectable woman of her class at the time, even for one who worshipped at the altar of Apollo and imagined herself as Lord Byron.

Schwabe may indeed have viewed Bosie as a friend and perhaps still a lover rather than as a mark. He may, however, have viewed him as a useful source of information on the whereabouts of more lucrative targets to blackmail and swindle. These two roles, friend and information source, need not have been mutually exclusive. It is possible, even probable, that Bosie, still infatuated to some degree with his 'darling pretty', was swindled by Schwabe and the Stallmann gang. Throughout Schwabe's storied career he remained on good terms with people who were conned by his associates. (And a number of his associates were notorious for seducing people in order to swindle them.) The blame rarely fell on Schwabe. Bosie certainly knew that Schwabe feasted with panthers (it was no doubt part of the allure), but he may not have realised Schwabe was one of the craftiest of the breed himself.[13]

In the early part of his marriage, The Douglases were continually harassed by blackmailers. It had happened occasionally while they lived on the continent, but it 'assumed a double fury' when they returned to England.[14] Can it be entirely a coincidence that Schwabe and blackmailers came back into his life at the same time?

After the Wilde trials, Arthur Newton had become Bosie's go-to solicitor for any embarrassing mishap. He considered him to be equal or even better than Sir George Lewis in 'settling awkward cases out of court and without public scandal'.[15] We can only guess how many times Bosie required these services. What he may not have known about Newton is that he often conspired with criminals to create the very situations from which he then extracted his clients.

The Stallmann gang employed attorneys. These lawyers performed a number of important tasks. Gambling debts were unenforceable under British law. The sharps got around this by having a friendly player cover the debts of a mark in exchange for an IOU. The IOU became an enforceable debt and the attorneys would call to collect them and receive a cut. They also negotiated settlements for blackmail. The way this worked was that the 'friend' who had done the wiring would come to the rescue of the victim recommending a good lawyer – a confederate. The lawyer would recommend that the victim pay the blackmailers and negotiate a settlement receiving both a generous fee from the victim and a cut from the criminals. The victims were usually relieved that the situation had been resolved without scandal and viewed the lawyer as their champion rather than their blackmailer, continuing to consult him whenever a legal need arose. There is ample evidence that Arthur Newton was one of the lawyers employed by the gang and that he helped carry out a number of these cons, with Schwabe and other confederates.

After his death, a former clerk called Newton 'a habitual and often insolvent gambler who routinely overcharged and blackmailed clients, put forward spurious claims and concocted defences,' but even so, according to legal analyst Martin Dockray, his 'culpability would not have been obvious to bystanders of the time.'[16] Bosie praised Newton both in his *Autobiography* and in letters to the American attorney and author Elmer Gertz. Given Bosie's later reputation for litigiousness it is interesting that he admired Newton most for his ability to avoid the courtroom.

26

The Odd Couple

The relatively peaceful period of Bosie's early marriage had not been a boon for him as a poet. He confessed in 1904, 'I hardly ever write anything now, only very seldom a sonnet with great effort.' Even when he did write, he was disappointed with the results.[1] His most prolific period up to then had been during his relationship with Wilde. The energy created by the love and rivalry of two arrogant men, both co-muses and competitors, had provided a fertile soil. Bosie instinctively sought out another strong, arrogant man to fill that void. That man was T. W. H. Crosland.

Two years older than Douglas, Crosland was a native of Leeds, and the son of a Nonconformist preacher. He was a poet and humorist best known for a series of books parodying various ethnic groups. His best seller was *The Unspeakable Scot*. He was a prolific, jobbing writer, churning out titles at a fast pace to keep the cheques coming. In October 1903, for example, *The Sphere* reported that Crosland had three books coming out, all satires, and all before Christmas; the first lambasting 'modern nonconformity,' the second a parody of Rudyard Kipling 'mildly insinuating that five is the precise number of ideas contained in Mr Kipling's verses' and the third on the 'general incapacity of our age in literature.'[2] Although Bosie admired him most as a poet, he had carved out a niche for himself as a man who could effortlessly produce articles that would 'create comment – and amusement.'[3]

Crosland and Douglas had different stories about their meeting, but both place the event in late 1904 or early 1905. In Crosland's version, he and Douglas met for the first time when Crosland was writing for Harris's paper *The Candid Friend*. At the time Crosland only knew of Douglas through 'the cropping up of his name during the Wilde trials.' Douglas was in one of his episodic friendly periods with Harris, and when Crosland stopped in at Harris's office he was introduced to 'a youngish-looking, clean-shaven man attired in a tight-fitting black overcoat, and a bowler hat and on whose face there was a gentle smile.'[4]

After a short discussion of the weather and 'the rotten state of letters' Douglas went on his way, and they did not meet again for a few months. When Crosland became the editor of *The English Review* a friend showed him some sonnets and asked his opinion of them. Only after he had praised them was he told they had been written by Douglas. Crosland invited Douglas to his office and they became friends.

Bosie, on the other hand, said he was introduced to Crosland by Hannaford Bennett, a friend of Leonard Smithers, at a music hall. Crosland told Douglas that he had been Grant Richards' reader in 1899, and that it had been he who advised Richards to publish Douglas's *City of the Soul* because it was 'far beyond any contemporary poetry.'[5] This story has a certain verisimilitude to it. It is unlikely Bosie, who at the time of this writing was asserting his upstanding moral status, would have invented a meeting at a music hall if the locale had really been a literary office. Crosland's high view of Bosie's poetry made a strong impression on him and 'from that day I saw a lot of Crosland ... He was, I think, at that time really fond of me, at least I try to think so ...'[6]

In 1905, Crosland, Douglas and Sutton took a trip to Monte Carlo. Crosland was a life-long gambler who went to Monte Carlo the moment he had some money to throw away. If Crosland's later court testimony is to be believed, Sutton tried to secure the services of a young German prostitute from a woman, and was scratched when the girl turned out to be unwilling. He came back to Crosland, borrowed money from him saying 'lucky at cards, unlucky in love.'[7]

Crosland believed he had a fool-proof system to beat the house and he persuaded Bosie to give him £150 to play it. 'He had a mania for laying down the law on matters which he did not understand,' Bosie told his friend W. Sorley Brown, 'His "system" and his methods of gambling where childish. I found also that such as his system was, he was quite incapable of sticking to it.'[8]

Crosland lost all his money, and before Bosie left he gave Crosland another £50 to try to win it back.[9] Bosie left his friend at his favourite hotel and headed to the Antibes. En route he was robbed and his wallet stolen. He lost a long complementary letter from the French poet Stephane Mallarmé, which he had treasured so much he carried it with him.[10]

Outwardly you could hardly find two men more different than Douglas and Crosland. Douglas was always perfectly dressed for the season and time of day. His manners (when not in a temper) were impeccable. He was youthful and vigorous. Crosland was gruff and sloppy and loved to use coarse language. His one affectation was a bowler hat, about two sizes too small, which careful observers could use to gauge his emotional state. When he was annoyed he would push the hat down over his eyes or up so that it perched on the back of his head.[11]

Temperamentally, though, they were very much alike. They had a similar sense of humour. They delighted in cutting, satirical criticism. Both were prone to mood swings and outbursts of temper and the most trivial things could set them off. The literary critic Patrick Braybrooke described them as being 'like two schoolgirls – they have a scrap and then kiss and are friends again.'[12]

Douglas complained of being 'the patient recipient' of Crosland's 'vomited abuse ... when you happen to be in one of your dog-like humours.' He seemed to be unaware that he was equally describing his own half of the friendship.[13] (As was often the case when Douglas criticised the personalities of others, expressions involving pots and kettles come to mind.)

For his part Crosland (who shared Douglas's habit of writing scathing letters when angered) called his friend 'Saint Simple' and 'a dirty Scotchman' when he was angered. He once wrote to Douglas, 'I have no use for a man who is my very good friend one day and my howling, bloodthirsty enemy the next, and nothing will induce me to have anything further to do with you again.' The mood passed, and within a few days Crosland appeared before Douglas in tears and Douglas patted him on the back saying, 'It's all right, old chap; let us forget all about it.'[14]

Crosland kept a bottle of brandy on his desk and took swigs as he dictated his articles.[15] In his biography of Crosland, Sorley Brown depicted the writer as ending quarrels by 'having, or pretending to have, a heart attack. Whereupon Douglas would at once calm down and bring his weeping and remorseful friend round with a glass of brandy.'

Crosland was always in poor health, a combination of diabetes, cardiac problems and alcoholism. He walked with two canes, but when they would walk together, he could forego one and use Bosie's arm instead. Bosie often had to rush to the hospital to visit his ailing friend at his bedside. Brown, who knew the writers many years later described a typical scene of Douglas and Crosland walking slowly together from Crosland's offices to the Café Royal. As they made their way, Crosland had a heart attack. He leaned over in obvious pain, 'but Douglas kept him from falling.' When he had recovered, Crosland took his walking stick, pointed it at a new building that was being constructed and said, 'Mr Brown, that is where, when the war is over, Lord Alfred Douglas and I are going to have our new office. Perhaps you will join us.'[16]

The 'bond of affection' between Crosland and Douglas was obvious to Brown, who saw that 'each thoroughly understood the other.'[17] Although few people would agree with Bosie, he believed Crosland 'lifted me clean out of cheap cynicsm ...' and that he was 'nearly always right in his views about people and things.' Crosland told Douglas he was 'the best and dearest friend I have ever had.'[18]

Many of Bosie's friends (including his mother) believed Crosland was using Douglas, hoping the association would bring him money. Crosland was always broke. His relationship to money was similar to Oscar Wilde's. When he had it, he spent it. In those times he was generous and charitable. He had periods of gaming, grog and great meals followed by periods of unseemly begging. He was addicted to gambling. He had read every book and article on roulette trying to find a way to game the system. He never did. Instead, he sent panicked telegrams to Bosie from casinos asking him to wire money. Once Bosie had to pay some creditors to keep them from seizing Crosland's furniture.[19]

In Crosland, Douglas found a rare friend who both shared his conservative political views and was willing to publicly stand by him and defend him. Friendship with Douglas was, in those days, a socially risky proposition.

As a result, Bosie adopted the attitude 'of avoiding even any appearance of making advances to other people, either in the way of friendship or love, or mere acquaintance. I was so sensitive to slights that my whole life was ordered on the basis of a line of conduct which would make it difficult, if not impossible for slights to be offered to me.'[20]

Crosland on the other hand was willing to stand in open court and declare that he believed Douglas was 'an honourable gentleman, a genius and a great man.' He said, for the record, and before the press that he was 'proud' of Douglas.[21] Crosland's loyalty to Douglas was such that he was frequently willing to take the fall for him when the need arose.

As tempting as it is to imagine Crosland and Douglas as secret lovers, Crosland's heterosexual bona fides are fairly secure. He was a married man with two children who he supported while openly living with his mistress. While they were almost certainly not lovers, their relationship at its peak had an unusual intensity. Bosie may well have been in love with Crosland. Bosie once wrote that his real drive was not for sex but 'the desire to be loved and admired.' These feelings 'which were perfectly natural to me, and which I could no more help than I could help the colour of my hair ... did exist and did operate in innumerable cases quite outside any avowed question of sex.'[22] And Crosland did provide Bosie with affection and admiration. One example is this sonnet, which Crosland wrote for Douglas. It ran in *The Academy* on 5 December 1908 under the title To 'A. D.'

> You took proud words and touched their meagre blood,
> You gave them wine and oil and the full grain,
> The rose of love, the sacraments of pain
> And Death and joy, and Beauty where she stood
> Ineffable, like a beatitude,
> And washed in silver dawns and golden rain;
> You would not stoop for praises or for gain,
> And you have wrought us nothing else but good.
> They see your soul, on flaming vans of song
> Flash past the prisons, and they shake their bars
> With rage and malice; where there is no light
> They sit contriving mockeries and wrong;
> They know you have possessions in the stars,
> And they must spit at you their little spite.[23]

Crosland was, in colouring and build, not entirely unlike Wilde in the years Douglas knew him.

'His appearance when he was "smarted up" and forced into evening dress, I myself having tied his tie and brushed his hair – a process which occasionally took place, with many groans and protestations on his part ... was really not bad at all,' Bosie remembered, 'and he had fine eyes.'[24] This was also the one physical trait that Douglas had admired in Wilde.

Crosland was also a brilliant wit and conversationalist. In fact, Douglas called him 'one of the wittiest and most amusing men I have ever met.'[25] Coming from someone who spent years dining with Oscar Wilde, that is saying a lot. Like Wilde, Crosland was 'not only witty himself but the cause of wit in others.'[26] He was also (grudgingly) willing to put up with his friend's unpredictable emotions. Douglas found him to be 'a strange and remarkable man' whose outer appearance and manners made it hard for people to see that he was really 'a sensitive soul' with a 'passion for beauty'.[27] People must have done a double take when they saw Douglas at a table in the Domino Room of the Café Royal gazing with rapt attention at a portly man, cheeks flushed from numerous whiskey and sodas, completely engaged in a long, involved story.[28]

Lady Queensberry told Brown that she never could understand her son's devotion to the 'selfish and grasping' poet. She 'disliked Alfred's connection with him from the beginning'.[29]

After a bitter falling out, which we will come to in due time, Douglas would write a poem about Crosland, which he considered one of his best works 'inspired by the tremendously strong creative force of grief and indignation combined'. (This combination of emotions was the one that would most reliably inspire Douglas to write.)[30]

The Unspeakable Englishman

You were a brute and more than half a knave,
Your mind was seamed with labyrinthine tracks
Wherein walked crazy moods bending their backs
Under grim loads. You were an open grave

For gold and love. Always you were the slave
Of crooked thoughts (tortured upon the racks
Of mean mistrust). I made myself as wax
To your fierce seal. I clutched an ebbing wave.
Fool that I was, I loved you; your harsh soul
Was sweet to me: I gave you with both hands
Love, service, honour, loyalty and praise;
I would have died for you! And like a mole
You grubbed and burrowed till the shifting sands
Opened and swallowed up the dream-forged days.[31]

When they were reconciled a number of years later, Douglas wrote an emotional letter to Crosland. He said he had been 'more wounded' by Crosland turning against him than by 'anything else which has happened to me.'

> There has never been a moment since the quarrel occurred when I would not have welcomed a reconciliation ... I am delighted that you came, for honestly, I am and always have been quite devoted to you, a fact which comes out even in the sonnet I wrote attacking you. It is perfectly true, as I said in the sonnet, that I loved you dearly and would willingly have died for you. It was just this that made me feel so bitter when you turned against me.[32]

Bosie, who had written in great detail about his relationship with Wilde and the problems with his marriage, could not bring himself to recount what caused the falling out with Crosland in any of his autobiographical works, even those written many years later.[33] He would call it 'one of the worst experiences of my life' and even suggest that it was worse than reading the full version of *De Profundis*. 'Do as I will I cannot pretend to forget or condone what [Crosland] did to me. He had none of Wilde's excuses. Wilde did suffer through me (although it was not my fault) ...'[34] Bracketing Wilde and Crosland in this way suggests that he saw these relationships as being of the same kind.

Whatever happened, it is clear that Douglas had very strong emotions about Crosland. If he was in love, it would go a long way to explaining a devotion most of his friends found inexplicable. Love might explain why Douglas sided with Crosland over one of his dearest friends in a libel action, a series of events we will come to shortly. Crosland is often painted as the villain of the piece. Douglas would come to view him that way, and at times to use him as a scapegoat. But for better or worse, he stood by Douglas and supported him emotionally through what was to be the most painful period of his life.

27

The Buckingham Gate Flat Incident

Bosie and Sutton's adventures into what Sutton called 'the lower strata of Bohemianism' came to an end in 1905. Schwabe was then sharing his Buckingham Gate flat with Stallmann. On one occasion, when Bosie does not seem to have been present, Sutton was invited by 'the baron' to play a draughts game called 'Fox and Geese.' Sutton finished the game £500 and a pearl pin poorer. When he told Bosie about the loss he immediately advised him to call Arthur Newton. Newton recovered the lost property.

According to Bosie's later court testimony, after this incident he warned Sutton that the Baron could not be trusted, but Sutton continued to socialise with him anyway.[1] The baron may have been a criminal, but his 'sharp, lightly ironic wit, alert intelligence, apparent social status, cultivated self depreciating manners – and generosity' made him a charming companion.[2]

Shortly thereafter, at the Buckingham Gate flat, Sutton also met a foreigner named Beaudemont. Sutton swore that Bosie made the introduction, but Bosie denied it. For £5, Beaudemont introduced Sutton to a fourteen-year-old prostitute named Maggie Dupont. Sutton allegedly kept a house in Soho in order to entertain this sort of guest, although he would strenuously deny this in court, calling the house an investment property. While he would admit that he paid the £5, and that she 'did this kind of thing' for a living, he would deny that she was under 21 (although he said he never knew her name so he can't have asked too many questions). He would also deny he did anything improper in the private room they shared.

Ten days after his encounter with the girl, he was contacted by a private detective who said he would make the information public if he did not pay. Sutton immediately called Bosie, presumably because he was older, wiser and had far more experience of being blackmailed. Bosie again advised him to contact Newton. Sutton paid £1,200 to Beaudemont through Newton to make it all go away.[3]

It seems that as late as 1905, in spite of his marriage and his own growing feelings of guilt and shame, Bosie had not mended his ways. (Although it is possible that he had started to explore his taste for women rather than men.) Without the famous writer at his side, however, he had become better at disguising this. Robbie was probably aware of this. We do not know if Robbie took advantage of Schwabe's recreations as well. If he did, it never became the subject of a lawsuit. But Schwabe remained part of Ross and Adey's social circle until the end of his life.

There are two ways to interpret the events at the Buckingham Gate flat. One is that Bosie knew about Schwabe's role in the enterprise and conspired with (or did nothing to prevent) the swindle. The second is that he was unaware of Schwabe's criminality and viewed Newton as an over-priced but effective fixer who would do whatever it takes (whether strictly legal or not) on behalf of his clients.

Stallmann had his pick of young gentlemen. There was at this time an entire generation of young men who had been raised with excellent manners, respectable titles and the sense of entitlement that came with them. These men had been raised, like Douglas, to assume that money came to one naturally, growing magically from the soil of the landed estates. They were never taught financial management, and they were often shocked at how quickly an inherited fortune could disappear. By the time they came of age, the estates had lost their value. Some industrious young adventurers, like Percy Douglas, sought their fortunes in the vast reaches of the empire, looking for gold in Australia and South Africa, or for oil or lumber in Canada. Their expectations were high, their fortunes often elusive. When a young man of breeding gambled away a family fortune in a night, he was frightened and ashamed, and could easily be recruited with the promise of a simple means to gain it back without a loss of face. It was harder to get out of the criminal enterprise than it had been to get in.

Bosie could have been swindled in this manner, and have arranged to pay off his own debt by delivering more aristocrats to be swindled. Bosie was no stranger to gambling. When he went bankrupt in 1913, his assets included a sizeable £800 gambling winnings.[4] There is one intriguing anecdote about Douglas being a bit of a card sharp himself. When Masolino D'Amioco was researching Douglas and Wilde's time together in Naples he came across an interview with the descendants of Villa del Giudice where they lived. It was later called Villa Douglas. The family claimed the original owner had lost the property to Douglas in a game of cards 'the five of diamonds being the instrument of Fate.' D'Amico, however, rejected this story as 'fanciful' noting that we have every reason to believe Wilde and Douglas had a hard time paying the rent.[5]

Sutton, even when he was at the lowest point in his relationship with Bosie, testified that he did not believe his friend had any involvement in the swindle.[6] There is no evidence that Bosie lived the lifestyle of the band of criminals, and he does not seem to have profited financially from any of the blackmail or swindles that sprung up around him during his relationship with Schwabe. As long as he had bad habits and aristocratic friends he was probably more valuable as a mark than as an associate who would share in the profits. Both he and Sutton seem to have been shaken by the close call. Sutton sold the 'investment property' in Soho and within a year, Bosie had immersed himself in High Anglicanism.

As long as Bosie continued to enjoy recreation with Schwabe, these types of troubles continued to plague him. Paganism was becoming less and less of a grand adventure. It had left Bosie vulnerable to physical violence, blackmail, regular humiliations and most painful of all, in Bosie words, was '... the cruel position of being, just because I was as God made me, the innocent cause of the ruin of my friend ...'[7]

Around the time of the Sutton blackmail incident, Bosie began to seriously question the wisdom of his lifestyle. As he moved away from Wilde's influence, he had become increasingly conservative. Yet he remained, for the next few years, still torn between devotion to Apollo and Christ. It is notable that years later he still spoke of Wilde's circle in religious terms as a 'cult' and a 'tradition' and with Wilde as a 'prophet.'

'Long after Wilde was dead,' he wrote in his autobiography, 'and after I was married and had utterly got away from the Wilde cult and tradition, I went on subconsciously believing that he was, more or less, a prophet and that his views about morals, whether one liked them or not, were based on abstract truth and were unanswerable and irrefutable. It was not until after Wilde had been dead at least eight years, and while ... I was still devoted to his memory, that it first occurred to me that he was a very wicked man ...'[8]

Meanwhile, back at the home front, after a 'radiant beginning' the Douglas marriage was beginning to feel the strain.[9] Bosie was often away. He would send letters from visits to family and from his hunting and fishing excursions. Olive was left at home, where she grew increasingly bored and miserable. She had imagined Bosie to be a fairy tale prince who would whisk her away to a land of artistic beauty. She had wanted to act out the Platonic ideal where two poets form an intellectual bond and create great works through a pregnancy of the soul. Bosie wanted a wife. So their union produced literal pregnancy, which left her feeling trapped in a traditional role she had never wanted to inhabit.

Olive did not take to motherhood. When the nurse dressed up little Raymond and brought him to his mother, she felt no emotional attachment. Whenever Raymond is mentioned in Olive's diary it is with a note of indifference.[10] By summer 1905, it was clear to Bosie that something had changed between them. Although he was still in love, she was not responding to his letters in the same adoring, playful way. Bosie knew something had to change. He was tired of the social slights, blackmail and secrecy. He wanted to settle down and live a simpler life. Henceforth he would be a better husband, and a better man. The first step was to get away from London and all its temptations.

28

Ownership of Oscar

Contrary to popular belief, the demand for Oscar Wilde's writing never dried up. If anything, his downfall had made him notorious and sparked curiosity about him. While it is true that respectable publishers in the first years of the 20th Century saw fit to publish only Wilde's clearly innocent fairy stories such as *The Happy Prince*, there continued to be a thriving underground community that wanted to read the notorious Wilde, and where is demand, there will be supply.

Filling this niche were two well-known pornographers who, between them, released pirate editions of nearly everything Wilde had ever written. Leonard Smithers in London and Charles Carrington in Paris coordinated their efforts to the extent that there was no overlap in their published offerings. Smithers put out seventeen Wilde titles, some of which were issued under the imprint 'Melmoth & Co'.

Charles Carrington was the pseudonym of Paul Ferdinando, one of the most successful purveyors of illicit books in the English language. He was a specialist in erotic titles, pirated editions and falsely attributed works supposedly by Wilde, but he was also for a time, the only legitimate publisher of *Dorian Gray* having purchased the rights to that dangerous title from the Official Receiver for £60. Both Carrington and Smithers catered to a particular educated subculture, who appreciated French verse, fine volumes and occasional vivid descriptions of illicit sex. Wilde had been a part of this culture long before his arrest, and that audience had only grown as it was forced further underground. Wilde's works were thus marketed alongside erotica, giving them a sinister hue. Until Ross was finally given an official role as Wilde's literary executor in 1906, no one was particularly concerned about the state of affairs.[1]

In the early part of the century, as Ross worked at the Carfax gallery and did occasional journalism, he continued to work on behalf of Oscar Wilde without any legal status. Even so, Ross believed two of Wilde's works, *Duchess of Padua* and *De Profundis,* were his personal property. In 1904, when Ross allowed Max Mayerfeld to publish a German translation of *Padua* the Board of Trade prosecuted him. (We'll deal with the *De Profundis* question in much more depth later.) Ross bought a few copyrights with money from his own pocket including *A House of Pomegranates, Intentions,* and *A Florentine Tragedy.*[2] For the most part, however, the copyrights remained both locked up and unused, at least by legitimate publishers.

174

Bosie was still happy to leave the literary business in Robbie's capable hands. He often referred questions about Wilde's works to Robbie. For example, in 1902, Bosie received a letter from a 40-year-old architect, art and music connoisseur and 'confirmed bachelor' named Walter Ledger.

Ledger had an extensive collection of Wilde material, which he'd been compiling since 1890, and thought it might be useful to compile a bibliography. He was nervous when he initially contacted Bosie but was gratified to receive a friendly reply saying he considered it an honour to be associated with Wilde. He suggested, however, that Ledger would do better contacting Robbie, who knew more about such things.[3]

Robbie soon found himself writing to yet another would-be biographer, Christopher Sclater Millard. Born in 1872, Millard was a graduate of Keble college Oxford. In the spring of 1895 when news of Wilde's arrest broke, he had been a student at Salisbury Theological College. (An institution from which he was soon to drop out.) The handsome twenty-two year old with wavy brown hair and dark eyes was then in a romantic relationship with another male student. Millard took the courageous step of writing a letter to *Reynolds* newspaper in protest. He argued that Wilde had been unjustly prosecuted for 'satisfying his natural passions.' He further argued that if the Crown was to be consistent it would have to arrest 'every boy in a public or private school or half the men in the Universities'.[4] The bold stance was characteristic of Millard. He was seductive, charming and completely unapologetic about his sexuality. Millard had been a teacher at Ladycross in Bournemouth, a Catholic preparatory school from 1895 until 1900 when he resigned, apparently following an incident of some kind involving a boy. In 1905, when he started corresponding with Ross, he was living in Iffley near Oxford and spending everything he had on the most obscure Wilde publications, photos, articles and letters.

Collecting Wilde in those days meant tracking down pirated editions in the back rooms of antique shops run by pornographers. Ledger and Millard were like the enthusiastic fans who trade bootleg tapes of unreleased tracks by their favourite musicians. Even when he officially became Wilde's literary executor and was trying to stamp out the bootlegs, Robbie embraced Millard and Ledger's efforts to collect and identify them. It was useful to him to know what was out there so he could put an end to the illegal editions and break the association of Wilde's name with pornography.

In this Robbie performed a delicate balancing act, one that only a 'discrete' homosexual like himself could have managed. As he worked hard to promote the image of the respectable Wilde, he also allowed the underground uses of the name Oscar Wilde to flourish by encouraging, sometimes tacitly, and sometimes more overtly the work of Millard.

For example, in 1906, Carrington published *The Trial of Oscar Wilde: From the Shorthand Reports*. It was an account of the Wilde trials, presented with titillating editorialising and speculation that could be read either as exaggerated shock or campy endorsement. Any account of the trials would do nothing to improve Wilde's standing in society, but it could do a great deal for the counter culture. So Robbie did nothing to discourage or prevent Millard from publishing his own, less sensational, account of the trials *Three Times Tried* under the pen name Stuart Mason a few years later.

Millard would go on to play an important role in Ross's life and in the Ross/ Douglas saga. While Ross would later claim that he had never met Millard in person at this time, and only corresponded with him on business matters, this was not true. Millard visited Ross in London to help him prepare Wilde's *Complete Works*. And they were friendly enough that Millard sent him a bouquet of wild flowers he had picked while walking in a meadow in Oxford.[5]

Meanwhile, as the Ross and Ives circles were opening doors for Freddie Smith, other doors were slammed in his face. Robbie often hosted and attended rehearsals of the church dramatic society and invited its members to dinner. It became apparent to some of them that for a boss and secretary, Smith and Ross were 'very, very friendly'. They behaved more like a father and son than an employer and employee. When Freddie was in a temper, as he often was, he would be 'very disagreeable' to Robbie. He was rude and seemed to be able to get away with whatever he liked. Where an employer would be expected to fire someone so insubordinate, Robbie responded with soothing affection. One member of the society even saw him put his arm around Freddie's shoulder and say, 'Oh my darling, do not be so angry.' Emma Roker, a member of the society, said it was 'as if [Freddie] were the master'.[6] The rumours reached the curate and Freddie's days as an acolyte came to an abrupt end. Although he continued, for a time, to perform with the church dramatic society, the cold shoulder nudged him towards a more daring theatrical group.

The New Stage Club presented controversial and avant-garde works to small, private audiences made up of of artists and intellectuals. As a private club they were able to circumvent official censorship and present plays with Biblical themes, something that was otherwise forbidden by official censorship. In 1905 they staged the first British production of Oscar Wilde's *Salome*. It was not destined to set the theatrical world on fire. *The Daily Mirror's* reviewer was inspired to say only that the performance 'by amateurs last night was not strikingly successful.'[7] It was, however, a step in the right direction. In 1905 the revitalisation of the literary Wilde was, if far from inevitable, at least plausible.

Meanwhile Bosie was making his own small efforts to revitalise Wilde's reputation. Around the time Crosland and Douglas met, he and Sutton had put up the money to allow Leonard Smithers to publish an edition of Wilde's poem 'The Harlot's House' with haunting illustrations by Althea Gyles, one of the most respected illustrators of the day.[8]

After his success with the *Ballad of Reading Gaol*, and the acquisition of two of Wilde's unpublished plays in 1899, Smithers had over-extended himself, publishing more titles than he could sell. The members of the Wilde circle tried to help as best they could. Edward Strangman, a friend of Ross and Rothenstein, came on board as a business partner and Percy Douglas and More Adey made investments in the company, but it was not enough. By September 1900, Smithers had gone bankrupt.[9] At that point, all of the copyrights he had purchased reverted to Wilde, and later to his estate. In 1900, however, Wilde promised Smithers the copyright to *Harlot's House* to compensate for the fact that he had already been given advances for works he never delivered.[10]

Bosie socialised with Smithers and Gyles in Paris when they dined with Wilde. He may even have been present at the 1899 dinner when the idea of publishing *Harlot's House* with Gyles' illustrations first came up. (Gyles and Smithers were then having an affair.) Wilde had seen Gyles' illustrations shortly before his death and he loved them.[11] By investing in the title, Bosie was facilitating the publication of one of Wilde's own concepts. Its presentation was a high-quality production, as Wilde had envisioned it, with fine typography, quality paper and the five 'weirdly powerful and beautiful' illustrations printed on plate paper. In his preface Smithers wrote that *Harlot's House* was 'undoubtedly Oscar Wilde's finest and most imaginative poem'.[12]

The book was issued by the new imprint Mathurin Press in 1905, but one of Robbie's first acts when he was officially granted the status of literary executor in 1906 was to sue to stop the publication.[13] The business conflicts behind their feud have not interested biographers as much as the romantic and sexual elements, but the episode bothered Bosie enough that he mentioned it in his *Oscar Wilde and Myself* as one of his grievances against Robbie. Where they had once shared the literary Oscar, Robbie was beginning to assert his exclusive control.

29

In Symbolic Relation

> If it was a forgery (and I have never been convinced) it was certainly a
> masterpiece.
> Robert Ross, *How We Lost the Book of Jahser, Masques & Phases*[1]

People who know nothing else about Oscar Wilde know this: When he arrived
at US customs to begin a lecture tour he was asked if he had anything to declare.
He replied, 'I have nothing to declare but my genius.'

There is only one problem with this anecdote. It never happened. Reporters
followed the exotic aesthete from the moment he arrived on American shores.
He was constantly interviewed, his manner of dress, his habits, his every thought
were recorded. His year-long tour of America produced more than five hundred
newspaper and magazine articles, yet not one contemporary journalist thought to
print what would become his most famous utterance.

The first time the tale appears in print is in Arthur Ransome's *Oscar Wilde:
A Critical Study*, which was written with the assistance of Ross. Ross did not
know Wilde yet when he was crossing the US border. It would be another several
years before they discussed Chatterton and Shakespeare's W. H. Maybe Robbie
heard this story from Oscar or someone else who would be in a position to
know what he had said. It is equally possible that Robbie simply made it up as a
splendid example of something Oscar would have said.[2]

To call this invention a 'lie' would be unfair. Robbie and Oscar had similar
ideas about the nature of artistic truth. It was, after all, Wilde who wrote in
The Critic as Artist, 'The one duty we owe to history is to rewrite it.' What
was most important about a story was whether it was affective, not whether it
was historically accurate. The fiction helped construct an image of a man that
was true to Robbie's memory of him. Wilde, in *De Profundis*, said he stood in
symbolic relation to his age. It would be up to Robbie to make this true.

Before we turn to Ross's work as Wilde's editor and literary executor, which
started in earnest in 1905, it is informative to take a moment to remember
another artist who died the same year. Simeon Solomon, born in 1840, was a
contemporary of Edward Burne-Jones, part of the aesthetic 'art for art's sake'
school with works featuring beautiful androgynous youths. He was a friend of
Oscar Browning, and a favourite artist among members of the Wilde circle. One
of the losses that Wilde regretted most when his possessions were sold were his
'Simeon Solomons'. In 1877, while he was still an undergraduate at Oxford,
Wilde had written an article for the *Dublin University Magazine* calling Solomon

'that strange genius.' Lionel Johnson's rooms on Fitzroy street were lined 'wall to wall' with Solomon's art. In his later years, Solomon was supported by Count Eric Stenbock with Ross acting as intermediary.[3]

A turning point in the artist's life came in 1873, when at the age of thirty-two and at the height of his artistic career he was arrested in a public urinal with sixty-year old stableman and charged with an attempt to 'feloniously to commit the abominable crime of buggery'. Solomon was released to the care of his cousin and was sent to two private lunatic asylums in an (unsuccessful) attempt to cure his unnatural urges. He later moved to France where he was arrested in a Parisian urinal with a male prostitute. He served six months in a French jail on a charge of 'outrage to the public decency'.[4]

After these events Solomon was shunned by polite society, his work suffered until he was producing worthless copies of the subjects of his glory days. He ended his life as a poor, friendless alcoholic. If this tragic tale of the brilliant artist destroyed by legal prosecution and social hypocrisy calls to mind the tragic last years of Oscar Wilde it is no coincidence. Both of those narratives were advanced by Robert Ross.

Ross wrote the most influential obituary of Solomon, which initially appeared in the *Westminster Gazette* in August 1905, around the time he was preparing to release the first published version of *De Profundis*. It was later re-published with slight changes in various publications including *The Academy*, his own collection of essays *Masques and Phases* and finally in *The Bibelot* in 1911. Carolyn Conroy, who wrote a dissertation on the life of Solomon after 1873, describes these obituaries as consisting of 'vividly constructed anecdotal and unsubstantiated tales'. Some of this, Ross claimed, was from first-hand knowledge. Ross wrote that he had 'the pleasure of seeing' Solomon as late as 1893.

It would not be out of character, however, for Ross to write something in the first person that he had not experienced. So his 'pleasure of seeing' Solomon could just as well be the 'pleasure of hearing about' him from someone who saw him directly at that time.

Ross described Solomon's post-arrest work as repulsive and ill-drawn. In the first version of the obituary, he said Solomon had not produced any work of value after 1887. *The Academy* version amended this to 1890. He claimed Solomon led an isolated, sordid existence but that he 'enjoyed himself in his own sordid way.' The Ross obituaries contain stories of Solomon breaking into a house to rob it while drunk and being admitted to an asylum by friends. Conroy investigated these claims and found that 'much of this information is, simply either incorrect or unlikely.'[5]

By contrast, Julie Ellsworth Ford, a New York socialite and children's book author, remembered Solomon in his later years as energetic, full of humour and enthusiasm and focused on his work. At the time Ross said Solomon was 'sunk in the lowest depths of drink and misery' Ford found him to be busy and light-hearted. Solomon's work had become popular in America from the 1890s. The American public seemed to be unaware of the artist's arrests and did not share Ross's view that he was an artistic shadow of his former self. If, as Conroy said, 'the language Ross used in relation to Solomon was very reminiscent of the public reaction to Wilde,' it is no coincidence. Ross was largely responsible for our understanding of both.[6]

Today we expect stories to wrap up with a happy end. In the 19th Century the great dramas were tragedies. Nobility went unrewarded and unknown to all but the reader, society destroyed the good and moved on with little notice. If Ross was inclined to exaggerate the tragic elements in the last chapters of his stories of Wilde and Solomon it served a greater purpose. It was through such tragedies that society might start to question whether it made sense to destroy great artists in the name of conformity. Was society really served by ruining its Solomons and Wildes?

Ross faced a daunting task in rehabilitating Wilde. The first order of business was to demonstrate to the public at large that there was nothing dangerous or corrupting in his writing. He tried to do the same in his obituary of Solomon, reassuring readers that they had 'no need to frighten' themselves by looking 'too curiously for hidden meanings.' Owning a Solomon did not make one a deviant, nor did an appreciation of the works of Oscar Wilde.

Ideally, he would also have to find a way to show that Wilde had been no Svengali. The greatest evidence for that was the personal part of *De Profundis*, which depicted its author as the victim of another manipulator. To use that material, however, was to sacrifice Douglas for the rehabilitation of Wilde. At this time Robbie was still on good terms with Bosie and was not yet willing to make that bargain.

He focused instead on the labour-intensive task of compiling a *Collected Works of Oscar Wilde*, which would not be completed until 1908. It is impossible to under-estimate the monumental accomplishment of this collection. Not only did Ross have to edit texts that sometimes existed in multiple versions or were entirely incomplete, he had to determine which articles that had run without a byline in his journalistic days had been penned by Wilde. He had to track down manuscripts that had scattered to the wind in the bankruptcy sale, and to secure copyrights for works that had been sold by the Official Receiver. It was a time-consuming act of love, which he carried out with little personal reward and with great modesty. This modesty was, in part, his nature. It was also a necessity. In order to effectively rehabilitate Wilde he could not be too personally associated with his 'cult.' He had to present himself as one of the respectable 'us' not one of the deviant 'them' and that meant keeping himself out of the spotlight.

He did not approach the task of editing Wilde's work the way a modern editor would. His guiding principle was not to show readers the most authentic Wilde, but the best version of Wilde. If that meant smoothing rough edges, harmonising what had been irregular, and removing lines that could be interpreted with a homoerotic hue, that is what he did.

'The very diligence with which [Ross] undertook the dual task of securing Wilde's reputation and freeing his estate from bankruptcy appears to have led most modern commentators to assume that he acted with integrity and transparency, faithfully reproducing both Widle's intentions towards his texts and his ambitions as a writer,' wrote literary scholars Ahmadgoli and Small, adding that '… the motives which governed his practices are certainly more complex, and often not quite so laudable as early commentators have generally assumed.'[7]

The scholars note that when it comes to the journalism, there is no way to corroborate or contest Ross's attribution of authorship on the various pieces he selected for his *Complete Works*. He had not met Wilde when many of the pieces were published and his criteria for selection may simply have been that he thought they sounded like Oscar. He made a good 3,500 changes in the *Pall Mall Gazette* texts, most of which were standardising titles, fixing accidental errors and so on, but there were also 'substantive and conceptual changes.'

While these changes were fairly minor, they resulted in a corpus that made Wilde appear to be 'a more scholarly and systematic writer' than he actually was and gave a coherence to different kinds of writing produced in extremely diverse circumstances. Thanks to Ross's editing, a cohesive Wildean style emerges throughout. In the case of Wilde's unfinished works, *A Florentine Tragedy* and *La Sainte Courtisane*, Wilde had left only blocks of text and snippets of dialogue were often not yet assigned to a character. To make it readable, Ross had to assign these speeches to characters and sometimes invent characters to speak the lines. Ross might well have heard Oscar tell these stories often enough to guide him in this, but there is no way to know.

Ross's approach was to give the posthumous Wilde the same type of editorial advice he would have given the living Wilde. (Except the dead Wilde could not reject his friend's suggestions.) Ross believed he was improving the work by cleaning it up and making his fixes invisible. Wilde may well have shared that editorial philosophy. The result is a 'polished homogenized author constructed by Ross' rather than a 'more unsettling figure' created when the works are displayed in all their inconsistency.[8]

If the polished, consistent literary Wilde was created by Ross, so too would be the mythological biographical figure of the doomed playwright. Now we come to his most fateful editorial choices of all, the handling of the manuscript that he would name *De Profundis*.

The only account we have of how Robbie came into possession of *De Profundis* comes from Robbie himself, and was written long after the ownership of the document had come into question. There is no reason to disbelieve that Oscar entrusted it to Robbie after he left prison. Whether he handed it to him on the dock as his first act of freedom is open to question.

From the day Wilde handed *De Profundis* to him until 1904, Robbie had kept the prison manuscript under wraps, but rumours of its existence had leaked. Bernard Shaw heard the rumours and so did Max Meyerfeld. By 1904, Wilde was enjoying popular success in Germany. Meyerfeld contacted Ross asking for permission to publish the fabled prison work. At first Ross was reluctant. It seemed too soon. He knew, as well, that it would have to be heavily redacted to avoid hurting Bosie who was now enjoying a relatively peaceful period of his life. Meyerfeld was persistent, however, and Ross finally agreed to give him a version 'suitable for publication'.[9]

The work was not pleasant for Ross, it brought back painful memories and he kept putting it off until Meyerfeld's persistent letters 'of which I frankly began to hate the sight' persuaded him to finish. After judicious pruning, the philosophical musings about Christ as Artist were in, the depiction of Bosie as the devil was out. What remained was a tale of redemption. In the harsh confines of prison, Wilde had learned the value of suffering and humility. Ross gave it the title *De Profundis*. (Wilde had half-jokingly called it *Epistola: In Carcere et Vinculis* — in prison and chains.) Ross's title was a reference to Psalm 130, known as *De Profundis* for its opening in Latin; 'De Profundis clamavi ad te Domine,' or in the King James version, 'Out of the depths have I cried unto thee, O Lord.' It is one of the most familiar penitential Psalms in the Catholic liturgy. Thus the title sets up the expectation for a theologically literate audience that this is the cry of the repentant sinner standing in awe of the forgiving nature of God.

The difficult process of revisiting the prison letter had a side effect. It was a vivid reminder of all of Bosie's mistakes, follies and faults. Robbie was now in a different place in his life. He was the older man in love with a beautiful but moody, demanding younger man. He was more inclined than ever to believe that a young man could place a spell on an older and drive him to extremes. As Robbie poured over the material again and again his feelings about Bosie were increasingly darkened. Robbie found it harder to forgive Bosie's personality flaws. Tensions between the old friends started to appear, slowly at first and then in a deluge.

Meyerfeld's translation was published in *Die Neue Rundschau* in the January/ February 1905 issue. Included were parts of four letters from Wilde to Ross while in prison. A year later, it was published in book form. Having already done the emotionally gruelling work of editing the manuscript, it was natural that Robbie should start to contemplate publication in England. He sent the new version of the manuscript to E. V. Lucas, a reader for Methuen and Company, asking his opinion on publication. Lucas thought it should be published, but suggested a few additional cuts, which he made himself. Lucas did not accept any payment for this work. He told Ross that he had always felt guilty that he had never reached out to Wilde and that he hoped he would have been as faithful to Wilde as Ross had been if he had been his friend.

Interestingly, in the Clark Library is a letter signed E. V. L. with handwriting that is suspiciously similar to Lucas's – the bibliographer of the Clark letters assumed was from Lucas and identified it as such. It reads: 'Dear Oscar, When am I to see or hear from you? I've been twice to St. James's Place but they could give me no information at all. I am dying to see you. Do write to me quickly & arrange a meeting. Your own loving EVL. Feb. 24 '94, 34 James Street, Buckingham Gate, S. W.'[10] Lucas's sense of guilt and responsibility, and the source of his admiration for Ross, may have sprung from a much deeper source than he was willing to admit.

The contract for *De Profundis* was signed on 23 November 1904. It was published on 23 February 1905 and was an immediate sensation. The day after its release Methuen wrote Ross to say they were already going to a second edition. Further editions came out in March, April and September and again the following March. The book was widely, and mostly positively, reviewed. The reviewers were doing something they had rarely done in his lifetime – taking Oscar Wilde seriously.

The unanswerable question about *De Profundis* is what was Wilde's intent? Oscar and Robbie had ample time to discuss the fate of the manuscript when they met in Dieppe. There is some reason to believe that Ross carried out Wilde's wishes, at least those which he had while still in prison and shortly thereafter. It was a document that had always been part personal letter, part public statement, part primal scream and part artistic fashioning; a text with multiple parts that imagined multiple audiences. In a letter to Ross of 1 April 1897, Wilde outlined his plans. The full manuscript was meant for Bosie's eyes, but there were parts that he thought would be of interest to other acquaintances who had been supportive of him in his time of need, people like Adela Schuster. The manuscript of *De Profundis* has a number of sections marked off in blue pencil and Ian Small notes that these correspond fairly well with the passages mentioned in this letter although 'there are some differences too.'[11]

There is still the unavoidable fact that the Ross did not follow Wilde's only written instructions on how to handle *De Profundis*. He did not send the original manuscript to Lord Alfred Douglas. In a statement for a lawsuit, Ross claimed Oscar gave him verbal instructions that contradicted his letter on the subject. Instead of sending the original, Robbie should keep it and send Bosie a typescript, which he claimed he did. (Bosie was capable of casting a long letter away in a fit of anger without realising what was in it, as he had with Robbie's 14 page explanation of the life interest.) Ross stated in a deposition that just before his death Wilde repeated his instructions to make sure *De Profundis* should one day be published.[12] (This would have been on the same occasion when Oscar broke down and cried to Robbie that he was dying and would never see 'him' again.)

Oscar's initial feelings when he had just finished writing *De Profundis* and was still in prison are clear. He wrote Robbie that it was 'the only document that really gives any explanation of my extraordinary behaviour with regard to Queensberry and Alfred Douglas.' He said he wanted the truth of his actions to be known 'not necessarily in my life time or Douglas's.' Following Oscar's lead, Ross regarded *De Profundis* as the one text that could make sense of Wilde's behaviour and earn him a measure of forgiveness. Ross clearly viewed it as an important work and one that he was determined to protect.

Wilde's feelings while he was still in prison, and three months later when he had reunited with Douglas, however, had been quite altered. Yet a prison letter from Wilde to Ross is the only correspondence that deals with *De Profundis* in any detail. In his extant letters to Ross, Wilde asks about the progress of the typing on the document, and then he never mentions it again.

The key here is the word 'extant.' It is possible that Oscar decided not to bring that particular document up for a while given the strain on his friendship with Robbie over his return to Bosie. It is equally possible that there *were* additional letters on the subject, but that they did not strengthen Ross's case for publication so he discarded them. As we have seen with the life interest and Ross's correspondence with Smithers over the *Ballad of Reading Gaol*, Robbie did not always follow Oscar's instructions when he disagreed with them.

The letter that spells out Wilde's intentions for *De Profundis* also happens to be the document in which Wilde asks Ross to be his literary executor. As the only document that gave Ross authority to make these literary decisions, he could not get rid of it. It would be much easier to explain why he had not followed the instructions in regards to *De Profundis* than to make a case that he had the authority to act on behalf of the Wilde estate without it. He could, however, discard *other* letters from Wilde on the subject of *De Profundis* if he wanted to. Only he would ever know.

There was nothing inevitable about Ross's appointment as Wilde's executor. Wilde left no will, and Ross was not a relative. He had no clear legal standing to publish his edited version of *De Profundis* in 1905. Therefore he was acting much as Douglas had with Smithers' *Harlot's House* – publishing first, sorting out the copyright issues later. From the point of view of the Official Receiver, Ross had put out a very successful pirate edition.

When the Official Receiver learned about the publication he sued Ross to claim the £1,000 that it had earned to that point. Ross fought this and the litigation continued for a year. The result was that on 14 August 1906, Ross was officially appointed administrator and executor of the Wilde estate. The Official Receiver agreed not to contest Ross's claim to be the owner of *De Profundis* as long as he agreed to devote its proceeds and those from other works at issue to paying off the bankruptcy.[13] This may, or may not, have been his intent all along. One thing that is clear is that Ross was determined to retain control of *De Profundis* long before he fell out with Douglas.

When the first edition of *De Profundis* was published, it included other letters from Wilde to Ross and this gave the clear impression that the long letter was also written to him. The *St James's Gazette*, which ran a series of articles on *De Profundis* and Oscar Wilde in 1905 wrote 'According to Mr Robert Ross, to whom the letter was addressed, it was the last prose work he ever wrote. It was also the first piece of self-revelation he ever wrote.' Ross did nothing to correct the misconception. The introduction to the 1908 edition implied it even more strongly, as it included above Ross's signature, a portion of the prison letter that said '... there is none for which I am more grateful than for his permission to write fully to you, and as at great a length as I desire.'[14]

Ross's claim of ownership of the text, before he was appointed executor, was hard to defend. It would have been even harder to defend if the Official Receiver, and the public, were aware that it was actually a letter written to someone else entirely. It cannot have been an accident that he made it seem the letter had been written to him.

From the beginning, there were those who were sceptical about the origins of *De Profundis*. Readers of the *St James's Gazette* wrote to say that a document like that could not have been composed in prison because prison rules would forbid it. (In most cases, they did.)

'Certain people (among others a well-known French writer) have paid me the compliment of suggesting that the text was an entire forgery by myself or a cento of Wilde's letters to myself,' Ross said in 1910. 'Were I capable either of the requisite art, or the requisite fraud, I should have made a name in literature ere now.'[15]

Ross received many letters of congratulations. Sherard, who read the full manuscript at the time of the Ransome trial, also agreed that Wilde's friend had done him a great service in his editing. 'I don't believe that if the whole manuscript, as it stood, had been published it would have gained a tithe of the universal appreciation which it now enjoys,' he wrote. 'Its beauties would have been swamped in the unloveliness of the peevish recriminations it contains, which are of no interest to anybody.'[16]

Crosland agreed that Ross's editing was the key to *De Profundis'* success, but unlike Sherard, he did not see it as a positive.

> It can be demonstrated out of the text that Mr Ross's selectings and puttings-together have, in the net result, entirely deceived the public, not only with regard to the nature and intentions of 'De Profundis' as a book, but also with regard to Wilde's own character and his attitude towards his own misfortune ...
> On literary grounds alone we are surely entitled to protest against such a dangerous violation of the normal editorial function. If we are to take 'De Profundis' for an approved precedent, a literary executor is justified in treating a dead man's inedited manuscripts in such a way that he is made to say only half of what he really did say, and so made to appear the direct opposite of what he really was.[17]

Douglas, who was an enthusiastic motorist, was invited to review the edited 1905 version of *De Profundis* for *The Motorist and Traveller*. Millard wrote to Walter Ledger and declared Bosie's piece an 'excellent review'. He spent far more than he could afford when he ordered six copies for his collection.[18]

Although Bosie always claimed he had no idea that *De Profundis* was a letter to him – and what else was contained in it – others did. Lilly Wilde wrote a letter to the *St James's Gazette* on 11 March 1905:

> ...it would be more entertaining to learn why Wilde took the extraordinary action against Lord Queensberry. Under whose advice did he take the proceedings? Was he sober at the time? Was 'A' [Lord Alfred Douglas] there? Who was responsible for urging him to such a fatal step ... the manuscript now published under the name 'De Profundis' ... in its present form offers no solutions to these problems. Wilde told me it contained all the answers to the questions I am

asking now. Will not Mr Robert Ross, who has so far ruthlessly exercised his editorial discretion oblige with further extracts?[19]

Max Beerbohm and Reggie Turner had seen the unpublished *De Profundis* not long after Wilde left prison and were familiar enough with its text to make inside jokes about it. A letter dated September 1897 is revealing not only in what it might say about Ross's handling of the manuscript but also in the friends' attitude toward Wilde's writing. They knew all of the principals, and they do not seem to have viewed his sentiments as sincere. They were amused at how Oscar blamed Bosie for his drinking and spending. They also found some humour in his depiction of Robbie as an angel.

'How funny your meeting must have been with Sebastian and the "Infant Samuel,"' Max wrote, a reference to Wilde's adopted name and a line from *De Profundis* where Wilde complains that Douglas is seen as holy while he is seen as evil. 'Did Oscar order any of those liqueurs about which he was so very bitter in the historic letter, and did he refer at all to "Bobbie's beautiful action" at the Bankruptcy court?'[20] Knowing, at an early date, exactly what was in the full version of *De Profundis*, and being sceptical about its sincerity, Turner was uncomfortable with Robbie making any of it public. The 1905 edition had been successful beyond Ross's wildest hopes, and Reggie attended a party where Ross read some letters he was getting from readers who had been moved by *De Profundis*. He was saying that these letters proved that he had been right to publish 'a private letter to someone else'. This was when Douglas walked in. As Stanley Weintraub recounts in his biography *Reggie*, 'He stood and fidgeted, while Ross read a note from Bernard Shaw which interpreted the letter as a gigantic *blague*, Wilde's prison pose for the benefit of the British public. Bosie agreed that it was insincere.' Ross and Bosie argued about whether *De Profundis* was sincere or not. The argument ended with 'Bosie's angry departure. First an inner door slammed, then an outer one; and the three who remained looked at each other, hoping someone else would find something to say.' Ross went back to reading congratulatory letters on the publication of *De Profundis*.[21]

30

Divergence

All excess as well as all renunciation, brings its own punishment.
Oscar Wilde, *The Picture of Dorian Gray*

Bosie and Robbie were always destined to drift apart. When they were not chasing boys together they had very little in common. A good illustration of their different directions can be found in the gentlemen's clubs each attended. Ross was a member of the Reform Club, which took its name from the 1832 Reform Bill, a set of electoral system reforms that were strongly opposed by the House of Lords. The Reform Club was an answer to the Carlton Club, which had been formed by Tories. Although the clubs had drifted from political to more social aims by the end of the century, they retained their liberal and conservative flavours. The Reform was 'the symbolic centre of Liberalism.'[1] It was the first of the gentlemen's clubs to admit women, albeit not until 1981. Among the influential contacts Ross cultivated at the Reform were H. G. Wells and Herbert Asquith. Winston Churchill was also a member, although he resigned in 1913 when a friend was blackballed. Wells and Ross nominated the novelist Arnold Bennett for membership. Bennett later embarrassed Robbie by showing up in a red and yellow waistcoat and smoking a cigar in the atrium.[2]

Bosie was a member of White's, the oldest and most elite club with a membership that included barons and princes.[3] (Prince Charles is a current member.) It was, however, an era in which the Reform, and not White's was ascendant, both politically and culturally. Burke's *Peerage* had been joined by a new volume, *Who's Who*, first published in 1897, which catalogued its notables not by family line but by success and accomplishment, and from 1905-1922 the nation had a series of Liberal prime ministers.

Bosie was conservative and always had been. He enjoyed the class system and his elevated place in it and had no desire to see society transformed. The only thing that made Bosie an outsider was his sexual orientation. As he moved away from Wilde's influence, he found his own voice and it was anathema to many in the Wilde set.

As Bosie wrote of one artist friend (the poet Wilfrid Blunt) in *Without Apology*, 'He took me up ... chiefly, I think, because of my having come into violent collision with "Society" over the Wilde affair. That, I think, was greatly to his credit ... he was sticking up for the oppressed ... if he turned against me ... it was simply because he was incapable of understanding my divergence from all his standards and the force of the spirit which impelled me on a road which he had never trodden himself.'[4]

(Oh yes, and there was also the fact that when they did disagree, Bosie fired off an angry letter to Blunt, calling him a 'crazy old gentleman' and concluding for good measure, 'being known as your friend or associate has always been something in the nature of a social handicap.')[5]

As 1905 became 1906, Bosie had decided to become a new man and claim the life he had always been destined to lead, that of a gentleman poet. One of the first steps in his transformation was to move to the country. He bought a beautiful brick farmhouse in Wiltshire called Lake Farm. The property had been recommended by his cousin Pamela Tennant.

Olive, in her imaginative moods, called the property 'Fairlyland'. Each room of the interior, with the exception of a pale-pink dining room, was painted white. There was a long south-facing drawing room for entertaining. The couple had separate bedrooms – this was common for families of their class at this time. Bosie's was, like all of the other rooms, white. Olive's bedroom had a green carpet and William Morris chintzes with rose, tulip and bird patterns. Her small dressing room was decorated with the same fabric. Bosie also had a den, a converted kitchen with exposed beams.[6] Olive decorated the walls with framed prints of Bosie's series of six love sonnets titled 'To Olive'.

The farm was a short way from the River Avon and Colonel Custance, who had begrudgingly accepted his son-in-law, shared his trout fishing expertise. Bosie developed a love of fishing to match his love of hunting and horses. The Douglases got on well with their neighbours the Tennants, the Stroubs (Stroub, Wavie and Toots) and the family of the brewer Joseph Lovibond.

In spite of this, Olive found country life dull and isolating and the Douglases continued to rent a house in Chelsea. It was an expense that Bosie did not feel they needed. When he had first proposed to move permanently to Lake Farm in January 1905, he and Olive argued. Bosie wrote the following letter to his wife who was in London to see a medical specialist.

My precious darling,

I can't say how much I love you and adore you. When you came back from that specialist and cried like that, my heart ached with love for you. I can hardly bear to be away from you for one night. I feel quite ill for the want of you. Every day I love you more.

My blessed sweet, you shan't go to the country unless you like. But you know I sometimes am a better judge and in this case I know it is the right thing to do and I know I can make you happy here and I do want you to come even if we are not certain of keeping on the house.

I am going to try myself to try and make you happy, my darling good little girl. I have often been selfish and horrid, but not really in my heart, and I have always tried to do what was best and to think of you before myself. But I know I fail and London is bad for me morally and physically if I have too much of it. I love it for a few months. I am longing to get back to you.

It is dreadful that you should be so tormented by illness and troubles. Every wound to you is a sharp knife to my heart. I hate to think that I cannot bear your hurts for you.

My darling dearest darling sweet,
Your loving devoted,
Boy.[7]

Bosie described his time at Lake Farm as the happiest period of his married life. The couple's conflicts were mild, limited to such dramas as a parlour-maid who drank too much and fought with the cook during dinner, forcing Bosie to fire her.[8] Staffing problems aside, their life was overall comfortable and peaceful.

Yet it seemed, somehow, the happier Bosie became, the more his wife retreated. Her life of dressing in lovely clothes and dining with lovely guests was pleasant, and she had moments of simple pleasure.

Mostly, however, she was bored. She missed seduction, flirting and being flattered and courted. She recorded the old pet names that her suitors had called her in her diary, (there were many) and she tried to elicit jealousy from Bosie by saying how much she would like the men in America.[9]

The playful child that Bosie had loved was more often than not in what he called a 'disconnected, tiresome mood' in which she would 'peek and pine.'[10] She worried about money, suffered from insomnia and began taking Veronel, a barbiturate. She had the servants bring her breakfast in bed instead of getting up. She started to realise that her husband was not the free spirit she had believed him to be. She was disappointed that he was 'just like other men.' Bosie described the problem:

> In the end, after we were married, I was more in love with her than she was with me ... But how could I know or guess that the very thing she loved in me was that which I was always trying to suppress and keep under: I mean the feminine part of me? As soon as I was married I deliberately tried to be more and more manly. The more manly I became the less attractive I was to Olive. I can see now, looking back at it all, that she was always desperately trying to recapture the 'me' that she had guessed and seen and loved, and only occasionally finding it concealed under various cloaks ... My only consolation, now that I at last understand, is that if she had married anyone else her disillusion would have been ten times more rapid, and quite as complete.[11]

Robbie's romantic life was faring a bit better. In January 1906, Freddie Smith packed his bags and moved permanently into his new home with Robbie. George Ives was hurt when Freddie left, but he had no ill-will towards Robbie. He recorded on 23 January about Freddie, '... he's a dreadful trial, and often very hard to put up with, but he has grown to be one of us.' He retained hope that Freddie would return to him, but that was not to be. Robbie and Freddie had become inseparable. Their 'marriage,' however, would prove to be just as complicated and bumpy as the Douglas's.

Robbie's cohabitation with More Adey had not raised eyebrows. This would not be true of his relationship with the attractive young clerk and amateur actor. When Freddie moved in with Robbie, he started to draw a generous salary of £120 a month as a personal secretary, a sum an unsympathetic judge would one day describe as 'beyond the dreams of avarice for this young man, considering the circumstances of his earlier life.'[12] (It was twice what Bosie was about to earn as editor of the literary journal *The Academy;* a salary that some found excessive even for the high-status job of editor.) Freddie's position as secretary created a plausible explanation for their shared living, but it did not convince many. It did not need to. For the most part, Robbie and Freddie maintained a circle of friends who were understanding and supportive of their relationship, but there were always those on the fringes who found their affection distasteful and troubling.

There are differing accounts as to the Ross family's reaction to the couple. According to a letter from Robbie's niece Ethel Jones Sprigge to Margery Ross written in 1949 all of the family 'had the same absence of feeling as to dear Robbie's idiosyncrasy' and accepted Freddie as a member of the family. Other letters show that Freddie was invited along to family Christmas celebrations and to spend time with Mary's family in the country.[13]

Borland, who wrote her biography of Ross in the 1980s, on the other hand, reports that Robbie's sisters, nieces and nephews were 'horrified by his blatant disregard of social conventions.' She reports that the family had a meeting and elected Mary's oldest son Edward (then just 28 years old) to confront Robbie about his lifestyle. The 'family all agreed that Robbie should be ordered to end forthwith the living arrangements with Smith.' Robbie did not appreciate being told how to live any more than Oscar or Bosie had. He never forgave Edward and cut off all communication with him and his sons.[14] If this family confrontation did happen they changed their point of view fairly quickly.

In the early years of their relationship, Robbie and Freddie occasionally socialised with Lord and Lady Alfred Douglas giving Bosie an opportunity to witness their dynamic. They often argued and in Bosie's view, the younger man dominated the older. An exchange years later in court between Mr Cromyns Carr and Ross reveals how Bosie had described their relationship to his legal team.

Q: He had complete control over your house?

A: When I was not there.

Q: And when you were there, I suppose?

A: I allowed him to use one of the rooms for his rehearsals.

Q: A great deal more than that. Did he not do what he liked and order what he liked?

A: He very often ordered the dinner.

Q: And ordered you about, Mr Ross, didn't he?[15]

In 1906, Robbie returned to his neglected writing career and starting contributing on an almost weekly basis to the literary journal *The Academy,* which was also a forum for both Douglases and Pamela Tennant. The journal was edited by Harold Child and P. Anderson Graham, a tall, absent-minded fellow who 'kept his desk like a haystack' and kept losing manuscripts. Because of Graham's Bohemian nature and disorganisation, it was Child who 'did practically all the work.'[16] Child was lavish in his praise of Ross's work.

Ross submitted articles that ran under his own name, without a byline and under the pseudonym 'Christian Freeborn'. His articles were often written in the first person, yet they were far from autobiographical, as Borland noted he 'chose which parts of his life to include, which to leave out, which parts to exaggerate, and which parts to belittle.'

Robbie also used the pages of *The Academy* to praise his lover's small role as 'Old Age' in Arthur Symon's morality play, *The Fool of the World*. He wrote that the part was 'rendered with marvellous skill by Mr F. Stanley Smith, who by a paradox very common on the stage was the youngest of the performers. I have heard him compared, not ineptly, with the child actor Salathiel Pavy, immortalised by Ben Johnson ...'[17]

In the early part of 1907, Child resigned from *The Academy* in order to join the staff of *The Times*. Pamela Tennant recommended her husband, Sir Edward 'Bart' Tennant buy it and appoint Douglas as editor. Accounts differ somewhat as to how this came about. Ross would later claim that the idea was his and that he not only recommended his friend, but travelled to the Tennants' home to discuss the matter, advise the family and their solicitors on the value of the newspaper and help them negotiate the price. In his *Autobiography*, Bosie did not mention Ross. In his account, his cousin Pamela campaigned for him because she wanted to keep the paper in the family.[18] Alice M. Head, who worked at *The Academy* before and after the transition did not mention Ross having any role in the appointment either. As she told it, the choice evolved out of a weekend visit by editor P. Anderson Graham to the Tennant's estate in Salisbury.[19]

In any case, Ross's intervention should not have been necessary. Pamela and Bosie had been playmates as children. The Tennants were the Douglas's neighbours and the entire family were frequent guests. Pamela had strong motivations of her own to want to help Bosie whenever she could. Back in 1894, when she was still a Wyndham, she had been courted by Bosie's brother, Francis, Viscount Drumlanrig. The family, in particular Alfred Montgomery, had been thrilled at the prospect. The Wyndhams were not as keen. They had gotten wind of the unseemly rumours about Drumlanrig and Rosebery – thanks to Queensberry's tirades all of society had been abuzz with it. Pamela had heard the whispers as well, and she was concerned about the 'opinion of the world'. At the end of the summer, she rejected Drumlanrig and he became engaged to someone else.[20]

After Drumlanrig's apparent suicide, the Wyndhams came to London for the funeral and then invited the grieving Douglas family to their home, Clouds House, in Wiltshire. It was a harrowing experience for Pamela. Sybil seemed to have disappeared into her mourning garb, Edith was 'simply dazed' and Bosie was 'thoughtful and gentle.' But the family member who affected her the most was Montgomery. He could not stop saying things to Pamela like 'He was so fond of you – he loved you so – how fond he was of you – let me look at you – ah my dear' & then breaking down.' The experience shook her to her core and 'felt like swords inside.' That night she was kept awake by the sound of Edith's sobbing.

Pamela sank into a well of grief and self-blame. She regretted that she had been 'blind and afraid' and swayed by other's opinions. If she had only married him, she told herself, everything might have been different.[21] She now had a chance to help his little brother when his own trajectory had been derailed by rumours and innuendoes. There was really only one thing she could do.

'... her action in getting me the editorship of *The Academy* was a piece of pure good nature and friendliness, which I have never ceased to appreciate of be grateful for,' Bosie wrote.[22]

Bosie was not the obvious choice for the job. His editorial experience was limited to his student days. Not only that, his politics were quite at odds with those of his benefactor who was a Liberal MP and brother-in-law to the next Prime Minister, H. H. Asquith. Bart Tennant was reluctant to put the paper into the hands of a 'Diehard Tory'[23] but he was persuaded that Bosie would keep the editorial focus of the paper on literature not current events, and for a time that was true.

Bosie's first act as editor of *The Academy* was surprisingly progressive for a man who actively campaigned against women's suffrage. He hired Head, a talented writer who had started in the typing pool and who was then working as Graham's secretary. He invited her to act not only as his secretary but also as his sub-editor. She would go on to be 'one of the most successful business women and magazine editors of her day.'[24]

The hiring led to a 'mild scene' when she accepted the offer before consulting Graham. He did not react well to the news, she burst into tears and they spent a day in 'constrained silence' before Graham finally came around and congratulated her on the great opportunity.[25]

In the early days of Douglas's *Academy* the mood was light. The difficulties he had faced in life had not robbed the editor of his personal magnetism. Head was impressed by his 'exceptional beauty,' his 'blue eyes,' 'perfect teeth,' 'schoolgirl complexion' and 'smile of infinite charm.' The staff at first consisted only of Douglas, Head and an office boy who referred to his boss as 'the Lord.' When he was asked to fetch the contributors' ledger, the young man would say 'The Lord's got it.'[26]

If Robbie, indeed, was involved in Bosie's appointment, he must have hoped that the journal would be, as *The Spirit Lamp* had been, a sympathetic outlet for literary homosexuals. In the early years of Bosie's editorship it was not only a forum for many of the members of the old Wilde circle including Ross, Adey and Turner, it also gave Freddie Smith his first publication.[27] *The Academy* published a Greek-themed poem by Charles Moncrieff dedicated to Ross. *The Academy* also published works by Frederick Rolfe (alias Baron Corvo) and was the first to publish many of the upcoming new writers known as the 'New Bohemians' and a then-unknown Siegfried Sassoon.

For a time Robbie was willing to overlook Bosie's growing political conservatism because he valued the association. When Bosie was editor of *The Academy* there was at least one journal that was consistently pro-Wilde. Interestingly, during the period when he was contributing regularly to *The Academy*, Ross never wrote about Wilde. The small glimpses that one could get from various prefaces that he wrote were 'purposely and deliberately concealed ...' The 'detached and patronising attitude' of Robbie's writings on Wilde sometimes annoyed Bosie.[28] He, on the other hand, made many positive references to Oscar in *The Academy*. He called Wilde a 'great artist,' a 'phenomenon in literature' and 'the poet whose immortality is assured as long as the English language exists.'[29]

Robbie knew he could count on Bosie as a fellow keeper of the Wilde flame. What he did not realise was that his friend was undergoing a dramatic transformation that would eventually lead him to renounce his youthful views.

One of the frequent contributors to *The Academy* was Arthur Machen, an author best known for tales of the supernatural. The Gothic horror and pagan sensuality of his *Great God Pan* caused a sensation when it was published by John Lane in 1890. Machen was part of the larger circle of aesthetes and decadents. He had dined with Wilde and his works were illustrated by Beardsley. In the early part of the 20th Century, Machen sought religion to help him through the his grief when his wife died from cancer in 1899. He embraced mysticism and briefly joined a ritual magic group called The Hermetic Order of the Golden Dawn.[30]

He developed, around this time, a literary theory that the defining characteristic of art was 'ecstasy ... Substitute, if you like, rapture, beauty, adoration, wonder, awe, mystery, sense of the unknown, desire for the unknown ... I claim, then, that here we have the touchstone which will infallibly separate the higher from the lower in literature, which will range the innumerable multitude of books in two great divisions, which can be applied with equal justice to a Greek drama, an eighteenth century novelist, and a modern poet, to an epic in twelve books, and to a lyric in twelve lines.'[31]

Slowly he began to meld his paganism with Christianity producing his own mystic Celtic form of the religion. His love of symbolism and ritual led him finally to High Anglicanism. It was as an Anglican that he began writing regular articles for *The Academy* on the subject of religion. Machen's conception of the church was compelling to Bosie. It was the perfect bridge from Apollo to Christ.[32]

As Bosie's marriage started to break down, he became increasingly attracted to the church. (Olive found church 'depressing'.) In a world where the only acceptable form of family was based on sexual attraction between a man and a woman, the church presented an alternative. As an undergraduate, Apollo had made Bosie part of an underground community. Wilde's disciples were united in their flaunting of convention and the fast intimacy that comes from risky pass-times and shared secrets. But this was a young man's game. As they grew to middle age, many of the former decadents naturally wanted more security than such a lifestyle could offer. After sowing their wild oats, heterosexual boys settled down with their beloveds and started families. Those who had sewn Wildean oats did not have such an option. When Bosie had tried to create a home with Oscar Wilde in Naples after the playwright's release from prison, all hell had broken loose. When he discovered he had the capacity to love a woman, Bosie thought this conflict had been resolved. He and Olive would have a home, a family and live happily ever after. But this was not working.

The church offered something his marriage could not: 'fictive kinship'. When Jesus's mother and brothers came to him, as recounted in Mark 3:31-38, Jesus rejected them and turned to his disciples and said, 'Here are my mother and my brothers.' Family, in Christian terms, was not defined by biology or sexual compatibility. All who accepted the doctrine became 'brothers and sisters in Christ'. And so as Olive continued to worship at the shrine of Apollo, Bosie was beginning to turn to Christ.

Years after Wilde's death, Robbie still had to fight back tears at the memory. His loss and grief was compounded by guilt. He had seen Wilde's family torn apart, his possessions sold to creditors, his manuscripts and letters pillaged by treasure seekers and scattered to the winds. He had watched as his friend had given up hope and seen his health erode until he died an early death. Deep in his heart he could not escape the thought that it had all been his fault. He had seduced Wilde into the life that led to his ruin. He would spend the rest of his years trying to repair the damage. He would work tirelessly to restore Wilde's literary reputation, to recover his lost letters and papers, to pay down his debts and to make sure his family was cared for.

Bosie dealt with his own grief and guilt in an entirely different way. He tried to cleanse himself of the shameful desire that had caused it all. Christianity offered absolution and forgiveness. As he would one day write about Wilde's deathbed conversion, 'The difference it makes in the way I am able to think of Oscar is, of course, tremendous; chiefly because the fact of his wishing to die a Catholic implies a certain state of mind which connotes a number of other things. For example, a man becoming a Catholic must *ipso facto*, if his conversion be genuine, 'forgive all those who have injured him and ask pardon of all whom he has injured ...' Christ was the answer to the line that cut both ways, 'each man kills the thing he loves.'[33]

The form of Christianity Bosie would come to embrace was intimately tied to notions of innocence, purity and being cleansed of sexual sin and shame. It was a struggle for Bosie to suppress his sinful desires. He lived in constant fear of a relapse. He immersed himself in the church with a zeal that was characteristic of the Douglas clan and believed it with a faith that was universally described as 'childlike.' *The Academy* began to reflect his new religious philosophy as enthusiastically as *The Spirit Lamp* had championed his old.

As Bosie was sublimating his desire for ecstasy into religious ritual, the members of the Ross circle were carrying on the culture that he had abandoned. Christopher Millard had returned to England and was working at a booksellers called Jacobs on Edgware Road, a cosmopolitan locale frequented by artists and inverts. The shop specialised in writers from the 'naughty nineties', especially Oscar Wilde.

Millard's lover, Charles Scott Moncrieff, was in his final year at Winchester College. He published a controversial short story in the *New Field*. *Evensong and Morwe Song* was the tale of a pair of public school boys. The older, Carruthers, seduces the younger, Maurice. Carruthers graduates and becomes headmaster of another school. He discovers a 'painful incident' similar to his own youthful behaviour and expels one of the boys, who is, by coincidence Maurice's son. The story was unsparing in its criticism of such hypocrisy. The authorities were not amused by the article, and suppressed it, but Moncrieff was not expelled.[34]

Throughout the rest of the year, Millard remained in close contact with Robbie as he worked on his ambitious complete bibliography, a labour of love which would consume his energies for a decade. While the estate was officially focused on presenting Wilde as someone it was respectable to read, Millard had another goal. Late in the year he oversaw the reprint of a story that had been used against Wilde at his trial, John Bloxam's *The Priest and the Acolyte*. Ostensibly, the purpose of the reprint was to make it clear that the story was not by Wilde. Of course, an article on the subject would have sufficed to make that point. Millard's real goal was to ensure that the Uranian works of the 1890s were available to a new generation. Its moral had appealed to Bosie when he first published it in the *Chameleon*, but it stood in stark opposition to what he now felt in his soul. 'There is no sin for which I should feel shame ... God gave me my love for him.'[35]

31

'I No Longer Wish to Associate with Persons like Yourself'

The only difference between the saint and the sinner is that every saint has a past, and every sinner has a future.

Oscar Wilde, *A Woman of No Importance*

The beginning of the end of Robbie and Bosie's friendship came in 1908. From here on out, Robbie and Bosie's account of events will invariably differ. What they agree upon is that the rift stemmed from a dispute over how Robbie's submissions were edited by *The Academy*. The trouble began when Crosland became Bosie's sub-editor.

After *the English Review* went belly-up, Crosland took over a magazine called *The Future*, which he used as a platform to criticise *The Academy*. Bosie must have been in a good mood when he read this. Instead of firing off a bitter letter, he responded by inviting Crosland to join his staff. Initially he came on board as a contributor, but it was not long before he was Bosie's right-hand man. Crosland could churn out copy quickly and easily, a marked contrast to Bosie's slow, methodical process. He was a great asset. Although Crosland is little remembered today outside of his connection to Douglas and the Wilde feud, he was at this time, a celebrated writer near the peak of his fame. Douglas respected Crosland as 'a good poet and easily the best article writer in London ... just as he learned from me how to write sonnets, I learned from him a great deal about literary work.'[1]

Crosland's motto, according to Siegfried Sassoon was 'Giving hard knocks and getting them in return – that's my game.'[2] Under Crosland's influence, *The Academy* took a new tone. There was more political commentary and the reviews and critiques became harsher and more pointed. Bosie discovered that controversy sells.

'Nobody likes *The Academy*,' Bosie wrote Olive a short time after Crosland became editor in October 1908. 'It appears to annoy and infuriate everybody, but on the other hand they all read it, and I don't care how angry it makes people as long as they read it. The circulation goes on rising, we are printing extra copies this week, and we have more adverts again.'[3] Or as a reader put it, 'I love *The Academy* even while it makes me twist and squeak like a soul in the lower parts of Hades.'[4]

Alice Head, who had stepped aside as sub-editor in favour of Crosland, found the relationship baffling. She could never understand how two men 'of such alien natures' could be so close. Yet in spite of all of their differences they were 'inseparable.' She expressed anger and frustration at the way Bosie eventually allowed Crosland to alienate most of his friends. What she saw as Crosland's negative influence on Douglas, and the tension created by the two men's regular arguments, eventually caused her to resign.[5]

Ross's business also brought him into conflict with friends. He was famously generous, and often put the interests of his artist friends above his own profit, but not always. Early in his tenure at the Carfax he had refused to accept a commission on one of Max Beerbohm's sales. As he became more established, he was more inclined to press his business interests even when they threatened to strain friendships.

Towards the end of his tenure at the Carfax, Lady Augusta Gregory visited her nephew the artist Hugh Lane and found him 'tormented, agitated and walking up and down.' He was being vexed by a lawsuit brought by the Carfax. Lane had displayed a work at the Carfax, which had gone unsold. A short time later someone who had seen it at the gallery contacted Lane directly and purchased without paying any gallery commission. Lane believed he was within his rights, and was 'very angry' that his friend Robbie would bring in the lawyers who, be believed 'found delight in prolonging the argument ...' The fracture was not permanent, however, and it was not long before Lane was inviting Ross to dinner again and recommending him for a post as a buyer for a gallery in Johannesburg.[6]

Ross was now doing well enough financially to put Millard on his payroll, allowing him to leave his job at the book shop and focus all his energies on research and writing. This work was invaluable to the Wilde estate, as Robbie worked to crack down on unauthorised editions. In June, Robbie published Millard's *Mr Stuart Mason's Memorandum of the Authorized Editions which May be Sold in the United Kingdom*. Ross and Millard had become quite close and wrote 'lively and racy' letters to one another as Millard carried on his work.[7]

Millard had been every bit as fascinated with the *Picture of Dorian Gray* as Bosie had. His new-found financial freedom gave him the time to compile *Oscar Wilde, Art and Morality: A Defence of The Picture of Dorian Gray*. Millard approached his favourite novel with a collector's eye. His book gave details of more than 140 editions and translations. This was followed by a large sampling of contemporary reviews, both positive and negative. It concluded by quoting the uses to which it was put in Wilde's trials. In all it was a subtle condemnation of 'The Puritans and the Philistines, who scented veiled improprieties in its paradoxes.'[8]

'You are such a brave disciple of Oscar's that there is no wonder you are going down to posterity,' Freddie Smith wrote to Millard after he published a defence of Wilde's poetry in the *Sunday Times* early that year. 'The cause' was alive and well in the Ross circle.[9]

Meanwhile, *The Academy* was advocating censorship. The book in question was the 1908 *The Yoke* by Hubert Wales published by a regular advertiser, John Long. It was, to be fair, a novel that even by modern standards is fairly creepy. *The Yoke* is the story of Angelica, a widow who had raised a boy called Maurice from the time he was two years old. When her husband was dying from cancer, his last words to her had been 'take care of the kiddie.' Now Angelica was forty and 'the kiddie' twenty-two. He had developed an unhealthy desire for prostitutes and so in order to save him, Angelica started sleeping with her stepson. This sets his course right (a friend who was not saved from the horrors of prostitution by the intervention of incest commits suicide) and Maurice finds a nice woman to marry. When Angelica sends him off to his new life, she calls out 'Take care of the kiddie.' Bosie decided to make this title the focus of a more general attack on 'wicked and unregenerate' catalogue of John Long. He had already been offended by two other novels by the firm, Victoria Cross's *Five Nights* and Cosmo Hamilton's *Keepers of the House*.

The Academy published a long article calling for the book's withdraw. The original editorial did not have the effect Bosie had been hoping. It made *The Yoke* a cause célèbre and boosted its sales. After that Bosie led the charge to have the book ruled obscene. He sent copies to Scotland Yard and to Francis Bourne, the Catholic Archbishop of Winchester. He was disappointed when the bishop refused to take a stand against the novel.[10]

In October, 1908 the court rejected a claim to rule on the novel. A month later, the French writer and poet Valery Larbaud published an unsigned piece in *Le Phalange* protesting *The Academy*'s actions. Larbaud noted that English literature was 'one of the richest in the world in what *The Academy* calls 'indecent works' and priapisms of all kinds.' Laraud then took the standard attack against *The Academy*'s editor, alluding to the Wilde affair and publishing two stanzas from one of Bosie's homoerotic poems.[11]

Bosie was not deterred, he continued his campaign in *The Academy* and the National Vigilance Society took up the cause. In December, John Long was finally brought to court to answer the charge of publishing 'a certain indecent, lewd, wicked, scandalous, obscene libel' containing 'diverse lewd, impure gross and obscene matters ... against the peace of our Lord the King, his Crown and dignity.' Instead of refuting the charge, Long agreed to discontinue the publication. He said he had 'been in publishing for twenty-five years and did not want his business to be the subject of prolonged police-court discussion.' The summons was withdrawn and the magistrate ordered the destruction of the seized books.

Ross and Douglas's 'causes' were now in opposition. This played a substantial role in their division, but just how central was it? One version of the story of the rift between Ross and Douglas has won out. In this case, it is Bosie's. The story goes that Crosland was on a moral crusade with a particular focus on the 'unnatural vice'. He had a passionate hatred of Oscar Wilde and everything he stood for. Thus he did not feel that someone with Robbie's moral character should be allowed to write for *The Academy* and he urged Bosie to ban him from the paper. Bosie was not yet ready to do this. In spite of their political disagreements and a growing coldness between them, he still considered Robbie his friend. But he told Crosland that he could cut anything out of Ross's submissions that he honesty disapproved of. Crosland took the blue pencil to anything that smacked of homosexual vice. Crosland's heavy-handed editing of Ross's work caused their relationship to fracture.

Bosie wrote his account long after he had decided Ross was his number one enemy. He never missed an opportunity then to tell the world Robert Ross was a sodomite and thus he over-emphasised the role that sexual morality played in the editing of Ross's contributions and the dispute that followed. (Although when asked on the stand if he had made references to 'unnatural practices' in his submissions to *The Academy,* Ross did not deny it.) In any case, it was Douglas, not Crosland who was a recent, zealous convert to Christianity and a champion of moral values.

Crosland was an equal opportunity curmudgeon taking on assignments, as he was paid, to write scathing satires of any group imaginable. He took down the Scots, the Irish, the English, the Welsh, the Japanese, the Americans, Jews, women, men, teetotallers, suburbans and the uncultured commercial class. He even, it is said, wrote an anonymous satire of himself, 'The Unspeakable Crosland.' In fact, his most consistent target was the bourgeoisie, whose striving for status through clothes, possessions and country vacations led to all manner of uncouth behaviour. This class 'knows nothing of noblesse oblige,' he wrote in his *Wicked Life*, 'having no noblesse to oblige.' A review of *Wicked Life* gives an idea of how seriously his pronouncements were taken by his contemporaries. 'It is not for the sober and serious reader, but for the man who likes a laugh whether with or at its author. It is amusing reading for a half hour.'[12] Homosexuals, however, had never been one of his targets.

On Crosland's religion, Douglas told Sorley Brown, 'It is all tommy rot about Crosland being a Methodist. He never set foot in a Methodist place of worship in the last years of his life.' Bosie would later occasionally drag Crosland to Catholic mass. Bosie would come to believe (as he believed of everyone he wanted to meet again in heaven) that in his heart Crosland was a Catholic, but 'on account of the life he led he preferred to keep out of any definite religious creed.'[13]

Rather than inspiring Bosie to engage in a moral crusade, it seems that Bosie, the convert, was drawing Crosland into his moral battles. Bosie set the editorial tone of his paper and it was increasingly a moral, High Anglican one. Crosland was not as concerned about moral purity as he was anxious to pick a fight. As Crosland was soon to say about Douglas on the witness stand, 'He is the master, and I am the man.'

Bosie's defenders have tended to shift the blame for his mid-life moralising and anti-Wilde stand onto his friend. Crosland has thus gone down in history as a rabid homophobe who had a personal hatred of Wilde and who steered Bosie in that direction. If this were true, it is unlikely that he and Bosie would have become such good friends in the first place. In 1905, when they met, Bosie was still a practising (if conflicted) pagan and one of the foremost champions of Oscar Wilde.

Before the lead up to the Ransome trial, which revealed the contents of the full version of *De Profundis*, Crosland had little to say about the Wilde cult. He had never met Wilde. Before he worked for *The Academy*, Crosland said he had never read anything of Oscar Wilde's and knew only what any member of the public did – that Wilde had been parodied by Gilbert and Sullivan in *Patience*, 'and that he had said something eminently idiotic about the Atlantic.'[14] In his 1905 *Wild Irishman* (an Irish version of the *Unspeakable Scot*) Crosland wrote that 'two of the very wittiest men of our own time have come to us from Ireland. One of them was the late Mr Oscar Wilde and the other is Mr George Bernard Shaw.'[15] He was the first to publish Douglas's memorial sonnet to Oscar Wilde, later known as 'The Dead Poet'. It appeared in *The English Review* as 'In Memoriam, O. W.'[16] Under Douglas's editorship *The Academy* had been consistently pro-Wilde, and it doesn't seem that Crosland had a problem with that. This was all about to change, but it had not happened yet. Nor did his anti-vice crusade continue after his legal actions against Ross were concluded.[17]

Crosland would one day pose on the stand as someone who had a long-standing horror of homosexual vice. As we shall soon see, there is little in

Crosland's testimony in that case that can be taken entirely at face value. He was also, as the testimony will reveal, sensitive to the idea that he might be painted as a sodomite himself. His outspoken campaign against homosexual vice after the revelations of the Ransome case can be read, in part, as a defence mechanism that allowed him to maintain and intimate public friendship with Douglas without falling under suspicion.

On the stand, Crosland would take credit for 'making excisions' from Ross's articles and claim that they were offensive because of their moral content. Crosland claimed he gave Bosie an ultimatum, either Ross goes or I go. This probably never happened. If he had been asked to chose between Ross and Crosland, Bosie would undoubtedly have chosen Crosland, but he did not ask Ross to stop submitting. Ross got tired of writing for him. Ross had never met Crosland personally and saw him for the first time at the Ransome trial although he said, 'Douglas spoke with great admiration of Crosland.'[18]

One of the editors of *The Academy* did have a reputation for altering copy in a way that changed its meaning, and that editor was not Crosland. In 1907, before Crosland joined the paper, the poet John Davidson wrote a letter to *The Academy* to complain about a cut that changed the meaning of his text. As it appeared in *The Academy*, Davidson's article said 'the more masculine and less delicate minds among men dislike women except in their sexual relations.' In the original the line had read 'in their sexual relations as mothers, wives, lovers, sisters'. Davidson complained that it had been 'done designedly and very meanly' and that the editor of *The Academy* should step down to 'Make room for some honester man.' The journal *The Freethinker* weighed in on the protest noting that instead of issuing a normal apology, the editor had congratulated himself on 'drawing this elegant protest' from the poet, 'we are not surprised at his perpetrating a gross outrage on Mr Davidson and chuckling over it afterwards – for Mr Davidson is a Freethinker, and the editor of *The Academy* is a Christian, and that is sufficient enough explanation.'[19]

Ross's account of their falling out (given in the context of a legal action) is probably more accurate, although it too has its problems. As Ross tells it, Bosie sent him a copy of a play by Maurice Baring and asked him to review it in *The Academy*. The published version, Robbie said, turned his critique into 'a vulgar and violent abuse of a great personal friend of mine who were [sic] dragged into the article and mercilessly attacked.'[20]

Ross usually received a byline for his reviews, but in this case his name had been removed. He sent his payment for the article back to the business manager with a note saying he would not accept payment as it was not his work, and that he no longer wished to write for *The Academy*. He also claimed he asked the manager not to tell Douglas anything about this because he wanted to avoid a quarrel.[21]

Ross's sympathetic chronicler Edra Bogle ran into some issues when she tried to fact check this story. She looked through the entire volume in question and the index and could find no references to Baring, nor anything in Ross's style and there were 'so many attacks on various persons that it cannot be identified by that.'[22] Ross's slip – 'a personal friend who were' – might indicate that he was creating one specific story as a stand in for the many cases in which he felt the integrity of his writing was compromised and his friends were unjustly maligned by Douglas's *Academy*.

Vincent O'Sullivan felt that he had been insulted in the pages of *The Academy*, and he wrote to Ross to ask him his opinion of a letter he had written in response. His letter is included in the collection of Ross correspondence *Friend of Friends*, where it is dated 26 February 1905. The date must be mistaken, the letter talks about the 'constant shrill hysterical vituperation' of *The Academy* and then follows this by saying *The Academy* is setting itself up as 'the only protector and promulgator of Wilde and his works' and then expressing surprise at a bit of 'brutal impudence' from Douglas, with whom he believed himself to be on good terms. It must have been written after Bosie became editor some time after March 1907. The letter shows that Bosie's editorial policies (and unpredictable temper) caused hard feelings between him and a number of his friends.[23]

Once Olive wrote to Crosland asking him for a 'SECRET FAVOUR'. She begged him not to write anything more about the poet and journalist Filson Young. 'For you see, if he is my friend he must not be my poet's enemy ... or yours!'[24] (Olive was quite close to Young, and Bosie would soon suspect them of having an affair.)

The final nail in the coffin of their friendship was the way Bosie responded, or didn't respond, to Robbie's greatest accomplishments, bringing the Wilde estate out of bankruptcy and seeing to publication Wilde's *Complete Works*. Given everything they had been through together, Bosie should have been Robbie's greatest cheerleader when he reached this monumental landmark. He was not.

The early months of 1908 were an exciting time in Wilde circles. *De Profundis* had been a best-seller, and spawned a new interest in the reading public for all things Wilde. When the twelve-volume *Complete Works of Oscar Wilde* was released Douglas wrote a glowing review under the title 'The Genius of Oscar Wilde'. While he was lavish in his praise of the accomplishment, he failed to mention the editor (Ross) by name.

> The publication in twelve volumes by Messers. Methuen of the complete works of Oscar Wilde marks, in a striking way, the complete literary rehabilitation which this author has achieved. When one considers that at the time of Oscar Wilde's downfall the whole of his copyrights could have been purchased for about £100, one cannot help entertaining grave suspicions as to the value of criticism in England.

Of course, Bosie had himself passed up the opportunity to purchase the copyrights for that sum. Ross would always believe that this was the real cause of Bosie's bitterness towards him, and there was certainly an element of truth in this.

While Douglas emphasised his own friendship with Wilde, he was quick to distance himself from his sin. 'It would be idle to deny that Oscar Wilde was an immoral man ...' These types of statements always stuck in Robbie's craw. He considered them to be the height of hypocrisy as if Bosie had forgotten that he had been a more-than enthusiastic participant in such 'immorality' only a few years before. It was, however, a sincere expression of Bosie's conflicted feelings at the time. His admiration and pride at having been the great man's friend shine through, even as he tries to distance himself from a philosophy he no longer believes.

Wilde, putting aside his moral delinquencies, which have as much and as little to do with his works as the colour of his hair, was a great artist, a man who passionately loved his art. He was so great an artist that, in spite of himself, he was always on the side of the angels. We believe that the greatest art is always on the side of the angels, to doubt it would be to doubt the existence of God ... It was all very well for Wilde to play with life, as he did exquisitely, and to preach the philosophy of pleasure, and plucking the passing hour; but the moment he sat down to write he became different. He saw things as they really were; he knew the falsity and the deadliness of his own creed; he knew that 'the end of these things is Death;' and he wrote in his own inimitable way the words of Wisdom and Life.

Perhaps thinking of the gulf that had grown between him and Robbie, Bosie urged his readers not to paint Wilde's admirers with a single brush. While he praised Wilde's literary disciples, he denigrated his Pagan philosophy and the men who would follow it.

Those who knew and loved him as a man and as a writer were men who had their own individualities and were neither his shadows nor his imitators. If they achieved any greatness they did it because they had greatness in them and not because they aped 'the master.' ... Wilde has his school of young men in those who copy what was least admirable in him, but from a literary point of view he has no school. He stands alone, a phenomenon in literature. From the purely literary point of view he was unquestionably the greatest figure of the nineteenth century ... The evil that he did ... was interred with his bones, the good ... lives after him and will live forever.[25]

Ross at this time had been working on a new edition of *De Profundis*, which would include more material than the previous version. In Bosie's declaration of intellectual independence he may have heard echoes of one of young Bosie's harsh statements, one that had become a bitter refrain in Wilde's prison letter: 'I owe you no intellectual debt whatsoever.'

While Bosie had failed to mention Ross by name in his praise of the *Collected Works*, he would not be so careless in the criticisms which ran the following week. It seems that Bosie had not examined the *Collected Works* too closely – or at all – when he wrote his review. Much of his article had centred on the 'greatest and most terrible moral lessons' in *The Picture of Dorian Gray*. The problem is, the novel had not been included in the collection. In a private conversation, Robbie had explained why. It seems that Robbie told him the President of Magdalen College, Thomas Herbert Warren, had complained of its immorality. This may have been a joke that Bosie took literally. In reality, the compiling of the *Collected Works* was a huge ordeal, as the copyrights had been sold and scattered requiring all sorts of purchases and negotiation. *Dorian Gray* was not included in the original release of six volumes because the holder of the English copyright, Charles Carrington, wanted £425 for permission to print the work. The only way Methuen thought they could make it economically feasible was to put it out with additional material and excerpts from Wilde's prison letters in a separate edition. It was released later as volume 11.[26]

Bosie, of course, had never taken correction well. As it happens he was also a bit miffed at Methuen for refusing to advertise in his paper. So on 18 July 1908 in a column headed 'Life and Letters', Bosie expressed his outrage at the act of censorship. (He approved of censorship, but not of works that he personally liked.)

> Wilde's masterpiece ... can be obtained, it is published, not by Methuen, but by Mr Carrington, of Paris ... It is regrettable that Mr Ross, the able and painstaking editor of this edition, did not select a firm of publishers more worthy of issuing this collection of a great man's works.[27]

Ross was willing to forgive Bosie's gentle criticism, but he was furious that he had used information from a private conversation to attack a firm with whom he was still in constant negotiations.

Bosie was not the only one who was critical of the decision to leave *Dorian Gray* out of the collection. The Scottish writer and scholar J. W. Mackail had also heard the rumour that *Dorian* was to be left out for moral reasons. He wrote to Robbie to say that it it would not do justice to Oscar and that there was 'no safety ... in half measures'.[28]

In August, The Douglases and Ross were invited to a dinner at the country home of Frank Lawson. The subject of *The Academy* inevitably came up, and Robbie expressed his frustrations at the way his works were cut and changed, the way Bosie attacked his friends, and his lack of tact in his critique of Methuen. Robbie said he 'told him that I thought he owed more courtesy to me as an old contributor to the 'Academy' and as the inventor of his becoming the editor.' Bosie flew into a rage. 'I did not lose my temper,' Robbie said, 'though I apologised afterwards to our host who told several people that he would never have us in the house again.'[29]

It fell to Olive to smooth things over. She asked Robbie to forgive Bosie his temper, as he had so many times in the past. Robbie invited Bosie to lunch at this club. 'That was the last time I spoke to him. We parted perfectly good friends.'[30]

The release of the handsome twelve-volume *Collected Works* was followed by what was sometimes referred to as 'the cheap edition'. It included various odds and ends. It was originally to have included Christopher Millard and Walter Ledger's bibliography as one of the editions, but Ledger wanted too much money and Millard had become controversial after his own arrest for gross indecency. Volume 14 of the *Collected Works*, called *Miscellanies*, included, for copyright reasons, a mish-mash of everything Ross could ascertain Wilde had written, including journalism, obscure essays and reviews. Ross actually considered it to be 'the most exciting of all the books' because they had discovered a number of previously unknown works. Ross gave his longest introduction to this volume. He admitted that Wilde would probably not have wanted some of the pieces to be included, but because there were so many articles falsely attributed to Wilde, he felt it was important to include everything known to be authentic. This time, Bosie did not limit his criticism to the publisher.

> The recent publication in book form by Messers Methuen of Oscar Wilde's scattered reviews and scraps of journalism is, in our opinion, to be regretted ... Wilde was a very good journalist no doubt, but he was also a great man of letters, and we cannot imagine that he would have relished the idea of seeing his unconsidered trifles of journalism brought again into the hard light of criticism. Anyone who knew Oscar Wilde must be aware that he was for ever

girding at journalists and journalism, and admitting that this was a fad, and not altogether consistent one, his feelings on the subject should have been considered.

One suspects that it is really Bosie's own feelings on the subject that he felt should have been considered. The review concluded:

> We are not in the least surprised that Messers. Methuen, having set out to publish Wilde, and having out of sheer stupidity, refused to include in their edition what is probably his finest book, should not hesitate to publish a collection of newspaper articles which cannot possibly add to Wilde's reputation, and may, even in the eyes of unthinking people, detract from it. What does surprise us is that Mr Ross should have consented to authorise such a publication, though we would not for a moment even appear to suggest that Mr Ross's motives were not beyond reproach. It strikes us as merely an error of judgement on his part.[31]

Robbie cannot have welcomed this critique from someone who, up to now, expressed little interest in Wilde's literary matters. His shouting from the sidelines was annoying but not as hurtful as what followed. In December 1908, Robbie was finally due to receive some long overdue recognition for his years of labour on behalf of the Wilde estate. Robbie's friends had arranged a congratulatory dinner for Ross to be held at the Ritz in London. The guest list was a who's who of the literary world. Among the more than 200 guests were most of Oscar's old friends, Max Beerbohm, Reggie Turner, More Adey, Ada Leverson, Frank Harris, Oscar Browning, George Ives, William Rothenstein, and Robert Sherard. Millard and Robbie's new friends were all there. Robbie's family was there, sitting happily with his lover Freddie Smith. Both of Wilde's sons attended.

Robbie gave a gracious speech, thanking all of the people who had made his success possible. He also announced that the estate had received an anonymous gift of £2,000 to pay for a monument for Wilde's grave. Although he did not reveal it, the benefactor was Helen Carew, an old friend of Wilde's who gave the money under the condition that the monument be designed by the artist Jacob Epstein.[32]

Bosie, in one of his disagreeable moods (perhaps a depression) had become petulant and refused to attend. While he had been prevented from living with Wilde, Robbie was living quite openly with Smith, and their standard of living was better than his own. Bosie had spent the past few years doing his best to lead a morally upstanding life and it had not put an end to the innuendoes and jokes at his expense. Most galling of all, his important role in Oscar Wilde's life had never been celebrated, only shamed. Ross was being canonised.

'There are many persons now alive who were friends with Wilde in the days of his greatness and prosperity,' Bosie wrote, 'and without a single exception, as far as I am aware, their friendship is reckoned to their credit, and in some instances, has proved highly advantageous to them from many points of view. Yet what was a virtue in these persons would seem to have been a crime in me.'[33]

He had, of course, been invited. Reggie Turner was one of the organisers. Yet even though he had excluded himself, he was bitter at being excluded. He wrote an ungracious letter to Turner saying he would not attend. Robbie was, in his words, 'deeply offended' to receive 'no word of acknowledgement or congratulation' from Bosie. Instead, Bosie made 'some very disagreeable remarks on the subject to various friends.'[34] Robbie would not hear of anyone trying to defend Bosie on the matter. Some time later he was having lunch with Reggie at the Reform Club. Reggie said something supportive of Bosie and Robbie 'became almost violent in his rage against Reggie.'[35]

Robbie had made his feelings known widely, which led to the only discordant note of the evening. Frank Harris made the audience uncomfortable with his speech by alluding to Bosie 'in a way that was not at all in the note of the evening.'[36]

Robbie and Bosie had once been united as two of the most loyal keepers of the Wilde flame. In his moment of triumph, the one person from whom Robbie should have been able to expect congratulations was Bosie. Even were this not the case, any real friend would have gone to celebrate another friend's milestone. It was an ungracious and thoughtless snub, one that hurt in proportion to the intimacy that they had once shared. Bosie had not behaved as his friend for some time, and Robbie had had enough.

A few weeks later, Olive invited Robbie to lunch. His response was stiff and formal. 'What have I done?' Olive replied, 'Do come and see me one day soon. You must know I always love to see you.' She added 'Because I am afraid you and Bosie are not friends just now, I am sorry.'[37]

In his response, Robbie explained that because he and Bosie now disagreed on so many topics, and Bosie had never learned to disagree in a pleasant way, any meeting would inevitably lead to yet more arguments. He gave his reasons for the split: 'I am with the opposite side on every controversial matter discussed by *The Academy*, which moreover attacks all the people who are my personal friends and most of the books and authors I happen to admire ... Alone of all my former friends, or I may say of Wilde's friends, he sent me no message of felicitation on the public celebration of the conclusion of what had been my chief occupation for eight years.' He concluded, 'I have no hostile feelings whatever because I know Bosie too well and have known him too long. But I decided some time ago to deny myself the privileges coincidental to friendship with him.'[38]

He suggested that perhaps he and Olive could meet without Bosie 'under the hospitable roof' of their mutual friend Helen Carew. Olive, of course, showed the letter to her husband, as Robbie must have known she would. Handling rejection with grace was never Bosie's strong suit. He responded in typical fashion with one of the infamous letters that he came to call a 'stinker.'

'As to your determination to forgo my friendship, as you have raised the point, I may say that the boot is very much on the other leg. I gave up going to your house because I disapproved of your views, your morals and most of your friends. My own views have changed and I do not care to meet those who are engaged in active propaganda of every kind of wickedness from anarchy to sodomy.'[39]

After this Bosie wrote an angry letter to More Adey expanding on this theme. He said he had detectives following Ross and that he knew about a number of his escapades including a tryst with one of the waiters in the Royal Automobile Club in Pall Mall and another with a servant at the Hotel Dieudonne in Ryder Street.[40]

Robbie consulted George Lewis about the letter, but he advised his client to take no legal action. Instead Robbie started gathering up evidence that would prove his nemesis was homosexual. He thought having these in his possession would ward off any attacks. It was a homosexual version of cold war and mutually assured destruction. This might have worked, but Robbie could not resist using his weapons. Robbie also realised that if he and Bosie were enemies, he had better take steps to shore up his claim on *De Profundis*. While he now had full control of the copyright, his claim on the physical manuscript – a letter addressed to someone else – was legally tenuous. He placed it in the British Library with the provision that it be kept under seal for fifty years.

In spite of all this, Bosie probably did not yet think his friendship with Robbie was finished. His friendships with Wilde and Crosland, and any number of friends, were punctuated with fights and reunions and there was every reason for Bosie to expect that their rift was temporary. He was oblivious to the massive trap that his former friend had laid.

Right: 1890 portrait of Robert
Ross by Charles W. Fuse.
(Courtesy British Library)

Below left: Lord Alfred Douglas,
age five. (From Lord Alfred
Douglas's *Autobiography*, 1928)

Below right: Lord Alfred Douglas
age 21; this was a favourite photo
of Oscar Wilde's. (From Lord
Alfred Douglas's *Autobiography*,
1928)

A young Robert Ross. (Courtesy British Library)

Robert Ross and Reginald Turner, c. 1895. (Private Collection / Photo © Tallandier / Bridgeman Images)

Above: A rare image of More Adey, art critic and editor.

Below left: Max Beerbohm considers the décor in this photograph taken in 1908 by Alvin Langdon Coburn in the Beerbohm family home in Upper Berkeley Street and reproduced in Coburn's *Men of Mark* in 1913.

Below right: The most famous image of Oscar Wilde and Lord Alfred Douglas.

Above: 'The Girl Who Asked for a Glass of Milk at the Cafe Royal' by H.M. Bateman.

Below left: Maurice Schwabe. (Courtesy Lance Banbury)

Below centre: Robert Sherard, as pictured on the flyleaf of one of his novels.

Below right: Frank Harris. (Library of Congress)

Above left: Lord Alfred Douglas in Egypt.

Above right: Sir George Lewis Snr in a contemporary newspaper.

Below left: Cartoon of Queensberry confronting Tennyson at a performance of *The Promise of May.*

Below right: Artist's impression of the sale of Oscar Wilde's effects from the *Illustrated Police Budget.*

Above: Illustration of the 'Separate System' of prisons c. 1860 showing the caps used to prevent communication still used in Wilde's day.

Below left: Oscar Wilde in Naples. (William Andrews Clark Memorial Library, UC)

Below right: A famous image of a soulful-looking Lord Alfred Douglas, 1903.

Above: The woman shown here kissing Natalie Barney has not been definitively identified, but she bears a striking resemblance to Olive Custance.

Left: Olive Custance, one of Lord Alfred Douglas's favourite photos from the period of their courtship. (From Lord Alfred Douglas's *Autobiography*, 1928)

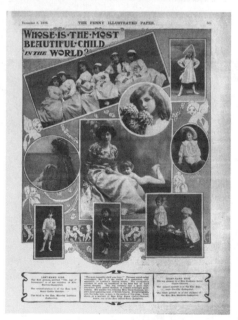

Above left: Olive Douglas is in the centre with her bonny baby Raymond.

Above right: Arthur Newton caricature from *Vanity Fair*, 21 September 1893.

A scowling
T.W.H. Crosland.
(From Sorley Brown's
biography of Crosland,
1925)

Above left: Christopher Millard. (Courtesy Bodleian Library)

Above right: Charles Garratt on the stand in 1914.

Left: 'Baron von Koenig', the conman and blackmailer Rudolf Stallmann, from the archives of Special Branch. (Courtesy Raymond Batkin)

Below left: Simeon Solomon, from Sorley Brown's biography of Crosland, 1925.

Below right: An illustration of the nefarious tricks used by the Stallmann gang as shown in a popular German magazine, 1931.

Sir George Lewis, Jnr from a
contemporary newspaper.

Justice Charles Darling portrait
by Charles W. Fuse. (From
The Life of Lord Darling by
Derek Walker-Smith, 1938)

Above left: A *Vanity Fair* caricature of a suitably ambitious-looking F.E. Smith MP, 16 January 1907. The caption reads 'A successful first speech.'

Above right: Sir Coleridge Kennard by Jacques-Emile Blanche, included in a 1924 exhibition of Blanche's work under the title *Le Portrait de Dorian Gray*. (Private collection, England. Courtesy of W. M. Brady & Co., New York)

Below left: T.W.H. Crosland, Lord Alfred Douglas and Freddie Manners-Sutton at the time of their libel action.

Below right: Principals in Douglas v Ransome and Others.

Cecil Hayes. (From Sorley Brown's biography of Crosland)

Robert Ross c. 1916. (Library of Congress)

Maud Allan as Salome. (Library of Congress)

Salome, *The Climax*, by Aubrey Beardsley, first published in 1894; one of sixteen illustrations commissioned by Wilde.

Lord Alfred Douglas with Father Wulstand of Greyfriars, Oxford, 1938.

The fateful document at the heart of the matter; Robert Ross with a copy of *De Profundis*.

32

Family Reunions and Divisions

One of the highlights of the celebratory dinner for Ross was the announcement that an anonymous benefactor had donated funds to build a monument to Oscar Wilde, who was still resting in a pauper's grave. The unnamed benefactor was Helen Carew, the mutual friend who Olive Douglas had hoped would facilitate a reconciliation between Bosie and Robbie.

Carew had remained on good terms with both Ross and Douglas. (She and her son are both mentioned in Olive Douglas's diary in 1907).[1] Her son by her first marriage Sir Coleridge Arthur Fitzroy Kennard, 'Roy' to his friends, was born in 1885 and was now an Eton educated dandy. He was wealthy enough to believe that authors who wrote books for money were not legitimate artists and also traditional enough that he had gone to the school of Mr Diptich Schoones in Garrick Street to cram for the Foreign Office exam and join the Diplomatic service.[2]

There Kennard became friendly with a fellow student, Wilde's son, Vyvyan who had been given a new family name, Holland, after the tragedy. Kennard invited him to dinner at his mother's house. It was the first time since his family fled England that Holland had heard his father mentioned with admiration. As the evening progressed Carew cautiously brought up the name Robert Ross. She was stunned to find Holland had never been told about the man who had done so much for his family.

Holland had a great curiosity about his father and was anxious to meet people who knew him and who held him in esteem. The following week, Carew hosted another dinner. This time she invited Ross, Max Beerbohm and Reggie Turner. Douglas was, of course, not invited. It would not have been appropriate to have 'the other man' there.

Ross set out to show Holland that his father had been widely loved and admired. He introduced him to some of Wilde's greatest supporters including Ada Leverson and Adela Schuster. All of his life, Vyvyan and his brother had been shuttled from place to place, their past spoken of in whispers. Carew and Ross had given him something precious. For the first time he felt that he was part of a community and part of a family with a heritage he could be proud of. It was life changing.

One episode in Robbie's relationship with Helen Carew can perhaps shed some light on one of the great debates of the Ross/Douglas feud. Ross had acted as an intermediary when Wilde was in prison, and handled his affairs afterwards. Could he have, as some of Douglas's supporters suggest, manipulated the situation to his advantage in order to eliminate a romantic rival?

When Oscar and Bosie were struggling to stay together in Naples, Bosie had become convinced that Robbie was conspiring against them. The fourteen page letter that he almost neglected to read had persuaded him otherwise, but after their falling out, Bosie came to believe that his first impression had been right and that Robbie had always been plotting against him. Some time after the Ransome trial, the writer A. J. A. Symons suggested to Bosie that perhaps Ross had acted out of jealousy, and tried to marginalise Bosie because of his 'first claim' on Oscar.[3]

This idea made sense to Bosie, and he would, from that point on, suggest it to others as Robbie's motivation. A jealous Robbie, plotting to take Bosie's place, became a standard feature of Douglas's sympathetic biographies. Robbie rarely spoke publicly about his own feelings or motivations. His intent may never be fully known. There was, however, one episode in which he clearly did conspire to separate a pair of lovers. It happened in 1909, Carew was concerned about the behaviour of her now twenty-four year-old son and she asked for Robbie's help.

Kennard's grandfather, who was also called Coleridge Kennard, had founded the *Evening News*, and on his death in 1890 he left an estate worth more than £380,000. His grandson was to inherit the bulk of it but not until he reached the age of 25 in 1910. Two months after passing the Foreign Office exam on 22 October, 1908, Kennard met and fell in love with a married woman with two children, Edith Cornelia 'Yoï' Buckley. She was a free spirit with a striking mane of flowing hair, a sweet, warm voice, and a great deal of personal charm. Buckley, who later wrote about the affair, did not record how they met but one possibility is that they were introduced by the Douglases. Olive's diary mentions visits by Helen Carew and Coleridge Kennard in 1907 and Yoï is also mentioned a number of times. (The most interesting, given future events, being the entry for 19 March 1908 in which she met Yoï to lunch with Maud Allen.)[4]

It was love at first sight. Within three months of their meeting Kennard asked Yoï to go away with him. They determined that she should get a divorce so they could marry. Carew believed Buckley was a gold-digger who was colluding with her husband to get her hands on her son's fortune. She also worried about the scandal if Kennard's name came up in a divorce proceeding.

In mid-March, a period, incidentally in which Yoï was socialising regularly with Olive Douglas, Carew went to the Foreign Office, where she had a number of personal friends and asked them to send Kennard to Rome right away instead of later as he would have been in the normal course of events.

Yoï believed Kennard had only joined the Foreign Office to please his mother and really wanted to spend his life with her making art. Until his inheritance became available, he needed to keep his mother happy. But once he inherited, he would be free to do whatever he wanted.

Before he left for Rome, he gave his beloved a gift of jewellery and promised that they would be together. While he was in Rome he wrote and telegraphed regularly asking Yoï to join him. Accordingly, she wrote to her husband to say she was leaving him. And Kennard sent regular telegrams begging her to join him, 'I cannot be without you.'

By the end of the month both Ross and Kennard were was back in England. Robbie tried to persuade him to end the affair, but his appeals had little effect. After that, the activity to end the relationship kicked into high gear. Carew and Ross, along with representatives of the Lewis & Lewis law firm intervened with the Foreign Office. Kennard was called to answer to Sir Charles Hardinge,

Permanent Under-Secretary of the Foreign Office. Ross's official capacity is murky, but letters in the Foreign Office files show that he corresponded with representatives on the matter and sat in on meetings.

Kennard would later write Buckley that Hardinge had given him a week to either finish with her or be fired. Ross and Carew could not move him, so they convinced the Foreign Office to take another route. Kennard was transferred to Tehran for a two year assignment in the hopes that the distance would put an end to the infatuation.

Buckley then received a visit from Ross. He explained that Kennard really had no choice in the matter and otherwise 'he would be dismissed in such a way as no one had ever been dismissed before.' They would both be disgraced so fully that they could never 'live in England or meet English people.' Once she was divorced, he would be allowed to come back. Given these assurances, Buckley did not try to persuade Kennard to stay.

Before he left England, Kennard and Ross came to her with a marriage settlement that drafted by Lewis & Lewis which gave Buckley an income of about £100 a month. She claimed she was reluctant to sign, as they were not yet married, but 'Ross ... urged this, against my objections.' Kennard told her not to worry, they would be married in a few months.

She would later say of her meeting with Ross that he 'had tried to make me believe evil of everyone surrounding me and after which I had fainted from sheer horror, Sir Coleridge Kennard said that never in all my life would he permit this man either to speak to me or see me again.'

On 23 July, the day he left London, Kennard wrote to Captain Buckley asking him to commence divorce proceedings. He instructed his solicitors to 'facilitate in every way' the granting of the divorce. 'We fear that there are a great many people working against Yoï.'

He wrote the next day to his solicitors asking them not to defend him (i.e. not to deny there was an affair) in the divorce case, ' ... if the divorce is thwarted I shall not hesitate to take any step for Mrs. Buckley's sake'. The same day he wrote to her solicitor saying 'Nothing will stop me from marrying Yoï when the divorce is granted ...'

He continued to send love letters, written on the train en route to Tehran. He warned her that people were plotting against them and told her not to believe anything he heard about his feelings for her unless it came directly from him. Kennard, Buckley said, specifically warned her against Ross. They made up a code word so she would know important letters really came from him. He would also sign letters Royoï, a combination of their two nicknames, to show that they were united.

While Kennard was in Tehran, Buckley's husband began divorce proceedings. Separated from her husband, with only the income from the marriage settlement, she endured great hardship for one of her class, 'After that my maid was the only servant I had.'

In autumn 1909 there was a flurry of activity behind the scenes, with the Foreign Office and the Carews anxious to end the relationship, while Kennard continued to write to Yoï saying 'nothing can alter me' and to his solicitors about 'our future.' In December, Kennard's letters suggested that his mother, grandmother and others were going to 'vile depths' to try to separate them and that he was afraid that people were telling her lies about him.

She was 'utterly perplexed' when telegrams that seemed to be ending the affair came in January 1910. More upsetting was that Carew's circle of friends seemed to know about the messages before she had even received them. According to

Buckley, Ross and Carew were telling everyone that the marriage settlement had been settled upon her in order to set Kennard free.

Something had transpired in January to change Kennard's mind, but Buckley could get no word as to what it was. She heard Kennard had told his solicitors to defend the divorce suit. Buckley could not believe it and she asked her solicitor to confirm. The answer was a telegram, signed with their code word, which said only 'Have had to.' She sent a telegram asking if he wanted her to go back to her husband, and there was no answer.

From correspondence between Buckley's solicitor Holman and Ross in the Foreign Office file, it seems as though something had come up regarding Mrs. Buckley's 'past life.' The information was not elaborated upon, however, it seems that it was more in the nature of gossip than anything tangible, for no evidence was ever produced.

Much like Douglas with the imprisoned Wilde, Buckley was not willing to accept that Kennard's feelings had changed without speaking to him personally. She sent a telegram saying that if he really wanted to end things he should write to her and tell her using their secret code.

On 7 February the divorce case came before the court. There was no defence, and the marriage was dissolved. Custody of the children was granted to Captain Buckley. Around this time, Ross was meeting with Buckley's solicitor, Allen, and they had a 'long interview.' Ross visited the solicitor two days in a row to impress upon him that Kennard had changed his mind. He referred to letters that Kennard had written to him and produced a telegram from Kennard. The reply said 'Feelings have changed. Find it impossible to marry her or continue present relations have no code to Allen (Buckley's solicitor) so I do not repeat.' Allen believed the telegram was a forgery.

Allen wrote to Kennard saying, 'I ask you as a man to man to write and tell me that you have changed your mind and intend to leave Yoï to face the fate which you have forced on her. Nothing short of this under your own hand, will ever shatter her belief in you.' There was no answer.

Buckley, through sheer determination, managed to get a face to face meeting with Kennard in March 1910. It was clear he had turned against her. Lancelot Oliphant, a witness to the meeting said she 'threw herself down in despair.' Kennard was not moved. He told her that his mother had given him absolute proof that she and her husband had colluded to try to get his fortune and that he was planning to take legal action against them. 'Thank Good,' she said. 'Now it will be proved false.' Kennard left the room. Buckley turned to Oliphant, and repeated, 'It will be proven I am innocent.' Oliphant described her tone as 'one of undying devotion to him.'

Buckley later wrote that 'those proofs were either forged or false witness … I now live to disprove it.' She also claimed Ross boasted to friends that he had arranged Kennard's Tehran posting so that he could put an end to their marriage plans.

The echoes of Bosie's correspondence with Robbie while Oscar was in prison are striking:

> I cannot believe that Sir Coleridge Kennard is a coward and a person devoid of all sense of honour. If he is, I ask him to tell me so himself – this is the only way by which I can believe it, and only by knowing that he has become an entirely different person … I can feel that I have now nothing in common with him … it is easier to believe that he is acting from some mistaken idea of renunciation, for his mother's sake or mine …

On 5 April, 1911, Coleridge Kennard married Dorothy Barclay, daughter of the British minister to Persia.

Buckley landed on her feet. She wrote a book about her travels, *A Year of Strangers*, under the name Yoï Pawlowska (her mother's maiden name). Filson Young, who was previously mentioned as the writer Douglas believed was overly intimate with his wife, reviewed Buckley's book for *Living Age*, saying her exile was 'chiefly through a piece of treachery and misconduct too sordid to be recounted here. It is interesting to the reader only because it was apparently the origin of the book, which is a record of the year which the writer thought to find the happiest of her life, but in which instead she wandered in lonely places and drank of bitter waters. And yet all that the public, ignorant of the inner story, will see is a charming book by a new writer.'

As Buckley was Lady Alfred Douglas's friend, Lord Alfred would have been well aware of 'the inner story'. The events may have influenced how Douglas remembered and thought about Ross's actions as an intermediary in his own relationship.[5]

The Kennard case provides more questions than answers. It shows that Ross did not need to be motivated by jealousy to take an active role in ending a relationship. It is not clear whether Ross worked so hard on Carew's behalf because he was convinced Buckley was colluding with her husband or whether, as Buckley believed, he was working against them on his mother's behalf using disinformation, manipulation and perhaps even forgery to attain her ends. There may be validity in both of the claims. Perhaps Ross did manipulate people's perceptions because he truly believed Kennard was being conned. Whatever his motivations (and Yoï's), his efforts were greatly appreciated by Carew and her mother.

33

Litigation Mania

> I knew then, instinctively, that if I got into the witness box I could carry a jury
> with me. I have proved it since over and over again.
>
> Lord Alfred Douglas[1]

With Crosland at his side, Douglas became increasingly confident at the helm of
The Academy. He was emboldened to share his views, whether literary, political
or social. After years of being marginalised, he loved the sense of power that came
with his position. This began a period in which Bosie would become more famous
for his litigation than for his poetry.

Crosland already had a reputation as a libeller and a litigant long before
he joined *The Academy*. In 1903, *The Sphere* reported that Crosland had 'no
fewer than three libel actions against newspapers in progress.'[2] He had lost
his most recent high profile libel complaint, in which he had sued The *Saint
James's Gazette* over a parody of his *Lovely Woman*, a book which did for
the 'gentler sex' what The *Unspeakable Scot* had done for the Scots. During
that trial, the counsel for the defendants described Crosland as 'a man who
obtained his means of livelihood by being a purveyor of libels with a catch
penny title.'[3]

While Douglas would, in later years, blame Crosland for getting him into
many of his scuffles, it is clear from his own writings that he enjoyed battling in
the courtroom and was proud of his ability on the stand. He even boasted about
his courtroom strategy, which he named 'Le Systeme Douglas.'

A number of motivations drove Bosie to the courts. One was self-defence.
It was not uncommon for newspaper men in those days to threaten to expose
embarrassing episodes from prominent men's pasts if they did not pay. Douglas
was a tempting target.

In *Without Apology*, Bosie accuses Frank Harris of trying to shake
him down. According to Bosie, in 1908 Harris was editing *Vanity Fair*.
A representative from that publication, Edgar Jepson, came to him and said an
article that discussed his role in the Wilde scandal was going to appear in the
next issue, but that it could be stopped for 'a small financial transaction, say a
couple of hundred pounds.' He told this person to go back to Harris and tell
him that he was prepared to sue him for libel. 'I also invited him not to forget
that I too had a paper, and that I was quite as capable of writing unpleasant
articles as he was.'[4]

This, Bosie would later tell Elmer Gertz, was he moment that he fell out with Harris. He could forgive him for swindling him in the casino matter, but he could not forgive his blackmail. After that he decided to fill the pages of *The Academy* with 'good-natured 'roasting' of Harris. 'For weeks I used to put paragraphs in my paper making fun of him and referring to him as "the world's greatest wearer of rabbit-skin coats."' This was part of a 'standing joke' about 'the world's greatest' this or that. Douglas and Crosland thought it was hilarious that magazines sometimes referred to H. G. Wells as 'the world's greatest novelist.'[5]

For his part, Harris believed Bosie was attacking him 'without rhyme or reason,' but he said, 'I thought he had been misled by Crosland, a malicious and disappointed journalist, and so I did not take the matter very seriously.'[6] It is entirely possible that Jepson was acting without Harris's knowledge or that the blackmail attempt was conveyed not directly, but through Crosland, who exaggerated it or even made it up. There was not much love lost between Harris and Crosland. Such forceful personalities seem almost designed to be in conflict. Crosland had written for Harris at *Vanity Fair*. Yet while he was cashing Harris's checks, he was also writing anonymous critiques of his editor in other publications.[7]

Before Crosland entered the picture, Bosie's life had a regular undercurrent of negative innuendo. More than a decade after the trial that had made him a household name, Bosie had moved on. Yet in the public imagination he remained frozen in time as Oscar Wilde's darling boy. Whenever anyone disagreed with his editorial choices in *The Academy* they would dismiss him by making a reference to the Wilde trial.

There was, for example, the time he insulted the American literary establishment by suggesting, in the pages of his paper, that their nation had no culture. *The Atlanta Constitution* responded by reminding its readers of the Wilde scandal and concluding 'Lord Alfred enjoys the advantage of occupying the unassailable position of the man who has no reputation to lose. He can't hurt himself by anything he says or writes. And he can't hurt anybody else.'[8]

To Bosie, it was the height of hypocrisy. He was well-placed enough to hear all the society gossip. He understood that the difference between himself and his accusers was not their superior moral behaviour but their superior ability to keep their foibles secret. Increasingly, in his middle years, he would respond to those who tried to throw Wilde in his face by reminding them of their own embarrassments.

One anecdote will suffice to illustrate this. At a garden party while Bosie was editor of *The Academy*, he met the American actress Maud Allan. Her performance as the Salome Dancer had made her the toast of the town. She was surrounded by admirers, and rumoured to be the favourite of the King. She was about to publish her autobiography *My Life in Dancing*.

Allan had received a harsh review in *The Academy*. The article, 'All We Like Sheep' was written not by Douglas, but by a Christopher St. John who argued that Allan was a pale imitator of Isadora Duncan. St. John viewed her as more of 'a hypnotist' than a 'genuine dancer.' She had, he concluded 'never learned to dance.'[9]

Seeing the editor of that disrespectful journal at the party, Allan delivered 'a gross insult' – presumably about the Wilde scandal. Without missing a beat Bosie replied, 'But your brother was a murderer!' This was true, but few people in England knew it. He had probably heard the gossip from his brother Sholto who was living in California and was able to follow the trial of her brother Theo in the local papers. Allan, who thought she had left this scandal back home, was shocked to have her family secret brought out in public. She struck the cheeky aristocrat across the face with her fan.[10]

Bosie viewed *The Academy* as a 'weapon of defence' against blackmail and insults. 'As long as I was in the powerful position which the editorship of a weekly paper bestows on a man, my enemies, of whom I had a great many, were afraid of me.'[11] Suing for libel was a way to advertise to the entire world that he was not afraid of blackmailers, and that he was willing to stand up and fight.

Although he would publicly deny it, Crosland was aware of Bosie's sexual history with Oscar Wilde. We know this because Bosie wrote that when they were working on *Oscar Wilde and Myself*, Crosland advised him that telling the truth would be 'equal to committing suicide.'[12] When Crosland became aware of the truth is never elaborated. But the fact remains that before Crosland joined Douglas at *The Academy*, Bosie had been reluctant to initiate libel suits. After Crosland became his sub-editor, Bosie lost that reluctance. The most reasonable explanation is that Crosland persuaded him that if he denied he had any knowledge of Wilde's vices, no one could prove otherwise. This probably happened some time before 1909, when Crosland filed his first libel suits on Douglas's behalf.

His first targets were not particularly threatening. In 1909, Bosie took on a pair of undergraduate magazines, Oxford's *The Isis* and *Cambridge Magazine*. Each had written articles on Wilde that referred to him in an uncomplimentary fashion. Crosland served a writ on both publications. They backed down, paid fifty guineas in damages and fired the editors. For the first time, Bosie felt as though he might have some control over his own reputation. It felt wonderful.[13]

What is more, suing his detractors and pushing for a settlement could be lucrative. 'The sums I got for compensation from persons who libelled me, and squealed for mercy when I writted them, were for a long time, in a small way, quite a source of income to me,' Bosie wrote. Most observers agree that money was Crosland's primary motivation.[14]

But Bosie had a deeper, more fundamental reason to prove his talent on the stand. By showing that he was a first-rate witness, he could prove that he had not led Wilde to his destruction. If he had only been allowed to testify in Wilde's libel case as he had wanted, everything would have been different.

In his own writings he repeatedly linked his later legal actions to the Wilde case. The most blunt expression of this came in a comment to Elmer Gertz, 'There is all the difference in the world between 'goading a man to his doom' and advising him to bring an action for libel,' he wrote, 'a thing I have done over and over again myself with complete success.'[15]

By now Bosie was a middle-aged man, and he looked back on the actions and attitudes of his younger self as if they belonged to another person. He had come to genuinely believe his youth had been misspent, his acts had been sinful, and the price for those sins had been heavy. As early as 1907, Robbie had a sense that Bosie had become unsympathetic to the cause. He warned Millard not to be so effusive in his praise of his lover Scott Moncrieff when he wrote for *The Academy*.[16]

Bosie became increasingly moralistic – although not nearly as moralistic as he would later be. Bosie reflected on this period some forty years later (in *Oscar Wilde: A Summing-Up*), 'Mr Justice Darling (who presided over the Ransome case) invariably foamed at the mouth, literally as well as metaphorically, whenever the subject of homosexuality came up in his court ... I think he did sometimes 'protest too much.' People who talk in that sort of way have only themselves to blame if they are sometimes suspected of trying to establish a moral 'alibi.' One of the things that I most regret in my life is that ... I myself was cowardly enough to take up, in some respects, the same attitude. It was a great mistake ... A man in such a case was practically forced to pretend that the mere mention of homosexuality drove him into paroxysms of horror.'[17]

As his social conservatism was alienating him from his Bohemian friends, his political conservatism was causing a rift with his benefactors. Bosie was no fan of Lloyd George and Winston Churchill who he saw as 'jointly responsible for the ruin of the country and the 'smash up' of almost everything that used to make life in England worth living,' but he saved his greatest rancour for Edward Tennant's cousin Herbert Asquith.[18] As a Christian, Bosie was highly critical of Asquith's suppression of a Catholic procession around Winchester cathedral. Originally the Eucharistic Congress had planned to carry the Host through the streets, but this was not allowed under the terms of the Catholic Emancipation act. Asquith allowed the procession to take place, but without a public display of the Host. This marked the beginning of Bosie's editorialising against him. But his determination to attack the Prime Minister may have come from a more personal source. It was Asquith, who as Home Secretary, had given the swift order to arrest Oscar Wilde.[19]

Whatever Asquith was for, *The Academy* was against. This was awkward for Tennant, and unpolitic of Bosie. As the Liberal MP was paying Bosie a generous salary of £300 per year, and hoping to be nominated for a peerage by Asquith, *The Academy* was editorialising against him in the strongest terms. Those sympathetic to the Wyndham cousins urged Bosie to tone it down, but he dug in his heels. (In his *Autobiography*, Bosie claims to have calmly offered to change his tone, but this would be, to put it mildly, uncharacteristic.) Bosie felt that he was 'constantly being found fault with' and he was 'indignant' when he received what he called 'an extremely offensive letter' from Tennant asking him to withdraw a particularly vituperative article on Asquith.[20] Bosie was sure he was about to be fired from his dream job and he was miserable.

Crosland came to the rescue. He knew Bosie well, and his technique for raising him out of a depression would be characteristic, and unfortunately, destructive. When Bosie was in the heat of a rage, there was nothing to do but to stand back and let it blow over. But after the storm had passed, Oscar Wilde the 'supreme consoler,' had been able to diffuse Bosie's residual anger and smooth conflicts over. Crosland took a different tack. When Bosie was down, Crosland stoked his sense of entitlement and outrage, urged him to see his adversary as an enemy, and to stand up and fight. He became a funhouse mirror, exaggerating all of Bosie's most unattractive traits.

In this case, Crosland bucked Bosie up by pointing out that Tennant, who was new money (his family's fortune came from the invention of a dry bleaching powder), was beneath his station. He persuaded Bosie that 'I was not just the poor dependent on the half-contemptuous whim of the millionaire *nouveau riche* who paid my miserable little salary, but editor of a powerful paper installed in a position from which, if I showed fight, it would be no easy job to oust me.'[21]

Crosland convinced Douglas that he was too soft, and that he should allow Crosland to negotiate on his behalf. In retrospect, Bosie would say that he did not approve of Crosland's 'quite unnecessary' bullying, but he was no doubt cheering him on at the time. The nature of the 'bullying' has not been elaborated, but given subsequent events, Crosland probably threatened to publish embarrassing articles about Tennant if he did not agree to his terms. The family had a whole host of skeletons in its closet, to which Bosie was privy. In the end Tennant decided to wash his hands of the whole thing. He gave the paper to Bosie along with £500 and wished him good riddance.

It was a Pyrrhic victory. It soured his relationship with members of his family who had once been among his most reliable supporters and left him with a property that was, financially speaking, almost worthless. Bosie would have had his hands full with the paper at any rate. The early 20th Century was a period in which literary journals were failing right and left, being replaced by small-scale and usually short-lived papers run on a shoe-string. *The Academy* had been losing money for some time, and now it was Bosie's responsibility to keep it going. He was about to discover that family money is not so quickly forthcoming when you have alienated the family.

Wilfrid Blunt had once been one of Bosie's most reliable champions. He'd known Bosie as a boy, the Wyndhams and Douglases played together as children at his house. He had been uncritical of Bosie's relationship with Wilde. He'd tried to find a bride for Bosie and had hosted a party for the Douglases when society was scandalised by their marriage. The Douglases had spent many enjoyable evenings with the Blunts.

When Bosie telegraphed him asking for money Blunt telegraphed back 'Just leaving for Clouds. You must not count on me in this matter.' The reference to the Wyndham home 'Clouds' made the reasons for his refusal entirely clear.

Bosie's response to the rejection was typical. He lashed out and tried to reassert his own worthiness. Unable, in this case, to rely on superior social class, he attacked his cousin's poetry. 'Did not count on you. I never count on anyone who can't write sonnets.'[22]

As Bosie revelled in his new sense of power, Olive was at home lamenting her 'gloomy and useless life.'[23] She fantasised about the kind of marriage she would prefer.

> they should live alone and have lovers – if they like – and look after their beauty … but they should never marry again … no woman ought to live with a man in the same house after she is twenty-seven … But I fear—at present—but few women would agree with me! It would be so charming if Bosie and I had two houses … and saw each other every day![24] [The ellipses are in the original.]

The last line, about the two houses, was prophetic. Olive would, in the end, have such an arrangement. For now, however, she was trying to play a role that did not suit her. Some of her happiest times were spent not with her husband, but with Freddie Manners-Sutton.

Olive accompanied Sutton on a house-hunting trip. They found a little panelled home in Church Row with a lovely garden. Olive was taken with the balustrade of carved oak and the Queen Anne-style windows. She encouraged Freddie to buy it. 'I wish I could take it,' she wrote in her diary, 'and live in it myself!'[25]

Olive was eventually able to persuade Bosie to buy the house and in February 1910, they moved to 26 Church Street, Hampstead. 'I hope I shall never have to move house again,' Olive wrote in her diary. By the time they settled in, however, her friendship with Sutton had been destroyed.[26]

34

Justify! Justify to the Hilt!

Perjury is often bold and open. It is truth that is shamefaced ...
Justice Charles Darling, *Scintillae juris*[1]

In the early hours of the morning of 6 July 1910, an unknown artist arrived at the Carfax Gallery, sat down in front of a Rembrandt with an easel, examined the details of the theme, the colours and the brush strokes. He began the work of imitation, learning about the artist's technique as he copied the image from one canvas to the other. Within a couple of days he had produced a painting so similar only a highly qualified examiner could tell the difference.

The unnamed artist was not, as we might call him today, a forger. He was a copyist, and in the days of aristocratic decline his services were increasingly needed. The current generation of Viscounts and Earls were in the painful position of having to sell the portrait of grandfather in order to maintain the estate he had built.

Original paintings could fetch high prices in Germany or America. A broke aristocrat did not necessarily care about the artist, he cared about the subject – his ancestor. The sales were arranged by a gallery, and part of the contract was that they would prepare an exact copy to put in its place.[2] Most of these losses were experienced only by the families themselves, but occasionally the symbolic value of a treasure made it a cause célèbre.

One such painting was Hans Holbein's *Christina of Denmark, Duchess of Milan*. It was the property of the Duke of Norfolk and had been on loan to the National Gallery since 1880. Its subject was a 16-year-old Danish widow who Henry VIII thought a good candidate to become his fourth wife. Although neither the painter nor the model was British, its history made it part of the 'British school'. Norfolk made a deal to sell the painting for £72,000. He had offers from Germany and America, but he gave the National Gallery a month to match the price.

The trustees of the gallery, aristocrats all, did not have that kind of cash on hand. The Gallery had recently received a large grant to purchase Franz Hals' *Family Group*. Perhaps they did not like the precedent it might set if they met the duke's price. For whatever reason, they announced they were not in a position to buy the painting. British art lovers were outraged and launched a campaign to 'save the Duchess'. The uproar was such that it inspired Henry James to write a light novel (his last), *The Outcry*, based on the affair.[3]

Ross wrote a letter to the *Morning Post* critical of the trustees. He pointed out that the Holbein was only the most famous example of the many paintings that had been refused after they were offered to the National Gallery for 'comparatively small sums'. He hoped the rejection was 'for lack of funds, not of taste'. He felt it was 'not surprising that collectors, compelled to sell for reasons into which I need not enter, should turn to dealers rather than to Trustees.'[4]

When the Duke of Norfolk decided to sell his painting to the highest bidder, he had no idea what he had unleashed. It was yet another episode that called the aristocracy into question. No longer, it seemed, did they have the wealth, the connections or the discernment to be effective stewards of the nation's cultural treasures.

As the public lost trust in the elite institutions associated with Bosie's class, new institutions were taking their place, and Robbie was central to this process. It had begun in 1903 with the foundation of the National Art Collections Fund, which ran on contributions from private donors, mostly from the educated middle class. Its mission was to buy works of art being jettisoned by the aristocracy, for the benefit of the public. Ross was a member, as were the artists associated with him at the Carfax and at *Burlington Magazine*. A short time later, Ross was instrumental in the formation of the Contemporary Art Society, which would buy the works by living artists, and in establishing the Arundel Club, which promoted the photographing of famous works to allow members of the general public to see them.

Andra Poole in *Stewards of the Nation's Art* has argued that Lloyd George was able to channel the high-profile controversy over the fate of the Duchess of Milan into a broader anti-aristocratic political message. In the end, donations from the public and one anonymous donor who gave £40,000, allowed England to keep the historic work of art. The people had done what the aristocrats could not.

In the wake of the Duchess of Milan dust-up, the laws regarding estate tax were revised to try to prevent important works being sold overseas. The new law required that works of cultural importance would not be subject to death duties unless they were subsequently sold. This required a valuation of the art left behind when a wealthy owner died. The job of Adviser to the Inland Revenue on picture valuation would need to have a unique skill set. He had to be an expert in art and its market value and to have the emotional grounding to deal with grieving families about financial matters at a sensitive time. Robbie was the ideal candidate. His warm, caring manner and genuine desire to be of service endeared him to many philanthropic widows. In the years that followed, Robbie relished the opportunity to match these wealthy patrons with deserving, underfunded artists. At the same time he was able to advise the National Gallery on works he believed they should acquire and advance his goal of keeping British art at home and making it available to the public.

Meanwhile, over at *The Academy,* the editors were not yet done biting the hands that fed them. In the summer of 1909, Crosland wrote a series of articles criticising W. H. Smith and Son's 'monopoly' in the news business. This was unwise as Smith's printed and distributed the paper. If Crosland had believed taking a hard line with the company would get him favourable rates he was sadly mistaken. In July, Smith's stopped acting as *The Academy's* distributor and refused to sell the paper in its stalls.

Crosland remained optimistic believing that a 'lord' with ties to rich and powerful families could always find 'stacks of boodle'. 'In about another couple of years this paper will be making at least £10,000 a year,' he said. 'You will hear people in the streets whispering: "Who is that fair youth?"And the reply will be: "That is the wealthy Lord Alfred Douglas, who owns *The Academy*." Then they will ask: "And who is that dazzling object by his side?" "That's Crosland," will be the reply.' The idea of Crosland as a 'dazzling object' elicited peals of laughter from Bosie, disrupted his malaise, and encouraged him to press on.[5]

The sense of 'you and me against the world' had always bonded Bosie to someone. It had bonded him to Oscar, when they battled his father, and it had bonded him to Olive, when they married against her family's wishes. Now the struggle of keeping *The Academy* bonded him to Crosland.

Personally, Bosie was kept afloat mostly through family money. From 1910 until his bankruptcy in 1913, his mother was providing him with an allowance of £500 per year.[6] His son Raymond's boarding school fees had been paid by Colonel Custance since the boy was old enough to go to school. In exchange, they agreed to let Raymond spend part of his holidays with his grandfather.[7]

Bosie tried to augment these income sources with gambling proceeds, but the results were predictable. The financial situation at *The Academy* was becoming dire, and they were having trouble paying their writers. (One contributor, Horace Wyndham claimed not to mind 'as the weekly privilege of reading Douglas's sonnets and Crosland's pungent paragraphs was quite a good return for the columns I laboriously filled with my jejune opinions.'[8])

Bosie had a friend he could call – Freddie Manners-Sutton, now a partner in the publishing firm Cope and Fenwick. Some time before, Sutton had said if *The Academy* was ever short of funds, he could find some investors to back it. Bosie took this as a promise. He could have raised the question with his son's godfather over a friendly dinner. Instead, he decided to send Crosland. By now, Bosie was well aware of Crosland's bullying tactics. Clearly something had changed in Sutton's attitude towards Bosie or *The Academy* since he first made his generous offer, and Bosie must have been aware of that. (An angry letter written by Bosie a short time later alludes to some quarrels. 'I believed, for the hundredth time, that I had misjudged you ...')[9]

Crosland sent Sutton a telegram saying he had to see him right away 'on urgent business'. Sutton would later tell Olive that he imagined Crosland was going to ask for a loan, but the urgency worried him. He was afraid that Bosie might have been involved in something serious and so he dropped everything to meet Crosland on short notice.[10]

Crosland asked Sutton for £500 in exchange for 500 debentures in *The Academy's* publishing company. Sutton refused. Crosland then suggested they settle on £150 for 150 debentures. Although Crosland's aggressive stance did not sit well with him, Sutton was a publishing man and considered it as a serious business proposal. He said he might consider backing the paper if they got their finances in better order. Specifically, he thought Bosie's salary of £15 per week as editor was excessive.

When this was relayed to Bosie, all he heard was that his friend believed he was not worth his pay. This triggered an explosion. On 10 June he wrote a furious letter complaining of Sutton's 'gross impudence and brutal insolence'. The letter concluded 'Consequently I beg to inform you that neither I nor Olive will ever speak to you again and that I forbid you to come to this house. Furthermore I will tell you quite plainly that I consider you to be a dirty, low, huckstering, Jew-minded pimp.'[11]

From this point on, Crosland and Douglas's motivations diverged. Crosland wanted the money, Douglas wanted revenge. In order to satisfy both of their needs, they went after Sutton. They played to win, and they did not play fair. On 12 June, two days after Bosie's violent letter, *The Academy* printed an unsigned blurb, written by Crosland, criticising an anonymous man who was at the same time the owner of a publishing firm that dealt in books with high-minded religious themes and a shareholder in a pornographic publishing house. While it had named no names, the article concluded with a barely veiled threat. 'We have a proper number of striking facts at our disposal with reference to this matter, but we will forbear for the time being.'[12]

The following week, *The Academy* published an even more detailed article on the subject, also unsigned, but written by Douglas. This article said it would withhold the names of the publishing firms in question for the time being but 'we shall revert to this matter on a future occasion, and, as it is one of obvious public importance and highly interesting from the point of view of letters, we shall leave nothing unsaid.'[13]

Sutton was not amused and he had his secretary write to *The Academy* demanding that a notice be placed in the paper stating that he was not the subject of the blurb. He received a menacing reply from Crosland:

> We do not propose to oblige you by stating that Mr Manners-Sutton is not the gentleman referred to Rather, at our own time and when we have completed our investigations, we shall be disposed to say that he is the gentleman. With regard to the action you threaten, we have only to remark that in our view Mr Manners-Sutton is a person whom it would be difficult for reasonable people to libel. At that same time, if he wishes to make a fool of himself we shall be quite pleased to receive the writ.[14]

Crosland received no reply, and on 8 July he followed with a more menacing letter:

> ... The writ has not arrived: consequently I must conclude that the solicitors' letter was a piece of bluff and that you yourself are a coward and a poltroon, besides being a person of no principle. I sought you in Paris the other week and found that you were at none of your numerous addresses. I shall be obliged if you will give me an address in France where I can see you.[15]

After this second letter Sutton decided to try another tack. He took Olive to lunch at the Bachelor's Club in the hopes that she might be persuaded to reason with her husband. The result was yet another 'violently abusive' letter from Bosie. 'If you succeed in getting rid of Crosland I shall still be there, and I will make it hotter than ever for you,' he told Sutton.[16] Sutton was convinced that Bosie was not in his right mind.

'I certainly believe 'Bosie' to be a little eccentric,' Sutton wrote to Olive in a last attempt to explain his point of view, 'but there are limits to human endurance, and although I am free from all feelings of malice, some curb must be placed upon his actions and also upon those of his remarkable lieutenant. You cannot possibly imagine that I obtain any pleasure or satisfaction in carrying on an expensive and unsatisfactory lawsuit with a bankrupt journalist. The whole affair is, I assure you extremely distasteful to me ... I am sorry to hear you are worried, and sorry that it should be necessary for you to consider me an unscrupulous and heartless villain and that, perhaps, because I am nothing of the sort.'[17]

On 21 July 1909 Bosie wrote to Olive, 'That little beast Freddie has summoned Crosland for libel and the case comes on today … There is nothing in it and Freddie has not a leg to stand on. Newton says that he thinks he can get the case dismissed right off.'[18]

The very presence of Arthur Newton should have given Sutton pause, as the man had been a party to his settlements involving Beaudemont, Baron von Koenig and the incidents at Schwabe's flat. At this point, however, the belligerent stances of both parties were a bluff. Neither wanted a trial. Crosland was still hoping that by not standing down he could get a big settlement. He knew at least some of his target's secrets, either because Bosie had told him, or as he would claim in court, because Sutton had shared them with Crosland himself. Sutton was counting on the fact that the bankrupt Crosland wanted a quick payout, and could not afford to go to trial.

Crosland, through Newton, tried to negotiate a settlement of £250 for Sutton to avoid an embarrassing plea of justification. Sutton stood his ground. He would not be blackmailed. They went before the magistrate, Sir Albert de Reutzen. He suggested that Sutton drop the charges if Crosland would agree to issue an apology. This would, indeed, have been the best for all involved. George Elliott, appearing for the prosecution, agreed to the terms and it seemed as though the matter was going to be settled. Unfortunately, Bosie, suffering a manic episode, was not inclined towards reasonableness. He shouted across the court room, 'Justify, justify up to the hilt!' Then turning to his old friend he said, 'Take him to the Old Bailey!'

After that outburst any chance of settlement was gone. Crosland was committed for trial at the Central Criminal Court. Bosie, on the way out the door, called the prosecutor's agent a 'swine appearing for swine' and threatened him with his walking stick. (He would later deny this in court. Marshall Hall asked him, 'Had you a stick?' 'Of course, I had a stick,' he said. Then referring to Hall's judicial robe and wig, 'You have a stick, I suppose, when you are not dressed up like that.')[19]

When he got home, Bosie fired off another letter to his former friend saying that he regretted he was 'still full of malice'. Sutton tried once more to reason with the unreasonable, 'You must know that I am not actuated by any malice or real vindictive feeling towards you, and I can only tell you that the whole business is very painful to me, and I should be glad if it can be ended, as you suggested, in an honourable manner.'

On the stand, Sutton was asked if he thought Douglas's 'Jew-minded-pimp' was not more offensive than Crosland's 'coward and poltroon'. He replied that Bosie's letter 'was so obviously written in temper that one could afford to take no notice of it. The second was more serious; it was written with more determination and deliberation.'[20]

In his *Autobiography,* Bosie would describe the Sutton case as a 'quarrel into which I was reluctantly forced' by Crosland. He said the whole thing came down to a 'fit of rage and temper' on Crosland's part. Crosland was always annoyed by 'Freddie's feline sarcasms and banter' and 'he was also very jealous of him with me.'[21]

On 15 October, Crosland entered his plea of justification. His legal team also filed affidavits claiming that a material witness for the defence was in America. Because of this, the case was adjourned to 9 February 1910. This latter filing was a combination stalling tactic and threat. The material witness was a prostitute. If the prosecution believed the girl could be found and would testify, they might be inclined to settle (with a payment) to avoid the spectacle.

Mr Marshall Hall, representing Sutton, said 'a more disgraceful document [than the plea of justification] never came from the hand of any member of the legal profession.' It detailed the events at the Buckingham Gate flat, the blackmail by Beaudemont, Sutton's 'rental property' and the events in Monte Carlo.[22]

Crosland was in the hospital recovering from a heart attack. *The Academy* continued its attacks on Sutton. It published an article alleging that a material witness was being hidden by Arthur Newton. The headline 'Where's Maggie Dupot' was printed in large type on posters to advertise the edition.

On 8 February 1910 the case against Crosland for maliciously publishing a defamatory libel concerning Henry Frederick Walpole Manners-Sutton opened. The court room at the Old Bailey was filled to capacity for the scandalous case between a peer's son and a famous author. The public was about to be treated to the entertaining spectacle of three men who had enjoyed illict sex, each indignantly proclaiming his virtue.

The prosecution opened by having Sutton recount the events at the Buckingham Gate flat. Sutton testified that this was the only time in his life that he had ever done such a foolish thing, that he had been influenced by the older Douglas, and that anyway, nothing improper had happened. The phrase 'certainly not' formed the basis of much of his testimony. He denied being an atheist and defended his publishing enterprises by pointing out that the publisher Crosland was calling a pornographer had actually put out books by both Douglas and Crosland.

On the second day, Mr Valetta cross-examined Sutton on behalf of the defence. He asked about the Buckingham Gate Flat incident and then in a flashback to the Wilde trial, Sutton was asked to read a passage from a book and comment on whether or not it was indecent. 'I do not think it indecent,' he said, 'but it is unintelligible.' He added that he had nothing to do with its publication.

In his cross-examination Marshall Hall emphasised that Douglas was seven or eight years older than the witness, and that at the time of the incident Sutton was only 25 years old. Taking off his pince nez style reading glasses, he said, 'I don't want to mention the name in open court, but I want to hand you a piece of paper and ask you to write down at whose house Lord Alfred Douglas introduced you to this man Beaudemont, so that his lordship and the jury may know it.' As in Wilde's libel trial years before, the name 'Maurice Salis-Schwabe' was written on a piece of paper and handed to the judge. Sutton ended his testimony by declaring that he had 'strong religious views' and 'a good character'.

After Sutton's testimony, the case took an unusual turn when Newton, who had represented Crosland in his preliminary hearing, appeared under subpoena to testify for the prosecution (Sutton). He testified that he had never met Crosland before the trial and that before he agreed to represent him, he had asked Sutton if he had any objections given their previous relationship. He testified that he had stopped working for Crosland – he did not explain why. After he had stopped officially acting as Crosland's solicitor, he heard from Mr Fynes-Clinton, Crosland's new solicitor. Fynes-Clinton had a hard time handling Crosland who was 'a very excitable person and wanted everything his own way'.

Both solicitors felt that it would be best if the matter was settled with an apology, but Crosland would not do so unless he was paid to cover his court costs. Newton visited Sutton to see if he would agree to the payment. After Sutton refused, *The Academy* published the attack on Newton saying he had gotten a witness away.

He admitted that he 'might have said in a casual manner to Mr Fynes-Clinton … that as the incident happened five years ago with a common woman' the chances of finding her were low, and that this may have been misconstrued and relayed back to Crosland. He said because there was no truth in it, he ignored the whole thing.

There are a number of curious things about this testimony. The first is that Douglas would have accused his own solicitor of colluding with Sutton in the first place. If Bosie believed this to be the case, you would expect Newton to feature prominently in his enemies list. He should have immortalised him with a poem that makes use of the metrical possibilities in the word 'Iscariot'. He did not. In fact, Bosie remained Newton's friend until his death, praised him in print and even sent a wreath for his funeral.[24] On the other side, Newton was strangely unperturbed that *The Academy* had publicly accused him of hiding a witness. Newton had experience with the charge. He had first made a name for himself by representing Lord Arthur Somerset in the Cleveland Street Scandal. Somerset was tutor to Prince Albert Victor, Heir Presumptive to the British Throne. Newton had stirred things up by suggesting that if his client were prosecuted the name of 'a very distinguished person' would be associated with the male prostitution ring at the center of the case.

After the trial, Newton was charged with 'conspiracy to defeat the course of justice' by helping his client and some of the witnesses flee the country to avoid prosecution. He pled guilty and was sentenced to six months in jail, although he did not lose his license to practice law. *The Academy* had accused him of committing the very crime that had sent him to jail. If he believed he had been libelled by Douglas, you might expect him to drop him as a client. He did not. He continued to do work for him (and his brother Sholto) long after his licence to practice law was suspended.

The initial libels published against Sutton in *The Academy* had been mild. The accusations about his publishing enterprises were not the type of thing that would put fear in a man's heart. They were the kind of barbed attacks *The Academy* often threw at their 'enemies' and which usually resulted in nothing more than a series of extremely literate complaint letters from angry poets. It was only Bosie's insistence on a blood feud that drove it further and forced a legal confrontation.

After the initial negotiations broke down with Bosie's 'Justify!' outburst, Crosland and Douglas needed something stronger to induce Sutton to surrender. Even Bosie admitted the 'plea of justification was very thin …'

Only two years before, Newton and Schwabe had conspired with the controversial racing man and publisher Robert Standish Sievier to extract money from a man Sievier routinely libelled in his paper *The Winning Post*. (Schwabe's involvement in the celebrated trial was revealed in newspaper accounts. Newton's name had been hidden from the public, he was identified only as 'solicitor x', but it is revealed in the case files.) In that case, Newton and Schwabe had approached Sievier's adversary J. B. Joel with a plan to 'lay a trap' for Sievier. While Joel believed they were working for him, they were actually working for Sievier. In *The Academy* libel case, Newton (and perhaps Schwabe) had found a new libel battle to exploit. Newton had few scruples about feeding false information to the press. He was about to be disbarred for doing just that. The Maggie Dupont story may not have been an attack *on* Newton, but an attack *devised by* Newton to put pressure on Sutton.[23]

In Valetta's opening statement on behalf of Crosland, he argued that his client was being made a scapegoat and that it was really a personal quarrel between

Sutton and Douglas. As the prosecution had argued that Douglas as an 'intimate friend' had used information 'which bonds of secrecy ought to have preseved', Valetta would seek to establish that Crosland had learned about the events in question from Sutton himself. He also announced that he would put Douglas on the stand to testify that Sutton had 'boasted to him of his degenerate ways.'

Crosland swore that Sutton had told him he had decided to spend most of his time in France after the Dupont affair because the French took a different view of such things. He recounted his version of the events in Monte Carlo. He also wrote down a filthy expression that he swore Sutton had uttered. He claimed his own delicate ears had never before heard the term. 'It is the most terrible filth, and I should leave it alone,' he said. It must have been quite a novel turn-of-phrase. Frank Harris once told a colleague that Crosland used the vilest language of anyone he had ever met.

Counsel was also sceptical that he had lived so many years without hearing such language. 'How old are you, Mr Crosland?'

'Forty. I may be forty-one. I don't know.'

Crosland swore that Rowland Strong had been present and that he could corroborate the story if he was called. Then, implying that the prosecution had hidden him, he added that he didn't know where Strong was, but Mr Manners-Sutton probably did. He cannot have looked very hard for Strong. He would have been quite easy to find as he was a regular contributor to *The Academy*.

Crosland claimed he had learned about the Dupont affair when Sutton sought his advice about Newton. According to Crosland, Sutton told him, 'I have reason to believe I have been severely had by Arthur Newton.' He said he didn't think that a simple working man would have demanded a sum like £1,000 and that it didn't seem as though Newton could be 'bluffed by a man who was merely working as a cabinet-maker or something of that sort'. He thought the solicitor must have pocketed most of the money.

About Maggie Dupont, Crosland expressed dramatic outrage. 'You do know where she is,' he shouted at the prosecuting attorney. 'Mr Manners-Sutton knows. He has got her safely tucked away, and he gives you a big fee to come here and make me out a liar.'

'Compose yourself,' said the Common Sarjeant, Sir John Bosanquet (whose nickname as it happened was 'Old Bosie.')

'It isn't a question of composing one's self, it is intolerable.'

'You won't do any good by tirades against the opposite party.'

'You say *The Academy* is used for literary purposes?' asked Marshall Hall.

'Literary and political.'

'*The Academy* is never used to fight its private battles?'

'Certainly, it is occasionally.'

'Are you responsible for what appears in *The Academy* or is Lord Alfred Douglas?'

'He is the master, and I am the man.'

'Who rules?'

'When you see Lord Alfred Douglas, you will see who rules.'

Crosland praised his business partner. He said he considered Douglas to be 'an honourable gentleman, a genius and a great man'.

With that, Crosland's testimony was concluded and Douglas took the stand. After a number of questions related to Maurice Schwabe (who Douglas mentioned by name) and Baron von Koenig, Crosland's attorney Mr Wing attempted diffuse what he knew was coming by mentioning Oscar Wilde first. 'You were a friend, a great while ago, of the late Oscar Wilde, were you not?'

'Yes, but may I say ...'

Valetta interrupted to caution Douglas, 'Not yet.' They had prepped the witness, and they knew how effective he could be on the subject of Wilde. They wanted to leave it to the plaintiff's counsel to try to attack him on the question.

'Was there ever anything that you have to regret or be ashamed of in your relations with the late Oscar Wilde?' asked Wing.

'No, none whatsoever.'

'Did you ever tell Mr Manners-Sutton that there had been?'

'Never.'

It was now Hall's turn to cross-examine and he made a serious tactical error. In an effort to show that Douglas was not a paragon of virtue, he took the bait and brought up the Wilde case. Crosland would later refer to this as the 'Buzfuz method'.[24] He was the first counsellor to attempt this tactic, but he would certainly not be the last.

'You declined to give up your friendship with Oscar Wilde, to which your father objected?' Hall asked.

'Yes, I did. I was young, and perhaps foolish then, and no one but a brute would drag it up now.'

'Of course at the time you knew nothing of Wilde's character?' asked counsel.

'I believed him innocent,' Douglas said emphatically.

'After Mr Wilde had been convicted, and came out of prison, did you join him at the Royal Hotel, Naples?'

Bosie would be especially proud of his answer to this question, and would write about it years later as the cornerstone of his 'Systeme Douglas'. He stood up straight and spoke in a loud voice, 'I did not join him, but I continued being friendly to him at the time that he died.'

'Did you go and live at the same hotel with him?'

'No, but I will admit a great deal more than that,' he said. 'I had a villa at Naples, and he came and stayed with me there. I am not a bit ashamed. When he came out of prison, he came out a broken and dying man saying I was the only friend he had. "If you leave me," he said, "I shall go to hell headlong." These were his exact words. He declared I was the only decent friend he had left.' When he died I paid for the funeral expense, and am not ashamed of it.'

'And you still believe in his innocence?' asked counsel.

Bosie now changed his response. 'No, I did not. But I didn't care. He had been a friend for years. I loved and admired him. My life was made a hell on earth because I did. I was abused and assaulted on every side by every kind of brute. I say a man who calls himself my wife's friend, and who has hired you to come and drag up the filth of 18 years ago is a brute.'[25]

The last part of his answer must have been shouted, for the Common Serjeant interrupted, 'Answer the questions please, quietly.'

'It is impossible for me not to feel emotional,' Douglas said. 'He is speaking about my dead father and my dead friend.'

Bosie was on less sure footing when Marshal Hall brought Schwabe into the conversation, 'Your friend, whose name is not to be mentioned in this case, was also acquainted with this unfortunate case, which occurred years ago,' Hall said.

Bosie claimed not to know that and then quickly changed the subject, 'I contend this has nothing to do with this case,' he said. 'He is trying to throw dirt at me.'

Valetta was strong in his closing argument. He said it was in the public interest that Sutton be 'prevented from disseminating foul and filthy literature, prevented from using his money for the purposes of buying defenceless children to gratify his beastly passions, prevented from associating his name with the name of the great pillars of the church, such as the Archbishop of Canterbury. Hall's closing was much weaker. He downplayed the fact that his client had paid £1,200 to paper over a scandal, and focused instead on Douglas's credibility. He mentioned that the solicitor who was instructing him had represented Queensberry in Wilde's libel suit and hinted that he knew things about Douglas that he could not mention.

The judge, however, sealed everything up in a bow for Crosland when he asked the jury to consider whether someone would really pay more than £1,000 to avert a scandal if he had only done what Sutton claimed. It took the jury two hours and ten minutes to return with a verdict of 'not guilty'.

Rowland Strong (the friend who could supposedly have confirmed that the Hon. Henry Frederick Walpole Manners-Sutton was foul-mouthed if he could only have been found) seems to have been following the case quite closely as well. His friend F. C. Philip, an author best known for the novel *As in a Looking-Glass*, was also a barrister. He attended the trial, sitting in the area reserved for members of the bar, and reported back to Strong after Bosie's cross-examination. 'My dear boy,' he told Strong, 'Douglas simply ate him, he *ate* him; there's no other word for it. I never saw anything like it in a law court before.'[26]

Later that year, Bosie gave Strong a valuable gift, an autographed presentation copy of *A Woman of No Importance* which had been signed 'Bosie from his friend, the author, Oscar Wilde, Nov. '94.' Bosie inscribed it underneath Wilde's signature, 'Given to Rowland Strong by Alfred Douglas, October 28th, 1910.'[27]

There was, incidentally, a curious sequel. After the verdict, the newspaper John Bull published a critical commentary on the case. It pointed out that all of the spectacular evidence of justification had not figured into the jury's deliberation. They had simply found that, because the articles in *The Academy* had not named names, and the most libellous text had been sent in a private letter not published, Sutton was not entitled to compensation. In the same edition there was an open letter to Crosland, signed John Bull, which began 'Notorious Confrere'. On the circumstances of Crosland's 'amazing acquittal,' John Bull wrote, '… I contented myself with pointing out that the jury probably attached very little importance to a libel coming from you – although I might have adopted the other alternative, that they were mad.'[28]

Crosland sued John Bull's publisher Horatio Bottomley, whose vulgarity and litigiousness outshone Crosland's own. The case was tried before Justice Charles Darling, who was to figure prominently in Crosland and Douglas's legal dramas to come. Known in some quarters as 'Little Darling,' he was a Tory MP who had beaten out Wilfred Blunt the liberal candidate for Deptford in 1885. He was one of the most celebrated judges in the country and one of the most flamboyant. A dandy who hid the most impeccable tailoring under his judicial robe, his manner was a showcase of erudition and breeding. F. E. Smith described his appearance as 'a very delicately fashioned cameo'.[29] One of his treasured possessions was a hawthorn walking stick with an inscribed silver band which read 'C. D. From E. C. 1894.' It was a gift from one of Darling's closest friends in the profession, Edward Carson, 'Old Ned,' from the Queensberry libel case. (Another of Darling's closest associates was Frank Lockwood.) Darling was not a great fan of Wilde's writing or his wit, but he did know quite a bit about his libel case because he was in chambers with Carson at the time of the trial.

Crosland was represented by Douglas's old friend Cecil Hayes, who was new to the bar and somewhat hampered in his efforts by the fact that his client didn't bother to show up to court. F. E. Smith, who would soon be acting against Douglas in the Ransome case, represented John Bull.

When Bottomley was asked if his open letter to Crosland had been in the public's interest, Bottomley replied, 'I think it will have the effect of doing good in helping to rid the journalistic world of one of the greatest vampires who ever existed.' The jury found for Crosland, but awarded him only three farthings damages.[30]

In spite of this, Bosie continued to believe that his talent on the stand had won the day. It would be some time before he would come to regret having attacked his good friend. They would be reconciled eventually, just two years before Sutton's death in 1918, thanks to Olive's efforts. Even so, Bosie's main takeaway from the case was the 'useful discovery that I was an exceptionally good witness.'[31]

Not everyone took such a rosy view of his performance. There were, of course, no recording devices in the court room. Reporters took handwritten notes with various levels of speed and attention, printing only what they thought the most newsworthy or interesting. The next day some newspapers, opting for consistency, reported only that Douglas had said he believed Wilde was innocent. Only a few reported that he had first said he thought him innocent and then changed his story and said he knew he was not and didn't care. Some reported that he had said he loved and admired Wilde. Many papers thought it more tactful to leave that part out reporting only that he 'admired' Wilde or going straight from 'I was his friend' to 'My life was made a Hell on Earth.' Based on his reactions to the testimony, Robbie, who was not in the courtroom, read an account that did not include Bosie's declaration that he knew Wilde was not innocent and didn't care, and probably did not include his expression of love and admiration either.

Still smarting from Bosie's snub at his celebratory dinner, Robbie was incensed when he heard Bosie declare that he was the only friend who had helped Wilde in his time of need. (In fairness to Bosie, we know Wilde wrote to him that he could only do beautiful work in his presence so it is entirely possible that Wilde did say what Bosie stated on the stand, or something very similar to it.) Ross immediately contacted Hall and offered to testify on behalf of the prosecution. As the prosecution had already closed its case, however, it was too late.[32] He was probably prepared to give the same information that was to surface a few years later in the Ransome trial, namely, *De Profundis*. A few days later he had dinner with Walter Ledger. He was still furious and asked him not to bring up the trial, 'I am not sane on the subject.'[33]

When Bosie heard that Robbie had contacted the prosecution he was furious. He wrote to Adey complaining that Ross's offer to the prosecution was 'an almost incredible act of villainy'. Adey would not be drawn into the quarrel. As he was no longer communicating directly with Ross, Bosie vented his spleen by writing nasty letters to a number of his friends saying that he had heard Ross was about to be arrested for sodomy.[34]

Those who had been attracted to Bosie for his youthful idealism and his sexual boldness no longer related to him, and as their feelings about him changed, in many cases so did their memories. The further Bosie moved from the homosexual community, the more they were inclined to blame him for Wilde's downfall. The narrative was slowly becoming conventional wisdom in the old Wilde circle. George Ives, who had slept with Bosie, went back and edited his diary writing 'Traitor!' on the Douglas entries. Andre Gide, who had contemporaneously written that Bosie had been 'depraved down to his bone marrow' by Wilde, had by 1903 come to believe that Bosie was responsible for Wilde's downfall. This new point of view was reflected in his *Pretextes* which had recently been published. (By the time Gide published his memoir *Si le grain ne meurt* in 1926 Bosie had been completely transformed from the corrupted to the corruptor. Victoria Reid, author of *Andre Gide and Curiosity* suggests that this about-face was because by the early 1920s Gide was 'no longer the young initiate, but the initiator of others and it suited him to view the younger man as corruptor.'[35] Bosie would be deeply hurt by the picture Gide painted of him in *Si le grain*.)

Robbie was now determined that the world should know the truth about Douglas. He wrote to Gide in March 1910. After complimenting him on his new book, he said he might publish Oscar Wilde's letters to him, which would confirm Gide's picture and put an end to Bosie's lies.

> ... You no doubt heard reported in a recent libel action that he swore in the witness-box that he was unaware of Oscar Wilde's guilt, and that he was the 'only decent friend who remained with Oscar Wilde'. You know perfectly well that Alfred Douglas was the cause of Oscar Wilde's ruin both before and after the imprisonment. I would like to have pretended this was not the case, out of old friendship and regard for Douglas: and the fact that I quarrelled with him personally would not have affected my determination to let the world think he was really the noble friend he always posed as being. But since he has taken on himself, in his new character of social and moral reformer, to talk about Oscar Wilde's sins (in most of which he participated) and has betrayed all of his old friends, there is no longer any reason for me to be silent.[36]

Bosie had betrayed Oscar Wilde. He had not abandoned him in Naples or when Wilde was in prison, as Robbie knew quite well, but these were mere historical details. What mattered is that Wilde had been betrayed. Robbie was determined that the world should know.

35

The Quality of His Admirers

While Sutton had been careful not to mention Schwabe by name in his court proceeding, Douglas had not. The appearance of his name in the newspapers connected with Baron von Koenig could not have come at a worse time. For in 1910, Stallmann was arrested and one after another his criminal associates across Europe were being hauled in by police. The noose was starting to tighten. In 1911, Schwabe changed his name to Maurice M. Shaw by deed poll.[1]

The newly-christened Shaw went into business with Gerald Hamilton, soon to be famous as the prototype of the charismatic conman in Christopher Isherwood's *Mr Norris Changes Trains*. He was born Gerald Frank Hamilton Souter on 1 November 1890 in Shanghai, the son of Frank Thomas Edward Souter, a merchant engaged in trade between China and Britain. Hamilton was a homosexual who was bullied at school and ended his academic career in disgrace. He was shipped off to China in 1908. The voyage was no more successful in curing Hamilton's bad habits than Australian exile had been with Schwabe's. In China, Hamilton adopted native dress, 'fraternised with houseboys' and blew his inheritance. His father disinherited him, at which point Hamilton dropped the name Souter.[2]

Even so, Hamilton continued to have access to family money thanks to his solicitor, Arthur Newton's son, Reginald.[3] Hamilton was such a fabulist that it is difficult to believe anything that he says about himself. It seems likely, however, that he met Schwabe in 1911. This is based on the circumstantial evidence that Hamilton said he met two of Schwabe's friends that year: Lord Alfred Douglas and Baron Von Koenig.

Hamilton was one of the few people who was on friendly terms with both Douglas and Ross in this era. He used to go on Sundays to a gathering of the old Wilde circle at a restaurant called Trevigilo. Hamilton wrote: 'I, of course, never knew Wilde, but every Sunday when we met, old More Adey, who had been a great friend of Wilde, acted as host. Amongst those who came was Millard, who on two or three occasions brought Robbie Ross to the party. I met the latter several times, but never knew him very well. Bosie Douglas was of course absent from these gatherings, for, although I knew him well, this was at the time there were lawsuits between him and Robbie Ross.'[4]

As Hamilton became Schwabe's business partner, it is reasonable to assume that Schwabe was also one of the 'friends of Oscar Wilde' who occasionally frequented the Italian eatery on Church Street. Millard on at least one occasion brought a young man named Charles Garratt along. Another young man who sometimes attended was Aylmer Gustavus Clerk, a solicitor, who may have sometimes come with an actor named Frank 'Fluffy' Hughes, who seems to have been his romantic partner. These names will become significant.[5]

Meanwhile Bosie was in the middle of a conflict with his father-in-law. He was sending increasingly libellous letters to Custance and his friends and associates trying to goad Custance into suing him for libel. Custance had no desire to embroil himself in a scandal, and was reluctant to respond. He started to give Bosie's numerous letters, unopened, to his solicitor, who happened to be George Lewis. (The George Lewis who acted in the Dansey matter and fixed the 'Oxford mishap' had retired in 1909. This was his son.) By early 1911, Bosie resorted to his old trick of sending his insults in telegrams and post-cards. The exhausted, harried Olive was stuck in the middle. One can only imagine the toxic environment of the Douglas house in early 1911. Bosie turned more and more to religion for solace.

In early 1911, Ross and Smith moved to 3 John Street in Berkeley Square where they spent the next six months. Their live-in staff consisted of a cook, a parlour maid and an Italian valet. They also maintained the Vicarage Gardens property. The Douglases were similarly staffed with a cook, a lady's maid, a parlour maid and a female 'servant', though Lord Alfred had to make do without a valet. He was perhaps feeling insecure in his role when he filled out the 1911 census form – he put quotation marks around his role as 'head' of the family. In June, Ross and Smith moved again to 13 Little Grosvenor Street in Mayfair. Reggie Turner, who had also been Robbie's neighbour at Sheffield Gardens, had an apartment there although his primary residence was in Paris. A year later, in the lead-up to the Ransome trial, Max Beerbohm would write to Reggie, 'It is a pity that the old botherationist Bobbie took those rooms underneath you, thereby leading you such a life of botheration.'[6]

In March 1911, Ford Madox Hueffer published a memoir, *Ancient Lights and Certain New Reflections*, which mentioned Wilde critically. What bothered Robbie about the book was not the depiction of Wilde as pathetic and broken, nor even the fact that Hueffer did not appreciate Wilde as an artist. It was where he placed the blame for Wilde's downfall: on the 'quality of his admirers, who demanded always more and more follies; when they had pushed him to his fall, they very shamefully deserted this notable man.'

This criticism hit close to home. Robbie once told Millard that the reason he was so driven to restore Wilde's literary reputation was because he felt responsible for what had happened.[7] Being blamed by the world at large was more than he could bear. He published a 'contemptuous review' in the *Morning Post*.[8]

Robbie had a document that could shift the blame from 'admirers' to a single 'admirer': Bosie, and Bosie alone, ruined Oscar Wilde. Robbie needed to make this known. At just this moment, Arthur Ransome came to him proposing to write a book about Wilde.

Ransome had just finished the first in what he hoped would be a series of critical literary studies for the publisher Martin Secker. The first had been on Poe. The books were to include a short biographical summary followed by a study of the writer's objectives, style and technique. Ransome had wanted to follow up with a book on Robert Louis Stevenson, but the sales on Poe had been disappointing, and Secker thought Wilde would be a more marketable subject.[9]

Ross was more receptive and helpful to Ransome than he could ever have imagined. Ransome found him 'delightful ... extremely amusing, alert, witty and selflessly devoted not only to Wilde but to any artist whose work he liked.'[10]

In a statement for the courts a few years later, Ross would insist that he had not let Ransome see the typescript of *De Profundis*.[11] Ransome told a different story.

Ross introduced Ransome to Wilde's sons, Ada Leverson, Millard, and Sherard. (Ransome found Sherard 'revolting'.) He also introduced him to Walter Ledger, but discouraged him from becoming too friendly with him saying he 'suffered from homicidal mania and was accustomed to have himself shut up.' Ransome later regretted heeding this advice. He got to know Ledger when he joined the Royal Cruising Club where the Wilde collector was also a member. He found Ross had exaggerated his 'quite harmless' eccentricities which 'brought a strange breath of salty air into the somewhat greenhouse atmosphere of the literary Nineties'.[12]

One person Ross did not introduce Ransome to was Douglas. It is curious that Ransome did not seek him out. Ransome never explained why he had not talked to Douglas before publication. The most likely explanation is that Ross steered him away from it, as he had discouraged the author from getting to close to Ledger.

Meanwhile, Harris had started writing his Wilde biography. Harris was, in many ways, an ideal biographer, a true friend of his subject, he knew and admired him without being blind to his faults. Unlike Douglas and Sherard, he'd played no role in encouraging Wilde's vices and therefore did not have to overcome any feelings of guilt. What is more, he could tell a story. Because he was also a well-known womaniser, he had no fear that he would be painted as a 'deviant of the Oscar Wilde sort' and could thus speak freely. This last point, however, would also be one of his shortcomings. He knew nothing of the homosexual side of Wilde's life. For that he relied on the assistance of Ross. Harris had begun his project at just the right moment, Robbie's bitterness over what he had seen in the Sutton case was raw and he was determined to let the world know about Douglas's role in Wilde's downfall. He showed Harris *De Profundis*, and Wilde's letters. These only confirmed Harris's negative opinion of Bosie who had only recently been engaged in seemingly unprovoked attacks against him in *The Academy*. Harris had Ross correct the manuscript of his Wilde. He found only a few minor factual errors but 'he seemed to have modified Harris's views of Douglas from beginning to end.'[13]

That September Robbie and Freddie Smith travelled to Hove near Brighton to spend some time at the home of Helen Carew's wealthy, widowed mother, Helen Wyllie. It had been just over two years since Coleridge Kennard's affair with Buckley had begun and Robbie had come to Carew's aid. The house in Hove was only one of the family properties. It had twenty-four rooms and was staffed by a team of servants that included a butler, cook, housekeeper and two footmen. This visit, just five months after Kennard had married someone other than Mrs Buckley, was probably to show the family's appreciation for Robbie's intervention.

Wyllie and Carew had become especially close to Freddie Smith during the ordeal and they took him in as something of an adopted son. Kennard's posting to Tehran had had some unintended consequences; he had started to write Persian poetry and he developed a taste for opium, which would haunt him for the rest of his life. His marriage was not happy for long, and they soon separated.

Not everyone was pleased with Carew's choice of friends. Kennard's son George in his memoirs described his grandmother as spending her last year 'prey to parasites whom she maintained at the expense of a disappointing son'. There is little doubt that he was referring to Ross and Smith for he followed this observation with a reference to her 'life-long affection of Oscar Wilde'.[14]

Not long after this visit, Wyllie made an extraordinarily generous gift to the couple. To Ross she gave £1,000 (about £106,000 in today's money), to Smith she gave £9,000 in stock (about £954,000).[15]

The most logical explanation is that Carew hoped that with money Smith would be in a position to move in the same circles and keep and eye on her prodigal son. The gift made Smith a man of independent means and while he would continue to be Ross's 'secretary' he no longer did regular secretarial work for him. Instead, Ross hired a grateful Millard. This was to have a number of unforeseen consequences. As Smith became financially independent and successful in his own right their dynamic changed. Ada Leverson once said of Robbie, 'I think he rather resented any friend who was not in actual need of help.'[16] Robbie, who needed to be needed, could not adjust to his lover's independence. They failed to make the Greek transformation from eros into platonic love between equals. This would not manifest itself right away, but over the next few years, their relationship cracked under mounting stresses. Ross increasingly confided in Millard about the growing tensions between himself and his lover. Ross's close association with a man who had been arrested for gross indecency would soon be fodder for his enemies.

On 2 June, 1911, Lord Alfred Douglas was accepted into the Catholic Church. Bosie's explanations for his conversion to Catholicism are vague and flat. In his 1929 autobiography, he described his conversion as an entirely intellectual process, which does not sit well with what we know of his personality. By his account, he came to the decision almost out of boredom. 'I felt in some ways that to become a Catholic would be a tiresome necessity.'[17]

Bosie's tone of inevitability suggests that he viewed Catholicism as some kind of rite of passage. This did not refer to a family tradition, rather it seems becoming Catholic was what all the 'artistic men' he knew did when they got to a certain age.

Indeed, an impressive number of the homosexuals from the Wilde circle eventually joined the Roman church. John Gray, for example, had been ordained to the priesthood in 1901. Many aesthetes were drawn to the church's rich symbolism and ritual. The artistry seems to have been what attracted Robbie. Arthur Machen, who had inspired Bosie to embrace High Anglicanism was likewise inspired by the symbolic language of the mass. The Catholic Church appealed to outsiders because it was an outsider religion. It aligned a poet with the cultures of Rome and continental Europe rather than England. The Catholic doctrine of original sin was also a paradoxical pull for homosexuals in particular. The doctrine pronounced all human beings stained by the very fact of their sexual creation. Within the walls of the church, being in a state of shame was unifying, not isolating. It did not matter which temptations one wrestled with, or what type of lust he needed to suppress, all that mattered was that he did not give into it, or that he went to confession when he failed. This aspect was especially appealing to Bosie who was racked by a deep sense of shame and a desire to be cleansed and purified.

The final document that made Bosie give in and become a Catholic was Pope Pius X's *Encyclical Against Modernism*.[18] Bosie never explained what in it had persuaded him, except to say that the process was intellectual rather than emotional. A careful reading suggests a few aspects that may have appealed to his lordship. First of all, anything 'against modernism' was sure to strike a chord with a monarchist who was against women's suffrage, reform of the House of Lords and the heresy of free verse. Bosie may also have been attracted to Pius's devotion to the Virgin Mary. Pius taught that the most direct route to renew all things in Christ was through the blessed mother. Bosie had long associated pure love with childhood and his own mother provided the closest thing to unconditional love he experienced in life.

His disappointment with married love eventually persuaded him that St. Paul had been right and that total celibacy was the ideal way of life. He would later write in his sonnet sequence *In Excelsis*, 'For love essentially must needs be chaste, /And being contracted to unchastity/(Even in marriage) knows essential loss ...'[19]

One of the first things Bosie did as a Catholic was to ask for forgiveness from those he had wronged. Around this time, he sent cordial letters forgiving and asking forgiveness of his 'enemies'. He was not a master of the art of apology and sometimes failed to grasp the fine distinction between contrition and justification. Olive received one of these letters dated 3 June 1911 marked 'very important'. Bosie wrote, 'I do still love you and for a short time I really did hate you. But I do understand that what you have done was forced on you by your father and that villain Lewis and I forgive you. Your loving boy.'[20]

He also wrote to Wilfred Blunt to apologise for the angry letters he had sent when he refused to provide money for *The Academy*. Blunt replied, 'Your trespass against me was a small matter and easy to forgive, but your sins against others of your friends in the last two or three years have been less forgiveable, and you must not expect me to condone them or give you any further countenance.'

Catholicism had done nothing to change Bosie's basic nature, and his spirit of generosity proved to be short-lived. When he received Blunt's reply he fired off a characteristically fiery missive. Blunt recorded in his diary that this was what he 'expected and intended, for I had rather have him as an enemy than a friend ... Whatever he may have done by becoming a Catholic, it has not brought him to the point of repenting his sins.'[21]

As Ross was quietly working to make Bosie's past known, Bosie was working to make the world forget. In November 1911, the *Mercure de France* requested permission to reissue his 1896 poetry collection but he refused. Part of his objection was aesthetic, he felt that he had matured as a poet and his early verse was not up to his new standard. More important, however, was that they expressed a point of view he no longer held. He was ashamed of his homoerotic verse and his pagan enthusiasms and no longer wanted his name associated with them.[22]

In the spring of 1912 Robbie lost his position as art critic at *The Morning Post*. The move was criticised by many in the art world, including his friends at *The Burlington Magazine*. As usual, he landed on his feet. He was invited to write for the *Westminster Gazette* and was soon asked to be the London director of the new Johannesburg Art Gallery. This was but a stepping stone. In August he became Valuer of Pictures and Drawings for the Board of the Inland Revenue.

Arthur Ransome meanwhile was fighting with Methuen over the use of copyright material. He did not take heed of the publisher's friendly advice to avoid any references to Oscar Wilde's personal life in his *Critical Study*.

36

'The Worst Experience of My Life'

> He had lived the delicate and luxurious life of a young man of birth and
> fortune, a life exquisite in its freedom from sordid care, its beautiful boyish
> insouciance; and now for the first time he had become conscious of the terrible
> mystery of Destiny, of the awful meaning of Doom.
>
> Oscar Wilde, *Lord Arthur Saville's Crime*

The first Oscar Wilde book published in 1912 was Christopher Millard's *Three Times Tried*, a verbatim account of each of the Wilde trials. It was billed as the first attempt to 'give a fair picture' of the events in question. He drew on descriptions from Wilde's friends, including Robbie (who was not there for the last two trials). While the text of the trials was presented without any editorialising, Millard did include an epilogue in which he criticised the verdict as being based on the evidence of 'two blackmailers and some hysterical servant girls'. He argued that the State should not be 'vindictive' and 'hound a man on to his ruin' and that there was a strong and widespread suspicion that the prosecution's methods 'did not square with an Englishman's notion of justice and fair play'. He drew on Sherard's description of people dancing and celebrating outside the court, and added his own twist. It was now 'harlots' who 'lifted their skirts and danced with delight' on the news of the verdict.[1]

On 16 February 1912 Ransome's *Oscar Wilde: A Critical Study* was released. The book opened with this acknowledgement, 'I wish to thank Mr Robert Ross, Wilde's literary executor, who has helped me in every possible way, allowed me to read many of the letters that Wilde addressed to him, and given much time out of a very busy life to the verification, from documents in his possession, of the biographical facts included in my book.'[2]

Bosie received one of the shocks of his life when he read the chapter headed 'De Profundis'. Ransome described the history of the document.

> The passages were selected and put together by Mr Robert Ross with a skill that it is impossible sufficiently to admire. The letter, a manuscript of 'eighty close-written pages on twenty folio sheets,' was not addressed to Mr Ross but to a man to whom Wilde felt that he owed some, at least, of the circumstances of his public disgrace. It was begun as a rebuke of this friend, whose actions, even subsequent to the trials, had been such as to cause Wilde considerable pain. It was not delivered to him, but given to Mr Ross by Wilde, who also

gave instructions as to its partial publication. It is not often possible to detect the original intention of rebuke in the published portions of De Profundis. I suppose that as Wilde pointed out his friend's share in his disaster, and set down on paper what that disaster was, he came to examine its ulterior effect on his own mind, for those pages that are open to us contain such an examination.[3]

Ransome went on to describe Wilde's reunion with the unnamed 'friend', a 'friendship [that] had already cost him more than it was worth ... whose conduct he had condemned, whose influence he had feared.' The friend, he said, left Wilde as soon as there was no money left. 'It was,' said Wilde, 'a most bitter experience in a bitter life.'[4]

Bosie sat down and wrote his first letter to Ross in three years:

It is true that the man Ransome does not mention my name but anyone reading the book carefully with a full knowledge of the circumstances would be led to infer that I was the 'friend' referred to. I now write to ask you whether it is true that the MS of De Profundis consists of a letter addressed to me, and if so why you have concealed this fact from me for all these years? I should also like to know why you published the letter as a book without my knowledge or consent. Hitherto I have always been under the impression that De Profundis was a letter written by Wilde to you but containing abusive or scandalous references to me which you had suppressed. Of course if this latter version of the affair is correct there is no more to be said. But if Ransome's version is correct, matters assume a very different and very serious aspect.[5]

Robbie must have known that there might be trouble, because instead of responding to Bosie himself, he had his solicitor answer. Lewis claimed Wilde had entrusted the manuscript to Ross 'with directions that he should not part with it but that he should send you a copy of the letter, which he did in the year 1897.' He further claimed the manuscript was published 'in accordance with [Wilde's] directions'.[6]

Olive urged Bosie to drop the matter, but she did not hold as much sway with him as did Crosland. Crosland had taken a job as editor of the Penny Illustrated Paper. With that move, his income fell to about £6 per week. His family was forced to sell their country house and relocate to a small cottage. Crosland had his eye out for any additional sources of income: a new libel suit, perhaps. So when Bosie contacted him asking his opinion on the Ransome book, he advised him to sue the author, the publisher and The Times Book Club, which circulated it. Bosie, however, was not yet looking for money. He only asked that the book be withdrawn and the libels removed. The publisher and the printer apologised quickly.

Ransome was reluctant to enter the fray, and was inclined to follow the publisher's lead. In fact, shortly after the book's release members of the Wilde family had objected to some aspects of it, and Ransome had been cordial. He apologised and agreed to change the text in future editions.[7]

Lewis urged Ransome not to do the same with Douglas. The case was important to Ross, he said, because if Douglas won he might have the basis for a future legal action against Ross for disseminating De Profundis. '... so I felt I had to go through with the thing,' Ransome wrote in his autobiography, 'much as I hated it.'[8] Because it was really Ross whose interests were at stake, he furnished Ransome with the 'best representation money could buy'.[9]

Although he claimed he was reluctant to enter the legal arena, Ransome did see some potential advantages. In a proposal to the literary agent Curtis Brown he wrote 'the success of the Wilde book, which will, of course, be enormously stimulated when my case ... comes into court, should ensure a very wide notice for it both here and America.'[10] Indeed, Ransome's *Wilde* was his first best-seller, going through five editions.

Ransome wanted to steer clear of any personal issues and focus on literary matters. His benefactor, Ross, had a different idea. He was preparing for total war. He had collected enough material to prove that Douglas was as guilty as Wilde of gross indecency and that he was a cad of the lowest sort.

Afraid that the coming storm might reflect badly on the estate, Ross wrote to Martin Holman, the solicitor who handled most of his literary legal matters, and asked him to 'take the necessary steps for relieving me of the administration of Oscar Wilde's literary estate at the end of this year.' He explained that his personal interests would likely conflict with his duties because of 'intermittent persecution from Alfred Douglas'.[11] Holman did not accept his resignation but he did not want the estate to be involved in any legal conflicts with Douglas. A few months later, when Bosie filed a copyright claim against Methuen over ownership of *De Profundis*, Holman turned over all of the records of the legal proceedings with the Official Receiver to George Lewis.[12]

Robbie had spent years trying to make the public forget the Wilde scandal and focus on his genius. Had he been thinking as executor at that moment, he should have encouraged Ransome to apologise and settle rather than risk a second round of exposure and outrage over Wilde's crimes. Something had become more important to him – setting the record straight. He was determined the world should know who the real villain of the Wilde drama had been.

Edmond Gosse urged Robbie to walk away. On 29 July 1912 he wrote to his friend:

> Your unhappy fondness for litigious struggles and fightings, sometimes, if you will forgive my saying so – causes you to lose a sense of the proportion of things. You say you are full of anxieties, and I daresay you are, and I am extremely sorry that you are, but you know that in your heart you have a love of fighting ... I wish you could lift yourself, for once and all, out of this circle of ideas and people. As to D. as a serious antagonist, or as to his grotesque and insane manoeuvrers, I regard them with contempt: and you should do the same. He is a criminal, but not a dangerous one, because his mind is loose and ragged.[13]

Gosse was not the only friend to observe this trait in Ross. The poet Siegfried Sassoon, who knew him during the war said there was 'an element in his nature that delighted in provoking opposition.'[14] Perhaps Freddie Smith was among the friends who urged Robbie to stay out of the matter. Whatever the spark was, something caused a major falling out between them, and Smith moved out. He went to the French Riviera to stay at the Carew's villa.

The first time Bosie read the unpublished portions of *De Profundis* was in the summer of 1912 when a typescript was sent as part of the 63-page particulars of justification for his libel action against Ransome. Crosland helped Douglas prepare for the trial by reading *De Profundis* out loud to Douglas, line by line, and asking him to respond to Wilde's charges.[15] This was a painful experience for Douglas, and one that Crosland would not forget. Crosland 'shuddered' as he read.'[16]

De Profundis struck at all of the pillars of Bosie's sense of self – his pride at being a male muse, his talent as a poet (which Wilde mocked) and the courage he had shown in sticking by Oscar Wilde through thick and thin. Wilde's description of their great love story shook Bosie to his foundations. His greatest fear had come to pass; the portrait in the attic had been exposed, and the foulness of his soul was on full display. To have such a blow delivered by Oscar was devastating. Only a few years before, Bosie had confidently written in one of his sonnets to his wife Olive 'The world is very strong, but love is stronger.'[17] He no longer believed it.

'I was nearly out of my mind with grief and indignation,' he wrote, 'and, I might add without exaggeration, misery. The shock of the revelation of Wilde's attack on me, after all I had done for him ... was the worst experience of my life. It shook me to the very core, and it altered me in one week from a young man, still full of gaiety and joie de vivre to a fierce and embittered man.'[18]

In this painful moment he burned the love letters he had received from Oscar Wilde. 'He rarely wrote a letter that was not full of delightful wit and humour, and he wrote some which would have melted a heart of stone. When I think that I sat in front of a fire in the year 1912 and threw one hundred and fifty of them into it, one after another, only keeping about thirty, I feel almost suicidal.'[19]

Bosie fired off a series of abusive letters to Ross accusing him of blackmail. 'You filthy bugger and blackmailer. My libel action against Ransome henceforth becomes and action against you and will be so conducted ... I am ready and willing to repeat publicly what I now say and justify my words up to the hilt.'[20]

Bosie fell into a deep depression and contemplated suicide. ' ... the storm burst upon me in 1912,' Bosie wrote. 'I weathered it solely because I was a Catholic, for if I had not been one, I would have inevitably decided that life was not worth living and would have taken the easy way out of it.'[21]

Crosland saw the devastating effect De Profundis had on his friend and like Queensberry and Wilde before him decided that he would act as Bosie's protector and defender. 'I then began to seriously consider the whole Wilde movement as engineered by Ross as a foul affair and dangerous from a public point of view, and I determined to do everything in my power to destroy it and get out the real facts,' Crosland told Sorley Brown.[22]

Crosland expounded at length as to why he developed a hatred for Wilde, and there is no reason not to accept his own explanation. His issue with Wilde was that he had published immoral works that influenced a circle of young men into accepting a philosophy that turned homosexual vice into virtue. Crosland felt the 'Wilde movement' needed to be stopped, and it was personal. He believed his friend was one of its victims. In reading De Profundis he found the deviant Wilde blaming his own victim in the harshest and most bitter terms, while all the while posing as a moral example. He was outraged.

There is a case to be made for Crosland's point of view. Uranian culture was not the same as modern gay culture. It specifically idealised the sexual mentorship of young men and boys by older men. Wilde was guilty of the crimes with which he had been charged. Much of his behaviour is disconcerting, even by modern standards. The witnesses against Wilde were youths. Walter Grainger (the boy who Wilde deemed too ugly to be kissed) was a 16 year-old servant when he was seduced by the 38 year old Wilde. In his witness statement, Grainger claimed Wilde threatened that he would be in 'very serious trouble' if he told anybody about their relations. Alfred Conway, neither a prostitute nor a servant, was also 16 when seduced by Wilde. Robbie Ross had been 17 when his relationship with Wilde began. Alfred Douglas was an immature college undergraduate. In Wilde's presence young Andre Gide said he had 'forgotten how to think' and he feared that Wilde was 'religiously contriving to kill what is left of my soul.' The practice of a middle-aged men sexually mentoring much younger men and boys continued in the circle that surrounded Ross, his own relationship with Freddie Smith was just one example. Another was Millard's relationship with Scott Moncrieff.

During his relationship with Oscar, Bosie had believed he had as much influence – or even more influence – on Oscar as the other way around. Now that he felt he had been deceived and betrayed he found it easy to imagine that the people who had tried to rescue him had been right all along. Wilde was a monster who had seduced him into an immoral culture, put his soul in danger, and led him to believe he was his great love, while all the while secretly conspiring with Robbie Ross to tarnish his reputation for future generations. With Crosland egging him on, Douglas would come to believe that the cult of Wilde needed to be stopped 'by so-called legitimate means or otherwise.'[23]

Crosland sprang into action. He wrote two long scathing poems condemning *De Profundis*. In 'The First Stone' he calls Wilde a 'flabby Pharisee' 'O Treachery! O damned And furtive Plotter! Thou Of whom the filthiest friend Might wish to wash his hands ...' Feeling he had not sufficiently made his point, Crosland followed this up with *The Second Stone*, in which he compared Wilde to the 'fetid leper of the Fiftieth Pit.' *The First Stone* also made a dig at Ross, mocking Oscar's fans who 'make swift trips to Dieppe/ When they think the police/ May call ...'[24]

Crosland had wanted to publish a book that would go through *De Profundis*, line by line, and respond to its claims, as they had done when preparing for trial. The plans were blocked by Robbie who would not permit Crosland to quote the copyright material. As Bosie became more and more frustrated at his powerlessness and inability to respond, he became increasingly mentally unstable.

In the wake of the twin stressors of the breakdown of his marriage and the Ransome trial, Bosie fell into a state of depression, unable to fully function. By the time Bosie got up from the punch, he had a new cause. He would fight against sexual immorality, especially homosexuality, and he would make sure everyone knew about the villainy of Oscar Wilde and Robert Ross. His mental state included delusions of grandeur and persecution paranoia. The Catholicism that sustained him became mystical. Bosie believed he was a martyr and angels were intervening and supporting him in his quest for justice. Bosie was on a mission to become a saint. Christ would finally vanquish Apollo.[25]

Before we examine these events, it is important to take a look back at the history of mental illness in the Douglas family. By the time Bosie was born, there had already been, in just a few generations five suicides or suspicious deaths among his kin. Queensberry had lost his own father to an apparent suicide at age 14. The circumstances of Archibald William Douglas' (Viscount Drumlanrig) death in a suspicious hunting accident were remarkably similar to those that took the life of Bosie's brother, the next Viscount Drumlanrig.

Queensberry's brother Lord James Douglas was three years old when their father died. James would live only thirty-three more years before taking his own life in 1891. James's 'eccentricities' were recorded on the police blotters. In 1888, he was arrested for harassing a 19-year-old woman named Mabel

Scott who had rejected his request for her hand in marriage. He was so persistent that the young woman had to get a court order forbidding him from having any contact with her. A particularly bizarre aspect of the story is that James sent the young woman a brooch bearing the Douglas crest. He then sent abusive letters to the young woman and her mother saying she was not entitled to wear the crest because she lacked moral character. The girl sent it back to him, at which point he sent it back to her, and this process was repeated twice.

When she finally got the courts involved, James tried to hide from the process servers but was eventually handed the legal documents while stepping into a hansom cab. He crumpled the order and threw it into the road. Believing, apparently, that tossing it away invalidated it, he proceeded to ignore it. He was three times arrested for trying to see Miss Scott and three times apologised profusely and promised not to do it again. The court was lenient with him. Finally, he went on a vacation to the Mediterranean and sent the object of his obsession a Christmas card 'of a character that most persons would have shrunk from sending to a young lady of 19.' This time, the court had tired of his lordship's excuses. He was sent to jail but released two weeks later.[26]

A month before his death, James had been charged with fraud for filling in his census form listing his wife as a 'cross sweep' and her son as a boy born in 'Darkest Africa' who worked as a 'shoe black.'[27]

After that his decline was rapid. He lashed out in violent rages and then drank until he passed out. Queensberry tried to help his brother by arranging a fishing holiday in Ireland. It did little to calm his frenzied mind. On his return from the vacation his behaviour was so strange that a police officer accompanied him. He was booked into the Euston Station hotel where he was discovered by the chamber maid the next morning lying in a pool of his own blood. This time there could be no question. It was a suicide. He had stood in front of the mirror and slit his throat from ear to ear.

To truly understand Bosie's state of mind leading up to and after the Ransome trial, we must look more closely at the specific manifestation of bipolar disorder in two members of the Douglas family. Lord Milo Douglas, the great-grandson of Bosie's brother Percy (Percy, incidentally, had an alcohol problem, which suggests he also suffered from the disorder and was self-medicating); and Bosie's father, John Sholto Douglas. With both of these men, stressful life events triggered depression followed by manic episodes with hyper-religious aspects.[28]

We'll begin with Lord Milo, whose struggles were charted by modern medical professionals and therefore give us some insight into how his earlier family members might have been diagnosed had these categories existed in their day. After a lifetime struggling with bipolar disorder, Milo took his own life in 2009 by jumping from a tower of flats.

Milo, a friend remembered, 'always had a few layers of skin less than most people,' but his serious difficulties did not start until he was 24 years old. That year a love affair with a young Italian man went sour. He was devastated by the break-up. Shortly thereafter he had his first manic episode.

'It manifested itself by classic behaviour,' said a family member. 'There were overwhelming religious aspects to his thoughts; he became hectoring about moral issues ... He would invite tramps back home and gave away his possessions and money to people sheltering under Waterloo Bridge.'[29]

He was treated with medication, but when he decided to stop taking it in 2008, the 'mild hypomanic symptoms' returned, including poor concentration and increased religiosity. He also experienced a 'psychotic depressive state' with hallucinations. In the depths of a depression, he came to believe two people working with his father were the devil.[30]

In John Sholto Douglas's day no one used words like 'bipolar affective disorder,' 'hypomanic symptoms' or 'hyper-religiosity' but look at how Queensberry's biographer described his 'long spiritual journey.' It had 'begun in 1865 with grief and confusion [and] would pass through a process of enquiry followed by enlightenment leading to bombastic certainty, missionary zeal and finally rage.'[31] In other words, the system of thought that Queensberry developed to get him through his depression became an irresistible compulsion during his manic episodes.

Queensberry started to develop his religion as his marriage was breaking down (as Bosie would turn to Catholicism to deal with the disintegration of his marriage). Meanwhile economic change was making landed estates less viable, and Queensberry was beginning to feel the pinch. At the time, Q was still mourning the death of his brother, Francis, who had been killed in a mountain climbing accident on the Matterhorn. Queensberry had climbed the mountain in an unsuccessful attempt to find his brother's body and he was humbled and awed by the enormity of nature.

At this time he discovered the works of Herbert Spencer, an advocate of the theory of evolution and the man who had coined the term 'survival of the fittest.' Spencer's *Social Statics* became Queensberry's 'poison book' shaping his thoughts as Pater had shaped Wilde and Wilde's *Dorian Gray* had shaped Bosie. He was so taken with it that he memorised the chapter 'Evanescence of Evil,' a feat that took him two weeks to achieve.[32]

The grand theory he developed became his lifeline. His activities were initially quiet and introspective. He wrote a long poem about the ever-developing soul of man. The letters he wrote to friends about his new ideas were not at all 'hectoring.' In 1876 he wrote the Earl of Rosslyn, confessing that 'I am turning into a very bitter unhappy man' and saying he knew his friend 'would not agree' with his views on religion but '... it is my faith & the only thing I do believe in, the ultimate perfectibility of mankind.'[33]

By the end of 1879, this belief had become an absolute obsession. Queensberry had an irresistible compulsion to spread his truth, and he would do so no matter how much damage it did to his personal reputation. He was energetic, erratic and single-minded. Some of his actions, like standing and shouting in the theatre during the production of 'Promise of May,' were devoid of any normal social constraint. He defended his actions to the *Daily News* by saying there was no tactic he would not try to advance his cause 'everything is fair in war; and this is war.'[34]

Absolutely nothing was going to stop him from his mission. He said he intended to write individually to all of his fellow peers (although he probably didn't), and when he was barred from making a speech defending his secularism before the Scottish house of lords he said he would make his speech all over England and 'all over the world.'[35]

While Queensberry's underlying theology was diametrically opposed to Bosie's strict Catholicism, the pattern of behaviour was the same. If mental illness was the cause of Douglas's visions, this in no way lessens the religious significance as he experienced it. He was persuaded to the core of his being by his mystical experiences that he had found the truth. He was on the side of the angels, and Robert Ross and Oscar Wilde were beasts from Hell. Ross, in particular, was behind every misfortune that befell him.

In his indignation, Bosie was transformed into his father. In a letter to Ross dated 1 November 1912, after boasting about his ability on the stand and expressing his hope that Ross will be a witness so he can be cross-examined, he tells him that he intends 'to give you a very severe thrashing and horse-whip. I am bound to come across you one day or another when occasion serves and you shall be whipped within an inch of your dirty life. Also there are other things in store for you but I won't go into them now. There is a time for everything. The mills of God grind slowly & yet they grind exceeding small.'[36]

That did not prove enough of a catharsis, and a day later he wrote again, warning that Ross's treachery in acting like his friend while keeping De Profundis from him would soon be known, 'Your name shall go stinking down the ages & I will make you so that no decent man or woman in England will sit in the same room with you.' He repeated that he planned to give Ross a whipping 'and other things.'[37]

Three days later there was another letter, where Bosie made it clear that he intended to lure Robbie into a libel action so he could expose everything he knew about him. On 17 November, Robbie sent a letter to Lewis recounting a visit by a strange man who had come to his flats asking the landlord a lot of questions about him and Freddie. He believed he was a detective sent by Bosie.[38]

At the end of November, Pamela Tennant, now Lady Glenconner, hosted an 'At Home Friday' to meet the Prime Minister and Mrs. Asquith. Robbie was friendly with the Tennants, and was sent an invitation. His first instinct was to decline, as he feared Bosie might show up, but George Lewis assured him that he would not be there. Robbie arrived and was chatting amiably to the novelist Mrs. Belloc Lowndes when Bosie entered the room. On seeing Ross he shouted, 'You are nothing but a bugger and a blackmailer!' Robbie did not want a scene and he went to Lord Glenconner asking if he might leave. Glenconner led him by the arm to his sister, Margot Asquith, and she whisked Ross away to 10 Downing Street. Douglas continued to rant to all within earshot about his grievances against Ross. He was not receiving a sympathetic reception, and he left after a short time.

Bosie's outburst did little to persuade anyone of the righteousness of his cause. Instead, it bonded the Asquiths to Robbie. The next day he wrote and apologised to his hosts saying that should they like an explanation of the quarrel they might ask Sir George Lewis, and that he would never have accepted the invitation if he knew Bosie would be there. Both Glenconner and Mrs. Asquith wrote him sympathetic letters. Asquith wrote, 'We all thought you behaved splendidly.'[39]

In early December, Bosie drew up a statement charging Robbie with 'committing unnatural offences' with Freddie Smith. This was done 'with the aid of a disbarred attorney' – undoubtedly Arthur Newton.[40] Newton had lost his license to practice law a short time before in a trial before Justice Darling. The Hawley Crippen murder case had fascinated the British public. When the police began to investigate the disappearance of Crippen's wife, he fled to the United States with his mistress, who travelled disguised as a boy. It was the first time wireless telegraphy had been used to intercept a criminal and the public had followed the developments as they unfolded.

Horatio Bottomley arranged to pay Newton, who was not only one of the most famous solicitors of the day but also a close personal friend, to defend Crippen. In return, he asked for sensational, exclusive copy. There is no evidence that Newton gave his client anything but a vigorous defence. After he was found guilty, however, Bottomley wanted a confession for his pages. He sent a letter to Crippen through Newton, asking 'Brother, how came you to do it? What demon possessed you? Relieve your burning brain, confiding to me the name of your accomplice.' Crippen had nothing to say to Bottomley's readers, so Newton dictated the reply himself. It was the beginning of the end of a once-stellar career.[41]

In the early months of 1913, Olive had had enough her husband's infamous temper. The violence of some of his rages terrified her.[42] Bosie came home one day, after a trip to visit his sister, to find that Olive had moved out and taken much of the furniture with her. He experienced this as a bitter betrayal. He was now fighting a two-front war, the battle to preserve his marriage and family and the libel suit. The new year did not bring any joys. On 14 January 1913 a receiving order was filed against him in bankruptcy court. The money lender who filed the petition was concerned that if he did not get his money now, and Douglas lost his libel suit, he might have to wait in line. As soon as he was declared bankrupt, he was struck off the list of members of White's Club. The bankruptcy, incidentally, would not be discharged until 1981.[43]

Douglas was preparing his case with the assumption that he would get Ross on the stand and could grill him about his own past. A few weeks before the Ransome case, Ross received a visit from an acquaintance named Norman Farr. Farr told him that he'd been contacted by Harold Benjamin, the junior counsel on the Ransome case. Benjamin had asked Farr if he'd had sexual relations with Ross. According to Ross, Farr said Benjamin promised he'd be well paid if he were to swear to it. Farr told Benjamin he hardly knew Ross and had only met him a few times.

Bosie would, in the course of their feud, accuse Ross of having sexual relations with a number of men and boys. Ross would deny it in every case, including Freddie Smith. Bosie used a number of coercive methods to try to get testimony from the men, as his father had in the case against Oscar Wilde. In that case, although Wilde had denied every accusation, most are assumed to be true. Thus Bosie could have tried to coerce witnesses to tell a truth that they would be reluctant to share, rather than to lie. We can safely assume that Ross did not take a vow of celibacy after his experience with Dansey in 1894. We can also assume that Douglas, who was still on good terms with Ross for some time after Wilde's death, knew about some of his partners. If any of the men who Douglas tried to bribe had actually been Ross's lovers, Farr is a good candidate. He met Ross in 1902 when he was a sixteen year old student at St. Paul's. They met at the Douglas's house.[44] Ross claimed he had only chatted with the boy about a teacher he knew at St. Paul's and that a few years later Farr bought some pictures to the Carfax to be valued.[45]

A few months later after his warning visit, Farr called Ross and told him that Digby Lamotte, a teacher at St. Paul's had been visited by Sir Charles Mathews, the Public Prosecutor. Mathews showed Lamotte a letter from Douglas that claimed Ross had corrupted boys at the school. Lamotte knew Farr was acquainted with Ross (a detail that seems to contradict Ross's story that he had only met Farr two or three times in passing) and sent for him. Farr gave Ross a written statement saying that Benjamin had tried to bribe him, but he did not want to testify. Farr was now a medical student at St. George's Hospital, and being connected to a case of this nature could be very damaging to him. As Farr was telling Ross about this, two Scotland Yard detectives arrived.[46]

On 23 December 1912 Max Beerbohm sent Christmas greetings to Reggie. He mentioned the upcoming Ransome trial. Although it was ostensibly a dispute between Douglas and Ransome, everyone familiar with the case believed it was really a battle between Douglas and Ross. Beerbohm believed Ross, 'the old botherationist,' had set it all in motion and that it was going to be a disaster not for Bosie but for Robbie. 'The outlook is decidedly bad for him—as we have often agreed,' he wrote. He hoped that somehow the case would not come to court. Even so, he wrote to Robbie wishing him luck with it.[47]

Douglas v. Ransome and Others

I believe the plaintiff will be heartily shamed for the rest of his life.
J. H. Campbell, on Lord Alfred Douglas.[1]

When Sherard published his Oscar Wilde memoir in 1905, Bosie had not been pleased to read his relationship described as 'the friendship which had brought ruin and disaster'. He consulted Arthur Newton who advised him against taking legal action and he demurred. Although he didn't like having other people say so, Bosie admitted himself, on many occasions, that he was the (indirect) cause of Wilde's ruin. Sherard had never claimed Bosie *abandoned* Wilde. In fact, he wrote that Wilde's unnamed friend had 'placed his house, a delightful villa at Posilippo and his purse at Wilde's disposal.'[2] So the accusation had not been as troubling to him as Ransome's.

Bolstered by Crosland and his inflated faith in his own ability as a witness, he thought his only option was to take the stand and defend his honour. Even with Wilde's *De Profundis* in evidence, Bosie had a strong case. He could prove he had not left Wilde of his own volition, and he could show that he helped Wilde financially before and after the trial.

Beyond that, he was misled by what was given to him in discovery. Initially, on the stand, he tried to deny that *De Profundis* was addressed to him. He would only have done this if the document he had seen lacked the salutation 'Dear Bosie.' Indeed, the typescript of *De Profundis* used by the Ransome defence team was recently sold to the Free Library in Philadelphia. It reveals that the salutation was not on the original court-prepared typescript. Counsel's copy had 'Dear Bosie' written in pen on a small slip of paper and tacked in to the first page. The lawyer for the Times Book Club even argued in his closing, based presumably on a copy of the typescript he had been given to prepare his case, that 'Wilde in the *De Profundis* letter had not mentioned the plaintiff's name.'[3] Bosie never saw the original hand-written manuscript until he appeared in court. He would have known, of course, from the details in the letter that he was its intended recipient, but until he saw the original manuscript he thought it could not be definitively proven.

The reading of *De Profundis*, however, as dramatic as it was, did not cause him to lose his case. Justice Charles Darling, in his summation urged the jury not to take the prison letter at face value. He called it a 'most remarkable and interesting document.' He said it should be taken as a study of what a bad man of genius had gone through in prison and its effect upon him. 'It would be a great mistake to take all that he said as Gospel truth. The document was an excuse and an apology.' If *De Profundis* had been the only evidence, Douglas would probably have won.

As we shall soon see, what swayed the judge, and caused him to direct the jury as he did, were damning personal letters provided by Ross that proved beyond a doubt Douglas was guilty of the same crimes as Wilde. The defence team had strategically held back the letters, saving them to use as rebuttal evidence in cross-examination. Thus they did not have to include them in the initial plea of justification. In a statement for a later legal case, Ross would claim that he had produced the letters 'under subpoena.' Perhaps. But if he had not made the decision to show them to the Ransome legal team, they would have had no way of knowing of their existence in the first place.[4] If Bosie had known what was about to be unleashed, even the litigious lord might have thought twice about bringing the action.

His biggest mistake, however, was in believing he was going to court to refute the charge that he had abandoned Wilde. Ransome's book had been heavily influenced by Ross. Ross and his circle blamed Douglas for disloyalty to Wilde. Greater society did not care about that. They blamed him for having been Wilde's lover in the first place. That would be the real focus of the Ransome trial.

Douglas would later try to explain how he could have lost the Ransome case. He said he was 'bound by a promise that I had given to Cecil Hayes, on my word of honour, that I would not attack the Judge however great the provocation he gave me. So I was simply a dumb lamb for the slaughter.'[5] I will leave it to you, gentle reader, to decide if this is a fair assessment.

The trial Douglas v. Ransome and Others opened on 17 April 1913 before Justice Charles Darling. Darling was, in his heart, a frustrated writer and he relished the opportunity to demonstrate his wit and word-play on the stage of his courtroom. The humour went over well in the gallery, but was often less appreciated by the people who were on trial for their lives and livelihoods.[6] He would be in great form during the Ransome case, injecting his humour and observations throughout.

In the front row Ross sat between Sir George Lewis and Arthur Ransome. Crosland (who Ransome described as Douglas's 'bulky friend') sat down nearby and gave him a menacing glare.

Sherard was also in the courtroom. He had been subpoenaed by the defence to testify about his Wilde biography, but he was never called to the stand. He spent most of his time sitting 'overwhelmingly bored and disgusted.'[7]

The Times coverage of the trial the next day took up almost the entirety of page four, the space reserved for coverage of the courts. There was only room for small blurbs for the other four stories of interest. The first was Lord Alfred Douglas's own bankruptcy going on in another courtroom. The second was a case in the Bow Street police courts. Solicitor Arthur Newton was on trial for fraud involving Berkley Bernard Bennet and the unindicted Count Andor Festetics, (A Stallmann associate) who had fled the country.[8]

Ransome and the Times Book Club had separate legal teams with their own legal strategies. Ransome's team, consisting of Mr J. H. Campbell and Mr McCardie would argue that the libel was true, while the Times Book Club's larger team, led by F. E. Smith along with Eustace Hills and W. G. Howard Gritten, would argue that they had distributed the book in good faith unaware that it contained a libel.

Born in 1872 in Birkenhead, Cheshire, F. E. Smith was a slightly younger contemporary of Douglas at Oxford. Douglas's first competition with Smith had been on the track. Smith had come in third in the University trials, just behind Douglas.[9] Outside of athletics, however, the undergraduates moved in different circles. Even as a student, Smith had political ambitions. He studied the great speakers, quickly shed his northern country accent, and earned a reputation as an excellent debator and a brilliant orator. He became president of the Oxford Union, one of the largest debating societies in the world. According to his son, Smith would often 'muse' about the 'decline' of Douglas after his glory days at Oxford.[10]

Smith's admiration for great speakers may be what led him to seek out one of the most celebrated talkers of his day, Oscar Wilde. Smith met Wilde at Oxford when the writer was visiting Douglas. He lunched with Wilde but was disappointed, finding not a magical wit, but an overweight, vain man with bad teeth surrounded by sycophants who sighed in appreciation at his every word.

As a barrister, Smith had many of the qualities that Darling admired in Ned Carson and, Darling's biographer wrote, 'there was nobody Darling liked to have appear before him more than the future Lord Birkenhead.'[11] Douglas could only afford the young and inexperienced Cecil Hays, who may have represented his friend pro bono.

He warned the jury that the defence would try to throw mud at his client, but they should ignore it. This would prove difficult for any jury, as the mud that was about to be slung was brilliantly distracting. Then Douglas took the stand to receive the friendly questions of his own counsel. He was well-dressed as always, arriving to court in his top hat and a neat cravat, but the events of the previous months had taken their toll on him physically. He was gaunt with pronounced cheekbones and dark circles under his eyes. Even so, he carried himself with great confidence and pride as he began his testimony.

He told the story of his acquaintance with Wilde, emphasising his literary tutelage, the fact that he visited the family home and was welcomed by his mother, the friendship between his mother and Constance Wilde and the fact that the Douglases had influential friends. Things seemed to be going well as Darling chimed in to note that the friendship of a man of Douglas's social class would be useful to a 'literary adventurer.' He seemed to be enjoying the play that was unfolding in his courtroom. Douglas showed his bank book to document all the money he'd given Wilde. Hayes concluded by asking his client if there was any truth whatever to the libel. 'None whatever,' was the reply.

Next J. H. Campbell stood to cross-examine on behalf of Ransome. When he asked if Douglas 'flew the country' when Wilde was arrested, Hayes objected, 'That is a most improper question.'

Douglas answered it anyway. 'So far from flying the country, I visited Wilde almost every day when he was in Holloway Prison.'

'The jury disagreed in the first trial. Did you fly the country before they disagreed?'

'Before they disagreed I went abroad.'

As delicate matters were starting to be discussed, Darling issued a warning to the press that they should report on the case 'as decently as possible' in order to avoid 'incalculable harm.' At this point the *Times's* coverage becomes vague. The Australian press went on to report in full on the Magdalen College blackmail, printing the 'Jack' letter referenced earlier. This was followed by a number of Wilde's letters to Douglas and some matters that even the Australian press declined to detail, the result of which was that Douglas admitted to knowing a number of the men and boys associated with Wilde's conviction. This was followed by some of the editorials and articles for French publications he had written to defend Wilde while he was in prison.

'Is your case today to try to suggest that all this degeneracy was brought about by your intimacy with Wilde?'

'I don't admit I was degenerate.'

'You called him a horrible man,' Darling said.

'He was a horrible man, an incarnate devil. I am very much ashamed of the letter. It was horrible—abominable. It shows what a frightful effect the beastly man had on me. I was writing what he taught me. I was trying to defend him. It does not show that I betrayed him and lived on him.'

Darling cross-examined again, 'You gave Wilde large sums of money and attended his funeral. Did you realise when he came out of prison the depth to which this 'beastly man' had betrayed you?'

'I did.'

'Why did you go near him again?'

'I was sorry for him. I thought he had had his punishment then. He had no friends. He was a genius, and I thought it was right that someone should speak to him in the interest of literature. I thought at that time that literature was more important than morals. Now I know that it was not. But that is why I went to him again.'

'How could you, knowing what he was, live under the same roof?'

'There did not seem to be anything wrong with that.'

The judge's imposition on this point stuck with Douglas. He would write many years later that Darling 'literally trembled with outraged propriety when I admitted I had invited Wilde to my villa at Naples. 'How could you?' he said, 'How could you, knowing what he was?' This, be it observed, although the case of my opponents was precisely that I had 'abandoned' Wilde and was responsible for his ruin. One would have thought that even Mr Justice Darling would have reflected that he could hardly have it both ways. You cannot logically at one and the same time accuse a man of 'abandoning' his friend and of receiving him as a guest in his villa!'[12]

Campbell continued, 'Is it not true that in some of your letters you addressed Wilde as 'Darling Oscar'?'

'Yes.'

Next the subject turned to Douglas's poetry and 'Two Loves' was once again a matter for the courts. (*The Times*, in its coverage, referred to it as 'the plaintiff's poem about 'Love in a Garden',') Campbell asked if 'Two Loves' did not 'advocate the sort of thing that Wilde was sentenced for.'

Douglas insisted that it was a beautiful poem and that 'it requires a person of counsel's mind to put another construction on it.'

Campbell, feeling he'd laid sufficient groundwork, asked Douglas directly whether he had ever been guilty of any sexual perversion. At this point Darling interrupted and told him not to answer as he had a right not to incriminate himself. Campbell instead read passages from a letter that Douglas had written to Ross in 1898 which was full of homoerotic innuendo.

'That was merely a joke in Wilde's own vein,' Douglas said. 'It proves nothing against me except that I was in this man's society and talking the jargon of his class and friends. I admit it. It is better that I should admit it now than that people should go on writing books upholding him as a martyr and attacking the people associated with him. In those days I had no religion, but for two years past I have been a Catholic. Because I am leading a decent and clean life and won't mix with them any longer, this is their revenge to rake up all this muck. That is what you are standing there for. I congratulate you.'

Campbell then dredged up the old family quarrell. Douglas admitted to having written nasty letters to Queensberry in response to his own, but he was not prepared for a letter he'd written to Ross in which he compared his father to Jack the Ripper. It brought laughter to the court and he claimed no memory of having written it.

Douglas would later recall, '... when it came out ... that I had given Wilde £360 just before his prosecution of my father, this was counted against me as a terrible example of unfilial conduct. Whereas if I had not given him any money at that time, I would doubtless have been held up to execration as a heartless brute who refused to help his friend in his need.'[13]

Darling openly mocked Douglas's childish letters, 'Where are the letters of Wilde's that you prayed over every night, and placed under your pillow?'

'I destroyed them a long time ago,' he said.

Then Campbell came to the heart of the matter. 'Does the unpublished part of *De Profundis* refer to you?'

'No,' Bosie answered.

With this Mr McCardie took over for the defence. They produced a document on loan from the British museum, twenty light blue foolscap folio sheets embossed with the prison seal, Oscar Wilde's usually expansive writing condensed to save paper, two handwritten lines for every ruled line.

Hayes initially objected to *De Profundis* being read at all, but when he was overruled, he insisted it should be read in its entirety to show Wilde's fluctuating moods. And so the reading of *De Profundis*, as described in our opening chapter, began.

Part way through, as Darling was reading, he became impatient. 'I have read pages and pages of it,' he told Hayes, 'It seems to me to be the same all the way along. It is impossible to go through this.' Hayes again insisted that the whole thing be read to show that Wilde was 'an exotic creature' who would write something one day and something entirely contradictory the next. 'If you want any more read you must read it yourself,' Darling said, but he continued reading himself for a few paragraphs anyway before handing the document on to Hayes.

As the first day's reading concluded Darling observed that it was clear Wilde had written the letter for publication because he 'gave himself the beau role all the time.' He asked Hayes to reconsider reading *De Profundis* in its entirety. The next morning, having duly considered the court's suggestion, Hayes again insisted that it be read. This was, undoubtedly, a mistake.

'Very well,' the judge said, 'Of course, it is your right. I looked ahead and it seemed to be the same as the rest – very dead water indeed.'

The jury foreman asked that they read it louder than on the previous day.

'Louder and faster,' Darling quipped. McCardie took over reading. It was some time before Darling noticed that Douglas was not in the court. He stopped the reading and asked where he was.

'He has not been there since the reading began,' Campbell said. 'And it has been read at the request of the plaintiff's own counsel.'

'I know,' said Darling. 'It is in order apparently that he may enjoy himself out of court. Stop reading it until he comes into court. Let him be fetched.'

As a court officer went to find the wayward plaintiff, the counsel discussed some matters of evidence. Hayes complained that not only had he not received advance copies of most of the letters in evidence, he still did not have copies.

'They are not bound to set out in the particulars everything they are going to cross-examine upon,' Darling said. He then decided that it was a waste of time to stop the reading to wait for Douglas, and he asked McCardie to continue.

A few minutes later Douglas arrived and sat in the witness box. The judge glared at him. McCardie paused, but Darling said to him, 'Go on.' When he had got to the end of the paragraph, Darling turned to Douglas, who stood up.

'I understand your lordship is annoyed with me?'

'Lord Alfred Douglas,' Darling said, 'is it by your instruction that the whole of this document by Oscar Wilde is being read?'

'Yes, my lord.'

'Then why did you absent yourself from the court?'

After the testimony recorded in the opening chapter, Darling sighed. 'Mr Hayes, do you want every word of this read? We're not even half way through yet.'

'No my lord,' Hayes finally said. 'I will accept your suggestion.' He said really he only wanted the jury to hear the last two pages.

'You read it then,' Darling said, gesturing to McCardie to give Hayes the manuscript. Hayes read the last two pages (Wilde's plans to reunite with Douglas) but by now everyone in the court was bored and annoyed and paid it no attention. Their attention was revived, however, by more scandalous letters.

By now, Douglas's patience was wearing thin, and the well-rehearsed responses to *De Profundis*, which he had practised with Crosland, were giving way to sheer frustration. Asked about Wilde's assertion that they only 'met in the mire' Douglas said, 'We generally talked about pictures and art. Wilde sat down and wrote that filthy letter, which a pack of lies with some half-truths, which I am supposed to admit, in order to cleanse himself and injure me and my family. He wrote it in order to curry favour with the prison authorities. It was quite irregular and contrary to regulations.'

Douglas was asked about a letter he had written to Ross in which he said 'I had great fun, though the strain of being a bone of contention between Oscar and Mrs. Oscar began to make itself felt.'

'I don't think it's fair to judge my relations with Mrs. Wilde from an expression in a single letter.'

'Listen,' Campbell said, 'In this letter to a friend you say, 'It is a commonplace among friends that everything should be in common. Oscar contributed everything, I had nothing to contribute. I remember the sweetness of asking Oscar for money: it was a sweet humiliation.' Now I ask you, do you still deny you lived on Oscar Wilde?'

'Yes. I may have borrowed money sometimes ... just as I should let him have it. I have paid it back fifty fold.'

When Campbell tried to interrupt him, Douglas said, 'You must allow me to finish my answer if you wish to get the truth; but perhaps you do not wish it.'

Darling responded, 'Don't be impertinent to the learned counsel.'

'I do not wish to be impertinent.'

'You are impertinent, whether you wish to be or not.'

'I was only about to ask a question.'

'You are not entitled to do so.'

'I accept your lordship's rebuke.'

'You will not only accept my view, but you will act on it.'

'I said your "rebuke."'

Darling snapped, 'Be silent until you are asked questions.'

This particular exchange was popular in the next day's press with a number of papers leading with 'Lord Alfred's impertinence'.

'Did you write this letter to Mr Ross – 'After the first shock of that terrible letter, I had a moment of deep bitterness against Oscar, now gone away never to return?' Had he not said, in his own letter, that he knew he had ruined Oscar's life?

'My own attitude has always been that since this catastrophe, I accept all responsibility, and have no wish to defend myself against any accusations.' (A singularly odd comment, given its context in his own libel trial.)

From Ransome's unique place in the eye of the hurricane, the scene was surreal. The trial had devolved into a sequel to the Wilde trials. It had nothing to do with his humble work of literary criticism. Ransome had the distinct impression his counsel had never even read his book. The judge, meanwhile, was enjoying the drama too much to reign it in.

Campbell continued asking Douglas whether he had written, 'The case was tried by a jury of shopkeepers. I should like to appeal to a jury of artists and young and generous people, who would have said, "This may be immoral and wrong but there is nothing mean or sordid in this tragedy of love."'

'Oh, that was Oscar Wilde all over.'

'It was Oscar Wilde, was it? Did you live under the same roof with Oscar Wilde?'

'I had invited him to.'

'You knew on his own confession what he was?'

'Yes, but I did not think that was any reason why I should refuse to have anything to do with him. I suppose other friends who knew him would have him under their roof. I did not see why not.'

Campbell then asked him if he knew that Wilde's decision to move in with Douglas cost him his annuity and if he was angry about it. 'I was angry at his surrendering all his interests for £150 a year.'

'Do you agree that it would have been in the interests of both that you should be kept apart?'

'Most certainly.'

'Then why did you write, "If Oscar only loves me half as much as I love him when he comes out, and even if he thinks he does not, nothing in the world can keep us apart. All the plots of friends and relations will go to the winds when I am with him again and I am holding his hand"?' This produced loud laughter from the gallery.

'That only shows what a faithful friend I was. In the book I am accused of not being his friend. You want to have it both ways. If I stick up for him I am a brute and a swine; if I don't I am a traitor.'

Darling tried to move things along, 'Mr Campbell, can you take your case much further? Is there anything that can advance it further? According to the plaintiff he is an apostle against vice, and here you have his letters.'

'They were written twenty years ago,' Douglas exclaimed.

Hayes said he thought his learned friend was wasting time. He wanted to get on to other parts of the case. After a few more questions about the annuity and the consequences of living together, Campbell asked, 'In spite of that did you force your way back to him?'

'I never forced myself on him.'

Campbell asked Douglas about a letter he said he had received from Wilde while he was in prison, one that was critical but which he said was too short to have been *De Profundis*. Douglas described it as 'awful'. Campbell asked if this awful letter did not persuade him that Oscar Wilde did not want to see him again.

'I thought he might have changed his mind,' he said. He further said that when he asked Wilde about it when he came out of prison he said 'I was mad with hunger and misery. I implore you to forgive me.'

When Campbell asked him a follow-up question on the letter, Douglas objected and said he could just stop answering if he wanted. He could quite easily move away.

'Don't you think it would be easy for you to go away,' Darling glared from the bench. 'I would soon have you back.'

'I did not mean that,' Douglas said.

'Do you know that Wilde said your leaving him when his allowance ceased was "the most bitter experience of a bitter life"?'

'Yes.'

'Were you surprised that all Wilde's friends as well as your own were doing their best to keep you apart?'

'I was not surprised.'

'You said that you would not be kept apart?'

'Yes.'

'At that time you knew of his past life?'

'Yes.'

'And with all the knowledge of Wilde's past life and his vice and sin, you insisted on returning to his friendship?'

'Yes.'

'And you enticed him by the offer of your villa?'

'I don't know about "enticed". I made him the offer to stay there.'

Counsel then resumed the questioning and turned his attention back to finances. 'Did not you suggest yesterday that you had shown great generosity to Wilde in 1897?'

'No. I said I paid his expenses and paid £200 when he went away.'

'Was this not a debt of honour?'

'No.'

Campbell went back to the 'bitterest experience' letter Wilde had written to Ross. He asked whether this letter did not confirm what Wilde had written in *De Profundis*.

'It was the most horrible document I have ever read,' he said. 'Here is a man deliberately sitting down in prison ascribing every kind of crime to me and trying to incriminate me. It is horrible meanness. This is the man I made all the sacrifices for and he tries to hound me down because I stuck to him. This letter he was keeping up his sleeve, and all the time he was living with me and pretending to be my friend. The thing is the height and depth of perfidy, meanness and treachery, and scoundrelism. There are all sorts of deliberate lies in the unpublished portion of 'De Profundis.' They were invented in order to blacken my character.'

'Is not the plain text of the *De Profundis* letter that you were the ruin of Wilde's life?'

'Yes.'

'Do you not admit that to be true? Had he not written that before?'

'Something like it. Through a sense of Quixotic generosity I let it pass.'[14]

He confirmed that he had, indeed, written that the Wilde trial was 'the greatest romantic tragedy of the age'.

'And this is the man who you yesterday spoke of as a monster and a vampire,' Campbell taunted.

'No,' the judge corrected. 'The devil incarnate.'

'Oh, but I have since read this manuscript,' Douglas said.

'Up to that time you thought he was a splendid hero and a martyr?'

'When I read the unpublished portion of *De Profundis*, I realised he was a fiend out of hell.'

Campbell read from a translation of one of Douglas's French articles. '"It may have been immoral or wrong, but there is nothing sordid or mean or dirty in this terrible tragedy of love." You did not think he was a devil incarnate then?

'I did not at the time.'

Campbell then read from a letter from Douglas to Ross describing his blasphemous poem about the devil. Douglas said it was 'a horrible thing to have written' but he was more upset that Ross had 'kept all of these things locked up while pretending to be my friend.'

'I suppose if you had known all these things were in existence you would not have come into court?' Campbell asked.

'Oh yes, I should. But they ought to have been disclosed so that I should have had an opportunity of preparing to meet them.'

As the questioning got more intense, Douglas found it impossible to maintain a polite demeanour. Twice as the judge discussed *De Profundis* with Campbell, he shouted that it was 'all lies'.

'Lord Alfred Douglas,' said Justice Darling, in the tone of a scolding parent, 'I shall not warn you again. Understand for once and for all that there is nothing in your position that entitles you to treat the court differently from any other person.'

'I am not ...'

'You are not entitled to insult counsel when he asks a question put to him by another counsel, and I will not allow you to.'

Chastened, Douglas sat quietly as Campbell read another of Wilde's letters and then finally passed the baton to The Times' legal team. Their only question was whether someone unfamiliar with the details of the Wilde trials would have recognised Douglas as the unnamed person in the text. He admitted that to recognise him a reader would have to already be familiar with the events.

Then Hayes stepped up to re-examine his own witness. He began by asking about his sporting successes as a student at Winchester and Oxford because one who was good at sport could hardly be guilty of the unmentionable vice. He followed this up by asking, 'Is there any truth in the suggestion that you are a degenerate?'

'I don't think so.'

'I should like to know,' Douglas asked of *De Profundis*, 'if it ever was a letter to me at all, why Ross never told me.'

Hayes then proceeded to read extracts from the published version of *De Profundis* and floated the idea that it and the letter were two different documents written at different times. There is something to that. *De Profundis* was not a simple letter written from beginning to end. There are sheets without prison numbering, added later, which do not lead into or out of the material before and after, even sometimes breaking mid-sentence. Small hypothesises *De Profundis* is actually 'an amalgam of several documents, one of which was a letter to Douglas which Wilde had been hoping to finish around February 1897, but which he had ended up expanding and developing by combining it with other material which he had been working on.'[15]

Bosie always admitted he had received *something* from Oscar through Robbie. He said the typescript he received had been made before Wilde left prison. Bosie's earliest published account of this was in *Oscar Wilde and Myself*. He claimed the letter came with a covering letter from Robbie apologising for having to send it, 'but that Wilde was apparently more of less out of his mind ... disposed to quarrel with everybody and that he (Ross) hoped that I should take no notice of what he was sending.'

Bosie said he read only a few lines and threw it on the fire (in a later version he tore it up and threw it in the river). In any case, he did not read much of it. He replied that 'if Wilde had anything to say to me he could say it in his own handwriting.'[16]

This all gibes with what he wrote to Robbie after receiving the letter from Lewis that claimed Ross had acted in accordance with Wilde's wishes: 'As you must be perfectly well aware, I have never, until I saw it stated in Ransome's book, had the slightest inkling that the MS of *De Profundis* was a letter addressed to me by Wilde or that there was any connection between the letter you sent me in 1897 (which I destroyed after reading the first half dozen lines) and the book. Had I been aware of this I should have used every endeavour to prevent the publication of the book by appealing to the sense of decency and honour which at that time I did not doubt you possessed.'[17]

'Why did you remain friends with Wilde after he came out of prison?' Hayes asked.

'Because before he went in he implored me to stick to him, and said it was his only hope of living through the time if I would stick to him.'

'If Ross had not told you not to, would you have written to Wilde in prison?'

'Certainly I should.'

Hayes concluded his re-examination by asking about the letters. Douglas said some of them had been entrusted to the law firm of Lewis and Lewis as his father's old solicitors and that their appearance was a breach of confidentiality. 'It is the office of a notorious blackmailer,' he said.

At this Campbell stood up to protest, 'Is there anybody else you would like to attack?'

'No, but if I did I should not wait for you to ask me.'

Campbell announced he was speaking on behalf of Sir George Lewis to deny the accusation. Hayes objected that it was improper for Campbell to make a statement from the well of the court, but the judge was not having it.

'The witness has said a very offensive thing,' he said, 'and if a solicitor, in such a case, does something irregular, I shall not restrict him.'

On Monday Adey was called to the stand on behalf of the plaintiff. Douglas's team had brought him in to testify that he had given Wilde £200 from Lady Queensberry when the Naples ménage broke up in 1897. But in cross-examination, he admitted that he and Ross both thought it would have been better if Wilde and Douglas had not reunited. More damaging was his claim that the £200 was not given in a spirit of generosity but as part of a £500 'debt of honour' to cover the costs of the Queensberry trial.

The £500 'debt of honour' comes from an 1898 letter from Wilde to Ross which also makes the false claim that Sibyl Queensberry had not given him any money when Bosie left. Robbie, who always felt Bosie had a moral obligation to help pay off the bankruptcy his father's action had caused, must have believed the 'debt of honour' existed and that Bosie had reneged on it. Adey, having seen the letter, must have believed the same. Bosie did not consider that there was any 'debt of honour,' but the £500 did refer to something. In court, he explained it away by saying Oscar always expected £500 from his brother Percy, but that he was not in a position to give it at that time. Years later, when writing *Without Apology* he seemed surprised to discover a reference to the £500 in a letter to his mother. 'Also if you possibly can, pay him the rest of the £500,' he had written when leaving Wilde in Naples. 'I cannot now, after all these years, give any explanation of this reference to "the £500". I can only assume that I had asked her originally go give him £500, and that she had told me that it was impossible, but that she could manage £200.'[18]

After the trial Bosie sent a letter to Adey, calling him Judas Iscariot:

> I wish you joy of what you have done, knowing as you do that I have for years led a clean, straight life, and have struggled hard to be a good Christian and a good Catholic, and knowing that Ross, who put up Ransome to write the book is a filthy beast and to this day a habitual corrupter of young boys. Our friendship is at an end. I shall never speak to you again. It is no business of mine to seek revenge on you or on Ross, but the reckoning will surely come sooner or later.

Then, rethinking his view on revenge he added the P. S. 'I am sending a copy of this letter to the Judge.' The judge found this move quite inappropriate.[19]

Many in Ross's social circle were delighted that Douglas was receiving his comeuppance. They shared their glee in seeing the moralist squirming at the sound of his lover's words. Millard wrote to a friend, 'The reading of *De Profundis* was most impressive and "sensational" (as a journalist would say).'[20]

Douglas was not in the courtroom as the third day of testimony began. This time, his presence was not required. The topic had finally returned to Ransome's *Oscar Wilde a Critical Study*. The Times Book Club's defence was short and sweet. Smith called Alfred Butes, the director of the club and asked him some preliminary questions about its selection process. In cross-examination Hayes got the witness to admit that he had not actually read the book in question, only glanced through. (Was Douglas the only person in England who actually read Ransome's book?) Hayes asked Butes if he had any young lady subscribers.

'Yes, but we exercise a certain amount of discretion as to sending a book to a subscriber.'

'If a book is in circulation, how can you prevent a subscriber from getting it whether a young lady or a male student?'

'In every case we have a right to substitute something else.'

'What do you mean?'

'He means,' Justice Darling imposed, 'that if a subscriber wrote for a copy of this book, and he thought it was not good for that particular subscriber, he would send Wordsworth.' This brought laughter to the courtroom.

'I would say our subscribers expect us to do that,' Butes said, to more laughter from the gallery.

Hayes read a passage from the book about Wilde's trial and asked Butes if he thought it was indecent and asked him to answer yes or no. The judge answered instead, 'You would not say that no one should write books except of the nature of The Lives of the Saints? ... Do you say that The Times Book Club ought not circulate any book except such as young ladies would be allowed to open?'

Hayes said he would not go so far.

'Then why say so much about young ladies unless you are prepared to say they must not issue any book which is not fit to be put in the hands of young ladies?'

In closing for the book club Smith took up Darling's own argument that being suitable for young girls was not the standard to which the club should be held. People did not get books on Oscar Wilde without knowing the facts of his life and a book on Wilde could not be expected to leave out all mention of those events. He argued, reasonably, that those who were not already familiar with the case would not know the passages in Ransome's book referred to Douglas, and those who were already familiar with Douglas's role would not learn anything new from the book.

He then suggested that because Douglas had, in the past, written in defence of Wilde's vices that it was he who had been a bad influence on Wilde and he should not be granted 'a farthing in damages.' He asked the jury to imagine that Ransome's libel was not that Wilde's friend had abandoned him but that Douglas had attempted to corrupt innocent persons. Essentially, he was asking the jury to ignore the actual facts of the case. He asked them not to give Douglas 'a vindication of character'.

Once again, 'Two Loves' was read in court. Smith submitted that Douglas's explanation of its meaning was 'palpably untrue'. Finally, he argued that Douglas had betrayed Wilde's memory by bringing this case to court and dredging up the past just as the public was starting to focus on the artist rather than the man's life.

Standing to make his closing statement on behalf of Ransome, Campbell agreed. He said Douglas had chosen 'with amazing stupidity' to bring the case. His story was exactly the one that Ross wanted to be told: 'Whatever might be said about Wilde and his unhappy career, he showed himself during the terrible days of his three trials to be a true and loyal friend to Lord Alfred Douglas. He never gave him away, though now Lord Alfred Douglas exhausted a vocabulary of abuse upon him. Wilde, to whom the plaintiff sent the deathbed message, 'Give him my undying love and affection,' was now described by Lord Alfred Douglas as the devil incarnate, a beast, a vampire. Those expressions were used by the plaintiff not on account of Wilde's alleged or real vices, but because Wilde wrote what was to be found in the unpublished part of *De Profundis* ... I believe plaintiff will be heartily shamed for the rest of his life.'

Wilde, said Campbell, 'was the man who sacrificed himself beyond all doubt, who screened the plaintiff from criminal proceedings, exposure and disgrace ... whom the plaintiff pursued with savage passion and devotion, and to whom on his deathbed the plaintiff sent a message of undying love. That was the man whom Lord Alfred had kept on a pedestal and worshipped as a sort of religious saint, a man who, in many aspects of his private life, was, I am afraid, a man of monstrous vicious habits. Now plaintiff has come here to dethrone and defame him, not that he differs from his views on life, but because Wilde, in the solitary seclusion of his cell at Reading, wrote that document which drew the veil aside of some of the facts that caused his ruin in to the abyss of which he sank.'

He said there was 'a good deal of stage-acting' on Douglas's part, but he believed his flight from the court during the reading of *De Profundis* revealed his true emotions. The reading 'seared his conscience. If the statements in that terrible indictment were true it was a terrible ordeal for him to have to undergo in the witness-box.'

He said in 1896, a year before *De Profundis* was written, Wilde wrote to Ross that Douglas had ruined him and that instead of denying it, Douglas had written in 'grovelling submission' saying 'I know I have ruined his life.'

Campbell argued that every line in *De Profundis* had been proven true and that Douglas had come into court 'thinking that time had destroyed most of the evidence against him.'

Campbell complimented Ross saying his only desire was to collect the poet's works so that 'the stigma of his private character might be palliated by the better demonstration of his literary greatness ... The plaintiff had got off scot free,' he said, 'while Wilde had stood by him and borne all the disgrace and punishment.'

In conclusion he, like Smith, told the jury that the most important evidence in the case was Douglas's letters. He did not deserve 'a shilling' in damages because he had brought the action only to blast the reputations of those with whom he had once been intimate, including the man to whom on his dying bed Douglas had sent a message of 'undying love and affection'.[21]

The case for the defence was concluded, and Ransome had never been called to the stand. This was a tactical move on the part of his counsel. He was not in a position to testify to the facts of Wilde's life from personal experience. All he could do was to say he had gotten his information from Ross, which would open the door for Ross to be called. Lewis had pressed Ransome not to drop the action in the first place because he was anxious that Ross's handling of *De Profundis* not be questioned. With Douglas threatening far and wide to throw all kinds of mud at his client, there was no way he was going to risk putting him on the stand. This seems to have thrown Hayes, who we can assume was armed with mud.

Next it was Hayes turn to make a speech. He said his client was 'fighting the battle of his life'. He thought the jury would agree that his client had acted with 'chivalry and courage in defying the opinion of the world' and lending his villa to a man who had been shunned by society. He began by reading poems to show the influence of Douglas's work.

He read Shakespeare's sonnet 20 with its line about 'the master-mistress' of his passion and a poem by Swinburne and concluded, 'these poets are to be congratulated that they did not have to be cross-examined by Mr Campbell.'

'Did Swinburne really write that?' asked the judge.

'Yes, my Lord; Here is the volume.'

'Well, it sounded to me like what you would expect to read in a Valentine.' There was loud laughter in the court. 'Do you mean the jury to infer that Shakespeare was guilty of the same practices as Wilde?'

'Certainly not,' said Hayes, 'I meant that Shakespeare's sonnets were perfectly innocent, and anyone is at liberty to write sonnets of the same kind without any meaning being attributed to them.'

He referred to the Times Book Club's portion of the case, and pointed out that Smith had devoted more of his closing argument to the question of Douglas's loyalty to Wilde than the question of whether his clients had disseminated a libel. He reminded the jury that in cross-examination Butes had admitted he had not bothered to read the book before circulating it.

He then asked why Ross, the man behind so much of the evidence, had not been called as a witness by the defence. Darling gave him the option to call Ross as a hostile witness. Ransome felt that the judge was hoping Hayes would call him, because he was enjoying the case and didn't want it to end.

'But the onus of proving their justification lies on the defendants,' Hayes said.

'Mr Ross is not a party to this action,' said Darling, 'It is my duty to protect him.'

'He ought to have been called by the defendants,' Hayes repeated. 'I could not cross-examine him as my witness and should be bound by his answers.'

'I have listened in vain for any reason why he should have been called. He was only Wilde's literary executor.'

Hayes speculated that the fact the defence did not call the one person who could give first-hand testimony to Douglas's supposed abandonment of Wilde meant he could not prove it. Was there any doubt, he wondered aloud, who was inspiring the defence in this case?

Darling was not persuaded by this, but repeated his offer to Hayes to put Ross on the stand and treat him as a hostile witness. Hayes was astute enough to fear what Ross might have to say unchallenged in the witness box so he was only able to pose his most pressing question rhetorically: 'How came the most damaging passages of the unpublished part of *De Profundis*, which was not to be published until 1960, to be reproduced in Mr Ransome's book?'

He then asked the jury not to give much weight to the lengthy text he had himself inflicted upon the court. *De Profundis*, he now argued, had nothing to do with the case. They were the words of a man who was 'either a maniac or was suffering from hallucinations'. He could not be cross-examined, and there was no way to know what the condition of his mind had been when he wrote 'that black indictment.'

'Gentlemen,' he concluded, 'you are now in a position to appreciate the full import of the words of this alleged libel. I think you will agree that I am not overstating the magnitude of this libel when I say that if the words are true, then Lord Alfred Douglas will be branded as a despicable man; he will be for all time not only destroyed in his life, but as long as the memory of his name lasts. On the other hand, if the words are untrue, I know you will agree that this constitutes a defamation the grossness and wickedness of which can not be surpassed.'

Darling continued, 'Mr Ransome's book was published because it was admitted on all hands – no one proclaimed it more loudly than the plaintiff – that Wilde was a great literary artist, a great manager of words. '*De Profundis* is a most remarkable and interesting document. It was, and must remain, a study of what a bad man went through in prison, of the effect of prison upon him.'

As to whether the statements in Ransome's book were true, he told the jury that as a member of the Court of Criminal Appeal, he knew that prisoners often made grossly unfair attacks on others in order to excuse their own actions. They 'should not dream' of taking *De Profundis* literally but 'it did not follow that it was all false.' He defended Ross for leaving everything related to Douglas out of the published version. The fact that the trustees of the British Museum agreed to take it proved that it was a valuable document. After bringing the case, Douglas could not now complain that the defence had produced *De Profundis* to show what Wilde's view was of their relations. Nor, he said, could Douglas complain that his old letters had been produced.

It was on those letters that Darling put the greatest importance. He read one that Douglas had written to Wilde in 1899. The press declined to print it, but Darling described it as containing a 'conversation which a decent pagan of the time of Pericles would not have referred to ... This letter was written by a man of 27. Lord Alfred Douglas came into this world with advantages such as nobody in this court had. He had every opportunity to do well: born into a high position which if he had behaved himself decently he would still occupy. At 27 what could he not have done? He had written things that showed he was, if not a man of genius, certainly a man of talent – a talent which could have placed him in a high position in the world of literature.'

Darling spoke of the attempts that had been made after Wilde's release from prison 'to enable him to redeem his past, and perhaps to still again become a great literary man if only he would give up his evil life. The plaintiff had referred to Oscar Wilde as a "devil incarnate". If it was true that Wilde was trying to lead a better life, what term might he not well apply to the man who had written that letter?'

Darling said he was glad Lady Alfred Douglas did not know the contents of those letters, 'I hope she never will.' He concluded by congratulating the British press for heeding his instructions and not printing 'the disgusting parts in this case'.

He said it had been proved that Douglas was the subject of the passage in Ransome's book, and that *De Profundis* proved that Wilde held Douglas responsible for his downfall. His final thought before putting the case to the jury was devoted to *De Profundis*. 'Oscar Wilde was writing this, and it is plain that he was writing it for his own glorification, whether it is true or not. That is quite plain.'

It took the jury only 45 minutes to find that the words in Ransome's book were libellous, but also true. They found that the Times Book Club was not negligent in making the book available. From then on there was no more talk of Wilde being driven to excess by 'admirers' in the plural. Douglas was now the only suspect in Wilde's ruin. The only question his supporters and detractors would fight over was just how culpable he was.

Bosie's description of himself and Oscar as 'merely ordinary people who are very fond of one another' had been replaced by a more compelling story, a reversal of Dorian Gray where the student corrupts the Svengali. This myth was combined with yet another, the story of the great man suffering for his art, as revealed in *De Profundis*.

Ransome was disgusted by the whole experience. He was annoyed 'at being congratulated on the result of a struggle that, win or lose, had meant nothing to me but thirteen months of wretchedness.'[22] He had the references to Douglas removed from future editions of the book, and refused to discuss the case again.

Millard wrote to Walter Ledger in a spirit of celebration. He sent him copies of a newspaper with pictures from the trial. 'Douglas is up tomorrow at the Old Bailey for libelling Colonel Custance, so he has got his hands pretty full, hasn't he?'[23]

Max Beerbohm had a different reaction to the proceedings, 'The case seems to me very cleverly constructed by Ransome's counsel,' he wrote to Reggie Turner on 3 June, 'But as the main part of this cleverness was in keeping Bobbie Ross out of the witness-box, certainly the victory was not of a glorious kind.' He went on to tell Reggie that Bobbie had written to him recently saying 'I daresay you know that for some seven or eight years I have been offended with you.' Beerbohm assumed he expected his friend to write back and ask why. 'But really I can't profess to feel any curiosity about, or any sympathy with, a grievance that hasn't prevented him from showing the most unctuous cordiality whenever we have met.'[24]

Perhaps it would have been better for Ross in the long run if he had taken the stand. Then he would have faced Douglas in a mitigated setting under the rule of law. As it was, Bosie's frustration at being unable to confront either of the men behind the attacks upon him drove him to extremes of behaviour that were indiscriminately destructive. Wilde was dead and beyond the point that Bosie could do him any real harm. Robbie would bear the brunt for both of them.

'He was the High Priest of all the sodomites in London,' wrote Douglas,

... and it was he who was held up to the world as the faithful friend of Wilde (out of the exploitation of whose cult he had made a fortune), the noble disinterested friend, the pure, the holy person, in contrast to the wicked and depraved Alfred Douglas who had 'ruined' Oscar Wilde and 'deserted' him. Flesh and blood couldn't stand it, and I swore the day after the Ransome trial that I would never rest till I had publicly exposed Ross in his true colours.[25]

38

By Legitimate Means or Otherwise

> Robert Ross – I am well aware I have to thank you for handing to Ransome,
> for production at the trial in his action, the manuscript of the letter Wilde
> wrote to me ... There are other things in store for you, but I won't go into
> them now. There is a time for everything. 'The mills of God grind slowly and
> they grind exceeding small.'
>
> Letter from Lord Alfred Douglas to Ross.[1]

Douglas had no time to rest between trials. He was back in court bright and early
on 24 April for publishing libels against Colonel Custance. Hayes had applied
to the recorder for a three- or four-day pause between trials, but his request was
denied. It probably did not help that his client had just been reprimanded for
sending libellous letters to a witness and the judge in the Ransome case.

Douglas sat on the bench behind counsel looking nonchalant in a 'tight-
fitting dark grey frock overcoat and a dark grey tie beneath a wing collar' as
he chatted with Crosland. He was in fairly good spirits because had decided to
plead guilty and leave it to Cecil Hayes to argue for leniency. He was bound
on his own recognizance of £500 with the promise that he would not pester
Custance or his peers with any more angry letters. This inevitably proved
impossible for him, but for the moment it was a great relief to put an end to
all the painful litigation.

Douglas would give various explanations for his failure to justify. He
sometimes said it was to spare his wife from having to give evidence against her
father. On other occasions he said he was simply too exhausted from Ransome to
put up a defence. Or perhaps it was the 'two large iron boxes of exhibits' placed
before the dock including 'several volumes of Oscar Wilde's *De Profundis*' that
dissuaded him.[2]

In any case, he had only a brief respite from the courts. There was still the
small matter of his bankruptcy to deal with. On 12 June he appeared before the
Official Receiver in a long, dry hearing about his losses running *The Academy*.
The yawning reporters heard nothing sensational until the very end when the
subject of *De Profundis* came up. The newspapers that covered the hearing
typically quoted Douglas saying that he thought *De Profundis* was worth £5,000,
that it was his property and that he was willing to help his creditors get it.
This creates the impression that he was obsessed with getting possession of *De
Profundis* and that his motivations were primarily financial.

Reading the transcript of the hearing, however, a different picture emerges. It becomes clear that it was not Douglas who raised the subject of the manuscript, although he did believe it was his property. The Official Receiver pointed out that Douglas had, on 27 May, filed a sworn affidavit claiming that the *De Profundis* manuscript was his property. The Official Receiver wanted to know why it had not been claimed as one of his assets. He replied, '… because it was only recently suggested to me [that it was his property]. It never occurred to me until someone pointed it out to me.' He did, however, say that he thought it was probably worth £5,000 and that he was willing to help his creditors get it.[3] He may not have been trying to make money from the manuscript, but rather to get it out of the hands of his sworn enemy, Robert Ross.

Robbie, meanwhile, was gathering evidence to attack Bosie or to defend himself – the lines were becoming increasingly blurred. He wrote to Ada Leverson on 29 July thanking her for the 'Oscar-Bosie letter, which may be very useful some day'.[4] He also gathered some letters that Bosie had written to a friend from Biskra in which he said 'I am staying here with a marvellous boy. You would adore him.' Millard sold typescript copies of these letters to AJA Symons in 1925. Millard would later regret not having the typescripts to show to Frank Harris as he worked on his Wilde biography, but told him that the original was in George Lewis's safe.

Bosie had his own plan. He had hired a private inquiry agent who called himself 'Carew'. He was determined to find enough dirt on Robbie to force him into submission. He would spread libels against his old friend until he was backed into the same corner Wilde had been; obliged either to go to court and risk exposure and possible jail, or give in to Bosie's demands. Once he had Robbie in this position, he would force him to give up *De Profundis* and his old letters, which he planned to destroy.[5]

Robbie's stress, and his own paranoia, were by now causing many of his friendships to fracture. His friendship with Reggie Turner was one of the notable casualties. Even in their youth, Robbie and Reggie's friendship had been punctuated by 'awful coolnesses'.[6] Things had become increasingly strained between them since Robbie published the first edited version of *De Profundis*. Reggie had never approved of it. As we have seen from their letters, as early as 1898 he and Max Beerbohm had felt Oscar's grievances were comically exaggerated and unfair to Bosie. When the *Collected Edition* came out in 1908 containing a fuller version of *De Profundis,* Reggie told Robbie that publication of any part of it in Bosie's lifetime, whether or not he was mentioned by name, was 'disgraceful'.

Bitter at the rebuke, Robbie wrote ending the friendship and proposed that 'for the convenience of common friends we greet each other on the rare occasions when we may meet. How rare they may be I do not care to anticipate. The contingency would only occur in London.'[7]

This was not the last word, however. They were reconciled, but never fully. As the conflict began to heat up between Bosie and Robbie, Reggie had tried to avoid taking sides. As both camps were insisting that their friends must declare allegiance, it became increasingly difficult. He decided to avoid the battle by going abroad. But the bickering was not the only thing that caused him to flee.

Bosie's man Carew had questioned Robbie's neighbours as part of his fishing expedition. Reggie must have known that he was at risk of getting dragged into the mess. Indeed, Turner was listed as one of Ross's suspected homosexual associates in Scotland Yard files. A year later, after another falling out, Robbie would write to Reggie, 'I am also aware of what a foolish mistake I made in going to Little Grosvenor Street, & I am really heartily sorry that I caused you that annoyance.'[8]

The stress of the litigation and constant threats from Bosie cannot have helped Robbie and Freddie's relationship either. Strained to the breaking point, they had a serious quarrel. The focus of their argument was Freddie's desire to shut up two rooms in their flat, an admission, perhaps, that he no longer wished to stay there.

'I have at last reduced Freddie by threats to conforming in some way to my wishes. Every other appeal was made in vain,' Ross wrote to Millard. 'He attempted every kind of subterfuge ... elaborately ignoring the causes of my indignation with him & pretending that I have some other motive.' Robbie said he could never 'resume the old terms of affection' with him.[9]

On 4 September Ross left for Paris en route to Russia to oversee a production of *Salome* at the Moscow Art Theatre. His stay in Paris was longer than he anticipated because there were no sleeper cars available and he planned to see Reggie and the artist Adolph Birkenruth, whose studio was known as a homosexual hang-out. Robbie landed in yet another quarrel with Reggie. According to some notes Ross made in a letter to Millard shortly thereafter, the argument had something to do with Birkenruth, his sister the artist Josephine Birkenruth and Bosie's private investigator.[10]

Based on Scotland Yard files not made public until 1991, one can make an educated guess as to what transpired. Douglas's investigation had resulted in widespread interviews of suspected homosexuals in Ross's orbit. Birkenruth was mentioned in a letter from Douglas's solicitors who called the artist an 'alleged habitual sodomite ...' The police, however, found nothing in their files to report to the legal team.

Birkenruth, however, must have been aware of the increased scrutiny and decided to stay abroad where Robbie said he was 'depressed' because he seemed to 'have no friends at all.' Millard conveyed a rumour to Robbie that Reggie had left Paris to avoid meeting him. This caused Robbie to grumble about some 'stupid remark' Reggie had made to Birkenruth. He decided it was much better that they avoid each other.'[11]

Robbie continued on to Moscow, where he stayed from 18 September to 12 October. He had planned to travel on to St. Petersburg, but he was still in a black mood, everything was expensive, the museums were closed, he couldn't speak Russian and very few people spoke German, French or English. If there were other homosexuals in Russia (as there must have been) Robbie did not recognise them. He wrote to Millard, 'You will be surprised (as indeed I am) but among the hundreds of people I have met here I have not seen any "purple" people or any who avowed they were or looked in the least like it. Nor does one see them in the streets. It is rather depressing.'[12]

Even the Russians' attempts to be welcoming rubbed him up the wrong way. He wrote to his brother, that his hotel room was 'a mass of expensive flowers' which made him feel like a 'popular prostitute'.[13]

He decided to cut his trip short and asked Millard to meet him but not to tell Freddie that he was coming. He planned to arrive when Freddie would not be there because 'His presence would merely upset me' adding that his 'artificial enthusiasm would annoy me.'[14]

Two months later, Robbie moved out of Mayfair Chambers and took an apartment at Georgian House in Bury Street. Freddie stayed in the flat they had once shared for at least six months. He was in the process of launching a new career for himself. On 23 October he published his first of many novels, *Elektra*, under the nom de plume Stanley Ford. It was the story of a beautiful, but amoral young woman who was plucked from a life as an orange seller by a cultured gentleman who educated her and nurtured her singing talent. Once she had learned to carry herself like a woman of a more gentle class, she started to compare her husband to the 'wonderful looking young men' of the city and was bored and annoyed by all of his little manners and habits and, in particular, the physical signs of his age.

One night, as she watched him in his sleep she decided she couldn't take any more and she poisoned him, after which she went off on a series of adventures with other men throughout Europe including to St. Moritz Switzerland, a significant locale for Freddie. He had visited Colerdige Kennard and Helen Carew there. A hint as to the cause of Robbie and Freddie's tensions might be found on the dedication page. *Elektra* was dedicated not to Robbie but to the actor Herbert Dansey.[15]

Meanwhile, although he was not yet aware of it, a new weapon against Robbie had entered the scene in the form of an attractive, tall young man with wavy auburn hair and feminine mannerisms. (*The Daily News* would one day describe him as 'a lad of effeminate appearance and a girlish voice'.)[16]

His name was Charles Nehemiah Garratt, but he went by Charlie, and occasionally, when it was convenient to hide his identity, as Charles Tuke or Alfred Richardson.[17] The seventeen-year-old was born around the time of Oscar Wilde's trials in Countesthorpe, a small town outside Leicester. He was the son of a farm worker who had died when he was five, leaving his mother Elizabeth to raise six children. She earned eight shillings a week as a charwoman, of which two shillings were set aside for rent. Garratt had worked as an assistant groom and gardener and finally in a fried fish shop. He used his aliases to disguise his activities on behalf of the Men's League for Women's Suffrage, a brother organisation to the Women's Social and Political Union. The WSPU's slogan was 'Deeds, not words.' In 1913, they had started to smash windows, vandalise property and send letter bombs.

In early 1913, the militant suffragists became highly active. Throughout January there were riots, marches and more vandalism of mailboxes. Garratt was inspired to take action himself. But his terrorist intentions outpaced his criminal ability. He stole envelopes from his then-employer the George Hotel, and tore off the flaps which identified their source. He took a bottle of disinfectant from the stables and poured it into an envelope before dropping it into a pillar box. He did the same the next evening with different boxes. When the police eventually caught him, they charged him with damaging the property of the Post Master General in the amount of one penny for a stamp that had been washed off one of the letters in the box. He was sent to the Church Army Home for one month for the 'diabolical mischief'. His criminal record remained on the books, causing him problems later on.

Although his mother was unaware of it, Garratt started to take occasional trips to London with the suffragists, handing out pamphlets and speaking on behalf of the cause. He also took advantage of his time in the big city to meet men. (He would one day have cause to deny that men paid him for sex, but the police were not convinced.)[18]

This is how he had met Christopher Millard as he was walking along Shaftesbury Avenue on 19 August 1913. Millard, who was sympathetic to the suffragists cause, was interested in the young man's WSPU badge. (At least, this is what he told the authorities when they asked what had piqued his interest in the young man.) He struck up a conversation and asked the youth to join him for a drink. They met up with a man named Pat, and after a few rounds Millard invited them both back to his house. Garratt drank whiskey, and he stayed the night. Garratt would later refuse to tell investigators 'whether Millard and Pat kissed me and messed me about or whether they got into bed with me and behaved immorally.'

While Robbie was away in Paris and Moscow, Millard was reunited with Garratt. He had come back to London and Millard spotted him from his taxi window and invited him to come to dinner with friends, after which they went back to Millard's house. Garratt stayed there until around midnight. They met again the next evening and Millard took him to dinner and a show, an adaptation of *Dorian Gray* at the Vaudeville Theater in the Strand. The date was a success, and Millard soon described Garratt to a friend as 'a beauty' who 'arouse[d] his passion.'[19] He started to introduce him to his friends at the Café Royal and The Avenue. (Whether Ross received an introduction would be the subject of prolonged litigation.) The circle of friends included a young academic Charles Leopold Boulenger, Cecil Howard Turner, Aylmer Clerk and Frank Hughes, who went by the nickname 'Fluffy'.

Turner would one day deny that he enjoyed it when Garratt 'threw himself on the sofa' where he was sitting and 'endeavoured to embrace him.' He claimed he 'knew nothing of this sort of thing' and that he 'nearly strangled Fluffy when he made a suggestion to him.' Yet he was seen walking arm and arm with Garratt, and Millard felt comfortable enough to speak 'quite openly to him about improper conduct with different boys' and to tell him that his only interest 'was sodomy'.[19]

On 13 September, Millard and Garratt went on a small getaway. They travelled with Clerk to the Queen's Hotel near Westcliff railway station. There they met Hughes, who was working as stage manager for a production at the New Palace Theater. Hughes greeted his friends with kisses. (Or perhaps he didn't, depending on whose legal testimony you believe.) They had tea in lodgings that Hughes had rented, consisting of a bedroom and a sitting room. Hughes took Garratt to see the closing night of a play called *The Little Damozel* by Monckton Hoffe while Millard and Clerk went out walking. They all met up after the play and had a late oyster dinner and then went back to Hughes' rooms. The police would spend years trying to find out more about the sleeping arrangements on that night, who touched who, and what the sheets looked like afterwards. It seems that Garratt and Millard shared a double bed. The sleeping arrangements of the other two fellows is more contentious.

On 17 September, Millard had a few friends to dinner. One of them was Garratt, the others were probably Hughes (he was described as an actor) and Scott Moncrieff (described as a student at Edinburgh). They drank copious quantities of champagne and 'played charades.' Instead of going straight to his lodgings when he left the party, the tipsy Garratt headed to Picadilly where police officers assumed he was a prostitute because he 'acted in an effeminate way and smiled up into the face of gentlemen.' They described him as having a powdered and rouged face and 'smelling very strongly of scent.'

When Millard learned of the arrest, he rushed to the court and agreed to speak on Garratt's behalf. He described himself as an Oxford graduate and secretary to a well-known literary gentleman. He admitted that Garratt had had too much to drink at his house, but he said he was not drunk when he left, nor was he wearing rouge or powder. After the hearing, Millard wrote to Garratt's mother. He did his best to conceal the truth about the charges against her son, implying his arrest was related to the suffragist movement. (Political vandalism being more respectable than sex with men.)

By the time the hearing resumed on 25 September, the prosecutors had unearthed Millard's criminal record and he was recalled to the stand. The magistrate warned Millard 'not to lead lads like this to that sort of ruin.' Millard argued that he was not trying to ruin him, but to keep him out of trouble.

'But why do you have anything to do with the boy? Why is he in your hands at all?'[20]

The magistrate decided to give Garratt a light sentence of three months hard labour because 'I feel that the lad has fallen because of coming under the influence of you and men like you.' Garratt was led away in tears to Pentonville Prison. Millard visited him there, and corresponded with his mother. Garratt, full of suffragist idealism, threatened to go on a hunger strike, but Millard talked him out of it.[21]

The incident had not escaped the notice of Lord Alfred Douglas. When he saw Millard's name in connection with Garratt's arrest in the newspaper, he clipped the article and sent it to George Lewis as a warning. There is a good chance that he received additional information on Millard and his circle through their mutual friend, Gerald Hamilton or his business partner Maurice Schwabe. When police questioned Aylmer Clerk the following July, they asked him if he knew Hamilton. (The police called him Gerald Souter.) Clerk confirmed that he knew a man of that name but said, 'I decline to give any information about him.'

When he was in the middle of his three month sentence, Garratt received a visitor. It was Cecil Holt who Douglas had hired to replace Arthur Newton when he went to jail. Holt showed Garratt a photograph identified as 'Walter Ross of Oxford.' He asked Garratt if he knew the man. He either said that he did or that he did not. The story changed depending on who was telling it and when.

Either way, Holt asked Garratt to make a statement implicating Millard and Ross in gross indecency. If he did, Holt promised that the people he represented would help him after he was released. He refused. Shortly thereafter Garratt received a second visit from a Mr Fairall, from Holt's office. He also asked Garratt to make a statement, but Garratt again refused. Before he left, Fairall told Garratt he would leave the address of the Holt law firm with the prison governor in case he changed his mind.

Crosland, meanwhile, was writing *Oscar Wilde and Myself* with information that had been supplied by Douglas during their conversations to prepare for the Ransome trial. Douglas wanted to include some of the letters Wilde had written him to prove he had never abandoned him. But Ross, as executor, obtained an injunction to prevent it. The legal action delayed the publication of the book.[22]

Ross also took steps to make sure that Douglas could not circumvent this by publishing in the United States. He arranged to have fifteen copies of the complete *De Profundis* published by an American firm, Paul R. Reynolds. This put the full text in copyright under US law. Two copies were deposited in the Library of Congress. At least one copy had to be put on sale to fulfil copyright requirements, so one copy was placed in a book store with a $500 price tag, almost $12,000 in today's money. Amazingly, a person who has never been identified walked in, paid the price and took it home. The remaining twelve copies were sent back to England where Robbie shared them with friends including Vyvyan Holland, Christopher Millard, George Lewis, More Adey, John Lane, A. L. Humphreys, Viscount Haldane, Edmund Gosse and Carlos Blacker.[23]

As he was doing his best to keep Douglas's book off the shelves, Ross was helping Harris who was about to publish his own *Oscar Wilde*. On 18 December 1913, Harris wrote to Ross asking for permission to say that his book was recommended by the Wilde estate and that he had received permission to publish Wilde's letters. Ross gave him permission to include the letters, but said he should not mention it in print or Douglas would try to get an injunction against it. Harris, who had not yet had a run-in with Douglas on the matter, thought Ross was paranoid and replied that he was 'unnecessarily disturbed', but he agreed not to mention the letters in any marketing materials.[24]

This highlights the fact that only Ross now had the authority to decide which of Wilde's words would be shared and which would be suppressed. He could, and did, permit the dissemination of 'he fills me with horror' while preventing the publication of 'it is only with you I can do beautiful work.' This did nothing to diffuse the escalating conflict, but it did strengthen the narrative that Douglas had ruined and abandoned Wilde and the increasingly vengeful, bitter and unstable Douglas was unintentionally becoming Ross's greatest ally in spreading that story.

Both parties to the dispute were becoming increasingly anxious and paranoid. Robbie believed Bosie's influential family was bankrolling his vendetta. This was true only to the extent that Bosie could always count on his mother's financial help. Bosie's paranoia was even more exaggerated. As Custance and Ross were both represented by Lewis, Bosie had become convinced that they were collectively conspiring to destroy his marriage. He sent abusive letters to that effect to Custances's neighbours, his cousin Admiral Sir Reginald Custance, and even to the King. Bosie would later justify his letter-writing campaign saying he had taken the step 'very deliberately after mature consideration ...'[25]

On 28 October 1913 he wrote a menacing letter to Lewis, 'The chain of evidence which I have been collecting against your friend Robert Ross is now nearly complete. It includes, in addition to a stack of his own letters, sworn statements from two of his victims. As soon as my investigations are completed I shall apply for a warrant for his arrest.'[26]

When Charlie Garratt was released from jail on 10 December, Millard was there to meet him. Garratt told him about his strange visitors. Millard immediately took him to see Lewis, who then reported to Ross. With no money, no prospects and the stigma of jail hanging over him, Garratt hoped one of these men would help him find a situation. Garratt told his story to Lewis, but he offered him nothing for it. So two days later, unbeknownst to Ross and Millard, he headed on to Cecil Holt's office setting in motion the most bizarre episode in the Ross/Douglas feud.

Holt sent for Douglas, who gave the young man his card, 'to show me what a superior person he was'. Garratt would later testify in court. The card had the address 'Church-Road Hampstead' struck out and the address 'Grosvenor Hotel' written over it in red ink. ('Did that impress you?' the barrister asked, bringing laughter to the courtroom.)[27]

On 12 December, Garratt had lunch with Douglas and Crosland. The young man ordered a meal and drank two beers. On this Garratt and Crosland agreed.

Beyond that, their stories have little in common. Crosland described Garratt as looking like he was fresh from school, not the 'kind of boy' he would have imagined based on his criminal record. The boy had come to them, he said, because he wanted help to report Millard and Ross.

In the Crosland version, Garratt said that when Millard took him to see Gorge Lewis they tried to get him to sign a document swearing he didn't know Ross, but he refused. Initially he was shy and reluctant to talk about what had happened to him, but Douglas reassured him, 'Mr Crosland is a friend of mine and you can talk freely before him.' So Garratt told them about his parties with Millard and his friends.

Garratt described Ross (according to Crosland) as 'a man with a bald head with a fringe of hair at the back, about Lord Alfred's height, but fatter. He has a mouthful of teeth.' He said Ross 'did not do anything to me like Millard and Pat did. All he did was to kiss me and mess me about.'

When Crosland asked him what he meant by 'messing about' he said 'He put his hand on me and wanted me to go with him but I always refused.' He described Fluffy Hughes as 'one of Ross's particular boys'.

After that Crosland proclaimed grandly that he told Garratt he had been treated in a 'shocking manner' and that he ought to go home to his mother and 'try to straighten out his life'.

Before Douglas took his statement, Crosland told the boy 'These are very serious statements that you are making. I suppose you know that they are serious.' He swore they offered Garratt no incentive beyond the pleasure of doing his civic duty. One incentive that Crosland specifically swore he did not offer was to help Garratt get a position at Selfridge's on Oxford Street. The boy responded that he had come to speak the truth.

Garratt told a different story. He testified that Douglas and Crosland knew he'd never met Ross but they pressured him to lie. Douglas called Ross a dirty beast and said that if Garratt would make 'just a little statement' Ross would be put in a position in which he would have to pay a large sum of money or lose his appointment as adviser to the Inland Revenue. 'In fact, the whole lot of them, including Millard and Ross would have to clear out of the country if the facts were brought to light,' Douglas said. He believed they could extract £1,000 from Ross to make the matter go away.

What is not in dispute is that at the end of the lunch, Douglas and Crosland had a statement written in pencil on a page torn out of a book. It implicated Millard and Ross in indecent offences. Garratt agreed to go with them to Scotland Yard to be interviewed by detectives. On the way there, according to Garratt, Douglas urged him to 'Rub it well in about Ross.'

There was some disagreement as to whether Douglas and Crosland composed the statement or whether Garratt dictated it. In any case, Douglas and Crosland were not in the room as Garratt reported to Sargeant Stephens over the course of several days. When he had finished, his statement was 37 foolscap pages long and Garratt signed it. Crosland testified that there were details in Garratt's Scotland Yard testimony he had been unaware of until it was read in court. He knew nothing, for example, about a part of the statement where Garratt claimed Ross burnt his lip with a cigarette while trying to kiss him.

On 12 December, Crosland, Douglas and an unidentified man (maybe Carew) dined with Garratt at the Grosvenor Hotel. According to Crosland, Douglas asked him to come because he didn't want to be alone at any time with the boy. According to Garratt, Douglas asked him if he had 'rubbed it in' and kept talking about the £1,000. In Crosland's version there was no mention of hush money but Garratt asked them to pay for his room and board, which they did out of kindness and compassion.

Garratt's story of the events of the following days was dramatic. The Saturday after his visit to Scotland Yard, he said, he dined with Douglas and Carew. They first went to the Wilton Hotel, but Douglas became paranoid that they were being watched. They checked out and changed taxis three times on their way to the next hotel in case someone was following them. The next day was Sunday, so Douglas paused to attend mass at Westminster Cathedral and took Garratt with him. They ate again at the Grosvenor Restaurant and Douglas got tickets for Kensington where Garratt was to repeat his statement.

'Lord Alfred told me that he gave me his word of honour that nothing would happen to me. I just had to pick up the Bible, he said, kiss it, and it would be all over,' Garratt said. 'I refused and walked away. Lord Alfred used some filthy language.' (According to the police files he said, 'You are no good except to be f-d at' and Carew called him 'Hosy Posy'.)

'He was in a frightful temper,' Garratt continued, 'and a man who was with us (Carew) caught hold of me and said "You do what Lord Alfred wants you to do. He will see you are all right."' (In the next phase of the trial this became 'You had better do all Lord Alfred tells you, my boy.') After his attempt to walk away they kept him prisoner in Carew's house near Earl's Court. He wanted to run, he said, but he found that the door was locked and his boots had been taken.

Two days after Garratt had made his statement, Douglas was already impatient. He wrote to Scotland Yard reminding them of their duty to take action against Ross and Millard. He also asked them to look into Hughes who 'frequents the streets & other places where stage people congregate'. He said Hughes was Ross's 'particular friend' and that he frequently dined with him and gave him gifts such as 'silver dressing things'. Everyone knew that Ross 'continually committed acts of immorality with him'.

Ross became frantic when he heard about Holt's overtures to Garratt. He wrote to Lewis saying he was determined to take the initiative and put an end to the threat of Alfred Douglas. He felt that he would have a better chance with a jury if he was defending rather than prosecuting. His plan was to give all of the background information he had gathered on Douglas to the Home Secretary to force Douglas to initiate a libel action against him. It would be no small libel, but one so grand that Douglas would lose all credibility before he ever stepped foot in court.

He was going to publish the personal parts of *De Profundis*. He knew what the consequences would be but he had nothing to gain from holding his peace or by 'hushing up a scandal which is not about me …' and the 'world would then know what I want it to know. What I would rather it did not know it either knows already or guesses.'

The next day he wrote to Methuen asking if they would like to publish the suppressed parts of *De Profundis*. They must have rejected it, for ten days later he was making the same offer to John Lane. His 23 December letter described the book as containing 'a very controversial preface' which he planned to write as well as a 'contentious' appendix related to the legal skirmishes between himself and Douglas. He promised that the book would contain 'nothing obscene' but 'much that is libellous.' In order to protect the publisher, he would back up every statement with documentary evidence and he would also assume financial responsibility for any legal consequences. Most important, he said, the book would have to be published in a special way: 'the book must not be announced beforehand but put on the market quite suddenly' so that it would sell in large numbers, 'before Douglas or his family were able to obtain an injunction.'[28]

Crosland and Douglas had been busy as well. On Christmas Eve, Ross received a 'writ of summons' based on a statement on her son's behalf by Elizabeth Garratt. Ross was charged with the indecent assault of Charles Garratt.

39

War

> Provide me with two thousand pounds and, with the help of the same
> solicitors, I will undertake to collect enough evidence to bring an action
> against all and sundry, high or low, from the Prime Minister downwards.
>
> Lord Alfred Douglas, 1895[1]

On New Year's Day 1914, Robbie had the shock of his life. He returned to his flat after a brief holiday in Scotland. He was immediately overtaken by the eerie sensation that something had been tampered with. George Lewis was still on holiday, so Ross decided to investigate the matter himself. After consulting with the hall porter, he learned that not only had strange people been inquiring about his movements, Douglas had been trying to bribe staff members to steal documents and had actually taken rooms in the same building to spy on his neighbour. After speaking to the proprietor 'who was quite charming', it was resolved that Douglas would be thrown out in the morning. Ross wrote to Edmund Gosse from the safety of the Reform Club, 'Tonight I pass the night under the same roof as Douglas who has come with the avowed purpose of suborning the servants ... This is AD 1914 and you will not think me either melodramatic or mock heroic when I tell you that I return to my rooms tonight with firearms.'[2] This sounds like one of Robbie's tall tales, but it was corroborated by a witness in Ross's libel suit against Douglas.[3] The next day Douglas left the building without making a scene, but he did, according to Ross, bribe a chambermaid to steal some of Ross's handkerchiefs on the way out the door.[4]

Bosie was learning, much to his chagrin, that it was actually not so easy to get someone arrested for gross indecency. Wilde's case had been an anomaly. Because sodomy was considered such a terrible offence and the social stigma attached to it was so great, the police were quite careful not to make arrests—at least of men of the respectable classes (Garratt could still be sent to prison for looking at someone the wrong way). Uncorroborated accomplice testimony would not stand up in court, nor would rumours and innuendoes.

At the end of 1913, the police had decided that Garratt's criminal record made him an unreliable witness and they would not proceed with any charges against Ross. It is not clear whether they communicated this to him. They did not communicate it well to Douglas, because he was still going about telling everyone that Ross was about to be arrested. He and Crosland had secured Garratt at his mother's home in Countesthorpe. They were paying his mother 10s a week to keep an eye on him. He was bored and miserable.

The first months of 1914 were a low point in the lives of both Ross and Douglas. Ross felt as though he was being watched at every turn, his nerves were on edge and fantasies of his own ruin occupied his thoughts. When he heard a rumour that Douglas was planning to distribute pamphlets outside the Reform Club accusing Ross of unnatural offences with Freddie Smith he started to panic believing he was going to lose everything and would never 'recover [his] prestige even on acquittal.'[5] He wrote to Gosse, certain he would be 'ruined ... no interference or kind word from those in high positions, could ever obviate the consequences of Douglas causing a pamphlet to be distributed outside the Reform Club.'[6]

Bosie had already been publicly shamed, his marriage had fallen apart, and his litigiousness had driven him to bankruptcy. He no longer had a club to be kicked out of. He could wage war with impunity because he had nothing to lose.

Under the increased tension and scrutiny, Freddie Smith found it amenable to spend an increasing amount of time abroad. Likewise, in early 1914, Olive Douglas started to enjoy the company of other men, (at least Bosie believed this was the case) and this caused Bosie to resume his letter writing campaign against Custance.

By now both Bosie and Robbie were employing detectives to spy on one other. Robbie's man was following Douglas and taking notes of the people he met at the Café Royal and various offices.[7]

Bosie and his man, Carew, were courting Millard, trying to persuade him that he was being treated badly by his employer and urging him to help them find incriminating information. Millard played along for a while, gathering intelligence and reporting back to Ross on Douglas's plans. He even accepted an invitation to discuss the matter as a guest at Bosie's house. The more Robbie learned, the more nervous he became. He started to worry that Millard's arrest and association with Garratt were a liability and he fired him as secretary. Millard wrote to Bosie complaining that he had lost his job on his account. He wrote that he hoped he was happy to have 'succeeded in ruining irretrievably a fellow Catholic who has done you no injury.'

'God forbid I should judge other people,' Bosie replied. 'If it were merely a question of yielding to temptation, I should sympathise with you and your ex-employer Ross, but it is a question of deliberate propaganda in the exaltation of vice.'[8]

Douglas, thinking that Millard would be bitter at being fired, arranged to meet him. According to Ross, he told Millard that he wanted to see the newspaper headline 'Arrest of Robert Ross,' and said he believed 'anybody would come forward for £5 and swear to anything.' Douglas asked Millard if he could get his hands on any compromising letters of Ross's, and offered to pay good money for them. His purpose was to arrange for an exchange to get his own letters back and to have the unpublished parts of *De Profundis* destroyed.[9]

Garratt eventually became so bored in the country that he agreed to help Crosland and Douglas by returning to London to make another statement to the police. Really, he was after the train fare. In London, he eluded his chaperones and was eventually arrested again for prostitution. Back in prison, and away from the influence of Crosland and Douglas, he recanted his story about Ross and told a clerk from Lewis's office that he had been bribed to lie.

In his other battle, Bosie, predictably, had broken the terms of his prior agreement by sending nasty letters to Colonel Custance and his friends. This gave Lewis the opportunity to take action against Douglas without Ross's sexuality being brought into the matter. Lewis advised Custance to bring a summons against Douglas. Custance filed his complaint in the first days of March 1914. At 5 PM on 4 March a man named Arthur Parlett knocked on the door of 19 Royal Avenue Chelsea to serve Douglas with the order. When he gave him the document, Douglas said, 'Very well, all right.' Immediately thereafter, he had his servants pack his cases. E. R. Thowl, a private investigator for Lewis & Lewis watched as he went to the Charing Cross Station bringing with him two portmanteaux, another small case, and, for some reason, a rug. He bought a first class single ticket to Calais, registered his baggage, and got on the train at 9:10 PM.[11]

The next day Douglas sent a letter from Calais to the Recorder of London explaining that he did not intend to appear in court because 'I am seriously and conscientiously convinced that I have no chance whatever of obtaining justice or fair treatment at the Central Criminal Court. I have done nothing at all which merits punishment at the hands of the law ... if I came into your Court tomorrow I should be simply putting my head into a noose. Consequently I am not coming.' He concluded by asking that if the recorder decided to describe this as an 'improper letter' that he read it in court. 'The word 'improper' conveys all sorts of meanings, and to leave a man under the stigma of writing 'improper letters' may be to give people the impression that the letters in question are mere filthy abuse.'[12] A few days later he wrote to Crosland giving him full authority to act on his behalf in the matter of the book *Oscar Wilde and Myself*.[13]

Millard was so thrilled by Douglas's departure that he asked a newsagent to give him the poster from *The Star* advertising the headline 'LORD ALFRED DOUGLAS GONE.' He put it up on the wall of his flat in Molyneaux House. He wrote to Walter Ledger that he had gone to the Old Bailey for the 'satisfaction of hearing the ushers calling through the corridors 'Alfred Bruce Douglas surrender!' He thought Douglas was a hypocrite because, interestingly, 'there has been no limit to his debauching of little girls.' He believed Custance had filed his action 'in order to give Douglas an opportunity of bolting ... and so saving face to some extent.' For his part, Millard hoped that Ross would not pursue any further legal actions now that Douglas had fled.[14] But the battle had not come to an end for either party. Far from it.

On 6 March Douglas's court date came and went and he did not appear. Douglas forfeited his £500 recognisances but as he was an undischarged bankrupt, the magistrate said, 'I don't suppose the Government will get very much out of that.' He applied for a warrant for Douglas's arrest.[15]

Meanwhile, from the safety of Paris, Douglas continued to lob insults. He produced a pamphlet *Letters to My Father-in-Law No 1* (anticipating there would be a second volume). The screed made shots about Custance's 'grocer ancestors' and claimed Lewis was using him 'as a catspaw' on behalf of the 'notorious Sodomite' Ross. But 'Sodom Ross' and his private secretary 'Gomorrah Millard' were going to get their comeuppance. He promised he would 'take every measure' to bring them to justice.[16]

Now that Garratt had come forward to say he had been bribed, Lewis felt there was enough evidence to prosecute Ross's nemises for conspiracy rather than libel. If they could prove that Douglas and Crosland had conspired to suborn perjury and manufacture evidence against Ross, his sexuality should not be an issue. (While this was legally true, it was a faulty social assumption.) Warrants were issued on 25 March 1914 for the arrests of Crosland and Douglas. Both were in France at the time, and the police were careful not to allow word of the impending arrest to leak to the press, for they feared that Crosland and Douglas might destroy documents.[17]

On 6 April a strange case appeared on Justice Darling's docket. Baron Guy de Chassiorn had filed damages for slander against Edwin Montague Calvert, a Norwich solicitor. This is relevant to our story for two reasons: Baron de Chassiron was a friend of Douglas and Edwin Montague Calvert was Custance's solicitor.[18]

Chassiron's mother, Caroline Murat, was the great-grandaughter of the first Napoleon's sister. In spite of this grand pedigree, he was raised in England and was for all intents and purposes an Englishman, a financially strapped one at that. In his 1912 bankruptcy, he stated that he had never had an occupation and he survived on gifts from relatives and friends.[19] As this bankruptcy was pending, Chassiron and Douglas, also about to be declared bankrupt, signed a joint promissary note for £160 payable in six monthly instalments for an advance of £100: Douglas got £80 and Chassiron £20. Chassiron was later questioned about this transaction in court.

'Did Lord Alfred Douglas ask you to put your name on that bill?'

'He said he wanted money.'

'Were you both in want of money?'

'He was more so.'

'Did he ask you to put your name to that bill?'

'Yes, he did.'

'At that time you must have known perfectly well that you could not meet the the promissary note for £100.'

'As a matter of fact Lord Alfred Douglas said he did not intend to trouble me.'

'Yes? Anyhow you put your signature to the bill?'

'Yes.'

After a few questions about the timing of this document it was put to Chassiron that he had no assets at all at the time he signed the note.

'Not actually, no.'

'Nothing at all, you had absolutely nothing had you?'

'No.'[20]

Chassiron was sent to jail for concealing assets from the Official Receiver, but Douglas never suffered any legal repercussions for his part in the fraud.

Chassiron was a friend and sometime house guest of Hylton North, Custance's newphew by marriage. Mrs. Custance was born Eleanor Joliffe and the North brothers, Hylton, Dudley and Roger were her sister Hylda's sons. The North boys each inherited £10,000 on their majority, but Hylton and Dudley had blown through their fortunes within a year. When Roger came of age in 1910, he had taken this as a cautionary tale, and executed a voluntary settlement that would keep most of his money in trust and provide a small regular income. The only way to break the trust was to marry and make a settlement on his wife.

By this time Hylton had become involved with a criminal organisation and was making his living introducing young men who had lost money at cards to moneylenders. Hylton and his confederates appear to have arranged to break Roger's settlement in order to get at his money. In 1912, Roger North married Alice Amy Le Gros, and made a marriage settlement with Hylton North and solicitor Frederick Stanley Parker as trustees. The marriage was witnessed by a woman named 'Tina'.

Roger immediately got a loan from moneylenders on the settlement. Within four and a half months £6,000 of it was gone. It had been spent in high living by Roger, his wife, Hylton, the baron and Tina. This caused Roger to go bankrupt, and he committed some offence in connection with the bankruptcy. He was arrested and taken to Norwich Gaol. It was Roger's first arrest, but it was not to be the last. He would go on to a long career including stealing a motor car, passing bad cheques, and other crimes, often while posing as a Lord or Viscount. Years later, when he was arrested for bigamy, he produced a written statement that 'extracted some sympathy' from the court, in which he said that his unfortunate marriage to Amy Le Gros had set him off on his life of crime.[21]

Roger's wife sought the help of Francis Hyde ('a young, clean-shaven man') and his wife and they consulted the solicitor Calvert. Hyde asked Calvert if Lord Guildford (his uncle from another side of the family) or Custance would help, and this is when Calvert was alleged to have uttered his slander against Chassiron.

In court, Hyde would claim that he never told Douglas about the slander, and yet somehow he knew about it because he wrote a letter to Custance about it the day after Chassiron filed his writ. Custance eventually did get involved in Roger North's business, challenging the marriage settlement as a fraud and a conspiracy. It would be alleged that Hylton North and Parker had specifically sought out a woman who was infertile to be Roger's bride so that there would be no children with competing claims on the marriage settlement.

When the slander suit came to trial, Chassiron arrived in court accompanied by his (and Douglas's) solicitor, Cecil Holt. The forty year-old was himself in a desperate financial position. The youngest of his five children had been born the previous May and he was just two months away from being declared bankrupt and three months from being jailed for using his client's money for personal expenses.[22]

The star witness of this slander trial, however, was Hyde. After recounting the details of the alleged slander, he was cross-examined by Ernest Wild, who asked about his relationship with Chassiron. Hyde said he had known him for about 18 months. He denied that he was a 'boon companion' to Hylton North and that he met with him frequently at the Café Royal. He testified that he was aware Douglas and the baron 'knew each other very well.'

'You knew they were always together?'

'Yes. I have seen them together.'

'At the Café Royal principally?'

'Yes.'

Hyde testified that he knew Douglas and Chassiron had the same solicitor, Cecil Holt, and that he sometimes met them together at the Café Royal, but he did not know Crosland. Wild then got Hyde to admit that he, too, had squandered his inheritance in a year and had gone bankrupt, that he had once been charged with being drunk and disorderly and had been accused of swindling tradespeople. Hyde was a 'traveller' for a wine and spirit merchant and worked on commission.

'That would be the reason for your going to the Criterion, the Café Royal and the Café Monico?'

'Yes.'

'And for drinking as much as you could?'

'Not as much as I could.'

'Did you go about with young men teaching them to drink and introducing them to moneylenders?'

'No.'

'Have they been unlucky at cards sometimes?'

'Not to my knowledge.'

By now Chassiron and Cecil Holt had left the courtroom. When this absence was noted, Darling quipped, 'Perhaps it is because the evidence has given him such a painful shock that he went out of court.'

Mrs. Hyde was called to the stand to corroborate her husband's statement and then the plaintiff rested its case.

'Are you not going to call the plaintiff to give evidence?' Darling asked.

'No. There is no plea of justification,' Vachell said.

'There is not the slightest evidence that he is the person you say,' said Darling, undoubtedly familiar with conmen of the Stallmann type. 'I shall have to tell the jury that we know nothing about this person. There is evidence that he is a bankrupt, but no evidence that he is a baron.'

In closing, Wild told the jury that it was 'a gross abuse of the courts of law that a gentleman of position should be brought there for the purpose of being persecuted by a gang of blackguards, blackmailers and bankrupts. This was a blackmailing action brought by a disreputable adventurer, brought partly as the vendetta of Lord Alfred Douglas.'

Darling's sarcastic summation brought peals of laughter to the gallery. The jury did not need to retire in order to return a verdict for the defendant with costs. The foreman added that the jury was of the opinion that the matter should never have been brought to court.

The meetings at the Café Royal that this case exposed between Douglas, Holt, Chassiron and possibly Crosland were gatherings of financially desperate men. There was no evidence in the forthcoming trials that Douglas or Crosland ever asked Ross or his solicitors for money to drop their attacks on him. Money cannot, however, be ruled out as one of a complex set of motives. Douglas was animated by a desire to set the record straight, to get revenge, and a desire to stamp out vice and make himself a saint. A big financial payoff in court would nevertheless be a welcome side benefit. Entirely convinced of the righteousness of his cause, he could justify almost any means to his ends.

On 12 April, 1914, Easter Sunday, Crosland was arrested while returning from visiting Douglas in France.

40

Ross v. Crosland

The preliminary hearing in Ross v. Crosland opened on 27 April and dragged on through June.

It was heard before magistrate Paul Taylor at the Marylebone Police Court. Ross's barrister was Ernest Wild, who had acted for Calvert in the Guy de Chassiron case. Crosland was represented by Comyns Carr.[1]

As with most court procedures, the process was maddeningly slow. Throughout the preliminaries, Robbie was 'nervous and jumpy'.[2] Crosland was out on remand and went to see Douglas in Boulogne on the weekends and corresponded with him regularly. On 27 April Douglas wrote, 'You know I was a good and faithful friend to that filthy beast Wilde when he got into trouble; so it would be a poor thing if I couldn't do as much and more for you, who are the only real friend I have ever had and especially as you are in all of this through me. In view of all you say, I shall not return to England until I can do so with safety. As long as you are clear about my motives and my absolute loyalty to you I don't care a row of pins what anyone else says on the point ... Don't forget the souls of the just are in the hands of God. Yours ever, Alfred Douglas.'[3]

In early May, Robbie had his final falling out with Reggie Turner. Robbie had gone to Paris for a few days and visited Maurice Gilbert who showed him a letter Turner had written which said, 'I had always thought that Ross provoked Douglas & I did not think Ross ought to have used documents in the Ransome case which he had received when they were friendly. However I wish him well. I know that Douglas attacked me but I don't think he should be treated like ordinary people.'[4]

The full letter no longer exists, so we do not know why Turner felt Douglas should not be treated 'like ordinary people'. In any case, Robbie was so incensed by one passage that he asked Millard to make several copies to show other people.

'I was aware that this was his attitude but did not realise he would state it in such cold blooded terms of snobbishness ... Is there no one who can be trusted?'[5]

Robbie wrote to Reggie ending their already fractured friendship. 'I suppose it was very stupid of me, but I did not realise before that you seriously took the side of Douglas & Crosland,' his letter began. 'I was aware of course that you were a severe critic of mine, as all my very intimate friends appear to be. I am also aware that as the years have gone on, & our meetings have been fewer (owing to your absences abroad) our sympathies were out of tune, & have often been in absolute discord. I am sure the fault was mine ...'

He believed that Reggie would find the fact that he stopped corresponding with him to be a great relief. 'It will I am sure be a still greater relief to you if I say now that I regard our friendship as having definitely ceased. The next eight weeks or so will be very momentous for me, & I write purposely before the issue is decided. If Crosland is convicted, you would have a different kind of temptation to which I would not care to submit you, & I would be tempted into some expression which I might regret all my life. It is therefore better to sever at once the thin link which has become thinner in the last few months.' He signed the letter 'Yours affectionately'.[6]

A year later, when a group of Ross's supporters gave him a testimonial and collected a £760 fund for him (he gave most of it to found a scholarship at the Slade School of Fine Art) Reggie discovered his name had been listed without his knowledge. Max Beerbohm had sent a small sum but later wrote to Reggie that 'I wouldn't have done this had I known that you were standing aside.' Although Beerbohm had never '"officially" or directly quarrelled with Bobbie' he was not on good terms with him.

He concluded, 'And I hope you won't let yourself be bothered with Bobbie or any of his concerns. He has been a nuisance in your existence, and you can well afford to let him pass. He has his good points; but to you he seems to have shown always his worst; and you are well quit of him.'[7]

In 1922 Turner proposed to the publisher Martin Secker that he write a book on the last years of Wilde's life. Turner thought it was important that at least one book be written about Wilde that was sympathetic to Douglas. 'I have always felt that he has been much wronged & had a very real grievance against all the people who have written about him in connection with Oscar Wilde,' he wrote, adding 'I don't think it would be a bad or offensive thing to have an independent book into which a future commentator might dip when writing about that period, to correct some of the statements which appear other books.' He said that he had not been in touch with Douglas for a number of years. Although he had never quarrelled with him, he worried that maybe he thought he was 'hostile' to him because he had not remained in contact. As Secker had published some of Douglas's poems, Turner asked if he might be able to ask him if he was sick of being connected to Oscar Wilde and if he would object to being mentioned even in a positive light. 'I don't propose to make my defence of him,' he wrote, 'he is only too capable of defending himself: I should only make my picture as I see it, in which he stands in a pleasing light.'[8]

Unfortunately, although they batted the idea about for a couple of years, the book was never completed.

On 2 May, the *London Mail* published, under the headline 'Things We Want to Know?' 'Whether all decent persons would not heave a sigh of relief if the Government decided to deport the unspeakable T. W. H Crosland and the more unspeakable Lord Alfred Douglas.'

This became the subject of a small legal skirmish when Crosland applied to attach the *London Mail* for contempt of court saying that the quip was meant to prejudice jurors. The publishers were called in front of a three judge panel consisting of Justices Rowlatt, Sherman and Avory. The justices essentially ruled that the paragraph was intended to prejudice the court, but that it probably was not a serious offence, just stepping over the line. They thought an appropriate penalty was for the *Mail* to pay costs. The only dissenter was the humourless Avory who said 'Nothing was more out of place than humour aimed at a man charged with a criminal offence.' He thought there should have been a more serious penalty, but he was overruled.[9]

Crosland wrote a letter to Douglas, 'It will now I hope be quite plain to you—as it is to everybody and has long been so – that we are not popular in judicial or legal circles.'

Next he turned to Garrett's recantation. 'Now as to Garratt,' he wrote, 'You will have seen how he has lied his soul away. I never heard him say in my life that he didn't know Ross. Not only did he always profess to know him, but he gave a very clear description of him.'

He told Douglas that he was going to ask Carr to get Garratt to swear that he had never met Ross. Then he should 'produce the boy's letter and ask him why he wrote saying he felt like asking Ross and Millard to take him 'back again.' Crosland believed this would prove he was lying when he recanted, not the first time and thus 'the whole fabric of lies tumbles to pieces ... What do you think? And have you a better suggestion?'[10]

He must have agreed. Carr used the strategy. In his testimony for the preliminary hearing, which began on 7 May and continued on 13 May with cross-examination by Carr, Garratt repeatedly swore that he had never met Ross and that that part of his statement 'was all made up out of Lord Alfred Douglas's own head.'

'You say that until you were here in Court last week you have never seen Mr Ross in your life?' Carr asked.

'I say so.'

Then Carr produced a letter that Garratt had written to Lord Alfred Douglas complaining that he was unhappy and had so little money he needed to sell his clothes. 'Dear Lord Alfred,' the letter began, 'I would not have come to this awful beastly place had I known. ... I feel just like writing to Ross or Millard and asking him to let me come back again.'

'Do you still swear you never told Lord Alfred that you knew Mr Ross?'

'Yes.' Garratt said he must have been referring to Millard and another friend. The case was adjourned.[11]

Robbie must have had trouble hearing some of the questions put to him in the preliminary hearing because the newspapers referred to him as suffering from 'nervous deafness' during his testimony. He talked about his friendship with Wilde. 'During his imprisonment I constantly visited him in prison,' he said.

At this point he was overcome with emotion. His eyes welled up, and he buried his face in his hands. His voice was soft and broken when he said, 'I was with him when he died in November 1900. He died a bankrupt.'

He then talked about the 1905 publication of *De Profundis* and how he cut out any reference to Douglas. '*De Profundis* has run to 25 or 26 editions,' he said with some pride. 'None of them had any reference to Douglas.'

About Millard, who he described as a 'scholar of considerable attainment,' he said he only gave him literary work after Millard gave him 'an assurance of amending his life'. He further stated that he had 'no social nor personal contact with him'.

On 19 May the court heard the testimony of the private inquiry agent Englebert Thale, who had been staking out the Café Royal on behalf of Lewis & Lewis. Baron de Chassiron was mentioned. The magistrate, Paul Taylor, described him as one of Crosland's co-conspirators against Ross, but this element of the case was dropped before the main hearing.

The remainder of the time was spent going over documents that Detective Inspector McPherson had found in his search of Crosland's flat. It included letters about the mysterious 'Carew' and a poem that Crosland had written for Douglas addressed to 'A. D. a disagreeable witness at the Old Bailey.' Its conclusion read:

Chiefly to you this victory by God's grace,
Most disagreeable witness; with the trust,
The name that was a name at Chevy Chace,
Shine on serene above the smirch and dust.[12]

'I must say,' said Taylor, 'it seems to me particularly fine work.'

'My client will, no doubt, appreciate that,' said Carr.

Next Ross was recalled so that his deposition could be read over. Taylor put a few questions to him about his relationship with Douglas. Ross said he had been 'a great friend' until 1908, but since then they had not spoken. 'I knew that he was the associate of blackmailers like Crosland, and I severed my friendship with him.'

Taylor asked how old Douglas had been when he 'was associated with' Oscar Wilde. 'Undoubtedly the proceedings in the criminal prosecution showed that the boy had been corrupted by the mature man.'

Ross smiled, 'It is how you look at it. It is not my reading of it.' He said Douglas's grievance against him was that he had coached Ransome, but he denied it. 'I only answered his questions,' he said, 'as I have answered questions for hundreds of Wilde's biographers.' (Unlike today, there were not yet 'hundreds' of biographies of Wilde in 1914.)

'One cannot help feeling in this case that here was a young man of twenty-five in the hands of a genius who was a man of most depraved personal habits,' Taylor said. 'There is no doubt to anybody who takes a practical, common sense view of the matter that the young man was the victim of the old.'

Crosland, unable to restrain himself, pointed to Ross and shouted, 'Why did not this man save himself?'

Crosland finally got the opportunity to tell his story on 29 May. 'I hold strong opinions with regard to Mr Ross's conduct to Douglas in the Ransome case,' he testified, 'I have held strong opinions with regard to Ross for 15 years.' This is highly improbable, as it would have meant Crosland had strong feelings about Ross back in 1899 when few people outside his immediate circle of friends knew who he was.

After a series of indignant denials that he had coerced a perjured statement from Garratt; 'a most scandalous and abominable suggestion', he explained his grievance against Ross: 'I felt it was a most dangerous thing that he should be writing prefaces to Wilde's works and having books dedicated to him wherein these things are all glossed over and made to be good things when everybody knows they are bad things.'

He became animated, speaking with a loud, angry tone and thumping the edge of the witness box. 'I have been trying to find a friend of his who will tell me that what I have heard about Ross is not true, but I cannot find anyone. If I could I would climb down in a minute.'

The magistrate interjected that there had been no actual accusations made against Ross.

'I have grounds and evidence for it,' Crosland said, still in a huff. 'I don't care if you give me ten years' penal servitude; I won't withdraw it. It is a fact. It is time the world knew of it.'

Carr tried to calm his client down, but he continued to pound on the witness box and bellow. 'I have been ten years trying to bring this thing about, and I am here now, very happy and comfortable.'

The magistrate reminded Crosland that Garratt had recanted his statement. He asked him if he had known how unreliable Garratt was if he would have put the same confidence in him.

'Well obviously I should not,' he replied, 'but if he is a liar why is he a witness against me now?'

The magistrate admitted that was a valid point.

In cross-examination the next day Wild asked Crosland if he was aware that Ross did not receive any payment for his work on the Wilde estate.

'I doubt that very much, sir,' Crosland said.

Wild asked him if he had ever heard otherwise from anyone besides Douglas, and Crosland was forced to admit that he could not name anyone. Still he insisted that he believed Ross considered *De Profundis* to be his property and that he received royalties from it, although he admitted he was not in a position to prove it.

Wild then asked questions that suggested Crosland and Douglas were motivated by money. Wild read passages from a letter from Douglas to Crosland in which he complained that the electricity and gas were about to be turned off for non-payment. Crosland said Douglas did not know what it meant to be hard up because he had a regular income of £800 a year from his mother and 'squealed if he had not £50 in his pocket.'

Then, as Wild was going over some details about Garratt's statement he referred to the young man as 'your dinner companion.' Crosland sensed an improper suggestion in Wild's tone.

'If you talk to me like that I will rattle you quick,' he said. 'You have no right to make suggestions to me. I am as big a master of sneers and jeers as you are. You keep your sneers to yourself.' Again he thumped the witness box with his fist. He said he would not answer any more questions until Mr Wild withdrew the remark.

'Then I won't ask any more,' Wild said, 'and it can be recorded that the defendant refused to answer any more questions.'

Cromyns Carr added, 'Having been insulted by counsel.'

'He was not my 'Dinner companion!' Crosland exclaimed.

'He was your dinner companion,' said Wild.

'Liar!' Crosland shouted.

The magistrate told Crosland he needed to answer any questions that Mr Wild put to him.

'I shall not until he takes that question back. It is an impudent sneer.'

The magistrate did not agree. Carr advised Crosland to answer Wild's questions but he was adamant, 'I will answer them if he will say this man was not my dinner companion in an evil sense.'

The magistrate said, 'He did not mean it in an evil sense.'

After that impasse, Wild sat down and let Carr calm his client. The preliminary hearing was concluded with the testimony of Sargent Stevens who described how Garratt made his statement at Scotland Yard and that neither Lord Alfred Douglas nor T. W. H. Crosland were present. Carr argued that with this evidence, there was no chance that the jury would believe Garratt's changed story and the case should be dismissed. The magistrate disagreed and Crosland was committed for trial.

41

Old Acid Drop

The trial opened on Saturday 27 June at the Old Bailey,[1] one day before the assassination of Archduke Franz Ferdinand. Freddie Smith, who had been abroad, came back to support Robbie. Crosland was represented, once again, by Cecil Hayes. Robbie had selected to act as his barrister F. E. Smith, who had represented the Times Book Club in the Ransome case. While Smith had a great rapport with Justice Darling, he seemed to annoy the judge assigned to the Crosland case, Justice Horace Avory.

Ross could not have drawn a worse judge. The severe, serious Avory was described in his *Time Magazine* obituary as '[s]crawny-necked, thin-lipped, slit-eyed and fearsome.' He was known as 'The Hanging Judge' and criminals who appeared in his court called him 'Acid drop'.[2] In spite of this reputation, he did not actually condemn more prisoners or give them harsher sentences than other judges. What made it appear that way was his unsympathetic attitude towards those who appeared in his court. He had, moreover, appeared as a prosecuting attorney against Oscar Wilde in his criminal trials. Not a few observers felt that it was 'at least an error in judgement' to allow Avory to preside in a case between Wilde's admirers and his critics.[3] Ross made the same tactical error that Douglas had in the Ransome case. He assumed his loyalty to Wilde would count for him, rather than against him. This would not be true at all with Justice Avory.

Smith started his opening statement for Ross by saying that he would liked to have been trying Crosland not only for conspiracy but also for inciting to commit perjury. He described his client as 'a man of birth and culture.' Because he had stuck by Oscar Wilde, he had 'been called upon to bear the opprobrium of sticking to a friend when he was down, and now had to clear his character of foul aspersions and a horrible conspiracy.'

He told the story of Douglas's relationship with Wilde and Wilde's arrest for 'a certain offence' then of Ross's friendship and loyalty to Wilde, his work on behalf of the estate and Wilde's family. Smith traced the beginning of the Ross/Douglas quarrel not to the Ransome case, but to Naples. 'On Mr Wilde being released from prison Mr Ross did everything in his power to prevent him from renewing his acquaintanceship with Lord Alfred Douglas, which fact aroused the greatest resentment on the part of Lord Alfred Douglas towards Ross.'

This line of argument was intended to distance Ross from Wilde and Douglas's vices. There were certainly letters Ross could produce to the effect that Douglas was angry at him for intervening with Wilde. Ross had, however, made it clear to

Douglas at the time that he had not actively tried to separate them. Douglas had accepted this and their friendship continued. Ross was either more instrumental in engineering their separation than he admitted to Douglas (Douglas would come to believe this) or he thought it made him seem more respectable to take that unambiguous position later. In either case, this testimony helped to advance the tale of a bitter love triangle with long-simmering resentment between Ross and Douglas which became part of the mythology of Oscar Wilde.

Douglas fled the country while Wilde was in prison, Smith said, while Ross visited him. He was 'equally a faithful friend in the days of [Wilde's] shame and adversity' as he had been in his days of prestige and prosperity. (The clear suggestion being that Douglas was not.) Smith highlighted his tireless work for the estate and for Wilde's family.

Crosland, Smith said, shared Douglas's 'violent hatred' for Ross. In the Ransome case, Ross provided certain documents for the defence and the result was that 'The jury found a verdict the effect of which was that the defendants had succeeded completely in a justification of their charges, so shocking and so grave, which they had felt in their duty to make against Lord Alfred. By that action Lord Alfred lost any shred of reputation as still survived in the minds of imperfectly informed people and Lord Alfred Douglas was destroyed.'

'From that moment,' Smith continued, 'there was a common purpose between Crosland and Lord Alfred Douglas to bring about the consummation of Ross's ruin and disgrace.'

After reading out offensive letters written by Douglas and Crosland, he said he would show that Ross was in Russia on the dates he was supposed to have been involved with Garratt. He described what he called the 'strange luncheon party' where the friends conspired against Ross. He concluded by saying 'that for vindictiveness Crosland and Lord Alfred Douglas fomented, or tried to foment, this charge without having any reason for believing it true, but on the contrary, having every reason for believing it false.'

The trial resumed the following day with testimony from a clerk at the office of Lewis & Lewis regarding the letter writing campaign against Ross. Hayes asked him why the firm took no action against Douglas.

'Coming from a person like Lord Alfred Douglas we should not take it seriously,' he said.

Next Elizabeth Garratt, Charlie's mother, was called to the stand. She described herself as a 'widowed charwoman.' She said Crosland had come to her and told her a terrible story about what had happened to her son. He said Ross and Millard had met Garratt on a street corner in London and greeted him by saying 'Hullo, young man, we have seen you before.' Garratt told them that he hadn't, but they insisted and asked where he was going. They took him to have a drink and after giving him what he believed to be a bottle of mineral water, he woke up at 3 AM and found he had been locked up dressed in women's clothing. He told her that her son got three months in prison when Ross and Millard should have been in jail instead. He told her that Millard and Crosland had lots of money and that they would probably pay £1,000.

A few days later she received a letter from Lord Alfred Douglas who wrote from the Grosvenor Hotel. His letter said her son had made a statement about Millard and Ross and that he had gone to Scotland Yard to make another statement. 'I write this letter so that there may be no misapprehension as to my motive for seeing your son.' He enclosed what purported to be a report from the Commissioner of Police about Garratt. Crosland visited her again and said he had a document for her to sign. He told her it would help her son find a situation.

Crosland told her there would be no expense to her, and that all of the money she needed to come to court would be provided to her as soon as she signed the statement.

Crosland visited her a third time and told her that they were trying to get Garratt to come back home so he would be away from the influence of Ross and Millard. They said she should go and get him and that if she did they would pay 10s a week for the boy's maintenance. He returned home and stayed there seven weeks and six payments were made.

On 24 December, Douglas wrote a letter to Mrs. Garratt saying Charlie 'must on no account leave home or have any communication with anyone except (the solicitor)' presumably Holt. He continued 'Tell Charlie I have received his letter, and that he is very foolish to wish to go back to London. If he does so he will ruin himself for life and lose all chance of getting damages from these men.'

Crosland visited her again on 5 February and said he wanted her and her son to go to London the next day. He said it would mean £1,000 for the two of them. They took her to the solicitor's office and she met Lord Alfred Douglas for the first time. She was asked to sign a paper. That evening the Garratts were taken to a 'picture palace' with a chaperone. She slept at the solicitor's office. The next day Garratt ran away. The unidentified man, who had taken them to the pictures, gave chase and he caught up with Garratt, but he refused to have anything more to do with the case.

When Douglas and Crosland arrived, she told them that Garratt had said he knew nothing of the case and would not stay. Mrs. Garratt testified that later that day in a cab to St. Pancras, Crosland told Douglas he could not go on with it now. He changed his mind, however, because a few days later, Crosland came to her house again and asked her to come to London and give evidence.

She said she signed a document, but she didn't know what it was about, but as Garratt was now over 18 years old, the magistrate told them that he could not take the mother's complaint. This angered Douglas who told her that Charlie was 'stupid' for running off. He complained that he had spent more than £50 on the matter, and he would not let it drop.

Mrs. Garratt also testified that one day in Countersthope Charlie had told her that the story about Ross was not true.

In cross-examination Hayes asked Mrs. Garratt if she did not think it was a wicked thing for her to go into a police court and ask for a summons against Ross.

She said, 'When I signed the papers I really did not know what it was signing for.'

'What did you think it was for?'

'I thought it was for the benefit of my son.'

'How did you think he would benefit?'

'Because Crosland and Lord Alfred Douglas said it would be the means of getting my son's character back and getting him out of this business.'

'When the boy told you it was not true, why did not you write to Lord Alfred Douglas or Mr Crosland or someone and say that the boy had told you it was false?'

'I didn't know whether to believe the boy or Crosland. When Mr Crosland told me it was so I believed Mr Crosland. When the boy told me it was not I believed the boy.'

'You have never until today said your boy told you in the country it was all false?'

'No.'

'Did you not think it was a wicked thing to continue to prosecute Mr Ross after what your boy had told you?'

'I had signed then,' she said. There was much laughter at this in the court. The judge joined in.

'You don't now suggest that Crosland asked you to sign anything that was false?'

'No, I believed Crosland to be right and Lord Alfred Douglas too, and I believed Mr Millard was right too.'

In re-examination by Smith, Mrs. Garratt said Crosland had mentioned the £1,000 for her son a number of times.

'You know Lord Alfred Douglas is a lord – have you ever had talks with a lord before?'

'Never.' With that, the court was adjourned for the day.

Bosie followed the trial via English newspapers which Sibyl Queensberry had sent directly to her son daily. Crosland wrote him feeling discouraged about how things were going. On 30 June Douglas replied, 'Thanks for your letter, which, however, had rather a depressing effect on us, as up till the time I received it we had judged merely by the reports in the papers, which seemed entirely favourable. I don't see that there is much case left to answer. I hope they won't stop the case before you get into the box. In case things go wrong you will, of course, immediately enter an appeal. This is important and my mother asks me to say that she requests that this should be done in case of an adverse verdict. Personally, I am betting 100 to 7 on you, with no takers. I hope you are not over-burdened by the heat. With all best wishes. Yours ever, Alfred Douglas.'[4]

On 30 June, Charlie Garratt was called to the stand. His testimony was substantially the same as it had been in the preliminary hearing. The judge refused to allow Garratt to testify to the contents of a telephone conversation with Douglas because he did not trust the new technology. 'The reckless way in which people swear to voices on the telephone nowadays is to my mind the most dangerous. Everybody knows that some of the most familiar voices cannot be recognised on the telephone at all.'

Garratt testified that the statements he made to Douglas, Crosland and the police were true except for the parts about Ross and about his own biography. He said Douglas and Crosland wrote down everything he said but 'put in the name of Robert Ross where the names of other people ought to have gone in.' This brought laughter to the gallery. The judge rebuked the spectators. 'Don't laugh at this,' he said. 'Those people who come here for amusement have come to the wrong place altogether.'

Garratt said he rarely drank alcohol before coming to the city but 'I have had drinks with heaps of people in London.'

He had to be pressed to recount the story of the 'alleged orgies' at Millard's flat. He said he would not give the names of the people involved 'because I don't think they have anything to do with this case.' Avory was not having any of that. He said, 'That is not for you to judge.' At this point Garratt's memory became foggy. He said he could not remember their names. He did not make a great impression on Avory.

Millard was called to testify on 1 July. Millard talked about his conviction for gross indecency, his work for Ross, and his relationship with Garratt. He swore Garratt had never been in Ross's company. Millard also testified that he was fired by Ross when the Garratt incident occurred. He talked about his correspondence with Lord Alfred Douglas and Douglas's attempts to compel him to incriminate Ross. Douglas had told him that he had only lost the Ransome case because he had not had a good lawyer and that he would not rest until he could see newspaper placards with the words 'Arrest of Robert Ross' on them.

When Hayes (who had acted for Douglas in the Ransome case) began his cross-examination, he said he would agree with Lord Alfred Douglas's assertion that he would have won his case in High Court if he'd just had better counsel.

Avory replied, 'That is the ordinary expression made use of by everybody who has lost a case. There is no member of the Bar who has not had it applied to him.' This brought laughter to the courtroom.

Hayes asked Millard if he had ever used names other than his own. He said he wrote books under the name Stuart Mason.

'Many of the books written in that name are connected with Oscar Wilde?'
'Yes.'

Oscar Wilde and Dorian Gray were once again put on trial. 'You knew that Oscar Wilde was sent to prison for two years?' Hayes asked.

'That is a matter of history,' Millard said.

'Do you think he was guilty?'

'I have no opinion about the matter at all.'

'You knew Ross was a friend of Wilde when he came out of prison and stayed and lived with him?'

'I did not know that.'

'Were you not Mr Ross's secretary?'

'Only from March last year.'

Asked about his own arrest for gross indecency he said he only pleaded 'technically guilty' to the charge on the advice of his counsel.

'It was the fault of your counsel was it?' the judge interjected.

Hayes asked, 'In the preface of 'Dorian Gray' it says – There is no such thing as a moral or an immoral book. Books are either well written or badly written, that is all.'

'Yes.'

'Do you consider that 'Dorian Gray' is an immoral book?'

'No.'

'The theme, in a word, is the love a man has for a younger man: is that so?'

'No, not in my opinion.'

'Do you quarrel with the word 'love'?'

'I don't see why I should be cross-examined on another man's book.'

The judge asked, 'Do you approve of the book as a moral book?'

'I see nothing immoral in it.'

'You wrote a book, *Art and Morality*,' Hayes asked Millard, 'which is a defence of Dorian Gray?'

'Yes.'

Hayes then read extracts from the novel and asked Millard if he considered them to be immoral.

'I don't see how printed words can be immoral.'

The judge said, 'You were asked if printed words could not have an immoral tendency.'

'That appears to be a hypothetical question, my Lord. I do not consider it would have an immoral effect upon me. I fail to see how printed words can have an immoral effect upon anybody.'

This opened the door quite naturally as to whether or not Millard had been effected. Hayes asked if the allegations made against him by Garratt were true or not. He refused to answer on the grounds that it might incriminate him.

Hayes asked if, when Garratt was convicted, the magistrate had not said he would have made the sentence heavier were it not for the boy falling under the influence of people like him. Millard said that was true. Hays then asked if he'd written to Garratt's mother saying that 'it was some consolation' that the boy had gotten a lighter sentence because he'd spoken on his behalf. 'Is that in the nature of a paradox,' Hayes asked, 'or is it the candid truth?'

'It is perfectly true,' Millard said.

'And that is called Oxford logic,' said the judge.

On Wednesday it was Ross's turn. He was, perhaps, over-prepared by his legal coach. His attempts to seem confident and trustworthy came across to the judge as arrogance. He would probably have fared better in Justice Darling's court, for Ross could not resist injecting humour into his answers, and this did not sit well with Old Acid Drop.

His main testimony consisted of his background, his falling out with Douglas, the abuse he had suffered at the hands of Douglas and Crosland, followed by a denial that he had ever met Charlie Garratt. Then it was time for the cross-examination. Hayes began by questioning him about his relationship with Millard. He wanted to know if he had continued to dine with him after he had been fired as his secretary. Ross admitted that he had, but said it was always on business

'Didn't you think it might give people a false impression?'

'No,' Ross said, 'because everybody knows what my character is. I can afford to dine with anybody.'

'Are you above suspicion?'

'Yes, like Ceasar's wife.'

'Leave Caesar's wife alone,' Avory snapped.

'Is not your object in this case to vindicate you character?'

'No, to punish Crosland.'

Ross went on to say that when he first knew Wilde 'his character, I believed, had not begun to deteriorate morally.' He dated the beginning of his moral degeneration to 1891 – the year he met Douglas. 'I charged Wilde with it,' he said. 'A great many people were talking about it.'

'You were horrified that a friend of yours would go in for such practices?'

'I was, frankly, rather appalled.'

'Did you say to him you were so appalled that you could not continue to know him?'

'No, I did not.'

'You still remained friends?'

'Yes, I always remained very intimate with him up to the day of his death.'

'Although you said you were appalled at the horrible vice?'

'No, I said I was appalled at what people were saying about him. I did not say I was appalled at the vice.'

'In other words, what annoyed you was that the world should have found out?'

'No, I was very pained that a man of his distinction should have that kind of reputation.'

The judge was confused by this answer, and asked Ross to elaborate. 'I was rather appalled at hearing from rumours and other sources that Oscar Wilde was credited with practising such offences.'

'You believed the rumours?' asked the judge.

'Yes, I did.'

'That did not make any difference to your friendship?' asked Hayes.

'No.'

'Did rumour say anything about you at that time?'

'Very likely.'

'You did not mind?'

'I minded very much.'

'Do you mean that it came to your knowledge that you were being suspected?' asked the judge.

'No, not at that time. Not until 1895 after Wilde's conviction. I admired Wilde so much that I don't think it would have affected me one way or the other.'

'When your people wrote to your brother and called you a "disgrace to the family, a social outcast, a son and brother unfit for society of any kind," did not that make you think you had a bad reputation?'

'I do not remember what I thought at that time.'

'What do you think now?'

'I do not think about it,' he said. 'There were many friends of the family who objected to my being seen with Douglas.'

Justice Avory was not charmed by Ross's answer to the question, 'Do you think there can be such a thing as an immoral book.'

'Yes,' Ross said. 'I know heaps of them. Lord Alfred Douglas's poems for instance.'

This answer piqued Crosland, who leaned across the dock and shouted out what *The Times* called 'an excited but incoherent protest'.

'The attitude of the witness to Lord Alfred Douglas is obvious,' said Avory.

Hayes next started to bring up the Dansey case, producing a letter that Ross had written to Douglas more than two decades before. Ross objected strongly to the introduction of a letter written in his youth. But his counsel's objections were overruled.[5]

'I make an appeal,' Ross said to the judge, 'not on my own behalf, but on behalf of the wretched men and women who have had the misfortune to know me, that their names should not be introduced into the case with which they have nothing to do.'

Avory refused, but the press was largely respectful in not printing the names. Ross's excuse for the incident was 'I was with Lord Alfred Douglas and I got into the mess. I was not implicated.' He explained that the boy had stayed with him for a night and then Douglas took him away for a whole week. 'Before the boy went I told him to be very careful of Alfred Douglas, who had not a very good influence. I also told Douglas that I hoped the boy would come to no harm.' After saying this, Ross seems to have thought better of it, and he told the judge he was sure there was nothing wrong in Lord Alfred's behaviour with the boy.

The witnesses for the prosecution were Detective Inspectors McPherson and Nicholls. Hayes helped the prosecution a bit in his cross-examination. He asked them if any more inquiries into the Garratt matter had been made after their initial investigation. McPherson said there had been but they had found nothing to support the charges. The prosecution rested its case.

Hayes had grown a great deal since the Ransome trial. In his opening statement he ingratiated himself to the jury by presenting himself as the underdog going up against three of the most eminent members of the bar. He warned them that F. E. Smith, especially, was very subtle and he urged them to carefully consider everything he said. 'He opened the case with deep sarcasm, and the case needed it,' he said. Were it not for Smith's cleverness, he said, 'I firmly believe the jury would have stopped the case at the end of the prosecution.'

He brushed aside the weakest aspect of his case – Garratt's recantation of his statement – by framing the question before them as 'Had Crosland reasonable ground for believing Garratt's statement?' Whether or not the statement was true, Hayes argued that Crosland believed it, and he had reason to be suspicious because Ross allowed his name to be associated with Wilde's. He explained that Crosland's friendship with Douglas was 'purely literary'. Crosland sympathised with Douglas's efforts to live down his past association with Wilde 'and his efforts to stop books containing references to Wilde from being foisted on the world'.

Crosland had been waiting for this moment for some time. He loved performing in a packed courtroom. He assumed the moral pose he had adopted in the Sutton case. His language was blunt, straight-forward and came across as truthful. He entertained the jury early by describing himself as 'A minor author'. He told a tall tale about how Douglas had sent him some of his sonnets and he refused to publish them until Douglas swore that there was no truth to the rumours surrounding him and Oscar Wilde. That was all there was time for, and the court adjourned once again.

The next day, answering questions from his own counsel, Crosland swore that he knew nothing about what Garratt had said in his statement to the Commissioner of Oaths. The boy, he said, was afraid to face his mother after the charges that had been brought against him. So Crosland went to Countesthorpe to make the case to Mrs. Garratt that her son was 'more to be pitied than blamed.' He said it was not him but Mrs. Garratt's son-in-law who brought up the idea of compensation and that it was only because Mrs. Garratt was afraid she could not afford to keep the boy at home that Douglas offered to give her 10s a week to help.

Crosland said he was disgusted by *Dorian Gray*. Wilde's expression, '"there is no such thing as an immoral book," is the stand-by for all people who write dirty books.'

With that, Hayes gave the floor to Smith. The showdown between the famously sarcastic barrister and MP and the equally cantankerous literary curmudgeon was what the packed gallery had been waiting for, and they would not be disappointed. Crosland, 'who had remained commendably sober' was at his pugnacious best throughout the proceeding, deftly deulling with the verbal master.[6] Crosland's retorts infuriated Smith and got the better of him. He was aided, in no small part, by an unsympathetic Justice Avory.

Smith's goal was to tear apart Crosland's public interest argument. That Crosland was a heavy drinker, a gambler and a bit of a rogue was no secret. Smith's aggressive questioning of Crosland's morals came across to the jury as a relentless attack. He began by trying to tear down Crosland's public interest argument. He submitted 'The Genius of Oscar Wilde,' Douglas's full-throated defence of *Dorian Gray* from *The Academy*. Crosland claimed he had not read it.

'Anyone who can maintain that *The Picture of Dorian Gray* is not one of the greatest moral books ever written is an ass,' Smith read.

'I am one of the asses,' Crosland said.

'I suggest that the literary vogue of Oscar Wilde did not cause you anxiety until the Ransome case.'

'You are quite mistaken.'

'There is another phrase ending "His influence is all for the good".'

'I think it has been all for the bad,' Crosland said. 'Two men on the same staff can have a difference of opinion on such matters.'

Smith asked him if he thought Douglas was 'a suitable colleague' in this cause, and Crosland said he did. Justice Avory must have had a sense of deja vu as Smith read out Douglas's poem 'Two Loves'.

'Have you any doubt that the reference contained in the last verse is to unnatural affection?' Smith asked.

'I regret to have to say my answer is no. I see the obvious meaning, and I am sorry it is so.' He pointed out that he did not yet know Douglas at that time.

'Your counsel referred to your wife and family. Are you now living with your wife?

'I lived with my wife for twenty years,' Crosland said. 'and would be living with her now if it weren't for legal matters.'

'Who is Mrs Parnell?' Smith asked.

'She is the tenant of the flat in which I live. I am sorry you put such a question. If you knew the circumstances you would not. In a case like this, I don't think a man should be ashamed of saying he has a mistress. He might even be proud of his relations with the other sex. It is disgraceful to put such a question: If you can't get a conviction you want to ruin me outright. My wife might take divorce proceedings against me. What do you care? It's just for wanton mischief.'

'Did your counsel recommend you to the jury as a married man?'

'He did. I may say that for six or seven months the lady you mention has been my mistress.'

Smith got Crosland to admit that he had taken the lady to Monte Carlo just after getting £75 from the Royal Literary Fund for financial hardship. 'Did you go to Monte Carlo, having got that, and take this woman with you?'

'You needn't talk about "this woman" as though she were something terrible.'

'Did you take this lady with you then?'

'I did not go with the money you spoke of.'

'Does it occur to you when complaining of the suggestion made against you that you have made charges against Mr Ross as ruinous to him?'

'These charges are made in the public interest. This man has brought me here to ruin me; he does not care two pence about the public.'

Smith tried to counter this by suggesting that Crosland and Douglas were motivated not by civic-mindedness but by money. 'Have you ever been in gaol for non-payment of a committal order?' he asked.

'I have never been in gaol in my life, and I hope I am not going to be.'

He then asked about Douglas's 'desperate hard-uppedness'.

'You have tried to make a quarrel between myself and my wife,' Crosland snapped. 'Now you want to make a quarrel between Lord Alfred and myself. Go ahead. I wish you joy. I am not going to say that my friend is a liar.'

'You would rather not answer?'

'It is not a case of rather not. I won't.'

Smith followed up by asking Crosland about his many previous libel actions. 'I now suggest ...' Smith began.

'You are suggesting that I am a rogue,' Crosland said, his speech became heated and animated. He spoke so rapidly that it was hard for Smith to get a word in to ask his questions. When Smith asked the judge to intervene, Avory said Smith had brought it on himself with the nature of his questions.

Crosland said he had brought many cases to court but objected to being called 'litigious' He countered that Ross had listed 'litigation' as his favourite pastime in *Who's Who*. In answer to another question, Crosland said he would never go to a shady solicitor as he might rob him.

'Well, he could not rob you of very much could he?' This opened the door to questions about his bankruptcy.

'You may take it from me that I have been hard up all my life, since I was born, and will never be rich.' There was laughter in the gallery.

Crosland said Ross's conduct towards Douglas in the Ransome case was 'damned treacherous. Posterity will bear me out!'

The judge said he could not allow such words to be used in court and the defendant must watch his language.

'I am very hard pressed,' Crosland said.

'I have made a great deal of allowance already for you,' the judge said, 'and you must not overstep the limit.'

'I am anxious that the jury should not be confused.'

Smith said, 'The jury can take care of itself.'

'I have no doubt they can,' said Crosland. 'I want them to take care of me. I am here to fight with one of the finest intellects in England, and I am going to fight. Two thousand quids' worth of counsel against a poor man.' This elicited laughter from both the jury and the judge, and seemed to win the jury's sympathy.

'You have got Mr Hayes,' Smith said. He returned to events surrounding the statements by Garratt, and after a few questions he asked Crosland if 'a certain man,' presumably Carew, was 'a paid spy'.

Crosland scored points with the jury by responding, 'When Lewis and Lewis bring a man he is an inquiry agent. When I bring a man he is a paid spy.'

After a few more questions about Garratt, Holt and Carew, Justice Avory jumped in to ask, 'Had you anything to do with the sending of the person to interview this boy?'

'Certainly not.'

By now the questioning had gone on for hours and Crosland declared, 'You go on browbeating me. If you go on for another five hours you will probably get me to say I murdered Queen Anne.'

Smith continued his line of questioning about the unindicted co-conspirators. He wanted to know why 'certain people,' presumably Holt and his clerk, had not been called to testify that Garratt had indeed identified Ross in the prison interviews.

'You have the power to bring them here,' Crosland said. 'Why don't you bring them and put them in the dock for conspiracy? You dare not do it.'

Smith switched tack and questioned Crosland about having a drink with Mrs. Garratt.

'I am a sociable man, and whenever I meet anybody I say, 'Shall we have a drink?'

'With charwomen?'

'I did not regard this woman as a charwoman. I regarded her as a human being and the mother of an unfortunate boy.'

'And a possible litigant?'

'She was not a possible litigant in my view at all.'

'Have you ever had a drink with a charwoman before?'

'I am afraid I have not.' He added that it was a cold December day and the woman had walked to the station and it seemed reasonable to buy her a drink.

Smith then asked Crosland about a letter he had written to Ross which said, 'How is Fluffy? How is Charlie? How is Scotland Yard? How is Lewis the Jew? How are you? How is Millard? How is the Wilde movement?' (Ross had testified that when he received the note he thought 'Fluffy' referred to Lady Alfred Douglas.)

'This excellent example of literary epigram and powerful and charming style was received on January 1, 1914,' Smith said.

'I am not proud of that letter,' Crosland said. 'We are not wise at all times like yourself, Mr Smith.'

Smith asked him if the letter was not vindictive. Crosland replied that it was 'a savage joke.'

'It is difficult to see where the joke is,' Smith said.

'The joke may be a bit savage,' Crosland said. 'I wrote it in a more or less joking spirit. Taking it altogether it was a severe sort of joke.'

In conclusion Crosland denied that he wanted to see Ross suffer. He said, grandly, that 'the public interest is greater than the suffering of anybody.' He said Ross and Millard had transformed Wilde from an insignificant author to 'one whose works they boasted had the largest sale of any.' This, he said, was 'most dangerous.'

Then Hayes re-examined Crosland, getting him to put a more positive spin on his trip to Monte Carlo with his mistress and the money he borrowed. Hayes asked if he had ever written anything which had been accused of having 'an immoral tendency.'

'Never. I have had miles of criticism, and angry criticism, but nobody ever said anything like that.'

'I daresay,' said Justice Avory, 'there were a good many people who did not like *The Unspeakable Scot*.'

'Yes,' Crosland agreed. 'Some were very furious.'

The final evidence in the case was given by Detective Sargeant Stephens of Scotland Yard who testified about taking Garratt's statement, but being unable to corroborate it.

'Was any observation kept on Millard's flat before you came to your conclusion?' Avory asked.

'Some observation was kept.' The defence rested.

In his closing statement, Hayes argued that the jury could not punish Crosland for being 'a man of ferocious dislike of vice.' He referred to the moment of the trial that had aggravated the judge, Ross's declaration that he was 'above suspicion.' 'Anyone who declares himself in a public assembly to be above suspicion is either a silly noodle or an impudent hypocrite. And I would never call Mr Ross a silly noodle.' He told the jury that it was reasonable of Crosland to believe Garratt's statement and asked them to keep in mind the parable 'Birds of a feather flock together.' He concluded that 'a verdict of guilty would give delight in all the worst resorts in the West End of London.'

Smith knew he had been beaten. His tone of defeat muted his argument that Crosland's prosecution of Ross had been 'cruel and vindictive' and that it was not in the public interest but 'a private quarrel with which the public had no concern.' He closed by saying that if the jury concluded that Crosland believed Garratt's statements then the prosecution had failed but that 'it was incredible that at any stage Crosland believed that the story told by Garratt was a true one.'

Avory was far from neutral in his summary. He accepted Hayes's framing, that the question was not whether Crosland had gone after an innocent man, but whether he had *knowingly* gone after an innocent man. He asked the jury not to be swayed by the fact that Lord Alfred Douglas had not come to court. He said 'Douglas probably knew more than Crosland' about Ross's vices and that was most likely the reason that Ross had waited to press charges until Douglas was out of the country.

He took the position that it was reasonable for a man to sound the alarm if he honestly believed someone propagating the ideas of Wilde was guilty of the same types of crimes. The judge dismissed the testimony of both Garratt and Millard saying that to accept the testimony of Millard as corroboration of Garratt was 'like asking it to accept that one broken stick would support another broken stick. I cannot help thinking that for the sake of his university Millard would have done better to have left out the fact that he was a graduate of Oxford.'

He instructed the jury that hey were not there 'for the purpose of admiring the advocacy of Mr Ross's learned counsel, and certainly they were not there to convict anyone merely because Mr Ross had the good fortune to have secured the service of one of the most eminent and most eloquent of the counsel at the English bar.'

The judge wondered why Douglas would have written to Garratt's mother telling her he had taken her son to Scotland Yard 'if they were the wicked conspirators suggested'. Finally, as to Ross, he said if 'a man allowed himself to be associated with such a person as Oscar Wilde' people were entitled to take that into consideration.

He concluded by telling the jury that there were only two questions before them 'Did Garratt give a certain statement to Crosland?' and 'Did Crosland believe it?' To take the word of Garratt against that of Crosland was 'an insult to the brain of a human being to be asked compare seriously' Crosland's word against the word of a 'wretched boy – whose very life was a lie and whose face was a lie.'

It took the jury only a half hour to come back with a verdict of not guilty. As obvious as Crosland and Douglas's attempts to coerce Garratt had been, they felt Crosland was reasonable in his belief that Ross's work to revitalise Wilde's reputation was dangerous. The judge suppressed a spontaneous burst of applause. Crosland looked relieved and 'much moved.' He bowed to the judge and stood in silence for a moment. Then walked out to a group of waiting friends who shook his hand and congratulated him.

The Daily News summed up public opinion by saying, 'The only feeling of decent people in connection with the verdict in the Crosland case will be satisfaction that the whole wretched business is finished, as far as the public is concerned. We hope we may now be spared any more contact with the malodorous subject.'[7]

The News cannot have been entirely correct on this, because the Australian publication *The Truth* noted that 'It may be a coincidence' but sales of Wilde's works had increased since the Crosland trial began.[8]

Millard was horrified by the verdict and especially Avory's summing up. 'I am still in a state of collapse and chaos,' he wrote to Ledger. 'Avory did for Crosland what his own counsel was incompetent to do: namely he made a violent bigoted and ignorant speech for the defence – it is a monstrous miscarriage of justice.'[9]

42

Only His Grave, His Body and His Letters

There's Charlie Garratt he's in jail
For offering himself for sale ...
There's Chris Millard, such a dear
You will like him; he too, I fear
Has done a little bit of time
For what the silly law calls crime.

Lord Alfred Douglas, *The Rhyme of F double E*[1]

The verdict, and the attitudes that made it possible, came as a depressing shock to Ross. He had spent most of his life in a friendly circle of artists and Bohemians, and such a short time after his triumph in rehabilitating Wilde and paying off his bankruptcy, it was a terrible blow to realise just how much hatred there still was for Wilde and his kind.

A day or two after the verdict, Compton McKenzie visited Ross to offer his support and found his friend in 'something like an hysterical condition.' Ross told him that he should not be compromising himself by visiting 'such a social outcast.'[2]

In the wake of the verdict, Ross had received a message that if he did not resign his high-status position as Assessor of Picture Valuations to the Board of Inland Revenue, he would 'risk the humiliation of being ejected.'[3] Freddie Smith took dictation of his resignation letter.

Oscar Wilde and Myself, Douglas's watered-down response to *De Profundis*, was finally released in July 1914. The book presented the case that Douglas had planned to make in the Ransome trial before his letters to Robbie had taken centre stage. He made up for his inability to quote from Wilde's prison letter by including some mean-spirited literary criticism from Crosland.

There was only one big, outright lie in *Oscar Wilde and Myself*, and that is the claim that Douglas knew nothing about Wilde's sexual practices and did not share in them. Few believed his protests, and it was widely seen as the bitter, self-serving document it was. Douglas would come to regret having published it.

It was the opinion, not the facts, that made the book distasteful to him. The problem was not that it was untrue. It was *a far too truthful* reminder of how spiteful he had become in the Ransome trial's wake.

'There is really nothing quite untrue even in that first book of mine and Crosland's,' Bosie would one day write to Bernard Shaw. 'I repudiated it because it conveyed a false and misleading impression on the whole. It is simply that there are at least two ways of telling the truth and in *Oscar Wilde and Myself* I told it in the bitterest and most uncharitable way.'[4] *Oscar Wilde and Myself* was untrue in the exact same way *De Profundis* had been untrue. But Bosie, unlike Oscar, lived to repudiate a work he wrote from the depths of pain.

'I deeply regret that the book was ever published,' he wrote.[5]

On 8 July 1914, Freddie Smith took dictation of a letter from Ross to Frank Harris asking him to use the Reform Club as his address in the future. He planned to be a bit more mobile, beyond the watchful gaze of Douglas and Crosland's spies.[6]

Ross was pleased that Harris's biography of Wilde was going to come out soon. He knew that Harris had adopted his own position on Wilde's downfall. He was, however, too distracted to check the proofs for accuracy, as he had agreed to do. He asked Harris to send the manuscript, instead, to Millard.[7]

Yet as he encouraged Harris, Ross was thwarting Ada Leverson in her attempt to publish a Wilde memoir. She had secured interest in the project from William Heinemann, and Robbie wrote to her in his role as executor saying he would not approve the use of any quotes from Wilde because Heinemann 'has behaved very badly to me … I would throw every possible difficulty in the way of his publishing anything at all.'

He elaborated on his control of Wilde, 'Oscar is of course public property: only his grave, his body, and his letters belong to me, and Heinemann shall certainly not make anything out of them while I am alive.'[8]

As Ross was writing these letters, Sir Matthew Nathan was responding to his letter of resignation. He thanked Ross for all of his good work, and said while he knew the verdict did not reflect on his character, 'in view of all the disagreeable features of the case which you thought it necessary to bring to trial it will I think be advisable in the best interest of the government department which I represent that you should do as you suggest. I am sorry that we should lose services which your great knowledge of art made so valuable to us.'[9]

Ross felt 'bitterness' at 'this further triumph for Douglas & his family' but he was gracious. He returned his unfinished cases and offered both his successor and his immediate supervisor any help he could give with the transition.[10]

That Saturday Robbie received 'an obscene post-card' from Douglas.[11] He retreated to his sister Mary's house in Berkshire to recuperate while Smith went back to Europe. He stayed in St. Moritz, where Helen Carew was also vacationing. Something happened there that upset Robbie. Whatever it was, he did not learn of it immediately. Smith would later confess to Arthur Clifton that he had been 'off his head' at the time.

Robbie was not, however, the social pariah he imagined himself to be. In fact, the unfairness of the verdict, especially the judge's summation, elicited a flood of outraged sympathy from friends and associates. Robert C. Witt was furious about Avory's summing up. 'I am ashamed of my profession,' he said. 'As for yourself it matters little. You have done your duty. You have been very brave. you have done all you could to right a wicked wrong & there the matter ends. But for your friends & those who believe in you it is only the beginning. And you must now help us to help you.'[12]

D. S. MacColl invited him to attend a meeting of the Board of the National Art Collections Fund on 16 July. He said if there was any talk of Ross being asked to resign, he was prepared to walk out himself. The artist Charles Ricketts, who was also on the committee said the verdict was 'the sort of beastly chance which might make a man turn to drink' and that the members were planning 'some sort of friendly act which I know will please you but, about this you are to know nothing at present. I am half blabing [sic] as the news may cheer you.' He also had a gift for his friend, an Italian ring with Nero carved on it.[13]

A few days later MacColl wrote again saying that the board had decided to take up a collection for Ross's legal expenses. 'You have no idea what devotion you have excited,' he wrote. On 27 July, he wrote to Asquith's secretary Maurice Bonham Carter suggesting that he appoint Ross administrator of the National Gallery. Asquith was open to the idea, but felt that it would be politically wise to wait a while before making such an appointment. He did, however, promise to discuss the matter with the gallery's trustees.[14]

Meanwhile, Douglas and Crosland were having one of their periodic spats. The cause was something Crosland had said about Lady Queenberry. 'The fact is that you have at the back of you a very nasty cross-grained spirit,' Douglas wrote. 'The fight is not half over yet, there is a heap more to do, and I should think you might keep your superfluous venom for Lewis, Ross & Co, instead of emptying it on me, whose only crime is that I was longing to see you and felt injured at your neglect.'[15]

By mid-July, Scotland Yard had decided they did not have enough evidence to prosecute Millard. A. H. Bodkin was careful to document the department's reasoning because Douglas was determined to 'ventilate' this matter, no doubt to revenge himself for the recent proceedings, in which Millard and Ross 'are on the same side ... the police action or nonaction in the matter may have to be justified ... should any question arise in the House of Commons or elsewhere.'

In a memo dated 19 July 1914 Bodkin said he believed 'that in all probability a part of Garratt's story is true – as indeed the police at first thought ...' Even so, there was little chance that a case could be made because the indecent activities had been conducted in private. 'It can hardly be supposed that this coterie of sodomites will be found to support the tale of one of the number against another member of the party ... To expose a nest of sodomites may from one point of view be desirable, but it is not the duty of the police, unless in the course of a serious prosecution deliberately undertaken and on satisfactory evidence of criminal conduct.'[16]

Yet the police continued to make inquiries. They interviewed a neighbour, who knew very little about Millard. They also tracked down the cleaner, a man named William Barber, who testified that he had never seen Charlie Garratt or Fluffy Hughes at Millard's flat and that when he saw Millard he was 'usually occupied with typing.' (At this time he would have been typing the full text of *De Profundis*, which he was preparing for Robbie, so that he could ensure it would be protected by US copyright.) The police also tracked down the landlady who let rooms to Hughes for a week. She said he did have guests, but she had no idea what their sleeping arrangements were and she found nothing unusual about the bed sheets when she made the beds after they left.[17]

The investigation of Millard continued into the early part of 1915, but after tracking down and interviewing most of the men who were allegedly involved, none was willing to confess to a crime. Finally the police were forced to conclude: 'Summing up the whole matter in a few words, we do not think we have ever had a case of this kind put before us to advise upon in which there was such a hopeless dearth of reliable & materially corroborative evidence.'[18]

In early summer, Robbie felt comfortable in London again and he took rooms at 40 Half Moon Street, Mayfair. His flat was a showcase of the art objects Robbie had collected over the years, 'the casual accumulations of an expert.' The soft yellow walls featured long windows that opened onto a balcony overlooking Piccadilly. Through the glass door of the bookcase one could spot autographed first editions, poetry and belles lettres. Robbie often stood before the fireplace as he spoke about artists, their art and their dramas with friends.[19]

On 4 August 1914 England declared war on Germany ushering in a profound sense of unease and loss. The chaos and bloodshed of war seemed to tear civilization itself to shreds. The civilization that one mourned depended a great deal on what one had valued before that terrible moment. All of the art that had been created, only a few months before, seemed instantly to have come from a bygone era and the dark new age that was replacing it was a complete unknown. One thing was clear, the world of Wilde, with its focus on beauty and art for art's sake felt irrevocably distant. Revivals of Wilde's society comedies were immediately shelved as the theatres rushed to stage patriotic plays like Shakespeare's histories, *Tommy Atkins* and *On His Majesty's Service*.

The outbreak of war brought Douglas back to England. On 2 September he boarded a ferry feeling 'gloomy' and 'depressed.' Throughout the journey he said the rosary. The moral of the story that follows is that if you are going to be arrested, you really ought to be an aristocrat. Douglas was met at the pier by a 'nice-looking and smartly dressed' detective in plain clothes who, after informing him that he was under arrest, offered to carry his bag. Douglas thought he was being arrested on the old bench warrant for the Crosland case, and was surprised to learn that Ross had filed new charges against him for libel. Douglas was hungry after his journey, so the friendly officer gave him a piece of cake before locking him in the holding cell.

After two or three hours another police officer arrived from London and read out the warrant. Douglas felt 'exhilarated' as he always did 'when the issue is definitely joined in any kind of fight.' He enjoyed the officer's company, and was pleased to see that he had collected his luggage for him. They travelled first-class to London, and the officer bought him a whiskey and soda. He found the officers at Paul Taylor's police court to be 'exceedingly kind and friendly.' They allowed him to send out for dinner, and set up a bed for him in the detention room so he would not have to sleep in the cell.[20]

The next day, although his cousin and an Anglican minister were prepared to provide bail, Lewis opposed it based on his previous flight. His lordship was sent to Brixton Prison in a taxi. When he was finally locked in, he began to panic. In this moment he had what he believed to be a supernatural experience.

> I went through about two hours of mortal agony, during which I called on God, and reproached Him for deserting me … At last I looked round in utter despair, and saw a New Testament, the only book in my cell. I snatched it up, and opened it and read these words:
>
> 'And when Herod would have brought him forth, the same night Peter was sleeping between two soldiers, bound with two chains: and the keepers before the door kept the prison. And, behold, the angel of the Lord came upon him, and a light shined in the prison: and he smote Peter on the side, and raised him up, saying, Arise up quickly. And his chains fell off from his hands,' etc … I felt convinced that somehow I would be saved.[21]

He believed this suffering was his 'Passion' and was an answer to his prayers. For when he sat alone in his house after his wife had left him, burning his letters from Oscar Wilde, the 'idea of devotion ... took hold' of him. 'I prayed hard that I might suffer with Christ, be betrayed by all my friends and those whom I loved (except my mother) and taste all the bitterness of His Passion.'

Meanwhile, Crosland was haunting the police court 'in a great rage over the arrest of his friend, Lord Alfred Douglas'.[22]

After five days in detention, Douglas was taken to the Old Bailey, where he was joined by Olive and a solicitor provided by Crosland. He was bound over on another promise to keep the peace with Custance, an ordinary event which he compared to St Peter being delivered by an angel. But before he could go back out into the world to resume his collection of evidence, he had one more trial to endure. Although he had a surety to provide bail, the court would not accept it without twenty-four hours' notice, and so he was confined for the night in Wormwood Scrubs in a cell in the hard-labour division. As he lay on the plank bed, he thought of Oscar and wondered how he had endured such conditions for two years. For that night at least, he felt sympathy.

The description of his short stay at Wormwood Scrubs in his *Autobiography* has the feel of a story polished by repeated telling at dinner parties. He found all of the people he met in prison, with the exception of one chaplain, to be friendly and compassionate. If his account is to be believed, they coddled him as if he were a lost boy. When one officer made him cry, he put his arm around Bosie's shoulders, apologised for shouting and told him he didn't need to do hard labour if he didn't want to. Then he cheered him up by telling jokes, and helped him make his plank bed, as Bosie wiped his tears. If it weren't for the inedible food, Wormwood Scrubs, as Bosie described it, sounds very little like the 'hellish place' he called it.[23]

After his single night in prison, he was ready to take on the world. He now had only five weeks to prepare for his grand battle with his nemesis. Both Arthur Newton and Cecil Holt were in jail, so he needed new representation. The first solicitor he engaged did not 'approve of his methods.' Comyns Carr agreed to draw up a plea of justification, but advised Bosie that he had no real evidence and would lose at trial. Bosie was frustrated. He knew the truth, but he couldn't prove it. Everyone he contacted refused to get involved. Finally Bosie found a solicitor who did approve of his methods. His name was Edward Bell and he called his firm Carter & Bell in spite of the fact that he had no partner. Bell appreciated 'the Douglas fighting blood and spirit ...'[24] He was willing to go on a fishing expedition, requesting police files for Ross's friends in the hopes that something relevant would be found.

As Douglas was having his adventure in jail, Charles Garrett checked out of the White Cross League Boy's Home for the last time and joined the army. The police tried to track his whereabouts, but they were unable to discern what unit or regiment he had joined.[25]

That autumn Ross made plans to travel to North America to see galleries in the United States and to visit family in Canada. His health had been deteriorating due to the prolonged stress and he ended up having to cancel the trip. Throughout the end of the year and into the next he suffered periodic attacks of asthma, bronchitis and painful eczema.[26] He continued to mention Freddie in his letters, first bitterly, and later with wistful nostalgia, but the romance was over. On 3 October, Ross made out a new will leaving most of his property to his brother Alex and to his nieces Lillian and Hilda who he named as his executors.

Around the same time, however, Freddie Smith was being written into the wills of Helen Wyllie and Helen Carew. Wyllie went back and forth in the summer of 1914, first naming Smith as her executor, then removing him in favour of Kennard, then changing her mind and naming him as executor again. In every version of the will, he was provided for generously. Smith featured in Helen Carew's will as well. Between them they willed Smith a genuine fortune.[27]

One intriguing possibility is that Wyllie and Carew provided for Smith not because he was like a son to them, but because he was like a son-in-law. Maria Roberts, who wrote a biography of Freddie Smith, while acknowledging Kennard's many heterosexual affairs, calls the rumour that he was bisexual 'at least plausible ... and rumours of this occasionally seem to have emerged.' In 1904 Carew had had a falling out with the artist Jacques-Emile Blanche over the depiction of her son in a portrait she had commissioned. Carew disliked the effeminate look given to her son, but Kennard was pleased. He wrote to Blanche, 'It has shown her the real Roy, whom in her heart of hearts she imagined quite different. You have seen into my future ...' The painting was finally exhibited in 1924 under the condition that the name of the sitter be suppressed. The cataloguer gave it the title *Le Portrait de Dorian Gray*. Freddie spent a lot of time abroad and Roberts suggests that he spent this time with Kennard at his villa in Antibes.[28]

Meanwhile the search for witnesses against Ross continued. The law firm of Carter and Bell sent requests to Scotland Yard asking if they could please provide the date of the proceedings against Reginald Turner at Marlborough Street. They believed the proceedings were taken in 1898 or 1899 with Turner being defended by Charles Mathews and discharged by the magistrate. The police found nothing in their files. They closest they could come up with was an arrest of an 18-year-old named Reginald Herbert Turner who had been arrested in 1907 for 'indecently exposing his person'.

They also inquired about a William Beavis (or Beaver) Adams, an artist's model, who was sentenced to three months hard labour in 1909 for 'importuning male persons for immoral purposes' at Piccadilly Circus. Adams was 'said to have been at one time associated with' Ross.[29]

None of these avenues panned out, but ten days before he was to go to trial, Douglas got word that a man named William Edwards, who had followed the Crosland case with interest, had written to Crosland to tell him his son was one of Ross's victims. Douglas considered this divine intervention. Douglas's *Autobiography* embellishes a rather ordinary episode of showing up at the wrong address with prayers to St. Anthony of Padua and an angelic child appearing to guide him to the right door. He believed it to be 'a supernatural experience ... mysterious and wonderful'. The boy 'had an angelic face and smile. And how did he disappear in the space of time, a few seconds, between when I let go of his hand and when I looked round again?'[30]

As all of this was happening, the united front of Douglas and Crosland was fracturing. Crosland had decided he did not want to testify on his friend's behalf in Ross's libel action. Douglas wrote expressing his incredulity that Crosland would not stick to him 'as I have always stuck to you.' His letter was more hurt than angry, and concluded, 'I don't wish to argue with you or even quarrel with you, though I can never again feel the same about you as I have hitherto felt.'[31]

As the date of the trial approached, Crosland wrote to Douglas again saying he would be willing to testify if Douglas would give him £50. Douglas 'told him to go to hell.'[32] In the end Crosland did testify, and he and Douglas were briefly reconciled, but these were the first fissures in a friendship that was soon to be wrenched apart for good.

43

Rex v. Douglas

> It took a good deal more libelling to bring Ross to the fighting point than it did to bring Wilde.
>
> Lord Alfred Douglas.[1]

If this were a Hollywood blockbuster, everything would lead up to the big moment when Ross and Douglas finally faced off in court leaving one the victor and the other destroyed. In real life, the showdown was anti-climactic for a number of reasons. Douglas did put together an impressive string of witnesses. Because of the Defense of the Realm Act, however, the newspapers were extremely judicious and careful not to print anything that might be bad for public morals. Thus the testimony of few of the thirteen witnesses for the defence made it into the papers at all. This was incredibly frustrating to Douglas, who had been relishing his coup for some time. The trial ended in an ambiguous hung jury and a settlement rather than a victory for either side. Thus Douglas remained stymied and blocked in telling his story, and he was never satisfied that he had really had a hearing. He would continue to re-litigate his grievances against Ross in books for the rest of his life.

The lack of detail in the newspaper accounts was, however, a blessing for Ross. He had many friends who were willing to support him whether he was homosexual or not. On the other hand, it is one thing to accept homosexuality in the abstract, another to be confronted with the vivid details. Many who were willing to give Ross the benefit of the doubt might not have if they had been treated to the spectacle of a trial like Wilde's in which the stories of one handsome, working-class boy after another with descriptions of 'painted faces,' playful nicknames and all male parties had been put on full public display.

The long-awaited showdown finally began on 19 November 1914. The F Double E was not available, serving as Recording Officer to the Indian Corps. So Ernest Wild and Eustace Fulton appeared for Ross. Douglas was represented by Comyns Carr and E. J. Purchase. Mr Justice Coleridge presided.[2]

Robbie began his testimony on the second day of the trial. He talked about his friendship with Wilde, saying that he 'visited him constantly' in prison. He talked about his accomplishments in bringing the Wilde estate out of bankruptcy and about his choices surrounding the *De Profundis* manuscript. He said he'd been receiving harassing messages from Douglas for some time, but that he was initially advised not to take legal action because it was not worthwhile 'against a man who made libelling a profession.'

He went on to deny that he ever tried to blackmail Douglas and to downplay his relationship with Millard. 'I have no doubt what Garratt said about Millard was true,' he said. 'I have doubts, but probably they are true. All the parts about myself are untrue.' This statement made an impression on the judge, who underlined it in blue in his notes. Ross claimed Garratt's testimony about him had been scripted by Douglas and Crosland. This, the judge wrote in his notes, 'the jury disbelieved.'

This may have been due to the letter Garratt had written from his mother's house about Ross letting him 'come back again.' It was used effectively to rebut Ross's testimony. In cross-examination Carr asked Ross if he did not think that a person who used his friend's personal letters for an indirect purpose might be called a blackmailer. Ross said he did not believe so.

He was forthcoming on his motives when he was asked why he had prevented Douglas from using extracts of Wilde's letters in his book. It was personal. In light of Douglas's attacks on him it seemed 'a fair and reasonable thing to do.'

He admitted also that by the time Douglas met Wilde the playwright had 'already made a habit of the vice for which he was convicted.' That he knew what Wilde's vices were at such an early date cannot have worked in Ross's favour.

Asked about the Dansey case, Ross claimed he was sent abroad not because of any wrong-doing with boys but to get him away from the bad influence of Douglas who his family thought was 'odd in the head.' This was all the newspapers were prepared to report about the Bruges incident. In the courtroom, however, it was discussed in detail. Ross claimed Douglas had been the bad actor, not him.

He was then asked about a party that had allegedly taken place on New Year's Eve 1911 at Mayfair Chambers. This would have been at Reggie Turner's flat at 13 Little Grosvenor Street, the same building where Robbie and Freddie moved the following June. There it was said 'twenty or thirty men danced together and kissed each other.' Ross was supposed to have sat on a boy's knee. He denied it all. Carr asked if the 1905 edition of *De Profundis* did not paint Oscar Wilde as a repentant sinner.

'No, because it is well known that he did not die a repentant sinner. He lived a very irregular life up to the last, I am sorry to say.'

After a quick interview with Detective Inspector McPherson, who testified about Douglas's arrest, the prosecution closed.

Douglas then came to the stand and claimed that when he asked Ross about *De Profundis* he told him 'You had better be careful or I shall publish the manuscript as it stands, which will finish you off.' He said he also threatened to publish his personal letters 'if you are not careful.' Douglas said he replied, 'If you talk in that way you are a blackmailer.' This testimony impressed the judge, who wrote on the opposite page of his notes 'blackmailer'.

Although it was not covered in the press, Douglas testified at length about the Bruges incident. In his version, Dansey was already late to return to school when he visited him at the Albemarle Hotel. He stayed one night, and then returned to class. Three weeks later, he said, Ross came to him and told him that he had 'got into an awful scrape.' The headmaster, Wortham, had investigated and accused Ross of debauching other boys including his own sons. The judge underlined this in his notes, and also underlined Douglas's assertion that Ross admitted the charges. 'Ross had often been at the school, I had not,' Douglas said. 'The schoolmaster never wrote to me or accused me. I never had to consult a solicitor.'

Next he described his relationship with Wilde. 'Apparently I was like some sacred object to him,' he said. 'I do not disguise it was a very unhealthy sort of sentiment. He had a very bad influence on me. He encouraged me to be dissipated and idle, and destroyed all my faith in religion. Of course I had never met anyone the least like him before. At first I was amused. He was the most extraordinarily brilliant talker I had ever met. At least I thought so then. I don't know whether I would think so now.'

In answer to Ross's assertion that his family had sent him away because they didn't approve of his relationship with him, Douglas said, 'On the contrary, without boasting of my social distinction, they were very pleased to have my company – in fact, tickled to death.'

He concluded by saying that during the time he was associated with Wilde he was 'constantly in the association of depraved men. Mr Ross used to say every distinguished figure in literature and art was depraved, and he saw no harm in it. I was so corrupted by the teaching of Wilde and Ross that I condoned it and got to think nothing of it at all.'

In cross-examination, Wild got Douglas to admit that he had condoned Wilde's conduct until 1901. Wild read an extract from the 1895 article in *Truth* that called Douglas 'an exceptional young scoundrel' who was 'outside the pale of decent human beings.'

'You brought no action with regard to that?'

'I was hardly in the position to bring any action.'

Wild then asked about the two letters he wrote in response to that article, which had also been put under scrutiny in the Ransome case.

'What made me write was the fact that I was accused of deserting a friend,' Douglas said. 'I said he could call me a scoundrel if he liked, but he could not say I deserted my friend.'

Douglas took issue with the idea that he had fled the country when Wilde got into trouble. He said it was Ross who fled, while he remained and visited his friend in prison.

'Mr Ross only remained away six weeks, whereas you were absent from the country for almost five years.'

Douglas said after the scandal he felt that he did not wish to see London again. After a number of questions about letters and articles he had written in his youth, about the prevalence of homosexual activity at Oxford, and in high society, he said his views at the time 'were the result of the teaching of Wilde and Ross and the pernicious books they had given me to read in their efforts to corrupt me and in which they partially succeeded.' He now thought his old attitude was 'pernicious' and he 'repudiated it'.

Wild asked, 'You put yourself in the class of Wilde's friends who did not practise his vice?'

'Yes.'

'And you put Mr Ross in the class of those who did?'

'Yes.'

Wild then read one of the letters that Douglas had written during his association with Wilde. Douglas replied that he was 'a young fool in those days.'

'You were a poet?'

'I was a poet, yes; but poets are sometimes fools, you know.'

'Are you still a fool?'

'Yes, but I am not a wicked fool any longer.'

After a few more questions about his youthful letters, Douglas said, 'I don't see why I should not have these letters back. How much longer are they to be used against me by this gang of people? I suppose if an old woman was run down in an accident they would be used against me.'

Wild then turned his attention to letters of a more recent vintage. He inquired about one of the letters to Colonel Custance, which referred to his 'grocer ancestors'.

'It shows that the witness is a snob,' remarked Justice Coleridge.

'Do you think it is right to call your King a puppet and a coward?'

Douglas admitted that it was not, but explained in mitigation that it was an angry response to the Parliment Act and a proposal to create peers. 'I have written to the King again since then and have had a polite acknowledgement, so that evidently it did not produce any great feeling in his Majesty's mind, or of those of his immediate circle.'

Douglas was asked about some of the nasty letters he had sent about Ross, including one to the Prime Minister. 'Did you know Mr Ross was a personal friend of the Prime Minister and Mrs Asquith?' he asked.

'Yes, I thought it was right Mr and Mrs Asquith should know Mr Ross's true character. He is no longer a friend of the Asquiths and is not received at their house now.'

'Are you admitted?'

'No, I am not a friend of the Asquiths. Lord Glenconner told me that Ross was no longer a friend there.'

'Do you know Ross lunched with the Asquiths a fortnight ago?' Point Ross.

This is what the newspapers were willing to print. Coleridge's notes reveal a bit more about Douglas's testimony. These were the judge's personal notes, rather than an official transcript, so he was not necessarily quoting verbatim. Douglas talked about the time in Rouen, when he, Ross, Adey, Turner and Charles Hickey were staying together as Wilde was in prison. The Judge has Douglas saying, 'We talked about sodomy.' Douglas said after Wilde was released from prison he and Ross 'talked openly about their adventures with boys.' He said he and Ross often wrote letters about boys, and that both of them at that time condoned 'the vice.' 'I ceased to condone sodomy after 1900,' Douglas said, according to the judge, in what may be an ironic paraphrase. 'I condoned it up to that date. I thought Oscar Wilde's conduct excusable. I now abhor sodomy and a practising sodomite.'

The most damaging testimony came from Detective Frederick West who patrolled the area surrounding Picadilly from January 1905 to June 1911. One of his duties, since the Vagrancy Act had been passed in 1908 was to keep watch on 'male persons and boys loitering for immoral purposes.'[3] The Vagrancy Act explicitly prohibited soliciting a male for illicit purposes. West testified that he was familiar with many regulars who 'frequent the neighbourhood.' He limited his responses mostly to 'Yes' or 'No' and did not offer anything more than was asked of him. He came across as honest, even reluctant to say anything that might incriminate Ross.

Carr asked Ross to stand up and then asked West if he had ever seen him before. West said he had seen him frequently in Piccadilly and Jermyn Street over a number of years.

'What was he doing?' asked the judge. 'I walk through Jermyn Street every night of my life.'

'Your lordship will never do it again,' quipped Wild.

'My next question is in the company of what persons?' Carr asked.

'I can only give you my opinion, sir.'

'That is what I am asking you.'

West was reluctant to characterise the nature of Mr Ross's company. It took a number of questions, both from Carr and from the judge to get him to agree he had 'formed an opinion' about the young men from 'their get-up ... their dress and their faces painted'.

Wild cross-examined asking if West had observed Ross doing anything that broke the law.

'It depends to what extent,' he said.

'Sufficient for any charge to be formed against him.'

'If he had committed himself sufficiently, I should have arrested him.'

'If there had been any question of sodomy or taking part in soliciting.'

'Taking part?' Coleridge asked.

'That would not be sufficient, sir,' said West. He explained that a gentleman might be innocently walking down the street and be 'accosted by a boy'. It happened frequently. Wild pointed out that Ross lived not far from the area where West patrolled and was a member of a West End club and concluded with the observation that West had never arrested Ross for anything.

Then Carr asked further questions of his witness. West explained that the policy was not to arrest an alleged male prostitute unless a gentleman complained. He said when the Vagrancy Act was first passed, they arrested both the prostitute and the client but that 'it was found impossible to sustain the charge.' He testified further, 'I remember two cases where the person and the importuner were both arrested but they were discharged and they were never proceeded against, and then the youth was charged only.'

'It was put to you that any man might walk through Jermyn Street and be importuned by one of those youths,' Carr said.

'Yes.'

'That is so.'

'Yes.'

'Is that the kind of thing you meant when you spoke of seeing Mr Ross there?'

'No, Sir.'

The newspaper accounts of the testimony of someone named Albert Edwards was edited to the point of incomprehensibility. Edwards testified that in 1908, his son William met a gentleman in Church Street, Kensington. He returned occasionally and Edwards noticed the name 'Ross' on his collars and shirt band. When he read the name 'Robert Ross' in the newspapers in connection with the Oscar Wilde tomb, he remembered that was the name he had seen.

Reading between the lines, it seems that Ross either knew William Edwards enough to give him gifts or Edwards had taken items with the name Ross on them in order to blackmail him. The criminal file which contains some documents relating to the case does not have a transcript of the testimony to shine more light on this, but the judge's personal notes reveal some useful details. William Edwards was seventeen years old at the time, and his father, Mr Edwards, knew about his relationship with 'the gentleman' because he found some incriminating letters.

Further testimony about William Edwards was given by his brother Gilbert, a trooper in the City of London Rough Riders. He said his family had been deeply concerned about his brother. It seems that the family was estranged from William because Gilbert could only say that he 'believed he died' in South Africa. He described William as 'a cause of anxiety and trouble' to his family. In his *Autobiography*, Douglas claimed Gilbert said he did not know where his brother had gotten the money to go to South Africa, implying that it had come from Ross or someone who wanted him out of the way. Gilbert was 'overcome with emotion' on the stand.[4]

One day, in 1899 young William did not come home and Gilbert went out to find him. He discovered him at the Marble Arch. They went to a restaurant on Copthall Avenue where his brother 'inquired for a certain person' but he was not there. Later Gilbert went back and met the gentleman there. 'Are you Robert Ross?' he asked him. The man said he was. He asked him where his brother was. 'Who are you? What is his name?'

'I am his brother, my name is Edwards.'

'You mean Willie? Is it money you want?' Ross allegedly said. Gilbert said 'No,' used very strong language (according to the judge's notes it was 'you dirty bugger') and said Ross 'ought to be horsewhipped.' Ross threatened to call the police and have him locked up, and he told him he was 'quite at liberty to get the police.' Gilbert said he made a sworn statement about the event to a police officer, but he never saw the man or his brother again. The judge asked Ross to stand up so he could be identified. The witness said the man he spoke to so many years ago bore a strong resemblance to Ross, but he could not swear that it was him.

Two witnesses who were erased from public memory were a man who the newspapers only referred to as 'Laurence'. Ross denied knowing him. This was probably Arthur Lawrence of Regents Park, whose testimony does not survive but whose name appears on a list of witnesses who 'should receive their conduct money and expenses daily.'[5]

Another witness not mentioned in the papers was Jack Denny Bower, then living in Great Yarmouth and referred to in the police file as 'one of the catamite class in his young days – now reformed.' Bower had made headlines himself in 1910 when he was 25 and filed a breach of promise of marriage suit against a 54-year-old widow named Jesusa Agnes Ebsworth. The newspapers dubbed it an 'amusing' breach of promise case because it was rare for a man to file such a suit against a woman. Ernest Wild had represented Bower in the action.[6]

Bower testified that Ross and Freddie Smith had been living together 'immorally' at both Sheffield Gardens and Vicarage Gardens and that Robbie had taken Freddie to a villa in the south of France. Freddie Smith's biographer suggests that in this Bower was mistaken, and that he was actually referring to Coleridge Kennard's villa.[7]

Witnesses to Ross's relationship with Freddie Smith made up a large amount of the (unreported) testimony of the case. Douglas could not get over the fact that this information had not been publicised and years later, in 1918, he induced Robert Sievier to publish a long account in *The Winning Post*. The article was written by 'Robert le Diable,' one of Sievier's pseudonyms, but the information was clearly provided by Douglas, the article reflects his opinion, and may well have been written by him.[8]

The article argued that it was relevant to dredge up the accusations against Smith because of his 'incredible after-history' including his receiving a fortune from a wealthy woman and becoming an honorary attaché to His Majesty's Legation in the Swedish capital, a post that should have been out of reach to someone of his background. The article complained that both Ross and Smith had seemed to benefit from being sodomites. The contrast of how the world responded to Bosie and Oscar and how it responded to Robbie and Freddie could not have been more stark.

In spite of his own criticisms of Bosie for denying his relationship with Oscar in the Manners-Sutton case, when his time came, Robbie described Freddie Smith as his secretary. He explained how he met Freddie and how he had come to live in his house.

'Did you always treat this boy with familiarity?' Carr asked.

'Yes, I called him by his Christian name.'

'And behaved in such a way that there could be no doubt that you were living with him in relations of sodomy?'

'No, that is a false suggestion on your part.'

He also denied the claim of Emma Rooker, a member of the dramatic society who said Ross and Smith were 'very affectionate'; Ross put his arm around Smith's shoulder and called him 'darling.'

'Certainly not.' He did, however, admit that he may occasionally have given Smith presents in addition to his outsized secretarial salary. It did not help Ross's case much that the secretary who he had chosen to replace Smith was Millard, a man who had been jailed for gross indecency.

Reverend Robinson testified to the reasons Smith had been dismissed as an acolyte. He also gave his opinion that Smith was not 'fit or competent' to act as the secretary to a literary man when he met Ross. A Mr Harry Lovitt testified as to Smith's improved financial circumstances. His upward social trajectory was presented as highly suspicious. Lovitt also testified that Smith 'painted and powdered his face.'

The prosecution had assembled an impressive string of character witnesses beginning with Alex Ross. He said the Ross family had objected to his brother's association with Wilde. He denied that Ross had been sent abroad due to scandal and said it was for his health.

According to the judges notes, Alex talked about his brother's 1896 kidney operation and testified that he 'afterwards became very bald.' It is unclear what the context was of these comments or why the judge found Robbie's baldness relevant enough to record in his personal notes. Alex's next recorded statement had to do with Ross's reasons for travelling to Davos. 'He was out of his mind,' Alex said, 'That was the only reason.' He lamented the fact that his brother 'resisted our endeavours to break off the connection' with Douglas. While he admitted he had received a letter from Wortham about an incident with his students, he said he had destroyed it. He claimed the letter was a complaint that Ross had introduced Dansey to Douglas.

H. G. Wells, who said he had known Ross for 12 years testified that he had frequently met Freddie Smith at Ross's house. He said there was nothing 'abnormal' about him, he had never seen him paint or powder his face and his relationship with Ross was what you would expect of a boss and a secretary.

'Have you come here as a supporter of conventional morality?' Carr asked in cross-examination.

'I have come here to give evidence for Mr Ross as to his moral character.'

'Do you remember when Lord Alfred was editing *The Academy*?'

'Yes.'

'You remember that in that paper there were attacks upon your writing – that it was suggested that you written an improper book called 'Ann Veronica?'

'Yes, there was an ill-mannered article of that kind.'

'Was it an accurate description of that book to say that it was a glorification of people living together as man and wife without being married?'

'No, it is a stupid rendering of the case.'

Wells denied writing a complaint to *The Academy* about the review and said he did not pay attention to 'silly little reviews' in 'obscure publications'.

'Have you not consistently written advocating the view that the ordinary ideas of marriage are nonsensical?'

'I have done nothing of the sort.'

Edmund Gosse was next to testify to Ross's high moral character. He described him as 'flighty' and 'quixotic to an absurd extent'. He also thought he had bad judgement of men but that he was 'a totally honest, unselfish and clean man'.

Next Squire Sprigg confirmed Alex Ross's testimony that Ross had gone bald following his kidney operation. He also backed up Alex's claim that Ross had gone to Davos in 1893 because of 'a nervous breakdown'.

Vyvyan Holland, who was now a member of the bar and serving in the army, made a good impression saying Ross was 'like a second father to him'.

The most surprising witness for the prosecution was Reverend Biscoe Wortham, the headmaster at Bruges who had launched the investigation into Ross's relationship with his sons. By now Claude Dansey was an intelligence officer with MI5 and Wortham's son Philip was a decorated military officer. In deference to the sensitivity of an accusation of that sort against officers in a time of war, none of Wortham's testimony, or even the fact that he was called to testify, was reported in the papers.

Wortham had been contacted by Carter & Bell, Douglas's solicitors. Records show that Wortham replied, but do not reveal the content of either letter.[9] He cannot have welcomed the inquiry. The whole point of making a deal with the 'gang of most brutal ruffians' in the first place was to cover the incident up and to go on as if it had not happened. Douglas, in bringing the matter before the court, had broken his end of the bargain.

The same forces that had kept the minister from pressing charges against Ross and Douglas in the first place, now compelled him to take the stand and say that there had been no suggestions of immorality against Ross, or anyone else, in regards to his sons. This is contradicted by the series of letters written at the time. He was, however, willing to implicate Douglas (who had brought this matter into the light) for misdeeds with Dansey. Wortham testified about Douglas's letters and presents to Dansey and claimed that he had only blamed Ross for introducing them. He also said he had informed Dansey's father about the letters and persuaded him not to press charges. He said Adey had acted as an intermediary in the dispute, but did not mention Oscar Browning.

The judge was not impressed by either party in the dispute. In his summing up he described Ross and Douglas both as people who 'fluttered around the brilliant but certainly unwholesome person of Oscar Wilde as moths fluttered around a candle.' He attributed their feud to their being 'clamorous to obtain all the notoriety that could attach to Wilde and his writings.'

He expressed surprise that Ross did not express the outrage you would expect of one accused of something as horrible as homosexuality. 'I waited and waited, but I waited in vain for any moral expression of horror at the practice of sodomitical vices ... and indeed, to be frank with Mr Ross, when he was asked whether he did not constantly introduce these things into ordinary articles in a magazine, all he could say was that he could not remember. It was certainly not so emphatic a denial as you would expect from a man with no leprosy upon him ... I don't recollect that there is a copy or extract which has been produced indicating that he disapproves or that he views this kind of vice with disgust ... I would say that is the attitude of the man towards this kind of perversion of sex.'

He also wondered why Ross had gone to the rescue of Millard, with whom he had said he was barely acquainted, when he was arrested for 'an unnatural vice'.

'... Heaven forbid that one should judge a person by that,' the judge said, 'it would be ... a grave injustice to say that persons who visit outcasts and criminals are outcasts and criminals themselves. They may visit to comfort, alleviate, to reform. But why did Ross choose out of the forty-five million people in this country, why did he choose Millard to go visit in prison? ... And Millard did not reform, apparently, because we know from Ross himself that Millard continued to carry out these practices, and Ross knows it ...'

The judge went through the four incidents he thought most relevant, the Bruges incident, and the stories of Garratt, Edwards and Smith and concluded with Inspector West's testimony, which the judge gave great weight. He instructed the jury that 'Such vices as are here impugned can of course seldom be established by direct irrefragable proof. They are always practised under the veil of secrecy.'

Even so, he cautioned the jury that 'bare suspicion, even strong suspicion' was not proof and that they could only assume guilt if evidence was 'inconsistent with an innocent interpretation'.

The jury was out for three hours and failed to agree on a verdict and the case was adjourned. They were in 'two diametrically opposed camps'. The evidence Douglas had amassed against Ross was largely circumstantial, yet together it painted a damning picture. Gosse and Asquith were concerned that a second hearing might give Douglas time to unearth something worse. They agreed that the best thing for Ross would be to enter a *nolle prosequi*, permission to drop the case. Asquith consulted with the Attorney-General John Simon about it. Simon was sympathetic to Ross, but advised that the case could not be dropped unless both parties agreed to terminate 'these most deplorable proceedings ...'[10]

When he was first contacted by Ross's legal team, Douglas would not agree. The Ross team countered with an offer to pay Douglas's legal costs, and they further agreed that Ross would not produce in court or publish any letters from Douglas to Wilde. Douglas was prepared to agree to this if they would not oppose any application he might make to the British Museum about the *De Profundis* manuscript. They agreed and the matter was legally settled, although the battle would never be fully over.

Douglas took solace in the notion that the fact that the case had not gone to a jury meant his plea of justification would remain in the files (although it doesn't seem to have) and that the police could use it to mount a criminal case. To his eternal frustration, however, the police had little inclination to do so.

44

Infighting

As the calendar flipped to 1915, Robbie and Freddie were once again at odds. Millard was becomming Ross's confidant rather than Smith, and this created some tension between the two former secretaries. Freddie apparently now referred to his replacement as 'stupid & unintelligent Millard'.

At a time when Ross was doing his best to publicly distance himself from Millard, their friendship was growing more intimate. Ross was now signing his letters to Millard 'ever yours affectionately.' Freddie on the other hand had become 'F. S.' Robbie complained that Freddie had been writing something offensive about him to mutual friends, including Vyvyan Holland. Ross was sure that Smith had written 'in a similar strain to various other people,' although he had not actually seen such letters. He complained that the newly rich Freddie was 'swaggering' around at the Automobile and Junior Constitutional Clubs 'with the result that some members have threatened to write to the committees ... I shall probably have to go to America to avoid the consequences of his folly! – one of life's little ironies.'[1] (The locations of his 'swaggering' were metaphorical rather than literal. The Junior Constitutional Club, once one of the most popular conservative clubs in London, had closed in 1904.)[2]

Smith's fast rise in social status in Ross's company had been an issue in the Douglas trial, and the large gift from members of Coleridge Kennard's family had raised some eyebrows. If, as Roberts speculates, Smith's indiscretion in the previous year had something to do with Kennard it might have given Robbie an additional reason to find the behaviour offensive. Millard apparently told Ross that he was not all that worried about Smith's behaviour, because he replied, 'with that egoism of mine (which Reggie [Turner] wittily said was too deep for me to show) I ascribed my own feelings to yourself.'[3]

His bitterness, however, was not abated. Ross dictated a letter to Millard, who had done the typing on Smith's book when they were still on good terms. He planned to include it as a cover letter to an insulting gift for Smith, a copy of Abbott and Seeley's *English Lessons for English People*.

'To the author of Etelka on his 30th birthday. A careful study of Messrs Abbott & Seeley's volume may possibly render superfluous in the future the assistance of the "stupid & unintelligent Millard" whose painful task it was to transmute the nonsense and vulgarity of an unknown language into the English idiom.'[4]

We can only hope that once Ross got that particular meanness off his chest, he failed to send it. It must have been cathartic because the tensions soon relaxed between them. In mid-March Freddie wrote to him apologising for whatever transgression had occurred the previous June and Robbie went back to calling him 'Freddie' rather than 'F. S.' in his letters to Millard.

Douglas, meanwhile, knew that his actions against Ross had led not to widespread social approbation but to a glowing testimonial, printed on 29 March 1915. The statement was signed by 300 supporters including the Asquiths. It praised the 'justice and courage' of Robbie's writing, his generosity and assistance to new talent and expressed 'esteem' for a 'brave, loyal and devoted friend'.[5]

Douglas's evidence against Ross had been suppressed by the papers and now he was being celebrated in them and even Freddie Smith was enjoying elevated social status. It seemed clear to him that there was a far-reaching conspiracy and one that he was more determined than ever to expose.

Douglas may have made a legal agreement not to attack Ross, but Crosland had made no such promise. Bolstered by his success in Justice Avory's court, he decided to go on the offensive and sue Ross for malicious prosecution. In April 1915 the case was heard in the King's Bench Division before Justice Bray. Cecil Hayes once again appeared for Crosland. Hayes tried to argue that the original case against Crosland had been 'remarkable for its impudence and for its audacity.' Audacious because Ross had tried to 'whitewash that reputation and character which he knew he did not possess.'[6]

Crosland did not stand a chance in the case as soon as the judge heard his correspondence with Douglas including Crosland's own taunts to Ross encouraging him to sue for libel.

'You now complain that Mr Ross did what you invited him to do,' said Bray.

This time the court did not accept Crosland as the sole champion of public decency against a growing Wilde movement. Bray would not even send the case to the jury. He found that Ross had been justified in bringing the action and assigned costs to Crosland.[7]

Crosland and Douglas's friendship came to an end shortly thereafter. The implement of destruction was a telegram. Given the talent of both parties to write abusive letters, its text was surprisingly anodyne. There are two accounts of the incident, one a partial letter Bosie wrote at the time, the second was his explanation written when they briefly reconciled in 1920. The telegram read 'Why did not you keep appointment—Alfred Douglas.' It was addressed to Crosland, without initials, and sent to his Woking address, the home he shared with his wife, not the one he shared with his mistress: '... you are idiot enough to suppose that when last Wednesday I sent you a wire to Woking, I was endeavouring to do something to 'upset' your wife. Whereas I did not even remember that you had a wife or think anything about any such person,' he wrote in the first of the letters. 'I took it for granted that she knew we were meeting daily,' he said in the second. He claimed to have only sent the telegram because he hadn't been able to reach him at the office on Mitcham Street.[8]

Douglas knew very well that Crosland had a wife. One suspects the gentleman protests too much. The telegram was a method both he and Crosland sometimes used to force a reaction when someone had stopped answering letters.

Why addressing Crosland without his initials, and the fact that they were meeting daily upset Mrs Crosland is a mystery the two men took to their graves. It provoked a violent reaction from Crosland, which Bosie answered with the snobbery he resorted to when most injured. 'I certainly agree with you that it is quite impossible that we should go on being 'friends ... I hereby invite you to go to your own place and find your friends among your own class,' he said, before insulting Crosland's writing, his mood swings and concluding that he felt sorry for him: 'You are a very ill-bred, ill-conditioned and low person. In fact, you are everything that you laboriously set up not to be. You are a frightful coward, and you disguise your cowardice by loud shouting and general Ancient Pistolling. You fondly imagine that the world turns around your axis.'[9]

Although the break was temporary, it was this episode, and the way Crosland behaved towards him afterwards, not their final parting, that pained Douglas the most. When they were eventually reconciled in the 1920s, Douglas called it a 'sort of ghost of our former friendship'.[10]

45

The Wilde Myth

Scorn not the 'literary executor'
He is 'officially condoned,' for he
Has rescued Oscar Wilde from obloquy
And planted him in our heart's innermost core ...
Lord Alfred Douglas, *All's Well with England*[1]

The war and the wave of moralism that came with it had not put an end to the community that congregated around Ross as the keeper of the Wilde flame. The soldier/poet Siegfried Sassoon called Ross's rooms in Half Moon Street 'an oasis' and Ross made him feel as though 'he was a central point in my existence.' He was one of many young artists who sometimes stayed at Half Moon Street when he was in London.[2]

Robbie was committed to providing a respite, mental and physical, from the war. He hated the war and its patriotic champions whom he called, borrowing a phrase Wilde had once used for Queensberry, 'screaming scarlet majors'. (The line, without the 'screaming' found its way into Siegfried Sassoon's famous poem 'Base Details.') The Bishop of London, who had said war would be a purifying fire for the souls of young soldiers, was a frequent target of his mockery.[3]

Sassoon remembered Ross surrounded by 'sprightly young friends ... connected with the art world.' Men of his own generation, 'middle-aged and rather war-weary' also stopped by. They enjoyed Turkish delight, brandy, endless cigarettes and challenging conversation. Aleck Ross was a frequent guest, sitting quietly and observing the goings-on and enjoying his witty and impulsive brother's 'refreshing though sometimes intolerant talk'.

Adey was a constant presence in those days. He would arrive late at night, and had such a comfortable relationship with Robbie that he could walk in without knocking, and enter a room without so much as a word of welcome. Sassoon found him to be a 'sallow, moody little man'. Robbie found it difficult to sleep, because he suffered from asthma, and so he and Adey would sit up together half the night. They had spent so much time together that they had the same mannerisms, though Sassoon thought Adey's were 'a blurred reflection of the original'.[4]

Ross had taken Sassoon on as one of his latest projects, promoting him, encouraging him, and introducing him to people he thought might advance his career or inspire his art. He encouraged him to write bitter and honest depictions of his war experience. Gosse, who had introduced the poet to Robbie, was shocked by some of the verses that satirised the war, but Robbie encouraged him to keep working in the same vein. He found the poet a patron among the philanthropic women he cultivated as friends. Lady Ottoline Morrell, an art lover and pacifist, was always interested in Robbie's opinion and she became one of Sassoon's greatest supporters. Sassoon was grateful, although occasionally overwhelmed, by Robbie's ardent support.

Along with Robbie's flat at Half Moon Street, homosexual soldiers on leave enjoyed rest and relaxation at Gerald Hamilton's Westminster flat and at Christopher Millard's place in Molyneux House. On 11 November 1915 Hamilton's flat was raided on suspicion of gross indecency. He was found in the company of two soldiers and the police confiscated rouge, powder puffs and incense as evidence. Hamilton was jailed under the Defence of the Realm Act, released in 1917 and quickly rearrested.[5]

Millard's flat was under police surveillance as well. One of the men who attended Millard's Christmas party was arrested and agreed to make a statement that men had sex there. Two officers were court-martialled and Millard was again charged with gross indecency and forced to flee London. He settled in Northumberland where he went by the name S. Millar.[6]

Shortly thereafter he enlisted taking his military training in Edinburgh. While there he sometimes attended mass at St. Peter's in Falcon Avenue where the priest was Oscar Wilde's former lover, John Gray. Robbie disliked Gray, and as he had a great deal of influence over Millard, the latter decided not to make any attempt to meet the former 'decadent'.[7]

In early 1916, Douglas and Crosland continued to quarrel. Most of the complaints and skirmishes are not worth elaborating upon. By the end of March, Douglas was writing to Crosland saying 'You cannot increase the contempt I already have for you.' He also sent Crosland a copy of one of his books with his sonnets corrected in red pen.[8]

Crosland was a bad influence on Douglas, but he had at least been a powerful force and an ally. Now that his best friend had turned against him as well, Douglas was isolated and prey to his own untrammelled thoughts. He was more persuaded than ever that there was no love in the earthly realm, that he had been singled out for redemptive suffering, and that his mission in life was to warn the world about the dangers of carnal vices, especially homosexualism. As he ruminated, with few countervailing forces, he was prepared to believe all manner of conspiracy theories.

Harris's *Oscar Wilde* was released in the United States in 1916 and immediately outshone any previous Wilde biography. Ransome's book had been a literary analysis. Sherard and Douglas had written apologia. Only Harris had written a story. While it was out of reach of British libel law in the United States, it was still the target of anti-vice crusaders who nevertheless did more to spread its fame than to quash its distribution. Max Beerbohm refused to review it because he was bothered by 'All that raking-up of the old Sodomitic cesspool', which had been continuously stirred 'by various lawsuits'. He felt it was 'a dis-service (however well-intentioned) to poor old O. W.'s memory.'[9]

There was widespread agreement among Wilde's old friends as to the strengths and weaknesses of Harris's biography. Reggie Turner, Robbie Ross and even Alfred Douglas agreed that Harris had done a good job capturing Oscar's personality but a terrible job recreating his speaking style. They all agreed, as well, that the book was designed to make Frank Harris its hero and that the long conversations he claimed to have had with Wilde were mostly fiction. What they disagreed on, quite sharply, was Harris's depiction of Bosie.

Harris's story was powerful and dramatic, and it was the first published book to follow the *De Profundis* 'big looming tragedy' narrative, in which Wilde's fate is sealed the moment Alfred Douglas enters the scene. The British press might have been diplomatic when dealing with living people, but the US had no fear of libel suits and had no trouble summing up Wilde's tragedy as they understood it from reading Harris. Wilde 'would listen to no one except that vain, domineering, insolent little rat.'[10]

Ransome made his accusation as a passing observation in a larger context of literary criticism. Harris's depiction would stick, because it was dramatised in the form of a wonderful, well-told story that in most other aspects rang true. Harris and Douglas spent years battling over the content of his book. Most of this feuding took place after Ross's death, but it is worth mentioning here for what it reveals about the competing narratives that Ross and Douglas were trying to advance.

In 1925, Harris wrote that he was persuaded by Reggie Turner that he had misjudged Douglas and he determined to meet with him and put things right. This was true insofar as it went, but Harris had an even more pressing reason for wanting to make peace with Douglas. As long as the litigious Douglas objected to his book, no British publisher was willing to take it on. This was especially true as Harris was the author of a scandalous book, *My Life and Loves*, and there was an outstanding warrant against him in England for contempt of court. He would be dead in the water in any legal skirmish with Douglas. This was a problem because the Wilde biography was his biggest potential money-maker.

Yet Harris had genuinely begun to have doubts about what he had written when he met Reggie Turner in Nice in February 1925. Harris asked him his opinion on his Wilde book. Turner told him that 'as a matter of taste' he wished Harris had not lingered so much on the scene of Oscar's death. The part that bothered Turner most was a line that said when Oscar died there was 'a loud explosion; mucus poured out of Oscar's mouth and nose.' Harris said that what he had heard from Ross had been even more vivid and he had toned his story down. Ross said Oscar's 'bowels came away', the smell made him violently ill and that he had left Turner to clean up and 'burn the bedding'.[11]

When Harris asked him why Ross would make up 'such a hideous story about his friend', Reggie answered, 'Ross was a strange person in some respects, and he was afflicted with a dramatic imagination,' but he said 'I loved Robbie Ross and did not wish to give him away or quarrel with him.'[12]

Many biographers, including Ellmann, have given preference to Ross's exploding body story because they can come up with no motivation for Ross to tell such a grisly story about someone he loved, whereas Turner might well have concealed the story to preserve Wilde's dignity. Ellmann notes that Augustus John claimed to have heard about the explosion from both Ross and Turner.[13] But Ashley Robins, a lecturer in clinical pharmacology and psychiatry who made an extensive study of the medical evidence surrounding Wilde's death, does not concur.

'Ross's description of Oscar Wilde's body "exploding" makes no sense medically and I don't know how he arrived at that statement,' he said. 'Wilde died after a brain infection consequent on suppurative middle ear disease. He lapsed into a coma and died peacefully, as Turner commented.'[14] The story also contradicts Ross's earlier account, which says that there was 'nothing horrible about the body until about 6:30 in the evening when decomposition set in rapidly.'

This was not the only grotesque story that Harris began to question. Ross had also shared a colourful story about the occasion when Wilde's body was exhumed to be re-buried in Pere Lachaise. He said when Wilde died, the doctors had advised him to put the body in quicklime which would consume the flesh but leave the skeleton. When the grave was opened, he found that the quicklime had instead preserved the body so that it was entirely recognisable, its deathbed explosion notwithstanding. His hair and beard had gone on growing, and he was otherwise exactly as he had been when he went in the ground. Ross was horrified, and sent Oscar's son away. Then in a scene right out of Shakespeare, he told the gravediggers to stop their work and he went down into the grave himself, and moved the body with his own hands.

The story of the state of the corpse would require a forensic scientist to prove or disprove. The rate at which a body breaks down inside a coffin can vary a great deal depending on the composition of the soil, the material of the coffin and any number of factors. Quicklime has, indeed, been shown to preserve bodies. What is more, the scientific tests that confirmed this were not conducted until after Ross's death. So this part of the story may be true. Hair growing after death, however, is an old wives' tale. It is worth noting that Ross was spinning this macabre yarn around the time of the sensational Crippen murder trial. One of the elements of the crime was that parts of a body had been found buried in quicklime, which instead of breaking down the body had preserved it.[15]

If Wilde's body was preserved in some fashion it is hard to imagine that it would be in a state that Robbie would want to carry it 'in loving reverence'. Even if it were, it is even harder to imagine the diminutive Ross lifting a body that Shaw had described as suffering from a form of giantism. (After a rare literary double reversal, Harris first decided the story was a fabrication, then, after a falling out with Bosie claimed he had reason to believe that 'Ross did move the head at least with his own hands.'[16] He did not say what his reason for believing this was.)

When Harris asked Kennard, who had attended the reburial, what happened he said simply, Ross 'left all that to the professional grave-diggers.'[17]

'In fine,' Harris concluded, 'Ross had misled me time and again – deliberately here and to his own glorification, there out of instinct to make a simple story dramatic and effective.'[18]

The punchline to this is that the conversation with Kennard was another fiction. In 1926, Kennard wrote to Vyvyan Holland and said he had never spoken to Harris about the burial and that the story was 'an entire fabrication'.[19] Holland could not confirm or deny any account of what went on at the grave because Ross 'did not allow him anywhere near' it.[20]

These tall tales led Harris to question other things Ross had told him, including the charge that Douglas had introduced Wilde to prostitution, and that he had abandoned him. On the second point, Harris came across some letters from Wilde to Douglas, which had been published in America. The letters revealed that Wilde was writing to Douglas with affection as he was writing to Ross with contempt. On the first point, Reggie Turner told Harris that it was Ross, not Douglas, who introduced Wilde to prostitution. Harris was, briefly, convinced that he had done Douglas a great disservice.[21]

He arranged a meeting with Douglas and they got on so well at this point that he persuaded Douglas to make unprecedented confessions about his sex life with Wilde. Bosie had his own reasons for allowing publication. The Wilde estate would not give him permission to quote from *De Profundis* to respond to its claims directly. Robbie had, however, given *Harris* permission to quote from it and from Wilde's letters, although these quotations often appear in disguised form as dialogue in Harris's book. If Harris was willing to let him respond to these passages, it would be the next best thing to the book he had always wanted to write. The result was that Harris agreed to publish a new preface in the next edition of the book, and Douglas agreed not to block its publication.

Harris and Douglas corresponded amiably about the new preface throughout much of 1925. It was to contain Harris's explanation of how he had come to write the book as he had, what had led him to believe he had made mistakes, and then to print a long letter by Douglas. It included his familiar complaints against his father, his reasons for encouraging Wilde to go forward with the libel action and his grievances about Sir Edward Clark's handling of the case. When Harris sent the new preface to his publisher in London, they insisted for legal reasons that the passages about Clark, who was still alive, be removed. By then Douglas and Harris had reached an impasse as to what a new release of the Oscar Wilde biography would look like. Harris had thought the preface would resolve the issue, but Douglas was insisting that the entire book be re-set with the lines he found libelous either cut or presented with explanatory footnotes. Douglas was too impatient to leave his vindication until these issues were resolved. He published the New Preface himself. Harris was furious that Douglas had stolen his work and the brief honeymoon was over.

Already angry with Douglas over his behaviour with regards to the preface, Harris consulted with some other authorities on Wilde, Holland and Millard among them. They had both learned about Douglas primarily from Ross and had been persuaded by the evidence in Wilde's letters to him. Holland was diplomatic, but backed Ross's interpretations. Millard, whose life had been upended by Douglas, was more forceful in his condemnation. He told Harris that he had a dossier full of evidence against him.[22] Harris came away convinced that 'Alfred Douglas had lied to me again and again.' In 1926, Harris wrote an introduction for a new edition of *De Profundis* in which he called Douglas a 'traitor'.[23]

Douglas had an uncanny ability to sabotage himself. As much as he wanted to be seen in the role, he was not a sympathetic victim. His self-centredness, impulsiveness and combativeness always rose to the surface, confirming many aspects of the depiction of him in *De Profundis*. The Ross narrative may not have been entirely accurate, but it was not entirely wrong either, and Douglas could not stop himself from proving that at every turn. Yet he was self-aware enough to know that he did not have the personality his defenders would have wished.

'No doubt if you had the job of creating me I should have been quite different,' Douglas wrote to an American correspondent, 'But I am as God made me, and I have never been able to soar to the great Yankee ideal of "too proud to fight".'[24]

In 1928, it was clear that Harris's *Oscar Wilde* was not going to be published in England. The financially desperate Harris approached the book dealer A. S. W. Rosenbach with an offer to sell the two letters in which Lord Alfred Douglas had elaborated on the physical aspect of his relationship with Wilde. Harris described them as putting 'in the crudest words' exactly 'what Oscar did to him.' ('He sucked me.') He found a buyer in William A. Clark, Jr.[25]

Returning to 1916, Douglas's sense of religious mission was reaching its height. Over the next few years he turned his focus to the wider world. He truly believed, as he would one day write in a new preface to the second edition of *Oscar Wilde and Myself*, 'I was born into this world chiefly to be the instrument, whether I would or no, of exposing and smashing the Wilde cult and the Wilde myth; and to fulfil this mission I have had to fight against "the rulers of the world of darkness".'[26]

Years later, when he had recovered from this mental state, he would have to come up with explanations for behaviour that he did not fully understand himself. There was an apologetic tone to his observations on his mindset in this period when he looked back almost 15 years later: 'I got to the stage of glorifying in the persecution I was undergoing, regarding it as a special sign of grace.' He embraced the role of a suffering martyr so fully that it seems he would not be satisfied until he ended up in jail. In retrospect, Douglas had doubts that his experiences had been supernatural. 'The wonderful feelings I used to have are gone. So have the supernatural experiences; and though a priest in confession told me that this was simply because I no longer needed them and it was a greater merit for me to go on simply being a good Catholic without them. I believe in my heart that this is not really what has happened.'[27]

One of the ways he intended to advance his mission was with a new book called *The Wilde Myth,* which would attack his enemies head on. His relationship with the publisher, Martin Secker, was fine until he delivered the manuscript. It eviscerated a long slate of enemies, and was full of conspiracy theories linking the Wilde movement to pro-German forces. If he had limited his attacks to Wilde, the book might have been published, but Douglas was determined to vent his spleen about living people — including Herbert Asquith.

Crosland, who read the manuscript at the publisher's request, agreed that the book was unpublishable. 'I am afraid the *Wilde Myth,* which I have read at your request won't do. The critical parts need not be discussed, but the personal parts bristle with dangerous innuendo, and as much as I might desire to see the people concerned take medicine, I cannot reasonably advise you to supply the spoon.'[28]

Although Douglas was furious at the time, Secker did him a great favour in abandoning the project. Because it was never published, and only two proofs are known to have existed, Douglas was able essentially to deny it had ever been written and to blame any views he wished to recant in *Oscar Wilde and Myself* on Crosland. He would have had a much harder time sustaining that claim if the public had been able to read his own text, 'Wilde was not a great artist, he was a small one. He acquired by practice the faculty of writing the sort of stuff that appeals to and tickles the minds of small people.'[29]

The book concludes 'The Wilde myth has devastated my life from every point of view. It devastated my life when I was a victim to its illusions, and it has devastated my life ever since I escaped from those illusions.'[30]

46

Kicking Oscar's Corpse

> Are any of you aware, I wonder, that at this present moment this country
> harbours in its bosom 47,000 aliens from Sodom and Gomorrah, all busily
> plotting peace? Does that seem too monstrous for belief?
>   Vernon Lee (Violet Paget), *Satan the Waster*[1]

Bosie had agreed not to attack Robbie personally, but he had made no promise
about 'the Wilde cult' and liberalism in general. The paranoia of war gave him
an opportunity to make his case on a grand stage. The next trial would be the
climax of what Croft-Cooke called Bosie's 'raging fever'.[2] The events of Bosie's
life from this point until he was finally sent to prison in 1924 often play as
theatre of the absurd. No episode more so than his involvement in the famous
Black Book libel case between actress Maud Allan and the conservative MP Noel
Pemberton-Billing.

In the depths of war, two old notions were combined. The first was that for a
nation to survive it must be a unified people, and to be a people everyone must
share a way of life. The second notion was that homosexuality was a dirty foreign
habit, and those who practised it were more aligned with another country than
their own. Therefore it followed quite naturally that the Germans were turning
the English gay and that was why England was not winning the war.

Billing's conservative publication, *The Vigilante*, raised the alarm about
Germany and its 'Jew-agents' who had created an 'army of prostitutes' more
damaging to men than bullets. Even more worrying was the 'Black Book'
in which the Germans kept a list of 47,000 sex perverts, which they could
use to blackmail prominent English politicians and generals into committing
espionage and treason. Billing was not the originator of the so-called Black
Book. That rumour was started by Harold Sherwood Spencer, an American who
had fought with distinction in Algiers but who had been dismissed from not
only the US but also the British army for mental instability. He had met Billing
at a meeting of the National Party and complained to him that the military
authorities refused to take his conspiracy claims seriously. Billing gave him a
platform in *The Vigilante*.

The idea of a secret list of prominent homosexuals was not new. Douglas's
Mercure de France article, written while Wilde was in prison, included the line:
'I know for an absolute fact that the London police have on their books the
names of more than 4,000 persons, many of whom occupy the most exalted

places in politics, in art, and society, who are known as habitual paederasts, and yet none of them are prosecuted.'³ While *the* Black Book was a fiction, *black books* did exist. Douglas knew of at least one, and this is one reason he was inclined to believe the conspiracy theory.⁴

As *The Vigilante* was sounding the alarm about soldiers being turned homosexual, homosexual soldiers were turning to the welcoming presence of Robert Ross. In November 1917, Siegfried Sassoon met a kindred soul in the Craiglockhart hospital. A twenty-four-year-old poet, Wilfred Owen, was recovering from the psychological trauma of battle. Owen's poetry up to that point consisted of competent, but derivative patriotic war poems and a separate dossier that he showed to a few close friends. This latter was full of Urianian verse including a poem he had written to a 13-year-old parishoner when he was a lay preacher. It described a romp in the woods where they 'lay in hawthorn glades'. Another work was called 'Love Poem to a Child' and other verses contained lines like 'I fall in love with children, elfin flair.'⁵

Sassoon recognised Owen's talent and encouraged him to combine his Decadent and Urianian themes with the gritty ugliness of war. When Owen left the hospital to visit London, Sassoon gave him an envelope with a ten shilling note, Robbie's address at Half Moon Street and a message that read 'Why shouldn't you enjoy your leave? Don't mention this again or I'll be very angry.'⁶

Robbie took Owen to the Reform Club and introduced him to Arnold Bennett and H. G. Wells. Almost all of the poetry for which Owen is now known was written or revised during his association with the Ross circle. It was also an active social period for Owen. According to Dr Matthew Barry, Owen took on the Maurice Gilbert role, being 'serially available' to Ross's friends.⁷

Meanwhile, a Dutch impresario, Jack Thomas Grein, a naturalised British citizen, decided to take the provocative action of producing Wilde's banned play, *Salome* at the Independent Theatre. The enterprise was organised as a 'theatre club' to get around licensing restrictions. While the play was able to be performed to subscribers, Grein also had visions of a larger office, and he had put in an application to the Lord Chamberlain to issue a licence. The reader, George Street, found 'nothing indecent' in the play except for some squeamishness about how realistic the severed head would be. *Salome* may well have been en route to its first public performances in Britain had Billing not made it a cause célèbre.⁸

Grein had a personal connection to Wilde as well. He had defended Alfred Taylor in his criminal trials. Most of the newspapers misspelled his name 'Grain' in their meagre accounts, and recorded only that his summing-up consisted of asking the jury not to believe the word of blackmailers and prostitutes. Grein's defence of Taylor had not been one of the great moments in the history of jurisprudence. He viewed the courts as a sideline to his dramatic career and there is no evidence he was ever called to the Bar.⁹ Grein was courting controversy with his decision to cast Maud Allan, known for risqué dancing. He advertised that she would be performing 'the dance of the seven veils.'

The Vigilante attacked the production with a notice than ran under the headline 'The Cult of the Clitoris'. Like any good moralist, Billing read the material he considered corrupting. The word 'clitoris' was not yet familiar outside medical circles and the pages of Krafft-Ebbing. When Allan and Grein filed their libel complaint, Billing argued that 'clitoris' was a medical term that could not corrupt anyone because it was only known to the 'initiated'.¹⁰

Billing implied that because the word 'clitoris' was only known to insiders, it was homosexual code. He backed away from the charge that Allan herself was a 'lesbianist' claiming that the charge was only that she was 'pandering to those who practised unnatural vice by this performance'. In other words, Allan was 'posing as Sapphic' (or Sampphic, perhaps).

The Black Book case was a spectacle from the first. There was a colourful cast of characters, the showboating MP who had decided to represent himself, the glamorous actress, and the theatrical producer who wanted to strike a blow for artistic freedom. All it needed was someone to step into the symbolic space of Oscar Wilde. Billing drew Douglas into this role quite easily by announcing that he planned to call Ross as a witness. Hearing this, Douglas offered his testimony at once.

There is often a thin line between the absurd and the frightening, and this was on full display in Charles Darling's courtroom. Billings filled the court with supporters who cheered, heckled and hissed and his defence made a mockery of the social conventions that give the court its authority. C. G. L. Du Cann, a friend of Hume-Williams, attended the trial for 'a little healthy excitement'. He described it as 'Pantomime, circus, farce'. The crowd was rowdy, reacting as if they were witnessing the music hall performance it appeared to be. They were about to be treated to a parade of what Humphreys called 'half-mad witnesses'.[11] In terms of sheer entertainment it could not be beat: sex, perversion, secret conspiracies, and celebrated eccentrics would make the nation forget the war, at least for a few days.

One of the highlights of the affair was when a bitter Bosie took the stand in a tragi-comic tone of haughty belligerence to tell the world how much he regretted ever having met Wilde. 'I think he was the greatest force for evil that has appeared in Europe during the last 350 years,' is the most quoted line of his testimony. This was no off-the-cuff observation. He had written the line in *The Wilde Myth* where it was followed by 'I do not know of any man who more truly and literally sold himself to the devil than he did.'[12]

He began his testimony in the measured tone of a gentleman, but as the questioning wore on, Douglas became increasingly hysterical. It is clear from the more lucid part of his testimony that he is trying to come to terms with his own sense that everything he had once considered beautiful and meaningful with Wilde had been a lie, and that the man he had once thought of as his protector had really been his ruin.

He described the culture he had once embraced, 'those sort of people always refer to revolting things under pretty names. They try to disguise the horribleness of the action by giving it such names; they say beautiful, classic, and so on ... They have a jargon.'[13]

He continued, 'whenever [Wilde] was going to do anything particularly horrible, it was always disguised in the most flowery language, and always referred back to Art ... he probably did call it spiritual. It was part of the jargon.' Douglas ranted that sexual immorality as expressed in Wilde's *Salome* should be suppressed whether through legal or illegal means. He challenged the trial judge to send him to jail for contempt. He shouted that he was willing to go to jail for what he believed in. He would eventually get his wish. Justice Darling, as had become his tradition when Douglas was in court, threatened to expel the witness more than once.

The prosecution, as was also a tradition, tried to discredit Douglas with his youthful letters. 'It is about the twentieth time it has been read in a public court in the last six or seven years,' he shouted. He threatened to tear up the letters if they were put in his hand, and so Darling asked the court to hold them up out of his reach so he could identify his handwriting.

Douglas's contempt of court was mutual. Counsel followed this outburst with, 'When did you cease to approve of sodomy?'

To which Douglas replied, 'When did I cease to approve of sodomy? I do not think that is a fair question. That is like asking: When did you leave off beating your wife?'

After his testimony, Douglas stayed to watch the remainder of the trial from a seat in the back of the courtroom, which gave him the opportunity to create a scene as others testified. He waved his arms and shouted throughout the court, 'You have no right to say that. It is a lie. You are a damned liar. I will prosecute you if you repeat it outside.'

Before Darling could say anything, two police officers grabbed Douglas and marched him out of the court to cheers and cries of 'Bravo!' His dramatic exit was marred by the fact that his bowler hat and walking stick had been left behind. As the testimony continued, his lordship could be seen through the glass door pleading in vain with the constable to let him retrieve his hat.[14]

Claude Cahun, the queer French artist and photographer who had once gone by the nom de plume Daniel Douglas in honour of Oscar Wilde's lover, covered the trial for the *Mercure de France*. She was sympathetic to Bosie, whom she described as 'an ageing, discouraged man who by now is at the mercy of anyone who comes along armed with the name of Wilde.'[15]

Bosie considered it a triumph. Newspapers around the English-speaking world led with headlines about Oscar Wilde being the greatest force of evil in Europe. *The Wilde Myth* had been shelved, but its thesis had been transmitted. The triumph, in Douglas's mind, partially exorcised Oscar's ghost. Until it landed him in jail a few years later, Douglas was newly content in the knowledge that he had a great calling, to report to the world what he had learned as a survivor who had escaped the Wilde cult.

On 13 June 1918 Ross summed up his view of the Black Book trial in a letter to Charles Rickets, 'When the trial began, everyone thought I was mad because I said Billing would be acquitted. The English, intoxicated into failure, enjoyed tearing poor Maud Allen to pieces, simply because she had given them pleasure, and kicking Oscar's corpse to make up for the failure of the Fifth Army.'[16]

He went on to say that 'Every American and provincial theatre company' cancelled their contracts. This was an embellishment. American newspapers had, indeed, covered the Billing trial, but to them it was curious and distant. When Americans were done being entertained by that story, they bought tickets to see *An Ideal Husband* which was being performed by the Russell Janey Players in Milwuakee or one of any number of local theatres across the country where actors and actresses did recitations of various Wilde works. (It is doubtful, however, that the estate received royalties on the recitations.) The prominent theatre moguls, the Shuberts, also announced in July 1918 that they would be opening the next season at the famous Shubert Comedy Theatre in New York with *Ideal Husband* with an all-star cast and an advance run in Washington DC.[17] The same month *Los Angeles Times* ran an interview with Alla Nazimova, the star of the Broadway production of *Salome*. 'Today nobody interferes with the production, now running along merrily in New York.'[18]

The only impact the Billing trial seemed to have on America's theatrical world that season was that it produced an elaborate burlesque of *Salome* presented as part of the Winter Garden production of 'The Passing Show of 1918'. It culminated with the head of the German Emperor on a platter. 'This fell flat with the audience.'[19]

The collapse of the international market for Oscar Wilde may have been exaggerated, but Robbie's feeling that his values and way of life were under siege was genuine and profound.

After the trial, Ricketts wrote, Ross was 'a little uncertain in mental and bodily health, as a consequence an old man before his time'.[20]

47

The End

On 3 October, 1918, Siegfried Sassoon was visiting Robbie. When he was leaving, Ross came to the door. 'He said nothing, but took my hand and looked up at me for a long moment. His worn face, grey with exhaustion and ill-health, was beatified by sympathy and affection.' Two days later, Ross died in his sleep. He was only forty-nine. Sassoon wrote, 'While resting before dinner, he died of heart failure. It seems reasonable to claim that this was the only occasion on which his heart failed him.'[1]

George Ives recorded the passage in his diary, 'Robbie was one of the noblest people I ever knew, brave and chivalrous, ready to take on a fight at any odds if moved by loyalty or conviction. His behaviour to martyred Oscar Wilde was magnificent ... I never for a moment forgot his high qualities, and in the midst of so many who seem utterly vile & venal, it does us good to look upon a grand man.'[2]

In his short life, Robert Ross had accomplished a feat that no one had believed possible. He had paid Wilde's debts, restored his literary reputation and built up an impressive literary estate. He was the father of many artist's careers, the preserver of Wilde's work and the creator of the mythic Oscar Wilde, whose operatic downfall was a rebuke to the Philistines. Were it not for Ross's efforts it is entirely possible that Oscar Wilde would be an obscure figure today. Even Bosie, writing in 1937, admitted that this sort of mythologising might have been a necessary first step in the preservation of Wilde's memory.[3]

Ross lived a short and largely secret life in the shadow of other great men. One of the many ironies of the battle between Ross and Douglas is that without Douglas's determination to expose the 'villainy' of his one-time friend, Ross and his many great works would have remained largely anonymous. Perhaps that is what he would have preferred.

A few days after Ross's death, More Adey wrote to their mutual friend, Cecil Sprigge:

> I am ten years older than dear Robbie and his vitality of mind and of resistance—
> especially—had in 30 years' close and devoted friendship communicated itself to
> me, and had prevented me from enclosing myself within a wall of impenetrable
> reserve. I see the effect of Robbie in everyone who knew him, as well as the
> strong feelings of affection which he inspired in all sorts and kinds of minds,

even when he was opposed to them with great acumen over business matters! ... I have never been able to make out why, but suffering by Robbie has always seemed to me more poignant to see than in anyone else ... No one can ever be to you what Robbie has been, no one can ever be to me what he has been, but I should like to make up to you, dear Cecil, whatever little I can of the loss, and you can always count on me as long as I live.[4]

Adey left his job at *Burlington Magazine* the following summer after a dispute with his co-editors, and retired to Wooton-under-Edge. He had an interest in archaeology, and had the grounds of his estate dug up in search of rare Roman coins. His mental health deteriorated, and he ended his life in a mental hospital where he died in 1942.[5]

The generous bequest from Helen Carew had allowed Freddie Smith to join the diplomatic service, a position which required all candidates to own property worth at least £400 a year. Perhaps Carew supported Smith so he could be put in a position to keep an eye on her wayward son, for he ended up at the British Legation in Stockholm, Sweden. There he worked alongside Kennard, who had been transferred there just a few months before. (Kennard was in charge of British propaganda and came up with the idea of winning Swedish hearts and minds with British variety entertainment. He was given 'almost a free hand' to create cabaret in defence of Empire.) The post allowed Smith to avoid military conscription. In the peaceful setting of neutral Sweden, he continued to write novels, which he published under the name Stanley Ford.

Bosie's outing of Freddie did not help his prospects with the diplomatic service, and Holland blamed Douglas for ending his career; but the diplomatic service may have been other people's capital idea for Freddie, and not his own. His departure from the service and return to London in 1919 coincides with Kennard being promoted out of Sweden. During Carew's last years, Freddie became indispensable to her. When she died in 1928, Freddie was named her executor. In addition to the £1,000 he received for that service, he was left £20,000 in cash (more than £1 million in today's money) and 'all my ivories and bronzes, my crystal cup and cover, and all my books' and she entrusted him to disperse sentimental items to her friends.[6] Instead of embarking on the glamorous life of a millionaire, however, Freddie bought a modest house next door to his sister in the suburbs. He died aged sixty-seven on 30 January 1953. In his will he described himself as a 'retired author.'[7]

Bosie outlived Robbie by 27 years. No longer constrained not to libel the dead, he occasionally created pamphlets airing grievances against Ross and the still very much alive Millard. He usually put them on sale at the kiosk at the Café Royal and sometimes persuaded his mother to help with the distribution. Millard had been arrested on the old charge of gross indecency in January 1918 and served twelve months in Wormwood Scrubs. In early 1919, Millard caught sight of Douglas in the coffee room of a hotel in Lewes. He stood up and shouted 'My God, it's that bugger Alfred Douglas!' There was an altercation and afterwards Millard told the proprietress that Douglas was a 'notorious blackmailer' and encouraged her to bar him from the premises.[8]

Millard, who had been left a pension of £50 a year in Ross's will, blamed himself for his death. Just before he died, Robbie had been planning a journey to Australia to make acquisitions for the National Gallery in Melbourne. Millard believed Ross had planned to go to Melbourne so that he would be away from London when he came out of jail. He believed Robbie had gotten himself so worked up over the medical exam that he would need to get a passport that he worried himself into the heart attack that killed him.[9]

Millard continued the work of building a positive legacy for Wilde. His collection provided the basis of one of the largest archives of Wilde materials, the William Andrews Clark Library, and thus shaped Wilde research for years to come. Late in his life, Millard arranged to send Clark his entire collection of Wilde photographs, an iconography, which created a visual narrative of his hero. It was notable in that it did not include a single photograph of Lord Alfred Douglas. This was a deliberate omission. Millard did not want the man he saw as Wilde's betrayer associated with him.[10]

With Crosland mostly out of the picture, Bosie needed someone else to be his partner in 'you and me against the world'. He chose poorly. Captain Spencer, the mentally unstable witness from the Billing trial, was on his side when it came to ridding the world of vice. Bosie trusted him, and therefore believed all of the fevered plots he shared. Over the next year, he made it his mission to warn the world that Winston Churchill was involved in a plot with international Jewish bankers to use battles to rig the financial markets. In sentencing Douglas for criminal libel, Justice Avory said, 'It is to be regretted that your undoubted literary abilities have been degraded to such purposes as this.'[11]

Like Oscar, Bosie wrote in prison. Prison rules had been relaxed since Wilde's day, but the exceptions that were made for Wilde, which allowed him to carry *De Profundis* out of prison, were not made for Douglas. He had to commit his sonnet sequence to memory and then recreate it when he got home. Influenced by the Catholic devotional *Imitation of Christ* of St Thomas a Kempis, which he read during his six-month imprisonment, he produced a sonnet sequence, *In Excelsis*.[12]

The title (which translates 'to the highest') was a deliberate contrast to the Ross-selected title of Wilde's prison letter *De Profundis* ('from the depths.') A passage that Douglas highlighted in his copy of *Revelations of Divine Love* by Julian of Norwich points to his theological intention. 'Then is this the remedy,' Julian wrote, 'to know them both and refuse the wrong.'[13]

The Catholicism *In Excelsis* describes is introspective and reverent but passages that rail against the evils of birth control make it more literal and dogmatic than mystical and lines that vilify 'the Jews' stand in stark contrast to the notion that it is Douglas who has taken the high road. A major theme of *In Excelsis* is the difficulty of finding divine love in the world, which spurs the quest for perfect love through spirituality. Reading biographically, *In Excelsis* makes it clear that Douglas has built his entire self-image on the courage he showed during the Wilde scandal, and his refusal to distance himself from his friend. From that formative experience, he has learned to distrust the wisdom of the world. This quality is admirable when it comes to defending an outcast friend, but unfortunate when he applies it to his belief that Winston Churchill is involved in a Jewish banking conspiracy, the charge that actually landed him in jail.

In writing *In Excelsis*, Douglas tries to reconcile his devotion and loyalty to Wilde, which is clearly his proudest accomplishment, with his new Catholic belief that sexuality is sinful and that Wilde's hedonistic philosophy led him astray. He conflates his current sentence with his actions during and after Wilde's trials. He is in jail for that fighting spirit, he concludes, for the desire to stand for what is right and not to be silenced. In this way, *In Excelsis* harks back all the way to Douglas's most famous early poem 'Two Loves.' In 'Two Loves' he laments the inability of same-sex love to speak its name. Now he has moved beyond that. He has spoken his truth, and willingly suffered the consequences.

Had he been jailed for his battles with Ross or some other crime he might have composed an enduring prison work. As it is, *In Excelsis* contains a stomach-churning endorsement of the anti-Jewish propaganda *The Protocols of the Elders of Zion*. (At some point after the publication of *In Excelsis* he learned that the Protocols were a fraud. A note in the 1924 publication endorses the Protocols, his 1935 collection of sonnets, which also includes *In Excelsis*, has added a note that calls the Protocols 'perhaps apocryphal'.)

Going to jail erased the great charge against him, that Wilde had suffered for their relationship and gone to prison while he had escaped. It also gave him a taste of what prison life meant, and the conditions under which *De Profundis* was created. This allowed him to forgive Wilde and freed him to remember their relationship in a more affectionate light. He came out of jail less quarrelsome and he would come to express regret at having been so hypocritical and judgemental and for many aspects of his moral crusade.[14]

Rather than retiring to write poetry, however, Bosie spent the better part of his remaining years trying to set the record straight through a combination of libel actions (increasingly rare once Crosland was out of the picture), letters to editors and biographers, and a series of three autobiographies. He was reconciled with Olive. They never lived together again, but they never divorced, and they remained close friends, seeing each other nearly every day until her death in 1944.

In 1929, after Douglas's first autobiography was published, Reggie Turner reached out to him and renewed their friendship.

Dear Bosie,

I want to tell you that I have been much touched by your kindly references to myself in your autobiography, and also to tell you that I have preserved my old affection and admiration for you amid all that has passed since we met. I have kept a fresh memory of many acts of kindness and chivalry towards me which you have forgotten or performed unconsciously.

I think you must know that I have never approved of, or encouraged, or in any way abetted, any attacks on you, and have been bitterly sorry for the unprovoked attacks on you. Indeed many years of my life have been poisoned by that horrible contest, when Queensberry rules were thrown to the winds, and I have never failed to say – and thereby endured much criticism – that you were the provoked and that the production of that unpublished part of *De Profundis* was a disgraceful affair which – I think, indeed I feel sure – would have deeply pained the author.

I have rejoiced in your conversion, and I have only deep regret that your most exceptional talents and personality should often have been warped and wasted on dead controversy. To my mind no one has ever had harder luck, partly – may I say so, as I want to be honest – due to the defects of your qualities, as I see them. I don't share – I am not criticising – many of your opinions, but I revel in your expression of them ...

I have written to you, though you may not care to have my letter, because I wanted to, and because I thought I ought to.

Yours ever,
Reginald Turner[15]

Bosie responded with equal warmth, lamenting the 'friendship and companionship we could have had,' adding, 'I always realised you were placed in a difficult position ...'[16] They continued to correspond until Reggie's death in 1938, but never met again face to face. In his last year of life, Florence, Italy, where Reggie was living, had been gripped by the dark forces of conspiracy that Douglas had once embraced. Reggie, who was half Jewish but a practising Anglican, was living in a country with a Fascist government that blocked the sale of books by Jews. The last time Reggie wrote to his life-long friend Max was after the death of Max's niece. Reggie wrote, 'I don't want to go yet myself, but it would only be decent of me to do so, and I don't want to suffer.'[17] Max outlived them all, drawing his last breath in 1956 at the age of 84.

One of the books that helped Douglas finally to come to terms with his inner sense of shame was *Revelations of Divine Love* by St Julian of Norwich. His copy was a gift from his wife who inscribed it 'Heaven protect our love.' In those post-prison years, it became, in Douglas's words, 'so thumbed that it is almost falling to pieces.' Like Pope Pius, Julian is inspired by the divine feminine. Her text repeatedly evokes the image of Jesus as mother. The book describes a mystical journey in which the author receives the revelation that suffering and sin are necessary to bring us self-awareness and humility. In a passage which Douglas highlighted, she wrote, 'Then were it a great unkindness to blame or wonder on God for my sin, since He blameth not me for sin ... He doeth away all our blame, and beholdeth us with ruth and pity as children innocent and unloathful.'

She reveals that for every sin, the same soul is given 'bliss by love' in heaven and that the type of heavenly reward is directly related to the individual's particular sinful desire on earth. She lists many of the great religious figures of the past who were no strangers to sin: 'it is to them no shame, but all is turned for them to worship.'

Bosie highlighted all of the passages quoted above.[18] It is easy to understand why they resonated with him. With the help of this book, he stopped questioning God for making him as he was. He maintained (or endeavoured to maintain, depending on whose account you believe) his vow of celibacy. Yet he was once again able to enjoy his (unconsummated) physical attractions and warm relationships with other men.

He re-evaluated Plato's *Symposium*, and renewed his appreciation for it. He came to believe that he had misinterpreted it when he read it at Oxford. It was true that Plato said the love of boys was a higher form of love than that of women, but this only referred to non-sexual love. Love between men represented purity, whereas the love of women represented lust. Therefore, it was entirely consistent with Catholicism.[19]

This would become the central theme of his *The True History of Shakespeare's Sonnets*, which embraces Oscar Wilde's theory that the W. H. who inspired Shakespeare's sonnets was a boy actor in the playwright's company. (It also argues that Shakespeare was a Catholic and shared all of Douglas's own religious views.) Douglas contrasts Shakespeare's beautiful and chaste love for W. H. with his impure, lustful relationship with The Dark Lady and finds the love between the two males loveliest. In singing the praises of Shakespeare's attraction to W. H., Douglas also recaptures his own pride at having been a male muse as well as the inspiration he had drawn as a poet from male beauty.[20]

In almost all of his later writings, Douglas argued for the decriminalisation of homosexual acts and for the beauty and purity of love between men, even as he maintained his belief that homosexual acts were a sin. (He used the term 'homosexualist' to distinguish between those with same-sex attractions and those who acted on them.)

One of the best observations written about Douglas was from the book *Poets of the Nineties: A Biographical Anthology,* edited by Derek Stanford. Watching Douglas, Stanford writes, 'We have the spectacle of a man struggling, with the support of his religion, against the family history of egoism, vanity and violence. Mostly he is observed falling down; but we cannot help but be impressed by the "final perseverance" which he shows in the long conflict with his own unruly nature.'[21]

He died on 20 March 1945 at the age of seventy-four. Three days later a Requiem Mass was held for him at the Franciscan friary in Crawley.

Epilogue

By the way I forbid you to publish my private letters after my death! It is quite
necessary to say that to you.
Letter from playwright Laurence Housman to Robert Ross, 5 February 1905[1]

The cache of incriminating letters that Robbie had assembled for the Ransome
trial outlived him. The last time they made an appearance was in a curious libel
case in 1921. On 4 February that year the *Evening News* published Lord Alfred
Douglas's obituary. The problem was Douglas was not quite dead. In fact, he
had another two decades before him. After describing a fictional death in which
the poet was found in bed by his maid after he had suffered from a chill that
led to heart failure, the obituary described Douglas as a man of poetic gifts
who squandered his promise with endless scandals and litigation. A subheading
read 'A Great Life Spoilt – How the Evil Genius of the Douglases Dogged Lord
Alfred.' It went on to describe the 'degeneracy' of the house of Douglas. 'Many
of them were violently eccentric to put the case mildly.'[2]

By the time the late edition came out, the *Evening News* was fairly certain it
had encountered some problems in the fact checking department, as Lord Alfred
had phoned himself with a correction. 'I am very glad to say I am in the best
of health,' he told a reporter. The paper's retraction expressed regret at 'having
given currency to the inaccurate statement'. It did not apologise, however, for
its bleak assessment of his life. Although you cannot libel the dead, the *Evening
News* was about to discover that you can libel the mistaken-for-dead. Rather
than print a full retraction, they decided to defend Douglas's libel suit with a
plea of justification. They argued that except for the small matter of prematurely
announcing his lordship's death, the article was 'true in substance and fact'. They
called on Sir George Lewis, who was more than happy to provide the binder with
Douglas's letters.

Douglas was represented by Cromyns Carr and Ignatius Kelly. The defendants
had Douglas Hogg, J. B. Melvill and Lawson Campbell on their side. The case
was heard before a special jury in November. Having a team of lawyers to press
the case that a man had led a worthless life did not make the defence team
sympathetic to the jury. This time Olive joined her husband in court, which
helped to make him appear to be a respectable, repentant sinner.

On behalf of Douglas, Carr complained about the word 'degenerate' which
implied that his client was 'mad or half-mad'. When the defence brought

up Douglas's relationship with Wilde, Carr asked 'How could anything that happened to a young man falling under such a man justify the defendants hunting a man down into his grave thirty years later with vile allegations?' Hogg's opening argument on behalf of the defence was that the *Evening News* had been generous to someone whose time in the public eye could have produced an obituary far worse.

The letters and the French articles in defence of homosexuality were read out in court for the last time. They brought with them the interruptions and judicial scoldings that were a feature of 'le System Douglas'. ('I am always the villain of the piece,' was one of his objections.) Hogg quoted a lesser known letter Douglas had written to Wilde, some time around 1900, agreeing that the boys in Rome were more beautiful than those in Naples. 'In fact, I think they come next to English boys.'[3]

There was also the letter he had written to Ross talking about a 'beautiful sailor boy' with whom he'd 'had adventures'. This evidence allowed Douglas to score one of the most gratifying points in his litigious career, although it was not reported in the newspapers. He argued that no one would think anything at all of his letter about the English boys if it had been written to someone other than Oscar Wilde. He went on to say that he only wrote in this way because he was writing to 'horrible people'.

'You were writing to paederasts?' asked Hogg.

'I am glad you admit Ross is a paederast,' Douglas said. 'It is the first time that Sir George Lewis has admitted it.'

Douglas was so pleased by this small victory that he underlined the line about George Lewis in his copy of the trial transcript. (He also corrected the spelling of 'paederast'.)[4]

It took the jury only fifteen minutes to return a verdict of guilty and to award Douglas £1,000 in damages. Even more gratifying was that a jury finally agreed that Douglas had been haunted long enough by the follies of his youth. They added a rider to their verdict which said 'in the opinion of the jury the original Wilde letters should be destroyed.'

The judge made no recommendation with regards to this last statement, and the fate of the collection of letters, last kept in Sir George Lewis's safe, is unknown. At one point during the *Evening News* case, Douglas made the point that 'whoever stole [his letters] took care to take the worst ones.'[5]

Very few letters from Douglas to Wilde still exist. At the time Hyde wrote his biography of Douglas there were only three that were known to have survived.[6] Those that do were retained by people who were building legal cases against them. It is not a surprise that the surviving letters contain lines that confirm the idea that Douglas was the pursuer in the relationship and was interested in Wilde for his money. One of the three letters, written on 22 July 1897, finds Douglas worried about money and saying 'I suppose it is no use asking you to send me a louis (which I think you owe me), but if you happen to have it ...' This becomes, in Ellmann, an 'attempt to extract a louis' from Oscar. Ellmann assumes that this is typical of their relationship.[7] It is legitimate to ask, if this letter was typical, why didn't Ross keep more examples? Why didn't more of his letters show up in court to prove the charge that Douglas was only interested in Wilde's money? A second letter, preserved by Ross, shows Douglas as the pursuer in the relationship with Wilde. He says that he wrote three times without an answer and that he spent 'the whole evening hunting for you'.[8]

The letters that Bosie wrote in the clutches of irrational anger and fits of malice became the subjects of litigation and were quoted in newspapers. There is no denying that this contemptible side of his personality existed and caused others and himself a great deal of pain and harm. Thanks to their wide dissemination, they formed his public image.

Rupert Croft-Cooke, who knew Bosie in his last years, says that his friend's 'turgid and self-justifying' books did not capture him. Those who write about him from his own autobiographies 'misrepresent him. They are writing of the autobiographer, not of the man. They miss the basic paradox – that as a public figure and as an apologist for himself Douglas was crude and arrogant while as a man he was loveable and modest.'[9]

Croft-Cooke realised that it would be difficult to convince his readers of this. 'It is of little use to say he was gay and engaging in conversation and companionship, that he gave one a sense of holiday and exaltation, as John Betjeman puts it, when the prose of his books is so often either flat or excitable, with no light and shade and little humour or grace. All one can do is point to the number and diversity of people who loved him and the greater number of those who, throughout his life, found happiness and inspiration in his company.'[10] As the last person who knew Douglas personally died in 2014,[11] we can only take his word for this.

It seems entirely out of character when we come across a line in one of Bosie's letters like the one he wrote to his wife, 'I wish could bear your pain for you.' While his relationship with Olive was different from that with Oscar, his letters to his wife give some indication as to how he wrote to someone he loved. Much of Bosie's generosity has been obscured by the fact that he lavished it on the disagreeable Crosland.

Douglas was a class snob, capable of great selfishness, petulant self-pity, and outbursts of irrational rage; but the man who would risk everything to stand by Wilde, who rushed to Crosland's hospital bed and paid his debts, who admired Wilde for all he'd done to help others and who wrote that he wished he could bear Olive's pain, was a more complex, multifaceted individual than he is often given credit for.

Late in his life, Bosie told Croft-Cooke that the thing that bothered him most about *De Profundis* was the overall tone, which made his relationship with Oscar into a 'solemn sort of thing, crossed with terrible quarrels. But we were laughing most of the time – often at one another.' [12]

In his last book, published in 1940, Douglas was still trying to make sense of the great drama that had ensnared him. 'Some explanation is needed of the strange posture of affairs which forced me into the cruel position of being, just because I was as God made me, the innocent cause of the ruin of my friend ...'[13]

The great irony of the battle between Ross and Douglas is that they were, at the most basic level, trying to tell the same story. Lord Alfred Douglas was not Oscar Wilde's victim. He was his partner. Ross wanted the world to know that Douglas was Wilde's partner in tragedy and his partner in vice. Douglas wanted the world to know that he was Wilde's partner in love and laughter. All of this was true.

Ross's ashes were buried alongside Wilde's remains in the elaborate tomb which Ross had commissioned. In 1962 the words 'wife of Oscar Wilde' were added to Constance Lloyd's headstone, restoring her legacy as central to the playwright's life. Lord Alfred Douglas is buried with his mother in a shared grave.

In 1960, The British Museum finally made the full text of *De Profundis* available to researchers. Two years later Rupert Hart-Davis published the text in *The Complete Letters of Oscar Wilde*. It would be another seven years before the law under which Oscar Wilde was tried and imprisoned was repealed. The Sexual Offences Act of 1967, which replaced it, finally decriminalised consensual homosexual behaviour between men over the age of 21 in England and Wales.

In 1895, sentencing Oscar Wilde and Alfred Taylor for the crime of gross indecency, Justice Wills said, 'People who can do these things must be dead to all sense of shame.'

In March 2014 same-sex marriage became legal in the UK. A little more than a year later it became the law of Oscar Wilde's native Ireland. In January 2017 Wilde was posthumously pardoned, along with 50,000 other gay men who had been convicted under a law that no longer exists.[14] It can only be hoped that we are finally entering an era when men who love men can, indeed, be dead to all sense of shame.

Notes

Abbreviations

Autobiography Douglas, Alfred Bruce, Lord. *The Autobiography of Lord Alfred Douglas*. London: Martin Secker, 1929.

Bogle Bogle, Edra Charlotte. 'The Life and Literary and Artistic Activities of Robert Baldwin Ross, 1869-1918.' Ph.D. University of Southern California. Ann Arbor, Michigan: University Microfilms, Inc, 1969.

Borland Borland, Maureen. *Wilde's Devoted Friend*. Oxford: Lennard Publishing, 1990.

Bosie Croft-Cooke, Rupert. *Bosie*. Indianapolis and New York: Bobbs-Merrill Company, 1963.

Brown Brown, W. Sorley. *Life and Genius of T. W. H. Crosland*. London: Cecil Palmer, 1928.

CL Holland, M. and Rupert Hart-Davis (eds). *The Complete Letters of Oscar Wilde*. Henry Holt and Co., 2000.

Custance Custance, Olive. *I Desire the Moon*. Caspar Wintermans, ed. Woubrugge, Avalon Press, 2004.

DP 1905 Wilde, Oscar. *De Profundis*. London: G. P. Putnam & Sons, 1905.

Ellmann Ellmann, Richard. *Oscar Wilde*. New York: Alfred A. Knopf, 1988.

Epistola Wilde, Oscar. Ian Small, ed. *The Complete Works of Oscar Wilde*: Volume 2 De Profundis 'Epistola: In Carcere et Vinculis'. Oxford: Oxford University Press, 2005.

Foldy Foldy, Michael S. *The Trials of Oscar Wilde: Deviance, Morality, and Late-Victorian Society*. New Haven: Yale University Press, 1997.

Friend of Friends Ross, Margery, ed. *Robert Ross, Friend of Friends*. London: Jonathan Cape, 1952.

Fryer Fryer, Jonathan. *Robbie Ross: Oscar Wilde's Devoted Friend*. New York: Carroll & Graff Publishers, 2000.

Harris. Harris, Frank. *Oscar Wilde*. New York: Carroll & Graff, 1959.

Hyde LAD Hyde, H. Montgomery. *Lord Alfred Douglas*. London: Meuthen, 1984.

Let Them Say Roberts, Maria. *Let Them Say: The Life of Frederick Stanley Smith*. Feed A Read, 2016.

MS Gertz Elmer Gertz Papers. Library of Congress, Washington DC.

Masques and Phases. Ross, Robert. *Masques and Phases*. London: Humphreys, 1909.

McKenna. McKenna, Neil. *The Secret Life of Oscar Wilde*. Basic Books, 2006.

Millard. Roberts, Maria. *Yours Loyally: A Life of Christopher Sclater Millard*. Feed A Read, 2014.

Moyle. Moyle, Franny. *Constance: The Tragic and Scandalous Life of Mrs. Oscar Wilde*. Pegasus Books. Kindle Edition, 2014.

Murray Murray, Douglas. *Bosie: A Biography of Lord Alfred Douglas*. New York: Hyperion, 2000

OW & Myself Douglas, Alfred Bruce, Lord. *Oscar Wilde and Myself*. London: Duffield and Company, 1914.

Plea Douglas, Lord Alfred. *Oscar Wilde a Plea and A Reminiscence. Introduced and Annotated by Caspar Wintermans*. Woubrugge: Avalon Press, 2002.

Robins Robins, Ashley H. *Oscar Wilde; The Great Drama of His Life*. Brighton: Sussex Academic Press, 2011.

Shaw Hyde, Mary, ed. *Bernard Shaw & Alfred Douglas: A Correspondence*. Oxford: Oxford University Press, 1989.

Stratmann Stratmann, Linda. *The Marquess of Queensberry: Wilde's Nemesis*. New Haven: Yale University Press, 2013.

Summing-Up Douglas, Alfred Bruce, Lord. *Oscar Wilde: A Summing-Up*. London: The Richards Press, 1940.

Without Apology Douglas, Alfred Bruce, Lord. *Without Apology*. London: Martin Secker, 1938.

Wintermans Wintermans, Caspar. *Alfred Douglas: A Poet's Life and His Finest Work*. London: Peter Owen, 2007.

Introduction

1. CL p. 873
2. Csikszentmihalyi, Mihaly. *Creativity*. New York: Harper, 1997.
3. Portions of this introduction were taken from an article previously published on my personal blog, 'Story & Self', which goes into greater detail on how Csiksentmihalyi's findings apply in the cases of Oscar Wilde and Lord Alfred Douglas. https://lauraleeauthor.wordpress.com/2014/08/30/the-complexity-of-creatives-the-case-of-oscar-wilde-and-lord-alfred-douglas/ accessed 27 November 2016.
4. MS Gertz
5. Bogle p. 3
6. Roth, Samuel, 'Dramatis Personae,' *Two Worlds*, (June, 1926).

Chapter 1: 'He Lieth For His Name is Shame'

1. Quoted in Hyde LAD p. 103
2. See Ransome Trial chapter 37 for source notes.
3. CL pp. 646-647
4. CL pp. 650-651
5. CL p. 651
6. CL p. 933
7. Passages from *De Profundis* here were printed in 'Libel Action by Lord Alfred Douglas,' *The Times* (London), 18 April 1913.
8. 'In Sarum Close' was included in Lord Alfred Douglas's *City of the Soul* published in 1899. It seems Wilde disliked it so much that he memorised it, for in *De Profundis* Wilde used the line 'grey twilight of Gothic things' which was a reworking of the third and fourth lines of this poem.

Chapter 2: Café Royal Days

1. Quoted in McKenna p. 243

2. Symons, Arthur. *The Café Royal and Other Essays*. Westminster: The Beaumont Press, 1923. p. 4
3. Cecil, David. *Max: A Biography*. London: Constable, 1965. p. 70
4. According to the Oxford English Dictionary, the first use of the word 'heterosexual' to denote desire between males and females was in a translation of Krafft-Ebing's *Psychopathia Sexualis* in 1892. The word would remain largely confined to writings on sexual pathology until around 1915.
5. Hart-Davis, Rupert, Ed. *Max Beeerbohm's Letters to Reggie Turner*. Philadelphia: J. B. Lippincott and Company, 1965. pp. 38-39
6. Ibid. p. 91
7. Shaw, George Bernard. 'My Memories of Oscar Wilde.' Published as an appendix to Harris, Frank. *Oscar Wilde*. New York: Carroll & Graff, 1997. p. 337.
8. McKenna. p. 242

Chapter 3: Robbie

1. Quoted in Bogle p. 4
2. Ross family history is from Bogle pp. 24-31 Bogle's source is an unpublished family history 'Memories of My Youth and a Sketch of the Family History of the Ross-Baldwin Families by Their Descendant' written by Mary Jane Jones (Robert Ross's niece) then in the possession of J. P. B. Ross.
3. 'The Literary Log,' *Bystander*, 23 November 1910.
4. Bogle p. 37. Ross never listed the schools he attended and was private about his youth, but Bogle uncovered some of the schools based on postmarks on letters from Robbie in the possession of the Ross family.
5. Bogle pp. 41-42
6. Description of the Passion Play is from 'Another Tyrolese Passion Play.' *The Tablet*, 12 June 1883. Quotes of Ross's reaction are from Bogle p. 42 from a letter to Mary Jones, 16 November 1885 then in the possession of Giles Robertson.
7. Masques and Phases p. 272
8. Alexander Galt Ross's name was alternately spelled Aleck, Alek and Alex.
9. Quoted in Bogle p. 22 and p. 39. The letter is described as 'Undated letter in the possession of Giles Robertson.' Bogle speculates that the resemblance between Ross's boyhood fantasy for his life and the career of Oscar Wilde's father Dr. William Wilde is too close to be a coincidence. William Wilde was an oculist who successfully operated on the cataracts of King Oscar I of Sweden receiving the Swedish Order of the Polar Star. She posits that perhaps Robbie heard about William Wilde through his Irish ancestors and that Oscar Wilde's father might have been one of Ross's heroes. Ross may well have been exposed to tales of famous eye doctors through his brother's eye problems.
10. Cecil, David. *Max: A Biography*. London: Constable, 1965. pp. 70-71
11. Moyle p. 119
12. Masques and Phases p. 277
13. Rothenstein, William. *Men and Memories: A History of the Arts 1872-1922*. New York: Tudor Publishing Company, 1931. p. 187
14. Sitwell, Osbert. *Noble Essences: A Book of Characters*. Boston: Little, Brown & Company, 1950. p. 115.
15. Gosse, Edmund. *Books on the Table*. New York: Charles Scribners's Sons, 1921. p. 46.
16. Davenport-Hines, Richard, 'Oscar Wilde and the Marvellous Boy,' *Spectator*, 9 May 2015.
17. CL pp. 407-408

18. Wilde, Oscar. *Oscar Wilde Complete Works Ultimate Collection*. (Kindle Locations 10390-10395). Kindle Edition.
19. Borland. p. 19
20. Adut, Ari, 'A Theory of Scandal: Victorians, Homosexuality and the Fall of Oscar Wilde.' *American Journal of Sociology*. July 2005.
21. Anstruther, Ian. *Oscar Browning: A Biography*. London: John Murray, 1983. p. 96
22. Quoted in Borland. p. 22
23. Quoted in Chaney op. cit. p. 180
24. Bogle p. 46. Bogle saw a copy in the possession of J. P. B. Ross in which Ross had marked his contributions.
25. Chaney. op. cit. pp. 180-181
26. Chaney. op. cit. p. 181
27. Quoted in Borland. p. 22
28. McKenna. p. 93
29. Quoted in Borland. p. 25
30. Borland p. 26
31. Quoted in Bogle. p. 38 from a letter in the possession of J. P. B. Ross.

Chapter 4: Bosie

1. Wilde, Oscar. *Oscar Wilde Complete Works Ultimate Collection* (Kindle Location 7972). Kindle Edition.
2. Without Apology p. 174
3. Edward Parry Warren quoted in Sox, David. *Bachelors of Art*. New York: Fourth Estate, 1992. p. 23
4. McKenna p. 148
5. Wintermans p. 25
6. William Rothenstein, *Men and Memories* (London: Faber & Faber, 1934), I, 147.
7. Without Apology p. 175
8. Beerbohm, Max. *Max Beerbohm's Letters to Reggie Turner*. Philadelphia: J. B. Lippincott, 1965. p. 91 The term 'narcissism' describing a personality disorder characterised by extreme self-love did not exist at this time. It was not until 1897 that the British sexologist Havelock Ellis used 'narcissus-like' in an article for a medical journal to describe sexual attraction to oneself. Freud in 1910 described the 'narcissistic libido'. His 'On Narcissism' published in 1914 popularised the term, although it would still be some time before it took on its modern connotations.
9. Douglas, Alfred Bruce, Lord. *True History of Shakespeare's Sonnets*. Port Washington, NY: Kennikat Press, 1933. p. 102 and Autobiography p. 9
10. Without Apology p. 232
11. Autobiography p. 15
12. Cannadine, David. *Decline and Fall of the British Aristocracy*. New York: Vintage Books, 1990 p. 2
13. Autobiography p. 4
14. Without Apology p. 165.
15. Autobiography p. 15
16. Without Apology pp. 171-172. In her comparison of the manuscript and the published version of *Without Apology*, Kathy Hall notes that the editors changed Douglas's and Turner's sleeping arrangements from 'contiguous beds' in the manuscript to 'adjacent beds' in the published version. 'It seems the beds could be next to one another, but that a dividing line had to be maintained between them. They could not become one.'
17. Without Apology p. 171

18. Douglas, Alfred Bruce, Lord. *The Collected Poems of Lord Alfred Douglas.* London: M. Secker, 1916. p. 24.
19. Wilde, Oscar, *Oscar Wilde Complete Works Ultimate Collection.* (Kindle Location 34259). Scientists have, incidentally, discovered a link between poetry and bipolar disorder. 'Poetic language is the language of the special faculties of the right hemisphere (of the brain), and the associations between manic-depressive illness and poets and their poetry reveals just this biological association,' wrote Dr. Michael R. Trimble. 'Poetic language is a marker of brain behaviour associations, a window into the role of the right hemisphere for certain aspects of language.'
20. Douglas, Alfred Bruce, Lord. *Collected Poems of Lord Alfred Douglas.* London. Martin Secker, 1916. p. 18
21. Autobiography p. 4

Chapter 5: Oscar and Bosie

1. Bosie pp. 93-95
2. Douglas, Alfred Bruce, Lord. *Halcyon Days. Contributions to the Spirit Lamp.* Francestown, NH: Typographeum, 1993. p. 17
3. Ellman p. 47
4. Pater, Walter. *Studies in the History of the Renaissance.* London: MacMillan, 1873. p. 210
5. Without Apology p. 177
6. Summing-Up p. 64
7. Bosie pp. 93-95
8. Summing-Up p. 64
9. McKenna p. 158
10. Bosie. p. 54
11. Cooper, John, 'Three Times Tried,' Oscar Wilde in America Blog. oscarwildeinamercia.wordpress.com/2016/03/01/three-times-tried Accessed 21 September 2016
12. Delay, Jean. *The Youth of Andre Gide.* June Guichnaud, trans. Chicago: University of Chicago Press, 1963. pp. 289-294
13. Holland, Merlin. *The Real Trial of Oscar Wilde.* New York: Fourth Estate, 2003. p. 134
14. Stratman. p. 211
15. Quoted in Murray p. 33
16. May, Simon. *Love: A History* (p. 41). Yale University Press. Kindle Edition. 17. *Autobiography* p. 618. 'Wilde's Sex Life Exposed in Explicit Court Files,' *The Guardian*, 6 May 2001.
19. Douglas, Alfred Bruce, Lord. *Oscar Wilde: A Plea and a Reminiscence.* Woubrugge: Avalon Press, 2002. p. 20
20. Millard, Christopher, Ed. (Stuart Mason) *Oscar Wilde: Three Times Tried.* London: Ferrestone Press, 1912. p. 271
21. Holland, Merlin. *The Real Trial of Oscar Wilde.* New York: Fourth Estate, 2003. p. 90
22. Roberts, Brian. *The Mad Bad Line.* London: Hamish Hamilton, 1981.
23. Pater, Walter. *Studies in the History of the Renaissance.* London: MacMillan, 1873
24. Hyde LAD p. 97
25. Bosie pp 61-62 and McKenna p. 190
26. 'De Profundis!' *The Truth* (Sydney, Australia) 25 May 1913.
27. Harris, Frank. *Oscar Wilde.* New York: Carroll & Graff, 1959. pp. 143-444.
28. Robins p. 42

29. Douglas, Francis Archibald Kelhead. (Marquess of Queensberry). *Oscar Wilde and the Black Douglas*. London: Hutchinson & Co, [No year listed in book] p. 29
30. Stratmann p. 210

Chapter 6: Devotion and Admiration

1. Borland p. 30
2. CL p. 526
3. Sitwell, Osbert. *Noble Essences: A Book of Characters*. Boston: Little, Brown & Company, 1950. p. 116.
4. Pezzini, Barbara, 'More Adey, the Carfax Gallery and The Burlington Magazine,' *Burlington Magazine*, December 2011.
5. Sitwell op. cit.
6. Sitwell op. cit p. 117
7. Hyde LAD p. 107
8. Sassoon, Siegfried. *Siegfried's Journey*. London: Faber and Faber, 1945. p. 51
9. Letter to Adela Schuster, 23 December 1900 quoted in Bogle.
10. Autobiography pp. 70-73
11. Bosie. p. 60
12. Autobiography p. 70
13. Borland p. 248
14. Diary of George Ives
15. James, Callum. *My Dear KJ ... The Letters of Frederick Rolfe to Charles Kains-Jackson*. Callum James Books, 2015.
16. Hyde LAD p. 45
17. Gagnier, Regenia. *Idylls of the Marketplace: Oscar Wilde and the Victorian Public*. Stanford, California: Stanford University Press, 1986. pp. 162-163.
18. P. C., 'The New Chivalry,' *The Artist and Journal of Home Culture*. 2 April 1894.

Chapter 7: The First Battle of Salome

1. Douglas, Alfred Bruce, Lord. *Halcyon Days. Contributions to the Spirit Lamp*. Francestown, NH: Typogrpheum, 1993. pp. 33-34
2. Downey, Katherine Brown. *Perverse Midrash: Oscar Wilde, Andre Gide, and Censorship of Biblical Drama*. New York: Continuum International Publishing Group, 2004. p. 11
3. Masques and Phases p. 28
4. Sturgis, Matthew. *Aubrey Beardsley: A Biography*. New York: Overlook Press, 1998. p. 129
5. Friend of Friends p. 29
6. Wilde, Oscar. *Complete Works*. Collins, 1966. p. 1174.
7. CL p. 692
8. Robins, Elizabeth, 'Oscar Wilde: An Appreciation,' ed. and commentary by Kerry Powell, *Ninteenth-Century Theatre*, Winter 1993.
9. Shaw p 58
10. Maguire, J. Robert. *Ceremonies of Bravery*. Oxford: Oxford University Press, 2013. p. 2
11. Hyde. LAD. p. 46
12. Quoted in Wintermans p. 37
13. Wintermans p. 33

14. Ibid p. 34
15. Ibid. p. 180 Letter to Lane at the Harry Ransome Humanities Research Center.
16. Daadler, Joosst, 'Salome, Confusion & Misattribution.' The Oscholars. https://oscholars-oscholars.com/special-issues/contents/daalder/AccessedAugust 8, 2015
17. Daadler, Joosst, 'Re-discovery of a Passage by Robert Ross on Salome,' *Biographical Society of Australian and New Zealand Bulletin*, 27, 2003.
18. Sturgis op. cit. p. 162

Chapter 8: Feasting with Panthers

1. CL p. 758
2. O'Brien, Kevin, H. F., 'Robert Sherard: Friend of Oscar Wilde.' *English Literature in Translation, 1880-1920,* Volume 28, Number 1, 1985. and Sherard, Robert. *Oscar Wilde: The Story of an Unhappy Friendship.* London: Greening & Co, 1905. pp. 36-41.
3. Ellmann p. 218
4. Moyle, Franny. *Constance: The Tragic and Scandalous Life of Mrs. Oscar Wilde* (p. 91). Pegasus Books. Kindle Edition.
5. O'Brien op. cit.
6. Oscar Wilde in Context (Literature in Context) (Kindle Locations 2030-2037). Cambridge University Press. Kindle Edition.
7. Cook, Matt. *London and the Culture of Homosexuality.* Cambridge: Cambridge University Press, 2003.
8. Wilde, Oscar. *The Complete Works of Oscar Wilde.* New York: Barnes and Noble, 1994. p. 874.
9. Tobin, A. I. and Elmer Gertz. *Frank Harris a Study in Black and White.* Chicago: Madelaine Mendelsohn, 1931. p. 295
10. Autobiography p. 76
11. Anstruther, Ian. *Oscar Browning: A Biography.* London: John Murray, 1983. p.139.
12. MEPOL 3/240
13. Lee, Laura, 'The Mysterious Mr. Schwabe,' *The Wildean,* July 2016. Vol. 49
14. Hyde, H. Montgomery. *The Three Trials of Oscar Wilde.* New York: University Books, 1973. p. 5.
15. Cocks, H. G. *Nameless Offences: Homosexual Desire in the Nineteenth Century.* London: I. B. Tarius & Co, 2003. p. 17
16. Robb, Graham. *Strangers: Homosexual Love in the Nineteenth Century.* New York: W. W. Norton, 2003. pp. 19-25
17. Ibid p. 29
18. Golden, Catherine J. *Posting It: The Victorian Revolution in Letter Writing.* University Press of Florida, Kindle Edition, p. 25.
19. Lee op. cit.
20. Croft-Cooke, Rupert. *Feasting with Panthers.* New York: Hold, Rinehart and Winston, 1967. p. 141.
21. Croft-Cooke, Rupert. *Feasting with Panthers.* New York: Hold, Rinehart and Winston, 1967. p. 269.
22. Ibid p. 269
23. Croft-Cooke, Rupert. *Feasting with Panthers.* New York: Hold, Rinehart and Winston, 1967. p 264.
24. Ibid p. 271
25. Letter from Lord Alfred Douglas to Maurice Schwabe, 9 March 1893. In the collection of the Library of New South Wales. http://acms.sl.nsw.gov.au/album/ItemViewer.aspx?itemid=947177&suppress=N&imgindex=1
26. McKenna. p. 211
27. CL p. 789

Chapter 9: The Perils of Respectable Society

1. Wilde, Oscar. *The Complete Writings of Oscar Wilde*. New York: Pearson Publishing Company, 1909. p. 52
2. Wilde, Oscar. Ian Small, Ed. *Complete Works of Oscar Wilde. Vol II*. Oxford: Oxford University Press, 2005. p. 45
3. OW & Myself p. 193
4. Without Apology p. 75
5. Robins p. 203
6. Bosie p. 73
7. State Library of New South Wales.
8. Millard, Christopher, Ed. (Stuart Mason) *Oscar Wilde: Three Times Tried*. London: Ferrestone Press, 1912. p. 53
9. State Library of New South Wales. op. cit.
10. Victoria Reid in *Andre Gide and Curiosity* discusses this type of relationship among Gide's social circle in France.
11. Hyde, H. Montgomery. *The Three Trials of Oscar Wilde*. New York: University Books, 1973. p. 304
12. The boy is identified as Claude Dansey in McKenna, Fryer and in Oscar Browning's biography by Anstruther. Ellmann identifies him as 'Danney.' Maureen Borland swam against the tide in identifying the boy not as Dansey but as Alfred Lambart, whom she describes as the son of Brig. General Allan Lambart. The notes of a judge who identified the boy by the initial 'D' argue against this identification, as does the fact that Lambart was the general's brother, not his son, and was eight years older than Ross. Borland suspected Lambart because he was supported financially by Ross throughout his life. She speculated that the reason Lambart was not called to testify for the defence in Ross's 1914 libel suit against Douglas, in which he claimed justification, was that he was serving a three-year prison term for 'false pretences' at the time and would therefore have made a bad impression as a star witness. This is probably a reference to Alfred Lambert who was also born in 1861 and who was arrested and sentenced to three years hard labour in 1913. Alfred John Lambert was of humble stock. He had been 'living the life of a blooming fighting cock' for a decade and had a long list of frauds to his credit. See 'Life of Fraud', *Diss Express*, 14 November 1913.
13. McKenna. pp. 264-265
14. Beerbohm, Max. *Max Beerbohm's Letters to Reggie Turner*. Philadelphia: J. B. Lippincott, 1965. p. 84.
15. That there were presents as well as letters is from Notes of Mr Justice Coleridge. Coleridge Family Papers. British Library. ADD 85784
16. McKenna. p. 265
17. Correspondence between Philip Wortham and Oscar Browning (OB/1/1831/C) King's College Cambridge.
18. Fryer p. 79
19. McKenna. pp. 265-266
20. Notes of Mr Justice Coleridge. Coleridge Family Papers. British Library. ADD 85784
21. Ibid
22. Nash, Jay Robert. *Spies: A Narrative Encyclopedia of Dirty Tricks and Double Dealing*. New York: M. Evans & Co, 1997.
23. Quoted in Borland. p. 36.

Chapter 10: Family Values

1. Bosie pp. 93-95
2. 'The Mal-Administration of Justice,' *Reynold's Newspaper*, 14 December 1872.
3. 'The Late Lord Queensberry.' *Cheltenham Looker-On*, 10 February 1900. Bering, Jesse.
4. Stratmann p. 137
5. Without Apology p. 240
6. Autobiography p. 72
7. Without Apology p. 237
8. Without Apology pp. 238-239
9. Stratmann p. 95
10. 'Perversions' Aeon Magazine. https://aeon.co/essays/perhaps-it-s-time-to-get-rid-of-the-word-pervert-altogether. Accessed 6 April 2016.
11. Bell, T. H. 'Oscar Wilde's Unwritten Play.' *The Bookman*, April/May, 1930.
12. 'The Marquis of Queensberry and the Election of Scottish Representative Peers,' *The Agnostic Journal and Eclectic Review*, 19 December 1885.
13. Stratmann pp. 157-158
14. McKenna p. 226
15. Longford, Elizabeth. *A Pilgrimage of Passion: The Life of Wilfrid Scawen Blunt.* New York: Alfred A. Knopf, 1980. p. 307
16. Quoted in Startmann p. 180
17. Bosie p. 349
18. Kingston, Angela. *Oscar Wilde as a Character in Victorian Fiction.* New York: Palgrave, 2007. p. 146
19. Hichens, Robert Smythe. *The Green Carnation* p. 36.
20. Quoted in Stratmann p. 181
21. Stratmann p. 164
22. Ibid pp. 165-168
23. Maguire, J. Robert. *Ceremonies of Bravery.* Oxford: Oxford University Press, 2013. p. 36
24. Reggie Turner was a young lawyer in chambers, working along side Travers Humphreys' son. He gave this explanation in a letter to a Dr Renier on 22 March 1933 according to Bogle p. 76. J. Robert McGuire in *Ceremonies of Bravery* suggests that the rift between Lewis and Wilde was caused by Wilde's intervention in a dispute between his friend Carlos Blacker and the Duke of Newcastle. See p. 36.
25. U. K. Civil Divorce Records, 1858-1914. Ancestry.com
26. Robins p. 6
27. Robins p. 8
28. Del Collo, Sarah, 'Wilde, Sex, Lies and Sir Edmund Trelawny Blackhouse,' *South Carolina Review*, Fall2010, Vol. 43 I.
29. Quoted in Robins p. 10
30. Mason, A. E. W. *Sir George Alexander & the St. James Theatre.* New York: Benjamin Blom, 1935. p. 77.
31. Borland p. 42
32. Robins p. 13

Chapter 11: Posing Somdomite

1. Frank, Jerome. *Courts on Trial: Myth and Reality in American Justice.* Princeton University: Princeton University Press, 1973.
2. Robins p. 15
3. Robins p. 16

4. CL p. 634 and Douglas testimony in Rex v Douglas. Notes of Mr Justice Coleridge. Coleridge Family Papers. British Library. ADD 8578
5. Holland op. cit. p. 15
6. Ibid p. 5
7. Stewart, A. T. Q. *Edward Carson.* Belfast: The Blackstaff Press, 1981. p. 5
8. Wratislaw, Theodore. *Oscar Wilde: A Memoir.* London: Eighteen Nineties Society, 1979. p. 12
9. Holland, Merlin. *The Real Trial of Oscar Wilde.* New York: Fourth Estate, 2003. pp. 294-295
10. Harris p. 108 and p. 119
11. Roth, Samuel,' Dramatis Personae,' *Two Worlds,* I (June, 1926) and Notes of Mr Justice Coleridge. Coleridge Family Papers. British Library. ADD 85784
12. Letter from Lord Alfred Douglas to Elmer Gertz, 9 June 1930. MS Gertz.
13. Mason, A. E. W. Sir George Alexander & The St. James Theater. New York: Benjamin Blom, 1969. p. 92
14. Sources: 'Enthusiastic Reception of Mr George Alexander,' *Dundee Evening Telegraph,* 8 November 1895; 'Mr George Alexander: A Serious Charge Dismissed.' *Bristol Mercury,* 5 November 1895; 'Mr George Alexander,' *Lloyds Newspaper,* 10 November 1895; and Pinero, Arthur Wing, ed. *The Second Mrs. Tanqueray.* Toronto: Broadview Editions, 2008. pp. 174-175
15. McLaren, Angus. *Sexual Blackmail: A Modern History.* Cambridge, MA: Harvard University Press, 2002. p. 19
16. Moyle, Franny. *Constance: The Tragic and Scandalous Life of Mrs. Oscar Wilde* (p. 261). Pegasus Books.

Chapter 12: Upon His Evidence

1. Darling, Charles. *Scintilae Juris.* London: Stevens and Hayes Law Publishing, 1914. p. 63
2. 'Queensberry Libel Case.' *St James's Gazette,* 3 April 1895
3. Majoribanks, Edward. *Carson the Advocate.* New York: MacMillian, 1932. p. 204
4. Information on the Victorian obsession with mesmerism is from Dudgeon, Piers. *Neverland: J. M. Barrie, the Du Mauriers and the Dark Side of Peter Pan.* New York: Pegasus, 2009. p. 137; Wilde's interest in it and quote from his *Woman's World* review from Thurshwell, Pamela. *Literature, Technology and Magical Thinking, 1880-1920.* Cambridge: Cambridge University Press, 2001; and information on the subject of mesmerism in erotica from Green, Matthew, 'The Secret History of Holywell Street: Home to Victorian London's Dirty Book Trade,' *The Public Domain Review,* accessed 30 December 2016. http://publicdomainreview.org/
5. Foldy p. 2
6. Holland, Merlin. *The Real Trial of Oscar Wilde.* New York: Fourth Estate, 2003. p. 37
7. Gagnier, Regenia. *Idylls of the Marketplace: Oscar Wilde and the Victorian Public.* Stanford, California: Stanford University Press, 1986. p. 147.
8. Majoribanks op. cit. pp. 212-213
9. 'Oscar Wilde Under Cross Examination.' *Yorkshire Post,* 3 April 1895.
10. Majoribanks op. cit. p. 216
11. Millard, Christopher, Ed. (Stuart Mason) *Oscar Wilde: Three Times Tried.* London: Ferrestone Press, 1912. pp. 87-88
12. Majoribanks op. cit. p. 221
13. Holland op. cit. p. 252
14. Ibid p. 252
15. Plea pp. 27-28

16. Holland op. cit. p. 258
17. Majoribanks op. cit. p. 222
18. Majoribanks op. cit. p. 224
19. Majoribanks op. cit. p. 226
20. Holland. p. 294.
21. Ibid p. 296
22. Quote from a theatre critic signed Silvio writing in the French Canadian drama magazine *Le Passe Temps*. Quoted in Robinson, Greg, 'Whispers of the Unspeakable: New York and Montreal Newspaper Coverage of the Oscar Wilde Trials in 1895.' *Journal of Transnational American Studies*, 2015.

Chapter 13: Criminal Trials

1. Foldy p. 55
2. Majoribanks p. 227
3. Plea p. 26
4. Hyde. LAD p. 161
5. Quoted in Fryer p. 104.
6. CL pp. 646-647
7. 'De Profundis,' *Truth* (Sydney), 25 May 1913.
8. 'Result is a Surprise,' *Chicago Tribune*, 26 May 1895.
9. CL p. 644
10. Hyde LAD p. 101
11. Speedie, Julie. *Wonderful Sphinx*. London: Virago Press, 1993. p. 85
12. Robins p. 203
13. O'Brien, Kevin, 'Robert Sherard: Friend of Oscar Wilde,' *English Literature in Translation, 1880-1920,* Volume 28, Number 1, 1985.
14. CL p. 211
15. O'Brien, Kevin, 'Robert Sherard: Friend of Oscar Wilde,' *English Literature in Translation, 1880-1920,* Volume 28, Number 1, 1985.
16. Moyle, Franny. Constance: *The Tragic and Scandalous Life of Mrs. Oscar Wilde* p. 91. Pegasus Books.
17. Quoted in O'Brien op. cit.
18. Sherard, Robert. *The Real Oscar Wilde*. London: T. Warner Laurie, 1916. p. 27
19. Sherard, Robert. op. cit. p. 102.
20. O'Brien, Kevin, 'Robert Sherard: Friend of Oscar Wilde,' *English Literature in Translation, 1880-1920,* Volume 28, Number 1, 1985
21. Ellmann p. 463
22. Hyde, H. Montgomery. *The Three Trials of Oscar Wilde*. New York: University Books, 1973. p. 7
23. Sherard, Robert. *The Real Oscar Wilde*. London: T. Warner Laurie, 1916. p. 168.
24. Hyde p. 87
25. Horan, Patrick. *The Importance of Being Paradoxical: Maternal Influence in the Presence of the Works of Oscar Wilde.* Cranberry, NJ: Associated University Press, 1997. p. 75
26. 'Wilde's Second Trial,' *Reno Gazette-Journal*, 20 May 1895.
27. Autobiography p. 112
28. Bristow, Joseph, 'The Blackmailer and the Sodomite: Oscar Wilde on Trial.' Feminist Theory, Vol 17, 41-62, 2016.
29. 'Result is a Surprise,' *Chicago Tribune*, 26 May 1895.
30. See for example Gagnier pp. 206-207 [quoting letter in the Clarke library]
31. O'Brien op. cit.

32. Sherard, Robert. *Oscar Wilde: The Story of an Unhappy Friendship*. London: Greening & Co, 1905. p. 192
33. *Illustrated Police News*, 1 June 1895
34. Robins p. 202

Chapter 14: While Wilde Was Away

1. Bogle p. 41
2. Fryer p. 110
3. Sox, David. *Bachelors of Art: Edward Perry Warren and Lewes House Brotherhood*. London: Fourth Estate, 1991 p. 138
4. Plea p. 19
5. McKenna p. 414
6. McKenna p. 415
7. Notes of Mr Justice Coleridge. Coleridge Family Papers. British Library. ADD 85784
8. Stokes, John. *Oscar Wilde: Myths, Miracles and Imitations*. Cambridge: Cambridge University Press, 1996. pp. 52-53
9. Speedie, Julie. *Wonderful Sphinx*. London: Virago Press, 1993. p. 96.
10. In a letter to his mother in December 1897, Douglas wrote that Wilde's ruin was 'chiefly, I admit, on my account and through my fault.' Without Apology p. 297
11. Plea p. 32
12. Wintermans p. 282
13. Bogle p. 90 This quote is from a letter from Aubrey Beardsley to Robert Ross written December 1893. Margery Ross, who was at pains to downplay Ross's sexuality, included the letter in *Friend of Friends* but edited out this phrase.
14. Bosie p. 135. Charles Tindall Gatty, art museum curator and an 1892 Liberal Home Rule candidate for West Dorset, was a good friend of Bosie's cousin George Wyndham, and a member of Wilfred Blunt's Crabbat Club. Gatty was, according to Wilde, one of Bosie's 'many admirers'. Bosie's poem *Impression de Nuit* was written in his flat. During his heated campaign against the incumbent Henry Richard Farquharson, Farquharson decided to smear his opponent's character in a number of speeches, accusing Gatty of 'offences against purity' and involvement with 'printer's boys'. Gatty lost the election, but shortly thereafter (on Whyndham's advice) sued Farquharson for libel. Gatty was represented by Frank Lockwood, instructed by Lewis & Lewis, and the defence was represented by Edward Clark. Clark did not enter a plea of justification on behalf of his client and Gatty and was awarded £5,000 in damages, later reduced on appeal to £2,500. Two years after the widely reported case, an Act of Parliament was passed allowing members who slandered others to be removed from their seats. Wilde's knowledge of this case was surely a factor as he weighed the risks and rewards of his own libel action.
15. Mouret, Francois. J-L. 'Quatorze lettres et billets inedits de Lord Alfred Douglas a Andre Gide, 1895-1929' *Revue de Littérature comparée*, 49, no. 3 (July-September, 1975), 483-502. Translation mine.
16. Speedie, Julie. *Wonderful Sphinx*. London: Virago Press, 1993.
17. O'Brien. op. cit.
18. Plea p. 10
19. Brotchie p. 72
20. Quoted in 'De Profundis,' *The Truth* (Sydney), 25 May 1913.
21. Mouret, Francois. J-L. 'Quatorze lettres et billets inedits de Lord Alfred Douglas a Andre Gide, 1895-1929' *Revue de Littérature comparée*, 49, no. 3 (July-September, 1975), 483-502. Translation mine.
22. Ibid.

23. Bosie pp. 137-138
24. Hyde LAD p. 95
25. Robins p. 194
26. Hyde. Aftermath. p. 201 and Robins p. 194. This was, incidentally, a crime. Prison regulations stated 'Persons attempting to clandestinely communicate with, or to introduce any article to or for Prisoners, are liable to fine or imprisonment and any Prisoner concerned in such practices is liable to be severely punished.'

Chapter 15: Pit of Shame

1. Robins p. 56 and Breslow, Jason M. 'What Does Solitary Confinement Do To Your Mind?' *Frontline*, 22 April 2014.
2. Crone, Rosalind. 'The Great Reading Experiment: an Examination of the Role of Education in the Ninteenth-century Gaol.' *Crime, History & Societies*, Vol. 16. no 1, 2012. pp. 47-74.
3. Stokes, Anthony. *Pit of Shame: The Real Ballad of Reading Gaol*. Winchester: Waterside Press, 2007. p. 80
4. Mead, Donald, 'The Pillage of the House Beautiful,' *The Wildean*, No 47. July 2015.
5. Epistola. p. 77
6. Robins p. 27
7. Wilde, Oscar. *De Profundis*. London: G. P. Putnam & Sons, 1905. p. 6
8. Hyde, H. Montgomery. *Oscar Wilde: The Aftermath*. New York: Farrar, Straus & Co, 1963. p. 34.
9. Hyde. Aftermath op. cit. p. 33
10. Ellmann p. 492
11. Robins pp. 27-28
12. Hyde Aftermath op. cit. p. 34
13. Although Wilde recorded the date of his transfer in *De Profundis* as 13 November prison records show that it was actually 20 or 21 November. See Stokes p. 80
14. DP 1905 p. 102
15. Jackson, John Wyse, Ed. *The Uncollected Oscar Wilde*. London: Fourth Estate, 1991. p. xiii
16. Jackson, John Wyse, Ed. *The Uncollected Oscar Wilde*. London: Fourth Estate, 1991 p. xiv
17. Robins p. 171
18. Quoted in Kohl, Norbert. *Oscar Wilde: The Works of a Conformist Rebel*. Cambridge: Cambridge University Press, 1989. p. 302
19. Friend of Friends p. 43
20. Ellmann p. 498
21. Moyle, Franny. *Constance: The Tragic and Scandalous Life of Mrs. Oscar Wilde*. Pegasus Books, 2012. Kindle edition, p. 289
22. Hyde Aftermath op. cit. p. 56

Chapter 16: Continual Longing

1. Douglas, Alfred Bruce. *Oscar Wilde: A Summing-Up*. London: The Richards Press, 1940. p. 120
2. Hyde. LAD. p. 84.
3. Summing-Up pp. 24-25
4. Douglas, Alfred Bruce. *City of the Soul*. London: John Lane, 1911. p. 131.
5. Friend of Friends pp. 39-42

6. Hyde. LAD. p. 100
7. CL p 655
8. CL pp. 669-670
9. Hyde LAD p. 102
10. From original transcripts in the private collection of John D Stratford.
11. Bogle p. 104
12. This letter was quoted in the Ransome trial. 'Lord Alfred Douglas Absent When MSS of Oscar Wilde's Book is Read,' *Dundee Evening Telegraph*, 18 April 1913 and in the account of Douglas's false obituary trial in the *Leeds Mercury 25 November 1921*.
13. Hyde LAD p. 103
14. Speedie p. 105
15. Friend of Friends p. 56
16. From original transcripts in the private collection of John D Stratford.
17. CL p. 678

Chapter 17: De Profundis

1. Plea p. 31
2. Wilde, Oscar. *De Profundis*. London: G. P. Putnam & Sons, 1905. p. 118
3. Gagnier, Regenia. *Idylls of the Marketplace: Oscar Wilde and the Victorian Public*. Stanford, California: Stanford University Press, 1986. p. 193-194
4. Epistola p. 44
5. Ibid p. 75
6. Hyde. Aftermath op. cit. p. 3
7. Ibid p. 154
8. Ibid p. 91
9. 'Will you say in answer to my questions, that in one of my Holloway letters I had myself asked you to try, as far was you were able, to set me a little right with some small portion of the world? Certainly I did.' CL p. 902. 'Will you give as your answer that in the days of my greatness and fame I had consented to receive the dedication of your early work? Certainly I did.' CL p. 905.
10. Epistola p. 155

Chapter 18: The Life Interest

1. Epistola p. 133
2. Robins p. 81
3. Speedie pp. 95-96
4. Robins p. 86
5. Robins p. 87
6. Robins pp. 87-88
7. Moyle, Franny. *Constance: The Tragic and Scandalous Life of Mrs. Oscar Wilde*. Pegasus Books, 2012. Kindle edition, p. 294
8. Robins p. 94
9. Robins pp. 96-97
10. CL p. 837

Chapter 19: A Curious Way of Expressing Disinclination

1. Pearson op. cit. p. 154
2. CL pp. 858-859
3. Strong, Rowland, 'Paris: Oscar Wilde's Condition and Plans for Work – A Talk with Rochefort on Art.' *New York Times*, 12 June 1897.

4. Stratmann p. 262
5. Mackie, Gregory, 'Publishing Notoriety: Piracy, Pornography, and Oscar Wilde.' *University of Toronto Quarterly*, Fall 2004.
6. CL p. 924
7. Mackie, Gregory, 'Publishing Notoriety: Piracy, Pornography, and Oscar Wilde.' *University of Toronto Quarterly*, Fall 2004.
8. Autobiography p. 145
9. CL p. 858
10. Ibid pp. 864-872
11. Ibid pp. 872-873
12. Ibid pp. 872-880
13. Ibid p. 1188
14. La Jeunesse, Ernest, et al. *In Memoriam Oscar Wilde*. Greenwich, CT: Literary Collector Press, 1905. p. 58
15. La Jeunesse, Ernest, et al. *In Memoriam Oscar Wilde*. Greenwich, CT: Literary Collector Press, 1905. p. 66
16. CL p. 881
17. Ibid p. 884
18. Ibid p. 886
19. Autobiography p. 151
20. Bogle p. 122
21. Hyde LAD pp. 107-108
22. Bosie. pp. 156-157
23. Bogle p. 123 Bogle notes that although Croft-Cooke, Bosie's sympathetic biographer quotes from the accusatory part of this letter he doesn't mention this paragraph.
24. Stratmann p. 262
25. Bosie. p. 157
26. From original transcripts in the private collection of John D Stratford.
27. Murray p. 104
28. CL pp 932-933
29. Bogle p.128
30. Carlston, Erin. *Double Agents: Espionage, Literature and Liminal Citizens*. New York: Columbia University Press, 2013. p. 31
31. Babini, Valeria P et al. *Italian Sexualities Uncovered, 1789-1914*. Palgrave MacMillian, 2015.
32. CL p. 943
33. Ibid p. 948
34. Ibid p. 949
35. Ibid p. 950
36. CL
37. Bogle p. 113
38. CL p. 961
39. CL p. 952
40. CL p. 963
41. CL p. 979
42. CL p. 988
43. CL p. 990
44. Denver. op. cit. p. 84
45. McKenna. p. 448
46. Without Apology pp. 297-298
47. CL
48. 'Libel Trial,' *Sheffield Daily Telegraph*, 15 February 1910. He repeated this assertion in the Ransome trial three years later.
49. 'The Extraordinary Libel Action,' *Yorkshire Evening Post*, 18 April 1913.
50. Without Apology pp. 304-305

51. Bell, T. H. 'Oscar Wilde's Unwritten Play.' *The Bookman*, April/May, 1930.
52. Murray p. 119
53. O'Sullivan, Vincent. *Aspects of Wilde*. London: Constable & Co, 1936.
54. Hart-Davis, Rupert. *The Letters of Oscar Wilde*. London: Harcourt, Brace & World, 1962. p. 729 note 2.

Chapter 20: Luxuriating in Tragedy

1. O'Sullivan, Vincent. *Aspects of Wilde*. London: Constable & Co, 1936. pp. 59-60
2. 'I went to see his lordship. He is less interested in other people than ever before, especially Oscar ...' quoted in Ellmann, Richard. *Oscar Wilde*. New York: 1988.
3. Neil McKenna. *The Secret Life of Oscar Wilde* (p. 449). Kindle Edition.
4. Ellmann p. 567
5. Mikhail, E. H. *Oscar Wilde: Interviews and Recollections*. New York: MacMillian, 1979.
6. Sherard, Robert. *The Real Oscar Wilde*. London: T. Werner Laurie, 1915. p. 410.
7. O'Sullivan op. cit. p. 48
8. Bogle p. 141
9. Ellmann p. 567
10. These letters no longer exist (or if they do they have been well hidden) but the testimony and evidence in the Ransome trial makes it clear that in 1898 and 1899 Bosie wrote Robbie letters that the court found shocking for their homoerotic content, and that he wrote to him about his continued love of Oscar Wilde. We can assume that the letters from Bosie that were read in court were only a sample from a regular correspondence, chosen for their value in the trial, and that there were similar letters in the other direction.
11. Hyde LAD p. 373
12. 'A' (Lord Alfred Douglas), 'Oscar Wilde: His Last Book and His Last Years.' *St James's Gazette*, 2 March 1905.
13. Jones, Nigel, 'A Tale of Two Scandals.' *History Today*, February 2011
14. Ibid
15. Hyde LAD p. 122
16. Sherard, Robert. *Twenty Years in Paris*. Philadelphia: George W. Jacobs & Co, 1905. p. 443.
17. Esterhazy quoted in Maguire p. 129
18. Chesson, Wilfred Hugh, 'A Reminiscence of 1898,' *The Bookman*, December, 1911.
19. O'Sullivan op. cit. pp. 135-136
20. Nicolson, Harold. 'Dear Robbie,' *The Observer*, 6 April 1952.
21. 'Lord Alfred Douglas Absent when MSS of Oscar Wilde's Book is Read,' *Dundee Evening Telegraph,* 18 April 1913.
22. Jones, Nigel, 'A Tale of Two Scandals.' *History Today*, February 2011.
23. Pearce, Joseph. *The Unmasking Of Oscar Wilde* pp. 380-381. Ignatius Press. Kindle Edition.
24. O'Sullivan op. cit. p. 37

Chapter 21: Oscar's Last Years

1. Hyde LAD p. 125
2. Bogle pp. 146-147
3. CL p. 1104

4. Ellmann p. 567
5. This description is from *Oscar Wilde and Myself*, a book credited to Douglas but written by Crosland. The language here is clearly Crosland's style rather than Douglas's.
6. For a psychological analysis of Wilde's writer's block see Robins. pp 69-74. Robins says '... there is no justification for invoking a direct causative link between Wilde's imprisonment and his subsequent loss of volition and creativity.'
7. CL p. 1132
8. Friend of Friends p. 62
9. Bogle p. 150
10. Milne-Smith, Amy. 'Queensberry's Misrule: Reputation, Celebrity, and the Idea of the Victorian Gentleman.' *Canadian Journal of History*, Autumn 2013.
11. *Lichfield Mercury*, 15 June 1900
12. Without Apology p. 235
13. Shaw p. xxiv.
14. Hart-Davis p. 653
15. Hart-Davis op. cit. p. 828
16. Harris p. 305
17. Ibid
18. CL pp. 1187-1188
19. Harris, Frank and Lord Alfred Douglas. *New Preface to The Life and Confessions of Oscar Wilde*. London: privately printed for Members of the Homosexual Society of London, 1961. p. 46
20. Harris p. 305
21. Harris, Frank and Lord Alfred Douglas. *New Preface to The Life and Confessions of Oscar Wilde*. London: privately printed for Members of the Homosexual Society of London, 1961. p. 46
22. Hall p. 32
23. Sassoon, Siegfried, 'Wilde's Downfall,' *The Observer*, 30 October 1949.
24. Ellmann p. 346
25. Ellmann p. 562
26. CL p. 1225
27. Autobiography p. 148
28. Bell, T. H. 'Oscar Wilde's Unwritten Play.' *The Bookman*, April/May, 1930.
29. Ibid.

Chapter 22: Either the Wallpaper ...

1. 'A' (Lord Alfred Douglas), 'Oscar Wilde's Last Years in Paris,' *St James's Gazette*, 3 March 1905.
2. Friend of Friends p. 64 and CL pp. 1195-1208
3. CL pp. 1212-1213 and Friend of Friends p. 65
4. Harris, Frank and Lord Alfred Douglas. *New Preface to The Life and Confessions of Oscar Wilde*. London: Privately Printed for Members of the Homosexual Society of London, 1961. p. 15
5. CL pp. 1218-1219
6. CL p. 1217
7. Mikhail, E. H. *Oscar Wilde: Interviews and Recollections*. New York: MacMillian, 1979.
8. Burke, Edmund. 'Oscar Wilde: The Final Scene.' *London Magazine*, May 1961.
9. CL pp. 1224-1225
10. CL p. 1220
11. Bell, T. H. 'Oscar Wilde's Unwritten Play.' *The Bookman*, April/May, 1930.
12. Harris op. cit
13. CL pp. 1211-1214
14. Bogle p. 153

15. Robbie repeated the 'me' version of the story in a letter to Adela Schuster written 23 December 1900. This appears to support the Bogle thesis that 'him' was a simple mistake. However, Robbie did substitute himself for Bosie in other stories, particularly when it came to *De Profundis*, which he implied was addressed to him. Oscar could well have been emotional about both of his friends, (which would make both *him* and *me* correct) and Robbie had good reasons to edit Bosie out of the story for his own protection.
16. Friend of Friends p. 65
17. Bosie pp. 189-190
18. 'Lord Alfred Douglas Robbed in Paris,' *Manchester Courier and Lancashire General Advertiser*, 27 October 1900 and Rouzier, Eugene, 'L'Or du Lord,' *Le Journal*, 26 October 1900. (Translation mine.)
19. Reynolds, Sian. *Paris-Edinburgh: Cultural Connections in the Belle Epoque.* Hampshire, England: Ashgate Publishing, 2007.
20. 'Lord A. Douglas Loses Suit.' *Register* (Adelaide, Australia) 27 May 1913
21. Quoted in Bogle p. 159. Bogle describes this as a letter in the possession of Giles Robertson.

Chapter 23: The Aftermath

1. Bell, T. H. 'Oscar Wilde's Unwritten Play,' *The Bookman*, April/May, 1930.
2. Bell op. cit
3. Bogle p. 155
4. Bogle p. 154
5. Holland, Merlin. 'Oscar Wilde's Clothes: Story of Writer's Last Shirt.' *Huffington Post*, July 18, 2013.
6. Bogle p. 158
7. Friend of Friends pp. 66-67
8. The information on the wreath from Ross is in *Friend of Friends* pp. 60-61 and on Harris's agreeing to pay the hotel bill on p. 64
9. 'Terms of great friendship' is from Autobiography p. 37. Paying for the funeral from 'A' (Lord Alfred Douglas) 'Oscar Wilde's Last Days in Paris.' *St James's Gazette*, 3 March 1905. The 'friend' who shared the costs with him may have been the attorney Martin Holman who wrote to Ross that Hargrove and Co 'very properly seemed to think it would be the client's duty in the interests of the children to provide a respectable funeral.' Edra Bogle quotes this letter from the Clark Library (pp. 155-156) but adds that she was unable to find any records as to whether they really contributed to the cost of the funeral or not. In later years, when Douglas and Ross were feuding and shoring up their own accounts, Douglas would claim he had paid for the costs of the funeral in full and Ross would increasingly downplay how much Douglas had contributed.
10. Croft-Cooke, Bosie p. 187
11. Bogle p. 157
12. Summing-Up p. 141
13. Murray p. 119
14. Bosie pp. 189-190
15. Ibid
16. Bogle p. 159. Described as a letter in the possession of Giles Robertson.
17. Borland p. 76
18. Borland p. 77

Chapter 24: Olive and Freddie

1. Wilde, Oscar. *The Portrait of Mr. W. H.* New York: Mitchell Kennerley, 1921 p. 76
2. Bogle p. 161
3. Bogle p. 162
4. Nowell-Smith, Simon, Ed. *Edwardian England 1901-1914.* London: Oxford University Press, 1964. p. 334.
5. Friend of Friends pp. 71-73
6. Wthout Apology p. 69
7. Murray p. 122 ad Tobin & Gertz p. 193
8. Longford, Elizabeth. *A Pilgrimage of Passion: The Life of Wilfrid Scawen Blunt.* New York: Alfred A. Knopf, 1980. p. 321
9. Autobiography p. 204
10. Autobiography p. 208
11. Autobiography p. 215
12. Although Colonel Custace's middle name is spelled 'Hambledon' in many books, Caspar Wintermans, in his notes to Olive Custance's diary, points out that this was probably a typographic error that got repeated as *Who's Who*, 1923 and *Burke's Landed Gentry* list him as 'Hambleton.'
13. Custance p. 19
14. An excellent analysis of Olive Custance's work is found in Parker, Sarah. *The Lesbian Muse and Poetic Identity, 1889-1930.* London: Pickering & Chatto, 2013.
15. Sewell op. cit. p. 337
16. Souhamie, Diana. *Wild Girls.* New York: St. Martin's Press, 2004. pp. 39-40
17. Ibid p. 40
18. Ibid p. 41
19. Rodriguez, Suzanne. *Wilde Heart: A Life.* New York: Harper Collins, 2003. p. 125.
20. Autobiography p. 197
21. Autobiography p. 189
22. Henri W. and Albert A. Berg Collection, New York Public Library. See also *The Autobiography of Lord Alfred Douglas.* London: Martin Secker, 1929.
23. May, Simon. *Love: A History.* Yale University Press, 2011. p. 41
24. Autobiography p. 214
25. 'Colonel F. H. Custance, C. B.' *Northern Whig*, 1 October 1915.
26. http://www.biodiversitylibrary.org/bibliography/23312#/summary
27. Sewell op. cit. p. 5
28. Hyde LAD p. 138
29. MS Berg
30. *Western Times*, 5 November 1901
31. Letter from Lord Alfred Douglas to Olive Custance dated 1 November 1901. New York Public Library. Berg Collection.
32. Wintermans p. 103
33. Letter from Lord Alfred Douglas to Olive Custance dated 13 November 1901 New York Public Library. Berg Collection.
34. 'Lord Alfred Douglas Here.' *Washington Post*, 17 December 1901.
35. Foldy p. 129
36. Strangers p. 31
37. 'Not Earl Nor Actor.' *Minneapolis Journal*, 9 May 1901.
38. 'Put His Head Through Hole,' *Democrat and Chronicle.* 11 May 1901.
39. 'Peer Expelled From Club.' *New York Sun*, 18 December 1901.
40. Hyde LAD p. 139
41. 'Lord Alfred Departs.' *Washington Post*, 18 December 1901.
42. Murray p. 128
43. Murray p. 130

44. Keller, Phyllis. 'George Sylvester Viereck: The Psychology of a German-American Militant.' *The Journal of Interdisciplinary History*. Summer, 1971.
45. Autobiography p. 193
46. Autobiography p. 195
47. Hyde. LAD p. 141
48. Hyde LAD p. 140
49. Elizabeth Longford, *A Pilgrimage of Passion. The Life of Wilfrid Scawen Blunt*. London: Weidenfeld & Nicolson, 1979, p. 373.
50. Autobiography pp. 198-199
51. Hall p. 104
52. Hall p. 105
53. Borland p. 84
54. Hall p. 107
55. Autobiography p. 199
56. Rodriguez, Suzanne. *Wild Heart: A Life*. New York: Harper Collins, 1995. p. 140
57. Hyde. LAD p. 163
58. Le Diable, Robert, 'The Story of Frederick Stanley Smith,' *Winning Post*, 16 November 1918.
59. Let Them Say pp. 44-48
60. Le Diable, Robert, 'The Story of Frederick Stanley Smith,' *Winning Post*, 16 November 1918. The accusation comes from the libel case between Robert Ross and Lord Alfred Douglas and the information was certainly provided to the legal team by Douglas. In 1903 when the relationship between Ross and Smith was developing, Ross and Douglas were still friends, Douglas may still have been engaging in homosexual activities himself, and thus it is likely that he would have had first-hand knowledge of the relationship. In his court testimony, although Ross denied knowing Reggie Smith or being aware that they lived in a basement, his responses indicate that he was aware that Freddie Smith was living with his female cousin in 1903, which supports the idea that they were already acquainted then.
61. Bogle p. 188
62. Cook, Matthew. *Queer Domesticities*. London: Palgrave MacMillan, 2014. p. 101
63. Ibid pp. 100-101
64. Lewis, Brian. E-mail correspondence with author 26 April 2016.

Chapter 25: The Return of Maurice Schwabe

1. Letter from Lord Alfred Douglas to Lady Alfred Douglas. 28 August 1902. Berg Collection. New York Public Library.
2. Cook, Matthew. *Queer Domesticities*. London: Palgrave MacMillan, 2014. pp. 78-79
3. Maurice Salis Schwabe Bankruptcy Filing. National Archives. BT 226/2549 (Schwabe probably actually left for South Africa on 3 September 1897, as there is a record for a Mr M. Salis-Schwabe on the Norman Castle from London to *Cape Town in The Colonies and India*, 4 September 1897.) Rupert Croft-Cooke reported that Schwabe was in England when Wilde was arrested and fled the country at that time. He includes Schwabe's name on a list of homosexual friends who left the country in the wake of the trials. Croft-Cooke may have heard that Schwabe went to Australia and made an assumption about the timing. Schwabe appeared in the Sydney society pages as a guest at a number of parties in September 1894 and his mother wrote to him there in October 1894. With a three-month sea journey, he could theoretically have been back in England as early as January 1895, but there would have been no need for Schwabe to lie about being in England during the trial years later in his bankruptcy hearing, so there is no reason to doubt his own account.
4. Pyke, Christopher. *My Search for Montagu Pyke, Britain's First Cinema King*. Snoek Publishing, 2008. p. 11

5. Police file on the expulsion of Baron von Koenig from France in 1902. Archives Nationales (AN) F/7/160062 (Translation my own).
6. Pyke op. cit. p. 44
7. Cullen, Tom (2015-07-30). *The Man Who Was Norris: The Life of Gerald Hamilton* (Dark Masters) (Kindle Location 639). Dedalus Limited. Kindle Edition.
8. McHarg, Farquhar. Pistoleros: T*he Chronicles of Farquhar McHarg: Vol. 1:1918*. Oakland, CA: PM Press, 2011.
9. 'Famous Card Sharp Again at Liberty.' *Washington Post*, 16 August 1913.
10. *Illustrirte* magazine. http://magazine.illustrierte-presse.de/en/the-magazines/werkansicht/dlf/73691/24/0/?tx_dlf[pointer]=
11. 'Reputed Decoy for Swindlers.' *The Evening Chronicle*, 27 September 1910.
12. 'Libel Trial,' *Sheffield Daily Telegraph*, 15 February 1910.
13. Lee, Laura, 'The Mysterious Mr Schwabe,' *The Wildean*, July 2016 and 'The Mysterious Mr Schwabe pt II,' *The Wildean*, January 2017.
14. Oscar Wilde and Myself p. 195
15. Autobiography p. 104
16. Dockray, Martin, 'The Cleveland Street Scandal 1889-1890: The Conduct of the Defense.' *Journal of Legal History*, v.17, no.n1, 1996 April, p.1-16.

Chapter 26: The Odd Couple

1. Murray p. 140
2. 'A Literary Letter,' *The Sphere*, 31 October 1903.
3. Crosland, T. W. H. *Lord of Creation*. London: Grant Richards, 1904. p. 9
4. Brown p. 185
5. Autobiography p. 226
6. Autobiography p. 228
7. 'Society Case,' *Sheffield Daily Telegraph*, 12 February 1910.
8. Brown p. 436
9. Brown p. 190
10. Douglas, Alfred Bruce, Lord. *Oscar Wilde et Quelques Autres*. Paris: Librarie Gallimard, 1930. p. 181
11. 'The Late Mr. T. W. H. Crosland,' *The Straits Times*, 29 January 1925
12. Braybrooke, Patrick. *Lord Alfred Douglas: His Life and Work*. London: Cecil Palmer, 1931. p. 124
13. Brown p. 385
14. Brown p. 421
15. Head, Alice M. *It Could Never Have Happened*. London: William Heinmann Ltd, 1939. p. 43
16. Brown p. 27
17. Brown p. 31
18. Autobiography p. 228
19. On Crosland's roulette mania: 'The Late Mr. T. W. H. Crosland,' *The Straits Times*, 29 January 1925. On his telegrams to Douglas: Braybrooke p. 124. on furniture: Without Apology p. 111
20. Autobiography p. 210-211
21. 'Charge of Libel,' *The Times* (London) 12 February 1910.
22. Autobiography p. 214
23. Crosland, T. W. H., 'To A. D.' *The Academy*, 5 December 1908.
24. Autobiography p. 231
25. Without Apology p. 113
26. Without Apology p. 101
27. Without Apology p. 99
28. Deghy et al. Café Royal. pp. 146-147
29. MS Magdalen College
30. Without Apology p. 114

31. Collected Poems p. 109
32. Brown p. 393
33. Without Apology p. 113
34. Without Apology pp. 114-115

Chapter 27: The Buckingham Gate Flat Incident

1. 'Charge of Libel.' *The Times* (London) 15 February 1910.
2. McHarg, Farquhar. Pistoleros: *The Chronicles of Farquhar McHarg: Vol. 1:1918*. Oakland, CA: PM Press, 2011.
3. Manners-Sutton's testimony is in 'Charge of Libel.' *The Times* (London) 12 February 1910 and Douglas's is recorded in 'Charge of Libel.' *The Times* (London) 15 February 1910.
4. B 9/780 Bankruptcy file of Lord Alfred Douglas
5. Sandulescu, C. George, ed. *Rediscovering Oscar Wilde*. Gerards Cross: Colin Smythe, 1994. pp. 76-77.
6. 'Society Scandal.' *Sheffield Evening Telegraph* 11 February 1910.
7. Douglas, Alfred Bruce. *Oscar Wilde: A Summing-Up*. London: The Richards Press, 1940. p. 126.
8. Autobiography p. 79
9. 'Radiant beginning' was Olive Custance's depiction from a letter to W. Sorley Brown dated 13 April 1929 in the Magdalen College archives.
10. Custance p. 20 and p. 27

Chapter 28: Ownership of Oscar

1. Mackie, Gregory, 'Publishing Notoriety: Piracy, Pornography, and Oscar Wilde.' *University of Toronto Quarterly*, Fall 2004.
2. Bogle pp. 204-205
3. Biographical information on Ledger from Millard. pp. 49-50.
4. Novak, Daniel. 'Picturing Wilde: Christopher Millard's 'Iconography of Oscar Wilde' *Nineteenth-Century Contexts*, 28 November 2010.
5. Millard pp. 64-66. Ross's statement is referenced in Bogle p. 211.
6. Le Diable, Robert, 'The Story of Frederick Stanley Smith,' *Winning Post*, 16 November 1918.
7. Let Them Say p. 52
8. 'Charge of Libel,' *The Times* (London), 12 February 1910. Caspar Wintermans identified Manners-Sutton as the unnamed friend mentioned in *Oscar Wilde and Myself* in end note #23 of *I Desire the Moon*.
9. Nelson, James G. *Publisher to the Decadents: Leonard Smithers in the Careers of Beardsley, Wilde Dowson*. University Park, PA: Pennsylvania State University Press, 2000. p. 222
10. CL p. 1202
11. Nelson op. cit. p. 274
12. Ibid.
13. Oscar Wilde and Myself p. 145

Chapter 29: In Symbolic Relation

1. Masques & Phases p. 25

2. Cooper, John. 'Dubious Quotation: I Have Nothing to Declare But My Genius,' Oscar Wilde in America. http://www.oscarwildeinamerica.org/quotations/nothing-to-declare.html Accessed 1 December 2016.
3. Ferrari, Roberto C and Carolyn Conroy. 'Simeon Solomon's Shame Free Art.' *The Gay & Lesbian Review Worldwide*, September-October, 2011.
4. Simeon Solomon Biography. Simeon Solomon Research Archive. http://www.simeonsolomon.com/simeon-solomon-biography.html Accessed 13 May 2016.
5. Conroy, Carolyn. 'He Hath Mingled with the Ungodly: The Life of Simeon Solomon After 1873, With a Survey of the Extant Works.' PH. D. Dissertation. University of York, December, 2009. p. 34
6. Ibid pp. 40-41
7. Ahmadgoli, Kamran and Ian Small, 'The Creative Editor: Robert Ross, Oscar Wilde and the Collected Works.' *English Literature in Transition 1880-1920*, Spring 2008.
8. Ibid.
9. Bogle p. 196
10. Bogle p. 199
11. Epistola p. 22
12. Ellmann p. 581
13. Bogle p. 205
14. *St James's Gazette*, 23 February 1905
15. Quoted in Borland p. 96. For those inclined to entertain the notion that Ross could have forged all or parts of *De Profundis*, it is worth noting that although Ross may not have had the 'requisite skill' to pull off such a forgery, he might have known people who did among the staple of artists employed by the Carfax Gallery to make exact copies of paintings for aristocratic clients. See: 'Originals and Copies,' Home Subjects. http://www.homesubjects.org/2015/11/18/originals-and-copies/
16. Sherard, Robert. *The Real Oscar Wilde*. London: T. Warner Laurie, 1916. p. 161
17. The source is the largely ghost-written *Oscar Wilde and Myself*. pp. 153-154 credited to Lord Alfred Douglas. Both the literary style and the argument are more Crosland than Douglas, hence the attribution here. Douglas's arguments, while often cogent, invariably had an aspect of personal pique and outrage that is lacking here. The phrase 'puttings-together' is also a feature of Crosland's style. Douglas also stated later that all of the literary analysis in *Oscar Wilde and Myself* was written by Crosland.
18. Millard pp. 55-56
19. *St James's Gazette*, 11 March 1905
20. Beerbohm, Max. *Max Beerbohm's Letters to Reggie Turner*. Philadelphia: J. B. Lippincott, 1965. p. 122
21. Weintraub, Stanley. *Reggie*. New York: George Braziller, 1965.

Chapter 30: Divergence

1. Milne-Smith, Amy. *London Clubland: A Cultural History of Gender and Class in Late Victorian Britain*. New York: Palgrave MacMillan, 2011. p. 27
2. Bogle p. 215
3. Douglas's membership in White's is mentioned in 'Lord Alfred Douglas's Bets,' *Yorkshire Evening Post*, 7 April 1909.
4. Without Apology p. 29
5. Hyde. LAD p. 175
6. Custance p. 26 and p. 29
7. Hyde LAD p. 147
8. Custance op. cit. p. 35
9. Ibid p. 34
10. Ibid p. 26 and p. 40

11. Autogiography pp. 215-216
12. Le Diable, Robert. 'The Story of Frederick Stanley Smith,' *Winning Post*, 16 November 1918.
13. Bogle pp. 219-220
14. Borland p. 106. This anecdote is unsourced in the text. Borland says it came from a conversation with one of her three main sources, Sir Rupert Hart Davis, John Paul Ross or Professor Giles Robertson and 'you can take what I wrote as gossip.' E-mail correspondence with author, 29 August 2016.
15. Le Diable op. cit
16. Head op. cit. pp. 38-39
17. Borland p. 110
18. Hyde LAD p. 152
19. Head op cit p. 43
20. Renton, Claudia. *Those Wonderful Wyndhams*. London: William Collins, 2014. p. 163
21. Ibid pp. 164-165
22. Autobiogrphy p. 220
23. Autobiography
24. Alice M. Head Obituary. *Times*, July 29, 1981.
25. Head p. 41
26. Ibid pp. 42-43
27. Let Them Say p. 73
28. Pearson op. cit. p. 157
29. Ross's lack of Wilde content is from Borland p. 118, quote from Bosie is from Plea p. 12.
30. The Friends of Arthur Machen. http://www.arthurmachen.org.uk/machbiog. html Accessed 27 September 2016.
31. Arthur Machen. *Hieroglyphics*. London: Grant Richards, 1902. Digitised by Project Gutenberg. http://www.gutenberg.org/ebooks/40241 no page numbers.
32. Autobiography p. 245
33. Autobiography p. 143
34. Moon p. 7
35. Millard p. 87

Chapter 31: 'I No Longer Wish to Associate with Persons like Yourself'

1. Brown p. 31
2. O'Brien op. cit.
3. Hyde LAD p. 154
4. Davis, F. S. Letters, *The Academy*, 31 October 1908.
5. Head op. cit. p. 43
6. Gregory, Augusta (Lady). Hugh Lane's Life and Achievement. London: John Murray, 1921.
7. Millard p. 89
8. Mason, Stuart (Christopher Millard). *Oscar Wilde: Art and Morality, A Defence of Dorian Gray*. London: J. Jacobs, 1908. Digitised by Project Gutenburg. http://www.gutenberg.org/ebooks/33689 Accessed 28 September 2016. No page numbers.
9. Let Them Say p. 71
10. 'The Yoke,' *The Academy*, 10 October 1908.
11. Radford, Andrew and Victoria Reid. *Franco-British Cultural Exchanges*. London: Palgrave MacMillian, 2012. p. 45
12. *The Publisher's Circular*, 1 July 1905
13. Brown pp. 243-244

14. Brown p. 185
15. Brown p. 171
16. Brown p. 186
17. Edra Bogle notes on p. 333 'If Crosland had devoted the rest of his life to such a crusade, perhaps this view would be tenable. But he did not.' Interestingly, Bogle goes on to say there 'could be no question' of Bosie having romantic feelings for Crosland. She does, however, speculate that perhaps Crosland's personal hatred of Wilde was due to 'a reason which he could not acknowledge even to himself ... bitter jealousy of the man whom Bosie had loved.'
18. CRIM 1-149-1
19. *The Freethinker,* 6 January 1907
20. Bogle p. 237. She cites 'Statement' pp. 9-10 and Croft-Cooke, Bosie pp. 215-218.
21. Bogle p. 237 and Hyde LAD p. 158
22. Bogle p. 237
23. Friend of Friends pp. 101-102
24. Letter from Olive Douglas to T. W. H. Crosland, 8 January 1909 quoted in Sorley Brown. Life and Genius of Crosland. p. 246.
25. A. D. (Lord Alfred Douglas), 'The Genius of Oscar Wilde,' *The Academy*, July 11, 1908.
26. Bogle p. 226
27. 'Life and Letters,' *The Academy,* July 18, 1908.
28. Friend of Friends p. 103
29. Bogle p. 238
30. Ibid
31. 'Life and Letters,' *The Academy*, 7 November 1908.
32. Robinson, James. 'Oscar Wilde's Friend and Benefactor, Helen Carew.' https://lessorfewer.files.wordpress.com/2015/01/oscar-wilde_s-friend-and-benefactor-helen-carew-c-1856-e28093-1928.pdf
33. Oscar Wilde and Myself p. 4
34. Bogle pp. 238-239
35. Weintraub. op. cit. p. 162
36. Ibid p. 164
37. Hyde LAP p. 159
38. Borland p. 142
39. Hyde LAD p. 160
40. Ibid

Chapter 32: Family Reunions and Divisions

1. Custance pp. 66-67
2. Robinson, James. op. cit.
3. MS Gertz
4. Information on the Buckley/Kennard affair from Buckley, E.C. and Edward Heron-Allen, Captain J. Buckley, Mrs. E. C. Buckley and Sir Coleridge Kennard: A Statement of Facts. Privately Printed, 1912; Foreign Office File FO 1093/113 and 'Buckley v. Buckley and Kennard,' *The Times* (London) 8 February 1910. The sources agree on the major points. I used Buckley's pamphlet primarily to describe her feelings and perspective. The legal correspondence, including that from Buckley's solicitor and the account of Buckley's last meeting with Kennard, given by Oliphant, are from letters and documents in the foreign office file. Portions of this chapter were previously published in an article I wrote for issue 51 of *The Wildean*, 'All Sorts of Influences Brought to Bear,' published June 2017.
5. Young, Filson, 'A Year of Strangers,' *Living Age,* vol 271. Boston: Living Age Co, 1911.

Chapter 33: Litigation Mania

1. Autobiography
2. 'A Literary Letter,' *The Sphere*, 31 October 1903.
3. 'Libel Action by a Libeller.' *Timaru Herald*, 12 March 1904.
4. Without Apology pp. 71-72
5. Without Apology p. 72
6. Harris, Frank and Lord Alfred Douglas. *New Preface to The Life and Confessions of Oscar Wilde*. London: privately printed for Members of the Homosexual Society of London, 1961. p. 17
7. Tobin, A. I. and Elmer Gertz. *Frank Harris a Study in Black and White*. Chicago: Madelaine Mendelsohn, 1931. p. 145
8. 'Titled English Editor Sneers at American Literary Tastes,' *Atlanta Constitution*, July 7, 1907.
9. Cherniavsky, Felix. *The Salome Dancer: The Life and Times of Maud Allan*. McClelland & Stewart Ltd, 1991. p. 171
10. Ibid pp. 19-20 Cherniavsky notes that the source of this anecdote was 'society gossip' but in spite of this 'It is very likely that this incident ... is true.'
11. Letter dated November 1932 explaining Douglas's conversion to Catholicism. John J. Burns Library of Special Collections, Boston College.
12. Autobiography p. 25
13. Murray p. 152
14. Autobiography p. 238
15. MS Gertz (Comment by Douglas on the manuscript of *A Study in Black and White*)
16. Millard
17. Summing-Up
18. Autobiography p. 220
19. Holland. Real Trials p. xxxi
20. Autobiography pp. 220-221
21. Autobiography p. 222
22. Murray p. 152
23. Custance p. 83
24. Ibid p. 84
25. Ibid p. 86
26. Ibid p. 94

Chapter 34: Justify! Justify to the Hilt!

1. Darling, Charles J. *Scintilae Juris*. London: Stevens and Haynes Law Publishers, 1914. p. 59
2. 'Originals and Copies.' Home Subjects. http://www.homesubjects. org/2015/11/18/originals-and-copies/ Accessed 5 November 2016.
3. Litt, Toby, 'James and the Duchess,' *The Guardian*, 30 November 2001.
4. Quoted in Poole, Andrea Geddes. *Stewards of the Nation's Art: Contested Cultural Authority. 1890-1939*. Toronto: University of Toronto Press, 2010. p. 119
5. Autobiography p. 230
6. 'Lord Alfred Douglas's Bankruptcy,' *Yorkshire Post*, 13 June 1913
7. Bosie pp. 232-233
8. Auberon, Reginald. (Horace Wyndham) *The Nineteen Hundreds*, London: G. Allen &Unwin Ltd, 1922. p. 258.
9. 'Charge of Libel,' *The Times* (London) 11 February 1910
10. Ibid
11. Ibid

12. Ibid
13. Ibid
14. Murray p. 154
15. 'Charge of Libel,' *The Times* (London) 11 February 1910
16. Ibid
17. Ibid
18. Hyde LAD
19. 'Libel Trial,' *Sheffield Daily Telegraph*, 15 February 1910
20. 'The Unspeakable Scot,' *Express and Telegraph* (Adelaide, Australia), 19 March 1910.
21. Autobiography pp. 232-233
22. Trial testimony is from the following sources: 'Charge of Libel,' *The Times* (London) 11 February 1910; 'Society Scandal,' *Sheffield Evening Telegraph*, 11 February 1910; 'Charge of Libel,' *The Times* (London) 12 February 1910 and 'Society Scandal.' *Sheffield Evening Telegraph*, 11 February 1910; 'The Unspeakable Scot,' *Express and Telegraph* (Adelaide, Australia), 19 March 1910; 'Society Case,' *Sheffield Daily Telegraph*, 12 February 1910; 'Not Guilty.' *Sheffield Daily Telegraph*, 16 February 1910.
23. Lee, Laura. op. cit.
24. Brown p. 240
25. This dialogue is a reconstruction based on reports in the *Sheffield Daily Telegraph* and 'Proud that He Knew Oscar Wilde,' *Lethbridge Daily Herald*, 5 March 1910, each of which had edited the testimony differently.
26. Autobiography p. 234
27. American Art Association. Sale Catalogue, 1920. Item #99.
28. 'Literary Men in Libel Suit,' *Vancouver Daily World* (Vancouver, British Columbia), 21 April 1911.
29. Walker-Smith, Derek. *The Life of Lord Darling*. London: Cassell and Company, Ltd, 1938. p. 105.
30. 'Literary Men in Libel Suit,' *Vancouver Daily World* (Vancouver, British Columbia), 21 April 1911.
31. Autobiography p. 234
32. Borland p. 149 and Bogle p. 283
33. Let Them Say p. 86
34. Bogle p. 283
35. Reid, Victoria. *Andre Gide and Curiosity*. New York: Rodopi, 2009. pp. 88-89
36. Borland p. 150

Chapter 35: The Quality of His Admirers

1. Ancestry.com. *UK, De Ruvigny's Roll of Honour, 1914-1919* [database on-line]. Provo, UT, USA: Ancestry.com Operations, Inc., 2014. Thank you to Julia Atkinson for making me aware of this document.
2. Lee, Laura. op. cit.
3. Ibid
4. Hamilton, Gerald. *The Way it Was With Me*. London: Leslie Frewin, 1969.
5. MEPOL 3/240
6. Max's Letters to Reggie p. 218
7. Robins p. 133
8. Letter from Philip Burne-Jones to Robert Ross dated 27 March 1911 quoted in Friend of Friends p. 210
9. Findlay, Kristy Nichol, Ed. *Arthur Ransome's Long-Lost Study of Robert Louis Stevenson*. Sufflok, UK: Boydell Press, 2011 pp. 9-10
10. Ransome, Arthur. *Autobiography of Arthur Ransome*. London: Jonathan Cape, 1976. p. 142
11. Bogle pp. 284-285

12. Ransome op. cit. p. 142
13. Tobin and Gertz p. 276
14. Kennard, George. *Loopy: An Autobiography.* London: Leo Cooper, 1990. p. 5
15. Let Them Say pp. 92-93
16. Leverson, Ada. *Letters to the Sphinx.* Adelaide: Michael Walmer, 1930. p. 48.
17. Autobiography
18. Autobiography
19. Douglas, Alfred. *In Excelsis.* London: Martin Secker, 1924
20. Hyde LAD p. 176
21. Quoted in Murray pp. 161-162
22. Murray p. 158

Chapter 36: The Worst Experience of My Life

1. Millard, Christopher, Ed. (Stuart Mason) *Oscar Wilde: Three Times Tried.* London: Ferrestone Press, 1912. pp. 465-466
2. Ransome op. cit. p. 9
3. Ibid pp. 157-158
4. Ibid pp. 182-183 and p. 196
5. AD to Robert Ross, 6 March 1912. Ross TS Clark. Quoted in Wintermans pp. 123-124
6. Murray p. 170
7. Findlay p. 11
8. Ransome op. cit. p. 151
9. Chambers, Roland. *The Last Englishman: The Double Life of Arthur Ransome.* Boston: David Godine, 2009. p. 68.
10. Quoted in Findlay, Kristy Nichol. *Arthur Ransome's Long-Lost Study of Robert Louis Stevenson.* Suffolk: Boydell Press, 2011.
11. Quoted in Bogle pp. 291-292. (Original in Clark Library)
12. Bogle p. 294
13. Quoted in Bogle p. 292. Bogle notes that although this letter was published in Margery Ross's *Friend of Friends* this paragraph was left out.
14. Sassoon, Siegfried. *Siegfried's Journey.* London: Faber and Faber, 1945. p. 29
15. Brown p. 302
16. Preface to *The First Stone.* Quoted in Brown p. 285
17. Wintermans p. 255
18. Without Apology p. 62
19. Without Apology p. 77
20. Hyde LAD p. 184
21. Letter dated November 1932 explaining Douglas's conversion to Catholicism. John J. Burns Library of Special Collections, Boston College.
22. Brown p. 283
23. Hoare p. 154
24. Brown
25. Douglas wrote about his mystical experiences and their timing both in his *Autobiography* and in the letter on his conversion to Catholicism in the Burns library.
26. 'Lord James Douglas and Miss Mabel Scott. Order of Committal.' *Western Daily Press,* 30 May 1888 and 'Release of Lord James Douglas,' *Dublin Daily Express,* 14 June 1888.
27. Milne-Smith, Amy, 'Queensberry's Misrule: Reputation, Celebrity, and the Idea of the Victorian Gentleman.' *Canadian Journal of History,* Autumn 2013. Also Douglas, James. Letter to the Editor. *London Evening Standard.* 13 April 1891.
28. In one study of bipolar I disorder (BP-I) by Jerrell and Shugart (2004) it was found that almost 19% of the adult patients showed hyper-religiosity as a symptom.

29. Brown, Mick. 'Should More Have Been Done to Save Lord Milo Douglas?' *Telegraph*, 30 May 2011.
30. Ibid
31. Stratmann p. 81
32. Stratmann p. 83
33. Stratmann p. 86
34. Milne-Smith, Amy, 'Queensberry's Misrule: Reputation, Celebrity, and the Idea of the Victorian Gentleman'*Canadian Journal of History*, Autumn 2013.
35. Stratmann p. 94 and *Shields Gaily Gazette*, 12 December 1885.
36. Quoted in Bogle p. 294
37. CRIM 1-149-1
38. Quoted in Bogle. p. 296 from a carbon in the possession of J. P. B. Ross.
39. Bogle p. 297
40. Ibid
41. Beerbohm, Max. *Max Beerbohm's Letters to Reggie Turner*. Philadelphia: J. B. Lippincott, 1965. p. 190
42. Walker-Smith, Derek. *The Life of Lord Darling*. London: Cassell and Company, Ltd, 1938. p. 137
43. 'I will always love Bosie, but I am afraid to live with him at present,' Constance wrote to Douglas's mother in a letter quoted in 'Lord and Lady Alfred Douglas. Application with Regard to Son. Remarkable Letters,' *The Manchester Courier*, July 1, 1915.
44. B 9/780 Bankruptcy file of Lord Alfred Douglas.
45. Bogle pp. 301-302
46. Bogle p. 302
47. Bogle p. 301
48. Beerbohm op. cit. p. 219 and Bogle P. 305 citing a letter then in the possession of J. P. B. Ross.

Chapter 37: Douglas v. Ransome and Others

1. 'Lord A. Douglas's Lost Suit.' *Register (Adelaide, Australia)* 27 May 1913
2. Quoted in Borland p. 181
3. 'Libel Action by Lord Alfred Douglas,' *The Times* (London), 23 April 1913.
4. CRIM 1-149-1
5. Brown p. 300
6. Hoare pp. 112-113
7. Sherard. The Real Oscar Wilde p. vii
8. The Newton story is 'The Case Against Arthur Newton,' *The Times* (London), 18 April 1913. The account of the Ransome trial here is taken from a number of newspaper articles including the series in *The Times* which ran on April 18, 19, 22, 23 and 25; the *Manchester Courier*, April 18, the *Dundee Courier* April 18, 19 and 22, the *Dundee Evening Telegraph* April 17 and 18, the *Nottingham Post*, April 18, the *Yorkshire Evening Post* April 17, 18 and 21, *Leeds Mercury* April 22, 1913, The *St. Lous Post-Dispatch*, April 18 and the Australian publications *The Truth* (Sydney) 25 May and the *Register* (Adelaide) 27 May. Because the direct quotes do not appear in exactly the same form, or the same sequence, in the various accounts I have used some editorial judgement in reconstructing the case from these sources.
9. Smith, Frederick (Second Earl of Birkenhead), *F. E.: The Life of F. E. Smith*. London: Eyre & Spottiswoode, 1960. p. 39
10. Ibid p. 201
11. Walker-Smith op. cit. p. 107
12. Without Apology pp. 314-315
13. Without Apology p. 315

14. *The Times* truncated this moment in the trial and its version of this dialogue has often been quoted in biographies reading 'Is not the plain truth of the *De Profundis* Letter that you were the ruin of Wilde's life ... Do you not admit that to be true?' 'Through a sense of Quxiotic generosity I let it pass.' In this version it is strange, as he had obviously not let *De Profundis* pass or he would not have been in court. In the longer version he is saying that he had received a critical letter prior to, or different from, *De Profundis*, which he let pass. This distinction has some relevance when trying to discern the history of *De Profundis* and what Douglas did or did not receive from Ross.
15. Epistola pp. 12-13
16. OW & Myself p. 147
17. Murray p. 171
18. Without Apology p. 304
19. Hyde LAD p. 190
20. Millard p. 109
21. *The Times* in its 22 April 1913 coverage has Campbell saying that Wilde had sent the message of 'undying love and affection' to Douglas from his deathbed. All of the other coverage I consulted has Douglas sending the message to Wilde.
22. Robertson, Graham. *Time Was*. London: Hamish Hamilton, 1931. p. 213
23. Ransome op. cit. p. 134
24. Millard. p. 110
25. Autobiography p. 42

Chapter 38: By Legitimate Means or Otherwise

1. Hyde LAD p. 184
2. 'Lord Alfred Douglas Tried for Libel,' *Yorkshire Evening Post,* 24 April 1913.
3. B 9/780 Bankruptcy file of Lord Alfred Douglas
4. Speedie p. 199
5. Millard letters from Bosie p. 112 and Millard p. 196 and Bosie's goal of forcing an exchange of incriminating documents Bogle p. 314
6. Beerbohm op. cit. p. 132
7. Bogle p. 330
8. Ibid
9. Let Them Say p. 108
10. Bogle p. 329
11. Borland p. 194
12. Bogle p. 306
13. Friend of Friends pp. 253-254
14. Let Them Say p. 111
15. Ibid
16. 'Convict's Work for Militants,' *Daily News*, July 1, 1914. The more neutral description of his colouring and complexion is from 'Great Conspiracy Case: Dramatic Evidence,' *The Express and Telegraph* (Adelaide, Australia) 13 June 1914.
17. 'The Crosland Trial,' *Manchester Courier and Lancashire General Advertiser*, July 1, 1914
18. Millard p. 116. Information on the Garratt case not otherwise cited is from CRIM 1/149/1 and MEPOL 3/240
19. Millard pp. 118-123
20. Ibid
21. Ibid
22. Bogle p. 315
23. Bogle p. 310, with the exception of the name Carlos Blacker; I drew this inference from references in *Ceremonies of Bravery* that indicate he read DP.
24. Quoted in Bogle p. 316 from carbon then in the possession of J. P. B. Ross.

25. CRIM 1/138/4
26. CRIM 1/138/4
27. See Note 1 Chapter 40
28. Quoted in Holland, Merlin. *Oscar Wilde: De Profundis. A Facsimile*. London: British Library, 2000. p. 11

Chapter 39: War

1. Plea p. 25
2. Quoted in Bogle p. 320 from original in the Brotherton Library, University of Leeds
3. *The Times,* 15 May 1914
4. Bogle p. 320
5. From a letter to Edmund Gosse dated 10 March 1914 quoted in Bogle p. 321.
6. Bogle p. 313
7. 'Crosland Trial,' *The Times* (London), 20 May 1914.
8. Millard p. 135
9. Bogle p. 313
10. Quoted in Bogle p. 328
11. 'Lord Alfred Douglas Goes to Paris,' *Dundee Courier*, 7 March 1914.
12. Quoted in Brown p. 307
13. Brown p. 308
14. Millard p. 138
15. 'Lord Alfred Douglas Goes to Paris,' *Dundee Courier*, 7 March 1914.
16. Millard pp. 139-140
17. MEPOL 3/240
18. The account of the trial and the information from it is from a number of newspaper articles. The reporters in most cases misspelled 'Hylton North' as Hilton and I have corrected this. Most detailed was 'Alleged Plot for No-Child Marriage,' *Express and Telegraph* (Adelaide, Australia), 16 May 1914. Other sources are 'Baron's Lawsuit,' *Sheffield Independent*, 7 April 1914. 'French Baron's Honour,' *Leeds Mercury*, April 7, 1914. 'Baron's Action,' *Birmingham Mail*, 6 April 1914 and 'Money Lenders and Bride,' *The Register (Adelaide, Australia)*, 11 May 1914.
19. BT 226/3725 Bankruptcy filing for Guy de Chassiron
20. B 917/66 Bankruptcy trial for Guy de Chassiron
21. The involvement of Bosie's nephews by marriage in crimes similar to those perpetrated by the Stallmann gang raises many questions, however I have not been able to uncover any connections between Baron de Chassiron, the Norths and Schwabe or his associates.

    For more on Roger North's criminal career see 'Plea of Loss of Memory,' *Lincolnshire Echo*, 20 January 1914; 'Airman Deserter Sentenced,' *Burton Daily Mail*, 29 July 1915; 'Alleged Pose as Dead Baronet,' *Portsmouth Evening News*, 10 October 1924; 'Alleged car Deal in Dead Man's Name,' *Edinburgh Evening News*, 10 October 1924; 'Engineer's Career of Crime,' *The Scotsman*, 13 November 1924; 'Remarkable Disclosures at the Old Bailey,' *Lancashire Evening Post,* 13 November 1924; 'Amazing Career: Earl's Nephew as Crime Expert,' *Taunton Courier*, 19 November 1924. The romantic ending to North's career of crime was that he was arrested for marrying Dorothy Murial Joan Berry under a false name while still married to Alice North (who, incidentally, was probably having an affair with Baron de Chassiron). When the deception was uncovered, the second wife vowed to wait for her husband and to 'make it legal' when he got out. The judge said that the love of Berry probably 'saved' Roger North. They had children together and appear to have lived happily ever after. See 'Monocled Man on Bigamy Charge,' *Nottingham Evening Post*; 'We

Are Going to Make it Legal,' *Portsmouth Evening News*, 1 March 1935 and 'Bigamist Saved by Wife,' *Nottingham Evening Post*, 5 March 1935.
22. 'Solicitor Sent to Penal Servitude,' *Scotsman*, 23 July 1914.

Chapter 40: Ross v. Crosland

1. Trial details and dialogue for Ross v. Crosland are taken from the following sources. CRIM 1-13-49-1, MEPOL 3/240, *The Times* (London) coverage which ran under the headline 'The Crosland Trial' on 20 May, 30 June, 2 July, 4 July, 6 July and 7 July 1914; the preliminary hearings were covered in articles in the *Manchester Courier and Lancashire General Advertiser* on 30 May, 1 June, 3 June, 30 June, and the final verdict in that paper on 7 July 1914.

   Also: 'Author Cries Liar!' *Daily Mirror*, 3 June 1914, 'Author's Emotion in Box,' *Daily Mirror*, 14 May 1914, 'The Crosland Case,' *Derby Daily Telegraph*, 1 June 1914, 'Crosland Committed for Trial,' *Birmingham Daily Post*, 3 June 1914, 'Crosland Conspiracy Case,' *Birmingham Daily Post*, 20 May 1914. 'The Crosland Prosecution,' *The Morning Advertiser*, 3 June 1914. 'Crosland Trial,' *Birmingham Post*, 4 July 1914, 'Crosland Trial,' *Western Times*, 3 July 1914, 'Mr Crosland Appears in Court,' *Yorkshire Post and Leeds Intelligencer*, 27 May 1914, 'Millard and Mr Ross,' *Birmingham Mail*, 1 July 1914, 'Mr Crosland Charged,' *Manchester Courier and Lancashire General Advertiser*, 1 June 1914, 'Mr Crosland Committed,' *Yorkshire Post and Leeds Intelligencer*, 3 June 1914. International publications: 'Oscar Wilde's Friend,' *Express and Telegraph* (Adelaide, Australia), 8 August 1914, 'Oscar Wilde's Friends,' *Express and Telegraph*, 6 June 1914, 'The Great Conspiracy Case,' *Express and Telegraph* (Adelaide, Australia) 13 June 1914, 'Crosland is Acquitted,' *New York Times*, 7 July 1914
2. Millard p. 140
3. Brown
4. Quoted in Bogle p. 329
5. Bogle pp. 329-330
6. Quoted in Bogle p. 330 from a draft in the Clark Library
7. Beerbohm op. cit. pp. 241-242
8. University of Iowa
9. 'Press Humour in the Crosland Case,' *Aberdeen Evening Express*, 8 May 1914 and Brown p. 312.
10. Brown p. 313
11. The Crosland Case. Cross-Examination of the Boy Garratt.' *Manchester Courier and Lancashire General Advertiser*, 13 May 1914.
12. Quoted in 'Crosland Trial,' *The Times* (London), 20 May 1914.

Chapter 41: Old Acid Drop

1. See note 1 in previous chapter for sources on both the trial and the preliminary hearing.
2. 'Tears for Acid Drop,' *Time Magazine*, 1 July 1935.
3. 'Mr Justice Avory,' *The Spectator*, 3 October 1935
4. Brown p. 320
5. Borland p. 221
6. 'Commendably sober' is from Smith, Frederick (Second Earl of Birkenhead), *F. E.: The Life of F. E. Smith*. London: Eyre & Spottiswoode, 1960. p. 203
7. 'Crosland is Acquitted,' *New York Times*, 7 July 1914.
8. 'Letter from London,' *The Truth*, 5 July 1914.
9. Millard pp. 144-145

Chapter 42: Only His Grave, His Body and His Letters

1. Quoted in Millard p. 145
2. Quoted in Bogle p. 344
3. Ibid
4. Shaw p. 80
5. Sherard. *Bernard Shaw, Frank Harris and Oscar Wilde*. p. xii
6. Borland p. 227
7. Quoted in Bogle p. 347 from a letter from Robert Ross to Frank Harris, July 8, 1914, original in the University of Texas Library.
8. Speedie op. cit. pp. 214-215
9. Quoted in Bogle p. 346 original then in the possession of J. P. B. Ross
10. From letter to Edmund Gosse July 13, 1914. Quoted in Bogle p. 349 and Bogle p. 346
11. From letter to Edmund Gosse July 13,1914. Quoted in Bogle p. 349.
12. Bogle p. 348
13. Quoted in Bogle pp. 351-352
14. Quoted in Bogle p. 325 from original then in the possession of J. P. B. Ross and Borland p. 227
15. Brown p. 383
16. MEPOL 3/240
17. Ibid
18. Ibid
19. Sassoon, Siegfried. *Siegfried's Journey 1916-1920*. London: Faber and Faber, 1945. pp. 30-31
20. Autobiography pp. 274-275
21. Autobiography p. 277
22. MEPOL 3/240
23. Autobiography pp. 283-285
24. Autobiography p. 285
25. MEPOL 3/240
26. Bogle p. 378
27. The figures and the fact that Ross and Smith received these funds comes from Diable, Robert, 'The Story of Frederick Stanley Smith,' *Winning Post*, 16 November 1918. *The Winning Post* article only identifies the benefactor as 'an 87-year-old lady'. She was identified as Wyllie by Maria Roberts in her biography of Freddie Smith.
28. Let Them Say pp. 163-164 and Roberts, Jane. *Jacques-Emile Blanche*. Montreuil, France: Gourcuff Gradenigo, 2012. pp. 98-100
29. MEPOL 3/240
30. Autobiography pp. 286-288
31. Brown p. 384
32. Ibid

Chapter 43: Rex v. Douglas

1. Harris, Frank and Lord Alfred Douglas. *New Preface to The Life and Confessions of Oscar Wilde*. London: privately printed for Members of the Homosexual Society of London, 1961. p. 39
2. Sources on trial details and dialogue include: *The Times* (London) November 24, 25, 26, 27, *Birmingham Daily Post,* November 24 and November 26; *Daily Telegraph*, November 28, 1914, *Derby Daily Telegraph*, November 20; *Dundee Evening Telegraph*, November 24 and November 26; *Liverpool Echo,* November 26; *Manchester Courier and Lancashire General Advertiser* November 25; *Liverpool Echo*, November 26, *Sunderland Daily Echo and*

Shipping Gazettte, November 26, *Yorkshire Post and Leeds Intelligencer*, 26 November 1914. All references to the judges notes are from: 'Notes of Mr Justice Coleridge.' Coleridge Family Papers. British Library. ADD 85784

3. Detective West's testimony is from MEPOL 3/240
4. Autobiography p. 290
5. CRIM 1/150/8
6. 'The Amorous Widow,' *Larne Times*, 30 April 1910.
7. CRIM 1/150/8 and Let Them Say p. 172
9. Borland p. 233
10. Bogle p. 370

Chapter 44: Infighting

1. Let Them Say p. 130
2. Antonia Taddei, *London clubs in the late nineteenth century* (Oxford University discussion paper, 1999)
3. Let Them Say p. 130
4. Let Them Say p. 131
5. 'Tribute to an Art Critic,' *The Scotsman*, 29 March 1915.
6. Sources on the malicious prosecution trial include: *The Birmingham Daily Gazette* of 14 April and 16 April 1915, *Western Mail*, 14 April 1915 and *Manchester Courier and Lancashire General Advertiser*, 17 April 1915.
7. 'King's Bench Division,' *The Times* (London). 16 April 1915 and 17 April 1915, and 'Mr Robert Ross Sued by Mr Crosland,' *Manchester Evening News*, 13 April 1915.
8. Brown pp. 385-393
9. Ibid
10. Without Apology p. 112

Chapter 45: The Wilde Myth

1. Hoare p. 110
2. Sassoon op cit. p. 29
3. Ibid
4. Ibid pp. 30-35
5. 'Westminster Flat Raid.' *The Times* (London) 25 November 1915 and 'Bail Refused in Strange Case.' *Aberdeen Journal*, 15 November 1915.
6. Millard p. 161
7. Ibid p. 169
8. Brown p. 388
9. Hall, N. John. *Max Beerbohm: A Kind of Life*. New Haven: Yale University Press, 2002. p. 35
10. Rascoe, Burton. 'Arnold, the Audacious,' *Chicago Tribune*, 8 June 1918.
11. Harris, Frank and Lord Alfred Douglas. *New Preface to The Life and Confessions of Oscar Wilde*. London: privately printed for Members of the Homosexual Society of London, 1961. p. 14
12. Ibid
13. Ellmann p. 584
14. Robins, Ashely. E-mail correspondence with author. 1 August 2016. Ross's description of the body releasing fluids and rupturing from a build-up of gas is consistent with what happens to a decaying corpse left for a number of days. No account of Wilde's death suggests that this happened.
15. Adam, Alison. *A History of Forensic Science: British Beginnings in the Twentieth Century*. New York: Routledge, 2016.

16. Bogle pp. 257-258
17. Harris, Frank and Lord Alfred Douglas. *New Preface to The Life and Confessions of Oscar Wilde*. London: privately printed for Members of the Homosexual Society of London, 1961. p. 17
18. Ibid
19. Bogle p. 258
20. Ibid
21. Unpublished 'Final Preface' in Gertz papers.
22. Millard p. 196
23. Tobin and Gertz op. cit. p. 289
24. Ibid p. 296
25. Gertzman, Jay A. *Bookleggers and Smuthounds*. Philadelphia: University of Pennsylvania Press, 1999. p, 152
26. Quoted in Sotheby's Catalog. http://www.sothebys.com/en/auctions/ecatalogue/lot.99.html/2004/oscar-wilde-l04414 accessed 22 October 2016.
27. Autobiography
28. Sotheby's op. cit
29. Ibid
30. Ibid

Chapter 46: Kicking Oscar's Corpse

1. Quoted in Wachman, Gay. *Lesbian Empire*. New Brunswick, NJ: Rutgers University Press, 2001. p. 19.
2. Bosie p. 284
3. Plea p. 27
5. Matthews, Barry, 'Dark Secret of a Doomed Youth,' *Daily Mail,* 8 November 2014.
6. Hoare p. 15
7. Matthews op. cit.
8. Hoare p. 62
9. Ibid p. 60
10. Ibid p. 93
11. Browne, Douglas G. *Sir Traverse Humphreys: A Biography*. London: George G. Harrap & Co, Ltd, 1960. p. 175
12. Bennett, Will, 'Oscar Wilde Denounced as the Devil by his Lover,' *Telegraph*, 4 October 2004.
13. The majority of the trial dialogue is taken from 'Verbatim report of the trial of Noel Pemberton Billing, MP.' London: Vigilante Office, 1918.
14. 'Mr Billing Not Guilty,' *Liverpool Daily Post*, 5 June 1918.
15. Quoted in Bristow, Joseph, Ed. *Oscar Wilde and Modern Culture*. Athens, OH: Ohio University Press, 2008. p. 194
16. Friend of Friends p. 334
17. *Washington Herald*, 14 July 1918, *Evening World*, 29 July 1918 and *Brooklyn Life*, 3 August 1918.
18. 'A Few Confessions from Alla Nazimova,' *Los Angeles Times*, 21 July 1918.
19. 'In Manhattan,' *Brooklyn Life*, 3 August 1918.
20. Friend of Friends p. 334

Chapter 47: The End

1. Borland p. 285
2. Diary of George Ives
3. Sherard, Robert. *Bernard Shaw, Frank Harris and Oscar Wilde*. New York: Greystone Press, 1937. p. XV

4. Borland p. 287
5. Pezzini op. cit.
6. Wills of Helen Wyllie and Helen Carew held by the Principal Probate Registry
7. Information on Freddie Smith's life after his split with Robert Ross is from *Let Them Say*. Information on Coleridge Kennard's posting in Sweden is from Lockart, R. H. Bruce. *Memoirs of a British Agent*. London: MacMillan. pp. 215-216
8. Millard p. 196
9. Millard p. 186
10. Novak, Daniel, 'Picturing Wilde: Christopher Millard's 'Iconography of Oscar Wilde,' *Nintheenth-Century Contexts*, 32:4, 2010.
11. Hoare pp. 215-216
12. Douglas wrote about the influence of 'Imitation of Christ' on *In Excelsis* in the introduction to the 1924 Marin Secker edition.
13. Douglas's copy of *Revelations of Divine Love* with his highlights and marginalia. Eccles collection 1309. British Library.
14. See, for example, Autobiography pp. 30-31
15. MS Gertz
16. Quoted in Reggie p. 235
17. Ibid p. 248
18. Eccles 1309
19. Summing-Up
20. Douglas, Alfred Bruce, Lord. *True History of Shakespeare's Sonnets*. Port Washington, NY: Kennikat Press, 1933.
21. Stanford, Derek. *Poets of the Nineties: a Biographical Anthology*. London: Pall Mall, 1965.

Epilogue

1. Friend of Friends p. 91
2. *Scotsman*, 25, 26 and 29 November 1921, *Chicago Tribune*, 25 November 1921, *Leeds Mercury*, 25 November 1921.
3. Murray p. 230
4. From original transcripts in the private collection of John D Stratford
5. Murray p. 231
6. Hyde LAD p. 121
7. Letter quoted in Hyde LAD p. 109. Interpretation in Ellmann p. 568
8. Hyde LAD p. 122
9. Bosie p. 15
10. Bosie p. 383
11. Donald Sinden 1923-2014
12. Bosie p. 364
13. Douglas, Alfred Bruce. *Oscar Wilde: A Summing-Up*. London: The Richards Press, 1940. p. 126.
14. McCann, Kate, 'Turing's Law: Oscar Wilde Among 50,000 Gay Men Granted Posthumous Pardons,' *The Telegraph*, 31 January 2017.

Sources and Bibliography

From the National Archives. British Library

Criminal and Legal Files
Metropolitan Police file related to the investigation of criminal libel of T. W. H. Crosland MEPOL 3/240
Central Criminal Court case against T. W. H. Crosland for conspiring to defeat the course of justice CRIM 1/149/1
Central Criminal Court case against Robert Standish Sievier for libel and demanding money with menaces CRIM 1/109/3
Central Criminal Court case against Lord Alfred Douglas for criminally libelling Hambelton Custance CRIM 1/138/4
Criminal investigation of Douglas for criminally libelling Robert Ross CRIM 1/150/8
Notes of Mr Justice Coleridge on Rex v. Douglas. Coleridge Family Papers. British Library. ADD 85784

Financial Files
Bankruptcy file of Lord Alfred Douglas B 9/780
Maurice Salis Schwabe Bankruptcy Filing. BT 226/2549
Bankruptcy filing for Guy de Chassiron BT 226/3725
Bankruptcy fraud trial for Guy de Chassiron B 917/66

Other Files
Lady Eccles Oscar Wilde Collection. Lord Alfred Douglas's highlighted and annotated copy of *Revelations of Divine Love*. Eccles 1309.
Foreign Office File related to the case of Coleridge Kennard FO 1093/113
Maurice Shaw's war service file. WO 339/32318
The Diary of Archibald Walker. City of Westminster Archives Centre. Accession 1257/1/

Other Archives

Magdalen College Archives. Letters to W. Sorley Brown from Sibyl Queensberry, Olive Custance, and Robert Sherard.
Archives Nationales, France: Police file on the expulsion of Baron von Koenig from France in 1902. France. Archives Nationales (AN) F/7/160062

Library of Congress: Elmer Gertz Papers. Folders 6 and 7 in box 414 contain Douglas's correspondence with Gertz regarding his biography of Frank Harris, including numerous letters and Douglas's marginal comments on the chapter which describes their feud.

University of Iowa: Viereck Collection. University of Iowa.

New York Public Library. Berg Collection. Correspondence from Lord Alfred Douglas to Olive Douglas.

George Cecil Ives Collection. Harry Ransome Center, University of Texas at Austin. Diary of George Ives.

John J. Burns Library of Special Collections, Boston College. Article by Lord Alfred Douglas on his conversion to Catholicism.

The Adelman Collection, Bryn Mawr College Library. Letters from Reggie Turner to Martin Secker discussing a proposed memoir about Oscar Wilde.

Correspondence between Philip Wortham and Oscar Browning (OB/1/1831/C) King's College Cambridge

Bibliography

Aberconway, Christabel. *A Wiser Woman?* London: Hutchinson of London, 1966.

Adams, Jad. *Madder Music, Stronger Wine.* New York: Victoria, 2000.

Adlard, John. Stembock, *Yeats and the Nineties.* London: Cecil & Amelia Woolf, 1969.

Adut, Ari, 'A Theory of Scandal: Victorians, Homosexuality and the Fall of Oscar Wilde.' *American Journal of Sociology.* July 2005.

Anstruther, Ian. *Oscar Browning: A Biography.* London: John Murray, 1983.

Aronson, Theo. *Prince Eddy and the Homosexual Underworld.* London: John Murray, 1994.

Bell, T. H. 'Oscar Wilde's Unwritten Play.' *The Bookman*, April/May, 1930.

Bentjeman, John. Green, Candida Lycett, ed. *Letters Volume Two: 1951-1984.* London: Methuen, 1995.

Beerbohm, Max. Max Beerbohm's Letters to Reggie Turner. Philadelphia: J. B. Lippincott, 1965.

Bogle, Edra Charlotte. *The Life and Literary and Artistic Activities of Robert Baldwin Ross, 1869-1918.* Ph. D. Dissertation. University of Southern California. Ann Arbor, Michigan: University Microfilms, Inc, 1969.

Borland, Maureen. *Wilde's Devoted Friend.* Oxford: Lennard Publishing, 1990.

Braybrooke, Patrick. *Lord Alfred Douglas: His Life and Work.* London: Cecil Palmer, 1931.

Bristow, Joseph and Rebecca N. Mitchell. *Oscar Wilde's Chatterton.* New Haven, CT: Yale University Press, 2015.

Bristow, Joseph, "The Blackmailer and the Sodomite: Oscar Wilde on Trial." *Feminist Theory*, 2016 Vol 17,

Bristow, Joseph, Ed. *Oscar Wilde and Modern Culture.* Athens, OH: Ohio University Press, 2008.

Bristow, Joseph, ed. *Wilde Discoveries: Traditions, Histories, Archives.* Toronto: University of Toronto Press. 2013.

Brogan, Hugh. *The Life of Arthur Ransome.* London: Jonathan Cape, 1984.

Brotchie, Alastair. *Alfred Jarry: A Pataphysical Life.* Cambridge, MA: MIT Press, 2011.

Brown, W. Sorley. *Life and Genius of T. W. H. Crosland.* London: Cecil Palmer, 1928.

Browne, Douglas G. *Sir Traverse Humphreys: A Biography.* London: George G. Harrap & Co, Ltd, 1960.

Campbell, James. *Oscar Wilde, Wilfred Owen, and Male Desire.* London: Palgrave MacMillan, 2015.

Cannadine, David. *Decline and Fall of the British Aristocracy*. New York: Vintage Books, 1990.

Carlston, Erin. *Double Agents: Espionage, Literature and Liminal Citizens*. New York: Columbia University Press, 2013.

Cecil, David. *Max: A Biography*. London: Constable, 1965.

Chambers, Roland. *The Last Englishman: The Double Life of Arthur Ransome*. Boston: David R. Godine, 2009.

Cherniavsky, Felix. *The Salome Dancer: The Life and Times of Maud Allan*. McClelland & Stewart Ltd, 1991.

Cocks, H. G. *Nameless Offences: Honosexual Desire in the Nineteenth Century*. London: I. B. Tarius & Co, 2003.

Cohler, Deborah. *Citizen, Invert, Queer*. Minneapolis: University of Minnesota Press, 2007.

Cook, Matthew. *London and the Culture of Homosexuality*. Cambridge: Cambridge University Press, 2003.

Cook, Matthew. *Queer Domesticities*. London: Palgrave MacMillan, 2014.

Cox, David J. et al. *Public Indecency in England: 1857-1960*. London: Routledge, 2015.

Crosland, T. W. H. *The Collected Poems of T. W. H. Crosland*. London: Martin Secker, 1917.

Croft-Cooke, Rupert. *Bosie*. Indianapolis and New York: Bobbs-Merrill Company, 1963.

Croft-Cooke, Rupert. *Feasting with Panthers*. New York: Hold, Rinehart and Winston, 1967.

Croft-Cooke, Rupert. *The Unrecorded Life of Oscar Wilde*. New York: David McKa Company, 1972.

Custance, Olive. *I Desire the Moon*. Caspar Wintermans, ed. Woubrugge, Avalon Press, 2004.

Cuthbertson, Guy. *Wilfred Owen*. New Haven, CT: Yale University Press, 2014.

Deghy, Guy and Keith Waterhouse. *Café Royale: Ninety Years of Bohemia*. London: Hutchinson, 1955.

Delay, Jean. *The Youth of André Gide*. June Guichnaud, trans. Chicago: University of Chicago Press, 1963.

Dockray, Martin, 'The Cleveland Street Scandal 1889-1890: The Conduct of the Defense.' *Journal of Legal History*, v.17, no.n1, 1996 April, p.1-16.

Douglas, Alfred Bruce, Lord. *The Autobiography of Lord Alfred Douglas*. London: Martin Secker, 1929.

Douglas, Alfred Bruce, Lord. *Collected Poems of Lord Alfred Douglas*. London. Martin Secker, 1916.

Douglas, Alfred Bruce, Lord. *Complete Poems of Lord Alfred Douglas*. London: Martin Secker, 1928.

Douglas, Alfred Bruce, Lord. *Halcyon Days. Contributions to the Spirit Lamp*. ed. and commentary by Caspar Wintermans. Francestown, NH: Typogrpheum, 1993.

Douglas, Alfred Bruce, Lord. *Oscar Wilde: A Plea and a Reminiscence*. ed. and commentary by Caspar Wintermans. Woubrugge: Avalon Press, 2002.

Douglas, Alfred Bruce, Lord. *Oscar Wilde and Myself*. London: Duffield and Company, 1914.

Douglas, Alfred Bruce, Lord. *Oscar Wilde: A Summing-Up*. London: The Richards Press, 1940.

Douglas, Alfred Bruce, Lord. *Oscar Wilde et Quelques Autres*. Paris: Librarie Gallimard, 1930.

Douglas, Alfred Bruce, Lord. *True History of Shakespeare's Sonnets*. Port Washington, NY: Kennikat Press, 1933.

Douglas, Alfred Bruce, Lord. *Without Apology*. London: Martin Secker, 1938.

Douglas, Francis Archibald Kelhead. (Marquess of Queensberry). *Oscar Wilde and the Black Douglas*. London: Hutchinson & Co, [No year listed in book]

Dowling, Linda. *Hellenism and Homosexuality*. Ithaca: Cornell University Press, 1994.

Downey, Katherine Brown. *Perverse Midrash: Oscar Wilde, Andre Gide, and Censorship of Biblical Drama*. New York: Continuum International Publishing Group, 2004.

Egermont, Max. *Siegfried Sassoon: A Life*. New York: Farrar, Straus and Giroux, 2005.

Ellmann, Richard. *Oscar Wilde*. New York: Alfred A. Knopf, 1988.

Epstein, Jacob. *Epstein: An Autobiography*. London: Vista Books, 1963.

Fido, Martin. *Oscar Wilde*. London: Hamlyn, 1973.

Findlay, Jean. *Chasing Lost Time: The Life of C. K. Scott Moncrieff: Soldier, Spy, and Translator*. Farrar, Straus and Giroux. Kindle Edition.

Findlay, Kristy Nichol. *Arthur Ransome's Long-Lost Study of Robert Louis Stevenson*. Suffolk, UK: Boydell Press, 2011.

Foldy, Michael S. *The Trials of Oscar Wilde: Deviance, Morality, and Late-Victorian Society*. New Haven: Yale University Press, 1997.

Freeman, Nicholas. *1895: Drama, Disaster and Disgrace in Late Victorian Britain* (Edinburgh Critical Studies in Victorian Culture EUP). Edinburgh University Press. Kindle Edition.

Freeman, William. *The Life of Lord Alfred Douglas: Spoilt Child of Genius*. London: Herbert Joseph, 1948

Fryer, Jonathan. *Robbie Ross: Oscar Wilde's Devoted Friend*. New York: Carroll & Graff Publishers, 2000.

Gagnier, Regenia. *Idylls of the Marketplace: Oscar Wilde and the Victorian Public*. Stanford, California: Stanford University Press, 1986.

Gertzman, Jay A. *Bookleggers and Smuthounds*. Philadelphia: University of Pennsylvania Press, 1999.

Goodway, David. *Anarchist Seeds Beneath the Snow*. Liverpool: Liverpool University Press, 2006.

Guy, Josephine and Ian Small. *Oscar Wilde's Profession*. Oxford: Oxford University Press, 2000.

Guy, Josephine and Ian Small. Studying Oscar Wilde. Greensboro: ELT Press, 2006.

Hall, N. John. *Max Beerbohm: A Kind of Life*. New Haven: Yale University Press, 2002.

Hall, Kathy. 'Lord Alfred's Editor: The Balancing Act of Editing Lord Alfred Douglas's Without Apology.' *International Journal of the Book*, Volume 7, Issue 1, pp.65-80.

Hanberry, Gerald. *More Lives than One: The Remarkable Wilde Family Through the Generations*. West Link Park: Collins, 2011.

Harris, Frank and Lord Alfred Douglas. *New Preface to The Life and Confessions of Oscar Wilde*. London: Privately Printed for Members of the Homosexual Society of London, 1961.

Harris, Frank. *Oscar Wilde*. New York: Carroll & Graff, 1959.

Hart-Davis, Rupert. *The Autobiography of Arthur Ransome*. London: Jonathan Cape, 1979.

Hart-Davis, Rupert. *The Letters of Oscar Wilde*. London: Harcourt, Brace & World, 1962.

Hart-Davis, Rupert, Ed. *Max Beeerbohm's Letters to Reggie Turner*. Philadelphia: J. B. Lippincott and Company, 1965.

Head, Alice M. *It Could Never Have Happened*. London: William Heinmann Ltd, 1939.

Hibberd, Dominic. *Wilfred Owen: A New Biography*. Chicago: Ivan R. Dee, 2003.

Hichens, Robert. Yesterday: *The Autobiography of Robert Hichens*. London: Cassell, 1947.

Hoare, Philip. *Oscar Wilde's Last Stand*. New York: Arcade Publishing, 1997.

Holland, Merlin, ed. *Oscar Wilde De Profundis A Facsimile*. London: British Library, 2000.

Holland, Merlin. *The Real Trial of Oscar Wilde*. New York: Fourth Estate, 2003.

Holland, Vyvyan. *Son of Oscar Wilde*. New York: Carroll& Graff, 1999.

Holland, Vyvyan. *Time Remembered: After Pere Lachaise*. London: Victor Gollancz, 1966.

Horan, Patrick. *The Importance of Being Paradoxical: Maternal Influence in the Presence of the Works of Oscar Wilde*. Cranberry, NJ: Associated University Press, 1997.

Hyde, Mary, ed. Bernard Shaw & Alfred Douglas: A Correspondence. Oxford: Oxford University Press, 1989.

Hyde, H. Montgomery. *Lord Alfred Douglas*. London: Meuthen, 1984.

Hyde, H. Montgomery. *The Love that Dared Not Speak Its Name*. Boston: Little, Brown and Company, 1970.

Hyde, H. Montgomery. *Oscar Wilde: The Aftermath*. New York: Farrar, Straus & Co, 1963.

Hyde, H. Montgomery. *The Three Trials of Oscar Wilde*. New York: University Books, 1973.

Hynes, Samuel. *The Edwardian Turn of Mind*. London: Pilmco, 1968.

Hynes, Samuel. *A War Imagined*. New York: Colier Books, 1990.

Jackson, John Wyse, Ed. *The Uncollected Oscar Wilde*. London: Fourth Estate, 1991.

Jarry, Alfred. *Days and Nights*. London: Anthony Rowe Lts, 1989.

Jullian, Phillippe. *Oscar Wilde*. London: Constable & Co Ltd, 1969.

Juxon, John. *Lewis and Lewis*. New York: Ticknor and Fields, 1984.

Katz, Steven; Landes, Richard. *The Paranoid Apocalypse: A Hundred-Year Retrospective on The Protocols of the Elders of Zion* (Elie Wiesel Center for Judaic Studies). NYU Press short. Kindle Edition.

Kaylor, Michael Matthew. *Secreted Desires*. Brno, Czech Republic: Masaryk University, 2006.

Kennrad, George. *Loopy*. London: Leo Cooper, 1990.

Kingston, Angela. *Oscar Wilde as a Character in Victorian Fiction*. New York: Palgrave, 2007.

Kohl, Norbert. *Oscar Wilde: The Works of a Conformist Rebel*. Cambridge: Cambridge University Press, 1989.

Koven, Seth. *Slumming: Sexual and Social Politics in Victorian London*. Princeton University Press. Kindle Edition.

Lago, Mary M. and Karl Beckson, eds. *Max & Will*. London: John Murray, 1975.

Lewis, Brian. Professor of History, McGill University. E-mail correspondence. April 25, 2016.

Lockhart, R. H. Bruce. *Memoirs of a British Agent*. London: Macmillian, 1932.

Longford, Elizabeth. *A Pilgrimage of Passion: The Life of Wilfrid Scawen Blunt*. New York: Alfred A. Knopf, 1980.

Mackie, Gregory, 'Publishing Notoriety: Piracy, Pornography, and Oscar Wilde.' University of Toronto Quarterly, Fall 2004.

Maguire, J. Robert. *Ceremonies of Bravery*. Oxford: Oxford University Press, 2013.

Majoribanks, Edward. *Carson the Advocate*. New York: MacMillian, 1932.

Mason, A. E. W. *Sir George Alexander & the St. James Theatre*. New York: Benjamin Blom, 1935.

McKenna, Neil. *The Secret Life of Oscar Wilde*. Basic Books, 2006.

McLaren, Agnus. *Sexual Blackmail: A Modern History*. Cambridge, MA: Harvard University Press, 2002.

Mikhail, E. H. *Oscar Wilde: Interviews and Recollections*. New York: MacMillian, 1979.

Millard, Christopher, Ed. (Stuart Mason) *Oscar Wilde: Three Times Tried*. London: Ferrestone Press, 1912.

Milne-Smith, Amy. *London Clubland: A Cultural History of Gender and Class in Late Victorian Britain*. New York: Palgrave MacMillan, 2011.

Milne-Smith, Amy. 'Queensberry's Misrule: Reputation, Celebrity, and the Idea of the Victorian Gentleman.' Canadian Journal of History, Autumn 2013.

Moore, T. Sturge. *Self-Portrait Taken From the Letters & Journals of Charles Ricketts*, London: Peter Davies, 1939.

Morton, James. *Gangland: The Lawyers*. London: Virgin, 2001.

Mouret, Francois. J-L. 'Quatorze lettres et billets inedits de Lord Alfred Douglas a Andre Gide, 1895-1929,' *Revue de Littérature comparée*, 49, no. 3 (July-September, 1975), 483-502.

Murray, Douglas. Bosie: *A Biography of Lord Alfred Douglas*. New York: Hyperion, 2000.

Negev, Eilat and Yehuda Koren. *The First Lady of Fleet Street*. New York: Bantam Books, 2011.

Nelson, James G. *Publisher to the Decadents: Leonard Smithers in the Careers of Beardsley, Wilde Dowson*. University Park, PA: Pennsylvania State University Press, 2000.

O'Brien, Kevin, 'Robert Sherard: Friend of Oscar Wilde,' *English Literature in Translation, 1880-1920*, Volume 28, Number 1, 1885

O'Sullivan, Vincent. *Aspects of Wilde*. London: Constable & Co, 1936.

O'Sullivan, Vincent. *Opinions*. London: The Unicorn Press, 1959.

Orens, John Richard. *Stewart Headlam's Radical Anglicanism: The Mass, The Masses and the Music Hall*. Chicago: Unviersity of Chicago Press, 2003.

Patterson, Gary H. 'Lord Alfred Douglas: An Annotated Bibliography of Writings About Him,' *English Literature in Translation. 1880-1920*. Vol 23. No. 3, 1980.

Pearce, Joseph. *The Unmasking Of Oscar Wilde*. Ignatius Press. Kindle Edition.

Pearson, Hesketh. *Modern Men and Mummers*. New York: Harcourt, Brace and Company, 1922.

Platt, Len. *Aristocracies of Fiction*. Westport, CT: Greenwood Press, 2001.

Pollard, Patrick. *Andre Gide: Homosexual Moralist*. New Haven: Yale University Press, 1991.

Poole, Andrea Geddes. *Stewards of the Nation's Art: Contested Cultural Authority. 1890-1939*. Toronto: University of Toronto Press, 2010.

Powell, Kerry. *Oscar Wilde and the Theatre of the 1890s*. Cambridge: Cambridge University Press, 1990.

Pular, Philippa. *Frank Harris*. London: Hamish Hamilton, 1975.

Raby, Peter, ed. *The Cambridge Companion to Oscar Wilde*. Cambridge: Cambridge University Press, 1997.

Radford, Andrew and Victoria Reid. *Franco-British Cultural Exchanges*. London: Palgrave MacMillian, 2012.

Ransome, Arthur. *Autobiography of Arthur Ransome*. London: Jonathan Cape, 1976.

Reid, Victoria. *Andre Gide and Curiosity*. Amsterdam: Rodopi, 1994.

Riewald, J. B. *Max Beerbohm's Mischevious Wit*. Assen, Netherlands: Van Gorcum, 2000.

Renton, Claudia. *Those Wonderful Wyndhams*. London: William Collins, 2014.

Riess, Curt. *Total Espionage*. New York: G. P. Putnam's Sons, 1941.

Robb, Graham. *Strangers: Homosexual Love in the Nineteenth Century*. New York: W. W. Norton, 2003.

Roberts, Brian. *The Mad Bad Line*. London: Hamish Hamilton, 1981.

Roberts, Maria. *Let Them Say: The Life of Frederick Stanley Smith*. Feed A Read, 2016.

Roberts, Maria. *Yours Loyally: A Life of Christopher Sclater Millard*. Feed A Read, 2014.

Robins, Ashley H. *Oscar Wilde; The Great Drama of His Life*. Brighton: Sussex Academic Press, 2011.

Rodriguez, Suzanne. *Wild Heart: A Life*. New York: Harper Collins, 1995.

Ross, Margery, ed. *Robert Ross, Friend of Friends*. London: Jonathan Cape, 1952.

Ross, Robert. *Aubrey Beardsley*. London: John Lane, 1909.

Ross, Robert. *Masques and Phases*. London: Humphreys, 1909.

Rothenstein, William. *Men and Memories: A History of the Arts 1872-1922*. New York: Tudor Publishing Company, 1931.

Rothenstein, William. *Since Fifty. Men and Memories 1922-1938*. London: Faber & Faber, Ltd, 1940.

Saint-Amour, Paul K. *The Copyrights: Intellectual Property and the Literary Imagination*. Ithaca, NY: Cornell University Press, 2003.

Sandulescu, C. George, Ed. *Rediscovering Oscar Wilde*. Gerrards Cross: Colin Smuthe, 1994

Sassoon, Siegfried. *Siegfried's Journey*. London: Faber and Faber, 1945.

Sewell, Brocard. *Olive Custance: Her Life and Work*. London: The Eighteen-nineties Society, 1925.

Sherard, Robert. *Bernard Shaw, Frank Harris and Oscar Wilde*. New York: Greystone Press, 1937.

Sherard, Robert. *Oscar Wilde: The Story of an Unhappy Friendship*. London: Greening & Co, 1905.

Sherard, Robert. *The Real Oscar Wilde*. London: T. Warner Laurie, 1916.

Simpson, Colin et al. *The Cleveland Street Affair*. Boston: Little, Brown and Company, 1976.

Sitwell, Osbert. *Noble Essences: A Book of Characters*. Boston: Little, Brown & Company, 1950.

Smith, Frederick (Second Earl of Birkenhead), *F. E.: The Life of F. E. Smith*. London: Eyre & Spottiswoode, 1960.

Souhamie, Diana. *Wild Girls*. New York: St. Martin's Press, 2004.

Sox, David. *Bachelors of Art: Edward Perry Warren and Lewes House Brotherhood*. London: Fourth Estate, 1991.

Speedie, Julie. *Wonderful Sphinx: The Biography of Ada Leverson*. London: Virago Press, 1993.

Stewart, A. T. Q. *Edward Carson*. Belfast: The Blackstaff Press, 1981.

Stratmann, Linda. *The Marquess of Queensberry: Wilde's Nemesis*. New Haven: Yale University Press, 2013.

Stokes, Anthony. *Pit of Shame*. Winchester, UK: Waterside Press, 2007.

Stokes, John. *Oscar Wilde: Myths, Miracles and Imitations*. Cambridge: Cambridge University Press, 1996.

Stokes, John. 'Wilde at Bay: The Diaries of George Ives,' *English Literature in Transition*, Volume 26, Number 3, 1983.

Stopes, Marie Carmichael. *Lord Alfred Douglas: His Poetry and Personality*. London: The Richards Press, 1949.

Sturgis, Matthew. *Aubrey Beardsley: A Biography*. New York: Overlook Press, 1998.

Symons, Arthur. *The Café Royal and Other Essays*. Westminster: The Beaumont Press, 1923.

Symonds, John. *Conversations with Gerald*. London: Duckworth, 1974.

Thompson, F. M. L *The Rise of Respectable Society*. NY: Fontana Press, 1988.

Tobin, A. I. and Elmer Gertz. *Frank Harris: a Study in Black and White*. Chicago: Madelaine Mendelsohn, 1931.

Tydeman, William and Steven Price. *Wilde. Salome. Plays in Production*. Cambridge: University of Cambridge press, 1996

'Verbatim report of the trial of Noel Pemberton Billing, MP.' London: Vigilante Office, 1918.

Walker-Smith, Derek. *The Life of Lord Darling*. London: Cassell and Company, Ltd, 1938.

Watt, Reginald J. J. *Robert Hugh Benson: A Captain in God's Army*. London: Burns & Oats, Ltd, 1918.

Weintraub, Stanley. *Reggie*. New York: George Braziller, 1965.

Weiss, Samuel A., ed. *Bernard Shaw's Letters to Siegfried Trebitsch*. Stanford, CA: Stanford University Press, 1986.

Wilde, Oscar. *The Complete Writings of Oscar Wilde*. New York: Pearson Publishing Company, 1909.

Sources and Bibliography

Wilde, Oscar. *Complete Works of Oscar Wilde*. New York: Barnes and Noble, 1966.

Wilde, Oscar. Ian Small, ed. *The Complete Works of Oscar Wilde*: Volume 2 De Profundis 'Epistola: In Carcere et Vinculis,' Oxford: Oxford University Press, 2005.

Wilde, Oscar. *De Profundis*. London: G. P. Putnam & Sons, 1905.

Wilde, Oscar. *Letters to the Sphinx*. Adelaide: Michel Walmer, 2015.

Wilde, Oscar. *The Portrait of Mr. W. H.* New York: Michell Kennerley, 1921.

Wintermans, Caspar. *Alfred Douglas: A Poet's Life and His Finest Work*. London: Peter Owen, 2007.

Wright, Thomas. *Built of Books: How Reading Defined the Life of Oscar Wilde*. New York: Henry Holt, 2008.

Wright, Thomas. *Table Talk Oscar Wilde*. London: Cassell & Co, 2000.

Wyndham, Violet. *The Sphinx and her Circle*. New York: Vanguard Press, 1963.

Acknowledgements

First and foremost I would like to thank Maria Roberts who has been more generous with her time, research skills and knowledge than I could ever repay. Without her help I would not have been able to consult nearly as many primary British sources. I have also benefitted immensely from her knowledge of the Robert Ross circle acquired while writing biographies of Christopher Millard and Freddie Smith.

When I first approached the Lord Alfred Douglas literary estate, I was a bit nervous that they might not be enthusiastic about a book that focuses on one of the least appealing parts of Douglas's biography. I am indebted to John D. Stratford, co-executor of the estate, who put those fears to rest and who has been tremendously helpful and supportive.

Lord Alfred Douglas unpublished materials are reproduced by courtesy of the Executors of the Literary Estate of Lord Alfred Douglas ©John D Stratford and John Rubenstein.

I owe a debt of gratitude to Kimery Campbell who took time from her busy schedule to offer editorial suggestions and feedback on the manuscript. She has been a great supporter and champion.

Dr Christopher (Cal) Lee has been an invaluable support both professionally and personally. I am grateful for research assistance and advice on bridging the worlds of popular writing and academic scholarship.

Thank you to Donald Mead, former editor of *The Wildean*, for making me feel welcome in the community of Wilde experts and enthusiasts (who collectively have a lot of PhDs) and to Robert Whelan, current editor, whose attention to detail and suggestions on my submissions have improved not only my articles, but the content of this book.

I am also grateful to Eric Maillard, in France, who provided me with primary source materials related to Maurice Schwabe and who shared his expertise on the criminal circle that he was involved in, especially on Baron Rudolph von Koenig.

Thank you to Brian Lewis of McGill University for making me aware of references to Robert Ross and Freddie Smith in the diaries of George Ives and to the Harry Ransome Center in Austin, Texas, for permission to quote from them. Also to Ashley Robins for sharing his expertise on the medical causes of Oscar Wilde's death and to Kevin O'Brien for discussing his research on Robert Sherard with me.

In a project like this, sometimes you spend years tracking down a source only to discover it yields nothing you can really use. Such was the case with the diary of Lucas D'Oyly Carte, but I am nevertheless thankful to J. Donald Smith and Marc Shepherd for helping me find it.

A work like this could not be completed without the help of many librarians and archivists. I am grateful to Dr. Robin Darwall-Smith at the Magdalen College archives. Bruce Kirby of the Library of Congress. The staff of the reading room at the New York Public Library's Berg Collection. Margot Riley at the State Library in Sydney. The dozens of unseen librarians who fielded hundreds of requests for inter-library loans through the MELCAT system, and the staff of the Rochester Hills Public Library where portions of this book were written. Plus dozens of librarians, too many to mention individually, who responded to my research questions over the years.

I am grateful to my editor Shaun Barrington not only for making me sound more polished (and more British) than I am in life, but also for staying with *Oscar's Ghost* when I delivered substantially more material than he had entirely expected.

There are a few people who have been there for me over the past six years as I worked on this book. First, to my mother Carol Lee, whose emotional and practical support have allowed me to pursue a literary career with all of its ups and downs. It is a debt that I could never repay and I cannot express my love and appreciation enough. To Jennifer Hunter who patiently listened to me ramble on about dead poets. To my sister-in-law Jennifer Lee and my wonderful niece and nephew Sophia and Emerson who always bring joy into my life. And to Valery Lantratov, with love. Valery has shared my great life adventures with me, and keeps me from taking myself too seriously.

Finally I would like to express my gratitude for the passage of time, which has spared me the ordeal of having to win Lord Alfred Douglas's approval of my editorial point of view.

Index